The Cambridge History of American Theatre is an authoritative and wide-ranging history of American theatre in all its dimensions, from theatre building to play-writing, directors, performers, and designers. Engaging the theatre as a performance art, a cultural institution, and a fact of American social and political life, the History recognizes changing styles of presentation and performance and addresses the economic context that conditions the drama presented. The History approaches its subject with a full awareness of relevant developments in literary criticism, cultural analysis, and performance theory. At the same time, it is designed to be an accessible, challenging narrative. All volumes include an extensive overview and timeline, followed by chapters on specific aspects of theatre.

Volume One deals with the colonial inceptions of American theatre through the post–Civil War period: the European antecedents, the New World influences of the French and Spanish colonists, and the development of uniquely American traditions in tandem with the emergence of national identity.

The Cambridge History of American Theatre

Volume One

The Cambridge History of American Theatre

Volume One:
Beginnings to 1870

Edited by

Don B. Wilmeth
Brown University

Christopher Bigsby
University of East Anglia

CAMBRIDGE
UNIVERSITY PRESS

PUBLISHED BY THE PRESS SYNDICATE OF THE UNIVERSITY OF CAMBRIDGE
The Pitt Building, Trumpington Street, Cambridge, CB2 1RP, United Kingdom

CAMBRIDGE UNIVERSITY PRESS
The Edinburgh Building, Cambridge CB2 2RU, United Kingdom
40 West 20th Street, New York, NY 10011-4211, USA
10 Stamford Road, Oakleigh, Melbourne 3166, Australia

First published 1998

Printed in the United States of America

Typeset in ITC Cheltenham Book

Library of Congress Cataloging-in-Publication Data

The Cambridge history of American theatre / edited by Don B. Wilmeth,
  Christopher Bigsby.

     p. cm.

  Includes bibliographical references and index.
  Contents: v. 1. Beginnings to 1870
  ISBN 0-521-47204-0 (hc)
    1. Theatre – United States – History. 2. American drama – History
and criticism. I. Wilmeth, Don B. II. Bigsby, C. W. E.
PN2221.C37   1998
792'.0973 – dc21   97-12097
                                      CIP

*A catalog record for this book is available from
the British Library*

ISBN 0 521 47204 0 hardback

Contents

List of Illustrations

Contributors

The Editors

CHRISTOPHER BIGSBY is Professor of American Studies at the University of East Anglia in Norwich, England, and is Director of its Arthur Miller Centre. He has published more than twenty books on British and American culture, including *The Black American Writer,* editor, two volumes (1966); *The Second Black Renaissance* (1980); *Contemporary English Drama,* editor (1982); *A Critical Introduction to 20th Century Drama,* 3 volumes (1982–85); *Arthur Miller and Company,* editor (1990); and *Modern American Drama 1945–90* (1992), together with studies of Edward Albee, Joe Orton, and David Mamet. He recently edited a companion to *Arthur Miller* for Cambridge University Press. He is also the author of radio and television plays and of three novels: *Hester* (1994), *Pearl* (1995), and *Still Lives* (1996). He is a frequent voice on BBC Radio, having interviewed many prominent writers, and is often called upon for reviews, program notes, and essays in newspapers, theatre programs, and journals.

DON B. WILMETH is Professor of Theatre and English and Honorary Curator of the H. Adrian Smith Collection of Conjuring Books and Magicana at Brown University, Providence, Rhode Island. He is the author, editor, or co-editor of a dozen books, including *The American Stage to World War I: A Guide to Information Sources* (1978), the award-winning *George Frederick Cooke: Machiavel of the Stage* (1980), *American and English Popular Entertainment* (1980), *The Language of American Popular Entertainment* (1981), *Variety Entertainment and Outdoor Amusements* (1982), and the *Cambridge Guide to American Theatre* (co-editor 1993 edition with Tice L. Miller; editor 1996 paperback edition). With Rosemary Cullen he co-edited plays by Augustin Daly and William Gillette, and currently he edits for Cambridge University Press a series, Studies in American Theatre and Drama. He is a frequent contributor to reference works and serves on the editorial boards of six journals. A past Guggenheim Fellow and president of the American Society for Theatre Research, he is presently Dean of the College of Fellows of the American Theatre.

The Contributors

PETER G. BUCKLEY is on the history faculty at The Cooper Union for the Advancement of Art and Science in New York City and is a Fellow of the New York Institute of the Humanities at New York University. Educated at the University of Sussex and at SUNY Stony Brook, he has focused his work on the development of popular culture, especially of New York City in the antebellum period, and is currently at work on a history of the Cooper Union.

JONATHAN CURLEY, a graduate of Brown University, is a former Fulbright recipient to Ireland and is currently a doctoral student in English at New York University.

PETER A. DAVIS has taught at the University of Oregon and Tufts University and is currently on the theatre faculty at the University of Illinois at Urbana-Champaign, where he teaches theatre history. Although a specialist in the cultural history of American theatre and widely published in this area, he has taught a wide range of courses, from classical theatre history to acting and directing to speech and communication theory. He currently serves as dramaturge for the Illinois Repertory Theatre.

MARY C. HENDERSON has had a multifaceted career as Curator of the Theatre Collection of the Museum of the City of New York, as Adjunct Professor of Graduate Drama at New York University's Tisch School of the Arts, and currently as a freelance writer of books about the theatre. She is well known for *The City and the Theater* (1973) and *Theater in America* (new edition, 1996), has completed a biography of designer Jo Mielziner, and is writing a history of the New Amsterdam Theatre for Hyperion.

BRUCE MCCONACHIE is Professor of Theatre Arts at the University of Pittsburgh and was formerly at the College of William and Mary. He has published widely on popular American theatre and theatre historiography, including *Interpreting the Theatrical Past* (co-edited in 1989 with Thomas Postlewait) and the award-winning *Melodramatic Formations: American Theatre and Society, 1820–1870* (1992). He was recently a Fulbright scholar in Poland.

DOUGLAS MCDERMOTT is Professor of Drama at California State University, Stanislaus. He has been a Fellow of the National Endowment for the Humanities and an Honorary Visiting Fellow in the School of Theatre Studies of the University of New South Wales, Australia. He has published articles in journals such as *Theatre Survey* and *Modern Drama* and contributed to several books, including *The American Stage* (Engle and Miller). His research focuses on the theatre as a function of regional culture.

GARY A. RICHARDSON is Professor of English at Mercer University, Macon, Georgia. He is the author of *American Drama from the Beginnings Through World*

War I: A Critical History (1993) and, with Stephen Watt, *American Drama: Colonial to Contemporary* (1995). He is currently at work on *Staging Ireland,* a study examining the representation of Ireland and the Irish on the Irish, English, and American stages.

JOSEPH ROACH is Professor of Theatre and English at Yale University and has held appointments at Tulane University, Northwestern University, New York University, and elsewhere. He is the author of the award-winning *The Player's Passion: Studies in the Science of Acting* (1985), *Cities of the Dead: Circum-Atlantic Performance* (1996), and articles in such journals as *The Drama Review, Discourse, Theatre Journal,* and *Theatre Survey.* With Janelle Reinelt he is co-editor of *Critical Theory and Performance* (1992).

SIMON WILLIAMS is Professor of Dramatic Art and Director of the Interdisciplinary Humanities Center at the University of California, Santa Barbara. He has published widely in the fields of European theatre history and opera of the eighteenth and nineteenth centuries. His publications include *German Actors of the Eighteenth and Nineteenth Centuries: Idealism, Romanticism, and Realism* (1985), *Shakespeare on the German Stage,* Volume 1 (1990), and *Richard Wagner and Festival Theatre* (1994). He is completing a book on romantic actors.

Preface and Acknowledgments

The study of American theatre and drama has never established itself securely in academe. Histories of American literature have regularly assigned the most marginal of roles to its accomplishments. Too few universities teach its development over the centuries or consider its role in a developing social, political, and cultural world.

It is as though American theatre came into existence as a sudden grace, with Eugene O'Neill and his suitcase of plays its only begetter. In fact, American theatre has a history going back to the first encounter of Europeans with what, to them, was a new continent and, in the form of Native American rituals and ceremonies, a prehistory.

The theatre, the most public of the arts, has always been a sensitive gauge of social pressures and public issues; the actor has been a central icon of a society that, from its inception, has seen itself as performing, on a national stage, a destiny of international significance. For students of drama, theatre, literature, cultural experience, and political development, the theatre should have been a central subject of study. It has, instead, been seen as largely eccentric to those concerns.

There are signs of change. New theatre organizations have been formed or reformed (older ones are prospering as never before), new journals have appeared, and national and international conferences now find space, as once they did not, for American drama and theatre. The very few histories of the American theatre, mostly published in the distant past, have recently been augmented. These three volumes, therefore, build on this renewed interest and are themselves an attempt to redress the balance.

The study of American theatre and drama, perhaps especially in the United States itself, has been inhibited, in part, by an institutional division between departments of theatre and departments of English, the one being devoted to a performed art, the other to a concern with texts. Such a division is logical, but it is also patently artificial. Drama is a performed art. It exists, usually, though not inevitably, as a text, but that text itself exists to be performed. This may sound like a statement of the obvious, and indeed it is, but the obvious often escapes attention.

For the purposes of this History we have chosen to use the word "theatre" to include all aspects of the dramatic experience, including major popular and paratheatrical forms. Contributors have been asked to address particular aspects of that experience – whether it be theatre architecture, stage design, acting, playwriting, directing, and so forth – but they have also been invited to stress the wider context of those subjects. Indeed, they have been invited to engage the context within which theatre itself operates. Hence, we have set out to produce a history that will be authoritative and wide-ranging, that will offer a critical insight into plays and playwrights, but that will also engage the theatre as a performance art, a cultural institution, and a fact of American social and political life. We have sought to recognize changing styles of presentation and performance and to address the economic context that conditions the drama presented. This approach may lead, on occasion, to a certain recrossing of tracks, as, for example, a chapter on playwrights invokes the career of particular actors, and a chapter on actors describes the plays in which they appeared, but this redoubling of material is both inevitable and desirable, stressing as it does the interdependence of all aspects of this craft.

The theatre has reflected the diversity of America and the special circumstances in which the theatre itself has operated in an expanding country moving toward a sense of national identity. The history of the American stage and the making of America have been co-terminous, often self-consciously so, and to that end each volume of this History begins with a timeline followed by a wide-ranging essay that attempts to locate the theatre in the context of a developing society.

The History could have run to many more volumes, but the economics of publication finally determined its length. The precise division between the three volumes and the strategies involved in structuring them, however, was a matter of serious debate, a debate in which the editors were assisted by others, in meetings that took place at Brown University in the United States and at York University in Canada. It is proper, in fact, to pause here and gratefully acknowledge the financial assistance for the Brown meeting of Brown University, its special collections, and Cambridge University Press. For the York meeting we are indebted to Christopher Innes, who served as an adviser to the editors, and the Social Sciences and Humanities Research Council of Canada, who helped fund the expenses. In Providence we were able to gather a notable group of experts: Arnold Aronson, the late Frances Bzowski, T. Susan Chang, Rosemary Cullen, Spencer Golub, James V. Hatch, Warren Kliewer, Brooks McNamara, Brenda Murphy, Tom Postlewait, Vera Mowry Roberts, Matthew Roudané, David Savran, Ronn Smith, Susan Harris Smith, and Sarah Stanton. In Canada the editors were joined by Innes and the authors of overview essays (Aronson, Postlewait, and Bruce McConachie). Two individuals invited to Providence were unable to join the group because of inclement weather (Mary C. Henderson and Tice L. Miller), but each sent written recommendations. We are indebted to these experts for their thoughtful and challenging ideas and recommendations.

Ultimately, of course, the editors accept responsibility for the present format, but without the preliminary discussions we would have doubtlessly floundered. In the final analysis, that we have chosen 1865 and 1945 as defining chronological parameters is, in part, an expression of our desire to relate the theatre to a wider public history but in part also a recognition of certain developments internal to theatre itself. Any such divisions have an element of the arbitrary, however, chronological periods doing damage to the continuity of individual careers and stylistic modes. But division there must be, and those we have chosen seem more cogent than any of the others we considered.

The organization of the three volumes does, however, still reveal a bias in favor of the modern, which this preface began by deploring. Yet it does not presume that theatrical history began with O'Neill but simply recognizes that the story of the American theatre is one of a momentum that gathers pace with time, while acknowledging the rich heritage and accomplishments of American theatre during its earlier periods.

The History does not offer itself as encyclopedic. Given the restrictions of space, this could never have been an objective. Those wishing to research details not found in these pages should consult the *Cambridge Guide to American Theatre* (1993, 1996), edited by Wilmeth and Miller, and *Theatre in the United States: A Documentary History* (Vol. I, 1750–1915), edited by Witham. Both texts having been published by Cambridge, this History was planned with them in mind as complementary to this effort. The reader will, however, find detailed bibliographies of further reading at the end of each chapter. What the History does aim to do is tell the story of the birth and growth, on the American continent, of a form that, the Puritans notwithstanding, in riverfront towns, in mining settlements, in the growing cities of a colony that in time became a country, proved as necessary to life as anything else originally imported from Europe but then turned to serve the purposes of a new society reaching toward a definition of itself.

Americans often had theatre before they had sidewalks or sewers. They sat in tents, on riverboats, in the open air, or in formal theatres, to be entertained, moved, disturbed, or reassured, by those who were often drawn to the North American continent by the same dreams that animated their audiences. A nation is constructed of more than a set of principles enforced by a common will. It builds itself out of more than contradictions denied by rhetoric or shared experience. The theatre played its part in shaping the society it served, as later it would reflect the diversity that was always at odds with a supposed homogeneity. Inevitably derivative, in time the theatre accommodated itself to the New World, and, in creating new forms, in identifying and staging new concerns, was itself a part of the process that it observed and dramatized.

Theatre is international. Today, an American play is as likely to open in London as in New York and to find its primary audience outside the country of its birth. Despite the restrictions imposed by Actors' Equity, actors move between countries, as do directors and designers. Film and television carry drama across national frontiers. Yet the American playwright still addresses realities, myths, and concerns born out of national experiences; the American theatre still stages the private and public anxieties of a people who are what they are because of history. The accomplishments of the American theatre are clear. This is an account of those accomplishments as it is, in part, of that history.

This project was undertaken with the urging of Cambridge University Press editors Victoria Cooper and Sarah Stanton, who, along with our press editors in New York – first T. Susan Chang and then Anne Sanow – have been a source of constant support and assistance. We are grateful for all their good services. The editors are also indebted to their respective institutions for financial and editorial support. At the University of East Anglia we are pleased to acknowledge support from the research committee of the Schol of English and American Studies. At Brown University we received generous support from the faculty development fund of the office of Dean of the Faculty, the Dean of the College, and the Graduate School.

Finally, we are pleased to recognize the editorial assistance of Robert Lublin, Jonathan Curley, and Diana Beck, who made many of our chores less arduous.

Introduction

Christopher Bigsby and Don B. Wilmeth

On 15 September 1752, in Williamsburg, the capital of Virginia, the first play performed in America by a fully professional company was presented. It was Shakespeare's *The Merchant of Venice;* its *Virginia Gazette* advertisement ended with the formulaic phrase "Vivat Rex." It is hard not to see a certain symbolic significance in this production. First, company, play, and actors were British, as, of course, was the audience. After all, this was a British colony, and the Revolution was still more than two decades ahead. The influence of the British theatre, indeed, would remain central, if a matter of growing contention, throughout the period covered by this volume. Second, it was notable that the performance took place in a southern colony, for the fact is that theatre did not find a ready home on a continent that to some was to be a new Eden, a world in which God alone would have the prerogative of invention.

The only Word, the only authorized text, was to be the Bible, and man's role was to be obedient to He who alone was the author of the human drama. The frivolous, the sensual, the illicit were to be shunned. Display was seen as unseemly, the aesthetic as suspect. Boundaries were to be respected, not transgressed, and the theatre, as the Puritans well knew, had always been about transgression. Those on board the Mayflower had not suffered the privations of sea crossing and winter storms to worship Dionysus. They had another God, who would not be mocked by those who seduced by their skills of mimickry or claimed a license to portray the proscribed. The actor implied a Protean world in which transformation was a central and vivifying principle. Those who landed on Plymouth Rock looked to something more permanent.

Theatre in America was born into an immediately hostile environment – physically demanding, philosophically suspicious, culturally uncertain. A communal art, it found itself in a society whose priorities had to do with subordinating the natural world and enforcing covenents that foregrounded spiritual or commercial imperatives. This was a society busy constituting itself, simultaneously attracted to and repelled by a mother country whose possibilities – personal and civic – seemed depleted. The first formal playhouse, in Williamsburg, was not built until over a century after the original settlement,

1

whereas the first theatre in Boston, epicenter of Puritanism, was constructed some fifteen years after the Revolution. Apart from anything else, a playhouse required a sizable population to support it, and before the Revolution there were barely half a dozen centers with more than ten thousand citizens. Boston itself could boast only twenty thousand in 1774. But theatre consists of more than buildings. The impetus to perform, the need for public entertainment, for a collaborative and social art, is plainly irresistible, and there is evidence for such from the earliest days of exploration and settlement. Theatre accompanied the colonizers. Even the Spanish took time out from their search for golden cities to distract themselves from their failed utopianism with dramatic performances.

Despite its origins in religious and civic ceremony, theatre has always been a tainted art. In Imperial Rome any soldier turning to acting was instantly executed, whereas actors were required to raise their children in the same profession to limit the spread of corruption. The Puritans attacked the theatre for its presumption in challenging God's power to create character, for its licentiousness, and for its inconsequence. They recognized a certain lubriciousness in a form that displayed intemperate emotions and placed the body at the center of attention. Beyond that, theatre validated assembly and provided the occasion for a promiscuous mixing of people. Nor were the Puritans wrong. For whether or not sexual adventures were conducted on the stage, they had certainly historically been conducted in the auditorium, which in America continued to be a place of assignation, both amateur and professional, until well into the nineteenth century. It is notable that we know of one of the earliest performances in America, that of *Ye Bear and Ye Cubb* in 1665, because of attempts to ban it.

The fact is that despite the hostility that it encountered, theatre resisted proscription and has always proved adaptable to shifting circumstances, fashions, and values – adaptable to and expressive of such changes. Any history of theatre must therefore perforce be a history of the society that produced it. But such a history is not easily reconstituted, or not as easily as other cultural forms.

The history of the novel is easily reconstructed. We can be reasonably certain as to the logistics of publication and the nature of its readership. Easily carried, the book could survive sea crossings and frontier adventures, be picked up and put down at will, integrated with ease into the shifting rhythms of daily life. The price of purchase, provided that it or the form itself was not seen as subversive (as the novel itself was in South America for several centuries), was the only cost associated with an experience that could be public but that was usually private. Being itself a new form, it could take the impress of new experiences and prove adaptable to change. Beyond that, and crucially, books themselves are permanent. They survive. The history of the theatre is harder to establish. We have accounts of productions but not the thing itself. Texts may have survived, but performances have not, and performances are by their nature difficult to recuperate. We read accounts that speak, for example, of "realistic acting" in the knowledge that definitions of stage realism change with each generation. We acknowledge the dominance of English playwrights, actors, and stage designers but know less of the cultural, social, and even political uses to which such influences were put, since each society transforms the products it acquires from abroad, making them serve new purposes whatever the nature of their origin, whether it be British working-class fish and chips repackaged as franchised fast food for the middle class of America or British soap opera transformed into "Masterpiece Theatre" solely by virtue of crossing the Atlantic.

The form and nature of the novel remained open and unvalidated. It was, as its name implied, a new form whose development was coterminous with the settlement of America and in which America might be thought to have a hand. Henry James's "baggy monster" was by its nature undefined, sufficiently loose and expansive to incorporate a shifting reality. The ambition to create the "Great American Novel" may have been an act of hubris, but implicit in that ambition was a recognition of the fact that the novel could bend itself to new experiences, being fluid and without definable parameters. The theatre, with the authority of a longer tradition, shaped by other necessities than those of an emerging society, and subject to the limitations implicit in the form, was not so easily shoehorned into a novel environment, or, at least, not at first. The conventions of theatre, while permitting an imaginative expansion in time and space, constantly grounded that expansiveness in its own conventions. America did in fact play a major role in defining the modern novel. The situation with respect to theatre was different. Its tradition was external to the country. The early dominant playwrights were European, as were the principal actors. Theatre buildings followed European models as did styles of production. However, theatre changed as it necessarily adapted to new priorities, new conditions, and new assumptions. Nation building is not only a matter of political exhortation and physical exploration; it is a search for and justification of distinctiveness. Pride in geography and the new realities of the American continent eventually resulted in a call for equally distinctive cultural products that spoke not of an abandoned world but of a world in the making. An immigrant culture looks for justifications for the abandonment of old personal and social ties. Nostalgia for familiar if relinquished places and habits is balanced by a need to insist on the self-evident virtues of the new.

Certainly, revolution provoked a revolt against more than political values. The surprise, perhaps, is that England contrived to exercise cultural hegemony for as long as it did. Audiences who had just staged a successful revolt against the crown then took pleasure in plays that focused on the very principle of royalty they had supposedly rejected, just as in the twentieth century Americans remained fascinated by a British royal family itself reduced to largely theatrical significance.

In one sense the history of theatre in America recapitulates the history of America itself, in the attempt to stage a drama of social change while retaining a stabilizing sense of order. Just as the new topography was linguistically assimilated to the old (New London being sited on the River Thames), so cultural transformations were accommodated to familiar forms, styles, and characters. Plays, actors, and companies were imported along with other necessities, being required to do no more at first than announce their port of origin to establish their value. But they were also in time suspected to be incompatible with a new sense of national identity and as such began to take on a local coloration.

America was from the beginning a theatricalized environment, a space to be filled with significant action. Americans stood self-consciously upon a stage and prepared to perform exemplary actions. The Puritans knew the risk implicit in theatre, with its personations and pluralism of voices, but, as Nathaniel Hawthorne appreciated, they were hardly innocent of deploying its power, and not merely in the dramatic monologues in which its ministers reveled or the constructed dialogues they deployed in their published texts. When the sinner Hester Prynne was to be publicly chastised for breaching their codes, in *The Scarlet Letter,* she was made to costume herself and offered a text to speak before an audience sensitive to the symbolic meanings enacted before them. She was required to play out a drama of humiliation and repentance on a stage devised and constructed for the purpose of national consolidation. Encouraged to read the world symbolically, the Puritans saw no event as arbitrary: Each was expressive of an imminent meaning, each was staged by God for the enlightenment of man. The Quakers, likewise, suspicious though they were of masquerade, nonetheless were equally aware of participating in a drama greater than that staged in their own churches when persons rose to their feet and declared themselves in possession of their individual conscience and hence of their destiny.

When the theatre was banned, it cloaked itself in the very moral arguments that had been invoked to secure the ban, just as moralists had borrowed the techniques of a form they affected to despise. Theatrical performances were forbidden? Very well, early audiences were invited to plays in Boston and elsewhere under the guise of "moral lectures" or, later, informed of a "Histrionic Academy," where they would hear dissertations on subjects "Moral, Instructive and Entertaining," presumably in that order. Failing that, they could enjoy "Moral Dialogues" of the kind Puritans themselves had ostensibly engaged in. When David Douglass, who married Lewis Hallam's widow and reorganized the Hallam Company, played in New England in 1761, he presumably presented *Othello* as just such "a series of moral dialogues." Such a transparent subterfuge, however, can have fooled few, but moral sanctions were often embraced at the level of legal injunctions and ignored at the level of actual performance. Nor were bans ever really effective. In 1709 the Province of New York banned acting, along with cockfighting. Six years later Robert Hunter, governor of New York, published *Androboros,* a satire on the Provincial Court and the lieutenant governor. Prohibitions, though, continued. In 1750 the General Court of Massachusetts banned the theatre. Nine years later, in 1759, the House of Representatives of the Colony of Pennsylvania passed a law forbidding the showing and acting of plays, with a penalty of 500 pounds. In 1762 the New Hampshire House of Representatives refused a group of actors admission to perform in Portsmouth on the grounds that plays had a "peculiar influence on the minds of young people and greatly endanger their morals by giving them a taste for intriguing, amusement and pleasure" (quoted in Hornblow, I, 24).

The first Continental Congress, meeting in Philadelphia in 1774, passed a resolution in which its members committed themselves to discountenancing and discouraging "every species of extravagance and dissipation, especially all horse-racing, and all kinds of gaming, cock-fighting, exhibition of shews, plays, and other expensive diversions and entertainments." Revolution was not, they thought, compatible with drama. More than that, the Congress resolved that "any person holding office under the United States who shall act, promote, encourage or attend such play shall be deemed unworthy to hold office and shall be accordingly dismissed" (quoted in Moses, *American Dramatist,* 41). This did not, however, prevent George Washington from patronizing the theatre, or various colonies – most notably Maryland – from continuing to enjoy plays. The British, meanwhile, determined that if the Congress could close theatres, they could open them. General Burgoyne, himself an amateur actor and playwright, sanctioned theatrical performances in Boston's Faneuil Hall during the Revolution. Others followed in New York, where the manager of the company was Dr. Beaumont, surgeon general of the British Forces, and Major Williams of the artillery played the tragic heroes and his mistress the heroines. Theatre thus became the arena for a battle otherwise fought in the streets and fields.

Two weeks before the soldiers opened their season at the John Street Theatre, a notice appeared in the press announcing that the theatre would open "for the charitable purpose of relieving the Widows and Orphans of Sailors and Soldiers who have fallen in support of the Constitutional Rights of Great Britain in America" (quoted in Jared Brown, 33). The connection between theatre and politics could hardly be clearer, even if the plays – including *Tom Thumb, The Beaux' Strategem,* and *The Suspicious Husband* – showed little evidence of that link. In Philadelphia, likewise, war and theatre came together as the Southwark Theatre was used first as a hospital for the wounded before staging, in January 1778, fourteen plays, including *Henry IV.* Reportedly, Major John André, who was later sent to negotiate with Benedict Arnold – traitor or loyalist depending on your nationality – painted the scenery at the Southwark. This was the same André who was to become the subject of a play by William Dunlap.

Theatre also had high-level support. As president, George Washington had a regular seat, first at the John Street Theatre and then the Chestnut Street Theatre in Philadelphia, as the nation's capital moved relentlessly south. Abraham Lincoln was also a keen theatregoer until his enthusiasm was blunted by a bullet. John Wilkes Booth, an accomplished theatrical regicide, killed the president of the United States and then justified himself in Latin, thus dignifying the assassination with a touch of linguistic hubris and establishing a link to Shakespeare with the Latin tag from *Julius Caesar.* The killing itself was thus offered as an act of theatre while proclaiming a natural relationship between the public arena and the stage. Where else should a nation's tensions be staged but in a theatre? Where more appropriate to ring down the curtain on the Civil War?

Assassination was, thankfully, a rarity, but general disorder was for a long time epidemic. Washington Irving's account of his visit to the theatre, in 1801, reveals it to have been a kind of bear pit (fittingly, since, back in England, the bear pit and the theatre were usually situated next to one another and occasionally in the same building), in which audiences displayed little interest in the play and a great deal in themselves, a behavior common enough, to be sure, in England. If Frances Trollope is to be believed, however, America took this propensity to disruption to even greater heights, or depths. Reporting on a visit to the theatre in Cincinnati, she objected to the audience's habit of spitting and bursting into choruses of "Yankee Doodle." Because Cincinnati only boasted a population of one thousand, and was the only western town of any size until steam navigation opened up the Ohio and Mississippi rivers, this might be thought to be evidence of a certain frontier rawness. But things scarcely improved in Pittsburg, population twenty thousand, where she heard the sound of tobacco juice hitting the floor as a counterpoint to the declamation of actors, or in Washington, where the redoubtable Mrs. Trollope observed a man in the pit who "was seized with a violent fit of vomiting, which appeared not in the least to annoy or surprise his neighbors" (quoted in Hewitt, 120–21). And why should it? Theatre was not a site of decorum or a place to seek moral enlightenment or uplifting experiences. It was a source of entertainment, a place of public display, a stage where local pride could celebrate its accomplishments, and a nation's pretensions could find a form commensurate with its new energies. Nor was the audience then, as now, expected to sit in reverential silence. People went to participate, albeit at times overenthusiastically. Musicians in Boston once felt compelled to complain to the newspapers at being singled out as the target for peanuts and pieces of fruit, criticism being yet to establish a more formal language.

Perhaps such Dionysian behavior explains why, in 1824, the president of Yale College remarked that "to indulge a taste for playgoing means nothing more or less than the loss of that most valuable treasure the immortal soul" (quoted in Hornblow, I, 24). The theatre, however, predictably, survived. What Dionysus proposes the president of Yale is unlikely to frustrate. He did, however, have the virtue of precedent. In 1756 a memorandum from the Yale faculty charged that a play had been acted and that students and townsfolk had lingered "until after nine of the clock." Such playmaking, it was declared, "is of a very pernicious nature, tending to corrupt the morals of the seminary of religion and learning, and of mankind in general, and to the mispence of precious time and money" (quoted in Moody, *Dramas,* 2). Puritan afront and Yankee prudence, it seems, were beginning to come into alignment. The students were fined eight pence and the actors three shillings, as ever the actors being required to bear the greater moral responsibility.

The question arises as to what is American about the American theatre at a time when theatre was contested as a form and the uniqueness of the American experience was far from being fully articulated? America was, for more than 170 years, a colony and displayed the characteristics of a colony, conceding cultural primacy to an imperial center. Yet, even with independence, in the world of theatre England was still liable to define content, style, and subject matter. The British also had the advantage of boasting the preeminent playwright-poet in the English language, in the form of William Shakespeare, and of offering superior roles for actors, nostalgia for an abandoned country, cultural primacy for an educated elite, and moral sanction for a suspect art.

English theatre did, indeed, carry its own cachet, as did English actors, a fact satirized by Mark Twain in *The Adventures of Huckleberry Finn.* Not only did Shakespeare predominate, but even new London plays made their way quickly to America. Oliver Goldsmith's *She Stoops to Conquer* opened at the American Company's New York theatre less than five months after its London premiere. The English theatre was also experiencing a revival at the very time the American theatre was emerging, with Joseph Addison, William Congreve, John Dryden, George Farquhar, and William Wycherley producing work of distinction. The British also had a vested interest in exporting their culture, not to mention themselves. In a habit that has never entirely been abandoned, they eyed America as a place where fortunes were to be made and culture could be transmuted into gold. Beyond that, certain actors were driven out by financial distress just as much as were people in other crafts and professions. The elder Booth wrote from England to his father in America in 1826: "The distress is so excessive . . . that men look upon each other doubtful if they shall defend their own, or steal their neighbor's property. Famine stares all England in the face. As for the theatres, they are not thought of, much less patronized. The emigration to America will be very numerous, as it is hardly possible for the middling classes to keep body and soul together" (quoted in Graham, 10).

The Americans, for their part, demonstrated something of that "cultural cringe" that Australians were later to accuse themselves of displaying toward the "mother country," ceding authority to those presumed to be guardians of the flame.

From time to time American playwrights even presented themselves in the guise of Englishmen, the badge of theatrical respectability. Even when Royall Tyler wrote a comedy, *The Contrast,* for the Old American Company in which he mocked the Anglophilia of one of his characters, he did so in a play whose model was plainly English.

Writing in 1828, James Fenimore Cooper addressed the question of why America had failed to produce playwrights of the stature of its novelists and poets and why the theatre seemingly had less purchase on the culture than other genres. His answer was that not only was competition more fierce but the prevalence of foreigners meant that the theatre exerted "little influence on morals, politics or anything else" (quoted in Henry Williams, 5). Such foreigners spoke out of alien experiences. Their art was generated out of other necessities, reflected other priorities, engaged a social world distant in time and space. For Edgar Allan Poe, the son of an actor and actress, the answer was revolution: "We must discard all models. The Elizabethan theatre should be abandoned. We need thoughts of our own – principles of dramatic action drawn not from the 'old dramatists' but from the Fountain of Nature that can never grow old" (quoted in Moses, *American Dramatist,* 86). When Poe attacked Mrs. Mowatt's *Fashion* as an echo of eighteenth-century English comedy, she replied that American audiences seemed to find it an acceptable "counterfeit of life." Perhaps they did, but the feeling was growing that the American theatre needed to discover its own form, its own subjects, its own writers. In 1827 James K. Paulding called for a national drama that would celebrate the nation and the national character.

For Walt Whitman, the classic works of literature "had their rise in the great historic perturbations," which in part they reflected and embodied. The problem was that they thus reflected times past and declared, if not their irrelevance, then at least their unfitness to address what he called "the spiritual and democratic, the sceptres of the future" (quoted in Moses and Brown, 67). The understandable power of Shakespeare failed only insofar as it fell short of "satisfying modern and scientific and democratic American purposes." It was a drama that could not match "Yellowstone geysers, or Colorado ravines," and when ordinary people made their appearance it was only "as capital foils to the aristocracy," or as "the divertissement only of the elite of the castle. The comedies," thus, were "altogether non-acceptable to America and Democracy" (quoted in ibid., 68). There was, however, more wrong with the American theatre than the failure of American drama to match the stature of American geography or to address the concerns of a democratic people.

In 1847, in *The Brooklyn Eagle,* Whitman wrote a piece under the title "Miserable State of the Stage – Why Can't We Have Something Worth the Name of American Drama!" Largely denouncing the coarseness of the New York theatres, he attacked even the best – the Park – for being "a third-rate imitation of the best London theatres" offering "the cast off dramas and unengaged players of Great Britain," dramas in which "like garments which come second hand from gentleman to valet, everything fits awkwardly." Beyond that, however, he attacked a system that was to survive, in another form, into the twenty-first century – the star system, by which some "actor or actress flits about the country, playing a week here and a week there, bringing as his or her greatest recommendation, that of *novelty*". . . (quoted in ibid., 71). These stars would travel the country where audiences, thin on the ground before their arrival, "would crush each other to get a sight of some flippant well-puffed star, of no real merit" (Hewitt, 145).

According to actor-manager William B. Wood, the chief characteristics of such stars was vanity: "One star is very tall, and will play with no person of diminutive stature. . . . The next is very short, and will play with no one of ordinary height" (quoted in ibid., 152). The star would simply arrive in a given community, and rehearsal would amount to little more than moving people around the stage, ensuring that the star remained as close to center stage as possible. Whitman took this as further evidence of British theatrical corruption and called for "some American . . . not moulded in the opinions and long established ways of the English stage" to take the high ground, "revolutionize the drama . . . encourage American talent," and "give us American plays . . . fitted to American opinions and institutions" (quoted in Moses and Brown, 72). But the fact is that the theatre did not attract the country's leading writers. Sometimes their books were adapted – as was the case with Washington Irving, James Fenimore Cooper, and Harriet Beecher Stowe. Robert Montgomery Bird even flirted with the theatre, only to abandon it, while William Gilmore Simms wrote *Norma Morice* (1851) and Henry Wadsworth Longfellow *John Endecott* (1861) and *Giles Corey of the Salem Farms* (1868). But there were no plays from Irving, Poe, Hawthorne, or Melville. Bird had a simple answer. In 1831 he berated himself for turning to drama: "what a fool I was to think of writing plays! To be sure, they are much wanted. But these novels are much easier sort of things, and immortalize one's pocket much sooner" (quoted in Moody, *Dramas,* 236). One reason for this was that the actor Edwin Forrest purchased Bird's plays, whose owner-ship thereby passed directly to the actor, who subsequently made a fortune with them. But beyond such concerns, no play did what *The Last of the Mohicans, The Scarlet Letter,* or *Moby Dick* could be said to have done: define the nature of the culture, its ambiguities, tensions, and codes.

This was not, however, for want of trying. Royall Tyler's *The Contrast* (1787), produced by the American Company at the John Street Theatre, was very self-consciously designed to Americanize British forms. "The sentiments of the play," observed the reviewer of *The Daily Advertiser,* "are the effusions of an honest patriot heart" (quoted in Moses and Brown, 24). It was a play that, for all its English origins, introduced a figure, in the form of Jonathan, who was to appear in many more plays over the years as the embodiment of American common sense and the democratic spirit. Tyler graduated from Harvard in the year of American independence, saw military service, and rose to be chief justice of the Supreme Court of the State of Vermont. Perhaps unsurprisingly, patriotism was his strong suit. The program for *The Contrast* at the Charleston Theatre in 1793 carried the subtitle *The American Son of Liberty,* and the author was given as "Major Tyler, a citizen of the United States." When the play had first been performed, he had omitted his own name. He rectified this swiftly when success became apparent. When it was published, the list of subscribers was headed by President Washington, fol-lowed by the secretary of war and the attorney general.

America, thus, entered the theatre at least at the level of character and subject matter. The Revolution was restaged, with its confused motives adjusted and its heroes brushed down and placed at center stage in such plays as Mercy Warren's *The Group* (1775) and *The Defeat* (1773) or John Lea-cock's *The Fall of British Tyranny; or, American Liberty Triumphant* (1776). The Native American became a protagonist of the theatre even as Native Ameri-cans were relegated from history in the emerging national drama: Major Robert Rogers's *Ponteach; or, The Savages of America* (1766), John Augustus Stone's *Metamora; or, The Last of the Wampanoags* (1829), Robert Mont-gomery Bird's *Oralloosa, Son of the Incas* (1832), and George H. Miles's *De Soto, the Hero of the Mississippi* (1852). According to Richard Moody, seventy-five Indian dramas were written in the nineteenth century.[1] But more often than not, the plays were self-consciously offered as works whose chief virtue lay, at least in part, in their national origin. Thus, when *Metamora* was first staged, the actor Edwin Forrest, who had effectively commissioned it, hired Prosper M. Wetmore to add a prologue, which read:

> Tonight we test the strength of native powers,
> Subject, and bard, and actor, all are yours –
> 'Tis yours to judge, if worthy of a name,
> And bid them live within the halls of fame! (Moody, *Dramas,* 201)

The man usually identified as America's first playwright, William Dunlap (1766–1839), however, predated John Augustus Stone by several decades. He came from a Loyalist family and, in 1777, at the age of eleven, attended the New York theatre run by British soldiers. Later he made up for such youthful indiscretions by painting Washington's portrait and working at the John Street and Park theatres in New York. His numerous plays were frequently composed by freely appropriating whatever caught his eye, but he put an American spin on his works which attracted praise from those looking for nativist drama. Critics praised *The Father; or, American Shandyism* (1789) for its "allusions to characters and events, in which every friend of our country feels interested . . ." (quoted in Moses and Brown, 26). When the president appeared in the audience of *Darby's Return* (1789), an inconsequential piece, political patronage achieved what the piece itself could not as "the audience rose, and received him with the warmest acclamations – the genuine effusions of the hearts of Freemen" (quoted in ibid., 27). He wrote a number of patriotic interludes to mark the Fourth of July, including *The Glory of Columbia*, which opened on Independence Day, 1803. The setting for this play, based on his *André*, was the Revolutionary War. Setting and action compelled attention:

> Yorktown – at a distance is seen the town, with the British lines and the lines of the besiegers – nearer are the advanced batteries . . . cannonading commences from the besiegers on the town – explosion of a power magazine . . . the troops advance and carry it at bayonet's point – while this is yet doing, the nearest battery begins to cannonade and the American infantry attack and carry it with fixed bayonets, striking the English colors – shouts of victory. . . . A transparency descends, and an eagle is seen suspending a crown of laurel over the commander in chief, with this motto – "IMMORTAL-ITY TO WASHINGTON." (Quoted in Moody, *Dramas*, 90)

The play was carefully calculated to appeal to the American mood. When it was presented in 1812, it was given a subtitle: "What we have done, we can do." As ever, patriotism paid 110 cents on the dollar.

In 1828 Dunlap wrote *A Trip to Niagara*, which existed largely to serve the interests of the scene painter and a new scenic device called the Moving Diorama, which unfolded a moving panorama of the Hudson River in which eighteen scenes were portrayed over an area of 25,000 feet. Here, before Whitman saw fit to complain, was a theatre event precisely designed to celebrate the American scene, albeit in a drama that could hardly be said to have challenged the preeminence of contemporary British playwrights, let alone Shakespeare. The play itself included an array of characters who together constituted a cross section of Americans or proto-Americans, from a Frenchman and an Irishman to a Negro, a Yankee, and a Leatherstocking, the last dressed "as described in J. F. Cooper's *Pioneers*," showing the degree to which art fed on art rather than life.

Only the year before, the writer James K. Paulding had called for something very like *A Trip to Niagara,* though it is doubtful that he had moving
wallpaper in mind. He called for a national drama and then helpfully defined
precisely what he meant:

> By a national drama, we mean, not merely a class of dramatic productions,
> written by Americans, but one appealing directly to the national feeling –
> founded upon domestic incidents – illustrating or satirizing domestic man-
> ners, and, above all, displaying a generous chivalry in the maintenance and
> vindication of those great and illustrious peculiarities of situation and char-
> acter by which we are distinguished from all other nations. We do not hesi-
> tate to say that, next to the interests of eternal truth, there is no object
> more worthy the exercise of the highest attributes of mind than that of
> administering to the just pride of national character, inspiring a feeling for
> national glory, and inculcating a love of country. (Quoted in Moses, 83)

In the context, resisting the temptation to relegate eternal truth to second
place seems like an act of genuine humility. Nonetheless, for all the brashness
that then and now can send non-Americans into fits of self-congratulatory
laughter, what else had Shakespeare been to the British but a celebrant of
national values? Even during World War II the British government made
money available for Laurence Olivier, whose knighthood itself allied theatre
and country, to make a film version of *Henry V,* on the basis that although the
military victories in that play were at the expense of the French, the sight of
the British beating anyone at all at that stage of the war was felt to be a helpful
boost to the war effort. No wonder, then, that a country so sure of its national
purpose and yet so uncertain of its identity should see the theatre as a mechanism for defining that identity and, as a communal art, a means to unite its citizens who were uncertain about many things but clear about their national
superiority – if someone would only spell out the nature of that superiority.
Democracy, certainly, had something to do with it, and democratic ways were
frequently celebrated on the stage as the ways of the nobility were mocked.
But there was surely something else: a geography that challenged and provoked an adaptable character, native inhabitants who on the one hand offered
a glimpse of Rouseauesque virtue and on the other a challenge to civilized
ways, the melodrama of physical privation and moral conflict, the excitement
of novelty, the emergence of new ways of thought, new ways of being. The
novel took us into this territory. Could the theatre not do likewise?

Poe, writing in 1845, on the occasion of a production of Mrs. Mowatt's
Fashion, proposed another reason for the paucity of good American drama,
one of which H. L. Mencken would have approved, when he suggested that
"the intellect of an audience can never safely be fatigued by complexity"
(quoted in Moses and Brown, 61). This, presumably, prompted his complaint
that the author had an evident and objectionable desire to explain the

actions of her own play. His judgment that it "is a good play – compared with most American drama it is a *very* good play," is deliberately two-edged, suggesting a continuing sense of defensiveness, the more especially when he concluded his review in *The Broadway Journal* by adding that "by the natural principle of dramatic art, it is altogether unworthy of notice" (quoted, ibid., 63). He lamented, moreover, that dramatic art had remained stationary "while all of its sisters have been making rapid progress" (quoted in Moody, *Dramas,* 309). In his view, drama had been stultified for a hundred years.

Eighty years later, and with the supposed advantage of considerable hindsight, Montrose J. Moses, one of the first critics to attempt a history of American drama, observed that "we have not yet fully learned to meet life in our own way on the stage. We are still bringing the European mould and trying to make it fit American expression" (7). Surveying two hundred years of playwriting, he could find no play that would endure or take its place in the body of literature. Indeed, he insisted that:

> We would sacrifice our whole native heritage in drama now for one Shakespeare, for one Molière, for one Sheridan. Insomuch as we have no such single example, we content ourselves by watching the hesitant way in which American Drama has felt for its native life. And it has felt for it in its own way, an unsophisticated way, a childish way – fearful lest its soul be seen, its hunger and inadequacy stand confessed – putting on a brave front – the front of extreme youthful mentality. (9)

Noting that the American theatre had necessarily been dominated by English playwrights and English actors who had access to a heritage once common and still dominant, Moses characterized the struggle of the American theatre simultaneously to learn by imitation and to adapt to new values and circumstances. To him this had had unfortunate consequences insofar as American audiences

> have always wanted the square deal, have always wanted conventional virtue to conquer. The large heart rather than the evasive thought, the tense answer rather than the veiled meaning have always compelled sympathetic interest in an American crowd. . . . The quality of "uplift" has oftenest been associated with the word "American" . . . and so in many of our plays our ethics become doubtful, our manners become vulgar.

We have, he insisted, "never seriously dealt with history . . . never dealt with politics . . . never seriously faced our business problems" (quoted in Moody, *Dramas,* 10). The complaint is familiar, if not entirely justifiable. There had been very serious attempts to address an unfolding American experience.[2] A competition for an American play produced the hugely successful *Metamora; or, the Last of the Wampanoags,* by John Augustus Stone, which in turn provoked further plays about the relationship between whites and Indians. The adventures of Davy Crockett made their way onto the stage, as did the question of race, Harriet Beecher Stowe's *Uncle Tom's Cabin* being adapted for the stage and running successfully for many years.

Indeed, it is possible to find evidence of enlightenment in the theatre not always evident in the society to which it appeals. In *A Dialogue Between an Englishman and an Indian,* by John Smith, dating from 1779, the Indian – Joseph Yannhoontough – denounces the cruelty of Spanish and British alike in a manner that must have sat increasingly uneasily with those who chose to present the Indian as cruel and wanton, and this long before James Fenimore Cooper:

> Did not the Spaniards exercise such acts of cruelty towards the Indians of Mexico and Florida, and South America, as must make every humane mind, that attests to their horrid massacres and devastations, shudder? They wantonly butchered near twenty millions of those natives, and plundered their countries of almost infinite wealth. Without provocation, they would cut off the noses and ears of the Indians and give them to their dogs. . . . Were the Indians ever guilty of barbarity superior to this? . . . In case it is decreed, by Divine Providence, that the Indians must be extirpated, ought not those who have opportunity and ability, to use vigorous efforts, to save them? (Quoted in Moody, *Dramas,* 8)

To be sure, there is condescension in tone, voice, and subject but the spirit of the piece is clear enough. Robert Montgomery Bird's *The Gladiator* (1831) showed a similar sympathy. Bird himself recognized the mood that increasingly favored native products – "An American feeling was beginning to show itself on the theatrical matters. The managers of the Arch St. Theatre were Americans, all the chief performers were Americans and the play was written by an American" (ibid., 233) – but he was aware that his drama of slave rebellion in Imperial Rome was not without its significance to slave-owning America. As Richard Moody has observed, Bird knew that if it were played in a slave state he and all involved would be likely to end up in jail, not least because when he was writing it, "six hundred rebelling slaves under Nat Turner [were] murdering, ravishing and burning in Virginia." As Bird suggested, "If they had a Spartacus among them to organize the half million of Virginia, the hundred thousand of the other states, and lead them in the Crusade of Massacre, what a blessed example might they not give to the world of the excellences of slavery!" When Spartacus calls out, "Ho, slaves, arise! it is your hour to kill! / Kill and spare not – For wrath and liberty! – / Freedom for bondmen – freedom and revenge!" (quoted in ibid., 240), it was an injunction whose ambiguous force must have been felt by many even as it was claimed as a new classic of native drama and a new vehicle for America's premiere actor, Edwin Forrest.

As the nineteenth century progressed, so American realities were increasingly portrayed onstage, the wonders of technology being recreated with steam trains and riverboats amazing audiences, the very mechanisms by which theatre spread across the continent. The fact is that theatre accompanied Americans on their political journey from colony to nation, on their physical journey from Atlantic to Pacific, and on their ontological journey toward a sense of national identity.

For Fanny Kemble, though, Americans' theatricalized imaginations led them less into theatre buildings or to an admiration of the accomplishments of dramatists than into habits of display and public performance in which they were full participants rather than detached observers. "Our American progeny are," she insisted, "as a nation, devoid of the dramatic element, and have a considerable infusion of that which is theatrical delighting, like the Athenians of old, in processions, shows, speeches, oratory, demonstrations, celebrations, and declamations, and such displays of public and private sentiment as would be repugnant to English tastes and feelings" (quoted in Moses, *American Dramatist,* 82). It is hard not to recognize the continuing truth of such an observation. America is, and always has been, a theatricalized society, staging itself self-consciously as a Great Experiment with a Manifest Destiny, a society free of history, inviting the world to be an audience to its birth and development. As Fanny Kemble suggests, America has simply displaced its theatricalizing impulse from the theatre into society. Perhaps that is why for so long America did not produce its playwrights but did produce the star actors to whom Whitman took such exception. For the actor was to become the paradigm of success, an exemplar of that ability to transform oneself that was a cultural and social imperative. He bestrode the stage as the American was to bestride the continent, reinventing himself in a gesture that had the sanction of national myth.

The first native-born American actor to prove successful at home and abroad fitted this role perfectly. Edwin Forrest was influenced by a British actor, Edmund Kean, who visited the country a second time in 1825 and with whom Forrest played in a number of Shakespearean tragedies. However, Forrest's style seemed entirely appropriate to a society still in the business of subordinating the natural world and confidently forging a new identity. Forrest was a physical actor who performed strenuous exercises (too strenuous, perhaps, as he died of apoplexy in his sixties while still insisting on submitting his body to daily trial) and had a powerful and dominating voice. At one point, when the role of the Indian chief in *Metamora* was a major part in his repertoire, he lived with an Indian tribe, "adopted their habits, shared their food, slept in their huts . . . left the print of his moccasins on the hunting ground" while "the crack of his rifle echoed along the rocky sides of the hills and lakes" (Wilson, *American Acting,* 24). His fight scenes were apparently so realistic and physical that other actors went in fear, and not unreasonably, for at least one of them reportedly lost several teeth in the course of combat. As one critic observed, "Give him a hero fired with democratic passions who slashed out at a tyrant, and he could arouse an audience to shouting" (ibid., 27). It was a muscularity and occasionally a crudity that some criticized but that plainly appealed to audiences whose direct involvement is equally underlined in the above observation. A culture constituting itself out of an assertive individualism requires its exemplary figures, and Proteus is no less a god of America than of acting. The audience, in other words, had a vested interest in the stars whom they conspired to create and who in turn granted them the absolution of reflected significance. The star actor may be granted a powerful role in other societies. In England he was eventually allowed provisional entrée into the ranks of the nobility. But in America that synchronicity with national ambitions for a reconstituted self, confidently in possession of destiny, guaranteed and continues to guarantee the actor a central function in the culture.

The theatre also served a double role. A blend of the Apollonian and the Dionysiac, it was simultaneously an arena of disorder, with the audience throwing apples and spitting, and an assertion of order, a cooperative enterprise in which the talents of the individual shone the brighter for their being deployed in a communal enterprise. It reflected frontier anarchy and invention on the one hand and civilized values on the other. The actor expressed a similar ambiguity. Always on the fringe of society, never quite wholly assimilated to its values, never quite governed by its principles, the actor was an embodiment of that freedom announced as a national birthright if denied by social constraints. The actors experienced both adulation and social ostracism. Like that other hero of American expansionism, the frontiersman, they were admired for their bravado, their theatrical posturing, but shunned for their asocial nature. Meanwhile, the theatre's aura of the illicit constituted part of its attraction, as emotions and actions proscribed beyond its doors were vicariously experienced within its bounds.

Part of the illicit power of the novel lies in its ability to carry the reader into places he or she might not otherwise venture, to hear and see what is otherwise concealed or forbidden, to gain vicarious knowledge of that which, outside the parameters of fiction, would be prohibited. But this at least is a private negotiation. Theatre is a public experience with the risk of mutual contamination and the implication of social sanction. It is more dangerous as we jointly observe the breachings of decorum and mores and thus are seen publicly to take enjoyment or satisfaction from such violations of the norm. The line from "legitimate" theatre to burlesque is therefore logical, as the Puritans would have affirmed, and indeed their descendants did in the guise of censors and committees of public decency.

The theatre was thus an arena in which society engaged its tensions and in some degree enacted its conflicts. And, as though to demonstrate the truth of this, it saw riots break out in its auditoriums and, as we have noted, a president assassinated by an actor who had honed his skills as an assassin by performing the same role on the stage. And if the theatre was not always inflammatory, it was certainly flammable. Theatres burned down with such regularity that fire companies formed a close relationship with them. The Jenny Lind Theatre in San Francisco burned down, was rebuilt, and burned down again two days later. The Bowery Theatre in New York was burned down no fewer than six times. At the very least you have to say that the American commitment to theatre was not easily diminished. Sometimes the connection with social friction was direct. Hallam and Douglass's New York theatre was burned down during an anti-British riot, and the Astor Place riot, in which many died, was inspired by rivalry between a British and American actor. More often the cause lay in lighting wooden buildings with candles, whose habit of dripping on theatregoers was irritating but whose incendiary properties lit up many a night sky, or unbridled gas cocks that created a combustible explosion. That the theatre was the scene of riots, however, was a reminder of its power to inflame passions and stage a national drama as the country moved from revolution to civil war.

Theatre spread with the population. The first play in English in California was performed by American soldiers in 1847. The first professional performance took place two years later in the Eagle Theatre, Sacramento. Its popularity can be judged by its box office prices: two dollars and three dollars, and this in the mid-nineteenth century. Two years after that, San Francisco, a lawless town, was also a theatre town, with three theatres, one of which was French. The Mormons took theatre first to their settlement at Nauvoo, Illinois, and then to Salt Lake City, where Brigham Young built a theatre in 1861. Not for them the Puritan distrust of drama.

And the reality of America did generate new forms. A rapidly expanding frontier created a demand for theatre that necessitated something more than conventional buildings. Americans had always had a capacity to construct these, and with incredible speed, but widely scattered and often small communities lacked the resources to erect them or the audiences to sustain them. This was not Europe. Where were the roads? How could you transport actors, scenery, and props over open territory? The answer was: anyhow you could. They traveled by wagons, by the river system, and by trains. By the mid-1850s several railroad lines had crossed the Mississippi, and the transcontinental line was completed in 1869, facilitating travel for companies and stars. In the case of rivers, though, this was something more than a simple means of transportation. The Americanizing of theatre, it became plain, meant a great deal more than the production of American-authored plays about American characters.

Noah Ludlow's flatboat, on which he and his company first drifted down the Allegheny, and subsequently the Ohio and Mississippi, provided a rudimentary theatre as well as a means to allow the ramshackle but grandly named American Theatrical Commonwealth Company to penetrate the interior of an expanding frontier. It was followed, though, by ever grander ventures. Philip Graham, in *Showboats: The History of an American Institution,* charts their rise, beginning with William Chapman and his family, driven from England by financial recession, who launched their Floating Theatre on the Ohio in 1831, a flatboat that drifted with no power down to New Orleans, where, lacking its own means of propulsion to attempt the return journey, it was to be broken up. Among the Chapmans' repertoire was William Dunlap's version of Kotzebue's *Stranger.* Eventually, the flatboat gave way to a steamboat, and a new era began.

Nor were the new showboats restricted to the rivers. As Graham shows, they also invaded the growing canal system – the Little Miami Canal in Ohio, the Wabash Canal, and the Northern Mississippi, as well as the Erie Canal, which opened in 1825. Theatre went wherever it could and by whatever means it could.

It is hard to re-create now the evident hunger for performance beyond the urban centers of the East Coast. Visiting writers, singers, lecturers, and circuses were seized upon with avidity. Religious meetings were charged with theatrical energy. It was partly a matter of distraction from the business of expansion and settlement, partly a desire to convince that distance had not severed them from the advantages offered by eastern cities. And, in a gesture that would ultimately itself be seen as a defining characteristic of the new society, those who brought shows to the interior did so by adapting familiar forms to new necessities. Thus the primitive flatboat, with its crew of frequently bedraggled actors, gave way to great floating theatres that staged everything from plays to circuses for audiences whose numbers frequently exceeded those that would have been accommodated in a conventional building. Spalding and Rogers's Floating Circus Palace, built in 1851, seated nearly thirty-five hundred people and was two hundred feet long. On the towboat in its wake, concerts were given and plays performed. Bear pit and theatre once again coexisted. In 1845 the showboat reached New York in the form of Chapman's Temple of the Muses, lit by gas specially manufactured on board and seating twelve hundred people. The boat moved from one "slip" to another along the river, thus making itself convenient to a number of different communities, before moving up river and then traveling more widely under what was known as "a coasting license."

There were, to be sure, conventional theatres that were the showboat's equal. New York's Bowery Theatre seated four thousand in 1845 but, then, New York City had a population, only five years later, of six hundred thousand. The river boats served the needs of a more widely scattered population, as did stock companies, which ranged throughout a country in which newly established towns grew with astonishing rapidity. It has been estimated that by 1850 there were more than fifty stock companies, and by 1880 thirty-five hundred towns in which plays were regularly performed, with some five thousand playhouses served by two hundred fifty companies and five thousand actors.

The theatre may originally have been treated with deep suspicion, particularly in the northern colonies. It may never entirely have purged itself of implications of the disreputable, the marginal, and the illicit. But the hunger for theatre was evident from the days when the injunctions of colonial authorities and even of the assembled dignitaries of the Continental Congress were disobeyed by the ordinary citizen and by the man who would be the first president of the United States alike. No barrier, political, religious, or geographic, would prove sufficient to prevent theatre's spread, along its rivers, railroads, and tracks, across a space that in time became a country whose invention itself was presented as one of the great public spectacles. And if that drama was frequently presented as a melodrama, in which freedom challenged tyranny, the virtuously new rejected the villainously old, and humans struggled against nature to achieve their destiny, then why should we wonder that melodrama eventually proved the natural mode of the American theatre in its formative years? The posturing actor, compelling attention, was a paradigm, a prototype, an ideal for a society that genuinely believed that the curtain had risen on a new epic in which human possibility would stand as an animating faith and Proteus be elevated to a central position.

Notes

1 See Moody, *Dramas,* 203. For an even more extensive list of plays about Native Americans in the same period, see Wilmeth, "Tentative Checklist of Indian Plays."

2 For a recent examination of the many conflicting cultural and academic reasons for the neglect and frequent dismissal of American drama as a legitimate literary form, see Susan Harris Smith, *American Drama: The Bastard Art.*

Timeline: Beginnings to 1870
Compiled by Don B. Wilmeth and Jonathan Curley

This chronological chart by years (only major events are ordered chronologically within each year) provides a quick overview of major events during the time period covered by this volume. More important, the inclusion of factual details here allows authors of individual chapters freedom to approach their topics with greater flexibility and without the contraints of a traditional chronological, encyclopedic history. Briefly noted in the timeline are the following: in column one, major theatrical events in the history of the American theatre; in column two, other colonial or U.S. cultural and historical events of significance, or representative data; and in column three, key historical and cultural events from other parts of the world (with special attention given to England because of its great influence on early American theatre), included in order to provide points of reference in a wider context and to suggest not only influences but advances that frequently differ significantly from similar phenomena in Colonial America or the early years of the United States.

DATES	THEATRE EVENTS IN AMERICA	SELECTED HISTORICAL/CULTURAL EVENTS IN AMERICA	SELECTED HISTORICAL/CULTURAL EVENTS THROUGHOUT THE WORLD
1000		Leif Eriksson makes three landfalls on North American continent.	
1485–1509			Reign of Henry VII, first Tudor king of England.
1492		Columbus explores New World.	
1493–94		Spain and Portugal divide southern New World.	
1494–1559			Italian Wars (Spain, France, and Holy Roman Empire clash over control of Italy).
1497		Cabot claims eastern North America for England.	
1509–47			Henry VIII is king of England.

1513	Balboa sights Pacific Ocean.	
1516	Ponce de León sails from Puerto Rico and discovers Florida (returns in 1521).	Thomas More's *Utopia*.
1517		Martin Luther posts 95 theses, sparking Protestant Reformation.
c. 1518		Italian writer Niccolò Machiavelli's play *The Mandrake*.
1519	Cortés conquers Aztec empire in Mexico for Spain.	Charles V elected Holy Roman Emperor.
1520–22		Magellan circumnavigates the globe.
1524	Conqueror Cortés brings puppet tradition with him to New World.	
1528–36	Jean Cabeza de Vaca explores American Gulf Plains (Texas to Mexico).	
1532	Pizarro conquers Peru.	Machiavelli's *The Prince*.
1533		Birth of Elizabeth I of England.
1533–84		Ivan IV the Terrible reigns as first Russian czar.
1534	Jacques Cartier discovers St. Lawrence River; catalyst for French exploration of river and of lands west to Great Lakes.	
1540–42	Coronado is first European to explore Arizona and New Mexico.	
1541	Hernando de Soto (who landed in Tampa, Florida in 1539) and men are first whites to see Mississippi River.	

DATES	THEATRE EVENTS IN AMERICA	SELECTED HISTORICAL/CULTURAL EVENTS IN AMERICA	SELECTED HISTORICAL/CULTURAL EVENTS THROUGHOUT THE WORLD
1543			Copernicus refutes geocentric theory of the universe.
1545–63			Council of Trent (Catholic reform).
1546			Francis I begins building Louvre as royal art museum in Paris.
1550			Nicholas Udall's English interlude, *Ralph Roister Doister.*
1553–58			Mary I is queen of England.
1556			Philip II becomes king of Spain, Netherlands, New World.
1558–1603			Elizabeth I is queen of England.
1562			Thomas Norton and Thomas Sackville's *Gorboduc,* first native English tragedy.
1564			Birth of William Shakespeare (d. 1616) and Christopher Marlowe (d. 1593).
1565		Spanish found St. Augustine, Florida.	*Gammer Gurton's Needle* performed at Christ's Church, Cambridge.
1567	Two comedias performed at Spanish mission in Tequesta, Florida (near Miami).		
1570s	Records of Corpus Christi festivities in Cuba.		
1572			Birth of Ben Jonson (d. 1637).
1584		Virginia named for virgin queen Elizabeth by Sir Walter Raleigh.	English writer Thomas Kyd's *The Spanish Tragedy* (perhaps written as late as 1589).

Year		
1586		Rose Theatre built in London.
1587	Lost colony of Roanoke settled.	Spanish Armada defeated by English.
1588		Marlowe's play *Edward II*.
1590	Comedias and interludes performed in Cuba.	Illustrated edition of Thomas Harriot's *A Brief and True Report of the New Found Land of Virginia* (unillustrated ed., 1588).
1592		Shakespeare's *Richard III*.
1595		Plague closes London theatres for two years.
1596		Poet-playwright Torquato Tosso dies (b. 1544).
1597		Shakespeare's *The Merchant of Venice*. Philosopher René Descartes born (d. 1650).
1598	Spanish comedia by Marcos Farfán presented (April) north of Rio Grande River in New Mexico (deals with Farfán's conquests there). Also religious plays by Juan de Oñate's band of colonizers.	Fyodor I of Russia dies; Boris Godunov elected czar by national assembly after seizing throne.
1599		London's first Globe Theatre built.
1600		Edmund Spenser dies (b. 1552). English East India Company founded. Thomas Dekker's play *The Shoemaker's Holiday*.
1601		Shakespeare's *Hamlet*. Marlowe's *The Tragical History of Dr. Faustus*.

DATES	THEATRE EVENTS IN AMERICA	SELECTED HISTORICAL/CULTURAL EVENTS IN AMERICA	SELECTED HISTORICAL/CULTURAL EVENTS THROUGHOUT THE WORLD
1603			Death of Queen Elizabeth I; accession of James I.
1604			Thomas Heywood's play *A Woman Killed with Kindness*. Shakespeare's *Othello*.
1605		French and Indian hostilities.	Guy Fawkes plot against James I. Cervantes begins *Don Quixote*. Shakespeare's *King Lear* and *Macbeth*.
1606	French masque, *The Theatre of Neptune in New France* by Marc Lescarbot, seen in November at Port Royal, Acadia (Nova Scotia).	Virginia Company of London granted royal charter; sends 120 to Virginia.	Birth of Pierre Corneille (d. 1684).
1607		Jamestown, Virginia, settlement.	Ben Jonson's play *Volpone*. Artist Rembrandt van Rijn born (d. 1669).
1609		Hudson River, sighted by de Verrazano in 1542, explored by Henry Hudson.	Composer Monteverdi's *Orfeo*. Galileo invents telescope.
1610		Hudson discovers Hudson's Bay.	Ben Jonson's play *The Alchemist*. Michelangelo Caravaggio dies (b. 1579).
1611		First Presbyterian congregation in colonies organized at Jamestown.	Publication of King James version of the *Bible*. Dutch begin trade with Japan. James I dissolves Parliament. Shakespeare's *The Tempest*.

1612	John Smith's *A Map of Virginia, with a Description of the Country; the Commodies, People, Government and Religion; The Proceedings of the English Colony in Virginia.*	John Webster's *The White Devil.*
1613	John Rolfe plants tobacco in Virginia.	
1614	Dutch trading post (New Amsterdam) in what becomes New York City.	Hope Theatre and second Globe open.
1616	Native American princess Pocahontas marries John Rolfe.	Shakespeare dies.
1618	Smallpox epidemic in northern New England.	Sir Walter Raleigh returns to England and is executed.
1618–48		Thirty Years' War (devastates Holy Roman Empire).
1619	First slaves in Jamestown.	Spanish playwright Lope de Vega's *Fuenteovejuna (The Sheepwell).*
1620	First representative assembly in Colonies (Virginia). Signing of Mayflower Compact; Plymouth, Massachusetts, Pilgrim settlement.	
1621		Burton's *The Anatomy of Melancholy.*
1622	Indian–English war in Virginia (ends 1625).	Birth of Molière (d. 1673).
1623	British establish first settlement at Nova Scotia.	First folio of Shakespeare's plays.

DATES	THEATRE EVENTS IN AMERICA	SELECTED HISTORICAL/CULTURAL EVENTS IN AMERICA	SELECTED HISTORICAL/CULTURAL EVENTS THROUGHOUT THE WORLD
1623			Thomas Middleton and William Rowley's play *The Changling*.
1624		John Smith's *The General History of Virginia, New England, and the Summer Isles*.	
1625		Fort Amsterdam founded (22 April) on lower tip of Manhattan Island by Dutch West India Company.	Philip Massinger's play *A New Way to Pay Old Debts*.
1627			Death of James I; accession of Charles I.
			Coliseo built in Mexico City.
1628		Captain Miles Standish of Plymouth attacks Thomas Morton and his group.	English writer John Gay's ballad opera *The Beggar's Opera*.
1629		Massachusetts Bay Colony established by Puritans led by John Winthrop.	
c. 1630			Spanish playwright Pedro Calderón de la Barca's *Life is a Dream*.
1631			John Donne (b. 1572?) dies.
1632		Boston established as capital of Massachusetts.	First London coffee shop opens.
		Calvert, Lord Baltimore, receives charter for Maryland colony.	John Locke (d. 1704) born.
1633			English dramatist James Shirley's play *The Gamester*.
1634		First Maryland settlement.	
1635		Boston Latin School founded.	
		Roger Williams flees Massachusetts with followers to Rhode Island; founds Providence.	

Year		
1636	Founding of Harvard College.	
1637	First Indian War; against Pequots.	French playwright Pierre Corneille's *Le Cid.*
		French philospher René Descartes presents his "method of doubt" in *Discourse on Method.*
1638	First Colonial printing press in Cambridge, Massachusetts.	New masquing house built in London's Whitehall.
1639	Roger Williams establishes first Baptist Church in America in Providence, Rhode Island.	Birth of French dramatist Jean Racine (d. 1699).
1642	Basic literary law in Massachusetts.	London theatres closed by Parliament; beginning of English Civil War.
	Sir William Berkeley governor of Virginia.	Cardinal Richelieu (b. 1585) dies.
1643–1715		Reign of Louis XIV of France.
1643	New England Federation founded.	
1644		Globe Theatre torn down in London.
1647	Peter Stuyvesant governor of New Amsterdam.	
1648		First Quaker Society in England.
1649	John Winthrop, governor of Massachusetts Bay Colony, dies.	Beheading of Charles I of England; Commonwealth (Lord Protector, 1653) till 1660.
1650	Anne Bradstreet's anthology of poetry, *The Tenth Muse Lately Sprung Up in America.*	Charles II proclaimed king in Scotland.
	First iron exported from Massachusetts to England.	

DATES	THEATRE EVENTS IN AMERICA	SELECTED HISTORICAL/CULTURAL EVENTS IN AMERICA	SELECTED HISTORICAL/CULTURAL EVENTS THROUGHOUT THE WORLD
1653–58			Protectorate under Oliver Cromwell (d. 1658).
1653			Taj Mahal built at Agra, India.
1655		Dutch end Swedish rule in North America by occupying Fort Casimir on Delaware River.	Cromwell dissolves Parliament.
1657		Quakers sent from New Amsterdam to Rhode Island.	
1660			Charles II restores English monarchy; theatres reopen with patents to Davenant and Killigrew.
			Vauxhall Gardens open in London; closes 1859.
			Samuel Pepys's diary (through 1669).
1661			The professional actress (rather than the boy player) introduced to the English stage.
1662			Boyle's law of gas pressure.
			Royal Society founded in England.
1663		First hospital in colonies (Long Island, N.Y.).	Opening of London's Drury Lane Theatre (Theatre Royal).
		Charters granted to Rhode Island and Carolina (eight proprietors).	Samuel Butler's *Hudibras* (completed 1678).
1664	Captive African slaves forced to sing and dance for crew of English slave ship *Hannibal*.	English control New Amsterdam, renamed New York.	Molière's comedy *Tartuffe* premieres at Versailles.

1665	Nonextant *Ye Bear and Ye Cubb* by William Darby staged in Accomac County, Virginia (Aug.). First recorded play in English presented in Colonies.	New Jersey colony founded.	John Dryden's *The Indian Emperor, or The Conquest of Mexico* staged at London Theatre Royal, Bridges Street.
1666			Great Plague of London and fire.
			Molière's *The Misanthrope* staged at the Palais-Royal, Paris.
1667		Conclusion of Anglo–Dutch War.	John Milton's *Paradise Lost*.
1668			Society of Friends (Quakers) founded.
			La Fontaine's *Fables* (completed 1694).
1669		John Eliot's *The Indian Primer*.	
1670		Founding of Charleston, South Carolina.	William Congreve born (d. 1729).
			British establish Hudson's Bay Company for development of territories in Canada.
1671		Quakers in Great Britain and America object to slavery of blacks.	
1672		Third Anglo–Dutch War.	Royal African Company (for slave trade) founded.
1674		Increase Mather's (1639–1723) sermon "The Day of Trouble Is Near."	New Drury Lane Theatre opens after 1672 fire.
1675		King Philip's War (Iroquois Confederacy vs. New England Confederacy).	English playwright William Wycherley's (1640?–1716) comedy *The Country Wife*.
1676		Jamestown burns.	
1677		Culpepper's Rebellion (to 1679); Carolina colony rebels against British taxation.	Jean Racine's play *Phèdre*.
			English author Aphra Behn's play *The Rover*, Part 1.

DATES	THEATRE EVENTS IN AMERICA	SELECTED HISTORICAL/CULTURAL EVENTS IN AMERICA	SELECTED HISTORICAL/CULTURAL EVENTS THROUGHOUT THE WORLD
1678		Anne Bradstreet, *Several Poems*, published posthumously.	John Bunyan's *Pilgrim's Progress*.
1680		Banister-back chair first appears in New England.	Comédie-Française established in Paris.
1681		William Penn receives charter for Quaker colony of Pennsylvania from Charles II.	Death of Spanish playwright Caldéron.
1682		Founding of Philadelphia as capital of Penn's colony.	Thomas Otway's *Venice Preserv'd*.
		Sieur de La Salle claims lower Mississippi Valley for France; named Louisiana after Louis IV.	
1685			Death of Charles II: accession of James II.
1687	Increase Mather's Puritan attack on theatre (with Judge Samuel Sewall, squelches attempt by John Wing to set up theatre in his tavern).	First Anglican church service in Boston.	Isaac Newton's theory of gravity.
1688			Glorious Revolution against James II of England (replaced by William and Mary).
1689		King William's War (to 1697) marks beginning of sporadic skirmishes between France and Britain for control of North American territories.	Accession of William and Mary.
		First U.S. secondary school founded in Pennsylvania.	
1690	*Gustavus Vasa*, by Harvard student Benjamin Colman, possibly first play by American, staged.	Highboy invented by adding short legs to chest of drawers.	English philosopher John Locke's *Essay Concerning Human Understanding* and *Two Treatises on Government*.

Year			
1691–95	Count Frontenac produces two plays in Quebec (perhaps by Corneille?).	First newspaper in Colonies, *Publick Occurrences*, printed in Boston 25 September but shut down days later.	Henry Purcell composes *The Fairy Queen*.
1691		First postal service in Colonies.	
1692		Salem, Massachusetts, witch trials.	
1693		Founding of William and Mary College in Williamsburg, Virginia. Postal service between Philadelphia and New York.	
1698	Interest in student dramatics mentioned in Harvard College President's diary.		Jeremy Collier's *A Short View of the Immorality and Profaneness of the English Stage* (London).
1700		Samuel Sewall's *The Selling of Joseph*, an antislavery book.	Congreve's *The Way of the World* premieres.
1701–13			War of Spanish Succession.
1701		Yale University founded.	English writer Nicholas Rowe's play *Tamerlane* at Lincoln's Inn Fields Theatre.
1702	"Pastoral Colloquy" recited for governor by students at William and Mary College.		Accession of Queen Anne in England.
1703	British actor Anthony Aston performs in Charleston (Jan.); claims to have written play on "subject of the country."		Nicholas Rowe's *The Fair Penitent* premieres at London's Lincoln's Inn Fields Theatre in May.
1705	Pennsylvania Assembly prohibits "stage-plays, masks, revels."		

DATES	THEATRE EVENTS IN AMERICA	SELECTED HISTORICAL/CULTURAL EVENTS IN AMERICA	SELECTED HISTORICAL/CULTURAL EVENTS THROUGHOUT THE WORLD
1706		Presbyterian Church established in America by Irish churchman Francis Makemie.	George Farquhar's *The Recruiting Officer* at London's Drury Lane Theatre.
1707			Birth of Italian comic writer Carlo Goldoni.
1709	Governor's Council in New York forbids "play acting and prize fighting" (6 May).		
1712		Slave revolt in New York City.	
1713			Joseph Addison's play *Cato*.
1714	Judge Samuel Sewall in Boston opposes proposal to stage play (unknown) in Council Chamber.		Alexander Pope's *The Rape of the Lock*. German physicist Gabriel Fahrenheit constructs mercury thermometer. Queen Anne dies, succeeded by George I of the House of Hanover.
1715	*Androboros*, by Governor Robert Hunter of New York, first known play written and published in America.		Jacobite Rebellion.
1716	Playhouse opens in Williamsburg, Virginia (contract dated 11 July); erected by William Levingston with Charles and Mary Stagg as leading actors.		
1718		New Orleans founded.	Quadruple Alliance formed.
1719			Daniel Defoe's *Robinson Crusoe*.
1720		Boston's population, 12,000; Philadelphia, 10,000; New York City, 7,000.	Little Theatre in the Haymarket, London, opens inauspiciously.

Year		
	Beginning of Great Awakening revival in Colonies, stimulated by Protestant evangelists such as Jonathan Edwards.	Jonathan Swift's *Gulliver's Travels*.
1721	Birth of Jacob Philadelphia (born Meyer), first native-born conjuror to gain international acclaim.	George II king of England.
1723	First smallpox inoculations given in Colonies.	John Gay's *The Beggar's Opera* at London's Lincoln's Inn Fields Theatre.
1724	Pauper schools established in Maryland.	Birth of German writer Gotthold Ephraim Lessing (d. 1781).
1725	First acting company in Philadelphia recorded.	Birth of playwright-poet Oliver Goldsmith (d. 1774).
1726	Acrobats and comedians appear at "New Booth" on Society Hill, Philadelphia, a makeshift playhouse. Considered by some the first circus act.	Henry Fielding's *Tom Thumb* opens April at Drury Lane Theatre.
1727–60	Puppet "Punch" introduced to Colonies (perhaps earlier).	George Lillo's *The London Merchant* at Drury Lane Theatre.
1728	First lion exhibited in Colonies.	
1729		
1730	Wallpaper becomes popular among wealthy Colonial merchants.	
1731	Amateur production in New York of *Romeo and Juliet*, first Shakespearean play on the American stage.	

DATES	THEATRE EVENTS IN AMERICA	SELECTED HISTORICAL/CULTURAL EVENTS IN AMERICA	SELECTED HISTORICAL/CULTURAL EVENTS THROUGHOUT THE WORLD
1732	*The Recruiting Officer* at "New Theatre" (6 Dec.) in New York (location unknown, possibly converted warehouse on Pearl Street).	Ben Franklin's *Poor Richard's Almanack* (continued through 1747) begins publication.	London's Covent Garden Theatre opens in December with Congreve's *The Way of the World*.
1733		English settlers move into Georgia.	
		The New York Weekly Journal launched.	
1735	First recorded production in Charleston of Otway's *The Orphan*, in courtroom (Jan.).		
1736	Dock Street Theatre, Charleston (Charles Town), opens (12 Feb.); burns 1840.		
	William and Mary students stage *Cato* (10 Sept.) and several Restoration comedies thereafter.		
	Flora; or, Hob in the Wall, first opera performed in Colonies (Charleston).		
1737		St. Patrick's Day (17 March) first celebrated in United States.	Passage of Licensing Act in England; requires licensing of plays by Lord Chamberlain and restricts authorized theatres.
1738–9	Early pantomime, tricks of Harlequin and Scaramouche, performed at Henry Holt's Long Room in New York City.		
1739		Slave revolt in South Carolina.	Venetian playwright Carlo Goldoni's *The Man of the World* premieres in March in Venice.
1740		Founding of University of Pennsylvania.	

Year			
1741	John Moody Theatre Company in Jamaica (David Douglass a member).	*American Magazine* begins in Philadelphia and leads to many others by mid-1800s.	Charles Macklin as Shylock on London stage; David Garrick debuts as Richard III.
1742		Room-heating stoves invented by Benjamin Franklin.	George Friedrich Handel composes *The Messiah.*
1745		Pennsylvania Quakers establish first elementary schools for blacks.	
1746		Founding of Princeton University (N.J.).	
1747			Actor-playwright David Garrick becomes manager of Drury Lane Theatre.
1748	Birth of playwright H. H. Brackenridge.		
1749	Walter Murray and Thomas Kean company present Addison's *Cato* in Plumstead's Warehouse, Philadelphia, the first recorded professional company with any history.	Founding of Washington and Lee University, Lexington, Virginia.	Birth of Johann Wolfgang von Goethe (d. 1832).
1750	Otway's *The Orphan* presented by two unidentified Englishmen in Boston Coffee House but melee leads to proscription of stage plays by General Court. Murray and Kean arrive in New York (Feb.); open with *Richard III* (5 March) in Nassau Street Playhouse (room in large building); perform until spring 1751. General Court of Massachusetts passes edict to "Prevent Stage-Plays and other Theatrical Entertainments."	Massachusetts produces rum from molasses, often sold to Puritan distillers by slave traders, in 63 distilleries. Stagecoach from Philadelphia to New York requires three eighteen-hour days.	Death of Johann Sebastian Bach. World population reaches 750 million. Thomas Gray's "Elegy Written in a Country Church Yard."

DATES	THEATRE EVENTS IN AMERICA	SELECTED HISTORICAL/CULTURAL EVENTS IN AMERICA	SELECTED HISTORICAL/CULTURAL EVENTS THROUGHOUT THE WORLD
1751	David Douglass performs in the West Indies. Murray and Kean Playhouse (crudely built wooden theatre) opens in Williamsburg (Oct.), initiating "Virginia Company of Comedians," which lasts twenty years.		Denis Diderot's *Encyclopedia* begun (completed 1772).
1752	Lewis Hallam (1714–56) and his London Company of Comedians first appear in Williamsburg (15 Sept.) in *Merchant of Venice* and the afterpiece, *The Anatomist*.	Franklin's electricity experiment with a kite occurs. Assigns terms positive and negative to different electral charges. All original thirteen colonies settled and organized (Virginia colony's population nearly 250,000).	Great Britain adopts Georgian calendar. First theatre company formed in Russia.
1753	Hallam in New York (2 July) and by 17 September opens season in rebuilt Nassau Street Playhouse that lasts until end of March 1754. Anthony J. Dugee and wife offer a slack-rope walking display in New York.	Conestoga wagon introduced by Pennsylvania Dutch settlers.	British Museum founded in London.
1754	Hallam (15 April) at "New Theatre" (Plumstead's warehouse), Philadelphia.	Founding of Columbia University. Jonathan Edwards's *Freedom of the Will*.	William Hogarth's painting *The Election*.
1755	Lewis Hallam Sr. dies in Jamaica; company disbands.	"Yankee Doodle" composed as British satire of colonials. British take control of Canada.	German playwright Gotthold Ephraim Lessing's *Miss Sara Sampson* premieres in Frankfurt. Samuel Johnson's *Dictionary of the English Language*.

	Theatre		
1756	*The Masque of Alfred* presented during Christmas holidays at the College of Philadelphia.	Seven Years' War, known in United States as French and Indian War (England and Prussia vs. Austria and France), begins. Independence Hall (Pennsylvania State House) is completed in Philadelphia.	Scottish playwright John Home writes *Douglas* (staged first in 1756).
1758–59	Hallam company reconstituted under David Douglass (husband of former Mrs. Hallam), with Lewis Hallam, Jr. as leading man; open at Cruger's Wharf, New York. Harvard student productions of *Cato*, *The Orphan*, *The Recruiting Officer*, and *The Drummer*.		
1759	Douglass at Society Hill, Philadelphia (5 April) in Southstreet Theatre (season until December).		Voltaire's *Candide*.
1760	New theatre in Annapolis opened by Douglass (3 March). Earliest review of play appears (written anonymously) in the *Maryland Gazette*.		Laurence Sterne's novel *Tristram Shandy* (published 1760). Captain James Cook claims New Zealand for Great Britain. Spectators banned from stage in Paris. George III king of England; reigns until 1820. Premieres of Viennese composer Franz Joseph Haydn's symphonies nos. 2, 3, 4, and 5.
c. 1760		Franklin invents bifocal lenses.	
1761	Douglass invades New England (Rhode Island) during summer. Douglass opens Chapel Street/Beekman Theatre, New York (18 Nov.).		Birth of German writer August von Kotzebue (d. 1819), popular writer of melodramas, later translated by William Dunlap.

DATES	THEATRE EVENTS IN AMERICA	SELECTED HISTORICAL/CULTURAL EVENTS IN AMERICA	SELECTED HISTORICAL/CULTURAL EVENTS THROUGHOUT THE WORLD
1762	Rhode Island Assembly passes legislation to prevent stage plays (Aug.). Francis Hopkinton, America's first poet-composer, writes "An Exercise: Containing a Dialogue (by Provost Smith) and Ode, Sacred to the Memory of the Late Gracious Majesty George II," which is recited at College of Philadelphia's commencement; similar tribute to George III composed for 1763 commencement.		Garrick bans audience from stage at Drury Lane. French philospher Jean-Jacques Rousseau's *Social Contract* and *Emile*.
1763	Douglass builds Queen Street Theatre (temporary structure) in Charleston. Dialogue on "The Military Glory of Great Britain" presented at College of New Jersey (Princeton).	End of French and Indian War. Pontiac's Rebellion.	
1764	*The Paxton Boys,* published anonymously, introduces Indians as characters.	Brown University founded by Baptists as Rhode Island College. Sugar Act passed by British Parliament, and Colonists protest.	Mechanization of textile spinning begins (completed 1769). Literary Club founded in London by Dr. Johnson and others. Horace Walpole's *Castle of Otranto.*
1765		Colonists protest British Stamp Act, first major step toward the Revolution. American artist John Singleton Copley's (1737–1815) portrait of John Hancock.	French painter Jean Fragonard's *The Storm.*
1766	American Company officially organized under Douglass and Hallam; renamed American Company in November 1763 from the London Company of Comedians.	Rutgers University founded in New Brunswick, New Jersey.	Scottish inventor James Watt's steam engine. Oliver Goldsmith's only novel, *The Vicar of Wakefield.*

	Theatre	History/Politics	Arts/Science
	Major Robert Rogers's *Ponteach; or the Savages of America* first published play by an American on an American subject.	Mason–Dixon Line drawn.	Vienna's Prater Park opens.
	Southwark Theatre on Cedar Street, Philadelphia, America's first substantial playhouse, opens 12 November.		English clergyman-chemist Joseph Priestley's *The History and Present State of Electricity* published.
	Stamp Act mob pulls down and burns Chapel Street Theatre in New York City.		
	William Dunlap born 19 February in Perth Amboy, New Jersey. See 1789.		
1767	*Prince of Parthia* (Thomas Godfrey) performed at Southwark on 24 April, is first American play professionally performed (produced after withdrawal of Andrew Barton's [pseudonym of Thomas Forrest] *The Disappointment; or, The Force of Credulity*, advertised as a comic opera).	Townshend Act places duties on imported tea, glass, paint, oil, lead, and paper in colonies. New York assembly rejects the quartering of British troops.	
	A Mr. Greville deserts studies at Princeton College and joins Douglass's company, becoming first native-born professional actor.	John Dickinson's *Letters from a Farmer in Pennsylvania* (first installment).	
	Irish-born actor John Henry (1738–94) has American debut (in *The Roman Father*) in Philadelphia (6 Oct.).	North Carolinian Daniel Boone goes through the Cumberland Gap, reaching Kentucky in defiance of King George's 1763 decree.	Sturm and Drang movement begins in Germany (till 1787).
	John Street Theatre, first permanent playhouse in New York, opens (7 Dec.) with Farquhar's *The Beaux' Stratagem*.		

DATES	THEATRE EVENTS IN AMERICA	SELECTED HISTORICAL/CULTURAL EVENTS IN AMERICA	SELECTED HISTORICAL/CULTURAL EVENTS THROUGHOUT THE WORLD
1768	William Verling's Virgina Company (sometimes using the name New American Company).	First Methodist church in United States dedicated in New York City.	Death of British actress Hannah Pritchard (b. 1711).
	Showman displays leopard in New England.		Joshua Reynolds's painting of David Garrick as Kitely.
1769	British playwright Isaac Bickerstaffe's *The Padlock* with black character "Mungo" seen in New York.	Dartmouth College founded in Hanover, New Hampshire.	Steam engine patented by James Watt.
		French defeated in battle of Quebec.	First Shakespeare festival held at Stratford-upon-Avon.
1770		Jefferson begins Monticello in Charlottesville, Virginia.	Philip Astley begins modern circus with his one-ring circus (largely equestrian) in London.
		First American public mental hospital, Williamsburg, Virginia.	
		Boston Massacre on 5 March; becomes incident to arouse Colonial rancor against British.	
1771–72	George Washington attends theatre at least nineteen times.		
1771	Douglass opens West Street Theatre in Annapolis.	Benjamin West's paintings, *The Death of General Wolfe* and *Penn's Treaty with the Indians.*	British novelist Tobias Smollett's *The Expedition of Humphrey Clinker.*
	Francis Hopkinson's dialogue "The Rising Glory of America" presented at Princeton.	Part 1 of Ben Franklin's *Autobiography.*	
	A Mr. Faulks performs feats of horsemanship in Philadelphia.		

1772	*The Candidates; or The Humours of a Virginia Election* is written by Robert Munford, winter 1770–71 (published 1798). *The Adulateur*, first play written by Mrs. Mercy Otis Warren, though, like all of her plays, most likely not staged; satire on New England Tories. New Jersey passes provision to curtail increasing proliferation of mountebanks as part of act regulating medicine.	Led by Samuel Adams, Committees of Correspondence formed.	Oliver Goldsmith's play *She Stoops to Conquer* premieres at Covent Garden.
1773	*The Defeat*, possibly by Mrs. Warren. Connecticut passes an "Act for suppressing of Mountebanks." Church Street Theatre opens in Charleston, South Carolina. American Company presents (17 Feb.) George Cockling's *The Conquest of Canada; or, The Siege of Quebec*, the most spectacular production in its history. Menagerie act, including a leopard, seen in Boston.	Colonists throw British tea into Boston harbor (in demonstration against new English Tea Act). American painter Charles William Peale's (1741–1827) *Peale Family Group*.	Johann von Goethe's *Goetz von Berlichingen*.
1774	Continental Congress (20 Oct.) discourages all extravagance and dissipation, including "exhibition of shews." Also anti-importation act to discourage use and dissemination of British productions, including theatre. English-born Thomas Wignell (1753–1803) joins cousin Lewis Hallam's American Company.	Quartering Act passed by British parliament updates a 1765 act and requires Colonists to house British troops in barns or public inns when barracks unavailable. First Continental Congress meets in Philadelphia 5 September (all colonies represented, save Georgia).	Priestley discovers oxygen. Edmund Burke's speech "On American Taxation."

DATES	THEATRE EVENTS IN AMERICA	SELECTED HISTORICAL/CULTURAL EVENTS IN AMERICA	SELECTED HISTORICAL/CULTURAL EVENTS THROUGHOUT THE WORLD
1775	Thomas Paine, *A Dialogue between General Wolfe and General Gage in a Wood Near Boston.*	Patrick Henry, quoting from Addison's *Cato*, delivers "Give Me Liberty or Give Me Death" speech (23 March).	British playwright Richard B. Sheridan's play *The Rivals* premieres at Covent Garden.
	The Group, the only play acknowledged by Mrs. Warren.	British and Colonists begin physical combat; skirmishes at Lexington and Concord (19 April); Battle of Bunker Hill (17 June).	Debut of British actress Sarah Siddons at Drury Lane.
	British general John Burgoyne organizes a theatre in Boston's Faneuil Hall.	Congress creates American Navy.	Pierre Beaumarchais's *The Barber of Seville* premieres at the Comédie-Française.
	Douglass/Hallam troupe leave 2 February for Jamaica to stay till end of conflict.	Society for Relief of Free Negroes Unlawfully Held in Bondage founded in Philadelphia.	
1776	Burgoyne's farce *The Blockade of Boston* (lost) performed in January in Boston.	Thomas Paine's *Common Sense* (Jan.).	David Garrick retires; Richard Brinsley Sheridan assumes management of London's Drury Lane.
	A Dialogue between the Ghost of General Montgomery, Just Arrived from the Elysian Fields, and an American Delegate, in a Wood Near Philadelphia.	Colonists declare independence from the British (4 July).	Scottish philosopher Adam Smith's *Inquiry into the Nature and Causes of the Wealth of Nations* published.
	Hugh Henry Brackenridge's play *The Battle of Bunkers-Hill* published.	The British capture New York.	First volume of English historian Edward Gibbon's *The History of Decline and Fall of the Roman Empire* published.
	The Blockheads; or The Affrighted Officers, inspired by Burgoyne play, by anonymous author (attributed by some to Mrs. Warren).	Washington defeats Hessians at Trenton, New Jersey.	Friedrich von Klinger's *Storm and Stress* premieres in Leipzig.
	John Leacock's *The Fall of British Tyranny, or American Liberty Triumphant* published; possibly performed at Harvard.	British navigator James Cook explores western North American coast for an Atlantic passage.	Bolshoi Theatre founded in Moscow.

Year			
	The Battle of Brooklyn, a Tory farce.	San Francisco, established by Spanish monks, has its beginnings as a settlement called Yerba Buena (good herb). Phi Beta Kappa Society founded at College of William and Mary.	Richard B. Sheridan's play *The School for Scandal* opens at Drury Lane. English artist Thomas Gainsborough's *The Watering Place*.
1777	John Street Theatre renamed Theatre Royal and operated by British (Sir William Howe's "Players") till 1783 (same true in other major cities, especially Boston and Philadelphia). British, with Captain Delancey and Captain John André as leaders, establish military theatre in Philadelphia. Brackenridge's *The Death of General Montgomery*. Robert Munford's *The Patriots* (date approximate) written.	Washington defeats British at Princeton, New Jersey, then loses at Brandywine and Germantown. Articles of Confederation approved by Continental Congress (15 Nov.); go into effect 1781. U.S. Independence Day (4 July) first celebrated.	English writer John Dryden's (1631–1700) tragedy *All for Love*. Milan's Teatro alla Scala opens (3 Aug.).
1778	American troops perform in Portsmouth, New Hampshire. Congressional resolution (6 Oct.) against "plays and other expensive Diversions and Entertainment." American military theatre opens on 15 April at Valley Forge with a fete in May (celebrating the French alliance), and on 11 May Addison's *Cato* performed, with Washington present. American officers reopen, briefly, Southwark (Sept.).	French become allied with Colonists. (Marquis de Lafayette commissioned major general previous year.) Washington's troops retake Philadelphia in June, after British occupy it, beginning Sept. 1777. U.S. artist John Singleton Copley's painting, *Watson and the Shark*. Prussian general Baron Friedrich von Steuben organizes American army into disciplined troops.	

DATES	THEATRE EVENTS IN AMERICA	SELECTED HISTORICAL/CULTURAL EVENTS IN AMERICA	SELECTED HISTORICAL/CULTURAL EVENTS THROUGHOUT THE WORLD
1778	Congress, meeting in Philadelphia on 12 October, passes resolution reiterating suppression of diversions; second one on 16 October, but neither effective. André in Philadelphia paints one of first known backdrops in United States.		
1779	Legislature prohibits all theatrical entertainment in Pennsylvania. John Smith's *A Dialogue between an Englishman and an Indian* presented at Dartmouth College. *A Motley Assembly*, a farce published anonymously "for the entertainment of the curious."	John Paul Jones's successful naval encounter off English coast (Sept.). Spain joins war on American side (June). Charle Willson Peale's painting *George Washington at Princeton*.	English writer Hannah More's *The Fatal Falsehood* opens in May at Covent Garden.
1780		Pennsylvania becomes first state to abolish slavery. Nashville, Tennessee, begins as fort on Cumberland River (named in 1784). British take Charleston (12 May). Benedict Arnold joins British (Sept.) after activities exposed by capture of go-between Major John André.	Invention of Argand lamp; patented 1784.
1781	Actor John Henry petitions authorities in Philadelphia to present *The Lecture on Heads*.	British bottled up in Charleston by autumn. Thomas Jefferson's *The Rights of British America*.	William Murdock patents gas manufacturing process. French philosopher Jean-Jacques Rousseau's *Confessions* published (written 1766–70).

German philosopher Immanuel Kant's *Critique of Pure Reason,* his major work, followed in 1788 by *Critique of Practical Reason.*

German playwright Friedrich von Schiller's *The Robbers* opens in Mannheim.

Composer Giacchino Antonio Rossini born (d. 1868).

Pierre Choderlos de Laclos's *Les Liaisons Dangereuses.*

Opening of London's Royal Circus, later the Surrey.

William Pitt becomes prime minister of England (until 1801).

British actor John Philip Kemble debuts as Hamlet.

Siege of Yorktown begins in August.

General Cornwallis surrenders 8,000 British troops at Yorktown on 19 October, yet bloody encounters continue until November 1783.

Peace talks begin in Paris; Netherlands recognizes American independence.

The Pennsylvania Evening Post, first U.S. daily, begins publication.

Hugh Blair published *Lectures on Rhetoric and Belles Lettres.*

Treaty of Paris (3 Sept.) ends American Revolution; Colonies unite under Articles of Confederation.

Boston Magazine founded.

Noah Webster's *American Spelling Book* published.

Economic depression, which lasts until 1787.

1782   Theatre professionals begin to return to United States (e.g., Thomas Wall in Baltimore).

1783   Wall joined by Mr. and Mrs. Dennis Ryan from Dublin.

DATES	THEATRE EVENTS IN AMERICA	SELECTED HISTORICAL/CULTURAL EVENTS IN AMERICA	SELECTED HISTORICAL/CULTURAL EVENTS THROUGHOUT THE WORLD
1784	Hallam's American Company returns to Philadelphia.	New York chosen as temporary capital of United States.	Sir Joshua Reynolds (1723–92) paints actress Sarah Siddons as *The Tragic Muse*.
	John Parke's play about George Washington, *Virginia*.	North Carolina cedes western territory to United States.	Death of Samuel Johnson (b. 1709).
	Peter Markoe's classical tragedy *The Patriot Chief* illustrates dangers of aristocratic government.	Thomas Jefferson's *Notes on the State of Virginia* (private and French editions).	French playwright Pierre Beaumarchais's *The Marriage of Figaro*, written 1778, premieres at the Comédie-Française.
	Barnabas Bidwell's *The Modern Mistake.*		
1785	John Henry joins Hallam to form Old American Company.	Benjamin Franklin writes "The Internal State of America" and "A Petition of the Left Hand."	Wolfgang Amadeus Mozart's (1756–91) opera *The Marriage of Figaro* premieres in Vienna.
	Equestrian Thomas Pool(e) employs clown to amuse spectators between his feats; in New York and Philadelphia (Boston in 1786).	Timothy Dwight's verse, "The Conquest of Canaan."	
	Bidwell's domestic tragedy, *The Mercenary Match.*	Congress establishes dollar as official currency, using decimal system devised by Jefferson.	
	Two splinter groups from Old American form troupes, one under Mr. and Mrs. Allen and one under Godwin and Kidd (who perform the same year in Savannah, Georgia).	University of Georgia founded at Athens.	
	Actor, clown, equestrian, dancer-pantomimist, and theatre artist John Durang (1768–1822) joins company at Southwark Theatre, Philadelphia.		
1786	Allen troupe plays in Albany, New York.	Statute for religious freedom passed in Virginia.	Death of Frederick the Great of Prussia (b. 1712).

1786–87	Benjamin Rush (1745–1813) publishes *Plan for the Establishment of Public Schools and the Diffusion of Knowledge in Pennsylvania.*	London gunsmith Henry Nock invents breach-loading musket.
	First U.S. golf club founded near Charleston.	Scottish poet Robert Burns's *Poems, Chiefly in the Scottish Dialect.*
	Shays's rebellion in Massachusetts attempts to stop farm foreclosures during economic depression.	
1786–1823		Regulations of Viceroy curtail theatre in Mexico.
1787	Congress enacts Northwest Ordinance.	Friedrich von Schiller's play *Don Carlos* premieres in Hamburg.
Royall Tyler's *The Contrast*, first native comedy professionally staged on 16 April at John Street Theatre; introduces first stage Yankee. Later in year wrote *May Day in Town; or, New York in an Uproar*, a comic opera.	U.S. Constitution drafted, sent for ratification to states.	French artist Jacques-Louis David's painting *Death of Socrates.*
The Modest Soldier; or, Love in New York, Dunlap's first play (not produced; now lost), with Yankee servant.	*Federalist Papers* published (through 1788; written by Alexander Hamilton, John Jay, and James Madison).	Mozart opera *Don Giovanni* premieres in Prague.
Birth of playwright Samuel Woodworth.		Russia begins second war with Ottoman Empire.
A performing quack named John Brenon is recorded as having offered variety acts in New York.		
1788	Over 800 structures burned in New Orleans fire.	Immanuel Kant's *Critique of Practical Reason.*
Samuel Low's *The Politician Out-witted*, a staunch defense of the new Constitution, written; published next year, though not performed until 1987.	U.S. Constitution operable after ratification by ninth state, New Hampshire.	Founding of Royal Swedish Dramatic Theatre in Stockholm.

DATES	THEATRE EVENTS IN AMERICA	SELECTED HISTORICAL/CULTURAL EVENTS IN AMERICA	SELECTED HISTORICAL/CULTURAL EVENTS THROUGHOUT THE WORLD
1788		Beginnings of Cincinnati, Ohio.	Opening of Astley's Amphitheatre in London.
1788–92		French sculptor Jean-Antoine Houdon's marble statue of Washington (in Richmond).	
1789	Dunlap's *Darby's Return*.	Washington becomes first president.	British writer-artist William Blake's *Songs of Innocence*.
	Repeal (2 March) of Pennsylvania law against theatre.	U.S. Constitution ratified by eleven of thirteen states.	French Revolution begins (ends 1802) with storming of Bastille.
	The Father; or American Shandyism, William Dunlap's first play produced (at John Street Theatre). Dunlap (1766–1839) called "Father of American Drama."	James Fenimore Cooper born (d. 1851).	English philosopher-barrister Jeremy Bentham promotes utilitarianism in *Introduction to the Principles of Morals and Legislation*.
	Actor-manager Thomas Wade West, founder of a southern theatrical circuit active until War of 1812, immigrates.	John Jay becomes first chief justice of Supreme Court.	August von Kotzebue's play *The Stranger*.
		David Ramsay's *The History of the American Revolution*.	Scottish economist and philosopher Adam Smith dies (b. 1723).
		University of North Carolina, Chapel Hill, founded; first state university.	British statesman Edmund Burke's *Reflections on the French Revolution*.
		Protestant Episcopal Church founded as independent branch of Anglicanism.	English painter Thomas Lawrence's *Queen Charlotte and Miss Farren*.
1790		Thomas Paine's *The Rights of Man*.	
		Philadelphia the nation's capital (until 1800).	
		First successful U.S. cotton mill, Slater Mill (Pawtucket, R.I.).	

1791	Mr. and Mrs. Kenna break from Old American Company to form theatre troupe. American-born John Martin debuts as native actor in Philadelphia, but his career fails to develop. Mercy Otis Warren's *Poems, Dramatic and Miscellaneous* published. Wignell retires from Old American Company and becomes partner with Alexander Reinagle in Philadelphia. First French language theatre in New Orleans (second in Charleston). Birth of actor-playwright John Howard Payne (d. 1852).	American dentist Josiah Flagg constructs first dental chair. First U.S. copyright to protect U.S. authors. Federal-style furniture appears (variation of European neoclassical), and Shakers begin to sell slatback chairs in New Lebanon, New York. First full circus in Mexico presented 9 July. First Bank of the United States incorporated. Vermont becomes first new state after original thirteen. U.S. Bill of Rights ratified. Beginning of American carpet industry.	Death of Wolfgang Amadeus Mozart (b. 1756). Birth of French playwright Eugène Scribe (d. 1861), author of well-made plays. James Boswell's *Life of Samuel Johnson.*
1792	Joseph Harper's "New Exhibition Room" opens in Boston; closed same year by sheriff. John Hodgkinson (d. 1805), "The Provincial Garrick," brought by John Henry (with his wife to be Miss Brett) to join Old American Company. Scene painter Charles Ciceri at the Park Theatre. *The Yonker's Stratagem, or Banana's Wedding* by J. Robinson with a pretend Yankee.	Duncan Phyfe opens cabinetry shop in New York City and employs new factory system. J. B. Lippincott and Co. publishers founded. Yellow fever outbreak, reappearing for several years thereafter. Kentucky admitted to the Union.	Egypt swept by plague; 800,000 die. Thomas Morton's *Columbus; or, A World Discovered,* first of many Columbus plays. William Pitt the Younger, prime minister of England, attacks slave trade. France declared a Republic.

DATES	THEATRE EVENTS IN AMERICA	SELECTED HISTORICAL/CULTURAL EVENTS IN AMERICA	SELECTED HISTORICAL/CULTURAL EVENTS THROUGHOUT THE WORLD
1792	English actor James Fennell brought by Wignell to Philadelphia; retires 1810; publishes memoirs 1814.	New York Stock Exchange opens.	Italian-born Francis II becomes Last Holy Roman Emperor, till 1806.
	French performer Alexander Placide first appears in United States at John Street Theatre.	Hugh Henry Brackenride's novel *Modern Chivalry* begun (completed 1815).	English author Mary Wollstonecraft publishes *Vindication of the Rights of Women.*
	First theatrical performance (13 Aug.) in Boston's Concert Hall (built c. 1750).	Jeremy Belknap's novel *The Foresters.*	
		The Farmer's Almanac founded by printer Robert B. Thomas.	
1793	Repeal of restrictive legislation in Massachusetts and Rhode Island; theatre opens in Newport, Rhode Island's old brick market (building still stands) under management of Alexander Placide.	Washington begins second presidential term; issues "Proclamation of Neutrality" in French–British War.	Birth of British actor William Charles Macready (d. 1893).
	Scotsman (?) John Bill Ricketts presents on 3 April first complete circus performance in America in Philadelphia (he tours from 1792 to 1799).	Eli Whitney invents the cotton gin.	Reign of Terror in France under Robespierre; Louis XVI and Marie Antoinette beheaded.
	Production of *The Tempest* in Charleston features early stage effects.	Federal fugitive slave law requires return of runaway slaves to owners.	German philosopher Immanuel Kant's *Theory and Practice.*
	British-born comic actor John Harwood brought to Philadelphia by Wignell.	Artist Gilbert Stuart's (1755–1828) portrait of George Washington.	Britain at war with France.
	British Actress Mrs. Charlotte Melmoth, cited by Dunlap as "best tragic actress" in New York, brought from England.	Large-scale exodus of French planters from St. Domingue to United States; many settle in Charleston, S.C.	Louvre Palace, Paris, opens as art museum.
		Elihu Hubbard's *American Poems*, first published anthology of native verse.	

1794	Federal Street Theatre, designed by Charles Bulfinch, opens in Boston (3 Feb.) under management of Charles Stuart Powell; demolished in 1852.	Boston repeals 1750 law prohibiting plays.	William Blake's *Songs of Experience*.
	Henry sells share of Park to Hallam for $10,000; drowns while sailing the following year.	Whiskey Rebellion in Pennsylvania.	French occupy Belgium.
	Chestnut Street Theatre ("Old Drury") opens in Philadelphia (17 Feb.) under management of Wignell and Reinagle.	First independent Methodist church for blacks established in Philadelphia.	British novelist Ann Radcliffe's gothic novel *The Mysteries of Udolpho*.
	Anne Kemble Hatton's *American Discovered; or, Tammany, the Indian Chief*.	U.S. Navy established.	
	Designer–scene painter Charles Melbourne works at Chestnut.	Publication of Thomas Paine's tract, *The Age of Reason*.	
	Mrs. John Oldmixon (d. 1835) recruited from England by Wignell and debuts 14 May as Clorinda in *Robin Hood*.	Charles Willson Peale opens museum in Philadelphia to popularize science.	
	London-born actor James Fennell (1766–1816) begins substantial U.S. career in Philadelphia.	John Trumbull's painting *The Declaration of Independence*.	
	English-born actress-playwright Susanna Haswell Rowson's best play *Slaves in Algiers; or, A Struggle for Freedom*.		
	Charleston Theatre on Broad Street opens under Thomas Wade West.		
	Wignell and Reinagle open Holliday Street Theatre in Baltimore.		
1795	Ricketts constructs permanent circus building in Philadelphia (Art Pavilion and Amphitheatre).	Richard Snowden's *The Columbiad; or, A Poem on the American War*.	End of the Reign of Terror in France.

DATES	THEATRE EVENTS IN AMERICA	SELECTED HISTORICAL/CULTURAL EVENTS IN AMERICA	SELECTED HISTORICAL/CULTURAL EVENTS THROUGHOUT THE WORLD
1795	English-born Joseph Jefferson I (1774–1832) has U.S. debut in New York.	U.S./Spanish Treaty of Lorenzo establishes boundaries of Florida.	John Keats (d. 1821) and Thomas Carlyle (d. 1881) born.
	What becomes Scudder's American Museum opens in New York.	Requirements for citizenship set by Naturalization Act.	
	The Triumph of Love; or, Happy Reconciliation by John Murdoch with character "Sambo" performed in New York.		
	William Dunlap dramatizes Ann Radcliffe's *Romance of the Forest* as *Fountainville Abbey.*		
	Harvard's Hasty Pudding Club founded; begins theatrical production in 1844.		
1796	Dunlap becomes manager of Old American Company and buys interest in John Street Theatre.	George Washington's "Farewell Address."	English physician Edward Jenner's smallpox vaccine.
	First elephant exhibited (briefly) in America by a Mr. Owen.	Tennessee admitted to the Union.	Buddhist revolt against Manchu rule in China begins.
	British-born actor Thomas Abthorpe Cooper (1776–1849), brought by Wignell; has U.S. debut in Baltimore before Philadelphia debut as Macbeth (9 Dec.).	St. George Tucker's *Dissertation on Slavery* published.	Spain allies with France against British.
	British-born William Warren the elder (1767–1832), later manager in Philadelphia, joins Wignell's company.	Gilbert Charles Stuart paints *George Washington (Athenaeum Head)*, the most popular of Washington portraits.	British writer M. G. "Monk" Lewis's gothic novel *The Monk.*
	Actress-manager Mrs. Anne Brunton Merry (1769–1808) joins Wignell (whom she marries in 1803) at the Chestnut Street Theatre.		Francisco de Goya's painting *Los Caprichos.*

Year			
	Charles Stuart Powell opens Haymarket Theatre in Boston (Dec.). Theatre demolished 1803.		Samuel Coleridge's *Poems on Various Subjects*.
	M. Audin oversees effects and scenery for afterpiece *Apotheosis of Franklin* in Charleston.		German author Ludwig Tieck's *Puss in Boots*.
1797	*Bunker-Hill; or, The Death of Gen. Warren* by John Daly Burk (d. 1808) produced at Boston's Haymarket Theatre 17 February and in New York in September.	John Adams inaugurated as second president.	
	Susanna H. Rowson's *Americans in England* staged at Boston's Federal Street Theatre, 19 April.		British statesman Edmund Burke dies (b. 1727).
	Cooper's New York debut (Pierre in *Venice Preserved*) on 23 August at Greenwich Street Theatre.	Forty-four-gun frigate *Constitution* launched.	Birth of German composer Franz Schubert (d. 1828).
	British Actor John Bernard (1756–1828) has U.S. debut in Philadelphia.	Caleb Bingham's manual, *The Columbian Orator*.	Poet Samuel Taylor Coleridge writes "Kubla Khan" (not published until 1816).
	Ricketts opens circus building on Greenwich Street in New York (this and Philadelphia circus burn in 1799).	Novelist Hannah Foster's *The Coquette*.	
	Amateur theatre society in Kentucky.		
1798	John Street Theatre stages last performance (*The Comet and Tom Thumb*) on 13 January.	With United States on brink of war with France, Congress passes the Alien and Sedition Acts (which puts a damper on political drama).	English poet William Wordsworth's "Ode: Intimations of Immortality."
	Park Theatre (or New Theatre), after designs by Marc Isambard Brunel, opens in New York (29 Jan.) with *As You Like It* under Dunlap.	First military engagement in Caribbean; Navy warships engage French off Guadeloupe.	Birth of philosopher Auguste Comte (d. 1857), founder of positivism and sociology.

DATES	THEATRE EVENTS IN AMERICA	SELECTED HISTORICAL/CULTURAL EVENTS IN AMERICA	SELECTED HISTORICAL/CULTURAL EVENTS THROUGHOUT THE WORLD
1798	Federal Street Theatre burns (2 Feb.), the first of many theatre fires in the United States. Cooper first appears in New York as Hamlet at the Park Theatre on 28 February. *André* by William Dunlap with Charles Ciceri scenery (at Park Theatre, 30 March), early attempt to write native tragedy (Cooper as Bland; Hodgkinson as André). Revised 1803. *The Stranger*, Dunlap's first adaptation of Kotzebue, seen at Park Theatre, 10 December. John Daly Burk's *Female Patriotism; or, The Death of Jean of Arc.* First U.S. theatrical periodical, *The Thespian Oracle*, published in Philadelphia.	Novelist Charles Brockden Brown's *Wieland.* Yellow fever plague in New York Mississippi Territory created.	French troops occupy Rome. René Guilbert de Pixérécourt's play *Victor*, his first theatrical success.
1799	Amateur Thespian Society in Lexington, Kentucky. British soldier turned actor, Gottlieb Graupner, sings "The Negro Boy" in blackface as entr'acte entertainment at Boston's Federal Theatre; John Bernard sings songs in blackface in New York. Dunlap's adaptation (from Kotzebue) *False Shame; or, The American Orphanage in Germany* presented.	Death of George Washington. Charles Brockden Brown novels: *Ormond, Edgar Huntly,* and *Arthur Mervyn.*	R. B. Sheridan's version of *Pizarro.* English chemist Sir Humphry Davy discovers nitrous oxide as anesthetic. Napoleon becomes First Consul in France (19 Nov.).

Year			
Early 1800s	Jones's Woods, a grove of some 150 acres along New York's East River, develops as venue for large variety of amusements.		
1800	Wignell and Reinagle open theatre (in a hotel) in Washington.	Washington, D.C., becomes capital of the United States; Library of Congress founded.	Schiller's *Maria Stuart* premieres at Weimar.
	Pizarro in Peru; or, The Death of Rolla, adaptation of Kotzebue by Dunlap.	First Methodist camp meeting (Logan, Ky.); "Great Kentucky Revival."	Electric battery invented by Volta.
	Hachaliah Bailey imports elephant (Old Bet) sometime between this year and 1810; exhibited until 1816.	First record of a merry-go-round in United States (Salem, Mass.).	Influence of French melodrama writer Guilbert de Pixérécourt (d. 1844).
	English pantomime adapted to American theme (*Harlequin Traveller and the Temple of the Sun*).	Northwest Territory divided into Ohio and Indiana territories.	John Philip Kemble becomes manager of Covent Garden, London (till 1817).
1801	Scottish magician John Rannie first appears in United States.	Thomas Jefferson is president.	United Kingdom (Ireland and Great Britain) established on 1 January.
	First theatre in Cincinnati, Ohio, opens.	Second yellow fever outbreak.	Czar Paul I assassinated; succeeded by Alexander I, emperor of Russia.
		Charles Brockden Brown's novels *Clara Howard* and *Jane Talbot*.	
		Tripolitan War (to 1802): United States fights Barbary pirates.	
		First U.S. suspension bridge, Uniontown, Pennsylvania.	
		U.S. population estimated at 5.3 million.	
1802	Washington Irving, under name Jonathan Oldstyle, writes early theatre criticism in the form of nine letters for *Morning Chronicle* (Nov.–Jan. 1803); later he writes for *Salmagundi* (1807) and *Select Reviews* (1815).	Georgia cedes its western territory to United States.	French politician-writer François-Auguste-René de Chateaubriand's *The Genius of Christianity*.

DATES	THEATRE EVENTS IN AMERICA	SELECTED HISTORICAL/CULTURAL EVENTS IN AMERICA	SELECTED HISTORICAL/CULTURAL EVENTS THROUGHOUT THE WORLD
1802	Joseph Croswell's *A New World Planted.* Dunlap's *Abaellino, The Great Bandit,* Park Theatre, 11 February. Snelling Powell successfully manages (until his death in 1821) Boston's Federal Street Theatre.	U.S. Military Academy founded at West Point.	Birth of Victor Hugo (d. 1885). Mme. Tussaud's wax museum opens in London.
1803	Dunlap transforms *André* into patriotic spectacle, *The Glory of Columbia, Her Yeomanry.*	Ohio admitted into Union (seventeenth state). Jefferson negotiates Louisiana Purchase; obtains from France all lands east of Mississippi to Rockies, excluding Texas, for $15 million.	Beethoven's Symphony no. 2 in D major premieres in Vienna.
1804		Lewis and Clark begin first expedition across the continent to the Pacific coast, returning in 1806. Nathaniel Hawthorne born (d. 1864). Painter Washington Allston's (1779–1843) *Rising of a Thunderstorm at Sea.* Aaron Burr kills Alexander Hamilton in a duel.	Napoleon crowns himself emperor. Napoleonic Wars begin, lasting until 1815. Composer Johann Strauss Sr. born (d. 1849). Gas lighting demonstrated at London's Lyceum Theatre.
1805	Dunlap bankrupt at Park Theatre. Park Theatre sold to John Jacob Astor and John Beekman.	Anglo-American Benjamin Latrobe, most influential architect of "Federal" Neoclassicism, begins Catholic Cathedral, Baltimore. Mercy Otis Warren's *History of the Rise, Progress, and Termination of the American Revolution.*	Napoleon crowned king of Italy. Lord Nelson defeats French at Trafalgar.

Year			
1806	John Howard Payne edits *Thespian Mirror* (Dec.–May 1806). Thomas Cooper becomes lessee of Park Theatre, with Dunlap as assistant manager. Mrs. Anne Merry Wignell marries William Warren the elder. John Bernard co-manages Boston's Federal Street Theatre (until 1810). Lewis Hallam Jr. retires; dies in 1808. Publication of magazine *Theatre Censor*. John Howard Payne's first play, *Julia; or, The Wanderer*, staged at the Park.	Zebulon Pike explores upper Mississippi River. Gas installed successfully for first time in streetlights (Newport, R.I.). Noah Webster's *Compendious Dictionary of the English Language*.	Master Betty begins in London a rage for child prodigies on the stage. Death of German playwright Friedrich Schiller (b. 1759). John Stuart Mill born (d. 1873). Ireland suffers partial failure of potato crop.
1807	James Nelson Barker's (1784–1858) *Tears and Smiles* features character Nathan York. Architect John Joseph Holland (who arrived in United States in 1796) does alterations on the Park Theatre.	Sailing of Fulton's first steamboat, the *Clermont*. Embargo Act passed by Congress. Trading of slaves outlawed by Great Britain and United States. Births of literary figures Henry Wadsworth Longfellow (d. 1882) and John Greenleaf Whittier (d. 1892).	German philosopher Georg Wilhelm Hegel's *Phenomenology of Mind*. Napoleon signs treaties with Russia and Prussia.
1808	Barker's *The Indian Princess; or, La Belle Sauvage*, first produced "Indian" play (about Pocahontas) by an American playwright. Stephen Price (1783–1840), America's first professional manager, buys an interest in the Park Theatre.	Congress outlaws importation of African slaves.	Part I of Johann von Goethe's *Faust* completed (Part II, 1833). Arc light invented by Sir Humphrey Davy.

DATES	THEATRE EVENTS IN AMERICA	SELECTED HISTORICAL/CULTURAL EVENTS IN AMERICA	SELECTED HISTORICAL/CULTURAL EVENTS THROUGHOUT THE WORLD
1808	St. Philip Street Theatre built in New Orleans for French plays and operas. Lewis Hallam Jr. gives final performance in Philadelphia and dies the following year.		Charles Lamb's *Specimens of English Dramatic Poets*. German composer Ludwig van Beethoven composes his Symphonies nos. 5 and 6 (*Pastoral*). London's Covent Garden burns; rebuilt next year, provoking Old Price Riots.
1809	Native-born actor-playwright John Howard Payne (1791–1852), "Juvenile American Roscius," debuts at Park Theatre (24 Feb.) as Young Noval. The future Walnut Street Theatre, Philadelphia, opens as arena for Pepin and Breschard circus; name changed in 1820. Publication of *Rambler's Magazine and New York Theatrical Register.* Royall Tyler's *Yankey in London.*	Edgar Allan Poe born (d. 1849). James Madison becomes president. Birth of Abraham Lincoln. Washington Irving's *A History of New York from the Beginnings of the World to the End of the Dutch Dynasty.* Creation of Illinois Territory.	Russia annexes Finland. Birth of Charles Darwin (d. 1882). German poet and critic August Schlegel's *On Dramatic Art and Literature.* Debut of German actor Ludwig Devrient. Birth of Alfred, Lord Tennyson (d. 1892).
1810	George Frederick Cooke, first major British actor in United States, begins starring tour (continues until death in 1812) at Park Theatre (11 Nov.). James Douglass troupe travels to Lexington, Louisville, and Frankfort.	Zebulon Pike's *Account of Expeditions to the Source of the Mississippi and through the Western Parts of Louisiana.* West Florida annexed to United States.	Composer Frédéric Chopin born (d. 1849). Composer Robert Schumann born (d. 1856).

	English pantomime adapted to American material (*Harlequin Panattahah; or, The Genii of the Algonquins*). Publication of Philadelphia's *Mirror of Taste and Dramatic Censor*. London-born Mary Ann Duff, subsequently known as "American Sarah Siddons," has U.S. debut as Juliet, 31 December (with actor husband John R. Duff).	Death of writer Charles Brockden Brown.	Napoleon, at the zenith of his power, annexes Holland.
1811	Richmond, Virginia, theatre burns (26 Dec.), with seventy-one fatalities. American magician Richard Potter (1783–1835), son of British tax collector and black slave, becomes touring star.	Henry Trumbull's *History of the Indian Wars* (revised 1841). Hugh Henry Brackenridge's verse "Epistle to Walter Scott." First steamboat service on the Mississippi.	Prince of Wales becomes Prince Regent after George III declared insane. Composer Franz Liszt born (d. 1886). English novelist Jane Austen's *Sense and Sensibility* published anonymously.
1812	Barker's *Marmion; or, The Battle of Flodden Field* adapted from Walter Scott poem. Death of Alexander Placide, manager of Charleston Theatre, followed by dormant period in that area. Walnut Street Theatre, Philadelphia, opens (renovated circus building, first called the Olympic; in 1820 name changed to Walnut Street Theatre).	United States goes to war with England (War of 1812). Louisiana admitted to the Union. First U.S. life insurance company founded.	Napoleon invades Russia but is finally forced to retreat. Beethoven composes symphonies nos. 7 and 8. Lord Byron's "Childe Harold's Pilgrimage." Fourth and final Drury Lane Theatre built in London
1813	Dunlap writes *Memoirs of George Frederick Cooke*. Albany's first theatre, the Green Street Theatre, opens under John Bernard.	Creek War. British navy blockades ports.	Birth of Richard Wagner in Leipzig (d. 1883). Birth of Giuseppe Verdi (d. 1901).

DATES	THEATRE EVENTS IN AMERICA	SELECTED HISTORICAL/CULTURAL EVENTS IN AMERICA	SELECTED HISTORICAL/CULTURAL EVENTS THROUGHOUT THE WORLD
1813		"Uncle Sam" used for first time as synonym for the United States.	Mexico declares independence.
			English novelist Jane Austen's *Pride and Prejudice*.
1814	Noble Luke Usher, Kentuckian and strolling player, serves as catalyst for frontier theatre.	Daniel Bryan's poem "The Mountain Muse."	Louis XVIII reigns as first king of restored monarchy in France.
	Death of playwright Mercy Warren.	British capture and burn Washington, D.C. (including the Capitol, White House, and most of Library of Congress).	Congress of Vienna (ends 1815).
		"The Defence of Fort McHenry" ("The Star-Spangled Banner") written by Francis Scott Key.	Edmund Kean debut in London (26 Jan.) as Shylock.
		Baptist General Convention founded.	Limelight invented by Sir Thomas Drummond
			Scottish writer Sir Walter Scott's *Waverley.*
1815	Professional theatre company under English-born Samuel Drake in Frankfort, Kentucky (Dec.), marks true beginning of westward movement of theatre.	Creek Indian War ends.	Spanish painter Francisco de Goya's *The Second of May 1808* and *The Third of May 1808.*
	Cooper leaves management of the Park Theatre and becomes traveling star.	Nicholas Biddle's *History of the Expedition under the Command of Captains Lewis and Clark to the Sources of the Missouri.*	Napoleon defeated at Waterloo, exiled to St. Helena.
		Jackson defeats British at New Orleans; end of War of 1812.	Treaty of Vienna creates postwar map of Europe.
		Beginning of major recession.	

	American theatre	American context	International
	Payne meets actor Talma in Paris; begins translating and adapting plays.	Percussion cap invented; makes possible breech-loading firearms.	Debut of actor Ludwig Devrient in Berlin.
	Vauxhall Gardens opens in Philadelphia; lasts until 1825.	Benjamin Latrobe begins rebuilding White House; building completed 1817.	Quadrille dances for first time in England.
		North American Review founded (ceases publication in 1939).	
1816	Gas lighting installed for the auditorium in Chestnut Street Theatre (25 Nov.).	American Colonization Society founded to return freed slaves to Africa.	Gioacchino Rossini's opera *The Barber of Seville* premieres in Rome.
	British-born actor (and subsequent manager) James A. Caldwell comes to United States to perform in Charleston.	Indiana admitted to the Union.	Jane Austen's novel *Emma;* Austen dies the following year.
	Evidence of some theatre in Detroit, Michigan.	Samuel Woodworth's novel *The Champion of Freedom.*	British actor William C. Macready debuts at Covent Garden.
	J. N. Barker publishes eleven essays on drama in the *Democratic Press* (18 Dec.–19 Feb. 1817).	Cold weather persists into summer, with heavy snowfall in Northeast in June and July.	
	C. E. Grice's *Battle of New Orleans;* produced at the Park Theatre in New York, 4 July 1816.		
1817	Noah Ludlow, who leaves Drake company and forms own troupe, most likely presented plays on keelboat on the Cumberland, Ohio, and Mississippi rivers, and begins theatre in Nashville, Tennessee (in old salt house).	Steamboat sails from Louisville to New Orleans, initiating steamboat navigation of the Mississippi River.	German philosopher G. W. F. Hegel writes *Encyclopedia of Philosophy.*
	Charles Gilbert becomes manager (until 1825) in Charleston, revitalizing old Placide circuit.	James Monroe elected president.	Founding of *Blackwood's Edinburgh Magazine* (to 1980).
		Henry David Thoreau born (d. 1862).	Samuel Taylor Coleridge's (1772–1834) *Biographia Literaria.*

DATES	THEATRE EVENTS IN AMERICA	SELECTED HISTORICAL/CULTURAL EVENTS IN AMERICA	SELECTED HISTORICAL/CULTURAL EVENTS THROUGHOUT THE WORLD
1817		First Seminole War (through 1818). Poet William Cullen Bryant's (1794–1878) "Thanatopsis." Novelist John Neal's (1793–1876) *Keep Cool*. Painter Benjamin West's (1738–1820) *Death on the Pale Horse*. Mississippi admitted to the Union.	Byron's "Manfred." J. P. Kemble retires. English playwright Tom Taylor born (d. 1880).
1818	First English-speaking theatre company in New Orleans under Noah Ludlow. John Howard Payne's *Brutus; or, The Fall of Tarquin* with Edmund Kean first staged at Drury Lane (3 Dec.); at Park Theatre 15 March 1819. British actor James William Wallack the elder's (1795?–1864) U.S. debut on 7 September (at Park Theatre) as Macbeth.	Andrew Jackson and U.S. forces attack Seminoles in Florida. *Savannah* first steamboat to cross the Atlantic. Publication of first joke book (jokes = jests). Convention of 1818 establishes border between United States and Canada. Illinois admitted into the Union. James Kirke Paulding's poem "The Backwoodsman."	English novelist Mary Wollstonecraft Shelley's *Frankenstein*. Birth of Karl Marx (d. 1883). London's patent theatres install gas lighting. Franz Grillparzer's *Sappho* premieres at Vienna's Burgtheater.
1819	Playwright-critic Isaac Harby's *Alberti*. Mordecai Noah's *She Would Be a Soldier; or, The Plains of Chippewa*, based on 1814 battle of Chippewa; written for actress Catherine Leesugg. Remains popular for fifty years.	Herman Melville (d. 1891) and Walt Whitman (d. 1892) born. Spain cedes Florida to United States (Adams–Onis Treaty).	Lord Byron's poems "Don Juan " (completed 1824) and "Mazeppa." Percy B. Shelley's play *The Cenci*.

1820	Birth of playwright-actress Anna Cora Mowatt (Ritchie).	Collapse of land values leads to first U.S. banking crisis.	John Keats's "Ode on a Grecian Urn" and "Ode to a Nightingale."
		Anti-Slave Trade Act passes.	Prado completed in Madrid.
		First Greek Revival building in United States, Philadelphia's Second Bank of the United States.	German philosopher A. Schopenhauer's *The World as Will and Idea.*
		Arkansas Territory organized.	Sir Walter Scott's *Ivanhoe.*
		Alabama admitted to the Union (twenty-second state).	Simón Bolívar becomes president of Venezuela.
	Nathan A. Howes becomes first American to own a circus.	New York's population 125,000; Philadelphia, 113,000. See 1860.	George IV crowned king of England.
	Chestnut Street Theatre burns (2 April).	Missouri Compromise provides for admission of Missouri as slave state and Maine as free state.	Shelley's *Prometheus Unbound.*
	Park Street Theatre burns (24 May).	Washington Irving's *Sketch Book* (including "Rip Van Winkle") published in Europe.	Thomas Robert Malthus's (1766–1834) *Principles of Political Economy.*
	Edmund Kean (1787?–1833) first seen in United States (New York City, 29 Nov.) at Anthony Street Theatre. Tour until summer 1821. In Boston Mary Ann Duff plays opposite him.	Lambert Hitchcock begins noted chair factory in Connecticut.	Playwright Dion Boucicault born in Ireland (d. 1890).
	Debut (27 Nov.) of young Edwin Forrest (1806–72) at Walnut Street Theatre in *Douglas.*	James Fenimore Cooper's novel *Precaution.*	c. 1820 Coal Hole Public House, Strand, London, opened, one of most famous song and supper rooms, predecessor of the music hall.
	English-born actor-manager James Caldwell comes to New Orleans and dominates theatre scene until 1840.	Maine admitted as twenty-third state.	

DATES	THEATRE EVENTS IN AMERICA	SELECTED HISTORICAL/CULTURAL EVENTS IN AMERICA	SELECTED HISTORICAL/CULTURAL EVENTS THROUGHOUT THE WORLD
1820	Mordecai Noah's *The Siege of Tripoli.*	Birth of Susan B. Anthony (d. 1906).	German playwright Heinrich von Kleist's (1777–1811) *Prinz Friedrich von Homburg.*
1821	Opening of new and dramatically enlarged Park Theatre (Sept.).	First U.S. high school founded in Boston.	
	U.S. debut of Junius Brutus Booth (1796–1852) in Richmond, Virginia; New York debut, as Richard III (2 Oct.) at Park Theatre.	James Fenimore Cooper's *The Spy.*	English scientist Michael Faraday explains theory that becomes basic principle of electric motor.
	English-born actor Henry John Wallack (1790–1870) has New York debut at Anthony Street Theatre.	First U.S. natural gas well tapped at Fredonia, New York.	English playwright William Thomas Moncrieff's *Tom and Jerry.*
	William Henry Brown founds The African Theatre in New York and stages *Richard III* in September with James Hewett, its principal actor. Because of white persecution and pressure from Stephen Price, theatre closes in 1823.		Augustin Fresnel works on polarized light, providing support for wave theory of light.
	Edmund Simpson (1784–1848) becomes acting manager of Park Theatre.		Greek War of Independence begins.
	Columbia Street Theatre, Cincinnati, Ohio, early midwestern theatre opens.		Mexico declares independence from Spain.
	English-born actor, manager, scene painter Joe Cowell (1792–1863) emigrates to United States and in 1844 publishes *Thirty Years Passed Among the Players in England and America.*		
	Theatre begins in Pensacola, Florida.		
	Mordecai Noah's *Marion; or, The Hero of Lake George.*		

1822	Opening of rebuilt Chestnut Street Theatre.	Clement Clarke Moore writes "'Twas the Night Before Christmas."	Michael Faraday demonstrates principle of electric motor.
	English actor Charles Mathews (d. 1835) makes first U.S. tour (debut 23 Sept.), becoming first actor to exploit stage Yankee. He returns in 1834. See 1824.	*S. S. Robert Fulton* completes first steamboat trip from New York to New Orleans.	Greeks declare independence from Turks.
	English-born actor Francis C. Wemyss makes U.S. debut at Chestnut Street Theatre, turning to management in 1827.		Rosetta Stone serves as guide to deciphering Egyptian hieroglyphs.
	Mordecai Noah's *The Grecian Captive; or, The Fall of Athens*, adapted from a French melodrama.		Hungarian pianist Franz Liszt debuts in Vienna at age eleven.
	City Theatre, formerly Vauxhall Gardens, opens in Boston.		
	Edwin Forrest acts in "western" theatres under Joshua Collins and William Jones in Pittsburgh, Lexington, and Cincinnati.		
1823	African Theatre presents William Henry Brown's *The Drama of King Shotaway*.	Monroe Doctrine proclaimed.	Bolívar revolution in Latin America ends, six countries gain independence.
	Henry Placide's adult debut at the Park Theatre as Zekiel Homespun.	Cooper's *The Pioneers* published.	Historically accurate costumes used in Charles Kemble's *King John* (London).
	Solomon Franklin Smith organizes troupe in the South.	Chickering piano company begins in Boston.	
	John Howard Payne adapts French ballet-pantomime into *Clari; or, The Maid of Milan* with music by Henry Bishop (including Payne's lyrics for "Home, Sweet Home." First seen at London's Covent Garden).	Philadelphia completes the first city water system.	

DATES	THEATRE EVENTS IN AMERICA	SELECTED HISTORICAL/CULTURAL EVENTS IN AMERICA	SELECTED HISTORICAL/CULTURAL EVENTS THROUGHOUT THE WORLD
1824	J. N. Barker's *Superstition; or, The Fanatic Father* deals melodramatically with destructive effect of bigotry and superstition (set in 1675 New England with background of witchcraft).	Presidential election ends without electoral winner.	Cuban poet José Maria de Heredia's "Niagara."
	Camp Street or American Theatre, built by James Caldwell, opens in New Orleans (1 Jan.) with gas illumination.	South passage through Rocky Mountains discovered by Jedediah Smith.	Beethoven's Symphony no. 9 (*Choral*) debuts in Vienna.
	Mordecai Noah's *The Siege of Yorktown* performed during visit of Lafayette to New York.	Cherokee-language alphabet perfected.	
	Theatre opened in Mobile, Alabama (24 Dec.) by Ludlow.		
	U.S. debut of English actor William Conway.		
	Chatham Garden Theatre built on site of temporary venue in New York by Hippolite Barrière as competition to Park Theatre.		
	Micah Hawkins's *The Saw-Mill; or, A Yankee Trick*, comic-opera featuring Yankee characters, produced at Chatham Garden Theatre in November.		
	Charles II by John Howard Payne and Washington Irving first seen at London's Covent Garden on 27 May and then at the Park Theatre, 25 October.		
	Canadian-born actor William Rufus Blake makes New York debut at the Chatham Garden Theatre.		

African American actor Ira Aldridge (1807–67) leaves United States to establish career abroad.

Howes and Aaron Turner's circus credited as first to perform under a canvas tent; however, more likely, J. Purdy Brown was first to do so in 1825 or 1826 in Wilmington, Delaware.

1825 Samuel Woodworth's two-act musical drama *The Forest Rose; or American Farmers* with one of first Yankee characters (Jonathan Ploughboy played by Alexander Simpson) to hold stage debuts at Chatham Theatre 6 October; includes song "The Old Oaken Bucket" and black-servant role of "Lid Rose."

Edmund Kean appears in United States on second tour (first on 14 Nov. at Park Theatre) and is driven from stage in Boston (Dec.) for insulting audience.

Early theatrical center shifts from Philadelphia to New York City.

Lafayette Theatre built in New York by General Charles W. Sandford; opens 4 July.

Henry J. Finn (c. 1790–1840) becomes noted for eccentric comic roles, including Sergeant Welcome Sobersides in his own *Montgomery; or, The Falls of Montmorency*, which opened the same year in Boston.

John Quincy Adams elected president by House of Representatives.

Congress adopts removal policy to transfer eastern Native Americans to territory west of the Mississippi River.

Erie Canal opens (links New York City to Lake Erie and the West).

Hudson River School of painting founded by Thomas Cole.

Alexsandr Sergeyevich Pushkin begins poem *Eugene Onegin* (completed 1831).

Decembrist revolution in Russia.

DATES	THEATRE EVENTS IN AMERICA	SELECTED HISTORICAL/CULTURAL EVENTS IN AMERICA	SELECTED HISTORICAL/CULTURAL EVENTS THROUGHOUT THE WORLD
1826	First recorded theatre in Nashville, Tennessee.	Cooper publishes *The Last of the Mohicans*.	German composer Felix Mendelssohn (1809–1847) composes *A Midsummer Night's Dream*.
	English star William Charles Macready first appears in the United States (again in 1843 and 1848) at Park Theatre.	John Adams and Thomas Jefferson die 4 July.	
	Bowery Theatre opens in New York in October (as New York Theatre) under the management of Charles Gilfert (1784–1829).	Lyceum movement in adult education stimulated by efforts of Josiah Holbrook.	
	Lion tamer Isaac Van Amburgh begins career with animal menagerie; first appears in a cage with wild animals c. 1833.	Lord & Taylor opens in New York City.	
	Till 1830 Stephen Price manages London's Drury Lane Theatre.		
	Gas lighting installed in New York theatres.		
	Forrest supports Kean during latter's second tour; has New York debut in *Othello*.		
1827	Tremont Theatre, Boston, opens 24 September; becomes Tremont Temple in 1843.	140 antislavery groups exist in United States.	Death of Ludwig von Beethoven.
	George Washington Dixon at Chatham and Bowery Theatres promotes what become minstrel stereotypes of plantation "darky" and city "dandy" with songs such as "Coal Black Rose" and "Long Tailed Blue."	Baltimore and Ohio Railroad chartered.	Greek independence from Ottoman Turks.

Early theatre in St. Louis, Missouri.	New York's first public transit facility (horse-drawn bus).	German poet Heinrich Heine's *Buch der Lieder.*
French dancer Mme. Céline Céleste has New York debut at the Bowery.		Debut of actor-manager Charles Kean.
George Washington Parke Custis's *The Indian Prophecy.*		Victor Hugo publishes his influential preface to *Cromwell.*
Shocked by her revealing costume, audiences walk out on French dancer Mme. Hutin in New York City.		Death of Thomas Rowlandson, English artist responsible for numerous theatrical portraits and caricatures.
First probable use of border lights at New York's Chatham Theatre.		
James Kirke Paulding makes early plea for "American" drama in *American Quarterly Review* (June).		
London-born actress Clara Fisher's triumphant debut at New York's Park Theatre.		
British-born actor George Holland's (1791–1870) U.S. debut at the Bowery Theatre.		
1828 T. D. "Daddy" Rice (1808–60), possibly in Louisville, Kentucky, originates his "Jump Jim Crow" song and dance, beginning popularity of "Ethiopian Delineators."	South suffers under high Tariff of Abominations because of tax on imports.	English Romantic painter J. M. W. Turner's (1775–1851) *Regatta at Cowes.*
Forrest establishes cash prize for best new play about an "aboriginal" (28 Nov.), first of nine playwriting prizes awarded.	Workingmen's Party established in Philadelphia in reaction to Jeffersonian Republican's policies (spreads to thirty-three cities).	Birth of Norwegian playwright Henrik Ibsen (d. 1906).
Philadelphia's Arch Street Theatre opens under Canadian-born William B. Wood (1779–1861) (later co-managed with William Warren the elder [1767–1832]).	Webster's *American Dictionary of the English Language* published after 28 years of preparation.	

DATES	THEATRE EVENTS IN AMERICA	SELECTED HISTORICAL/CULTURAL EVENTS IN AMERICA	SELECTED HISTORICAL/CULTURAL EVENTS THROUGHOUT THE WORLD
1828	First stage version of *Rip Van Winkle* in Albany, 28 May, with Thomas Flynn in title role.	Painter Gilbert Stuart dies (b. 1755).	
	Stable converted into summer theatre (San Souci, later Niblo's Garden) by New York tavern keeper.		
	A Trip to Niagara; or, Travellers in America, Dunlap's final play, opens at the Bowery Theatre.		
	James H. Hackett (1800–1871), dialectician, first plays Falstaff, considered the finest of his day, and begins career as Yankee specialist starring in vehicles such as his own adaptation of George Colman's *Who Wants a Guinea?* titled *John Bull at Home; or, Jonathan in England*, first seen at the Park Theatre, 3 December.		
	Bowery Theatre burns for first time (of six).		
1829	John Augustus Stone's *Metamora* (first Forrest prize winner) opens 15 December at Park Theatre.	Spoils system introduced by Andrew Jackson.	Honoré de Balzac's first novel, *Les Chouans*.
	James Murdoch's (1811–93) stage debut at the Arch Street Theatre, Philadelphia.	Andrew Jackson becomes president.	French designer-photographer Louis Daguerre goes into partnership with J. N. Niépce.
	Richard Penn Smith's *William Penn* emphasizes need to domesticate Native Americans.	Mountain man Jedediah Strong Smith is one of first to cross Sierra Nevada and Great Salt Desert from west to east.	Rossini's opera *William Tell* premieres at Paris Opéra.

1830			
Theatre established in Memphis, Tennessee.	First railroad in United States (in England, 1825).	Victor Hugo's *Hernani* stimulates French Romanticism.	
James Kirke Paulding's *The Lion of the West* wins playwright prize from actor James H. Hackett, who creates role of frontiersman Colonel Nimrod Wildfire.	Tremont House, first modern hotel, opens in Boston (Oct.).	Revolution in Paris.	
Daniel Emmett writes "Old Dan Tucker."	Passage of Removal Bill, establishing Indian Territory in what becomes Oklahoma, forcing 92 percent of all Indians living east of the Mississippi to the west.	Accession of Britain's William IV, following death of debauched George IV.	
George Washington Parke Custis's *Pochantas; or, The Settlers of Virginia* produced at Walnut Street Theatre in January.	Church of Latter-day Saints (Mormon Church) founded by Joseph Smith 6 April.	Madame Vestris begins management of London's Olympic Theatre.	
Thomas S. Hamblin secures lease of Bowery Theatre and for most of the next twenty years controls its operation.	Poet Emily Dickinson born.	French novelist Stendhal's *The Red and the Black* published.	
	Artist George Catlin (1796–1872) begins first of three trips to the West (completed in 1832) to record at least seventeen Indian nations through his sketches.		
	South Carolina Canal and Rail Road offers first regular steam railway service.		

1831			
Harry Isherwood, with company of Joseph Jefferson I, emerges as early American scenic designer.	U.S. population reaches 12.9 million, including 3.5 million black slaves.	Pushkin's poem *Eugeni Onegin*.	
Robert Montgomery Bird's *The Gladiator* (another Forrest prize winner, performed thousands of times during career) 26 September at Park Theatre.	Cyrus McCormick invents reaper (automatic reaper patented in 1834).	English landscape painter John Constable's (1776–1837) *Salisbury Cathedral.*	
William Chapman's "Floating Palace or Theatre," first intentionally designed showboat, is launched in Pittsburgh.	Nat Turner's insurrection; fifty-seven whites killed before suppression.		

DATES	THEATRE EVENTS IN AMERICA	SELECTED HISTORICAL/CULTURAL EVENTS IN AMERICA	SELECTED HISTORICAL/CULTURAL EVENTS THROUGHOUT THE WORLD
1831	Nathaniel Deering's (1791–1881) play *Carabasset; or, The Last of the Norridgewocks* defends the Maine Indian leader.	*The Liberator* founded by William Lloyd Garrison.	English author Frances Trollope's *Domestic Manners of the Americans* published.
	Regency British pantomime brought to New York by Charles Parsloe with little success.	American Joseph Henry and Englishman Michael Faraday discover independently electromagnetic induction.	
	Weekly *The Spirit of the Times* founded in New York; features sporting and theatrical news (lasted until 1902).	E. A. Poe's *Poems* published.	
	Richmond Hill Theatre, New York, opens in November; remote location spells its doom.		
	Living pictures (or *tableaux vivants*) introduced to New York stage by Ada Adams Barrymore (illustrate painting *The Soldier's Widow*).		
1832	Bird's *Oralloosa, Son of the Incas.*	First horse trolley runs in New York City.	Irish playwright James Sheridan Knowles's *The Hunchback* premieres at Covent Garden (5 April); opens at two New York theatres in June.
	Founding of Boston Academy of Music.	Black Hawk War (Illinois and Wisconsin).	
	Dunlap's *History of the American Theatre* published.	Jackson reelected; vetoes U.S. Bank.	Donizetti's *The Elixir of Love* at Milan's La Scala.
	Appearances by Charles Kemble (1775–1854) and daughter Fanny (1809–1893), first at Park Theatre.	Cholera epidemics in major American cities.	
	T. D. Rice performs full evening of black-face songs at Bowery Theatre.	Lyrics to "America" written by Boston Baptist minister Samuel Francis Smith.	

American Amphitheatre built in Boston; opens 27 February.	Virginia legislature narrowly defeats a bill for the gradual emancipation of the slaves.	British end slavery throughout empire.
Danforth Marble begins successful career as yankee storyteller (best known as Sam Patch).		
Actor William Warren Jr.'s debut at Arch Street Theatre.		
First appearance of child actor Joseph Jefferson III as miniature "Jim Crow" with T. D. Rice.	Jackson's second term.	Edmund Kean dies 15 May in England.
Joseph S. Jones's *The Green Mountain Boy*, with character Jedediah Homebred.	American Antislavery Society formed by William Lloyd Garrison in December.	Dramatic copyright law passed in England.
Italian Opera House opens in New York; opera fails, and venue becomes National Theatre.	First penny daily newspapers serve as step toward mass-oriented publications.	
The Kentuckian; or, A Trip to New York, William Bayle Bernard's version of Paulding's *The Lion of the West* (1830).	(Nathanial) Currier and (James Merritt) Ives become "Publishers of Cheap and Popular Pictures."	
Irish actor Tyrone Power first appears in United States, settles here in 1840.	Oberlin College (Ohio) founded; becomes first coeducational college in 1838.	
G. W. P. Custis's *North Point; or, Baltimore Defended*, followed next year by *The Eighth of January*, both dramatize events from War of 1812.		
Thomas Hamblin presents sensational equestrian drama *Mazeppa* at the Bowery Theatre.	Penny press begins with *New York Sun*.	
Edwin Booth born on Maryland farm (13 Nov.).	Philadelphia's Olympic Ball Club plays early version of baseball (from English "rounders").	

1833

DATES	THEATRE EVENTS IN AMERICA	SELECTED HISTORICAL/CULTURAL EVENTS IN AMERICA	SELECTED HISTORICAL/CULTURAL EVENTS THROUGHOUT THE WORLD
1834	Bird's *The Broker of Bogota* (12 Feb. at the Bowery), his best play.	Whig Party founded.	Polish poet Adam Mickiewicz's *Pan Tadeusz*.
	F. C. Wemyss becomes manager of Philadelphia's Walnut Street Theatre.	Department of Indian Affairs established.	English novelist-playwright Edward Bulwer's novel *The Last Days of Pompeii*.
	Dunlap's *History of the Rise and Progress of the Arts of Design in the United States* published.	Beginning of boom period in cotton prices, land sales, and property values.	French Romantic painter Eugène Delacroix's (1799–1863) *Oriental Lion Hunt*.
	First National Theatre opens in Washington, D.C.		Spanish civil war begins; Portugal ends its six-year civil war.
	Josephine Clifton, who debuts in 1831 at the Bowery, becomes first American actress to star in London.		
	English actor William E. Burton's (1804–60) American debut at Philadelphia's Arch Street Theatre.		
	Record of exhibition of fire-eating for money in a private Chicago home.		
1835	Caldwell opens St. Charles Theatre in New Orleans.	Mark Twain born.	German writer Georg Büchner's play *Danton's Death* written (not produced until 1903).
	Nathaniel Bannister (who arrived in New Orleans the previous year and married John Augustus Stone's widow) presents his play *The Adventures of a Sailor* at the Camp Street Theatre, 14 March.	St. Petersburg, Florida, begins as settlement at Old Tampa Bay.	Alexis Charles Henri de Tocqueville's *Democracy in America* published.
	Frontier pioneers Noah Ludlow and Sol Smith form company (until 1853) operating theatres in Mobile, New Orleans, St. Louis, and other settlements.	Second Seminole War (to 1842).	

1,098 miles of railroad in operation.

December fire in New York destroys 674 buildings.

Russian playwright Nikolai Gogol's *The Inspector General* premieres in St. Petersburg.

Chartist disturbances in Great Britain.

Charles Dickens's novel *Pickwick Papers* published serially (completed 1837).

Ludlow and Smith build St. Emanuel Street Theatre in Mobile, Alabama.

Louisa Medina's *Last Days of Pompeii* sets record (29 performances) for longest run to date at the Bowery Theatre.

P. T. Barnum enters show business by exhibiting Joice Heth, billed as "nurse" of George Washington.

Franklin Theatre opens in New York; is reopened in 1848 as the Franklin Museum.

Zoological Institute founded to control competition in circus business. Its building, opened in 1833, became Bowery Amphitheatre for circus and equestrian performances; later a minstrel hall and as Stadt Theatre (1854) a German-language venue.

Irish actor Tyrone Power (1795–1841) is popular on frontier circuit until his death.

The Alamo falls in March; Santa Anna is defeated in April at San Jacinto; Texas declares independence.

New York's Astor House opens, setting standard for hotel luxury.

1836

Barnum serves as secretary-treasurer and ticket seller with Aaron Turner's Circus.

Acting debut of Charlotte Cushman (1816–76) as Lady Macbeth in New Orleans, followed by New York debut at Bowery Theatre.

E. L. Davenport (1815–77) begins acting career in Providence, Rhode Island.

DATES	THEATRE EVENTS IN AMERICA	SELECTED HISTORICAL/CULTURAL EVENTS IN AMERICA	SELECTED HISTORICAL/CULTURAL EVENTS THROUGHOUT THE WORLD
1836	Forrest appears for first time in London (debut as Spartacus at Drury Lane in October).		
	Irish-born actor Barney Williams (1823–76) first appears on the New York stage.		
	Yankee actor George Handel "Yankee" Hill (1809–49) takes his speciality to London (and again in 1838).		
	Dan Marble has unique success in *Sam Patch; or, The Daring Yankee*, coauthored with E. H. Thompson.		
	French mimes, the Ravel family, perform first in the United States at the Park Theatre, appearing frequently at Niblo's Garden through 1860.		
	Lion Theatre opens in Boston 11 January; structure stands until 1952.		
	English actress Ellen Tree tours for three seasons.		
	Richard Emmons's *Tecumseh.*		
	Alexander Macomb's *Pontiac.*		
1837	T. A. Cooper's last theatrical engagement (in Albany).	Martin Van Buren becomes president.	Victoria crowned queen of England; reigns until 1901.
	First free circus parade dates from about this time (Albany?).	Hawthorne publishes *Twice-Told Tales*.	Charles Dickens's *Oliver Twist* begun (completed 1838).

Barnum tours South, for one year, with his own circus, "Barnum's Grand Scientific and Musical Theatre."	Bird's novel *Nick of the Woods.*	German playwright Georg Büchner's *Woyzeck* (not produced until 1913).
First legitimate theatre activities in Chicago recorded.	John Deere perfects steel plow.	London debut of actor Samuel Phelps.
Ballad singing debut of English-born entertainer Henry Russell at the Brooklyn Lyceum; soon his solo vocal programs aimed at the common man became enormously popular.	Proctor and Gamble, manufacturers of soap and candles, established in Ohio.	Hector Berlioz's "Requiem" premieres in Paris.
Critic-playwright Epes Sargent's *The Bride of Genoa* written for actress Josephine Clifton.	Major financial crash (Panic of 1837) followed by depression after period of prosperity.	English actor-manager Charles Wyndham born (d. 1919).
Nathaniel Parker Willis wins Josephine Clifton's $1,000 play competition with *Bianca Visconti; or, The Heart Overtasked* (Park Theatre, 25 Aug.).	Artist Alfred Jacob Miller (1810–74) makes first trip to the West.	
	Ralph Waldo Emerson delivers "The American Scholar" address at Harvard, calling for intellectual independence from Europe, the past, and obstacles to originality.	
	First U.S. women's college, Mount Holyoke, founded in Massachusetts.	
	Horace Mann begins educational reforms in Massachusetts.	
1838 Louisa Medina's *Nick of the Woods* performed at the Bowery (burns this year and rebuilt the next).	Cherokee nation removed from Georgia to Indian Territory.	Charles Dickens's *Oliver Twist.*
John Robinson Circus uses first rail travel, from Forsythe to Macon, Georgia.	Introduction of Morse Code.	Edward Bulwer's play *The Lady of Lyons* at Covent Garden.

DATES	THEATRE EVENTS IN AMERICA	SELECTED HISTORICAL/CULTURAL EVENTS IN AMERICA	SELECTED HISTORICAL/CULTURAL EVENTS THROUGHOUT THE WORLD
1838	Summer saloon opened at New York's Vauxhall Garden.		Victor Hugo's *Ruy Blas* premieres in Paris.
	U.S. premiere of British writer Edward Bulwer's (Lytton) *Lady of Lyons* with Edwin Forrest and Charlotte Cushman.		Eugène Delacroix's painting *Medea* completed
	William E. Burton becomes manager of Philadelphia's Chestnut Street Theatre, remaining until 1848.		Beginning of Chartist movement.
	Joseph Jefferson II company plays Chicago in makeshift facility.		Hungarian composer Franz Liszt (1811–86) composes piano Concerto no. 1.
	Avenger of Blood; or, Richard Hurdis and the Idiot Girl: William Gilmore Simm's unsuccessful dramatization of his novel at Walnut Street Theatre (10 Oct.).		Regent's Park opens in London.
1839	J. S. Jones's *The People's Lawyer* with Yankee character Solon Shingle at Boston's National Theatre (6 May).	Poet Henry Wadsworth Longfellow's "The Village Blacksmith."	Development of Daguerre's photographic process and Fox Talbot's negative-positive process.
	Olympic Theatre built in New York in 1837 (stood until 1850) managed by English-born actor-manager William Mitchell (1798–1856) and operates for eleven years without stars.	By chance vulcanized rubber discovered by Charles Goodyear.	Chartist riots in England.
	John Gilbert's (1810–89) New York debut.	Antirent Troubles in United States (through 1847).	First production of Edward Bulwer's (Lytton) *Richelieu*.
	English actors Charles James Mathews tours United States with his manager-wife Madame Vestris, returning in 1857–58.		
	N. P. Willis's *Tortesa, the Usurer* opens at New York City's National Theatre (8 April) with James Wallack.		

Cushman first appears as Nancy Sykes (7 Feb. at the Park Theatre).

Castle Garden, previously indoor tropical garden, becomes large theatre after extensive reconstruction; 1847, remodeled into opera house. 1896, became city's aquarium (until 1940).

Death of William Dunlap and birth of James Herne.

1840 Edmund Simpson becomes sole lessee of the Park Theatre upon death of Stephen Price; manages it until his death in 1848.

C. A. Logan's *The Vermont Wood Dealer* with hero Deuteronomy Dutiful.

H. J. Conway's *The Battle of Stillwater* celebrates Revolutionary battle of October 1777.

Barnum manages variety acts in the saloon of New York's Vauxhall Garden.

First use of "vaudeville" in United States in Boston when "Vaudeville Saloon" advertises a variety program.

Ethelbert A. Marshall begins theatrical empire with Walnut Street Theatre, Philadelphia.

First play by Cornelius Mathews, termed "Father of American Drama" in his obituary, *The Politicians* (not performed).

Viennese dancer Fanny Elssler begins tour; introduced polka to United States.

John James Audubon completes his bird paintings.

U.S. population at 17 million (90 percent rural).

U.S. railroad tracks at 3,328 miles (compared to 1,818 in all of Europe).

Cooper's *The Pathfinder* published.

First U.S. iron-truss bridge, Frankford, New York.

World's first dental college opens in Baltimore.

Printed valentine cards orginated.

Publication of lawyer-writer Richard Henry Dana Jr.'s *Two Years before the Mast*.

Edward Bulwer's (Lytton) play *Money*.

Russian novelist Mikhail Yuryevich Lermontov's *A Hero of Our Time*.

Worldwide cholera epidemic begins; lasts through 1875.

Britain declares war on China (Opium War).

Scribe's *The Glass of Water* opens in Paris 17 November.

Polish actress Helena Modjeska born (d. 1909).

DATES	THEATRE EVENTS IN AMERICA	SELECTED HISTORICAL/CULTURAL EVENTS IN AMERICA	SELECTED HISTORICAL/CULTURAL EVENTS THROUGHOUT THE WORLD
1840s	First variety theatre opens in New York by William Valentine.	More than 200 steamboats on the Mississippi (double number in mid-1820s). 1.7 million immigrants in decade (from 599,000 in thirties).	Potato famine in Ireland; 1.5 million Irish emigrate, many to United States.
1841	Barnum buys John Scudder's American Museum on Broadway and Ann Street in New York and becomes proprietor on 27 December.	Emerson's *Essays* (also 1844 ed.).	English historian-essayist Thomas Carlyle's *On Heroes, Hero-worship, and the Heroic in History.*
	Boston Museum and Gallery of Fine Arts (begins as "an exhibit of curiosities") established by Moses Kimball.	William Henry Harrison dies a month after election as president; succeeded by John Tyler.	Macready assumes management of Drury Lane (to 1843).
	Boucicault's *London Assurance* (possibly with first box set) at Park in October (Jan. premiere in London).	Cooper's *The Deerslayer* published. E. A. Poe's *The Murders in the Rue Morgue* published.	
	Actress-playwright Anna Cora Mowatt begins performance career with readings in Boston.	*New York Tribune* begun by Horace Greeley.	
	J. S. Jones's *Amalek the Arab; or, The Scourge of Algiers*, Boston's Tremont Theatre, 15 March.	State fair tradition begins in Syracuse, New York.	
	Lee's Saloon, Boston; becomes Washington Theatre in 1845.		
1842	Richard Sands (d. 1870 of yellow fever while touring Cuba) develops his circus, the first American show to travel to England (1843–45); also invented color printing from wood blocks on rag paper.	Western settlement facilitated by opening of Oregon Trail.	Hamburg, Germany, largely destroyed by fire.

1843

Theatre	America	World
Irish-born actor-playwright John Brougham comes to American and appears at the Park Theatre.	John Charles Frémont expedition to California.	Robert Browning's "My Last Duchess."
Cushman manager (till 1843) of Philadelphia's Walnut Street Theatre.	Dorr's Rebellion in Rhode Island.	
James Rees's *Amaldi; or, The Brigand's Daughter*, Arch Street Theatre, 14 April.		
First U.S. costume house, Dazian's, opens in New York City.	Millerites, organized evangelists, begin to travel the "sawdust trail" along the western frontier.	
British-born George Vandenhoff begins U.S. career at the Park Theatre as Hamlet.	American surgeon Crawford W. Long first uses ether for anesthetic.	England's Theatre Regulation Act abolishes patent theatres' control.
Birth of theatre visionary Steele MacKaye.		Danish philosopher Søren Kierkegaard, founder of existentialist philosophy, writes *Either/Or*.
The Virginia Minstrels, founded by Dan Emmett (1815–1904), debut in New York (6 Feb.), staging first true minstrel show.	Forty-one-mile Old Croton Aqueduct completed in New York to supply water for New York City.	
Dan Bryant, minstrel and manager, debuts as dancer at New York's Vauxhall Garden.	First ship driven by screw propeller, the *Princeton*, launched.	Cigarettes first appear in France.
Barnum hypes midget General Tom Thumb (formerly Charles S. Stratton) and buys Peale's New York Museum, six months later integrating exhibits into American Museum. In August stages buffalo hunt in Hoboken, New Jersey, and later in Camden.	Yellow fever sweeps Mississippi Valley (13,000 die).	
Boston Museum begins dramatic presentations with resident repertory company.	Popular song "Columbia, the Gem of the Ocean" written by Thomas à Becket.	

DATES	THEATRE EVENTS IN AMERICA	SELECTED HISTORICAL/CULTURAL EVENTS IN AMERICA	SELECTED HISTORICAL/CULTURAL EVENTS THROUGHOUT THE WORLD
1843	James Caldwell, forced into bankruptcy, relinquishes control of New Orleans theatre.		
	Ben DeBar (1812–77) becomes manager of theatres in New Orleans and St. Louis, settling in St. Louis at outbreak of Civil War.		
	Matinee performance recorded in New York City.		
	William Charles Macready first appears in United States, supported by Charlotte Cushman.		
	Joshua Silsbee (1813–55) plays his first Yankee role.		
1844	Barnum and Tom Thumb tour Europe for three years, appearing before heads of state, including Queen Victoria.	U.S. treaty with China opens ports.	French novelist Alexandre Dumas père's *The Count of Monte Cristo.*
	Beginning of rivalry between American actor Edwin Forrest and British star Macready.	Samuel F. B. Morse perfects telegraph. First telegraph line strung between Washington, D.C., and Baltimore.	Samuel Phelps assumes management of London's Sadler's Wells (to 1862).
	William H. Smith's *The Drunkard; or, The Fallen Saved* opens in Boston on 12 February; seen first in New York in 1850.	Charles Goodyear obtains basic rubber vulcanization process patent.	Birth of French actress Sarah Bernhardt (d. 1923).
	Putnam, the Iron Son of '76, popular spectacle by Nathaniel Bannister (1813–47), opens (78 performances) and exploits feats of horse Black Vulture.	Transcendentalist feminist Margaret Fuller's *Summer on the Lake* published.	
		Death of architect Charles Bulfinch (b. 1763).	

1845		
America's most famous early native-born clown, Dan Rice (1823–1900), most likely debuted as a clown.	American Art Union established; makes original paintings available to middle-class consumers.	Richard Wagner's *Tannhäuser* opens in Dresden
Anna Cora Mowatt's (1819–70) *Fashion* opens at New York Park Theatre (24 March). Reviewed twice in *Broadway Journal* by Edgar Allan Poe.	Margaret Fuller's *Woman in the Nineteenth Century*.	Famine kills 2.5 million from Ireland to Moscow.
Debut of Mowatt as actress, June 1845, as Pauline in *Lady of Lyons*.	James Polk becomes president.	
Dan Rice becomes star circus clown.	Western land areas annexed (through 1860), including Texas in 1845; Mexico severs relationship with United States.	
Black minstrel dancer, William Henry "Juba" Lane, performs with white minstrels, but emigrates to England in 1848.	Mass emigrations from Ireland due to famine.	
Charlotte Cushman opens at London's Princess Theatre (13 Feb.); remains in England five years. In June first appears in London as Meg Merrilies in *Guy Mannering*.	Smithsonian Institution founded.	
Second Bowery increases capacity from 3,500 to 4,000. Burns and is rebuilt.	E. A. Poe publishes *The Raven and Other Poems*.	
Boston's Howard Athenaeum opens, burns, and second Howard opens next year (5 Oct.); structure stands until 1953.	George Caleb Bingham's painting *Fur Traders on the Missouri* (c. 1845).	
English actor-manager Charles Kean tours for two seasons (with new wife, Ellen Tree), creating impetus in United States for antiquarianism in production.	Southern Baptist Convention splits over slavery and doctrinal and procedural disputes from General Convention.	
James Rees publishes *The Dramatic Authors of America*.	Fire in New York City burns over 1,000 buildings.	

DATES	THEATRE EVENTS IN AMERICA	SELECTED HISTORICAL/CULTURAL EVENTS IN AMERICA	SELECTED HISTORICAL/CULTURAL EVENTS THROUGHOUT THE WORLD
1846	Cornelius Mathews's *Witchcraft; or, The Martyrs of Salem* (see 1840).	Mexican War begins 13 January (to 1848).	Felix Mendelssohn's oratorio *Elijah* premieres at Birmingham, England.
	William Warren Jr. (1812–88) debuts at New Boston Museum (opened 2 Nov.).	Elias Howe invents sewing machine.	Britain's Corn Law repealed; removes Ireland's favored status as supplier to British market.
	Julia Dean (1830–68) considered leading American tragic actress.	First baseball team, New York Knickerbockers, formed.	
	Walt Whitman writes theatre criticism for the *Brooklyn Eagle* (1846–48).	Charles Scribner's Sons Publishers is founded.	
	E. L. Davenport begins seven-year stint as leading man to Anna Cora Mowatt.	Boundary between Canada and United States established as a result of the Oregon Treaty (15 June).	
	King John and *Richard III*, presented as part of Charles Kean's 1845–46 tour; introduces historical accuracy and antiquarianism in scenery and costume and antiquarianism to United States.	William F. "Buffalo Bill" Cody born 26 February in Iowa.	
		American Medical Association founded.	
		Indian mounds in Mississippi Valley explored.	
		New York's Trinity and Grace Episcopal churches completed.	
1847	*Metamora; or, The Last of the Pollywogs*, satire of Indian play, by John Brougham (1810–80).	Melville's *Omoo* published.	Charlotte Brontë's *Jane Eyre* published.
	J. B. Rice constructs first permanent theatre in Chicago.	Mormons migrate to Utah, establishing Mormon Trail and founding Salt Lake City.	Emily J. Brontë's *Wuthering Heights*.

George Dibdin Pitt's popular melodrama *Sweeney Todd* premieres at London's Britannia Theatre.

British actress Ellen Terry born (d. 1928).

Economic depression in England

Michigan abolishes death penalty, the first state to do so.

Migration from the Netherlands to the Middle West begins; New York's first Chinese immigrants arrive in July.

Longfellow's poem "Evangeline."

Frederick Douglass begins abolitionist newspaper (the *North Star*).

Christy Minstrels debut at Mechanics' Hall in New York, setting format for subsequent minstrel shows.

James Kirke Paulding's *The Bucktails; or, Americans in England,* written shortly after War of 1812, published and produced.

Lester Wallack (1820–88) debuts at Broadway Theatre in *Used Up.*

William Warren the younger's fifty-year career with the Boston Museum stock company begins.

Mowatt's *Armand, the Child of the People* (Park Theatre, 27 Sept.).

Astor Opera House opens; sold in 1854 to become library and lecture hall (Clinton Hall).

A Dr. Colyer with his "Living Models" exhibits facsimiles of classical scuptures on the stage (poses plastiques).

Broadway Theatre (second with this name), modeled on London's Haymarket, opens and tries to replace Park Theatre, though not with complete success (torn down in 1859).

Palmo's Opera House introduces "living pictures" featuring scantily clad women and production shut down by New York officials.

First English-language performance (*The Golden Farmer* by Benjamin Webster) recorded in California (American soldiers in Sonoma).

DATES	THEATRE EVENTS IN AMERICA	SELECTED HISTORICAL/CULTURAL EVENTS IN AMERICA	SELECTED HISTORICAL/CULTURAL EVENTS THROUGHOUT THE WORLD
1848	Stephen Foster's "Oh! Susanna" and "Old Uncle Ned" published (other popular minstrel songs by Foster, such as "Camptown Races" and "Old Folks at Home" follow).	Mexico City occupied by U.S. forces (puppet government cedes California, New Mexico, Arizona, and Colorado through Treaty of Guadalupe Hidalgo).	Second Republic in France (Louis Napoleon, later Napoleon III).
	Burton's Chamber Street Theatre (remodeled 1844 Palmo Opera House) opens (10 July) in New York.	Gold discovered in California.	Revolutions in Paris, Vienna, Venice, Berlin, Milan, and Parma.
	Benjamin A. Baker's *A Glance at New York in 1848* opens 15 February at the Olympic and popularizes Mose the Bowery B'hoy, especially as impersonated by Frank Chanfrau.	"Bloomer" trousers for women introduced by Amelia Bloomer.	*Communist Manifesto* by Karl Marx and Friedrich Engels predicts collapse of capitalism.
	Macready tours the United States and competition with Forrest escalates into class as well as nationalistic conflict.	Liberty Party (antislavery) nominates candidate for president.	English novelist William Makepeace Thackeray's *Vanity Fair*.
	First known theatre in California converted from Monterey lodging house.	Women's Rights Convention at Seneca Falls, New York.	Royal British theatricals begin at Windsor Castle.
	Actor McKean Buchanan (1823–72) begins career with amateur Histrionic Association in New Orleans.	New York passes legislation allowing married women to own real estate.	Pre-Raphaelite Brotherhood formed by artists John Everett Millais, Dante Gabriel Rossetti, and Holman Hunt.
	Fox Sisters of Rochester, New York, with their production of strange sounds, help launch a distinctive American branch of performance related to spiritualism.	James Russell Lowell's *A Fable for Critics*.	
	Ethelbert Marshall controls 4,500-seat Broadway Theatre in New York City.	Yale lock invented by Linus Yale.	
	Calaynos, first play by George Henry Boker (1823–90).	Power loom for carpets invented by Erastus Bigelow.	
	Park Theatre burns in December.		

1849			
Dan Rice establishes his own circus.	Zachary Taylor becomes president.	Revolutions in Dresden and Baden.
Barnum's Museum boasts 600,000 curiosities and presents plays in its Lecture Room, beginning in September.	Edgar Allan Poe dies 7 October at age forty.	Death of Polish composer Frédéric Chopin (b. 1810).
Astor Place Opera House Riot (10 May), culmination of Macready–Forrest feud, leading to fragmentation of stage entertainment into more obviously popular and elitist forms.	*Lily*, a women's rights and temperance journal, published.	Birth of August Strindberg (d. 1912).
Debut (10 Sept.) of Edwin Booth (1833–93) in Boston as Tressel in *Richard III*.	Henry David Thoreau's *On Civil Disobedience*.	European revolutions ultimately suppressed.
Kate and Ellen Bateman, as child prodigies, appear in Shakespeare for first time in New York.	Department of the Interior established.	
The Bandit, first professional production in California, at Eagle Theatre (first structure built as theatre), Sacramento, which opens 18 October.	Gold rush to California under way.	
First theatrical performance in San Francisco, *The Wife*, performed by Eagle Theatre actors at Washington Hall.		
Joseph Andrew Rowe's Olympic Circus first in West (in San Francisco).		
Varieties Theatre opens in New Orleans; new theatre on same site in 1855 called Gaiety.		
Actor's Order of Friendship organized in Philadelphia as first theatrical club (lasts until 1944).		

DATES	THEATRE EVENTS IN AMERICA	SELECTED HISTORICAL/CULTURAL EVENTS IN AMERICA	SELECTED HISTORICAL/CULTURAL EVENTS THROUGHOUT THE WORLD
1850	W. R. Derr's *Kit Carson*.	Millard Fillmore becomes president.	Russian author Ivan Turgenev's play *A Month in the Country*.
	Barnum increases "Lecture Room" capacity to 3,000 for *The Drunkard*.	Henry Clay's Compromise of 1850 avoids break between slave and free states.	Elizabeth Barrett Browning's "Sonnets from the Portuguese."
	Concert saloons open in New York.	Nathaniel Hawthorne's *The Scarlet Letter* published.	Crystal Palace, designed by Sir Joseph Paxton, built in London.
	Comedian-pantomime artist George L. Fox manages National Theatre, New York, until 1858.	Fugitive Slave Act.	First and second Laws of Thermodynamics formulated by German physicist Rudolf Clausius.
	Barnum promotes Jenny Lind, the "Swedish Nightingale," beginning 11 September (until June 1851). Also buys Peale's Museum in Philadelphia, dividing holdings with Moses Kimball at Boston Museum.	First national women's rights convention held in Worcester, Massachusetts.	Charles Kean begins management of London's Princess's Theatre (to 1859).
	Value of photography to the theatre first exploited during Lind tour.	*Harper's Magazine* founded (as *Harper's New Monthly Magazine*).	Britain enters "Golden Age" of prosperity.
	George Henry Boker's *The Betrothal* staged at Philadelphia's Walnut Street Theatre, 25 September.	California becomes thirty-first state.	Dickens's *David Copperfield*.
	A. H. Purdy establishes Purdy's National Theatre, previously Chatham Theatre (1839).	Mathew B. Brady (1823–96) rises in prominence for his portrait photography.	
	At mid-century Russell Smith becomes chief scenic artist at Philadelphia's Academy of Music.	Stephen C. Foster composes "De Camptown Races."	
	Burton scores in New York City as Micawber in version of *David Copperfield*.	New York's population reaches 700,000 (20 percent foreign, mostly Irish).	

88

1851

First professional performances in San Francisco.

Mormons begin to present plays at Navoo, Illinois.

As many as fifty theatre companies throughout the country.

Barnum's Great Asiatic Caravan Museum and Menagerie begins four-year tour.

Beginning of Gilbert Spalding and Charles Rogers's "Floating Circus Palace" with circus, minstrel shows, and museum of curiosities; they became partners in 1848.

Irish-born actress Matilda Heron's debut at Walnut Street Theatre, Philadelphia, on 17 February as Bianca in *Fazio*.

Yankee Robinson completes first tenting tour in the fall.

First professional troupe (from New Orleans) appears in Minnesota at St. Paul's Mazourka Hall.

Irish-born actress Lola Montez's U.S. debut in *Betley the Tyrolean* in New York City.

American Theatre opens in San Francisco.

Henry O. Pardey's *Nature's Nobleman*.

Uncle Tom's Cabin by Harriet Beecher Stowe published as serial (novel published 20 March 1852).

Indian treaty, signed at Fort Laramie, Wyoming, gives United States permission to build roads and forts in Indian Territory in exchange for annuities.

Herman Melville's *Moby Dick* published.

First evaporated milk processed by Gail Borden.

(I. M.) Singer sewing machines successfully manufactured.

Hawthorne's *House of the Seven Gables*.

George Caleb Bingham's (1811–77) *The Trappers' Return*.

San Francisco fire destroys three-quarters of city.

Second Law of Thermodynamics articulated by Lord Kelvin.

Verdi's opera *Rigoletto* premieres in Venice.

Louis Napoleon (as Napoleon III) proclaims himself emperor of Second Empire.

Gold discovered in Australia, prompting international gold rush.

Eugène Labiche's *An Italian Straw Hat* premieres in Paris.

DATES	THEATRE EVENTS IN AMERICA	SELECTED HISTORICAL/CULTURAL EVENTS IN AMERICA	SELECTED HISTORICAL/CULTURAL EVENTS THROUGHOUT THE WORLD
1851	Burton produces first Shakespeare at his New York theatre (*The Winter's Tale* on 22 Sept.).	Fire destroys thousands of volumes in the Library of Congress.	
	Infamous divorce trial (Dec.) of Edwin Forrest and Catherine Sinclair (married in 1837).	*The New York Times* begins publication in September.	
1852	Wallack's Lyceum Theatre, originally John Brougham's Broadway (1850), opens 8 September under James W. Wallack.	Anheuser-Busch brewery founded.	Play version of *La Dame aux Caméllias* by Alexander Dumas fils first performed in Paris.
	Edwin Booth and father (J. B.) arrive in San Francisco in July.	Harriet Beecher Stowe's *Uncle Tom's Cabin* published (20 March), following serialization in the *National Era* (1851–52).	Boucicault's *The Corsican Brothers* first seen.
	J. B. Booth's final performance on 19 November at New Orleans's St. Charles Theatre; he dies soon thereafter.	Elisha Otis develops safety elevator.	Charles Morton, "Father of the halls," opens Canterbury Hall, a prominent music hall in London's Lambeth.
	Burton runs spectacular production of *A Midsummer Night's Dream* (Oct. to Jan.).	School attendance mandated in Massachusetts.	Ibsen appointed stage director and dramaturge at Bergen, Norway.
	Joseph S. Jones writes his most lasting play, *The Silver Spoon*.	Pennsylvania Railroad completes track linking Philadelphia and Pittsburgh.	
	First "Concert Hall" opens in Seattle, Washington.		
	George H. Miles's *Desoto*, popular for a decade, is produced by James Murdoch.		
	C. W. Taylor's *Adrian Grey; or, The Redemption*, New York's National Theatre, 9 August.		

1853

Van Horn Costume Company established in Philadelphia.

First Chinese theatre opens in San Francisco.

Lewis Baker and Alexina Fisher (husband and wife) run theatre on a stable basis in San Francisco for first time.

Boston Music Hall opens and structure still exists (though it has changed names four times).

Dublin-born John F. Poole becomes house dramatist at the Bowery Theatre.

George Aiken's adaptation of *Uncle Tom's Cabin*, first seen in Troy, New York (27 September 1852), with the Howard family, opens 18 July at Purdy's, in New York City, for 325 consecutive performances.

Barnum's produces "pro-Southern" version of *Uncle Tom's Cabin*.

Metropolitan Theatre, San Francisco, opens under Catherine Sinclair, 24 December; dominates until 1869.

Experiments with railroad circuses (Den Stone a pioneer by following year).

Edwin Booth appears as Hamlet for first time (in San Francisco, 25 April).

Dion Boucicault's first year in New York; seven of his plays seen that fall season.

Actor Edwin Adams debuts in Boston.

Franklin Pierce becomes president.

Gadsden Purchase treaty signed with Mexico.

Free Soil Party founded; against extension of slavery into the territories.

Potato chips developed in Saratoga Springs, New York.

Samuel Colt opens Hartford armory.

Foster composes his most popular song, "My Old Kentucky Home, Good Night."

DATES	THEATRE EVENTS IN AMERICA	SELECTED HISTORICAL/CULTURAL EVENTS IN AMERICA	SELECTED HISTORICAL/CULTURAL EVENTS THROUGHOUT THE WORLD
1853	*The New York Clipper* founded by Frank Queen begins publication as sporting and theatrical paper (absorbed into *Variety* in 1924).		
	Philadelphia's first all-minstrel theatre built by Sam Sanford.		
	William "Billy" Florence and bride Malvina Pray begin successful career as team, often in Irish-American roles.		
	First production of *Camille* (refined and chaste) in United States with Jean Davenport (9 Dec.), Broadway Theatre.		
	Actor Joshua Silsbee appears in *The Vermont Wool Dealer*.		
	Thomas Maguire founds the San Francisco Minstrels.		
1854	Boston Theatre opens in Boston on Washington Street.	Republican Party established by former Whigs, Free Soilers, and antislavery Democrats.	Japan opened by Commodore Perry; trade agreement signed with United States.
	Academy of Music opens in New York.	Thoreau's *Walden* published.	Crimean War; continues until 1856.
	Professional debut of John Wilkes Booth at Charles Street Theatre, Baltimore, as Richard in *Richard III*.	Kansas-Nebraska Act leads to fights over the legality of slavery in western territories.	Alfred Lord Tennyson's "Charge of the Light Brigade."
	Playwright-director-actor James A. Herne begins his career as an actor in San Francisco.	Know-Nothing party emerges to stop immigration.	Jean-François Millet's painting *The Reaper*.
		The Life of P. T. Barnum, Written by Himself first published (many subsequent editions; over a million copies sold during his lifetime).	

Boucicault's *Andy Blake* seen at Boston Museum, 1 March.

Anna Cora Mowatt makes last appearance as Pauline at Niblo's Garden (3 June).

Death of Charles Burke (b. 1822), half brother of Joe Jefferson III, noted for elegant, artificial roles.

Stadt Theater opens in New York City featuring first successful German-language company.

Timothy Shay Arthur's novel *Ten Nights in a Barroom and What I Saw There* (see 1858).

Russian playwright Aleksandre Ostrovsky active at Moscow's Maly Theatre.

1855 George Henry Boker's (1823–90) Romantic drama *Francesca da Rimini* with E. L. Davenport at Broadway Theatre in New York; title role created by English-born actress Madame Ponisi. *The Bankrupt* also staged at the Broadway, 3 December.

Boucicault appears in United States for the first time in his play *Grimaldi* (Cincinnati).

Actress-manager Laura Keene opens Laura Keene's Varieties Theatre in New York, followed in 1856 by New Theatre.

John Brougham's burlesque, *Po-Ca-Hon-Tas; or, The Gentle Savage*, at Wallack's, 24 December.

London-born playwright T. B. DeWalden's (1811–73) *Wall Street* makes fun of speculation.

Whitman's *Leaves of Grass* published.

"Bleeding Kansas" site of violence between pro-slavery forces and abolitionists.

Longfellow's "The Song of Hiawatha."

Leslie's Illustrated Newspaper begins in New York.

French painter Rosa Bonheur's *The Horse Fair.*

DATES	THEATRE EVENTS IN AMERICA	SELECTED HISTORICAL/CULTURAL EVENTS IN AMERICA	SELECTED HISTORICAL/CULTURAL EVENTS THROUGHOUT THE WORLD
1855	John Ellsler (1822–1903) becomes manager in Cleveland.		
	Dan Emmett opens first minstrel hall in Chicago. Also North's National Amphitheatre, devoted to equestrian shows, opens.		
	Matilda Heron (1830–77) first appears as Camille in New Orleans and two years later at Wallack's.		
	Sam Sanford builds Eleventh Street Opera House in Philadelphia as minstrel venue (until 1911).		
1856	First American copyright law (18 April), expedited by Dion Boucicault, gives author sole right to print, publish, act, perform, and present own plays.	Stowe's novel *Dred, or Tale of the Great Dismal Swamp* published.	*Madame Bovary* by French novelist Gustave Flaubert published.
	American circus adds candy and lemonade concessions and invents calliope; Spalding and Rogers Railroad Circus.	Melville's *Benito Cereno.*	Birth of George Bernard Shaw (d. 1950).
	Mrs. Sidney Bateman's (1823–81) *Self,* satire on New York society and business methods.	James Buchanan elected president.	
	Critic-playwright Edward G. P. Wilkins's contemporary comedy *My Wife's Mirror.*	Wabash and Erie Canal opens.	
	Birth in Philadelphia of Frederick Eugene Powell, later master of large-stage magic illusions.	Western Union chartered.	
	Edward Wilkins's satire *Young New York.*	Railroad service extended to Chicago.	

	French poet Charles Pierre Baudelaire's *Les Fleurs du Mal* published.
	English novelist Anthony Trollope's *Barchester Towers*.
	Aniline dye industry begins in England.

Mountain Meadows Massacre in Utah Territory.

Atlantic Monthly established in Boston.

U.S. Supreme Court in *Dred Scott v. Sandford* legalizes slavery in U.S. territories; finds 1820–21 Missouri Compromise unconstitutional.

Short-lived Panic of 1857.

1857

James Pilgrim's *Americans Abroad*, Burton's, 28 June.

Wallack's Theatre presents Indian burlesque *Hiawatha; or, Ardent Spirits and Laughing Water* by Charles M. Walcot.

(James H.) McVicker's Theatre built in Chicago.

Maltilda Heron's *Camille* at Wallack's (23 Jan.) with E. A. Sothern as Duval.

The Poor of New York (based on Brisbarre and Nus's *Les Pauvres de Paris*) as adapted by Boucicault, 8 December at Wallack's.

Early extant "variety" program using that term at the Santa Clause Concert-Saloon on Broadway in New York.

Edwin Booth's New York debut in May at Burton's Chambers Street Theatre.

Maguire's Opera House built by Tom Maguire in San Francisco.

Lawrence Barrett, who debuted in 1853, has first important New York appearance as member of W. E. Burton's Metropolitan Theatre Company.

George Fox Bailey, son of Hachaliah, assumes control of Howes and Turner's circus; becomes the Grand Metropolitan Quadruple Combination (Bailey's Herr Driesbach's Menagerie, G. C. Quick's Colossal Hippotamus, and Sands, Nathans, and Co.'s Performing Elephants).

DATES	THEATRE EVENTS IN AMERICA	SELECTED HISTORICAL/CULTURAL EVENTS IN AMERICA	SELECTED HISTORICAL/CULTURAL EVENTS THROUGHOUT THE WORLD
1857	Dan Bryant and brothers found Bryant's Minstrels, quickly becoming New York's premiere minstrel show.		Britain takes direct control of India.
	William Wells Brown reads his play *The Escape; or, A Leap for Freedom* on abolitionist platforms.		French composer Jacques Offenbach (1819–80) debuts *Orpheus in the Underworld* in Paris.
	British-born actress Emma Waller's American debut at Philadelphia's Walnut Street Theatre as Ophelia.		Death of French actress Rachel (b. 1820).
	Irish-born John McCullough (1832–85) debuts at Philadelphia's Arch Street Theatre.		
	German-speaking presentations seen at St. Paul, Minnesota's Athenaeum Theatre; continue through 1886.		
	John Brougham's burlesque *Columbus, El Filibustero! A New and Audaciously Original Historico-Plagiaristic, Ante-National, Pre-Patriotic, and Omni-Local Confusion of Circumstances* (a call for reconciliation between North and South).		
1858	Francis Leon begins career as female impersonator (star into the 1880s).	Rotary-action washing machine patented.	
	William V. Pratt's *Ten Nights in a Bar-Room* opens at New York's National Theatre. See 1854.	Laying of first transatlantic cable begun, completed in 1866.	
	Laura Keene first produces English playwright Tom Taylor's *Our American Cousin* in New York with English-born E. A. Sothern (1826–81) as Lord Dundreary.	Oliver Wendell Holmes's "The Chambered Nautilus."	

	Theatre	American events	World events
	J. G. Burnett's *Blanche of Brandywine*, Laura Keene's Theatre, 22 April.	Minnesota admitted as thirty-second state.	Anglo-Chinese War, begun 1856, ends.
	William Henry Hurlburt's *American in Paris*.	United Presbyterian Church of North America formed; follows conservative Scottish Presbyterian pattern.	
	Boucicault's *Jesse Brown; or, The Relief of Lucknow*, 22 February at Wallack's.	Congress refuses to admit Kansas to the Union under its pro-South constitution.	
	Joe Jefferson III joins Laura Keene's New York company, wins distinction as Asa Trenchard in *Our American Cousin* (written for Joshua Silsbee in 1851 but not produced then).	R. H. Macy Co. opens in October in New York City.	
	Burton closes his theatre in October and withdraws from management; dies in 1860.	New York's Central Park opens in autumn.	
1859	Boucicault's *The Octoroon; or, Life in Louisiana* opens at the Winter Garden 5 December.	John Brown's raid on Harper's Ferry.	*Origin of Species* by British naturalist Charles Darwin.
	Clifton W. Tayleure's *The Boy Martyrs of September 12, 1814* staged at Baltimore's Holliday Street Theatre.	Comstock Silver discovery in Virginia City, Nevada.	Italian actress Eleonora Duse born (d. 1924).
	Dan Emmett credited as composer of "Dixie," which premieres 4 April by Bryant's Minstrels in New York.	First oil well drilled (in Titusville, Pa.).	Franco-Austrian War.
	First dramatic agency likely founded in New York.	First sleeping car in train introduced for passenger service.	Wagner composes *Tristan and Isolde*.
	Charles Blondin crosses Niagara Falls on a tightrope 30 June.	Oregon admitted as thirty-third state.	Dickens's *A Tale of Two Cities*.
	New York–born actress-singer Charlotte Crabtree (Lotta) captures California and heads east.		English philosopher John Stuart Mill's major statement on individual liberty in *On Liberty*.

DATES	THEATRE EVENTS IN AMERICA	SELECTED HISTORICAL/CULTURAL EVENTS IN AMERICA	SELECTED HISTORICAL/CULTURAL EVENTS THROUGHOUT THE WORLD
1859	G. L. Fox and James W. Lingard open New Bowery Theatre.		
	The Melodeon, concert saloon, opens in New York City.		
1860	Boucicault's *The Colleen Bawn* at Laura Keene's Theatre, with John Drew, 29 March.	Frederick Douglass emerges as abolitionist leader.	Italy unified by Garibaldi (continued until 1870).
	Second Wallack's Theatre opens (25 Sept.); remains brilliant stock theatre until renamed The Star in 1881.	Democratic Party splits into pro-slavery and compromise factions.	British novelist George Eliot's (Mary Ann Evans) *The Mill on the Floss* published.
	Jefferson performs his version of Rip in New York on 24 December without success.	Lincoln nominated by Republicans.	Birth of Russian playwright Anton Chekhov (d. 1904).
		U.S. population 31.4 million (New York over 800,000; Philadelphia exceeds 500,000).	
		U.S. Government Printing Office begun.	
		Pony Express organized by Russell and Majors (lasts one year; first transcontinental telegraph line makes it obsolete).	
		South Carolina secedes (ten others within a year).	
		First Japanese embassy in United States.	
		Ralph Waldo Emerson's "The Conduct of Life."	
		Martini invented by San Francisco bartender.	

Year			
1860s	Term "Variety" entertainment becomes commonplace.	First pocket ten-cent joke books printed.	
	Davenport Brothers become first successful stage mediums.	Levi Strauss markets denim jeans in San Francisco; ladies blouse-skirt combination introduced.	
	Augustus Pitou becomes major manager of New York theatres.	Newspapers suffer censorship during Civil War.	
1861	Adah Isaacs Menken first appears as "Naked Lady" in *Mazeppa* in Albany at the Green Street Theatre.	Abraham Lincoln becomes president.	Serfdom abolished in Russia by Alexander II.
	Tony Pastor (1837–1908) establishes his first variety theatre in New York.	Beginning of American Civil War. Confederacy established at Montgomery Convention (4 Feb.), and Jefferson Davis becomes president on 9 February.	Victor Emmanuel creates Kingdom of Italy.
	Charles Gayler's *Bull Run; or, The Sacking of Fairfax Courthouse* opens in New York 21 July.	Wartime needs produce business boom.	First Oxford Music Hall opens in London.
	Brigham Young erects Salt Lake Theatre in Utah.	Mathew Brady and others hired by him begin photographic record of Civil War.	George Eliot's *Silas Marner* and Dickens's *Great Expectations* published.
	Mrs. John Drew becomes manager of Philadelphia's Arch Street Theatre.	Southern Presbyterian Church formed, a result of split with northern branch over slavery.	
	Brooklyn Academy of Music opens first theatre on Montague Street (burns in 1903).	Yale awards first Ph.D. degree granted in United States.	
	English actor Charles Fisher (1816–91) becomes leading man in Wallack's company (till 1872).	Richmond becomes capital of Confederacy.	
	Edwin Booth begins first English tour.	First battle of Bull Run (21 July); second, August 1862.	

DATES	THEATRE EVENTS IN AMERICA	SELECTED HISTORICAL/CULTURAL EVENTS IN AMERICA	SELECTED HISTORICAL/CULTURAL EVENTS THROUGHOUT THE WORLD
1861	John T. Ford (1829–94) builds Ford's Theatre in Washington, D.C. (after Lincoln's death managed theatres in Baltimore and Washington).	Union captures Forts Clark and Hatteras (Aug.) and enforces naval blockade of Confederacy.	
	New Wallack's Theatre opens in New York City.		
	Maggie Mitchell (1832–1918) first appears in title role of *Fanchon, the Cricket* (St. Charles Theatre, New Orleans).		
	Actress Clara Morris begins apprenticeship at John Ellsler's theatre in Cleveland (through 1869).		
	Birth in Iowa of comic singing star Lillian Russell.		
	Seattle's Yesler Hall built as first permanent performance space in that city.		
1862	George L. Fox stages pantomimes at the Bowery Theatre, until 1867.	Julia Ward Howe's "Battle Hymn of the Republic."	Victor Hugo's *Les Misérables.*
	Leah, the Forsaken by Augustin Daly (1838–99) presented at Howard Athenaeum in Boston (8 Dec.) and on 19 January 1863 at Niblo's Garden, New York City.	Homestead and Pacific Railroad acts passed by Congress, granting Indian land to whites, in order to clear way for transcontinental railroad.	Debut of French actress Sarah Bernhardt at Comédie-Française.
	Fanny Davenport's adult stage debut at New York's Niblo's Garden Theatre.	John D. Rockefeller invests in what becomes Standard Oil Company.	Bismarck prime minister of Prussia.
	Colonel Jack H. Haverly organizes his first minstrel show, opening his first theatre two years later in Toledo, Ohio.	Richard Gatling invents first machine gun.	Norwegian playwright Bjørnstjerne Bjørnson's *Sigurd the Bad.*

Salt Lake Theatre opens in Utah under ownership of Brigham Young.

After management chores in Philadelphia, William Wheatley becomes manager of New York's Niblo's Garden, where in 1866 he produced *The Black Crook.*

Piper's Opera House built in Virginia City, Nevada; by 1865 five light-opera theatres, six variety houses there.

German-born actor Daniel Bandmann first acts in English at Niblo's Garden, New York City, 15 January as Shylock.

Charles W. Witham begins career (in Boston) as scenic artist and becomes most prominent designer of century.

East Lynne (Clifton Tayleure play version of Mrs. Henry Wood's novel published that year) begins long history in Brooklyn (26 January) as one of the most popular plays in U.S. history.

Lester Wallack's *Rosedale.*

Mrs. John Wood (not author of novel) becomes manager of Olympic Theatre (for three years).

Oneida Football Club founded in Boston.

James Abbott McNeill Whistler's (1834–1903) *The Little White Girl.*

Federal land grants initiated to aid agricultural colleges.

First battle of ironclad warships 9 March (*Monitor* vs. *Merrimac*).

Lincoln issues Emancipation Proclamation on 1 January.

Draft riots in New York (July) following Military-conscription law (3 March).

Battle of Gettysburg (1–4 July).

First rotary press fed by continuous roll of paper is invented by William Bullock.

Poet John Greenleaf Whittier's "Barbara Frietchie."

Thanksgiving Day made a national holiday (first proposed in 1789 by Washington).

Ivan Turgenev's *Fathers and Sons* introduces term nihilism.

Workers' Party founded in Germany.

French realist painter Jean-François Millet's *Man with the Hoe.*

English Pre-Raphaelite painter Dante Gabriel Rossetti's (1828–82) *Beata Beatrix.*

French pre-Impressionist painter Edouard Manet's (1832–83) *Luncheon on the Grass.*

Birth of Russian director Constantin Stanislavsky (d. 1938).

DATES	THEATRE EVENTS IN AMERICA	SELECTED HISTORICAL/CULTURAL EVENTS IN AMERICA	SELECTED HISTORICAL/CULTURAL EVENTS THROUGHOUT THE WORLD
1863	G. L. Fox offers burlesque version of *Camille* (*With the Cracked Heart*), 17 November, followed by Bryant's Minstrels burlesque on 23 November (with the pulmonary heroine).	National banking system established.	
1864	Booth brothers (Junius Jr., Edwin, John Wilkes) appear together for only time in careers in *Julius Caesar* in New York (25 Nov.).	U.S. Grant becomes commander of all Union armies (9 March).	Louis Pasteur develops germ theory in France.
	Augustin Daly begins career as theatre critic (first *The Evening Express*, then *The Sun, The New York Times,* and *The New York Citizen*). Continues until 1867.	Cheyenne and Arapaho families, existing in peace under U.S. protection, slaughtered by Colonel John Chivington at Sand Creek, Colorado.	*War and Peace* by Russian novelist Count Leo Tolstoy begun (completed in 1869).
	English-born actor John E. Owens (1823–86) first appears as Solon Shingle in *The People's Lawyer*.	Sherman's "March to the Sea" (14 Nov.–22 Dec.).	
	Edwin Booth begins 100-night *Hamlet* (26 Nov.) and manages first Winter Garden Theatre until 1867.	Lincoln reelected president in November.	
	Lester Wallack becomes head of Wallack's Theatre upon death of James W. Wallack.	First railroad sleeping car built by George Pullman.	
1865	Boucicault's *Arra-na-Pogue*.	Robert E. Lee, made commander of all Confederate armies in February, surrenders last major Confederate army in April at Appomattox Courthouse.	First experiments in genetics by Mendel published.
	Barnum's American Museum burns down 13 July; new museum opens 6 September.	Civil War ends. Union losses almost 360,000 dead; Confederacy, about 258,000.	English author Lewis Carroll's *Alice's Adventures in Wonderland*.

Adam Forepaugh begins his first circus.

San Francisco Minstrels begin nineteen-year stay in New York.

Joseph Jefferson III (1829–1905) plays Rip Van Winkle (in Boucicault version) for the first time (4 Sept.) in London (Adelphi) and the following fall in New York (Olympic).

First ornate circus wagon imported from England by Seth B. Howes.

Charles B. Hicks's Georgia Minstrels, one of the earliest black troupes, founded.

Tony Pastor opens his New York variety theatre, Tony Pastor's Opera House, 14 August.

New York debut of Agnes Booth, leading lady on New York stage in 1880s.

Chicago's Crosby Opera House opens 20 April.

William Winter becomes critic for *New York Tribune* (there till 1909).

George Goodale becomes city and dramatic editor of the Detroit *Free Press* (writes criticism until his death in 1919).

Abraham Lincoln assassinated by John Wilkes Booth on 14 April at Washington, D.C.'s Ford's Theatre.

Thirteenth Amendment abolishes slavery. Freedmen's Bureau established to assist former slaves.

Andrew Johnson becomes president.

Ku Klux Klan organized at Pulaski, Tennessee.

Winslow Homer (1836–1910) paints *Prisoners from the Front.*

Stetson "ten-gallon" hat created in Philadelphia.

First train robbery in Ohio.

Birth of Irish poet-playwright William Butler Yeats (d. 1939).

The Bancrofts (Marie Wilton and Squire Bancroft) begin management of Prince of Wales Theatre, London (to 1879). Stage T. W. Robertson's *Society,* 11 November.

Franz Schubert's "Unfinished" symphony premieres in Vienna.

DATES	THEATRE EVENTS IN AMERICA	SELECTED HISTORICAL/CULTURAL EVENTS IN AMERICA	SELECTED HISTORICAL/CULTURAL EVENTS THROUGHOUT THE WORLD
1866	The lavish *The Black Crook*, forerunner of musical comedy and American burlesque, opens (then tours widely and is often revived) 12 September at Niblo's Garden, running for a record 475 performances. First extensive use of limelight.	Winslow Homer paints *The Morning Bell* and *Prisoners from the Front*.	Russian novelist Fyodor Dostoyevsky's *Crime and Punishment*.
	Concert saloons begin offering matinees twice weekly for women and children, neither of whom attended nightly shows where liquor was served.	Race riot occurs in southern cities.	
	After retiring as a consequence of Lincoln's assassination, actor Edwin Booth returns triumphantly as Hamlet (3 Jan.).	United States opposes French installation of Archduke Maximilian as king; General Philip Sheridan sent to Mexican border to show disfavor.	French Impressionist Edgar Degas's (1834–1917) *Woman Drying Her Foot*.
	Italian actress Adelaide Ristori begins first of several U.S. tours.	Winchester repeating rifle introduced.	
	Thalian Dramatic Association founded at Brown University, one of earliest student producing groups.		
	G. L. Fox presents pantomime *Jack and Jill* (19 Feb.).		
	First circus owned by Adam Forepaugh; continues with his name until his death in 1890.		
	Fourteenth Street Theatre, opens as the Théâtre Français in New York City.		
	Forrest, on decline, makes grand tour of California.		

1867	T. W. Robertson's *Ours* staged at Wallack's (11 Dec.) for forty nights. Daly's melodrama *Under the Gaslight* opens 12 August at New York Theatre. Pence Opera House, Minneapolis, Minnesota, opens in June. Lotta Crabtree stars in dual roles in *Little Nell and the Marchioness*, John Brougham's dramatization of Dickens's *The Old Curiosity Shop*. Rose Eytinge appears for the first time in her best-known role, Nancy Sykes, in *Oliver Twist*, opposite E. L. Davenport's Bill Sykes. Edward Harrigan first appears on stage as an Irish comic singer in San Francisco. Eaves Costume House founded in New York. Winter Garden Theatre destroyed by fire.	Horatio Alger's *Ragged Dick* published. Congress passes Reconstruction Acts. United States purchases Alaska from Russia for $7.2 million. Canada granted dominion status. First practical typewriter made. Whitman's poem "When Lilacs Last in the Dooryard Bloom'd" published.	*Das Kapital* (completed 1894) by German philosopher Karl Marx. English playwright T. W. Robertson's cup and saucer drama *Caste* staged at the Prince of Wales Theatre, 6 April. Ibsen's play *Peer Gynt* written; staged in Oslo in 1869. Dostoyevsky's *Crime and Punishment*. Alfred Nobel invents dynamite. English poet Matthew Arnold's "Dover Beach." French Impressionist Camille Pissarro's (1831–1903) *Still Life*. Modern antiseptic surgery begins with sterilization and antiseptic procedures of Joseph Lister.
1868	Daly's *A Flash of Lightning* opens 10 June at Broadway Theatre; followed on 12 October by his *The Red Scarf* at Conway's Theatre, Brooklyn, New York. George L. Fox's pantomime *Humpty Dumpty* opens at Olympic with Fox as Clown, which he plays until his death in 1877.	Second Fort Laramie treaty creates Great Sioux Reservation. President Johnson impeached. Ku Klux Klan terrorizes blacks and supporters of Reconstruction.	English novelist Wilkie Collins's *The Moonstone*. French painter Jean-Baptiste-Camille Corot's (1796–1875) *The Sleep of Diana*. French Impressionist Claude Monet's (1840–1926) *The River*.

DATES	THEATRE EVENTS IN AMERICA	SELECTED HISTORICAL/CULTURAL EVENTS IN AMERICA	SELECTED HISTORICAL/CULTURAL EVENTS THROUGHOUT THE WORLD
1868	Lydia Thompson and her British Blondes appear in New York, first in *Ixion; or, The Man at the Wheel*; help combine burlesque with pulchritude in tights (leads to "leg show").	Fourteenth Amendment to U.S. Constitution is ratified.	Edouard Manet's *Zola*.
	Barnum's New American Museum burns down.	Bret Harte's California stories and poems appear in *The Overland Monthly* (through 1871).	Maxim Gorki born (d. 1936).
	George Wood renames building opened the preceding year by John Banvard as a museum, Wood's Museum and Metropolitan Theatre.	Burlingame Treaty signed between United States and China.	
	Dan Castello's Circus becomes first to make transcontinental tour.	Celluloid developed by inventor John Hyatt.	
	The Lottery of Life, John Brougham's sensational melodrama.		
	Henry Austin Clapp (1841–1904) begins career as theatre critic with the *Boston Daily Advertiser*.		
	The Benevolent and Protective Order of Elks begins in New York as charitable organization with a theatrical connection, which is lost by turn of the century.		
	Publication of Sol Smith's *Theatrical Management in the West and South for Thirty Years*.		
1869	Booth's Theatre, New York, opens at Sixth Avenue and Twenty-Third Street on 3 February with *Romeo and Juliet*.	Ned Buntline's *Buffalo Bill, the King of Border Men* published (first of more than 550 dime novels about Buffalo Bill Cody).	Suez Canal opens.

Augustin Daly assumes management of Fifth Avenue Theatre (dates from 1865); opens 16 August with Robertson's *Play*.

Mrs. George H. Gilbert begins thirty-year engagement with Daly, becoming one of the "Big Four," as does actor James Lewis.

Daly presents his first Shakespeare production, *Twelfth Night*, 4 October.

California Theatre opens on Bush Street in San Francisco (18 Jan.) under management of John McCullough and Lawrence Barrett.

Sam Lucas initiates long career as distinguished black performer.

Actress Kitty Blanchard marries Arthur McKee Rankin; they begin twenty-year touring career.

J. K. "Fritz" Emmet (1841–91) appears in his first Charles Gayler "Fritz" play, *Fritz, Our Cousin German*.

Magician Alexander Herrmann first seen in New York.

Actor-playwright Steele Mackaye studies in Paris with François Delsarte.

Actor Frank Mayo's New York City debut.

Ulysses S. Grant elected president.

Battle of Summit Springs (Fifth Cavalry defeat Cheyennes led by Tall Bull, in Colorado).

Susan B. Anthony becomes president of the National Woman Suffrage Association (organized by Anthony and Elizabeth Cady Stanton).

Cincinnati Red Stockings becomes first professional baseball team.

Transcontinental railroad completed with driving of golden spike at Promontory, Utah.

Chewing gum patented.

First intercollegiate football game played between Princeton and Rutgers.

First processed-food factory opened by Henry J. Heinz.

Mark Twain's *The Innocents Abroad*.

Bret Harte's *The Outcasts of Poker Flat*.

Vienna's Staatsoper opens.

DATES	THEATRE EVENTS IN AMERICA	SELECTED HISTORICAL/CULTURAL EVENTS IN AMERICA	SELECTED HISTORICAL/CULTURAL EVENTS THROUGHOUT THE WORLD
	Theatre critic Andrew Carpenter Wheeler (A.K.A. Trinculo and Nym Crinkle) begins career as New York reviewer with the *Sunday World*.	Louisa May Alcott's *Little Women* published.	
	British actor Charles Wyndham appears in *The School for Scandal* at Wallack's.	National Prohibition Party founded.	
	Daly's first major success, *Frou-Frou*, adapted from French play by Meilhac and Halevy, opens 15 February.	First blacks elected to U.S. Congress.	Franco-Prussian War (ends 1871); Siege of Paris.
	Clara Morris joins Daly's company; leaves in 1873.	Salt Lake (Utah) connected with East and West coasts (becomes favorite touring stop).	Birth of Marie Lloyd (d. 1922), music-hall star.
	Mme. Rentz's Female Minstrels (renamed Rentz-Santley Novelty and Burlesque Company) created by Michael B. Leavitt, credited as first American burlesque show.	Fifteenth Amendment ensuring citizenship to former slaves and prohibiting Confederates from holding public office ratified.	Bismarck becomes first chancellor of German empire.
	Across the Continent (James J. McCloskey) premieres at Park Theatre, Brooklyn, starring Oliver Doud Byron.	Atlantic Refining Co. is incorporated.	Completion of unification of Italy.
	Publication of "Colonel" T. Allston Brown's (1836–1918) *History of the American Stage*.	Standard Oil of Ohio is incorporated, with John D. Rockefeller as president.	French writer Jules Verne's *Twenty Thousand Leagues under the Sea*.
	Kate Claxton (called "the Sarah Bernhardt of America") begins acting career with Lotta Crabtree.	Railway track mileage exceeds 53,000 miles nationally.	
	Drama critic L. Clarke Davis becomes editor of *The Philadelphia Inquirer*.	Grant attempts to annex Santo Domingo and Dominican Republic; blocked by Senate.	

1869	Premiere of T. B. DeWalden's successful version of *Kit, the Arkansas Traveler,* vehicle for F. S. Chanfrau.	First headquarters established for Weather Bureau.
	London-born actor Charles Fechter (1824–79) has U.S. debut.	Boston Museum of Fine Arts chartered.
1870	Bronson Howard's first major play, *Saratoga,* produced.	Congress readmits four remaining southern states to the Union.
	Former actress and playwright Olive Logan publishes *Before the Footlights and Behind the Scenes.*	
	Merced Theatre in Los Angeles opens.	

1

American Theatre in Context, from the Beginnings to 1870

Bruce McConachie

Introduction

Theatrical performances do cultural work of historical significance through their repeated circularity over time. A performance genre, the interplay of conventional actions and responses, is repeated for a few years until groups of performers and spectators find other modes of interacting that are more entertaining. Theatre historians have traditionally jumped in to explain this ongoing circular process at the many points of production, but the moments of reception – the points at which the feedback loop is complete – also require explanation. Explaining audience response necessarily leads the historian to embed performance events into their social and cultural milieu; spectator response, in turn, is potentially the most important key to historical context. Consequently, this summary chapter on the context of American theatre from 1600 to 1870 focuses on historical audiences and the major genres they enjoyed.

Because the most relevant context for theatre audiences is frequently other types of performances, this overview will also include comments on sporting events, religious rituals, and other kinds of public performances beyond the theatre. All American cultures enjoyed a range of performance events, only some of which ever found their way onto a stage. Many historical groups, of course, had neither the cultural inducements nor the material necessities to establish theatre as a separate institution. Of the three major cultures in North America after 1600, only white Europeans began with an itch for "theatre" as it is usually understood; Native Americans and Africans had institutionalized other modes of performance. A history of the American theatre limited to performances in a European language on a raised stage automatically excludes the performance traditions of many Americans.

Two major questions organize this chapter: Who was in the audience for these significant performance genres, and why did they enjoy the show? A host

111

of minor questions follow from these two: How did individual spectators group themselves according to normative divisions of race, class, gender, and other historical categories; what aspects of their backgrounds and daily lives carried over into their performance experiences; and among those social groups in attendance, which exercised the most authority at performance events and in their historical societies as a whole? Regarding enjoyment, what was it about these performance genres that animated the desires and concerns of these spectator groups; how did spectator participation in these events help them to justify celebrating, marginalizing, or erasing the cultures of other Americans?

Investigating possible answers to questions about audience composition, background, and cultural authority is sometimes difficult but relatively straightforward in approach. Several theories and methods, however, might be used to understand the subjective responses of groups of playgoers and how they became a part of the many kinds of cultural work done in performance. I approach this area of inquiry through cultural systems analysis. Such an approach involves understanding the major genres of performance within the cultural systems that gave them significance for their audiences – that is, the systems of discourse and action that shaped and were shaped by their historical participants. Christianity, for instance, is a cultural system (with many subsystems) that continues to be constituted in the United States by an immense variety of texts and actions, some of which have been based in performance. Cultural systems organize behavior and belief in the body, the family, the community, and larger social institutions. They generally cut across conventional divisions of gender, class, and race, although cultural systems invariably help to facilitate the super- and subordination of particular social groups derived from these divisions. This chapter emphasizes the boundaries of cultural systems, especially as they helped to construct the dimensions and dynamics of class, race, and gender in American history.

Each of the major genres organizing performers and spectators spilled into several cultural systems but were typically anchored in only one or two. The equestrian acts of the early circus, for example, often involved their spectators in the cultural systems of republicanism and gentility but were rooted, through their primary image of a hero on horseback, in the cultural system of patriarchy. In no period of U.S. history has theatrical performance connected with all of the major cultural systems in the country, but during a number of eras the theatre has been a part of several important ones.

This overview comprises three major sections. "Folk and Elite Performance, 1600–1770" begins with the performance traditions of Native Americans on the eve of English imperial incursions into North America. Despite wide diversity among tribes, most Indian performances rested within a version of the Native American cultural system of reciprocity. Next, this section traces the survival of some folk performances from Europe and the emergence of new ones in the Spanish, French, and, primarily, the English colonies. The section concludes with the brief efflorescence of English colonial theatre, which was dominated by the merchant and planter elite and which primarily reinforced their cultural systems of patriarchy and gentility.

"Popular Performance in the New Republic, 1770–1830" starts by asking why many English colonists in the late 1760s turned against the theatre and other forms of performance that they had previously enjoyed. What motivated the intense antitheatrical prejudice of the revolutionaries, and why did it continue through most of the 1780s? By the 1790s, popular performances began to flourish as never before, partly because the social base for auditors at theatres and other performance venues broadened to include more professionals, artisans, and women from all classes. Many of the performances they enjoyed – including militia parades, gothic thrillers, circus horsemanship, and domestic melodramas – helped to organize their beliefs and behavior within American republicanism, a new cultural system, and within paternalism and sentimentality, derivations from the previous systems of patriarchy and gentility. As unwilling immigrants to America, Africans had begun to develop a cultural system of collective mutuality during the Middle Passage. By 1800, African Americans, both slave and free, had modified their African past to elaborate distinctive performance genres within this system in an effort to allow them to maintain their dignity and individuality in the midst of white oppression.

"Commercial Performance, 1830–1870," looks at the emergence of many different audiences as better transportation and more populous cities encouraged capitalists to develop a wide range of profit-making performances. Star-struck Jacksonians, Irish immigrants, Protestant women and men, rowdy urban workers, German Americans, and the new Victorian business class patronized a range of performances, from Indian plays and minstrel shows to Italian opera and sensation melodramas. For a while, various of these performance events continued the traditions of republicanism, sentimentality, and paternalism, but others involved the spectators in a cultural system relatively new to American theatre – rationality. By 1870, the experiences of rationality and respectability in American theatres had helped to transform the dominant culture of the United States from the republicanism of the Revolutionary era to bourgeois Victorianism. As before, but through different means, the performances enjoyed by white Americans continued to marginalize or erase the black and "red" Americans also living on the continent.

Folk and Elite Performance, 1600–1770

Tribal societies from Siberia were the first immigrants to North America, crossing a land bridge between forty and fifteen thousand years ago and gradually moving south. By 9000 B.C., these Paleo-Indians had spread through-out the Western Hemisphere. Many groups of Native Americans began sup-plementing their hunting, fishing, and gathering practices with agriculture; eventually, complex societies based on the production of corn and other crops arose in several areas of both continents. In 1500, roughly 7 to 10 mil-lion American aborigines were living north of present-day Mexico. Although their societies, languages, and cultures differed widely, trade and warfare facilitated an ongoing exchange of social practices and technologies. Further, their common heritage in circumpolar culture ensured that their belief sys-tems, and hence many of their performances, shared striking similarities.

Ethnohistorians interested in understanding the significant performance traditions of Native American peoples before their contact with Europeans face many obstacles. Chief among them is the lack of documentation; the Indians kept no written records, and early reports from European explorers are vague and riddled with ethnocentric assumptions. Further, Native Ameri-can performance practices continued to be historically dynamic. Because many performances originated in dreams and visions as well as "tradition," the Indians began altering their performances to accommodate their new cir-cumstances soon after their encounters with Europeans. Nevertheless, eth-nohistorians can assume that many performances in Indian communities probably changed little over time, especially in those rituals in which it was sacrilege to alter fixed patterns of behavior. This opens up their investiga-tions to oral history and contemporary observations as well as to some later reports by European travelers. Archeological digs, understood in the context of other cultures deriving from circumpolar peoples, are also helpful. Together, these sources allow ethnohistorians to paint a colorful picture of precontact Indian performance that focuses on continuity and similarity amid much intertribal variety.

Preencounter Indian performance in North America ranged from casual sto-rytelling to week-long rituals. Most tribal members were welcome at all perfor-mance events, although children and menstruating women were excluded from some rituals. Since Indian children were generally expected to learn con-formity and self-control, it was important to include them as observers unless the performance was restricted to members of a sect or special group. Sex as well as age determined the division of labor in a tribe and thus the kinds of roles that women might play in tribal performances. Although apparently no tribe allowed women to become shamans, women participated as musicians, dancers, and designers in many rituals. Samuel de Champlain reported an Algonquian victory dance in 1615 that featured wives and daughters as the primary performers. For shamans and chiefs, performing rituals and speeches maintained and might even enhance their leadership in the tribe. For all par-ticipant-spectators, performance events gave them an opportunity to improve their standing among other tribal members. Much of life in Native American societies centered on prestige, rather than on property or power. This partly accounts for the many rituals in which gift-giving played a significant role; the more one could give away, the more prestige one acquired.

Enhancing prestige through gift-giving was an important part of a larger cultural system in most tribes that centered on reciprocity. The mutual exchange of gifts, of conversation, of articles in trade, and of performance techniques helped tribes to maintain solidarity despite often great differences in power and status among individual tribal members. Many of their rituals, stories, and sports legitimated a general notion of reciprocity. In Native American understanding, nature was a web of interdependent powers within which humans had to share their bounty with animals, trees, ghosts, and other forces. To maintain cosmic harmony, Indians believed they had to conciliate the powers of nature. Conciliation took a variety of forms; the horticultural tribes of the Southwest had very different concerns and rituals than the hunting tribes of the North, for instance. But most ritual dancing in both areas aimed at restoring a natural and spiritual equilibrium that had somehow fallen out of balance. Propitiating the sun or the spirit of the bear served the same general ends in southern and northern tribes.

Thus religious practice, with its emphasis on interdependence, usually bolstered customary tribal ways and maintained traditional disparities of prestige within tribes. This cultural system and its performances also allowed Indians to demonize nonconformists, who might be banished for causing sickness and death. Outsiders beyond their tightly knit tribes might be vilified too, as potential destroyers of the cosmic equilibrium on which their physical and spiritual lives depended. In dealing with outsiders, most Indians hoped for reciprocity, but they prepared for war. Indeed, reciprocity was not the only cultural system shaping Indian lives. Native American reciprocity functioned through eight major genres of traditional ritual performance, according to ethno-historian Ake Hultkrantz. Death rites, unification and bundle rituals, initiation ceremonies, hunting and fertility rites, New Year rituals, and rituals performed by shamans either in a quest for guardian spirits or to heal the sick were widespread in North America in 1600. All tribes practiced mourning rites and burial rituals, although extensive ancestor rites were not a part of North American cultures. Unification rituals among southwestern and southeastern tribes, for example, derived from the aborigine notion of a dual cosmos; the Indians danced to secure the unity of their divided universe, typically the union of earth and sky. Rituals centered on the celebration of sacred bundles were especially prevalent in the Great Plains area. The Cheyenne practiced a tribal ritual involving the bundling of sacred arrows, for instance.

Separate clans and secret societies within tribes danced initiation ceremonies; entire tribes sometimes used them to establish friendship with foreign groups. One of the first Spaniards to arrive in Texas in 1527 reported that the local natives (from a Hokaltecan tribe) danced all night to prepare for their sacrifice. In the morning, he was surprised when they insisted on the reciprocal giving of food and hospitality instead. An Algonquian circle dance involving the exchange of gifts greeted French travelers in 1709. This was probably a calumet or "peacepipe" dance, practiced by tribes from the Plains to the St. Lawrence to initiate strangers. Typically, these ceremonies began with a parade to greet the recipients of the ritual and ended with a gift give-away, the smoking of the pipe, and a feast to celebrate their initiation as temporary tribal members. Within tribes, members were initiated as male warriors or marriageable women in similar festive rites of passage.

The belief that animals share many of the same physical and spiritual attributes as humans anchored most hunting rites among the aborigines of North America. Bear ceremonialism, common among many cultures deriving from Ice Age circumpolar tribes, was meant to appease the spirit of the slain bear, usually by returning some part of it to nature, so that hunters might kill other bears for food. Many tribes along the North Pacific coast honored the first salmon caught during the season for similar reasons. Often the women of eastern tribes played a prominent role in hunting rituals; Captain John Smith was shocked when thirty Powhatan females in Virginia emerged from the woods nearly naked and danced near him, one fitted with deer horns and others carrying bows, arrows, and clubs. Several seventeenth-century explorers in New England and the Plains noted the use of elaborate makeup and costuming to represent the interplay between stalking Indians and animals in the wild.

The agrarian cultures of the Southwest practiced some of the most complex fertility rites, but by 1600 similar rituals had spread from the Sioux in the Plains to the Iroquois in the North and the Creek in the South. Two travelers among the Creeks in the eighteenth century gave an extensive account of their Corn ritual, the most important of their six seasonal ceremonies during the year. This ritual of reciprocity began in August with the maturing of the corn crop and lasted for a week or longer. After burning their old belongings and drinking a strong emetic meant to purify their bodies and spirits, the Creeks fasted for three days before dancing. The travelers reported a variety of songs and dances accompanied by tambours, rattle-gourds, and flutes and the ritual distribution of new fire by the priests, gift-giving, tobacco smoking, and visiting with friends from neighboring towns. One of the most dangerous fertility dances practiced in the Southwest was the snake dance of the Hopis. Seeking their ancestors' assistance in bringing rain, select fraternities in Hopi tribes danced with live rattlesnakes, symbols of their ancestors, who, like the snakes, were believed to have emerged from under the earth.

Many native New Year rituals were similar to seasonal fertility rites. A New England colonist in 1674 reported a year-end harvest dance in an Algonquian tribe that centered on individual dancing, elaborate gift-giving, and visits with neighboring tribes; the Indians, he added, committed "much impiety" at these reciprocity revels. Most New Year rituals represented tribal notions of cosmic creation. Often, the lodge house used for these ceremonies was laid out to symbolize the universe; the length of the ritual usually corresponded to the time of cosmic creation. The Hupa and Karok Indians of northern California, for example, constructed a new sweat house every year to recapitulate the creation of the world. The Sun Dance of the Plains' Arapaho centered on an offerings pole, meant to represent the World Tree. This symbol connected the lower world (the place of creation) to humankind on the earth's surface and ultimately to the sky gods. To recreate the time it took to shape the world, the Arapaho performed the Sun Dance in four days.

Tribal shamans generally derived their powers from dreams, visions, or ecstatic states induced through the use of tobacco and other drugs. In his quest for a guardian spirit, the shaman often attempted to reciprocate, through mimicry, the attributes of the animal whose protective spirit he sought. One of the most colorful of such rituals was the Thunderbird Dance performed by Kwakiutl shamans in the Northwest, who dressed in a costume of eagle feathers replete with a carved wooden mask to represent the bird. Most shamans invoked war or peace spirits, counseled tribal leaders, and worked as "medicine men" to cure physical and psychological illness. Shamanic healing rituals might last for several days; Navajo shamans performed a nine-night curing ceremony. Iroquois shamans invoked spirits, represented by carved facial masks worn during the ritual, to drive away disease. Most shamans exerted substantial power within their tribes. By 1600, organized priesthoods shaped the lives of many Indians in several tribes of the Southeast and Southwest.

Other performance events besides ritual dancing helped to constitute the reciprocal cultural systems of North American aborigines. Storytelling and speechmaking, usually in situations facilitating the sharing of many stories and speeches, played significant roles in all Indian tribes. Many stories related cosmological myths, such as those among tribes in the Southwest, which centered on the actions of the sun. Some mythic tales served institutional purposes, narrating how an ancient hero instructed tribal ancestors in making canoes or houses and regulating tribal affairs. Other stories, although told primarily for entertainment, instructed tribal members in modes of excess and buffoonery; a whole series of tales told among Plains tribes focused on a trickster figure renowned for his sexuality, greed, and treachery. Mastering persuasive public speaking was especially important for shamans and chiefs, since most Indian communities made decisions by consensus. John Smith noted that Powhatan elders spoke to tribal members with such vehemence and at such length that they were exhausted and hoarse when they finished. Sporting events featuring balls, sticks, racquets, and hoops were also popular in many tribes. Typically, their games were another form of ritual reciprocity in which gifted athletes, prepared by shamans, competed to placate spirits as well as enhance their prestige. At least forty-eight native tribes played a version of lacrosse.

Despite some early instances of reciprocity among Native Americans and European invaders, the encounter experience was a catastrophe for Indian populations and their cultures. The Spaniards needed conquered natives to labor in their mines, provide food for their missions and military outposts, and increase their count of saved Christian souls. After nearly a hundred years in Florida, New Mexico, and California, Spanish wars, diseases, and missionary work had reduced tribal populations by over 90 percent and had Christianized many Indian rituals. To facilitate their fur trade from Quebec to New Orleans, French males married into many tribes. Several generations of "mixed bloods" rose to prominence in what remained of the Huron, Illinois, and Choctaw tribes. Over time, the "mixed bloods" altered their traditional Indian cultures, including their performance practices, to accommodate French trading interests. Epidemic diseases decimated Indian populations near Dutch and English settlements along the Atlantic. The Second Powhatan War of 1644–46 and "King Philip's" War in 1675 opened up vast territories in Virginia and New England to land-hungry English colonists.

Most tribes in contact with French and English imperialists intensified and altered their ritual performances to ward off the ravages of European gunpowder and disease. After a century of Jesuit missionary work, several Algonquian tribes in Canada changed their burial rites and began elaborating a concept of the afterlife in their storytelling that included a Christian notion of hell. Following an initial drop in the Indian population of New England from around 125,000 to less than 10,000 in 1675, Puritan missionaries established nearly thirty "praying towns" of Native Americans in their colonies. These Christianized Indians were dispersed and herded into reservations, the first in the "new world," or forced to work for the colonists after the Puritan–Indian wars of 1675–76.

Not all of the intercultural traffic in ritual change went one way, however; occasionally, the colonists had to accommodate themselves to Native American performances. Perhaps the most important instances of this were the Condolence Councils of forest diplomacy, practiced first among the Five Nations of the Iroquois Confederacy and later extended to regulate the fur trade among Indians and colonizers from France, Holland, and England. In what were essentially initiation ceremonies, colonial governors and Native American *sachems* sang, exchanged gifts, celebrated kinship ties, and mourned their tribal ancestors to gain mutual understanding and negotiate treaties. One of the most solemn events of this ritual of reciprocity was the linking of arms among Indians and colonizers to form a covenant chain, the physical embodiment of their interdependence. A Condolence Council provided the foundation for four Iroquois *sachems* to visit London in 1710 to plan for the Anglo-Iroquois invasion of French Canada. The Iroquois used Condolence Council rituals to hold the balance of power between France and England, thus gaining decisive leverage for more than a hundred years with these rival imperialists.

No western or northern tribes, however, could stop the flow of Indians pushed out of the East by the advancing whites. By the mid-eighteenth century, shamans from eastern tribes relocated in the Ohio Valley began to form prophetic movements in response to the decline of reciprocal gift-giving from the British, a decrease in sources of game, and pressure to cede more territory. One Delaware prophet, Neolin, elaborated new rituals, called for the repudiation of European culture, and preached pan-Indian military cooperation to drive the white devils from their lands. This sparked a war against the British and led to a partial Indian victory in the English Proclamation of 1763, which recognized existing Indian land rights west of the Appalachian crest. (Because the Proclamation limited westward expansion, it also exacerbated anti-British feeling along the frontier and ensured that most western settlers would support the Revolution twelve years later.) By 1770, then, European imperialism had forever changed many of the performance practices of eastern and southwestern Native Americans.

From the Indian point of view, the cultural performances among the early colonists probably appeared paltry as well as pointless. Unlike Native Americans, Europeans separated the secular from the spiritual and celebrated man's domination of nature in many of their performances. Although the early European settlers carried in their heads a rich folk tradition of performance, their departure from stable communities and their initial struggle for survival forced them to settle at first for simple sports, hearty songs, humorous stories, and earnest speeches. Some performances from the rich legacy of English country fairs and vocational and religious holidays would appear later on in English colonial life, but others, like morris dancing and the feast of St. Crispin's, could not survive the dispersal of the immigrant population into isolated farms and tiny villages.

Traditions of religious performance, however, better weathered the transatlantic passage. This was especially true in New Spain and New France, whose missionaries used Catholic rituals and occasional religious dramas to convert the Indians. Probably the first European play in continental North America was performed in 1567, when Spanish settlers and soldiers staged a religious drama in Florida to celebrate the feast day of St. John the Baptist. French Jesuits in Canada were performing plays with and for Native Americans as early as 1606. In the English colonies by the 1660s, religious services blended into the seasonal rituals of frontier agricultural life. These included harvest dances, winter sewing circles, barn raisings, and sporting competitions at occasional community gatherings for fairs, elections, and militia drills. Seventeenth-century English settlers were especially adept at inventing or adapting community rituals that combined work with pleasure. Though very different from Indian performances, several of these dances, worship services, and community activities – especially those drawing on peasant traditions – did recognize and celebrate relations of interdependence among various "tribes" of early English colonists. Other seventeenth-century rituals, however, drew the settlers into the more modern European cultural systems of nationalism, Puritanism, and/or patriarchy.

By the beginning of the eighteenth century, two distinctive and often antagonistic orientations toward performance were shaping colonial life in America. Both orientations had deep roots in English tradition. White men of all classes in the South tended to draw their notions of enjoyable performance from the English aristocracy and peasantry; they wagered on blood sports like cockfighting, practiced competitive debates in their schools and taverns, and sought to enhance their honor through drinking bouts and fist fights or duels. Gentlemen in the Chesapeake region, for instance, celebrated their leisure time with extravagant show and vigorous competition. And because African slaves had replaced white indentured servants as the primary work force, some southerners had more leisure to enjoy than before. Indeed, the economic success of slavery devalued earlier performances related to work and reciprocity, turning the culture toward performances that celebrated leisure and elaborated patriarchal power.

Many settlers in New England and the Middle Colonies also recognized the importance of sports, convivial drinking, and debate, but counseled moderation in these matters. The religious dissenters among them – not only Puritans, but also Dutch Calvinists in New York and Quakers in Pennsylvania – rejected the aristocratic culture of competitive ceremony and honor. Their religions inclined them to look inward for signs of salvation, to find their moments of ecstasy in spiritual regeneration, not in worldly rewards. The rituals of the dissenters, including sermons, covenant renewals, and public executions, focused attention on individual sin, the need for humility and industry, and the demands of community service. Southern performances tended to value self-assertion and personal honor and took delight in ceremonies of social role-playing. Most New Englanders and many in the Middle Colonies prized performances that rewarded self-control and work, and they questioned the morality of self-representation.

These two orientations to performance would significantly shape each region's response to the arrival of new performance genres from England, including the theatre. A Massachusetts law banning theatrical shows in 1699 was reinforced in 1750, and the Quaker-dominated city council of Philadelphia refused permission for a troupe to perform in the same year. Colonists in Virginia and Maryland, however, never enacted legislation against performers and encouraged a variety of theatrical fare after 1700.

By the 1740s, the success of tobacco and slavery solidified the dominance of a planter elite in the Chesapeake, the most populous region of the South. Three distinct classes had emerged among whites: the gentry, whose members owned more than fifty slaves and a thousand acres of land; a larger class of slave-owning yeoman farmers and town merchants; and a mass of laborers, tenants, and servants, constituting perhaps three-quarters of the white population. The yeoman farmers and merchants deferred to their "betters" in the gentry, who controlled the courts, the tobacco trade, the sale of western lands, and the flow of credit from England.

With slave labor producing most of the necessities of life on their plantations, gentry such as Robert Beverly and George Washington were free to pursue politics and entertainment. The patriarchs of the great families presided over festive balls at their estates; at political occasions linking their dominance to a hierarchy descending from the king of England; and at "Publick Times" events, when the business of the courts and the assembly brought in thousands of visitors to Williamsburg, Annapolis, and other centers. During these events, the gentry sponsored competitions in shooting, fiddling, dancing, juggling, and other performance activities; their show of magnanimity in the awarding of prizes further legitimated their authority. Chesapeake planters also built quarter-mile tracks and established week-long events to make thoroughbred horse racing the most popular spectator sport in colonial America.

The Hallam "Company of Comedians from London" established its reputation in the midst of elite social life in the Chesapeake. A variety of amateur and semiprofessional efforts, including playreadings at the College of William and Mary (see Timeline), had already whetted the appetites of the Chesapeake gentry for professional theatre when Lewis Hallam arrived with his troupe in Williamsburg in 1752. From the start, Hallam depended on the patronage of the Virginia elite; one of them interceded with the governor to reverse his initial refusal of permission to perform. Although the Hallam company also performed in New York and Philadelphia, its success through the mid-1760s was tied to the habits of the southern gentry; wealthy slaveowners provided the most reliable audience for the first truly professional theatre in America. (Of course, many of the elite in northern colonial audiences also owned slaves.) After the troupe returned from Jamaica in 1758 under the new management of David Douglass, it established a circuit throughout the Chesapeake, stopping to perform for a few days or several weeks at scheduled assembly days, public times, and race weeks.

The southern audience for the Hallam–Douglass troupe was predominately male, since gentry women traveled far less frequently to town. George Washington, an avid theatregoer, rode long distances to watch the players but rarely took his wife. Slaves required to wait on their masters saw many productions, usually from the gallery balcony seated next to a scattering of white artisans and laborers. Most gentry sat in the boxes along the side of the auditorium, but some took bench seats among yeoman planters and merchants in the pit, the present-day orchestra. Wherever they sat, which occasionally included the stage, the gentry dominated theatregoing with the same ease with which they controlled other activities at public gatherings. So popular was the theatre among the Chesapeake elite and their clients that the Virginia Company, a troupe begun by actors deserting from Douglass, was able to flourish in the region for a year and a half in the late 1760s while the "Company of Comedians" performed up North.

As in the South, Hallam and Douglass needed the permission of royal governors to perform in New York and Philadelphia. To secure it, the troupe sought assistance from key members of a proprietary elite of town merchants and professionals. The population of both seaports was small; New York contained about seventeen thousand in 1760 and Philadelphia only eighteen thousand by 1765. Nonetheless, the few hundred elite in both cities were enjoying a culture of leisure in the 1760s, partly spurred by profits from imperial wars between Britain and France. Their luxurious lifestyle (by eighteenth-century standards) segregated them from the artisans and laborers lower on the social hierarchy and brought them closer to their upper-class cousins in the South. Elite leisure activities in New York and Philadelphia, which took place in townhouses, assembly rooms, and taverns, included dancing, blood sports, and occasional performances by traveling musicians, acrobats, and jugglers. Wealthy New Yorkers were especially keen on horse racing; in 1736 they built the first indoor track in America. Like the gentry of the Chesapeake, elite townsfolk who were not religious dissenters looked to London for the latest fashions and reveled in the conspicuous consumption of mansions, carriages, and fine clothes.

Despite initial strong resistance, Douglass and his troupe, having made firm alliances with the local gentry and built new theatres, were enjoying longer and more profitable seasons in New York and Philadelphia by the mid-1760s. Although the evidence is skimpy, it is likely that audiences were somewhat more diverse in the North than in Charleston or the Chesapeake. Although spectators remained mostly male and upper class, it is probable that more women attended, because a trip to the playhouse did not involve long-distance travel. Gallery audiences seem to have been larger and also more mixed socially. In a 1772 letter to the editor, one Philadelphian complained of "some ruffians in the Gallery" who had interrupted the performance and committed "repeated Outrages" upon other theatregoers (quoted in Rankin, 170–71). Attending the playhouse was expensive for most artisans and journeymen, however; gallery prices ranged from two to five shillings per ticket, and the typical journeyman tailor earned only four shillings a day in 1762. Further, the fashionable and convivial atmosphere of the playhouse conflicted with the sober ways of most artisans. Differences in lifestyle as well as enormous disparities of income kept theatre attendance a predominately elite activity during the colonial era.

Theatregoing, along with many other activities of the colonial elite, derived its primary audience from two major cultural systems, patriarchy and gentility. Patriarchy, the rule of mature males, was the dominant form of authority throughout the colonies, as it was in Europe. Domestic patriarchies, in the form of large plantations and small farms, were the primary social and economic units of life throughout eighteenth-century rural America. Town life, with its greater social complexity, somewhat modified the rule of the fathers, but most wealthy men in New York and Philadelphia exercised substantial authority over their servants and families. Women had few public rights, and grown-up children typically deferred to their fathers as long as they were alive. Whereas elite townsmen in the Middle Colonies shared political and economic power with men in other classes, the local and regional authority of gentry patriarchs in the South went virtually unopposed. All the significant ritual occasions of Chesapeake life – the militia muster, "Public Times," Anglican church ceremonies, and the pomp of court and assembly days – buttressed patriarchal power.

Colonial theatregoing was part of this patriarchal culture. Rich men ruled in the playhouse, as they did at most other public events. If a respectable woman desired to see a play, she needed to be escorted by her husband or father. As at elections and cockfights, where the gentry mixed with other classes of men, the pursuit of common pleasures cemented the authority of all males. On the other hand, relations between men of different classes in the theatre probably tended toward formality, closer to cross-class relations in the courthouse than in the tavern. Spikes separating pit benches from stage seats and the gallery from the upper boxes encouraged this formality in the Williamsburg and Philadelphia theatres. Perhaps Douglass wanted to be sure that the lower-paying "pittites" and "gallery gods" would not clamber into higher-priced seating, but the effect was to embed class lines into auditorium architecture. As in England, theatregoing males treated the actors like servants. Men throughout the playhouse had the presumed right to shout down, talk over, or ignore the players; patriarchy typically made for noisy performances.

For their part, the actors worked within conventions that encouraged a servant–master relationship. By playing for "points," moments of high energy when actors expected applause, they reinforced their dependence on their spectators. When an actor in the Virginia Company expressed his resentment at being hissed at during a performance in 1769, he was reprimanded in newspaper print. The writer, shocked by the actor's "sovereign contempt" for his superiors, cut him down for this "violation of decorum" (quoted in Rankin, 149). All regular actors in theatre companies also relied, as in Europe, on yearly benefits, when they were allowed to keep the proceeds of one evening's performance, minus managerial expenses. Performers who pleased the male elite could count on a strong house on their benefit night to supplement their meager earnings. Wealthy patriarchs expected obedience, deference, and gratitude from those dependent on their generosity. In the theatre, as in their houses and public assemblies, they generally received it.

The cultural system of gentility reinforced colonial patriarchal authority in many areas of life but qualified it in others. In America as in Europe, gentility gave cultural authority to men and women of delicacy, sensibility, and "taste." Those who separated their lives from coarse behavior, who freely expressed the sentiments of sorrow and gratitude, and who recognized beauty in nature and art might become arbiters of genteel culture. Thus gentility fostered both the cult of sentimentality and the "scandal clubs" of censorious wit in the mid-eighteenth century. The primary stage for genteel performance was the town mansion or plantation house, where the rituals of dining, conversing, and dancing separated the truly refined from the pretenders. The successful performance required a clean, white body, emphasized through smooth clothes, an erect posture, and behavior that mixed decorous formality with casual ease. If the central image of patriarchy was a powerful male on horseback, porcelain figures of a man and woman dancing the minuet might stand as the essence of gentility. Gentility and patriarchy reinforced each other in numerous ways, not the least of which was the necessity of wealth and social position required to shine in both arenas. Yet gentility provided many more roles for women and significantly softened the rule of the fathers in everyday life.

Located firmly in both realms, colonial theatregoing mixed the behaviors and attitudes of patriarchy with those of gentility in roughly equal proportions. For the male patrician, going to the playhouse was something of a cross between a cockfight and a dress ball. Hallam understood the importance of a genteel image. His initial advertisement in the *Virginia Gazette* boasted "scenes, clothes, and decorations . . . furnished in the highest taste." He also promised playgoers that they "may depend upon being entertained in as polite a manner as at the theatres in London" (quoted in Rankin, 50–51). Defenders of the theatre often used the language of gentility in newspaper letters. "Dramaticus" in the New York *Gazette* in 1767, for example, applauded play performances for their "tendency to refine and polish the manners of the audience" (quoted in Young, *Famous American Playhouses,* I, 19).

Most of the Hallam–Douglass repertory paraded the power of patriarchy and the proper sentiments and wit of gentility, either together in a single play or separately in individual shows. Almost anything by Shakespeare passed muster in both cultural systems. The Company of Comedians opened with *The Merchant of Venice* in 1752 and performed *Richard III, King Lear, Macbeth,* and other patriarchal histories and tragedies throughout its stay in North America. Other plays featuring stalwart heroes and sexist values included Thomas Otway's *Venice Preserved,* Joseph Addison's *Cato,* and Dryden's *All for Love.* Images of gentility crossed the stage in their productions of *The Conscious Lovers,* the comedies of George Farquhar, current hits by David Garrick, and "she" tragedies like Nicholas Rowe's *Jane Shore.* The actors, trained in London, knew they had to be adept at genteel speech and body language. Indeed, when they were not rehearsing or performing, many of Douglass's troupe gave lessons in dancing, music, and French. In addition to reaffirming the joys of male camaraderie, men went to the playhouse to see and hear the latest in genteel behavior.

As in other provincial English troupes, the white actors in Douglass's company "blacked up" to perform roles in *Othello, The Padlock,* and other plays featuring African American characters. Native Americans were already facing dramatic erasure as well; *Ponteach; or, The Savages of America,* the first play by a colonist on a native topic, was published in 1766. Playwright Robert Rodgers based his neoclassic tragedy on Pontiac's rebellion but stuffed his Indian chief with patriarchal European virtues, effectively erasing genuine Native American culture. Long before the Hallam–Douglass troupe arrived, the decimation of Indian populations and the institution of slavery had effectively ensured that Anglo-American culture would continue to practice the racism of the mother county. And the enormous distance separating the Indian performances of reciprocity from the rituals of patriarchy and gentility evident in the theatrical, sporting, and political performances of the colonists meant that Anglo-American images of the Indian would remain unchallenged. These, together with condescending images of black slaves, helped the English colonials to construct a contrasting image of whiteness that would allow them to justify their continuing oppression of both races.

Compared to many other kinds of performances in eighteenth-century North America, the colonial professional theatre was provincial, ephemeral, and elitist. Occurring sporadically and centered in the gentry-dominated cultures of patriarchy and gentility, it likely made little impact on the general shape of American colonial life. Insofar as it may have influenced its audiences, it primarily drew elite Americans to emulate models of belief and behavior in London, the center of imperial culture. Despite Douglass's best efforts, the geographic reach of the professional players was limited to a few population pockets along the Atlantic seaboard; they never established more than a foothold in New England or penetrated the frontier. And many groups of Americans remained suspicious – some, downright contemptuous – of players and playgoing. Antitheatrical prejudices increased after 1770, most Americans spurning the entertainments of the gentry as a corruption of republican virtue.

Popular Performance in the New Republic, 1770–1830

Most American historians agree that the Revolution was the single most important event in American history. This insight is as true for the American theatre as it is for many other areas of American life. The "revolution" in the American theatre, however, had to wait until the 1790s. When it came, it effected major changes in audiences, architecture, theatrical genres, and acting styles. No longer a leisure activity primarily for the elite, the American theatre became by 1800 an arena for popular entertainment and public politics, two developments that were nearly unthinkable a few decades before.

The main reason for the delay of this theatrical revolution relates to American republicanism, the chief cultural system shaping the revolutionary era. Politically, republicanism derived from the ideology of the Radical Whigs during the Commonwealth era of English history. In their belief that good government rested upon the virtue of its citizens, the radicals emphasized the need to subordinate private interest to the public good. According to this tradition, the virtuous male republican citizen must be socially and economically independent, capable of sustaining himself and his family without relying on employment or patronage from others. Colonial republicanism was socially communitarian and suspicious of imperial power; the republicans assumed that continuous vigilance was necessary to prevent the crown from compromising the traditional rights of all British subjects. In the theatre, traditional republicanism helped to make Addison's *Cato* one of the most frequently performed plays in the colonies. Republican planters and merchants applauded Addison's neoclassical tragedy about the rebellion of a stoic Roman against a potential tyrant in numerous productions by amateur groups and occasionally by professionals.

Yet many colonial republicans also condemned the theatre. If the virtue of its citizens was the foundation of a legitimate republic, any institution that might corrupt virtue was suspect. To many traditional republicans, the elite colonial theatre fostered a desire for luxury, destructive emulation, dependence on the crown, and class division. In this regard, republicanism tended to reinforce the antitheatrical prejudices of Puritans, Quakers, and other religious dissenters, even though it derived from different principles. By the 1760s, those American colonials who lived much of their lives within the cultural system of republicanism – a group that included many merchants, artisans, and planters

– were pulled in ambivalent ways when it came to theatregoing. Even as they hoped for a theatre that would propagate republican values, they feared that playgoing would corrupt their own and others' civic virtue.

During the revolutionary era from 1765 until 1788, their fears generally overruled their hopes. A harbinger of events to come was the Chapel Street Theatre riot in 1766, when a New York City mob pulled down and burned the Douglass troupe's playhouse during the Stamp Act crisis of 1765–66. Anglo-Americans had long recognized rioting as a justifiable protest against a situation deemed immoral by aroused citizens. And Republicans understood this form of street performance as a legitimate means of protecting the communal welfare from the incursions of the crown. In the 1766 protest, as in other Stamp Act riots, a plebeian mob attacked a symbol of English tyranny, immoral luxury, and class division. There was little Douglass could do to unhitch the image of his troupe from these antirepublican attributes. Even though he had renamed his troupe the "American Company," his success depended on the favors of royal governors and the habits of the colonial rich. For the next twenty years, the primary form of theatre in America would be amateur republican performance in the streets, not professional playing on conventional stages.

Republican street theatre drew from three overlapping folk traditions with a long history in the European past: the charivari, rituals of misrule, and rites of passage. Also known as a "skimmington" or "rough music," the charivari was a shaming ritual deployed against miscreants, such as wife beaters and stingy employers, who acted outside of community norms. The revelers ridiculed the offenders with a mocking, raucous concert of pots and pans, screams, and shouts. Rituals of misrule, related to European traditions of carnival, turned the social hierarchy and normal patterns of behavior upside down. Usually these celebrations involved role reversals, such as the elevation of a mock king during Pinkster Days, a colonial holiday. Like the other folk performances, rowdy rites of passage among groups of young men were an accepted part of colonial life; most townsfolk tolerated the noisy drunkenness, window smashing, and other assaults on property and propriety that came with the passage from youthfulness to manhood. At some colonial events, such as Pope Day or New Year's Eve, these three performance traditions converged: Drunken celebrants serenaded their neighbors with rough music and turned the world upside down with effigy processions and bonfires. (See also Chapter 6.)

These traditions, evident in the Chapel Street Theatre riot, shaped republican street theatre from the Stamp Act crisis through the Revolution. As had the Sons of Liberty in the 1760s, the Committees of Safety and Correspondence in the seventies refigured the conventions of riotous performance to suit their overtly political purposes. They substituted effigies of royal governors for effigies of the pope in the Pope Day parade, for example, and tricked out traditional maypoles as liberty poles to oppose the Townshend Duties (1770) and the Tea Act (1773). The Boston Tea Party, in fact, followed the scenario of a ritual of misrule, complete with the overturning of a "civilized" custom (tea drinking) by "uncivilized" savages. These public spectacles were more important than the written word in animating Americans toward revolution, especially in northeastern seaports. One of their unexpected consequences was to push the Revolution toward more egalitarian goals. Because these street demonstrations required cooperation across class lines, patrician leaders began to envision more inclusive notions of governance. And by 1776, most laborers, artisans, and sailors assumed that a revolution would give them a more equal voice in determining all forms of authority. Despite the class tensions that these performances sometimes provoked, they pulled many plebeian and patrician patriots into the cultural system of revolutionary republicanism.

The republican theatre flourishing on the streets helped to banish the indoor theatre of patriarchy and gentility on the stage. The nonimportation pact of 1768 among merchants and planters politicized playgoing; productions by Douglass's English troupe became one of many consumer goods to be boycotted. More important than economics, however, was the republican fear that conspicuous luxury was undermining American civic virtue. By the early 1770s this concern had fostered a vigorous debate about the role of the arts in society (not unlike similar debates in the 1990s). As historian Gordon Wood explains in *The Creation of the American Republic,* the American Revolution was as much a movement for the moral regeneration of America as it was a repudiation of English tyranny. Banishing the theatre and other forms of English dissipation could be an important step toward making America into the "Christian Sparta" that Samuel Adams and other patriots hoped to attain. In the fall of 1774, the Continental Congress called on the states to discourage "every species of extravagance and dissipation, especially all horse-racing, and all kinds of gaming, cock-fighting, exhibition of shews, plays, and other expensive diversions and entertainments." Tarred as a symbol of English corruption, Douglass's "American Company" left for Jamaica in February of 1775.

Although professional playing ceased, soldiers on both sides presented plays during the war years. The British troops in New York City and elsewhere were particularly active. Wintering at Valley Forge, George Washington approved of a production of *Cato* among his officers. But even this tried-and-true paean to neoclassical republicanism was intolerable to fearful members of the Continental Congress, who promptly forbade acting in the army. Amateur street theatre also continued during hostilities, primarily to root out loyalists and protest the British occupation of cities and towns.

Not surprisingly, the triumph of revolutionary republicanism in the outcome of the war retarded the return of professional theatre during the 1780s. In addition, an economic depression, the difficulties of the new national government, outbreaks of violence on the frontier, and the return of many of the social divisions that had troubled townspeople before 1776 led many Americans to question whether the Revolution had really been a success after all. They wondered whether Americans possessed the requisite virtue to sustain a republican government and society. Many doubted it, and, turning to the usual republican suspects, redoubled their attacks on the corruptions of luxury. These fears led to new antitheatrical statutes. A Philadelphia law in 1785 and a 1787 Vagrancy Act in Charleston effectively outlawed theatrical production in those towns. The "American Company" had returned in 1784 and was struggling to find audiences and acceptable venues, but many Americans were rightly suspicious of the company's loyalty to the new nation. For a time in the mid-1780s, the theatre was legal in only Maryland, Virginia, and New York. Few could have predicted the theatrical rebirth and revolution that would occur in the next decade.

Before that could happen, however, republicanism itself had to be modified. The experience of the Revolution and of popular sovereignty during the 1780s broke the traditional linkage between patriarchy and republicanism. With the ratification of the new Constitution in 1787, most citizens believed that they had crafted forms of representative government that rested on the sovereignty of the people. Now, many hoped, power would flow upward, from the citizens to the state, not downward from traditional republican patriarchs to the people. Further, many in the gentry who read *The Federalist Papers* agreed with Madison that groups of citizens in political conflict would counterbalance each other, thus preventing what many feared would be the excesses of unrestrained democracy. These notions of popular sovereignty and of a balance of tensions among conflicting groups moved traditional republicanism toward political democracy. They also provided the foundation for a popular theatre of political contentiousness.

A more serious problem with classical republicanism for many Americans was its bias against capitalism. The republican argument against open competition in the economy ran this way: If citizens pursued selfish economic interests, how could they preserve their virtue and work for the good of all? The profit motive, with its inducements of power and luxury and its divisive consequences, contradicted the communitarian ideal. Yet, individual farmers, merchants, and small manufacturers had been pursuing profits for years. Still, there were few justifications for free-market capitalism. Many American gentry were suspicious of Adam Smith's assertions in *The Wealth of Nations* (1776) that the market did not require government control. Conventional playgoing, seen by many in the mid-1780s as a corrupting luxury of the rich, could only flourish if the strictures of republican communitarianism were loosened and individual capitalist enterprise given more breathing room.

During the 1790s the Democratic Republicans, the citizens favoring Jefferson and Madison over the Federalist policies of Washington, Hamilton, and Adams, reconciled several aspects of republicanism with the dynamics of capitalism. Although both sides in these disputes agreed that republican virtue must guide America, they differed widely in the strategies they advocated to attain this common end. Less fearful than the Federalists of the temptations of luxury, the Jeffersonians pointed out, for instance, that it would be unjust to deny virtuous citizens the fruits of their labor. Further, the Democratic Republicans asserted that the American farmer was right to pursue his economic self-interest, because it guaranteed his republican independence. In answer to Federalist concerns about the decline of civic virtue over time, Jeffersonians celebrated the extension of a republican economy in space, especially into the West. The Democratic Republicans were aided in their gradual success by a booming economy, stoked by the revival of trade during the European wars following the French Revolution. The election of Jefferson to the presidency in 1800 signaled the victory of a new, more popular republican vision that now accommodated American capitalism. Nevertheless, the tensions between older and newer versions of American republicanism would remain a part of the nation's civil religion and a source of antitheatrical prejudice to the present day.

Theatre practitioners did not wait on the sidelines while these forces fought over the nation's future. Indeed, the managers, playwrights, and actors of the late 1780s and 1790s played an active role in modifying American republicanism to reconcile it with theatrical entertainment. Performances of Royall Tyler's *The Contrast* in 1787, for instance, honored traditional republican virtues while edging its gentry audience toward an accommodation with a more individualistic future. At the moral center of this social comedy is Colonel Manly, late of the Continental Army, who attacks the luxurious corruptions of his sister and protects a maiden from the lecherous advances of a decadent Anglophile fop. Manly honors patriarchal authority and warns Americans that unless they are careful, they will repeat the decline of ancient Greece, where "the common good was lost in the pursuit of private interest" (Quoted in Moody, *Dramas,* 49). In some tension with these traditionally republican actions and precepts are the comic doings of Jonathan, Manly's servant, and the Knickerbocker materialism of Van Rough, the maiden's father. Jonathan's foolish provincialism and his eagerness for "girl huntry" undercut Manly's patriotic praise of natural American virtues. And Van Rough's constant injunction to "mind the main chance" nearly elbows aside the decorous republican moralizing at the end of the play. Despite (and partly because of) such contradictions, *The Contrast* was a hit in Philadelphia,

New York, and elsewhere. More important, the play joined theatrical entertainment to nationalistic republicanism, effectively trumping those critics
who believed such a match to be impossible.

As traditional republican anxieties withered in the 1790s, new theatre
troupes, mostly populated by imported actors from England, sprang up in the
larger towns of the nation. Initially, three major companies established
regional circuits and built theatres along the eastern coast: the remnants of
the old American Company, centered in New York City and soon traveling to
New England; the Chestnut Street Theatre Company in Philadelphia, which
toured to Baltimore and eventually to Washington, D.C.; and Thomas Wade
West's Company, which started in Charleston, South Carolina, and expanded
to include the towns in the Chesapeake region visited by Douglass's troupe
before 1775. All three companies soon met with vigorous competition. By
1800, there were seven major troupes, including a circus and two companies
of French-speaking actors (in Charleston and New Orleans), as well as innumerable minor companies. Most of the major companies continued, with a
few additions to their ranks, into the mid-1820s.

The new theatres built to house these players were generally much larger
than colonial playhouses, reflecting the optimism of theatre managers and
playhouse owners that republican drama and spectacle would draw popular
crowds. The Chestnut Street Theatre, for example, could accommodate
around two thousand spectators at its opening in 1794, with only nine hundred of those seats for patricians in the boxes. In Charleston, however – more
firmly in the grip of gentry control than cities in the North – boxes outnumbered other types of seating at the new playhouse of 1793. When the Providence Theatre opened its doors in Rhode Island in 1795, the motto over its
proscenium arch announced the happy union of entertainment and republicanism: "Pleasure the means; the end virtue" (quoted in Young, *Playhouses,* I,
47). Sometimes republican politics motivated the construction of a new playhouse. In 1796, Democratic Republicans, angered by what they took to be
pro-British performances at the Federal Street playhouse in Boston, raised
money to construct the Haymarket Theatre and started their own company.
The larger auditoriums and stages of these new theatres accommodated a
more spectacular theatre than had been possible before.

The audiences that flocked to these playhouses from the mid-1790s until
around 1815 were much more diverse than during colonial times, especially
in the North. Male patricians continued to populate the boxes, but more of
their wives and daughters now accompanied them to the theatre. Whereas
gentry women generally perched on box seats, working-class women sat in
the gallery and were occasionally seen in the pit. By the 1800s, most theatres
were reserving the top tier of boxes for prostitutes, but they could be found
throughout the playhouse. Theatregoers throughout the country remarked

on the cigar smoke, bad language, and drunkenness they encountered at the playhouse. Although more women of every kind were attending plays, the theatre remained a predominately male preserve.

The class composition of the pit audience was more mixed than before. An English visitor, Henry Faron, in 1817, noting the relative affluence of American workers, was surprised to discover the pit of a New York playhouse filled with "men that, if in London could hardly buy a pint of porter – and should they ever think of seeing a play must take up their abode among the gods in the upper gallery" (86). Whereas before the Revolution entrance to the pit had set most journeymen back about a full day's pay, by the 1790s the cost had shrunk to only a third of their daily earnings. Artisans were doing better, and managers, to fill their large theatres, were charging less. Professional people also frequented the pit, like the editor of *Rambler's Magazine,* who wrote in 1809 that he enjoyed the closer view it gave him of the female actors. The pit continued to attract the rowdy as well as the respectable, despite the inconveniences of dirty benches and dripping candle wax from above.

The rowdiest part of the playhouse was the gallery. Sailors, apprentices, servants, and other "gallery gods" shouted out tunes to the orchestra, demanded encores from the actors, and bombarded the pittites with fruits and nuts. Letters to the editor constantly urged managers to hire more and better constables to police the gallery, but to little avail. When African Americans, whether free or slave, attended the theatre they were usually required to sit in the gallery.

These diverse groups of citizen-spectators did not always get along in the theatre, and few expected that they would. Indeed, by 1800 most Americans viewed the playhouse as a legitimate arena for the clash of political factions. Disturbances and occasional full-scale riots erupted, usually led by plebeians in the pit and gallery and involving symbols of aristocratic privilege and/or English tyranny. In effect, the republican street theatre of the revolutionary era had been brought inside. The political disputes that led to the building of the Haymarket Theatre in Boston had earlier sparked a riot that destroyed the benches, doors, and windows of the Federal Street Theatre in 1796. As in earlier demonstrations, playhouse mobs might destroy property and burn effigies, but they rarely attacked people. Nonetheless, their shaming rituals could inflict other kinds of scars. For several nights at the Chestnut in 1802, Democratic Republicans hissed at a British actor who had replaced a favorite American star; finally driven from the stage, the actor committed suicide. Federalists in the Philadelphia audience struck back in 1803, hissing at an actor for toasting President Jefferson. Spectators in New Orleans rioted during the 1803–1804 season because the orchestra was not playing enough patriotic tunes. Although rowdy plebeians usually started such protests, most Americans, regardless of their class, recognized them as a valid means for virtuous republicans to express their grievances. After all, hadn't they just fought a Revolution to ensure such rights? The widespread toleration of playhouse conflicts was a function of the dominance of the cultural system of popular republicanism.

By the early 1800s, underneath the partisan squabbling and vindictiveness of national politics, there was broad agreement among white American males that the shift to popular republicanism had been right for the nation and themselves. Most merchants and planters had come to believe that some loss of their previous authority was more than made up for by the solidity of a national government based on popular sovereignty. Besides, the new republicanism retained the old social hierarchy and facilitated the profitability of their commerce, land speculating, and slave trading. For artisans, popular republicanism continued to idealize the independence of the craftsman. At the same time, the new emphasis on economic individualism led journeymen and apprentices to believe that they could rise in the social hierarchy through their own efforts and merit. Republicans of all political stripes praised white male farmers as the backbone of the republic. And after the Louisiana Purchase in 1803, citizen farmers throughout the country assumed that the Indians would be swept aside to provide them with an endless supply of cheap land in the West.

A variety of performances beyond the playhouse helped to constitute and sustain popular republicanism in the new nation. Many of these occurred during national and local holidays – Washington's Birthday, spring militia musters, the Fourth of July, fall elections, Evacuation Day (when British soldiers left town during the Revolution), local harvest festivals, and Christmas and New Year celebrations. These occasions often featured parades, street performances, and copious oratory, giving celebrants ample opportunity to engage in partisan rowdiness and to elaborate the myth of republican nationhood. As with other modern nationalisms, this myth centered on the idea of a chosen people, the elaboration of a glorious historical past, and a national messianic purpose for the future. The Grand Federal Procession in 1788, for instance, celebrated Philadelphia's political progress since Independence and linked it to the city's producer artisans, a republican version of a chosen people. Harvest festivals and rural elections typically named the American farmer as God's anointed. In Philadelphia and other cities, volunteer militias demonstrated their ties to a glorious revolutionary past through close-order drills, cavalry maneuvers, and gunnery salutes, often to the tunes of fife and drum. Patriotic speeches were well suited for prophesying a future in which America would stand as a model of republican virtue for the world to emulate.

A new style of oratory at these occasions made the rhetoric of popular republicanism sing in American ears. The decorous discourse of neoclassicism spoken among the gentry at public events before 1776 gave way to what

Kenneth Cmiel terms a "middling style" (55). This mode of political address, initiated by Patrick Henry's vigorous denunciation of the Stamp Act and the straightforward locutions and accessible vocabulary of Paine's *Common Sense,* became popular during the Revolution. The key to the success of middling rhetoric for its republican speakers was a willingness to indicate sympathy with one's listeners, not authority over them. Thus familiarity replaced genteel distance, appeals to the heart took the place of rational ethics, and blunt sincerity won out over elaborate indirection. The middling style did not prevent republican rhetoric from wandering into bombast, euphemism, and mindless sonority; then as now, many a Fourth of July speech made better sound than sense. But middling rhetoric did encourage an eloquent language for public affairs distinct from the discourse of the English aristocracy.

In the theatre, the popularity of middling oratory meant that playwrights and managers would have little success addressing their audiences in neoclassical cadences. *Cato,* long a favorite of traditional republicans, was rarely performed after 1790. William Dunlap authored one of the best constructed neoclassical tragedies of the era in *André,* but its 1798 production in New York was a failure. Written in serviceable if not inspired blank verse, *André* tells the story of an honorable British officer during the Revolution who is captured and condemned as a spy. Several noble characters, including André's wife, plead for his life, but Washington, though deeply moved, decides each time that he must follow his patriotic duty; in the end, André goes stoically to his death. The play's elaborate rhetoric and its refusal to embrace sincere emotion over genteel ethics put it at cross purposes with the middling style of address popular in public discourse. Dunlap salvaged parts of the tragedy and recycled them in *The Glory of Columbia – Her Yeomanry!,* an 1803 potboiler that shrank the André plot and added patriotic farmers, a humorous Irishman, several songs, and lots of flag waving. The show was a hit when it opened on the Fourth of July, but later managers trimmed back the *André* material even more in subsequent productions.

The Glory of Columbia was typical of the aggressive patriotism that dominated the American theatre during this period, as managers and playwrights turned every performance genre within reach into celebrations of republican nationalism. Perhaps as many as half of the plays and spectacles written by Americans between 1790 and 1815 reinforced the cultural system of popular republicanism. Authors reworked the conventions of English pantomime, for instance, to march to Yankee Doodle patriotism. A new French company in Charleston earned its stripes when it opened in 1794 with a pantomime entitled *The Attack on Ft. Moultrie,* based on an incident during the war. Similar pantomimes gained immense popularity as the nation was preparing for the War of 1812. Following the example of *The Contrast,* sentimental comedy led many national symbols of romantic virtue down the aisles. Robert Minshull's

Rural Felicity, With the Humor of Patrick and Marriage of Shelty, staged in New York in 1801, brought together farmers and woodcutters to sing the praises of their country, their heroes, and themselves. Opera roared to the defense of American virtues as well. Opening at the John Street Theatre in New York in 1794, *Tammany; or, The Indian Chief* used a Native American as a symbol of the nation. Even feisty farce, ever popular as a one-act afterpiece, vindicated American ways by landing satiric jabs on English society. Several of the titles of American farces reveal their nationalistic purposes: *The Federal Oath; or, Americans Strike Home* (1798), *He Stoops to Conquer* (1804), and *Love and Friendship, or Yankee Notions* (1807).

Perhaps the most reliable dramatic battleship to fight for American freedom was the heroic melodrama. *Bunker Hill; or, the Death of General Warren,* written by John Daly Burk in 1797 to open the radical Haymarket Theatre, was the most popular of these warhorses. As a Democratic Republican newspaper editor, Burk had sharpened his quill on partisan rhetoric and patriotic bombast. His General Warren denounces a British officer before the battle in language that recalls the sentiments, though not the concision, of Tom Paine: "What are kings? . . . They are the Manichean demons, who undo / The good which heaven has done: / They waste with fire the purple vintage, and the waving grain; / Their butcher hordes they send out to destroy . . ." (quoted in Moody, *Dramas,* 81). Like other flag wavers onstage, *Bunker Hill* pushed the middling style into purple poetry! The show climaxed in a spectacular battle scene lasting over twelve minutes with drums, distant cannon, the illusion of a town ablaze, and musket fire from more than thirty soldiers. In a letter to the manager, Burk cautioned him to be sure to open the theatre's windows after the battle to let out the smoke.

While bashing the Brits played a large role in defining republican nationalism, especially by evoking an heroic past, these performances also helped to specify which Americans might be among the chosen people. As in all modern nationalisms, Americans defined the ideal citizen partly on the basis of what he – and "he" is the relevant pronoun here – was not. Women were placed on the margins of republican citizenship, but African and Native Americans were excluded altogether. In republican eyes, Americans were white; "reds" and blacks, as creatures of instinct, were incapable of rational, independent judgment, and hence would never make good citizens. Much of this racism simply continued the prejudices of the colonial era, but with new emphases. Audiences at several playhouses enjoyed James N. Barker's *The Indian Princess; or, La Belle Sauvage,* which centered on the romance between Pocahontas and John Rolfe. Spontaneous and innocent, the title character not only saves Captain John Smith but rescues the English from the machinations of evil priests and a warring tribe. The Indian as child of nature and helpmate to the white man flourished as a national wish fulfillment at the same time as famine, disease, and frontier violence continued to decimate the eastern tribes.

The Declaration of Independence had professed that "all men are created equal," but most republicans simply ignored its implications for African Americans. Nonetheless, the Constitution did set a time limit on the slave trade. Most northern states adopted gradual abolition, and several southern states eased the laws allowing masters to grant manumission during the 1780s. By 1790, 8 percent of black Americans were free. The small progress made by African Americans began to be reversed in the 1790s, however, as several states stripped free blacks of voting rights and Congress passed a Fugitive Slave Law that denied African Americans many of the legal protections of the Bill of Rights. On the stage, white actors in blackface were a common sight during this period; well over a hundred plays and afterpieces, and probably more than a thousand performances, featured foolish and degrading images of black characters. Even playwrights who had reason to depict African Americans with some humanity did not avoid stereotypes. John Murdock, a Quaker author in Philadelphia, for instance, wrote *The Triumph of Love* with a servant named Sambo who, though clever and perceptive, wholly lacked self-respect and independence. Audiences were left in no doubt that the proper republican citizen was male and white.

As the dominant cultural system of the 1790–1815 period, republicanism not only defined American nationalism but also massively reshaped patriarchy and gentility, the two cultural systems that had contained much of American performance before 1770. Although the Revolution had been antipatriarchal, most American theatre, like American society, remained dominated by men. Men outnumbered women by at least two to one at most performances, and when a disturbance was anticipated, women stayed away entirely. As before, all males, regardless of their class, exercised their right to command actors as servants. Yet because the playhouse was now a contested arena of political factions among males, female spectators probably had more opportunity than during colonial times to assert their wishes. However, female actors generally had less freedom within an acting troupe than previously. Managers, invariably male, gained more power over all performers when companies moved from profit sharing to wages in the 1790s. Further, from the point of view of most men and women in the audience, the "actress" – simply because she dared to parade herself in public – was little better than a prostitute. While many women accepted their lower status as actors, others resented their loss of public respectability. At least they had the solace of knowing that they were receiving wages significantly higher than most other working women in the nation.

This secondary, marginalized position of women in theatre companies accorded with a republican understanding of their general role in society.

From the start, traditional republicanism had been embedded in patriarchy; the foil to the courageous, reliable, and virtuous male citizen was the timorous, unpredictable, and lustful woman. Especially with regard to affairs of state, women were foolish Ophelias, voluptuous Gertrudes, or conniving Gonerils. Although the Revolution undercut the conventions of obedience and deference among men, it actually reinforced traditional republican patriarchy in male–female relations. Thus, the new political order produced no new rights for women and left intact a social system that had long kept them in subordinate roles. In the new republic, women could participate on the periphery of events as republican mothers, guarantors of the virtues of their sons and husbands, but their property rights were unequal and they could not vote or hold political office.

Unsurprisingly, then, audiences applauded young female characters in *Bunker Hill, The Glory of Columbia,* and other patriotic rituals who were primarily passive victims, not active heroes. Older women onstage might be social climbers, supportive mothers, or farcical shrews, but they typically had little that was positive to add to the necessary action of the play. Several of the most successful women actors, including Mrs. Eliza Kemble Whitlock and Mrs. Anne Brunton Merry, worked within a style shaped by their famous contemporary on the London stage, Mrs. Sarah Siddons, who alternated between passive reserve and passionate abandon, seemingly swept by forces beyond her control. The few female authors who wrote for the stage rarely challenged conventional passivity for sympathetic female characters. Susanna Rowson, also an actress, drew her American heroine as a helpless woman trapped in a harem for her *Slaves in Algiers* (1794), for example.

Equestrian acts in circus entertainment also did the cultural work of patriarchy. Many individual circus acts had been popular in colonial times, including equestrian performances. When Philip Astley founded the modern circus in London in the mid-eighteenth century, he centered it on horsemanship, long a passionate interest of the male gentry. Performers familiar with Astley's circus began appearing in the United States after the Revolution, and in 1793 John Bill Ricketts opened an indoor "Circus" like Astley's in Philadelphia. Although he added other acts of balance and skill as well as elaborate pantomimes to his popular shows, feats of equestrian daring remained Ricketts's specialty. Equestrian performer and clown John Durang, for instance, remembered riding at full speed on two horses pounding around a ring, playing such characters as a foxhunter, a drunken soldier, and a frightened woman. Ricketts secured his ties to images of republican patriarchy through his cultivation of President George Washington. Widely regarded as the best equestrian of his time, Washington endorsed Ricketts's circus and even sold his Revolutionary War horse, Jack, to the circus master in 1797.

Already celebrated as the "father of his country," Washington evoked a symbolic aura that joined republican images of patriarchy and nationalism. Yet republican patriarchy's shaping of male relationships had changed from earlier times. Male citizens after 1776 still needed a father surrogate to replace George III as the head of the national family, but Washington and the other "founding fathers" could no longer assume that position by commanding obedience; instead, in their public behavior and writing as in their oratory, they had to instill respect, inspire confidence, and even induce affection. In short, republicanism continued to soften symbolic figures of male authority from distant patriarchs into generous paternalists, a process already begun in Anglo-American society well before the Revolution. When American men went to the playhouse after 1790, they still celebrated political heroes who commanded awe and duty; General Warren in *Bunker Hill,* for instance, remains a patriarchal leader of old despite his fervent republican principles. But increasingly – especially in social comedies and domestic melodramas – they warmed to affectionate fathers more inclined to forgive than to condemn.

Although changes in republican patriarchy partly account for the new images of fatherhood, this alteration in the theatre was given a bigger boost by a massive shift in the cultural system of gentility. Colonial theatregoers generally believed that only the genteel had the capacity for sentiment; those below the elite lacked the refinement necessary for sympathetic identification with the lives of others. The Revolution democratized gentility, opening up the national culture to the recognition that all people could experience empathy and sensibility. (For Americans today, when U.S. cultures have been swamped by excesses of sentimentality, it is difficult to appreciate what this revolution in feeling meant to ordinary citizens at the time.) In the theatre, this cultural-systems shift led to the emergence and immense popularity of two new theatrical genres, domestic melodrama and the gothic thriller.

Older forms of gentility did continue to shape some aspects of theatregoing in the republican era. Theatre architects modeled their designs on English originals, and London productions still set the standards for American actors and managers. Before 1830 audiences watched perhaps ten times more English than American plays because Shakespeare, Farquhar, and Sheridan were English, and the new imports from London were cheaper to do and had even been pretested before an audience. To venture far beyond these cultural forms was simply unthinkable for most American spectators and playwrights. In addition to the weight of the Anglo-American tradition, there was also the influence of postcolonial inferiority. Because of the newness of the nation, Americans had no prestigious intellectual and cultural formations to rival the accumulated authority of the English. The result was often the continuance of a genteel way of thinking and acting that aped, often unconsciously, its British betters. Even with regard to the democratization of sentimentality, influential changes in English moral philosophy prepared the way. The moral-sense philosophers, led by John Locke and Adam Smith, sidestepped rational theories of the mind to argue that our innate, instinctual ability to sympathize with other human beings is the basis of human morality. As these beliefs began to appear in novels and plays, they gradually replaced the idea that only a gentry possessing enlightened rationality could hope to act in ethical ways.

But if moral sensibility were a part of human nature, all people must be capable of it. This revolutionary implication, impelled by the events of 1776 and 1789, shaped the sentimental comedies of the German playwright August von Kotzebue, whose plays achieved immense success in every country where popular audiences longed for emotional empowerment. Kotzebue's weepy dramas emphasize the pathos of ordinary people and celebrate their sentimental feelings as the key to a finale of family togetherness. When the American Company under William Dunlap presented Kotzebue's *The Stranger* in 1798, "the effect of the pathetic scenes," according to one newspaper, "was beyond any former example within our remembrance" (quoted in Hewitt, *Theatre U.S.A.*, 54). The success of the production saved the company from bankruptcy that year. During Dunlap's 1799–1800 season, fifty-two of the company's ninety-four performances of full-length plays were adaptations or translations of Kotzebue. At performances of *The Stranger, Lovers' Vows, Pizarro in Peru,* and other Kotzebue plays, common people validated their natural inner virtue by weeping for surrogates of themselves. His sentimental comedies, and many others modeled on them, remained popular in the United States through the Civil War.

Because they generally lacked villains to motivate their action, Kotzebue's plays were not true domestic melodramas. The French playwright Guilbert de Pixérécourt was the first to popularize the injection of villainy into domestic situations and thus to create a form that, through several permutations, would dominate American theatre for most of its history. His success and that of his English imitators on the American stage before 1815 was wide-ranging. *A Tale of Mystery, The Forest of Bondy,* and *The Fortress* were direct steals from the French master, whereas many others, including *Abaellino, The Mountaineers,* and *The Maid and the Magpie* bore the imprint of his formula. These plays typically follow a circular pattern in which a heroine is hounded by villainy from her happy home, endures trials and torments, and is finally rescued by a benevolent father figure. The success of domestic melodrama was directly related to the experience of revolution; audiences who had witnessed the machinations of political conspiracy and dreamed of egalitarian utopias could relive these experiences through melodrama. Most domestic melodrama, however, traded on reactionary nostalgia; it sought to return its spectators to an illusionary image of prerevolutionary bliss when families lived together in faith and peace. And to achieve the social perfection demanded by the moral clarity of the form, domestic melodrama promoted the belief that evil could be banished forever. Ironically, dramas celebrating a democracy of feeling often ended up rejecting the messiness of republican politics that had made possible such sentiment.

Likewise, melodrama rejected the reforming impulse of the Enlightenment. Unlike sentimental comedy, domestic melodrama rarely satirized social excesses; nature and intuition had become better guides to moral behavior than reason. Melodramatic nature spoke through beautiful scenery, through the homey songs and local wisdom of common folk, through the insights of children and chaste lovers, and of course through the tears of the heroine. And many Americans were eager to listen. In a letter to John Adams, Thomas Jefferson recognized that the postrevolutionary generation was rejecting all knowledge that was not innate and "starting on the new ground of intuition" (quoted in Grimsted, 211). Indeed, for many Americans intuition was becoming entitlement. In courtship, the young were increasingly relying on romantic affection in choosing a marriage partner. In seeking professional advice, many citizens were rejecting the council of educated lawyers, clerics, and doctors. And in religion, thousands of Americans were walking away from traditional churches to embrace the more emotional experience of evangelical faith. Yet if evil were unnatural, why did it persist in the real world? Moral philosophy, domestic melodrama, and other changes in the cultural system of gentility might satisfy utopian desire, but they had a harder time explaining evil. Into this yawning breech created by the success of democratic sentimentality stepped the gothic thriller. During colonial times, sermons and confessions – many performed at the foot of the gallows – focused the attention of the culture on the potential for evil within all mankind. But by the 1790s, with clerics losing their monopoly on the public discourse about sin and murder, popular trial reports about murder were attempting to explain evil in sentimental terms as an aberration of nature, not a part of God's plan. Since their sentimental philosophy could neither fully explain nor resolve the problem, spectators sought surprise, terror, and revulsion from gothic literature and stage productions. The waning of traditional explanations of evil created a hunger for horror.

The rage for gothic thrillers on the American stage began in the mid-1790s. Among the most popular were two British imports, *The Castle Spectre,* by Matthew Gregory (Monk) Lewis, and *Blue Beard; or, Female Curiosity,* by George Coleman the Younger. Both are replete with the standard gothic features: a tormented, lustful villain-hero, castle dungeons hiding gory secrets from the past, and a ghost who helps to save the heroine. Their success spawned numerous American imitations, including *Bethlem Gabor* (1807), *The Mysteries of the Castle* (1806), and *The Wood Daemon; or, The Clock Has Struck* (1808). James N. Barker joined gothicism to republican nationalism in

Marmion (1812). Although based on Walter Scott's poem about Scotland's fight for independence from England, the play rejects Scott's endorsement of aristocratic chivalry. The title character is an English libertine who throws aside mistresses and fights with ghosts in his plot to undermine Scotland's cause. Although the play stands foresquare for independence (with Scotland the analogue of America), like most gothic thrillers it remains deeply ambivalent about its villain-hero, Marmion.

Much of the revolutionary energy of gothicism in the theatre came from its refusal to provide complete moral closure. Gothic playwrights typically mixed together elements of tragedy, romance, and melodrama to move audiences beyond conventional responses and into extreme states of human experience in which firm ethical judgment was impossible. Standing astride the boundaries of melodrama and tragedy was the gothic villain-hero, usually a dynamic, passionate, and grotesque figure akin to Shakespeare's Richard III, who might feel remorse but rarely renounced his desire for lust and revenge. Indeed, the most electric star of the period, George Frederick Cooke, colored his portrayal of Richard, Macbeth, and Othello with the shocking hues of gothicism in his performances. One observer, describing Cooke's "truly appalling" death scene as Richard III, recalled that "the expression of his eyes – as they for a moment vividly rolled, then became fixedly glazed, and all vision seemed gone – was peculiar, and thrilled the audience" (quoted in Hewitt, *Theatre U.S.A.,* 83). Like Cooke's Richard, all villain-heroes died, usually at the hands of a representative of the common people, but their charisma and horror lingered on. As with trial reports and other forms of gothic fiction, gothic theatre presented images of abnormality without fully explaining them; "unnatural" images such as rolling eyes resisted the closure of melodrama.

Recognizing their threat to conventional morality, conservative critics denounced gothic plays. Joseph Dennie, the Anglophile editor of *Port-Folio,* attacked gothic drama as a jumble of dramatic forms, their confusion rendering them "impossible to develop or understand." For the English poet Coleridge, gothic plays were "the modern jacobinical drama"; he equated gothicism on stage with the Jacobin Reign of Terror during the French Revolution.[1] Coleridge was right: gothic sensationalism offered to liberate audiences from the bastilles of an oppressive past through an experience closer to the rituals of misrule and other kinds of revolutionary street theatre than to any of the rational dramatic forms on the eighteenth-century indoor stage. Much more than domestic melodramas, gothic thrillers in America built on the leveling energy and moral confusion of the Revolution. They also explored the flip side of the cultural system of sentimentality, a fascination with "unnatural" evil that keeps their legacy alive today.

The theatrical innovations in the cultural systems of republicanism, paternalism, and sentimentality in the 1790–1815 period continued with few major changes for the next fifteen years. Republican nationalism dominated as before, with productions of heroic melodramas and comedies based on incidents from the War of 1812 being especially popular. Some of the best crafted American plays from the 1815–1830 period were by John Howard Payne, who gained success in London with several dramatic forms before returning to the United States. His domestic melodramas, such as *Clari, The Maid of Milan* (1823) and *Thérèse, The Orphan of Geneva* (1821), won the hearts of thousands of American theatregoers through their combination of sentimentality and paternalism. *Clari* launched the success of "Home, Sweet Home," a favorite in American parlors for the rest of the century. Many pantomime-ballets during the period, like *Cherry and Fair Star,* used fairy-tale transformations to pluck at the same domestic heartstrings. Gothic thrillers remained strong, especially since English stars like Edmund Kean continued to perform in them. One of the best was *Altorf* (1819), written by the outspoken feminist Frances Wright. Wright depicts a somewhat more sympathetic villain-hero than usual, made so, in part, by the love of his strong, forbearing wife.

The social basis for the continuing success of republican theatre across class lines was beginning to fall apart, however. Journeymen had been optimistic that an expanding market would elevate many of them into the master ranks, but instead many artisans saw their careers stagnating or moving backward as expansion benefited only a few masters. After the Panic of 1819, the income gap between these new capitalists and most middling artisans widened even further. Political coalitions committing artisan votes to Jeffersonian republicans began to disintegrate in several towns. In 1828, a Workingmen's Party emerged in Philadelphia, spread to other cities in the Northeast, and gained some electoral success. The new party demanded that the republican promise of equal opportunity implicitly made during the revolutionary era be kept. Others higher up on the social ladder, however, who had been moving into cultural systems more sympathetic to concentrations of wealth, found such demands old-fashioned. Although the Workingmen's Party met the fate of all third parties in the United States, its existence testified that the ideological glue that had held together groups from several classes during the republican era was coming unstuck.

Artisans continued to attend the same theatres as merchants, professionals, and other classes, but in relatively reduced numbers. City populations expanded rapidly during the period – New York's grew sixfold from 1790 to 1830, from 33,000 to 197,000 – and real estate speculators built several new playhouses to profit from the increase. Moreover, most new theatres reduced the previous proportion of seats in the pit and gallery to those in the more profitable boxes. In Philadelphia, the new Chestnut Street Theatre of 1822, for example, could hold more than two thousand spectators but accommodated only three hundred in the gallery and four hundred in the pit. When the Chatham Garden and Lafayette theatres were built in New York in the 1820s, gallery seating was eliminated altogether. Playhouse camaraderie among males continued much as it had before, with occasional riots led by plebeians and tolerated as legitimate, though not usually endorsed, by patricians. But political disputes of the kind that had animated Federalists and Jeffersonians in earlier playhouses – as distinct from class-based ones – nearly ceased. In short, the theatre of the 1820s was less popular and less political than it had been before 1815.

Throughout the 1790–1830 period, theatre companies had been moving west with white settlement, but there was little that was fundamentally different between the theatre enjoyed by western spectators and that back east. Western theatre, too, celebrated republican nationalism, modified traditional patriarchy with paternalism, and embraced the democracy of feeling in the new melodramatic and gothic plays. By 1830, touring professional players, mostly following Ohio and Mississippi river routes, were performing in Pittsburgh, Lexington, Cincinnati, Louisville, St. Louis, and Memphis, as well as in smaller towns along the way. (New Orleans, more an international port than a frontier town, had professional theatre by 1791.) Other performers opened up northern New England, upstate New York, and interior towns in the South.

Though proud of their frontier courage and hardiness, western townsfolk looked to the East for images of gentility and usually appreciated even the most ragged, understaffed, and overacted productions that these struggling companies could deliver. Frontier actor and later manager Sol Smith recalled a production of *Pizarro in Peru* staged by the Samuel Drake Company in the Ohio Valley in 1820. Kotzebue's spectacle was written for a dozen actors, plus many extras, and required a practical natural bridge for the climactic scene. The Drake Company performed it with four men, two women, and a couple of children on a flat, eight-by-ten-foot platform. At one point in the show, Smith played the entire Spanish army! However ridiculous these shows might sometimes appear, frontier townspeople were glad for a break from the isolation and rough conditions of their lives. Enthusiastic oratory from even a mediocre actor might remind the auditors of a recent religious revival and provided a welcome contrast to the usual recreations of drinking and rough sports.

While most white settlers in the West could afford to enjoy frontier theatre, African Americans throughout the country had to make do with performances intended for white spectators, if they were allowed into a playhouse at all. The one exception to this general rule occurred during the brief existence of the African Grove Gardens and African Theatre in New York. Retired steward William Henry Brown founded the African Grove in 1816 as a pleasure garden for the Sunday afternoon entertainment of free blacks; he modeled it on the whites-only Chatham Gardens nearby. When the city shut down the African Grove in 1821, he moved his occasional performances inside and began a small theatre company. So many white New Yorkers began to attend his productions that Brown was pulling patrons away from the nearby Park Theatre. The manager of the Park colluded with the city Sheriff, a Tammany politician attempting to secure Democratic power by raising the restrictions on black voting, and they closed Brown's theatre. Brown continued performing illegally in various spaces – even staging his own play, *The Drama of King Shotaway,* about a slave rebellion – before closing completely in 1823. Apparently the example of the racist persecution of William Henry Brown was not lost on other free blacks in the United States; African Americans began no other theatre companies until after the Civil War.

Instead, black Americans turned to each other to cultivate folk performances that would help them to shape a collective identity and to foster individual self-respect in the midst of white oppression. These performances had deep roots in the African past but drew as well from interactions with whites in the crucible of slavery. Although the West Africans exported to America as slaves came from several tribes with distinctive cultures, they shared many social institutions and cultural orientations. Because their tribal societies had emphasized kinship, for instance, Africans sought stability through family ties in America, despite the breakup of families in the Middle Passage and through subsequent slave trading. Most West Africans had been relatively open to additions to their culture from other groups, and this orientation encouraged new slaves to borrow features from white culture that would help them to survive and flourish in their new circumstances. Indeed, the early experiences of slavery taught African Americans to cherish adaptability and innovation; they expected change and learned to value it.

By 1800, native-born African Americans had developed a distinctive, semi-autonomous culture in the slave South. The transformation of Africans into African Americans, begun with the Middle Passage, was speeded during the Great Awakening and after the Revolution when white evangelicals converted many Africans to Christianity. In general, the rule of the masters set outer limits to the slave culture that emerged but did not determine its inner contents. Although whites sought to separate their own culture as completely as they could from the expressive practices of their slaves, so as to justify their power over these "inferior others," much cultural interpenetration did occur. Given the close interaction of the races in relations of work, recreation, and sexuality, mutual borrowing was inevitable. In this regard, blacks came to accept the paternalism and aristocratic ethos of southern society and built their culture within its codes of courtesy, honor, and shame. They also used southern notions of the personal nature of authority and the need for reciprocity in the performance of duties for their own benefit. As inflected by the slaves, these same values and practices also allowed African Americans to draw strength from their African heritage, in which various forms of reciprocity, personal assertiveness, and patriarchal authority were also prized. Whites had contained black culture, but they could not control it.

Much of their culture helped African Americans to resist the degradations of the slave system. Actions and beliefs affirming the value and spiritual strength of the slave community were especially beneficial to people whose sense of self worth was frequently assaulted and undermined. Thus many performances functioned to constitute and maintain a cultural system of collective mutuality, celebrating each person's responsibility for the good of all. In black spiritual singing, for example, the antiphonal call-and-response structure put individuals in dialogue with the rest of the community. The slaves intensified the communal effect of their spirituals by repeating the tune, increasing the tempo, and adding new sounds, such as hand clapping, to build them to a powerful collective conclusion. Often these were songs that had been introduced into slave culture by white evangelicals in the eighteenth century, but African Americans made them over to suit their own needs.

Spirituals were one of many religious practices that affirmed collective values while, at the same time, allowing for individual expressiveness. Slave preachers were accorded a great deal of freedom in their use of highly metaphorical language, but the call-and-response structure of the services ensured that their preaching connected directly to the emotional lives of their congregations. Many sermons, songs, and prayers centered on Old Testament stories, emphasizing the community's sense of itself as a Chosen People willing to endure temporary persecution for the promise of eventual salvation. At black funerals, typically held at night, the entire congregation met to mourn the passing and to celebrate the coming glory of the deceased. Here again, a collective ritual encouraged a variety of individual expressions. In one 1819 funeral in New Orleans involving two hundred African Americans, for example, a distressed white visitor described a carnival of rude noises and actions that greeted the moment when the body was metaphorically "cut loose" from its earthly toils, a moment celebrated by songs, dances, and jokes. What the visitor had witnessed was the beginnings of the New Orleans jazz funeral.

The religious services of many groups build community, of course, but black religion tended to be much less individualistic than its white counterpart. Following traditions of West African belief, African Americans of faith had little use for the doctrines of original sin and the Apocalypse. White evangelicals, on the other hand, focused much of their religious energy on affirming individual sinfulness and preparing for the Day of Judgment. In contrast, black worshipers in several areas of the South practiced a communal "ring shout" to gain spiritual power and induce new conversions. In this ecstatic, rhythmical dance, clapping African Americans shuffled and stamped in a circle as single worshipers moved into its center to express their spiritual release through highly individual riffs. In effect, new converts were invited to shape themselves to the rhythms of the group while adding their own contribution to the collective. While religious whites practiced individual bodily restraint and emotional inhibition, black rituals moved in the opposite direction, toward communal release. As one black preacher noted, the religion of white evangelicals made them "fiery mad," while African American church services made blacks "fiery glad" (quoted in Genovese, 341).

Likewise, African Americans expressed collective mutuality at their holiday celebrations. The former slave and abolitionist leader Frederick Douglass believed that the masters used festive events for social control by keeping the slaves' minds on eating, drinking, and courtship instead of insurrection. No doubt this was partly true. But as in their religious performances, many holiday events also strengthened slave communities and stiffened black resistance to the system. Despite onerous work schedules, most plantation slaves had a three-day holiday at Christmas time and several Saturday-night parties during the year, in addition to time-off on most Sundays. At the holidays and parties, blacks from nearby plantations would visit for a feast provided by the master that might feed them the only meat they had eaten for a couple of months. When the slaves could borrow or make instruments, banjos, gourds, or fiddles accompanied satirical songs and social dancing after dinner. More often, their dancing was "patting juba," in which they patted out a rhythm with their feet and sang as they danced. As with other folk performances in African American life, there was little distinction made between performers and spectators during these holidays; all joined in the fun.

At one of these events, corn-shucking festivals, whites and blacks enjoyed themselves together. Although these harvest celebrations involved a form of collective mutuality that crossed racial lines, blacks and whites looked to corn-shucking parties for very different pleasures. For the slaves, they were a time to show off their work abilities, practice their singing and dancing, recognize black leadership, and enjoy each other's company – in short, primarily to affirm their communal culture. From the planter's point of view, a lot of harvest work was done quickly while he and his family enjoyed the performances of happy slaves, always a spectacle to brighten their self-image as benevolent paternalists. The shucking itself was usually set up as a contest between two teams of slaves, each captained by a black man who led his team in work songs. Typically, the victorious team carried the master of the plantation around his house on their shoulders while singing a mocking song (the probable origin of the minstrel term "walkaround"). A feast followed, with singing and dancing far into the night. No doubt many African Americans realized that corn-shucking festivals helped their masters to justify their bondage. But their ethos of collective mutuality often led them to cooperate with slaveowners if they knew it would benefit their community in exchange.

While collective mutuality contained and reinforced many African American performances, some cultural practices among blacks modified this cultural system. In part this was because mutual cooperation, though comforting and often empowering, could hardly be a guarantee of self-respect or even survival under slavery. Other performances, then, instructed African Americans in modes of self-reliance that occasionally contravened the morality of their community. Chief among these were trickster tales, related by storytellers in the slave quarters to children and anyone else who cared to listen. Tales about animal tricksters like B'rer Rabbit were abundant, but tricksters could be human too. In narratives that clearly paralleled many a slave's experience with his master, a powerless but wily trickster would typically outwit a strong aggressor. Far from celebrating the joys of community, these tales frequently focus on an amoral, self-seeking protagonist with no family or wider social network. Mutual protection and affirmation have no place in the trickster's world of violence and duplicity. When the culture of collective mutuality failed them, African Americans needed other strategies for survival and success.

Commercial Performance, 1830–1870

The commercial and industrial revolutions of the nineteenth century significantly increased the amount and variety of U.S. theatre and permanently altered its modes of production and reception. In the place of an all-purpose stock company performing plays, opera, pantomime, and variety acts in the same playhouse, with occasional visits from stars and circuses, several of these genres gained their own sites for performance. With the advent of the star system in the late twenties, play production became more rationalized, and audience response shifted toward hero worship. Stars and impresarios, the new capitalists of show business, shed the remaining vestiges of elite patronage to produce new genres, such as minstrelsy and burlesque, and to charge customers what the market would bear. These initiatives, in concert with profound social changes, gradually created distinctive audiences that enjoyed different performance genres in specific ways. Following the emergence of a new business class in the 1840s based on the cultural systems of rationality and respectability, the commercial theatre became increasingly divided between "respectable" fare for pacified bourgeois spectators and unrespectable entertainments for rowdy workers. This division along the class line, which would shape the American theatre for the rest of the century, hardened with the collapse of stock company production in the 1870s and its replacement by a mode of production dominated by the national industrial bourgeoisie. Specialization, both in production and reception, marked the enormous growth of the American theatre in the 1830–70 period.

Manager Stephen Price along with actor T. A. Cooper of the Park Theatre in New York and London actor George Frederick Cooke began the practice of starring itinerants in 1809 when they struck an agreement for Cooke to appear in America. During the teens and twenties, Price had a monopoly on transatlantic stars; Edmund Kean, Clara Fisher, Henry Wallack, and others toured through his circuit and paid him a percentage of their profits. Soon other managers began to offer American stars like Edwin Forrest for a fee and altered their stock companies to provide support for a succession of starring engagements. As a system, starring emerged during the minor theatrical depression of 1828–30, when overbuilding and competition in New York, Boston, and Philadelphia shifted the balance of power in negotiating starring engagements from local managers to stars. Just as managers were breaking free from elite interference in the internal affairs of their theatres, the stars and their impresarios exerted new controls over their season selections and hiring practices. After 1830, the national star system (continually reinforced from abroad) dominated the business arrangements of most local theatres. The next major star maker after Price was Ethelbert A. Marshall, whose empire at its height in 1850 stretched from London, through the Broadway Theatre in New York, to Cincinnati and New Orleans.

Stock actors sought independent stardom as the reward of republican industry and talent. For the audience, however, the popularity of the stars rested on hero worship, a new relationship between actors and spectators throughout the West that derived from the breakdown of traditional patriarchy and the rise of gothicism and sentimentality during the revolutionary era. Unlike the respect and admiration accorded previous premiere actors in the eighteenth century, audiences invested Kean, Forrest, and other male stars with the kinds of charismatic appeal that had shaped their worship of Washington and Napoleon. The democracy of feeling let loose by revolution circulated easily between national symbols and the stage; belief in the power of male virtuoso stars became a source of democratic pleasure. As Thomas Carlyle understood, people sought to worship heroes because they symbolized, paradoxically, a more intense and heightened version of their own uniqueness. International stars like the violinist Paganini, the French actor Frédérick Lemaître, and the romantic poet Lord Byron reversed the traditional relationship between artist and patron; the male artist now became the source of aristocratic and heroic powers. Indeed, such charisma produced distinctly undemocratic results. Bonded to a star, the spectator became less subject to other social relationships and more easily controlled.

In the theatre, three new conventions confirmed the sublimity of star power: the curtain speech, the floral tribute, and the play contest. Kean began the American practice of speaking directly to spectators after the show on his two tours in the 1820s. By the mid-1830s, audiences looked forward to the opportunity to "meet" the star directly and bask in his uniqueness. Spectators presented male as well as female stars with floral tributes and other tokens of their gratitude; often these presentations preceded the star's curtain speech. The demand for heroic uniqueness sent the stars in quest of new plays, which led to the play contest. Early stars used the heroes of Shakespeare and other canonized playwrights to build their images, but audiences wanted to see their luminaries in characters that collapsed their stage role into their public persona. Edwin Forrest held the first play contest in the United States in 1828; it netted him *Metamora; or, The Last of the Wampanoags,* which became the most popular vehicle of his career. Many stars followed with similar contests in the 1830s and 1840s. Critics complained that these star vehicles limited dramatic interest to only one character, but this singularity, of course, was the main source of their popularity. If hero worship was to occur, audiences needed to see their star elevated far above the other figures on stage.

This specialized form of dramatic writing, coupled with the charismatic uniqueness of stardom, led to changes in the stock company. Although stock actors were still expected to be proficient in a variety of roles, managers now hired them primarily to support the visiting stars. And because audiences enjoyed watching their heroes command a large army or address a stage full of citizens, managers also hired many more supernumeraries than before. As in many other artisan trades in the 1830s and 1840s, the multilayered hierarchy within stock companies was giving way to a system in which a capitalist (the star) hired workers (stock actors and supernumeraries) for productive labor. Although this transformation would not be complete until the 1870s, the labor relations of the star system were already moving in this direction.

American actors and audiences learned much from English romantic stars, who outnumbered and easily dominated most of their U.S. counterparts in the 1820s and 1830s. After Cooke, James W. Wallack was the next significant star to cross the Atlantic, in 1818; he moved back and forth several times for the next thirty-five years. Praised for the grace of his melodramatic roles and his vivacity in comedy, Wallack, said one critic, "dazzled the observer by the opulence of his enjoyment." His several tours influenced a generation of American players of romantic comedy. On Kean's two trips to the United States, he impressed Americans with the intensity of his passions. Kean's sharp emotional transitions, which jolted spectators, shaped the technique of the young Edwin Forrest, who performed with him briefly in Albany. Possessed of much of the same fire and abandon as Kean was Junius Brutus Booth, who came to the States in 1821 and stayed. His most popular role was Richard III, in which, according to one observer, he "never failed of producing an electrical effect."[2] Billed occasionally as "The Mad Tragedian," Booth's power and apparent loss of control affected the playing style of Forrest, Augustus Addams, J. R. Scott, and many others. Charles Mathews, best known in London for the mimicry, wry humor, and comic inventiveness of his storytelling, toured twice to the United States. On his first trip in 1822–23, Mathews recognized the comic potential of the New England Yankee; his imitations of Yankee storytelling spawned the enormous success of American Yankee performers from the late 1820s into the 1850s. The charismatic appeal of these stars, especially the tragedians, thrilled American audiences and challenged U.S. actors.

Until the 1840s, the social construction of stardom denied most women stars from England and America the same status and appeal as males. Because republican culture blocked influential public roles for women, female stars were not generally accorded the same kind of high-voltage hero worship as men. London-born Mary Ann Duff achieved recognition in the 1820s for her grace and magnetism as Lady Macbeth and other strong women, but she continued the Siddons tradition of alternating between refined power and helpless emotion. The response to Clara Fisher, the most affecting player of innocent heroines in domestic melodramas in the late 1820s and early 1830s, was typical of that evoked by most women stars. Her vulnerability and spunkiness garnered paternalistic admiration from her mostly male audience until she married in 1834, when, significantly, her popularity plunged. Fanny Kemble, however, began to change the patriarchal assumptions of gendered stardom. When she toured with her father, Charles Kemble, in 1832 and 1833, she played dutiful-daughter roles but outshone him in public acclaim. In fact, onstage and in public, Fanny Kemble created sensations; she exchanged letters with President Jackson, gained worshipful admiration from politicians and judges, and stood as a symbol of self-confidence and achievement for feminists like Margaret Fuller. Her success helped the young Josephine Clifton, then an emerging U.S. star, to shape a public image that recognized her power. And Kemble had a formative influence on Charlotte Cushman, who modeled her strong-willed, passionate style on that of the English actress. Yet Cushman would not gain stardom until 1845. It would be another decade after Kemble's appearance before women stars in the United States could claim the same charisma as men.

As inspirers of hero worship, English stars reinforced the cultural system of gentility and its revolutionary-era offspring, sentimentality and gothicism. To the eyes of their adoring fans, stars were the new aristocrats, setting standards of behavior that status-conscious Americans hoped to emulate. Despite his commitment to Jacksonian democracy, the journalist William Leggett said of Charles Kemble, "We doubt if our stage has ever witnessed so fine a picture of unaffected courtliness; of the gallant and the finished gentleman. We think

Mr. Kemble's appearance in America will do a service to the art; that it will raise and refine its style . . ." (quoted in Hewitt, 111). Similar accolades greeted nearly all male and female British stars on their tours but seldom welcomed home-grown luminaries. Americans of middling status sought refinement, and they turned to foreign idols – in addition to etiquette books and sentimental fiction – to achieve it. Postcolonial anxiety and the rich legacy of English culture continued to structure many Americans' response to the London theatre.

But not the response of all citizens. Working-class rioters often targeted English stars and managers, who figured in seven major disturbances and many more threats and protests between 1825 and 1849. Styling themselves the defenders of national pride, workers typically demanded redress for some "insult" to America from the British stars. When Kean refused to perform before a small house on his first American tour, artisan patriots remembered the affront on his second tour in 1825 and staged riots in New York and Boston. In the early 1830s, working-class demands for apologies for alleged insults from Fanny Kemble, Charles Mathews, and Tyrone Power (Irish-born but identified as British by plebeian audiences) almost led to rioting, but strong support from genteel Americans averted mob action. Working-class riots against Joshua Anderson, Henry and Mrs. Wood, and George Farren, other theatrical imports from Britain, however, caused major property damage.

The class tensions underlying these riots climaxed in the infamous Astor Place Opera House riot of 1849. With its wealthy subscribers and exclusive dress code, the Opera House affronted the republican egalitarianism of New York City workers. Their specific target was William Charles Macready, the reigning tragedian of the English stage. New York artisans dubbed him the pet of princes; indeed, his studied acting style and ongoing quarrels with Forrest set him up as an appropriate scapegoat for working-class revenge. Forrest's supporters challenged the English star on his first night by throwing rotten eggs, wooden shingles, and even chairs onto the Astor Place stage during his performance. Macready decided to return to England but changed his mind when his elite advocates in the city – many desiring a confrontation with the riotous workers – persuaded him to continue his engagement. Following arrests and stone throwing the next day in front of the opera house, the state militia fired into the crowd, killing twenty-two people, most of them bystanders.[3] This was the first time that such deadly force had been used in a theatre riot, and it marked a turning point in class relations in the theatre. Workers, increasingly alienated from mixed-class theatre before 1849, turned more fully to their own entertainments. Managers of "respectable" playhouses, backed by court decisions extending private property rights, expanded their control over audience behavior. Previously understood as legitimate, if extralegal, forms of political expression, riots were now branded by the dominant culture as indecorous and criminal behavior. As the gulf between "respectable" and "unrespectable" theatre widened after 1850, rioting almost completely disappeared from bourgeois playhouses.

As well as extending the culture of gentility in the lives of the American business class, the star system advanced the careers of several American stage heroes who embodied notions of Jacksonian republicanism. Such stars included James E. Murdoch and Augustus Addams, but the chief proponent of these values was Edwin Forrest, the most popular American star in the 1830–50 period. Contemporary critics praised Forrest's herculean build and booming voice. They often compared his passionate outbursts to Kean's but found his overall style to be more straightforward and muscular than the English star's. Forrest capitalized on all the conventions of the new star system to build his hero-worshiping audience, milking curtain speeches, pumping his play contests for maximum publicity, and charging managers half of the gross receipts for his engagements. Early in his career, Forrest appealed to nearly all American theatregoers. By the time of the Astor Place riot, the elite scorned him, and other business-class Americans were turning to new stars. His core audience of republican workers, however, gave him packed houses and standing ovations almost to the end of his career in 1872.

Forrest relied primarily on his popular prize plays to create his public persona as a Jacksonian hero of the people. In *Metamora* (1829) by John Augustus Stone, *The Gladiator* (1831) by Robert Montgomery Bird, and *Jack Cade* (1835) by Robert T. Conrad, Forrest played champions of republican liberty – an Indian chief, a rebellious slave, and the leader of a peasant revolt, respectively – fighting aristocratic oppression. These heroes were more primitive, innocent, and belligerent than similar heroes during Jeffersonian times, reflecting a fusion of sentimentality and paternalism with republicanism that also shaped the public image of Old Hickory. Near the beginning of each of these prize plays, God speaks to his chosen agent through nature; "Red man, arouse! Freedom! Revenge or death!" he commands Metamora (quoted in Moody, *Dramas,* 215). Next, Forrest's hero mounts a revolution against aristocratic rulers who are forcibly preventing "the people" from returning to their ancestral home. "The people," however, betray their protagonist, the aristocrats regain control, and the hero dies a martyr for republican freedom. As this plot summary suggests, the Indians, slaves, and peasants for whom the hero fought did not deserve his sacrifice. Although these plays spout copious rhetoric about community and public virtue, they actually undercut the democratic side of republican culture to elevate a natural hero of Napoleonic authority and providential destiny. Coupled with the charismatic appeal of Forrest himself, performances of these star vehicles did more to enhance antidemocratic hero worship than the democratic values of republicanism. Significantly, the campaign oratory and tactics of Jacksonian Democrats, centered on hortatory speeches and militarylike parades, reflected many of the same dynamics.

In addition to furthering and modifying paternalism, gentility, and republicanism, the star system increased the reach of a cultural system relatively infrequent on the American stage: rationality. The belief that man's rational mind could control his will, shape his environment, invent systems of law and philosophy, draw up contracts, and direct others in useful employment was hardly new in western theatre and culture, of course. But although this cultural system gained influence in the Renaissance and Enlightenment, and shaped the American gentry's creation of a national constitution, it was not deeply embedded in the lives of most westerners; "common sense," paternalistic and republican habits, and traditional religion provided reason and system enough. In America, the revolution in politics, followed by revolutions in commerce and industry in the early and mid-nineteenth century, altered these older patterns of life irrevocably for many citizens, especially urbanites. First newspapers and post offices, then telegraphs and penny presses democratized the flow of information. Common people made laws, agreed on contracts, extended credit, and made rational plans about their futures. As the economic age of water and wood gave way to the age of steam and iron, capitalists and workers devised complex systems for organizing new means of production and distribution. Rationality reached into schools, government offices, and train schedules, channeling resources and energies in ways increasingly dictated by considerations of efficiency and social or economic profit. By the 1840s, for example, mass-produced clocks were everywhere, regulating work and leisure in the home, on the farm, and in the shop.

The star system itself was a part of the rationalization of American life, providing a more efficient mode for the distribution and enjoyment of theatrical talent than had been possible before. What made the system work, in addition to a hunger for heroes, was the widespread availability of new networks of information and transportation. Further, some of the plays performed by the stars began to reflect and construct Americans' response to the new constraints and freedoms of rationality. Complicating this response, however, were the conflicts between rationality and the cultural systems already embedded in theatrical entertainment. From a republican point of view, rational systems of law and contract could never countermand one's duty to oppose aristocratic privilege and fight for traditional rights. Paternalists and sentimentalists had a very different problem: how to square their new desire for system and profit with the older demands of the heart for warm authority and romantic love. In pre-1830 melodramas, for instance, characters relying on reason and angling for gain were invariably villains.

The first significant star vehicles to wrestle with these problems were the Yankee plays, written for a new breed of American comic, the stage Yankee.

These embodiments of republican virtues told stories with a New England twang and balanced rationalistic calculation with sentimental action. Yankee characters had appeared in farces, nationalistic melodramas, and sentimental comedies since the Revolution; Jonathan in *The Contrast* was an early example. The boom in Yankee theatre began in the mid-1820s, however, and by 1850 well over a hundred plays, most of them farces, had been crafted for several major performers, with George Handel "Yankee" Hill and Danforth Marble among the most prominent.

Although not written as a vehicle for a specific star, *The Forest Rose* (1825) was one of the earliest and most enduring of the Yankee plays; Hill and Marble performed it often. Like many later Yankees, Jonathan, "a little in the marchant way and a piece of a farmer besides," occupies a secondary position in the cast. With an eye on the main chance, this concoction of capitalist trickster and rural fool takes bribe money from a city-slicker villain to assist him in abducting the heroine. This puts Jonathan in a profits-versus-sentiment bind that afflicted Yankee characters in many of these vehicles and led to much of their comedy. "I don't calculate I feel exactly right about keeping this purse," he says. "And yet I believe I should feel still worse to give it back. Twenty-three dollars is a speculation that ain't to be sneezed at . . ." (quoted in ibid., 160, 168). In the end, Jonathan keeps the money but tricks the villain out of his prize, a compromise resolution appropriate enough for secondary characters in comedy or farce but impossible in straight melodrama. Americans enjoying *The Forest Rose* and struggling with their own conflicts about speculation and morality could laugh at their problems without having to resolve them, a sure-fire lure for comedy.

As the example of *The Forest Rose* suggests, Yankee calculation was usually laughed with as much as at in these vehicles. Dan Marble's character in C. A. Logan's *The Vermont Wool Dealer* (1838), Deuteronomy Dutiful, however, was generally the butt of the jokes. He chases after a rich girl but then sentimentally buys champagne for her wedding to another. Two generations of Yankee stars performed Joseph S. Jones's *The People's Lawyer, or Solon Shingle* (1839), in which a garrulous old farmer delays and finally frustrates the machinations of a courtroom villain by complaining about his missing barrel of applesauce. The Yankee is the comic counterpart of the heroic lawyer of the title; both uphold the sanctity of law and contracts to ensure justice. Hill's vehicle, Jones's *The Green Mountain Boy* (1833), like *The Forest Rose* and many Yankee plays, features a conflict between the shrewd easterner and a black character. These recurring contests pitted calculation against stupidity, independence against slavishness, and civilization against instinct – and the Yankees always won. Like several earlier stage symbols of the nation, Yankee stars played a large role in the social construction of whiteness. Dan Marble, in fact, performed most of his roles in clothing that resembled the later costume of Uncle Sam. Although accommodating the values of republican simplicity and sentimental virtue, the stage Yankees actually advanced the cultural system of rationality and the whiteness it assumed.

Other star vehicles also worked toward this end. The most popular play of the 1840s, outdistancing even *Richard III,* was *The Lady of Lyons* (1838), by Edward Bulwer-Lytton. The English dramatist had written his social comedy as a vehicle for Macready, who played it successfully, but women stars like Anna Cora Mowatt ensured its popularity for the next thirty years. The rationalizing realities of contracts, money, and the law lie beneath the sentimental surface of the play. At its climax, the heroine has promised to marry the villain to pay her father's debts, but the hero, formerly poor but now rich, rips up the marriage contract and gives her father twice the amount owed him to win the girl. U.S. stars also gravitated to two other of Bulwer-Lytton's plays, *Richelieu* (1839) and *Money* (1840), which recognized even more overtly the realities of power and position on which the house of sentiment was built. Among American plays, *The Broker of Bogota* (1834) by Robert M. Bird, written for Forrest, and *Tortesa, the Usurer* (1839) by Nathaniel P. Willis, performed occasionally by James W. Wallack, also gave legitimacy to the increasing power of rational principles in dramatic worlds that remained predominately sentimental. Rationality was emerging as a popular cultural system in the theatre of the 1830s and early 1840s, but republicanism and sentimentality still qualified and contained its effects.

Most stars during these years reached across regional, class, and gender differences to appeal to a broad American audience. The commercial revolution in society and the theatre, however, was already producing more specialized groups of spectators. The first to coalesce, in the mid-1830s, were urban audiences of mostly artisans and laborers. Located in the working-class districts of Boston, New York, and Philadelphia, the most populous centers of commerce in the nation, this group enjoyed variety acts, spectacular melodrama, and American – but rarely English – stars. Joining the workers at their theatres were a group of men that styled themselves "sports." Like traditional workers, "the sporting fraternity," which included men from many classes, shared an interest in prize fights, racing, blood sports, and other forms of gambling and rough camaraderie.

Thomas S. Hamblin, manager and owner of the Bowery Theatre in New York for most of the 1830s and 1840s, pioneered the innovations that established working-class theatre as a separate form of entertainment. Hamblin broke many of the traditions of genteel theatre: He built his stock company and production shops for spectacular melodrama; he experimented with gas lighting, aquatic staging, and special fire effects; he advertized new shows extravagantly and pushed them toward long runs; and he controlled the careers of several minor stars, including, for a while, Junius Brutus Booth.

The companies of Hamblin and his cohorts in other commercial centers of the East played before a mostly male audience that prized republican liberties, subjected women to traditional patriarchal codes, and attacked any perceived violation of their honor. Though generally indifferent to the emerging system of rationality – except when it touched their jobs or their masculinity – this audience resented the strictures of genteel respectability, correctly sensing in them a new mode of class domination.

Amid the American stars, animal acts, ballet dancers, and blackface minstrels appearing on working-class stages was a new kind of melodrama that spoke directly to the desires and fears of this audience. Drawing much of its energy from the gothic tradition, apocalyptic melodrama typically enrolled the villain-hero of gothicism in the defense of republican honor. In J. S. Jones's *The Carpenter of Rouen* (1837), for instance, the title character avenges the murder of his wife and the honor of the artisan class by killing a French Catholic nobleman who engineered an historical massacre of Protestants during the Reformation, when the play is set. The defense of family honor and free land in the West turns Reginald Ashburn into "the Jibbenainosay," a crazed avenger who slaughters Indians in *Nick of the Woods* (1838), adapted by Louisa Medina from the novel by Robert M. Bird. Unlike Bird's plays for Forrest, however, these melodramas were not written for a star and did not elevate a superhero over the people. In fact, they tended to emphasize the need for working-class solidarity in overcoming evil; *Carpenter,* like many of these shows, features several scenes of male bonding through secret rituals that help to contravene the often supernatural power of aristocratic villainy. Like several of the riots many workers started and enjoyed, these melodramas ended in a conflagration that symbolically consumed the evils that oppressed them. One of the most apocalyptic of these melodramas was an adaptation, again by Medina, of *The Last Days of Pompeii* (1835) that challenged Hamblin's carpenters and stage machinists to produce an erupting volcano, an earthquake, and a fire for the finale. Working-class audiences in eastern cities enjoyed several dozen of these apocalyptic plays through the mid-1850s.

Working-class delight in variety initially found a home at the Bowery and other playhouses featuring melodramas and stars but by the 1840s overflowed into more specialized venues. Apart from the minstrel houses, these theatres played to mixed-class audiences, though workers and "sports" formed the core of the spectators. William Mitchell's Olympic Theatre in New York began the trend in 1839 by offering musical travesties, local-color farces, and burlesques of popular plays and stars. Mitchell's success sparked competition in New York and imitation elsewhere. Probably the most gifted of the burlesque writers was John Brougham, whose comic exaggerations of popular plays and performers, including a delightful deflation of Forrest's bellowings in *Metamora,* amused New Yorkers throughout the 1850s. Variety theatre also spawned the success of Frank Chanfrau, who built his stardom on a single character, Mose the fireman, first seen at Mitchell's Olympic in *A Glance at New York* in 1848. This local-color piece by Benjamin Baker strung together farcical incidents with jokes, songs, and monologues centered on Mose, whose Bowery B'hoy mix of belligerence and sentiment connected directly to the lives of much of Mitchell's audience. City workers made up most of the volunteer fire companies by the 1840s and competed fiercely to be the bravest in the face of a blaze. Chanfrau contracted for other vehicles (*Mose in China, New York as It Is, Mose in California,* among them), toured them widely in working-class playhouses, competed with several imitators, and extended the Mose fad for three and a half years.

By the mid-1840s, German and Irish immigrants also constituted semiseparate audiences, predominately working class, for urban theatre. Over a million and a half Germans emigrated to the United States between 1830 and the Civil War. Although most of these became farmers, nearly a third of them settled in cities, and many of them took up the skilled crafts they had practiced in Germany. Disdained and envied by many native-born Americans for their modest success and clannishness, urban German Americans built their own institutions, including newspapers, singing groups, gymnastic clubs, and theatres. By 1860, German-language theatres had been established in New Orleans, Baltimore, St. Louis, Cincinnati, New York, San Francisco, and Chicago. Like their community singing groups, German-language theatre functioned primarily to separate German Americans from other social groups by celebrating traditional practices and values, but it also provided some theatrical experiences that assisted their audiences in coping with American life. The Stadt Theater Company in New York, for instance, produced much of the same fare found on midcentury stages in Germany, including operetta, Kotzebue, Schiller and other German romantics, and lots of farces. These were mixed with occasional comedies about immigrant life, such as *Anton in New York, oder Faust's Soll und Haben.*

The Irish, many of them fleeing the potato famine of the 1840s, constituted more than 2 million immigrants by 1860. Most came to the United States poor and unskilled, settled as best they could in city slums, and entered the work force at the bottom, where they encountered "No Irish Need Apply," even for ditch-digging jobs. By the Civil War, native-born Protestant Americans generally assumed that the Irish were a "race" apart, doomed by nature to indolence, stupidity, violence, and Catholicism. Nativist political movements in the 1840s, especially popular with groups of workers and small businessmen, tried to pass temperance and immigration laws to limit or discourage Irish immigration.

Unlike German immigrants, the Irish, despite their numbers, never established separate theatres. Many Irish Americans, of course, could not afford the price of a ticket. Those who attended the playhouses encountered the legacy of British imperialism in the stereotypical Irish trickster, especially common in farce. As played by the Anglo-Irish star Tyrone Power in the 1820s and 1830s, these characters were lovable clowns, overfond of drinking, fighting, and lying, but essentially children in need of paternal supervision. By the 1850s, Irish American stars like Barney Williams and William Florence had taken over Power's vehicles, but also added a few of their own. These new shows, many designed to appeal both to Irish Americans and to a wider audience of native-born citizens often hostile to the Irish in their midst, began to change the stereotype. The title role in *Shandy Maguire* (c. 1851), for instance, continues many of the trickster's traditional shenanigans, but drinks in moderation, foils a greedy villain, and rescues a heroine. On the other hand, most playwrights (including John Brougham, who created several sympathetic Irish characters), defined the "Irishman" as qualitatively different from the "American." Irish Americans could applaud favorable and even heroic images of themselves on stage by the 1850s, but these images were often tainted by a racism that defined the Irish as inherently "other."

More often, Irish Americans enjoyed another kind of racism in the theatre, the minstrel show. In 1843, Dan Emmett and three other blackface entertainers organized themselves as the Virginia Minstrels and shaped their individual variety numbers of music, dancing, and comic foolery into a single production. By 1850, dozens of minstrel troupes were performing throughout the country, predominately to urban working-class males, who would remain their primary audience through the Civil War. The conventions of white performers "blacking up" for public displays derived partly from elite colonial theatre, but mostly from the folk rituals of common people – the charivari, rituals of misrule, and rites of passage – that played such a central role in Revolutionary-era street theatre. Many Irish Americans, important in minstrelsy not only as spectators but as performers, had learned about similar ritual practices in Ireland. Before 1843, individual blackface performers such as T. D. Rice and G. W. Dixon, who appeared as specialty acts at the Bowery Theatre and other working-class houses, used this republican tradition to level pretentious aristocrats and mock oppressive figures of authority. These variety performances before the 1840s were only incidentally about African Americans; the black mask had long been used to signify a trickster figure in folk rituals of inversion. To be sure, Emmett, Dixon, and others advertized themselves as authentic "Negroes," and Rice even claimed to have taken the costume and dance for his wildly popular "Jim Crow" act from an old black man possibly in Louisville, Cincinnati, or even Baltimore. But the tunes they used were mostly Celtic in origin, the point of their entertainment generally a republican attack on other whites, and their images of blacks – though frequently demeaning – more benign than those of black characters in Yankee plays and other dramatic pieces. Significantly, working-class mobs in the 1830s often put new verses to "Jim Crow" and sang it as an accompaniment to their riots.

With the creation of the minstrel show in 1843, however, blackface performance became more overtly racist. This occurred even as white performers were borrowing heavily from African American street dancers in the North and slave festivities in the South to fashion new conventions for their shows. Corn-shucking rituals on plantations provided ready cultural capital for whites in the North eager to profit from the enormous popularity of minstrelsy. White performers had already adapted some musical instruments played by slaves during these festivities (the banjo and the bones), plus slave dances ("patting juba" and black jigs), and these were quickly incorporated into the new genre. Minstrels also altered the corn-shucking "walkaround" parade to begin and end their productions and elaborated the banter among blacks during the festival into comic exchanges between minstrel endmen "Tambo" and "Bones." After the musical numbers and jokes of the first part of the show and the specialty acts of the second, a one-act comedy, parody, or farce frequently ended the production. Many of these pieces were set in the midst of plantation festivity, and several featured parodies of corn-shucking. Although white minstrels borrowed heavily from African American performers, they repaid the debt through mockery and degradation. For most of the show, the minstrels portrayed their black characters as physically grotesque, foolishly inept, and animalistic in their habits and desires.

The minstrel show's embrace of aspects of the cultural systems of sentimentality and patriarchy somewhat qualified but also extended its racism. Minstrels sentimentalized southern plantations as happy homes for childish Jim Crows, Earth Mother mammies, and feminized old uncles. Yet, because they were also places where masters could attack beautiful "yaller gals" and separate slave husbands from wives, minstrelsy evoked some sympathy for slaves as victims. For the most part, though, such events provided occasions for weeping, not action. Stephen Foster, the master of minstrel sentiment and nostalgia, focused on dead slaves and departed lovers in many of his songs. "Old Folks at Home," like much of his music, invited his auditors of transplanted farm boys, rootless journeymen, and homesick Irish Americans to return to an imaginary home of childhood pleasures and paternal protection. Foster's immense popularity from the late 1840s through the early 1860s created an audience for the ideology of minstrelsy far beyond those who went to enjoy its shows.

The lure of old-fashioned paternalism was especially strong for male workers, whose traditional masculinist values were being undermined by the wages and attitudes brought home by their sisters, wives, and sweethearts. Encouraged to imagine themselves as slave owners, many working-class men could enjoy what minstrelsy and southern apologists held to be the familial basis of slavery. On the other hand, such identification could also create a conflict in the spectators' minds with their sentimental attachments to separated lovers and runaways, a minor but significant theme in minstrelsy during its first ten years. Despite this contradicton, the demands of masculinist pride also led minstrels to create "wench" characters, typically females with ridiculous features and engulfing appetites, to reassure their audiences of masculine superiority through laughter. Since minstrel troupes were entirely male, men played "wench" roles as well as the seductive "yaller gals." As Eric Lott has noted, these characterizations, played before a mostly male audience, "created an atmosphere of polymorphous license that could blur conventional gender outlines . . . [but probably] produced the reassertion of masculinity in misogynist representations" (27). Like other forms of male, working-class entertainment in this era, minstrelsy provided opportunities for homosocial and occasionally homosexual enjoyment. These moments, however, were usually wrapped in the sexist values of traditional paternalism.

Blackface variety had its beginnings in rowdy republicanism, and this cultural system, though altered and diluted, continued to inform minstrelsy through the Civil War. Minstrels still parodied aristocratic pretensions, most engagingly through the contortions of the urban dandy Zip Coon, and during the war they targeted for satiric attack corrupt businessmen and a draft law that discriminated against the poor. As had republican entertainment in the past, minstrelsy provided a rallying point for working-class solidarity. Irish and German Americans, rural folk from the countryside, and even competing gangs of native-born firemen could laugh and weep together at the same show; the minstrel mask mediated many intraclass conflicts. By temporarily identifying with the excessive and often erotic enjoyment of this symbol, spectators could even imagine a time when white and black workers might stand together to fend off the new codes of respectability and oppose the restrictive encroachments of rationality. In the end, however, white working-class groups built their camaraderie on the backs of African Americans; Irish immigrants, for instance, could shed their ethnicity and become "true Americans" by emphasizing their whiteness through minstrelsy. By 1865, most white urban workers assumed that the minstrels were providing them with an accurate picture of black people. Minstrelsy excluded free black workers from solidarity with others of their class and indelibly linked the consciousness of white workers to a shared sense of their "race."

The construction of whiteness also pervaded "respectable" Victorian theatre, which began to draw a distinctive business-class audience in the mid-1840s. The class divide was already separating the leisure activities of many urban Americans; the production and enjoyment of theatrical entertainment specifically aimed at the new business class simply recognized and capitalized upon social reality. Mid-century Americans used the distinction between physical and mental labor, a gap that had been widening since the 1820s, to separate workers from the bourgeoisie. Explained one Protestant reverend in 1857, "The business class [included] not the merchant and the trader only, [but] all those whose vocation it is to organize and direct the industrial forces of the community – the manufacturer, the master mechanic, the contractor, or the superintendent, in the various enterprises of production, accommodation, or improvement" (quoted in Blumin, 136). The good reverend might also have included himself, along with doctors, journalists, and other professionals. Allied with the leaders of this new class were thousands of intermediaries, salespeople, clerks, and others who earned yearly salaries, not weekly wages, and cultivated personal tastes and habits to avoid being classed as "unrespectable" by their superiors. By 1860, roughly 35 percent of the urban families in most large towns or cities of the Northeast belonged to one or another stratum of the new business class.

The theatres appealing to business-class spectators drew nearly equal numbers of men and women to their playhouse doors. Before the mid-1840s, theatregoing of all kinds had been a predominately male activity, with men enjoying the sociability of each other in a setting that included liquor and prostitutes. This tradition continued in working-class venues for the rest of the century. Entrepreneurs of the new museum theatres, however, challenged these norms of theatregoing. They encouraged the patronage of "respectable" women by placing their entertainments in educational environments, adopting regular matinee performances, advertising the propriety of their offerings, and banning temptations to male immorality. Although other managers had tried these policies intermittently, Moses Kimball at the Boston Museum and P. T. Barnum at the American Museum in New York pushed through this minor revolution in theatregoing. In 1843, Kimball began to offer theatrical fare in the midst of his museum curiosities, scientific displays, and educational lectures. Barnum was the better publicist, promoting midgets and "feejee mermaids," and promising moral entertainment for the whole family and ice water for patrons who wanted a drink. From 1845 to 1855, during the same decade that "unrespectable" minstrelsy rapidly expanded, "respectable" museum theatres became established in all the major cities of the Northeast. By encouraging female patronage and instituting new norms of audience decorum, the entrepreneurs of museum theatre laid the basis for the success of business-class theatre.

In addition to women, Barnum, Kimball, and their imitators increased the attendance of moderate-income families, many new to theatregoing, by playing on their class anxieties. A multitude of social forces in the 1840s were quickening the consciousness of urban Americans about the widening gap between the "respectable" and the "unwashed": urban riots, slum conditions, and massive immigration, on the one hand, and newly segregated housing patterns for the bourgeoisie, distinctive clothing fashions, and the ability to afford and furnish a front parlor, on the other. People near the class line sought reassurance about their respectability, and museum capitalists were happy to provide it, for a price. Some of their "freaks," for instance, demonstrated the apparent democracy of the norms of respectability. If high-status oddities of nature could command the respect and attention of the elite – Barnum had engineered an audience between Tom Thumb and Queen Victoria, for example – then surely all Americans who entered a museum could count themselves among the genteel. Other exotic curiosities, such as a "monkey man," the "Aztec children," and waxwork tableaux showing the horrors of drunkenness, induced a gothic response, allowing museum spectators to congratulate themselves on their own decorum and civilization. All of these exhibits were set in the midst of a parlorlike environment; the furniture, paintings, knickknacks, and picture books assured museum patrons, even those who could not afford such trappings in their own homes, that they were among the respectable.

So too did the kinds of plays produced on museum stages. Barnum, Kimball, and the other museum impresarios stayed away from genres of entertainment specifically identified with working-class tastes – apocalyptic melodramas, Irish plays, and rowdy minstrel shows – although Barnum did feature cleaned-up minstrel acts in the summertime. The overall repertory of museum theatres was actually close to that of other playhouses in the 1840s whose managers sought to draw audiences from all classes. Nonetheless, the public soon came to identify museum theatre with moral-reform melodrama because museum capitalists successfully advertised their long runs of these shows. Museum playwrights modeled these melodramas on eighteenth-century bourgeois tragedies such as James Shirley's *The Gamester* and George Lillo's *The London Merchant,* both still performed on antebellum stages. Like their predecessors, the dramatic allegories of the 1840s and 1850s pushed individualist values and humanitarian reforms, such as antislavery and urban vice laws. Temperance plays like *The Bottle, The Drunkard's Warning, Aunt Dinah's Pledge,* and *Ten Nights in a Barroom* were especially popular on museum stages.

By the time Barnum opened his new theatre in 1849 with a production of *The Drunkard,* Kimball's actors had already performed the piece more than 150 times. Of the dozens of popular temperance plays, this was one of the earliest and most widely produced; it became a model for several others. Written by William H. Smith in 1844, *The Drunkard* traces the hero's decline into dipsomania, the awakening of his conscience by a temperance reformer, and his eventual salvation. His reward, evident in the setting of the final scene, are the material symbols of respectable bourgeois family life:

Interior of Cottage. . . . – Edward discovered near music stand, R. – Julia [his daughter] seated on low stool on his L. – Mary [his wife] sewing at handsome work table, L. – Elegant table R. 2E. with astral light not lighted – Bible and other books on it. – Two beautiful flower stands . . . Bird-cages on wings . . . Covers of tables, chairs, etc. all extremely neat and in keeping. (Quoted in Moody, *Dramas,* 307)

The moral was clear: Exercise self-control, practice your duties to your family, apply your spiritual beliefs to attaining success, and you too could live in domestic bliss. These mandates – self-control, familial duty, and practical spirituality – were the central components of bourgeois respectability. They derived primarily from the cultural system of gentility, as modified by sentimentality and gothicism, but emphasized cultural practices available to the Victorian bourgeoisie. Ironically, this business-class version of gentility undercut some of the values that had boosted the bourgeoisie into positions of dominance in the first place. The aristocratic rewards of leisure and consumption end *The Drunkard* – Edward can now play his flute and display an astral lamp – rather than the republican virtues of democratic governance and productive work. Indeed, the new bourgeoisie increasingly abandoned the cross-class values of republicanism to urge forms of culture that reinforced the class divide.

Moral-reform melodramas also helped to constitute rationality as the twin pillar, next to respectability, of business-class life. H. J. Conway's version of *Uncle Tom's Cabin,* the adaptation of Stowe's novel most popular in museum theatres, celebrated the behavior of rational men of principle and the dynamics of the capitalist market even as it urged reform of the slave system. Where Stowe criticized the rationality of market relations for supporting slavery, Conway's melodrama ignored the capitalist basis of the slave system. In the play, though not the novel, two men of principle promise to free Uncle Tom from slavery; by the end of the melodrama, both deliver on their promises. This demonstration of promise making and promise keeping reinforces the contractualism necessary for rational calculation in market capitalism. Indeed, the action of many moral-reform melodramas centers on protagonists who make or break moral contracts – to take a temperance pledge, to live up to a promise made to a dying parent, to maintain one's virginity, and so forth. In these allegories of contractualism, the protagonist's rational will power to keep promises determines the dramatic shape of his or her fate. The dramatic carpenters of these pieces underlined the importance of rationality by contrasting men of principle with fools and villains who act irrationally. In *Uncle Tom's Cabin,* for instance, the slaves are minstrel buffoons, and Legree acts out of sheer malice, not rational calculation – characterizations at odds with Stowe's novel. The Yankee plays had accommodated rationality to the superior demands of sentimentality. In most moral-reform melodramas, the bias ran the other way; the audience might weep for victims of slavery or drunkenness, but it was rational principles, not sentimental tears, that saved them.

The respectability and rationality of museum theatres and moral-reform melodramas helped to shape the business class, but these cultural systems required fuller elaboration and wider dissemination to become socially dominant. Most interior theatre architecture in 1845, for instance, continued to divide a rowdy pit of workers from boxes meant for the elite. Where was the new business class to sit? After 1845, architects and refurbishers of business-class theatres began to replace pit benches with comfortable chairs. They called this new seating area the parquette, a term borrowed from opera houses designed primarily for the elite. They also cut back the number of side boxes in the first two tiers and entirely eliminated the third tier, the previous haunt of prostitutes and their customers. Following the mandates of respectability and rationality, prices for parquette chairs were higher than those for the older pit benches, and seating in this area was individualized and numbered, allowing for reservations and the orderly entrance of spectators into the auditorium. The new Boston Theatre in 1854, for example, featured a large semicircular parquette and commodious first balcony with folding theatre seats (the first of their kind), plus a second and third balcony of cheaper seats. Only four private boxes remained, and the pit had been eliminated altogether. In effect, the Boston business class had erased distinctions between themselves and the older elite and had removed respectable workers, if they cared to attend at all, to the margins of the playhouse. Box-pit-and-gallery seating had organized the interiors of English and American playhouses since 1660. By 1860, however, a mere fifteen years after the changes began, most business-class auditoriums reflected these new class arrangements.

Radical changes also occurred in the theatrical genres popular with business-class audiences. Unsophisticated playgoers unsure of their respectability might applaud moral-reform melodramas, but those confident of their class position needed plays that spoke more specifically to their own hopes and fears. For a while they found them in social comedies like Bulwer's *Lady of Lyons* and Anna Cora Mowatt's *Fashion* (1845), a comic attack on the pretensions of the parvenu – a character all too familiar to many in the new business class. By the mid-1850s, however, a different kind of melodrama was replacing conventions that had shaped the genre for more than fifty years. The new sensation melodramas borrowed notions of plotting and characterization from well-made comedies, a French genre that began to appear with regularity in England in the 1840s. The new melodramas derived from these plays recognized that chance occurrences often played a greater role in bourgeois lives than villainous conspiracy; poorly worded wills, missed communications, and financial panics might wreak unintended havoc on business-class families. Given such situations, God-given intuition or straightforward heroic action were no longer enough to ensure a happy ending, as they had been in most melodramas since the French Revolution. Uncovering the web of happenstance and deceit trapping melodramatic victims now took rational detective work. Thus, in substituting chance for villainy as the primary engine of the melodramatic plot, sensation melodramas increased the importance of rationality and downgraded the need for sentimental identification and republican heroism; in the process, they reversed long-standing cultural values implicit in melodramatic construction.

Dion Boucicault, an Irish-born London dramatist who wrote, produced, and acted in his plays in America from 1853 until the Civil War, was the most successful practitioner of sensation melodrama. His 1857 play *The Poor of New York* demonstrates the dominance of bourgeois respectability and rationality in sensation melodrama. The action centers on the Fairweathers, an upwardly mobile family temporarily derailed from the tracks of success and happiness by the Panic of 1857. Despite their economic reversals, the plot makes it clear that the family remains respectable; a working-class family, for instance, though better off economically, continues to defer to the Fairweathers as their betters. Although the title of the play suggests that the lower-class victims of the Panic deserve sympathy, the *real* poor of New York, according to Boucicault, are professionals who are "obliged to conceal their poverty with the false mask of content" (quoted in McConachie, *Melodramatic Formations,* 223). Lawyers and others who need to hide their temporary poverty have a greater claim on public sympathy than workers and beggars, the play asserts, because the code of respectability mandates a proper appearance. By play's end, a detective in the police department has rescued a receipt from a blazing building – the sensation scene of the play! – to reveal the villain and assist the Fairweathers in achieving economic justice. But unlike most previous villains, this one is allowed to reform and to appear with the good characters in the final tableau. Like many other sensation melodramas, *The Poor of New York* pushed the importance of rationality and encouraged its business-class audience to turn its back on class-based economic inequality. By the 1870s, Boucicault's melodramas were second only to Shakespeare's plays in overall popularity.

Other new performance genres pointed to an altered construction of gender relations for American bourgeois audiences. After 1845, melodramas of primitive female passion – their popularity built partly on the increased number of women theatregoers – electrified spectators. The stardom of Charlotte Cushman initiated and helped to sustain this trend. Cushman had been performing since the mid-1830s but did not achieve star status until 1845, when she triumphed in London (overshadowing a disgruntled Edwin Forrest on the same bill). Most of her major characters were powerful, primitive women. Cushman's Meg Merrilies, for example, swooped into the action of the dramatization of Scott's *Guy Mannering* like a gypsy Cassandra with womanly nurture and exotic knowledge to rescue the hero. As the prostitute Nancy in *Oliver Twist,* Cushman painted a "portrait of female depravity" that, for one critic, was "fearfully natural, dreadfully intense, horribly real" (quoted in Dudden, 89). Cushman was also widely celebrated for her "breeches" roles, male characters that she played in male attire. Her Romeo was one of the period's most erotic performances, a display of sexual attraction allowed between "pure" women because Victorian culture assumed that women could not become aroused by each other. Thus Cushman in performance was able to channel her strong attraction to other women in socially acceptable ways. Although she provided a model of strength for many female spectators, Cushman also helped men to imagine that women were more uncivilized and emotional than themselves.

By the mid-1850s, after Cushman's semiretirement from acting, many women stars specialized in characters typed as passionate, primitive, and natural by the cultural system of paternalism. One of the most famous was Matilda Heron, whose Camille, the dazzling French courtesan who dies for the love of a respectable young man, thrilled audiences with its emotional magnetism. Anna Cora Mowatt, better known as an actress than a playwright, moved spectators with the physiological naturalness of her performing. Playwright (and later manager) Augustin Daly wrote several melodramas of primitive female passion for stars in the 1860s, including *Leah, The Forsaken* for Kate Bateman and *Under the Gaslight* for Rose Eytinge. Many of these kinds of melodramas linked primitive emotion to domestic duty, suggesting that "natural" women were capable of the most untamed passion when family and/or motherhood was at stake. In Daly's *Under the Gaslight,* for instance, Eytinge's character Laura Courtland rescues a man tied to railroad tracks, because her sister's welfare is involved. The deleterious effects of this construction of womanhood by the system of paternalism were perhaps most apparent in the managerial career of Laura Keene. Despite recurrent but unfounded attacks on her vanity and instability as a woman, Keene successfully competed in the New York theatre scene from 1855 to 1863. Finally, a prejudicial press, financial problems, and the discouragement of having to mount spectacles employing lots of female flesh to stay in business forced her to close.

Cushman and other passionate female primitives succeeded for much the same reason that Keene failed: The cultural system of Victorian paternalism viewed women as inherently chaotic, emotional, and uncivilized. Men were destined to dominate women, according to paternalism, because they were orderly, rational, and civilized. One consequence of this cultural system was the belief that men were naturally more sensitive than women. This led to male stars whose construction of masculinity was very different from the strutting republican manliness of Edwin Forrest. Business-class audiences

praised the spiritual, idealized acting of Edwin Booth, the son of Junius Brutus. To establish himself as the tragedian of his generation, Booth played
Hamlet for 100 straight performances in 1864, winning accolades from the
bourgeois press as the most refined actor in America. Other male stars
worked for sensitivity and sentiment in their performances – notably Joseph
Jefferson, whose Rip Van Winkle was celebrated for its beauty and pathos.
Later critics would rail against the "feminization" of male stars, but in the
1860s most cheered for male spirituality.

Moreover, both male and female stars bolstered spectators' sense of possessing an authentic self beneath the social mask imposed by Victorian rationality and respectability. Bourgeois propriety mandated rigorous self-control
in public, but it also enjoined those in the business class to represent themselves to others with transparent sincerity. The necessary public image of
sincerity clashed with the anxieties and anger generated by home and business life. Alienated from their own feelings by the rationalization of the self,
however, American Victorians were hobbled in their attempts to understand
and resolve this double bind. Culturally, these conflicts produced some great
books and paintings to induce bourgeois self-examination. But the business
class also sought temporary relief from these burdens by turning to stage
images that reassured them that authenticity and multiple role playing were
not mutually exclusive. The power and authority of stage stars provided
seeming confirmation that individuals could play many roles but still remain
unique and coherent. Perhaps the best evidence of this was the widespread
circulation, after the mid-1860s, of photographs of the stars costumed as
their favorite characters. Audience adulation of the stars continued, but it
was increasingly tempered by emulation; the bourgeoisie needed models of
respectable role playing more than republican heroes. Whereas Forrest had
been a romantic symbol of the nation, Rose Eytinge and Edwin Booth became
refined and unique models of feminine passion and masculine sensitivity.

Not surprisingly, the desire to worship and emulate stars altered other
genres of Victorian performance by the Civil War. Star clowns and animal
tamers as well as star equestrians delighted American audiences in touring
circuses. Isaac Van Amburgh, the first performer to put his head in a lion's
mouth, owned his own circus, as did Dan Rice, a star clown who borrowed
his costume and much of his act from the stage Yankee tradition. Foreign
stars such as Marietta Alboni and Adelina Patti dominated operatic production and touring, offering the gentility of Italian opera to thousands of Americans. When the Lyceum lecture circuit advertised known stars like Daniel
Webster, Charles Dickens, and Charlotte Cushman, their audiences and profits soared. Romantic ballet produced its first superstar in the 1840s in Fanny
Elssler, who, like her female counterparts in drama, injected more erotic
power into her performances while remaining within the idealized images of

womanhood conventional to the genre. Of course, P. T. Barnum continued to be the master star maker of the era, refashioning himself as well as his celebrities to fill the vast desire of Victorian America for images of individual uniqueness and power. Barnum's star-making reach extended over all genres of performance, from circus animal acts to the operatic singing of Jenny Lind. The "Swedish Nightingale," as Barnum billed her, was nearly unknown in America, but the impresario puffed her as a religious songbird of surpassing purity, and her concerts dominated bourgeois culture throughout her 1850–51 tour. The cultural systems of respectability and rationalization had increased and extended the psychosocial need for stars. Entrepreneurs like Barnum fashioned strategies and institutions to fulfill that desire.

These systems and institutions of Victorianism worked their way into the lives of white southerners, whose traditions of republicanism and patriarchy shifted to accommodate them more gradually than in the North. By 1860, the South had its own bourgeoisie among planters and merchants, as well as many others who allied themselves with the new business class. The national and international star system helped to spread Victorian culture to the cities of the South. Traveling stars such as James W. Wallack, Forrest, Dan Marble, Cushman, Macready, Mowatt, and Edwin Booth played in New Orleans, Richmond, and Charleston during the thirty years before the Civil War. The stars of circuses and opera companies also circulated among the larger southern cities, inculcating the same desire for individual success and fame as that evoked by the actors. Although the plantation South had helped to shape the minstrel show, minstrelsy was much less popular in southern than northern theatres, primarily because fewer workers attended. Managers of theatres in the South generally followed the reforms of playhouses in the North, but there were regional differences, mostly due to slavery. The transition to parquette and balcony seating in southern theatres, for instance, usually left a special upper gallery for the seating of blacks. And in New Orleans, the Creole custom of white men taking educated *mulattas* as mistresses altered attendance patterns; for one night a week at the Camp Street Theatre, white women were barred from the playhouse so that some of their husbands could entertain their black mistresses without embarrassment.

Much of the success of the antebellum southern theatre, indeed of the South itself, rested on the profitability of cotton in world markets. And cotton profits, together with the spread of the slave system, were tied to the widespread availability of cheap land. President Andrew Jackson claimed thousands of southern acres for white Americans with the passage of the Indian Removal Act in 1830, which allowed federal troops to evacuate the Cherokees, Creeks, Chickasaws, and Choctaws west of the Mississippi. In response to these events and to the immense success of Edwin Forrest in *Metamora,* audiences attended plays about Indian–white relations in increasing numbers. This enthusiasm, which lasted until the mid-1840s, was centered in the East, where writers distant from the realities of the frontier struggled to justify American racism and imperialism. The unquestioned virtue of spreading republicanism across the continent provided the usual moral cover. In the West, most land-hungry Americans had few qualms about their appetites and actions.

Eastern justifications invoked two stereotypes that had served American interests in the past: the vengeful killer and the noble savage. Stone's *Metamora* had used both, with Forrest's hero only turning to vengeance after nobility got him nowhere with the duplicitous English colonists. Most other Indian plays, lacking a star for the title role, leaned toward the more negative characterization of Native Americans. These included *Pontiac* (1836), *Nick of the Woods* (1838), and *Putnam, the Iron Son of '76* (1844). But even those like *Carabasset* (1830) and *Oralloosa* (1832), which provided sympathetic portraits of noble savages, painted them primarily as doomed innocents – in need of Christianity, agriculture, and refinement – and easy prey to rapacious white conquerors. Both stereotypes allowed audiences to witness the advance of American imperialism in the South and West as inevitable republican progress; the Indians standing in the way either deserved to die or could be mourned as tragic symbols of lost ties to unfarmed nature.

The Pocahontas plays from this period generally worked within the same system of republican imperialism, but with a southern twist. Earlier dramatizations of the Pocahontas story had often included the marriage of the Indian princess to John Rolfe. After 1830, however, eastern writers fearing miscegenation – as much with regard to black–white as white–"red" relations – carefully avoided that part of the story. *Pocahontas; or, the Settlers of Virginia* (1830) ended with the princess's rescue of Captain John Smith, well before the interracial romance. *Pocahontas; or, an Historical Drama* (1837) recognized the love between the Virginian and the Indian but left the relationship unconsummated. Overall, the Indian plays, like much of the art and literature of the period, allowed the United States to exterminate the Native Americans or herd them into reservations with a clear conscience. As the French visitor Alexis de Tocqueville remarked, Americans had generally contrived to destroy the Indians "with singular felicity, tranquility, legally, philanthropically, without shedding blood, and without violating a single great principle of morality in the eyes of the world" (quoted in Takaki, 81).

Native Americans countered this deadly racism with written appeals, occasional counterattacks, and performances of their own. In New York City in 1828, when pressure for Indian removal was mounting, Red Jacket of the Seneca nation addressed an audience at Masonic Hall, after which Seneca warriors danced and sang. Red Jacket staged this performance, in part, as a response to a display at Peale's Museum in which two Onondaga Indians enacted what was billed as a scalping ritual. The desire of Native Americans to control their own performances was apparent as well in the refusal in 1836 of Chief John Ross and the Cherokee delegation to Washington to take part in a revival of *Pocahontas; or, the Settlers of Virginia* at a D.C. theatre. The manager had advertised their collusion in staging a "real INDIAN WAR DANCE, exhibiting, Hate, Triumph, Revenge, etc." (quoted in Bank, 483) for white American enjoyment. In 1843, after the southern tribes had settled north of Texas (in what would become Oklahoma) and made treaties with Native Americans on the Plains, four thousand delegates from seventeen Indian nations staged ceremonies pledging peace and friendship. The ceremony provided the basis for the contemporary southern variant of the intertribal powwow.

With the removal of the eastern tribes, white Americans encountered little resistance to western expansion until the mid-1840s. So rapid was the influx of settlers that fully a third of the population lived west of the Appalachians by 1840. By 1850, theatrical companies with visiting stars were flourishing in Chicago, St. Louis, and Mobile. Family companies performing on showboats along the banks of the Ohio and Mississippi often preceded the establishment of permanent troupes in river towns.

When Texas secured its independence from Mexico in 1836, some Americans began to dream of a transcontinental United States. Mexican territory, however, still stood in the way. Although soldiers and priests sponsored and acted in occasional play productions in mission villages, theatrical culture in the Mexican Southwest was irregular and amateur at best. With a firm belief in the "Manifest Destiny" of white Americans to own the continent, President Polk initiated a war against Mexico in 1846; the land grab netted the United States all of the territory between Texas and the Pacific. During the Gold Rush that soon followed the war, U.S. citizens seized thousands of acres that had belonged to Mexicans.

Ironically, the defeat of Mexico, the Gold Rush, and the stealing of land led to a population boom that created an audience for Hispanic theatre. An English-language newspaper reviewed a Hispanic production attended by Mexicans and U.S. soldiers in 1847, setting a precedent for interethnic audiences and criticism that would continue into the 1860s. By the mid-1850s, the Estrella troupe had emerged as the major Hispanic touring company in California. They mounted mostly melodramas popular in Spain, along with farces, songs, and dances, for family audiences. Like other Hispanic companies, the Estrellas occasionally rented theatres in San Francisco owned by Anglos. These Hispanic troupes had begun a tradition of performing and touring in the Southwest that would continue up to the middle of the twentieth century.

Hispanic theatre was only one of many non-English-speaking theatres operating in San Francisco in the decade after the Gold Rush. As the main supplier of miners and prospectors in the interior, San Francisco was bursting with mostly male immigrants from around the globe by the early 1850s. Especially numerous were Irish, Chinese, French, and Italians. Eager entrepreneurs built over fifty theatres, variety halls, and circus structures between 1850 and 1859 to entertain them; most of these venues burned down. Performers at Chinese opera houses, minstrel shows, and playhouses for French, German, and Italian drama played cheek by jowl with grand opera stars, variety acts at Barbary Coast cabarets, and occasional appearances by the likes of Edwin Booth. Several of the most popular performers came to San Francisco after touring the mining camps. Lola Montez, for instance, had achieved notoriety through her affair with King Ludwig of Bavaria – a liaison that culminated in his forced abdication. Beautiful and charming but with little acting talent, Montez performed a seductive spider dance that wowed the prospectors and shocked proper San Franciscans. Her protégé (or so she claimed), Lotta Crabtree, also danced and added singing and banjo playing to her personality act. Crabtree got her start in the gold fields and rose to minor stardom in plays especially crafted for her energetic charm. With the completion of the transcontinental railroad in 1869, the colorful early days of San Francisco theatre came to an end. As in other major U.S. cities, its Victorian elite increasingly proscribed the business class from attending the kinds of entertainment that had given San Francisco theatre much of its allure.

In between the California coast and the Mississippi River still lived an estimated 360,000 Indians at midcentury. Many continued their traditional performances, but white incursions onto their lands, proselytizing by Christian missionaries, and the massacre of the Buffalo herds radically reshaped their ceremonies. Most Plains tribes continued to practice the Sun Dance, for instance, in which young braves cut pieces of their flesh and danced around a central pole to effect the ritual restoration of nature through their cultural system of reciprocity. Buffalo skulls, however, were necessary for the proper performance of the Sun Dance. American sportsmen, scouts, and settlers were destroying the major resource of Indians' social, economic, and cultural lives. By the 1860s, the federal government had begun to force all western tribes onto separate reservations. Some Native Americans accepted their fate, but many others, including the Cheyennes, Arapahos, and western Sioux, resisted. The final battle for the West would not be over until Wounded Knee in 1890, but the outcome was never in doubt. Occasionally the white man's theatre played a role in the war against the Indians. After the Colorado militia massacred a band of peaceful Cheyennes and Arapahos encamped at Sand Creek in 1864, the citizens of nearby Denver proudly displayed the Indian scalps on the stage of their local opera house.

The cultural systems of respectability and rationality taught the dominant business class in the East to view Native Americans primarily as an impediment to their economic progress, when they thought about them at all. Fighting the Civil War, however, and securing the reconstruction of the South occupied most of their energy and attention in the 1860s. The war itself, although it did not change the major contours of Victorian culture, had brought certain problems to the fore. Publicly recognizing and controlling sexual desire was one of them. Having constructed women as inherently primitive and passionate, the men of the dominant culture worried that female sexuality might bound out of control. Victorian men had compounded this problem because, with the loosening of previous sentimental restraints on their own public expressions of sexual desire, they had begun to enjoy more overt displays of female flesh on stage. In the 1850s, increasing numbers of bourgeois males had gone to working-class concert saloons to applaud the songs, dances, and "living picture" poses of scantily clad women. This form of entertainment achieved respectability with the emergence of a new performance genre, the musical extravaganza. Deriving from the parodies and comic sketches of the variety stage, the extravaganza added the extra attractions of lavish spectacle and ballet dancers in small costumes and fleshling tights. Laura Keene staged one of the first of these pieces: *The Seven Sisters* ran for 253 performances in 1860–61 and saved her theatre from ruin. Musical extravaganzas gained popularity during the war years and reached their dubious acme in *The Black Crook,* an 1866 farrago of parodied gothicism, Offenbach-like music, and a troupe of French ballerinas. It played for 475 performances and grossed over a million dollars. The Civil War, rife with images of forceful masculinity, had lowered previous restrictions on the public expression of sexual titillation and desire.

This trend alarmed some Victorians, but it also emboldened a few women to take control of their own careers and push bourgeois hypocrisy about sexuality to new limits. In 1861, Adah Isaacs Menken, a darkly beautiful woman with an ample body, appeared "naked" strapped to the back of a galloping horse in the melodrama *Mazeppa.* Actually, "the Menken" wore flesh-colored tights and a light tunic for her famous ride, but the effect was sensationally erotic. Like Barnum, Menken had manufactured her own notoriety. Her *Mazeppa* ran for eight months on Broadway, and an 1863 tour of the gold fields and San Francisco earned her over a hundred thousand dollars. The next major shock to refined Victorians was the introduction of what would become the modern burlesque show with the 1868 tour of Lydia Thompson and her "British Blondes." Thompson's all-female troupe used suggestive poses and topical dialogue to strut their sexuality and mock masculine authority. To many Victorians, the monstrous femininity of the British Blondes mixed the images of the prostitute and the lady, thumbing its nose at the class and gender distinctions that upheld bourgeois propriety. Victorian males were both fascinated and repulsed, but the guilty pleasures derived from Thompsonian burlesque were finally less important than controlling the eruption of female assertiveness that it represented. The arbiters of Victorian paternalism declared burlesque unrespectable. For the rest of the century, a modified form of Thompsonian burlesque flourished as working-class entertainment; not until the twentieth century would it again cross the class line. Of course, the banishment of burlesque did nothing to stop the success of future leg shows that did not challenge male paternalism.

As burlesque was sinking into the mire of unrespectability, minstrelsy was rising out of it. Minstrelsy had been changing since the 1850s, becoming more respectable and less rowdy as several minstrel entrepreneurs strove to broaden their audiences. By the Civil War, some business-class urbanites were attending, although spectators for the genre remained predominately working class. Several troupes began to incorporate attractions used in other performance genres, such as Barnum-like freaks, extravaganza's spectacle, and even – following the success of Thompson's British Blondes – leggy women. By 1871, what had previously been an all-male form of entertainment now had eleven all-female troupes performing in whiteface. The public emergence of representations of sexual desire changed minstrelsy in another way as well: The female impersonator playing the wench role became a star in many companies. Following Francis Leon, the most famous of the impersonators, these primadonnas, as they were billed, played "yaller gals" in light makeup and expensive costuming, winning praise for their authentic femininity. In part, bourgeois anxiety about gender distinctions and role playing accounted for the popularity of these stars, but their success was also due to male homosexual titillation and female interest in high fashion.

By 1870, although many workers still attended minstrelsy, the concerns of the bourgeoisie were crowding out the oppositional republicanism of the earlier entertainment. These concerns were focused on issues of class and gender. Although minstrelsy remained casually racist, matters of race no longer agitated most white Victorians; for them, blacks remained inherently inferior, and the "Negro question" had been settled by the war. Thus, minstrel troupes composed of black performers, which had begun to appear before the Civil War, rapidly increased during and after it. Most Victorians understood black minstrelsy as an authentic display of natural impulses, and the black troupes, to increase their popularity, usually advertized themselves in this way. Because black companies could claim to be representing real plantation life, white troupes were forced to move even further from the traditional conventions of the minstrel show. The historical stage was set for J. H. Haverly, one of the most ambitious of minstrelsy's entrepreneurs, who would further shape the minstrel show to the norms of Victorian culture in the late 1870s.

These changes in burlesque and minstrelsy corresponded to larger shifts in American society as the new bourgeoisie consolidated and expanded its immense power during the 1860s. An economic depression in the late 1850s had increased the concentration of wealth into fewer hands. The new Republican party and the power of the national government, broadened during the war, further enhanced the political and economic reach of the national industrial business-class. In the 1860s, employment in manufacturing rose by 53 percent in Philadelphia, Boston, and New York. And despite the war, the percentage of the total labor force of the United States engaged in nonagricultural production during the decade jumped from 41 to 47 percent. The bourgeoisie expanded private property rights and the power of corporations. In cities, they rationalized and reinforced police protection and modernized benevolent societies to better control the poor and the discontented. The business class founded major cultural institutions – libraries, museums, and symphony orchestras – during the same decade, which bolstered the legitimacy of their domination.

By 1870, the norms of respectability and rationality regulated audience behavior in all the theatres "above" the class line. Audience members relied on new codes of politeness to greet one another in the lobby before moving decorously to reserved seats in the orchestra (as the parquette, or parquet, was beginning to be called) or in one of the balconies. Loud cheering and hissing, common in all theatres before the mid-1840s, had ceased. Riots were a thing of the past. The gas lighting in the auditorium, previously ablaze so spectators could see each other as well as the show, had dimmed. Increasingly, watching a play, a minstrel show, or a musical extravaganza had become a private, individual experience. The manners of the genteel parlor, first enforced regularly in museum theatres in the 1840s, had overtaken theatregoing by 1870.

This pacified, privatized bourgeois audience – by 1870, probably more female than male in overall composition – enjoyed theatrical entertainment produced by a system that was more rationalized than ever before. Like the factory system that was coming to dominate industrial production, fewer theatre people were in control, and the lines between management and labor had hardened. The stars, star-making impresarios, and a few theatre managers shaped the pace and marketing of theatrical production; star touring had flattened the company hierarchy up which stock actors had gradually moved into positions of shared responsibility and greater control. Stock actors lost an important strike in New York in 1864, when managers successfully fought their attempt to gain higher pay and a return to traditional ways of producing theatre. On the national level, Union Square in New York City had become the nucleus of the star system, a home to booking agents, costumers, photographers, script publishers, and others useful to the star system. This further consolidated the domination of the theatre capitalists – the stars and impresarios – at the center of the system. Within stock companies and among stars, the long run of a single production had replaced the repertory system of many shows throughout a season or on tour. This was partly in response to the drawing power of stars playing their best-loved characters, but also a result of the increased costs of more lavish spectacles. The long run, and its counterpart the hit show, helped to commodify audience enjoyment. Spectators could no longer count on seeing the same production over the course of several years; they had to purchase a ticket when the show was in fashion, like buying a new hat.

These processes of theatrical consolidation, rationalization, and commodification moved into high gear during the depression years of the mid-1870s. By 1880, the star system had effectively erased the stock company as the primary basis of theatrical production in North America. Although stars and impresarios had manipulated stock companies to serve their needs, local managers had continued to employ actors, build shows, and book stars for their seasons. In 1873, when the depression began, there were over fifty stock companies playing dramatic theatre throughout the country. By 1880, only seven remained. In their place, theatre capitalists formed combination companies – a star "in combination" with a troupe of actors, plus all production necessities – and toured the county. This shift occurred earlier for minstrel theatre; several blackface troupes had been touring as separate production units in the 1850s. By 1870, there were few purely local troupes remaining, and combination companies had long been standard procedure for the circus and opera. With a longer tradition of stock production and more investment in its continuance, capitalists of the legitimate theatre had been reluctant to alter the old system. When several stock companies failed during the depression, however, theatre capitalists created combination shows to fill the breech. The process snowballed because the combos no longer needed the surviving local companies for support. In 1886, there were 282 combination companies on the road.

By 1870, then, the hegemony of the American business class pervaded the theatre. The shift in productive relations to combination touring exacerbated the gulf between theatrical workers and capitalists. Former stock actors had to move to New York to find temporary work on a per-show basis; the remnants of their rights in traditional companies now lost, they had become the proletariat of the profession. Leg shows, dramatic theatre, and, increasingly, minstrelsy worked within the cultural systems of respectability and rationality. Pacified audiences were easier to manipulate and, in any case, could take no collective action against entertainment they found offensive. The dominance of the new bourgeoisie in the theatre and elsewhere had transformed the American stage.

Notes

1 Dennie is quoted in Meserve, *An Emerging Entertainment* (230) and Coleridge in Cox, *Seven Gothic Dramas, 1789–1825* (17).
2 Winter, quoted in Young, *Famous Actors and Actresses of the New York Stage* (1114) and Gould, in Hewitt (100).
3 Estimates of the fatalities are as high as thirty-one dead and a hundred to two hundred wounded, mostly bystanders. The figure cited here and elsewhere can be verified with the specific names of the fatalities.

Bibliography: American Theatre in Context

There are four divisions to this bibliography: a general listing of sources that I have used in writing two or more of the three sections of the above chapter and specific bibliographies for each of the three parts. Within the latter three divisions, I have tried to group the sources listed to correspond with specific portions of the chapter.

General Sources

The following general histories and bibliographies have been useful: Boyer et al., *The Enduring Vision: A History of the American People;* Brownlee, *Dynamics of Ascent: A History of the American Economy;* Hanson, *The Democratic Imagination in America;* Wiebe, *The Opening of American Society: From the Adoption of the Constitution to the Eve of Disunion;* Silvestre, *United States Theatre: A Bibliography;* Wilmeth, *American Stage to World War I;* and Zelinsky, *Nation into State: The Shifting Symbolic Foundations of American Nationalism.*

Several social and cultural histories of particular regions and urban areas have helped to link events in the theatre to their wider context: Collins, *White Society in the Antebellum South;* Greenberg, *Masters and Statesmen: The Political Culture of American Slavery;* Jaher, *The Urban Establishment: Upper Strata in Boston, New York, Charleston, Chicago, Los Angeles;* Monkkonen, *America Becomes Urban: The Development of U.S. Cities and Towns, 1780–1980;* Warne, *The Private City: Philadelphia in Three Periods of Its Growth;* Wyatt-Brown, *Southern Honor: Ethics and Behavior in the Old South.*

Changes in American notions of class are dealt with in insightful ways in these books: Blumin, *The Emergence of the Middle Class: Social Experience in the American City, 1790–1900;* Boyer, *Urban Masses and Moral Order in America, 1820–1920;* Laurie, *Artisans into Workers: Labor in Nineteenth-Century America;* Tyrrel, *Sobering Up: From Temperance to Prohibition in Antebellum America, 1800–1860;* and Wilentz, *Chants Democratic: New York City and the Rise of the American Working Class, 1789–1860.*

Useful studies of women in American society, a rapidly expanding field in the past two decades, include Cott, *The Bonds of Womanhood: "Woman's Sphere" in New England, 1780–1835;* Ryan, *Women in Public: Between Banners and Ballots, 1825–1880;* Smith-Rosenberg, *Disorderly Conduct: Visions of Gender in Victorian America;* and Stansell, *City of Women: Sex and Class in New York, 1789–1860.*

Changes in the American theatre were often reflected in similar alterations in the other arts. The following books provide a starting point to understand these changes and relationships: Bercovitch, ed., *Reconstructing American Literary History;* Harris, *The Artist in America: The Formative Years, 1790–1860;* and Patterson, *Authority, Autonomy, and Representation in American Literature, 1776–1865.*

Finally, regarding the general category of social and cultural history: On matters of race, see Berkhofer, *The White Man's Indian: Images of the American Indian from Columbus to the Present* and Takaki, *Iron Cages: Race and Culture in 19th-Century America;* on the history of sexuality and romance, see D'Emilio and Freedman, *Intimate Matters: a History of Sexuality in America* and Lystra, *Searching the Heart: Women, Men, and Romantic Love in Nineteenth-Century America;* on developments in material culture, see Bushman, *The Refinement of America: Persons, Houses, Cities;* and on a perceptive foreigner's view of the United States, see Tocqueville, *Democracy in America,* edited and abridged by Hacker.

For general sources on American theatre to 1870, the following guides, anthologies, and histories were useful: Brown, *The Theatre in America During the Revolution;* Engle and Miller, eds., *The American Stage: Social and Economic Issues from the Colonial Period to the Present;* Fisher and Watts, eds., *When They Weren't Doing Shakespeare: Essays on Nineteenth-Century British and American Theatre;* Grimsted, *Melodrama Unveiled: American Theater and Culture, 1800–1850;* Hewitt, *Theatre U.S.A., 1665–1957;* McConachie, *Melodramatic Formations: Theatre and Society, 1820–1870;* Moody, *America Takes the Stage;* Trussler, *The Cambridge Illustrated History of British Theatre;* Wilmeth and Miller, eds., *Cambridge Guide to American Theatre;* Young, ed., *Documents of American Theatre History: Volume I, Famous American Playhouses, 1716–1899;* and Young, ed., *Famous Actors and Actresses of the New York Stage.* (Other general sources will be found in succeeding bibliographical essays, especially those for Chapter 3, "Plays and Playwrights to 1800," and Chapter 5.)

On general theatre history in New York City, see Henderson, *The City and the Theatre: New York Playhouses from Bowling Green to Times Square,* and Odell, *Annals of the New York Stage.*

The following are suggested histories of theatrical production, including management, major companies, acting, and touring: Burge, *Lines of Business: Casting Practice and Policy in the American Theatre, 1752–1899;* Conolly, ed., *Theatrical Touring and Founding in North America;* Cross, *Next Week – East Lynn: Domestic Drama in Performance, 1820–1874;* Durham, ed., *American Theatre Companies, 1749–1887;* Donohue, ed., *The Theatrical Manager in England and America;* and Wilson, *A History of American Acting.* (See additional sources in Chapters 2 and 5.)

There are several books on early American playwrights. I relied extensively on two general sources: Moody, ed., *Dramas from the American Theatre, 1762–1909,* and Richardson, *American Drama from the Colonial Period Through World War I: A Critical History.* (See additional sources in Chapter 3.)

For specific social groups of Americans and the theatre, see Dudden, *Women in the American Theatre: Actresses and Audiences, 1790–1870;* Hatch, *The Black Image on the American Stage;* Hill, ed., *The Theatre of Black Americans: A Collection of Critical Essays;* Johnson, *American Actress: Perspective on the Nineteenth Century;* Kanellos, *A History of Hispanic Theatre in the United States; Origins to 1940.*

No general history of American theatre audiences exists. Many of the sources above have information on audiences and changing modes of spectatorship. I have supplemented these with Buckley, "To the Opera House: Culture and Society in New York City, 1820–1860," and Henneke, "The Playgoer in America (1752–1952)."

Several histories of other kinds of performances have also informed my essay: Click, *The Spirit of the Times: Amusements in Nineteenth-Century Baltimore, Norfolk, and Richmond;* Culhane, *The American Circus: An Illustrated History;* Davis, *Parades and Power: Street Theatre in Nineteenth-Century Philadelphia;* Dizikes, *Opera in America: A Cultural History;* Dulles, *A History of Recreation: America Learns to Play;* Gorn and Goldstein, *A Brief History of American Sports;* Hamm, *Music in the New World;* Jowitt, *Time and the Dancing Image;* Levine, *Highbrow/Lowbrow: The Emergence of Cultural Hierarchy in America;* and Roach, *Cities of the Dead: Circum-Atlantic Performance.*

Folk and Elite Performance, 1600–1770

Of the many fine books on Native American culture and performance, the following are worth consultation: Bierhorst, *The Mythology of North America;* Frisbie, ed., *Southwestern Indian Ritual Drama;* Galloway, ed., *The Southeastern Ceremonial Complex: Artifacts and Analysis;* Heth, ed., *Native American Dance: Ceremonies and Social Traditions;* Hultkrantz, *Belief and Worship in Native North America* and *Native Religions of North America;* Josephy, *500 Nations: An Illustrated History of North American Indians;* Laubin, *Indian Dances of North America: Their Importance to Indian Life;* Radin, *The Trickster: A Study in American Indian Mythology;* and Vecsey, *Imagine Ourselves Richly: Mythic Narratives of North American Indians.* On Indians and Europeans, see Axtell, *The Invasion Within: The Contest of Cultures in Colonial North America;* Cronon, *Changes in the Land: Indians, Colonists and the Ecology of New England;* Dowd, *A Spirited Resistance: The North American Struggle for Unity, 1745–1815;* Fitzhugh, ed., *Cultures in Contact: The Impact of European Contacts on Native American Cultural Institutions, A.D. 1000–1800;* Jennings, *The Invasion of America: Indians, Colonialism, and the Cant of Conquest;* Jennings, ed., *The History and Culture of Iroquois Diplomacy;* Meinig, *The Shaping of America, Vol. 1: Atlantic America, 1492–1800;* and Weber, *The Spanish Frontier in North America.*

The following books are helpful on the society and culture of colonial America before 1740: Bailyn, *The Peopling of British North America: An Introduction;* Greene, *Pursuits of Happiness: The Social Development of Early Modern British Colonies and the Formation of American Culture;* Hall, *Worlds of Wonder, Days of Judgment: Popular Religious Belief in Early New England;* Hawke, *Early Life in Everyday America;* and Stout, *The New England Soul: Preaching and Religious Culture in Colonial New England.* (For related sources on religion, see Chapter 6.)

Regarding the cultural systems of patriarchy and gentility in colonial life, several of the books in the general bibliography are useful, as are the following: Carson, *Colonial Virginians at Play;* Goodfriend, *Before the Melting Pot: Society and Culture in Colonial New York City;* Kulikoff, *Tobacco and Slaves: The Development of Southern Culture in the Chesapeake, 1680–1800;* Isaac, *The Transformation of Virginia, 1740–1790;* Nash, *The Urban Crucible: The Northern Seaports and the Origins of the American Revolution;* and Rankin, *The Theatre in Colonial America.*

Popular Performance in the New Republic, 1770–1830

For interpretations of the political, economic, and social dynamics of the revolutionary and early national periods, the following are suggested: Appleby, *Capitalism and a New Social Order: The Republican Vision of the 1790s;* Gilje, *The Road to Mobocracy: Popular Disorder in New York City, 1763–1834;* Larkin, *The Reshaping of Everyday Life, 1790–1840;* McCoy, *The Elusive Republic: Political Economy in Jeffersonian America;* Morgan, *The Stamp Act Crisis: Prologue to Revolution;* Rock, *Artisans of the New Republic: The Tradesmen of New York City in the Age of Jefferson;* Schultz, *The Republic of Labor: Philadelphia Artisans and the Politics of Class;* Watts, *The Republic Reborn: War and the Making of Liberal America, 1790–1820;* and Wood, *The Creation of the American Republic, 1776–1789.*

Several of the authors in the above paragraph also discuss American republicanism. Their discussions can be supplemented with the following: Appleby, ed., *American Quarterly, Special Issue: Republicanism in the History and Historiography of the United States;* Bailyn, *The Ideological Origins of the American Revolution;* Beeman, *Patrick Henry: A Biography;* Boorstin, *The Americans: The National Experience;* Cmiel, *Democratic Eloquence: The Fight Over Popular Speech in Nineteenth-Century America;* Fliegelman, *Declaring Independence: Jefferson, Natural Language, and the Culture of Performance;* Hatch, *The Democratization of American Christianity;* Higonnet, *Sister Republics: The Origins of French and American Republicanism;* and Shaw, *American Patriots and the Rituals of Revolution.*

The following scholarship has been helpful in understanding the cultural systems of paternalism and sentimentality during the revolutionary era: Davidson, *Revolution and the Word: The Rise of the Novel in America;* Eagleton, *The Ideology of the Aesthetic;* Hoffman and Albert, *Women in the Age of the American Revolution;* Jordan, "'Old Words' in 'New Circumstances': Language and Leadership in Post-Revolutionary America"; Kerber, *Women of the Republic: Intellect and Ideology in Revolutionary America;* and Longmore, *The Invention of George Washington.*

In addition to the previous general works on theatre history, the following books and articles were used to locate the white American theatre within the three cultural systems discussed: Anthony, "'This Sort of Thing . . . ': Productions of Gothic Plays in America"; Butsch, "American Theatre Riots and Class Relations, 1754–1849"; Cox, "Introduction," *Seven Gothic Dramas, 1789–1825;* Davis, "Puritan Mercantilism and the Politics of Anti-theatrical Legislation in Colonial America"; Fearnow, "American Colonial Disturbances as Political Theatre"; Garrett, "The Flexible Loyalties of American Actors in the Eighteenth Century"; Meserve, *An Emerging Entertainment: The Drama of the American People to 1828;* Ranger, *'Terror and Pity Reign in Every Breast': Gothic Drama in the London Patent Theatres, 1750–1820;* and Stoddard, "The Haymarket Theatre, Boston."

From the rich scholarship on African American culture and performance, I have drawn on these sources: Abrahams, *Singing the Master: The Emergence of African American Culture in the Plantation South;* Epstein, *Sinful Tunes and Spirituals: Black Folk Music to the Civil War;* Genovese, *Roll, Jordan, Roll: The World the Slaves Made;* Hatch, "Some African Influences on the Afro-American Theatre" in *The Theatre of Black Americans: A Collection of Critical Essays;* Hay, *African American Theatre: A Historical and Critical Analysis;* Isaac, *The Transformation of Virginia, 1740–1790;* Levine, *Black Culture and Black Consciousness: Afro-American Folk Thought from Slavery to Freedom;* Mintz and Price, *The Birth of African-American Culture: An Anthropological Perspective;* Raboteau, *Slave Religion: The "Invisible Institution" in the Antebellum South;* and Stuckey, *Slave Culture: Nationalist Theory and the Foundations of Black America.*

Commercial Performance, 1830–1870

Several works have traced the social and cultural developments that led to the worship of stars during the Jacksonian era, including the following: Bell, *The Development of American Romance: The Sacrifice of Relation;* Braudy, *The Frenzy of Renown: Fame and Its History;* Dyer, *Heavenly Bodies: Film Stars and Society;* Kohl, *The Politics of Individualism: Parties and the American Character in the Jacksonian Era;* Pessen, *Jacksonian America: Society, Personality, and Politics;* Ward, *Andrew Jackson: Symbol for an Age.*

On the influence of the cultural system of rationality, see Brown, *Knowledge Is Power: The Diffusion of Information in Early America, 1700–1865;* Chandler, *The Visible Hand: The Managerial Revolution in American Business;* Haskell, "Capitalism and the Origins of the Humanitarian Sensibility"; O'Malley, *Keeping Watch: A History of American Time;* Rodgers, *The Work Ethic in Victorian America, 1850–1920;* and Schudson, *Discovering the News: A Social History of American Newspapers.*

In addition to many of the books already mentioned under general sources, the following on working-class life and culture have guided my own investigation: Bergquist, "German-Americans," in *Multiculturalism in the United States;* Clark, "Irish-Americans," also in *Multiculturalism in the United States;* Denning, *Mechanic Accents: Dime Novels and Working-Class Culture in America,* Knobel, *Paddy and the Republic: Ethnicity and Nationality in Antebellum America;* Leuchs, *The Early German Theatre in New York, 1840–1870;* Miller, *Emigrants and Exiles: Ireland and the Irish Exodus to North America;* Reynolds, *Beneath the American Renaissance: The Subversive Imagination in the Age of Emerson and Melville;* Stott, *Workers in the Metropolis: Class, Ethnicity, and Youth in Antebellum New York City;* and Thernstrom et al., *Harvard Encyclopedia of American Ethnic Groups.*

Much of the scholarship on star theatre, the rise of rationality on stage, and working-class theatre has already been cited elsewhere. In addition, I recommend Hodge, *Yankee Theatre: The Image of America on the Stage;* McConachie, "The Cultural Politics of 'Paddy' on the Midcentury American Stage"; Meserve, *Heralds of Promise: The Drama of the American People in the Age of Jackson, 1829–1849;* and Senelick, *The Age and Stage of George L. Fox, 1825–1877.*

The scholarship on minstrelsy is extensive. (See also sources in Chapter 6.) I drew primarily from Cockrell, *Demons of Disorder;* Lott, *Love and Theft: Blackface Minstrelsy and the American Working Class;* Roediger, *The Wages of Whiteness: Race and the Making of the American Working Class;* Saxton, "Blackface Minstrelsy and Jacksonian Ideology"; and Toll, *Blacking Up: The Minstrel Show in Nineteenth-Century America.*

Regarding Barnum, his star-making success, and the respectability of his entertainments, I used many of the sources already mentioned, plus Bogdan, *Freak Show: Presenting Human Oddities for Amusement and Profit;* Butsch, "Bowery B'hoys and Matinee Ladies: The Re-Gendering of Nineteenth-Century Theater Audiences"; McConachie, "Out of the Kitchen and Into the Marketplace: Normalizing *Uncle Tom's Cabin* for the Antebellum Stage"; and Saxon, *P.T. Barnum: The Legend and the Man.* (See related sources in Chapter 6.)

The following books, in addition to several already discussed, are helpful in charting the political and economic rise of the American bourgeoisie: Foner, *Free Soil, Free Labor, Free Men: The Ideology of the Republican Party before the Civil War;* Hobsbawm, *The Age of Capital, 1848–1875;* Norton, *Alternative Americas: A Reading of Antebellum Political Culture;* Pessen, *Riches, Class, and Power Before the Civil War;* and Trachtenberg, *The Incorporation of America: Culture and Society in the Gilded Age.*

There's an enormous amount of good scholarship on the system of Victorian respectability. Some of the best of it includes Halttunen, *Confidence Men and Painted Women: A Study of Middle-Class Culture in America, 1830–1870;* Kasson, *Rudeness and Civility: Manners in Nineteenth-Century Urban America;* Mintz, *A Prison of Expectations: The Family in Victorian Culture;* and Rose, *Victorian America and the Civil War.*

Many sources already mentioned discuss Victorian paternalism and gender roles. In addition, I suggest McPherson, *Battle Cry of Freedom: The Civil War Era;* Russett, *Sexual Science: The Victorian Construction of Womanhood;* Ryan, *The Empire of the*

Mother: American Writing About Domesticity; Smith and Judah, eds, *Life in the North During the Civil War;* and Tompkins, *Sensational Designs: The Cultural Work of American Fiction, 1790–1860.*

On the history and theatre of the American West – and representations related to Indian-white relations – see Bank, "Staging the 'Native': Making History in American Theatre Culture, 1828–1838"; Berson, *The San Francisco Stage, 1849–1869;* Carson, *The Theatre on the Frontier;* Horsman, *Race and Manifest Destiny: The Origins of American Racial Anglo-Saxonism;* Rogin, *Fathers and Children: Andrew Jackson and the Subjugation of the American Indian;* Slotkin, *Fatal Environment: The Myth of the Frontier in the Age of Industrialization, 1800–1890;* Tilton, *Pocahontas: The Evolution of an American Narrative;* and Wilmeth, "Noble or Ruthless Savage?"

Other sources useful in understanding Victorian entertainments include Allen, *Horrible Prettiness: Burlesque and American Culture;* Bode, *The American Lyceum: Town Meeting of the Mind;* Felheim, *The Theatre of Augustin Daly;* Frick, *New York's First Theatrical Center: The Rialto at Union Square;* Hogan, *Dion Boucicault;* Knight, *Form and Ideology in Crime Fiction;* Mankowitz, *Mazeppa: The Lives, Loves, and Legends of Adah Isaacs Menken;* Seymour, *Lola Montez, A Life;* Wilmeth and Cullen, "Introduction," *Plays of Augustin Daly;* and Zeidman, *The American Burlesque Show* (New York: Hawthorn Books, 1967).

2

Structure and Management in the American Theatre from the Beginning to 1870

Douglas McDermott

Introduction

There are two areas of management (decision making) in the theatre. Artistic decisions about the physical setting (scenery and costumes) and the actors' performances occupy the foreground and are normally made by the appropriate artists in terms of current conventions (styles). These change over time because of innovations introduced by individuals who find current practices unacceptably restrictive. The discussion of these sorts of decisions and changes belongs to other chapters of this book.

The background is occupied by a context of other conventions by means of which the theatre operates as a social institution. It is these nonartistic conventions and their changes that are the subject of this chapter. This goal of social management is to organize the relationship between performers and the public in such a way that it provides the theatre personnel with a living. In a commercial (nonsubsidized) theatre such as that in the United States, the management must arrange for the performance of something attractive to an audience at a convenient time in a convenient place at an acceptable price, so that the gross box office income at least equals (and preferably exceeds) the gross cost of creating the performance.

Obviously there is a middle ground in which the two areas of management meet. When artistic decisions require the spending of money they affect the cost of the performance and therefore its possibility of profit. Any decision to spend more money on theatres, scenery, costumes, or actors must be justified in terms of its potential to increase revenue more than it increases cost and thereby increase net income.

The task is complicated by limitations in artistic ability and audience taste. Not all actors are good in all roles, and not all audiences like all plays. Even if a manager finds a successful combination of actors, plays, and audience taste, it will not remain permanently successful. Audience taste will change. Either population growth or shift will alter the nature of the audience and its taste, or a stable audience will grow tired of the same experiences. Thus, even the most successful manager must change plays, players, or places from time to time. Prosperity is never assured.

The critical element in social management of the theatre, therefore, is an understanding of the nature of the community of which the theatre is a part, and communities are shaped primarily by geography and economy. It is in this context that one can understand the large-scale structural shifts in the American theatre between 1752 and 1870. To better comprehend why the institutional conventions of theatre were the way they were at any time, and why they changed as they did, it is helpful to understand the changing structure of the society.

In seventeenth-century England wealth and civil rights were still largely the result of the ownership of land, as they had been since the Norman Conquest. For all the changes in politics and economics over seven hundred years, the majority of the people were still excluded from ownership of land and from an effective political voice. From this point of view, the landscape that became the United States was a vast tract of arable land devoid of prior European settlement and ownership, constituting, therefore, the greatest possible attraction to the dispossessed, the dissatisfied, and the ambitious. Whether an ambitious individual whose goal was to own land or a religious congregation whose goal was to govern itself, immigrants intended to create for themselves lives that were improved versions of the ones they had left. Even the most radical visions were expressed in terms of the context of the home culture.

Because removal to the new territory was difficult and expensive, individuals entered into contracts with one another in order to emigrate. Such contracts were recognized by the crown in grants, patents, and indentures. Although each settlement was independent, certain forces compelled them to seek union with each other. First, the colonies had to defend themselves against attack by hostile natives, and their individual vulnerability was exposed by the French and Indian wars. The need for security forced them to cooperate. Second, individual colonies had no success in representing their own interests to the British government. Only as a group did they achieve recognition as a political entity. Thus, the tendency in America before the Revolution was to unite individual entities into larger cooperative organizations for the common good.

This, then, was the model of social organization with which the United States began: an autonomous group of adults contracting to cooperate for their common good in creating a better version of the culture they had left.

Members were accepted on the basis of common qualifications and interests, and management was placed in the hands of a few members on behalf of the whole. This model held for business partnerships, new colonies, and religious congregations. The single professional theatrical company that dominated the American colonies before the Revolution was of this sort, organized and managed according to contractual provisions common in the English theatre.

The Eighteenth Century: General Conditions

At the outset (1752), theatres were organized as companies of actors hired by the year to play groups of parts in a rotating repertory of plays either in a single place or in a geographically contiguous group of places. The acting manager, usually the leading actor, was the proprietor of the company. He not only hired the actors, he also hired local inhabitants as musicians for the orchestra and ushers for the theatre. He chose the repertory, provided actors with their parts, and furnished the musicians with the music to be played during the performance. He arranged for a theatre, investing in a new or renovated building or leasing one from its owners, and he provided the scenery for it. He paid for handbills and for their posting to advertise the performances, and he paid for candles to light the theatre. Finally, he paid the cost of moving the company from one town to another. In return, he recovered nightly expenses from the gross receipts and then shared in the net, both as actor and manager.

It was the actor-manager's responsibility to devise those policies that sustained the company's popularity and profitability. He had to balance a particular audience's desire for novelty against their appetite for the repetition of standard pieces, and he had to consider any specific local conditions, such as a faltering economy, political unrest, or epidemic disease, that might affect attendance. He could change the plays and the players, as well as the times, days, and prices of performance. He could also move the company to another town; but he had to weigh the trouble and expense of such a move against the possibility of greater income in the new location. In short, the eighteenth-century provincial acting manager had a substantial investment in his company, significant responsibility for its success, and limited means of ensuring it.

There could be from one to two dozen actors in such a company, usually twice as many men as women, hired on seasonal contracts to play specific lines of business. Lines were classified by genre, sex, and importance, such as first and second lines for both men and women in tragedy and comedy. There were also recognized specialties, such as low comedy, old men, and old women. Other speaking parts were played by so-called "walking" ladies and gentlemen, whereas nonspeaking parts were played by supernumeraries recruited from the local population. Actors provided their own costumes and were paid in shares of each performance's net receipts. The most important received full shares; less important ones were given half or quarter shares. Actors were also allowed benefit performances at the end of a season for which they kept the net receipts. Major players got individual benefits, less important ones had to divide benefits among themselves.

Actors normally played no more than three nights a week, but each was a full one: a five-act main piece and a two- or three-act farce or musical after-piece, with songs and dances by members of the company between plays and sometimes between acts. A provincial company would have a repertory of at least two dozen main pieces and half as many afterpieces, any combination of which could be performed on a day's notice. The main pieces included three to six Tudor and Stuart plays, as many as eight others had been written between 1700 and 1750, and ten or more were recent London successes. The afterpieces were normally all of current authorship. Provincial companies did not, except in rare cases of local authorship, introduce new plays. The actors were seldom perfect in their parts, and the prompter, located off-stage, nor-mally read the script aloud, one line ahead of the performers.

America's theatrical pioneers faced difficulties that their provincial English counterparts did not. The audiences were small, isolated, and wary of admit-ting players to their midst. The population of the Colonies, while it grew from eighty thousand in 1660 to one-and-a-half million a century later, was scat-tered along a thousand miles from Georgia to Massachusetts, and travel, either by ship along treacherous shores or on primitive roads and trails, was made more difficult by hostile natives. The two largest settlements were Philadelphia and Boston. The Quakers of the former and the Puritans of the latter were opposed to theatre, and even the more liberal settlements, such as New York, Williamsburg, and Charleston, carefully regulated the profession of playing.

The colonial attitude toward theatre was not unreasonable. In isolated areas where money was scarce and social stability precarious, strolling players were disruptive. In an economy organized to produce material goods, they created no product, and they took some of the money they earned away with them. Not only were performances unproductive in them-selves, they were an occasion for assembly during which members of the audience performed no work either, and a gathering of people always increased the chance of disruptive behavior and the spread of disease. Moreover, originating with the seventeenth-century English clergyman Jeremy Collier, the perception was widespread that many of the plays offered examples of socially undesirable behavior.[1] Thus, any season of playing was a potential source of both economic loss and social disruption, and in order to succeed the players had to create as little disturbance as possible in the order of colonial life.

The Hallam–Douglass Company, 1758–1774

The earliest record of theatrical performance in English was 1665; the first professional actors, Walter Murray and Thomas Kean, arrived in 1749, and there is fragmentary evidence of others. However, the first company of professional players about which substantial information exists was managed by Lewis Hallam, the elder, and arrived in 1752. The theatrical history of the Colonies before the Revolution is primarily the story of this company as managed by David Douglass from October 1758 through May 1774. However, a juncture occurs during the season of 1766–67.

The company originated from the combination of two others. After an initial tour of the Colonies, Hallam had taken his company to Jamaica, where he died. His widow married David Douglass, the manager of a company already there, and she and her son, Lewis Hallam Jr., performed with Douglass and his company for three years in Jamaica.

The North American Colonies, however, offered better prospects because of their growing population. Consequently, Douglass brought the company to New York in October 1758 and began a series of alternate northern and southern campaigns that lasted for sixteen years. Like any good provincial manager, Douglass divided his territory, moving from one part to another as conditions indicated. Movement was the iron law of provincial playing. Audiences were small, and the manager could not afford to change the actors and the repertory often enough to give sufficient variety. Time and distance were the only strategy that worked, and the manager had to consider the vagaries of climate, transportation, and local conditions in deciding when and where to go next.

The company's first northern campaign, which consumed all of 1759, was divided between a converted sail loft on Cruger's Wharf in New York and a theatre just outside the city limits of Philadelphia on Society Hill. Douglass then took them south for eighteen months to Annapolis and Williamsburg (from March 1760 to May 1761). From Virginia they went north for a second campaign. For the first time actors ventured into New England to take advantage of Newport, Rhode Island's popularity as a resort for southern planters (from 7 September to 3 November 1761). After a winter season in a new theatre on New York's Chapel Street, Douglass returned to Rhode Island, but the season ended abruptly on 30 August 1762, when the legislature approved "An Act to Prevent Stage Plays and Other Theatrical Entertainments."

Leaving New England, Douglass initiated a second tour of the South, beginning in Williamsburg in November 1762. According to George Washington's diary, the company was still there in May 1763, but by June they were playing in Petersburg. They arrived at Charleston in November and played from mid-December through early May 1764. Then, for almost two years there is no record of them in America. They had retreated to Jamaica.

The 1760s were not propitious years for players. The country was gripped by a severe depression begun in 1761 and intensified in 1765–66 by the Stamp Act crisis. The militant, nationalistic Sons of Liberty waxed as the economy waned. The depression was attributed to English domination, the cure for which was independence. Because they were British, the players served as convenient scapegoats for the political radicals. Against these sentiments Douglass fought back as best he could, changing the name for his troupe from the London Company of Comedians to the American Company during their Charleston season. However, rebel sentiment remained hostile, forcing the company to stay away from the colonies during much of 1765 and 1766. When they returned, they initially avoided New York, where a mob had burnt their theatre during an anti-British riot.

While his companions were performing in Jamaica, Douglass had spent some of the time in England arranging for new plays, players, and scenery, so the company that opened in Philadelphia in November of 1766 was greatly changed. From the outset the actors had been distinguished by their stability and adherence to tradition in both organization and style of performance. In 1758 only Mrs. Douglass and her son, Lewis Hallam Jr., remained from Hallam's original company. The other members were Douglass's players, principally the manager himself, his partner Owen Morris, and Mrs. Morris. This nucleus controlled the principal lines of acting. Mrs. Douglass retained her line as leading tragic actress. Her counterpart was her son. Mrs. Morris played the chief supporting roles in tragedy and the leading ones in comedy. Owen Morris performed both low-comic and old-men roles, whereas Douglass played the second line in tragedy. Almost immediately after forming the company, Douglass added new players, expanding it to some dozen men and half-a-dozen women to accommodate a changing repertory. The only change in lines, however, came after 1761 as Mrs. Douglass gradually resigned younger roles to her niece, Nancy Hallam, and to Miss Cheer. Besides Mrs. Douglass, only Mr. and Mrs. Allyn had appeared on the London stage. All the others seem to have learned their craft in Jamaica and the Colonies.

The initial repertory contained twenty-two main pieces. Shakespeare formed the principal tragedy (*Hamlet, Lear, Macbeth, Othello, Richard III, Romeo and Juliet*), to which were added Nathaniel Lee's *Theodosius* and Thomas Otway's *The Orphan* and *Venice Preserved*, Nicholas Rowe's *Tamerlane, Fair Penitent,* and *Jane Shore*, John Home's *Douglas*, George Lillo's

George Barnwell, and Susannah Centlivre's *The Gamester.* George Farquhar supplied the comic material of the repertory with *The Beaux' Stratagem, The Constant Couple, The Inconstant,* and *The Recruiting Officer,* to which were added Colley Cibber's *The Provoked Husband,* Benjamin Hoadley's *The Suspicious Husband,* Joseph Addison's *The Drummer,* and John Gay's *The Begger's Opera.* Over the next eight years Douglass added mostly comedies to the repertory: Robert Howard's *The Committee* and William Congreve's *Love for Love* from the Restoration, Richard Steele's *The Conscious Lovers* and Centlivre's *The Busy Body* and *A Bold Stroke for a Wife* from the first quarter of the eighteenth century.

All of the repertory's plays had established their popularity in London before 1750, the most recent being the comedies by Cibber and Gay (1728). This repertory harked to an older British culture, that to which many of the audience had belonged and to which they must have still felt strongly attached. These people thought of themselves as natives of England, and the plays spoke clearly and consistently of the British values of social stability and respect for proper authority. The most often performed were *The Provoked Husband* (nine times), *Romeo and Juliet* (seven), *Douglas* (six), and *Hamlet, The Beaux' Stratagem,* and *The Recruiting Officer* were performed five times each. The tragedies depict the evils of rebellion and civil discord, whereas the comedies uphold the authority of fathers and husbands. The increase in frequency of performance of comedy possibly reflected the audience's increased desire for prosperity and stability as the political crisis with England intensified.

The changes that mark the period from 1766 to 1774 suggest that Douglass abandoned the policy of replicating an older British culture in favor of depicting an emerging one. The success of his management can be measured by the company's increased number of performances, longer seasons in each place, and the investment in new actors and plays, permanent theatres, and new scenery.

With the repeal of the Stamp Act and the consequent reduction in anti-British sentiment, Douglass must have felt it safe to resume his American monopoly. The company played in a new, larger theatre in the Southwark section of Philadelphia from November 1766 to July 1767. He then arranged for a similar theatre to be built during the summer on John Street in New York City, which the company opened on 7 December 1767. They then alternated between these two theatres until June 1770, with a brief excursion to Albany during the summer of 1769. A combination of renewed political turmoil and increased expense from operating the new theatres seems to have caused financial problems.

In the summer of 1770 the company headed south to what had always been a friendlier climate. They stayed in Maryland and Virginia for slightly more than two years, where they played a spring season in Williamsburg during the meeting of the legislature, and a fall one in Annapolis during the racing season, and short seasons in between in Dumfries, Fredericksburg, and Norfolk. They then returned to Philadelphia and New York (October 1772 through August 1773). A subsequent southern tour ended in Charleston, where they played their longest season ever (they had last been there nine years before) from 22 December 1773 through 19 May 1774.

Apparently confident of his company's place in America, Douglass planned a major northern campaign for the next two years. Lewis Hallam Jr. was sent to England to recruit new talent, the Charleston theatre was advertised for rent, and the company dispersed during early June. Douglass was in New York by the end of the month, probably to welcome actor Thomas Wignell, coming from England to join them. It was there in October that Douglass received notice from Peyton Randolph, president of the Continental Congress, of its resolution discouraging entertainments for the duration of the imminent conflict. He and his companions returned to Jamaica, where he sold his interest in the company to Hallam Jr. and the actor John Henry, becoming a printer, probably a trade he had learned before turning to the stage.

To accommodate a larger, more current repertory, Douglass added more and better performers after 1766. The number of men remained constant at about twelve, but nine women were normally needed. The major new faces were John Henry and the Storer sisters. Tall and handsome, Henry came from Dublin to Jamaica. He quickly became an audience favorite as a romantic leading man in both comedy and tragedy. Ann, Fanny, and Maria Storer accompanied him to America, and all three succeeded as comic actors and singers. These players lifted the company to a level at which it could be favorably compared to the larger English provincial ones.

The repertory was sharply updated. Although the most popular plays from before 1766 retained their relative popularity, about half of the plays, both the main pieces and the farces, were new. The principal plays of Richard Cumberland, David Garrick, Oliver Goldsmith, and Hugh Kelly were produced. The popularity of these spoken comedies was exceeded by the ballad operas of Isaac Bickerstaffe and the semioperatic adaptations of Shakespeare's *The Tempest* and *Cymbeline*. New plays were relatively inexpensive. No effective copyright law existed, so the manager had to pay only for one complete copy of the play, plus the cost of copying the actors' parts.

Seeming to seek symbolic control over a world approaching revolution, clearly, the audience maintained their preference for the order and security of comedy as augmented by music and spectacle. Perhaps as an intentional consequence of the increased performance of comedy, Douglass's company gave fewer performances of traditionally royalist, authoritarian tragedies. They condemned revolution less, if only by omission. It also seems clear, however, that the audience now preferred more recent comedies, perhaps because such plays validated the cultural maturity of colonial culture. They now consumed what London did, not what London had known a generation before.

Further evidence of Douglass's policy of updating the theatre to conform to the audience's perception of its cultural maturity can be found in the theatre buildings themselves. Not only were the Southwark and John Street facilities larger than those he had built before 1766, but they were permanent structures. Douglass was confident enough of their stability to use them repeatedly, and he was sufficiently successful that he could afford to leave his capital tied up in the buildings. New scenery was regularly advertised in this period, some by local artists such as Jacob Snyder and William Williams, some by Nicholas Thomas Dahl[2] and John Inigo Richards, leading scene painters at Covent Garden.

In other respects Douglass maintained a steady policy of playing three evenings a week, at six in the winter and six-thirty in the summer. Such curtain times seem calculated to give the gentry time enough to have supper before the theatre but exclude the working class. Such exclusion is reflected in the relatively high prices. Before 1766 Douglass regularly charged five shillings for a box seat, three shillings for the pit, and one shilling for the gallery. Just before the Revolution, these had risen to eight shillings, five shillings, and three shillings, respectively, and in Virginia the theatres had no galleries. When these policies are seen in the context of play selection and of Douglass's frequent reference to his membership in the Masons and to his benefits for local charities, a clear profile emerges of a manager astutely appealing to the interests of the propertied class, aligning his theatre with the colonial power structure.

Social Change after the Revolution: General Conditions

Political independence unleashed social and economic forces in the United States for which there was no precedent in European history. No longer simply a colony to be exploited by the home country, America expanded. Between 1790 and 1870 the land area increased from 865,000 to 2.9 million square miles, while the population increased from 3.9 to 39.8 million. Hundreds of thousands crossed the Appalachians to create new states, which formed a solid mass as far as the Mississippi River and, in a sharp flanking movement, included the Pacific Coast. Apart from insisting upon uniform surveys so that land titles could be registered, the federal government allowed practically unrestricted internal and external migration, and, except when political considerations interfered, new states were admitted swiftly and easily. Not surprisingly, the process was disorderly and frequently violent. Perhaps surprisingly, it produced economic prosperity: The consumer price index actually declined while the cost of living rose only by about one-third.

The consequence, however, was separation rather than union. As settlements dispersed, local interests invariably took precedence over national ones. America was the place where one could own land and prosper, and nothing must get in the way of one's ability to do so. In this context the development of conflicting interests in the newly formed nation could be seen as having a twofold development. First, geographic regions had different needs because differing geography produced different economic organizations. New England had navigable rivers that provided both easy transportation and cheap hydraulic power for industrial development. By contrast, the level, loamy soil of the Ohio Valley promoted the formation of self-sufficient family farms, whereas the relatively poor soil in the South encouraged large holdings and a cash-crop economy that required large amounts of cheap labor. Second, in addition to these sectional differences, a rapidly growing population and a developing economy led to the accentuation of class differences and reinforced sectionalism. Tensions finally erupted over the issue of slavery and were so strong they could only be resolved by civil war. Ultimately, the victory of the Union forces determined that the nation founded in 1776 would remain one.

The Structure of the Star System

What was true for the nation was also true for theatre. Theatrical organization responded to the growth of both regional and class differences. Before the Revolution America had been a single theatrical territory divided into two circuits, both monopolized by a single company organized by lines of business and shares of the net receipts. Between 1785 and 1870 America became a set of circuits, one around each large city outside of New York City: Boston, Philadelphia, Baltimore, Washington, Cincinnati, Louisville, New Orleans, St. Louis, Cleveland, Chicago, Detroit, Denver, and San Francisco. In these cities there was also separation among theatres. Each developed a specialized repertory and a group of actors intended to appeal to a particular segment of the audience. By the 1830s it was possible to identify certain New York City theatres by class interest, and that was true for other cities by 1870. At one extreme were theatres that emphasized manners comedy and the social problem play, appealing to that segment of the audience with the most education and disposable income, and at the other extreme were theatres devoted to forms of variety entertainment, appealing to those with the least. Somewhere in between were those theatres that specialized in sensation melodrama or musical burlesque and extravaganza. Outside these cities, however, social classes were neither large nor distinctive enough to support specialized theatres, and successful companies played the entire spectrum of the repertory so as to appeal to the broadest cross section of the population.

Expansion created new audiences and therefore new opportunities for actors. By itself, however, this only proliferated the eighteenth-century provincial mode of operation. Determined actor-managers created resident companies in various cities and carved out subsidiary circuits among neighboring towns. At the same time, however, something else happened that was new: Because population growth and expansion produced a demand that quickly exceeded the supply, leading actors began to exploit the possibility of playing with different resident companies during a single season. Certain advantages of such an arrangement were soon evident. First, changing leading actors within a standard repertory offered audiences a new source of variety and therefore increased the income of the theatre. Second, it was easier and less expensive to move single players from place to place than it was to move whole companies. Third, because income increased more than expense, both the proprietors of the companies and the traveling actors made more money than before. The result was the star system.

The star system represents the shift from autonomous, self-governing communities to industrial entrepreneurship, in which individuals compete with each other for the loyalty of supporters or consumers. Like politicians and revival preachers, stars represent the aspirations and values of those whom they serve. The star not only speaks for a constituency (whether in the theatre, the legislature, or the church) but models the upward social and economic mobility that was the path to prosperity in the expanding nation.

The manager of a theatrical company either contracted with a star directly or with the luminary's agent to play the manager's theatre, supported by the resident company, which was still organized as in the eighteenth century. Stars temporarily displaced those hired to play leading parts, but because the repertory remained relatively stable there was little other dislocation. A star often arrived the day before the first performance and rehearsed with the company the morning before playing each role. Having played all of his or her roles at least once, the star departed for the next engagement while the company played without a star until the next one arrived.

There were stars of various styles and sizes. Most played within an expanding tragic repertory built around *Hamlet, Othello, Macbeth, Richard III, Romeo and Juliet,* and *The Merchant of Venice* (approximately in that order of frequency). To these were added two adaptations from August von Kotzebue, *The Stranger* (Benjamin Thompson, 1798) and *Pizarro* (Richard Sheridan, 1799) (both later adapted by Dunlap as well), Thomas Dibdin's *Fazio* (1816), R. L. Sheil's *Evadne* (1819) and *Damon and Pythias* (1821), John Howard Payne's *Thérèse; or, the Orphan of Geneva* (1821), James Sheridan Knowles's

The Hunchback (1832) and *The Wife* (1833), Edward Bulwer-Lytton's *Richelieu* (1839), Victor Hugo's *Lucretia Borgia* (J. M. Weston, 1843), G. M. Lovell's *Love's Sacrifice* (1829) and *Ingomar* (1851), and Charles Selby's *The Marble Heart* (1854). The same actors also appeared in contemporary domestic and sensation melodrama. Dion Boucicault was the most prolific and successful writer of this genre, and his slavery play, *The Octoroon* (1859), vied for popularity with his Irish pieces, *The Colleen Bawn* (1860) and *Arrah-na-Pogue* (1864). The popularity of his plays was matched by Douglas William Jerrold's *Black-Eyed Susan* (1829), George Aiken's dramatization of *Uncle Tom's Cabin* (1852), the various versions of Dumas fils's *Camille* (1852), Augustin Daly's *Under the Gaslight* (1867), and Lester Wallack's *Rosedale* (1863).

Foremost among the starring men were William Charles Macready, Edwin Forrest, and Edwin Booth. Among the women, Charlotte Cushman, Matilda Heron, and Julia Dean were stars of the first magnitude. There were scores of others of lesser stature who played the same repertory successfully in provincial cities but not in New York (for example, McKean Buchanan and Mrs. D. P. Bowers).

Comic performers worked outward from a small core of standard plays to a fringe of specialties. At the center of the comic repertory were the plays of R. B. Sheridan (*The Rivals*, 1775; *The School for Scandal*, 1777), Oliver Goldsmith (*She Stoops to Conquer*, 1773), and George Farquhar (*The Beaux' Stratagem*, 1707), to which were added those of Edward Bulwer-Lytton (*The Lady of Lyons*, 1838; *Money*, 1840), Boucicault (*London Assurance*, 1841; *Old Heads and Young Hearts*, 1844), and Tom Taylor (*Masks and Faces*, 1852; *Our American Cousin,* 1861). At least two farces were as popular as most manners comedies: George Coleman the younger's *Heir-at-Law* (1797) and J. B. Buckstone's *Rough Diamond* (1847).

With the exception of Joseph Jefferson III, comic actors specialized within this repertory, such as Tyrone Power (Irishmen), James H. Hackett (Yankees and frontiersmen), and Frank Chanfrau (Bowery B'hoys). Others, such as Lotta Crabtree and Caroline Chapman, specialized in variety entertainment (primarily minstrelsy after 1842) or in roles tailored to fit their particular abilities in dancing, singing, and mimicry. Finally, there were child prodigies, such as Kate and Ellen Bateman, who astonished by preciosity more than talent.

The appeal of the star repertory was its celebration of individual emotional expression. Stories were constructed to create situations that, however improbable, justified extreme emotional response by the characters. The greater the range and intensity the better. The star's exploitation of the possibilities of the self was similar to those described in the adventures of Huck, Ahab, Henry David Thoreau, and Walt Whitman. In an age in which the repetitive factory task was becoming the norm, stars expressed the lost cultural ideal of unlimited personal possibility. Moreover, the star's expansiveness validated or was validated by the constantly expanding, shifting population within America. The function of the repertory was to provide a cue for energy, and the theatre as a social institution was its setting.

Initially the star was paid a flat rate for performing, regardless of receipts, but that rate was much higher than members of a stock company earned (between five and fifty dollars a week). By 1850 stars normally got either a flat rate or half the gross receipts, whichever was larger, plus at least one clear benefit for a week's engagement. Thus, while Edmund Kean was paid two hundred dollars a week in 1821, Edwin Forrest got either two hundred dollars a night or half the receipts in 1846. Even on these terms profits could be substantial because Kean averaged nine hundred dollars a night, and Forrest could top two thousand dollars. By contrast, a stock company without stars averaged perhaps three hundred dollars a night; and a manager's expenses, which included salaries for actors, musicians, and nonperformers; the cost of advertising, printing, and copying; and the rent on the building, were relatively constant and seemed to run between two hundred and three hundred dollars a night.

As changed in 1857, copyright law recognized plays as property. Ability to claim ownership of a popular drama made it possible for playwrights to emerge as stars in their own right. Previously, dramatists either sold texts outright to actors or kept them for their own use as actors. Under the amended law Dion Boucicault was the first writer to lease plays to actors for royalty payment instead of selling them.

Most of the other changes in management practices that took place after 1810 were responses to the star system. Stock company actors were still hired by lines or types of parts, their conduct was governed by a strict set of rules with fines for infractions, and they continued to play in more than one place, except in the largest cities. To maximize the earning potential of stars (necessarily present in any one company for only a limited time) the seating capacity of theatres was increased from less than a thousand to as much as two or three thousand, and the auditorium altered to increase the proportion of expensive seats. The pit was renamed (first as the parquette, then as the orchestra) and the price raised to the maximum, along with the price of the dress circle (the first balcony or the front of the single balcony), which replaced most of the boxes. A less expensive admission was then created for the seating under the balcony on the main floor, which was called the family circle. These changes restricted the cheapest tickets to the gallery, either the back of the single balcony or a second balcony. They also allowed theatres to increase income while maintaining the same ticket prices (typically a dollar-fifty, seventy-five cents, and fifty cents, but higher by fifty cents each in California) for almost the entire century.

At the same time, the repertory system of playing began to be replaced as certain popular plays were offered for as many consecutive performances as possible, with or without stars, and the number of performances was increased to six nights a week, with Saturday matinees becoming increasingly popular. In the 1860s some stars pioneered the combination system that was to dominate the American theatre after 1870. They began to travel with either a core group of actors or a complete company with a handful of plays, which they played in each place for as many consecutive performances as possible.

Transition to the Star System

These changes could not have been imagined by Lewis Hallam Jr. and John Henry when they returned from Jamaica to the John Street Theatre. Styling themselves the Old American Company, they resumed activity in November 1785. Creatures of an older theatre, they continued as before, and their inability to change ruined them. For seven years they operated in the old manner, playing in New York City during the winter, with short seasons in late spring and summer in one or more of the following: Philadelphia, Baltimore, Annapolis.

Unintentionally, Hallam and Henry created the conditions that forced them out of management and led their successors to the star system. They owned the company, controlled the principal lines in both tragedy and comedy, and their wives (Miss Tuke and Maria Storer) were ambitious to do the same. Their unwillingness to employ Thomas Wade West, his wife Margaretta, their daughter Ann, and her husband John Bignall (established provincial favorite) in 1790 resulted in West and his family creating their own theatre in Charleston and gradually dominating Virginia and the Carolinas.

Hallam and Henry could have survived the loss of the South if they had retained Philadelphia, but their possessiveness cost them that territory too. By 1791 the company's popularity depended on the low comic Thomas Wignell, and on Elizabeth Walker, the second wife of Owen Morris, who played first-female parts in both tragedy and comedy. Hallam and Henry attempted to replace her with their ladies, Morris appealed to Wignell for help, and Hallam threatened to fire Wignell. The upshot was that Wignell and the Morrises entered into a partnership with musician Alexander Reinagle in the summer of 1791 to establish a new theatre in Philadelphia.

Wignell hired a larger, better acting company than any Americans had seen. Six of the new company's principal players were established English favorites. Unfavorable comparison with Philadelphia and consequent confinement to New York City spelled ruin for Hallam and Henry. The establishment of a rival company in Boston and New England after 1794 added insult to injury, and by 1798 both Hallam and Henry had sold out to the aspiring playwright William Dunlap, who inadvertently invented the star system.

He did not mean to. All he was trying to do was turn a profit. That, however, was difficult. Not only did Philadelphia have better actors, but it had a large, new theatre, The Chestnut Street. Consequently, Dunlap agreed to rent a new theatre on Park Street from the private investors who built it. About the same size as the Philadelphia theatre, it cost more to build, and Dunlap paid twice as much rent as Wignell did. Dunlap discovered that he only showed a profit when he offered either John Hodgkinson (principal actor from Bath) or the leading tragic couple from Philadelphia, Thomas Abthorpe Cooper and Anne Brunton Merry. In 1803, when the two men undertook starring engagements elsewhere (Hodgkinson in Charleston, Cooper in London), Dunlap went broke. The theatre's owners made Cooper the manager and allowed him to star elsewhere as well.

In 1808 lawyer Stephen Price purchased a share of the management and began exploiting the economic potential of the starring actor. At Price's advent Cooper was playing Mondays and Wednesdays in New York, Fridays and Saturdays in Philadelphia. The theatre deducted the evening's expenses from the gross receipts and split the net with the star. Since Cooper grossed an average of seven hundred dollars a night, while the stock companies without him grossed between two hundred and three hundred dollars, there was more profit with him than without him. There was more profit for him as well, since leading players got paid no more than $100 a week at the time.

Not only did Cooper become the first star, at Price's direction he negotiated the appearance of the next one, George Frederick Cooke, since 1800 the leading tragic actor at Covent Garden. Receipts were highest when he played Richard III to Cooper's Richmond, Prince Hal to Cooper's Hotspur, Shylock to Cooper's Antonio, and, above all, Iago to Cooper's Othello. He played five engagements in New York, two each in Philadelphia and Boston, one each in Baltimore and Providence. Not only did the Park profit by about twelve thousand dollars from his first engagement there, but it took a share of his receipts from the other cities as well, netting perhaps as much as five thousand dollars from his first engagement in Philadelphia. Almost certainly, Price and Cooper would have followed with more London imports, but the war intervened, and the star system did not get under way fully until the season of 1818–19.

By then anti-British feeling caused by the war had abated, and a steady stream of English actors began starring at the Park Theatre and were then franchised to other managements as Cooke had been. By 1823 other managers were dealing directly with stars, bypassing Price, who eventually moved to London and managed Drury Lane from 1825 to 1830 as a means of assuring the Park a steady supply of new leading actors.

The Star System in Practice

Although the starring actor became the center of theatrical organization until 1870, the ways in which managers utilized stars were many. In a sense, therefore, the star system was a system only insofar as the principal player was the most important single element. Otherwise, it was unsystematic and is best described by a series of case studies that explore the range of managerial possibilities. The first three cases describe typical managements: John Potter's in the small towns and on the frontiers of settlement was essentially unchanged from the previous century; John Ellsler's in a provincial city was conservative and respectable; and the Wallack family ran a fashionable urban theatre for a fashionable audience. The last two cases describe innovations that indicate developments in structure and management after 1870: Tom Maguire's commercial monopolization and exploitation of entertainment in California and Laura Keene's pioneering of the combination system, a form of management that allowed her access to an audience that supported her particular talent.

Frontier Management: John S. Potter

John Sinclair Potter was a legend in his own lifetime. The stories appear to have been written down first by Sol Smith in 1868, but alternative and elaborated versions continued to appear for forty years. Potter was said to have opened (and closed) more theatres in more places than any other manager in the United States. He was notorious as a manager for never paying salaries or repaying loans, and, as an actor for appearing in multiple parts in the same play, changing only his wig. A survey of recoverable facts suggests that his myth had a foundation in truth. For thirty years he managed theatre companies in the small towns of America's rural and frontier regions, covering nearly the entire nation, and his goal and methods did not differ significantly from those of David Douglass a century earlier.

According to T. A. Brown, Potter was born and first went on the stage in Philadelphia, but his first professional engagement was with William Forrest and Edwin Dean in Cincinnati and Louisville (*History of the American Stage,* 294). He was an active manager in the South continuously from 1835 through 1846 and during 1850 and 1851, the intervening years being spent managing in the northern Ohio Valley, Canada, and New York State. He arrived in San Francisco in 1855 after three years as an actor in New Orleans, and for five years toiled in the gold mining region of the Sierra Nevada Mountains. From 1860 through 1865 he managed in the Pacific Northwest (Oregon, Washington, British Columbia, and Idaho), and during the last four years of his life he moved slowly eastward through Utah, Montana, and Nebraska, dying during an engagement in Morris, Illinois.

Potter's peregrinations were purposeful and adhered to a consistent pattern that had been followed by other managers on population frontiers since the eighteenth century. Establishing himself in a city to which stars normally came, he recruited his players and established a circuit of neighboring small towns in which the company would play rotating seasons of several weeks each. The goal was to develop a sufficient audience to support the company for at least forty weeks a year, year after year.

The movement from region to region was caused by failure to achieve this goal. The reasons for failure seem to have been a different combination of factors in each case. First, the economies of the communities were precarious and easily disrupted. Second, there was competition from similar companies. Potter was always immediately preceded or succeeded by another company of about the same quality offering similar attractions. Finally, these two factors affected his ability to engage the stars upon whom he depended.

Enough information exists to substantiate this pattern in at least three instances. From 1838 to 1843 Potter seems to have based his operations in Nashville, Tennessee, from which he traveled on a circuit that included Port Gibson, Grand Gulf, and Jackson, Mississippi, but that explored in other directions as far as Memphis, Tennessee; Little Rock, Arkansas; and Natchitoches, Louisiana. His company played in stables, warehouses, and storefronts, but worked with local citizens to raise money to construct theatres in these communities. Such efforts resulted in the City Theatre, Jackson, a building that measured 140 feet by 60 feet, seated twelve hundred, and opened on 9 December 1839.

To augment his company, which normally contained about ten men and four women, Potter was able to recruit such provincial stars as Mrs. Alexander Drake, Augustus Addams, and Edwin S. Conner, but his most reliable attraction was Estelle (erroneously identified as Esther by T. A. Brown) McCormac, whom he married in January 1842. Like most tragic actresses of the period, her roles included Shakespeare's Queen Margaret (*Richard III*) and Desdemona (*Othello*), Sheridan Knowles's Julia (*The Hunchback*) and Virginia (*Virginius*), Sheridan's Elvira (*Pizarro*), Pauline in Bulwer-Lytton's *The Lady of Lyons*, Mrs. Haller in *The Stranger*, and the title roles in *Evadne, The Wife, a Tale of Mantua*, and *Thérèse; or, the Orphan of Geneva*.

For reasons that are unknown, Potter shifted his management to Cleveland in 1848. Beginning in April, he played almost continuously until the end of June 1849, the longest season in Cleveland's history. In the spring of 1849 he built the Water Street Theatre at a cost of six thousand dollars. It was a wooden rectangle, 57 feet wide and 75 feet long, seating no more than fifteen hundred. Two local men secured their contributions with mortgages on the building and eventually took it over, forcing Potter out shortly before the theatre burned in September 1849. He claimed his loss in costumes, scripts, and scenery was three thousand dollars.

Although there was an almost complete personnel change during the course of the year (except for Mr. and Mrs. Potter), the Cleveland company seems to have included ten men and seven women. The tragic repertory was essentially the same as in the South because Mrs. Potter remained the starring actress, partnered by stock actors Charles Webb and George Ryer or paired with tragic stars A. J. Neafie and Augustus A. Addams. She was replaced by Julia Dean for one engagement. Potter varied his repertory by alternating tragic engagements with those of dialect comedians Dan Marble, Barney Williams, and Joshua Silsbee in their specialized Irish and Yankee pieces. Potter seemed determined to give the audience as much variety as possible.

His reasons for going to California are obvious: Its gold rush offered the greatest single opportunity to strike it rich in American history. Although Estelle continued to star under her husband's management in California during 1855 and 1856, the domestic situation seems to have deteriorated. She was billed as "Miss Potter," and she divorced him in 1857 to marry C. B. McDonald. During those years, however, Potter tried to establish a circuit among the mining towns, a pattern similar to earlier efforts in and around Mississippi. The base of all California theatricals in the 1850s was San Francisco, and Mrs. Potter had a single starring engagement there at the Metropolitan Theatre, 2–8 April 1855. From then on she toured with companies assembled by her husband. Complete cast lists were not printed, but her repertory required a minimum of ten men and three women. Though they played in Stockton and Sacramento, their principal circuit embraced any and all settlements that lay between the towns of Marysville, Nevada City, and Placerville. There was no need to build theatres because most places in California's gold fields had some form of public hall (seating from eight hundred to fourteen hundred), and all depended on visits from companies like Potter's for their formal entertainment.

The local papers were uniformly enthusiastic about Estelle Potter and usually gave high marks to her support. As *The Mountain Democrat* (Placerville) explained, "A California audience is generally not a very severe or critical one. . . . The great requisite . . . is, that they should *try to please;* and whenever it is apparent that they are *doing their best,* a few blunders and imperfections are readily overlooked" (10 October 1857).

Potter was hard-pressed to replace her, though he tried with Mr. and Mrs. E. S. Conner, Mary Provost, Marie Duret, and Mr. and Mrs. J. B. Booth the younger. His departure from California coincided with the resumption of her career in 1859. Although he still recruited in San Francisco, his last attempts at managing a stable circuit were rooted in the Pacific Northwest: Victoria and New Westminster, British Columbia; Port Townsend and Steilecoom, Washington (1860–63); and the Oregon Trail towns between Portland and Boise, Idaho (1864–65).

The suspicion that Potter always operated on the edge of solvency is confirmed by events in this period. In February 1861 he was jailed for debts, and James Stark, who was starring for him, designated his final performance (Shylock) as a benefit for Potter. The three hundred and twenty-five dollars discharged the debt, but a little over two years later Potter published a long explanation of "my inability . . . to make a living for myself and company for the past two seasons," even though he had "labored long and hard for the establishment of a permanent and respectable theatre in the city of Victoria." It was, he said, the result of "two or three diabolical plots, formed by designing and evil-minded men to speculate upon our labor, while the money that should have belonged to us was squandered by others" (*The Daily Colonist*, 15 April 1863). In spite of his troubles, *The Golden Era* (12 March 1865) concluded that "The Northern Circuit . . . acknowledges the veteran John S. Potter as the Master spirit in that managerial sphere. During the past year Mr. Potter has evinced indominable [*sic*] enterprise, and catered very liberally for the lovers of the drama."

A large part of that success lay in his ability to persuade stars popular in the West to tour with him. In addition to Stark, a major Western star, Potter imported such luminaries as Mr. and Mrs. W. C. Forbes, Mr. and Mrs. George Waldron, Julia Dean, Fanny Morgan, and (in the spring of 1865) Estelle McDonald; but his most consistent leading actor was Lambert F. Beatty. At its largest, the whole company numbered fourteen men and four women, and there were wholesale changes of supporting personnel about every three months. In spite of Potter's mythic inability to pay salaries, he never had trouble hiring either actors or stars, so it is likely that these changes were a management strategy designed to provide his audience with reasonable variety.

His stars played an expanded version of the repertory from the 1830s and 1840s. In short engagements (one to three weeks) there were hardly any repetitions, but during the longest stand of which there is detailed record – 88 nights in Victoria, from 8 October 1860 to 11 February 1861 – the company offered over forty main pieces, plus farces. The theatres ranged from modest playhouses, such as the Victoria Theatre (129 feet by 45 feet) to spaces such as the one in New Westminster, described as "an extended wooden shack" (Herring 66–67). About the only thing that changed significantly was the price of admission (seventy-five cents to two dollars).

John Ellsler, Cleveland

Outside of New York City the most important managers were William Warren and William Burke Wood (Chestnut Street Theatre, Philadelphia, 1803–26;

then Warren alone through 1831), James Caldwell (Camp Street Theatre, New Orleans, 1823–33), Alexander Drake (Louisville/City Theatre, Louisville, 1825–33), Noah Ludlow and Sol Smith (St. Louis Theatre, St. Louis, 1835–51 and St. Charles Theatre, New Orleans, 1835–53), Moses Kimball, E. F. Keach, and Robert M. Field (Boston Museum, 1843–93), Ben DeBar (Grand Opera House, St. Louis, 1855–78), John Ellsler (Academy of Music, Cleveland, 1855–85), James McVicker (McVicker's Theatre, Chicago, 1857–71), Louisa Lane Drew (Arch Street Theatre, Philadelphia, 1861–76), Benjamin Thayer and Orlando Tompkins (Boston Theatre, 1864–85), and John Barrett and John McCullough (California Theatre, San Francisco, 1869–79).

Cleveland was a small city (92,000 in 1870), but it was located on a primary transportation route, linking the emerging industrial heartland between Pittsburgh and Detroit. Cleveland had seen traveling companies such as Potter's since the 1830s, and Charles Foster, the manager in Pittsburgh, had built a theatre there in 1852. John Ellsler, one of his actors, settled in Cleveland in March 1855 and managed almost continually until 1885. As an actor Ellsler specialized in old men, while his wife was a leading lady. They had wide experience, having played in New York City and toured the South in management with Joseph Jefferson III.

Cleveland had barely thirty thousand people when he settled there, and so until the season of 1866–67 Ellsler played Cleveland from September to early January and again from April to mid-July, with an intervening six weeks in Columbus during the sitting of the legislature. Summers often saw tours to such interior towns as Akron and Canton, as well as Meadville, in the developing oil region of northwestern Pennsylvania. By 1867 Cleveland's population had nearly tripled, so Ellsler confined the company to forty-week seasons there.

Although Ellsler thought of his company as a family, about half the two dozen actors were new every two years. Only fourteen players lasted five or more consecutive seasons in the stock company. Four of those (Effie Ellsler, Mrs. G. H. Gilbert, James Lewis, Clara Morris) became stars by 1870. Necessarily, the emphasis was on the stars who occupied leading roles about two-thirds of the time. While almost every major star of the period played for Ellsler at one time or another, the Cleveland audience had its favorites: Charles Couldock, Joseph Procter, and Mrs. D. P. Bowers among the tragic players; Sallie St. Claire among the comediennes.

Although Ellsler observed the traditional lines of business, there was considerable flexibility within the company. An actor could refuse a role in his or her line, forcing the manager to press one of his four ballet girls into the part. Such substitution was Clara Morris's upward path, especially since Mrs. Ellsler disliked appearing as second lady to visiting female stars.

The principle of respectability was the key to Ellsler's management. His most popular offerings were holiday extravaganzas: *Aladdin, The Black Crook, The Naiad Queen,* and *Humpty Dumpty.* Melodramas such as *Uncle Tom's Cabin, Jack Sheppard, The Willow Copse, Camille, Nick of the Woods* (Louisa Medina, 1838), and *The Octoroon* were the most frequently performed non-musical pieces. The traditional tragic repertory accounted for about the same number of performances but consisted of a larger number of plays: *Hamlet, Macbeth, Romeo and Juliet, Richard III, Othello, The Merchant of Venice, Richelieu, Ingomar, The Hunchback,* and *The Stranger.* Modern come-dies, such as *The Lady of Lyons, London Assurance,* and *Our American Cousin,* were augmented by a single old comedy, *The School for Scandal.* The Cleve-land Theatre, built in 1853, was expanded and called the Academy of Music after its remodeling in 1859. It seated two thousand on the second and third floors of a block-square building and featured a typically large metropolitan stage, 40 feet deep by 65 feet wide. The renovation included replacing the pit with the more expensive dress circle, and at the end of the Civil War prices were raised to thirty-five cents for the gallery, seventy-five cents for the dress circle, and a dollar-fifty for reserved box seats, further restricting the theatre to the city's middle and upper classes.

Wallack's Theatre, New York City

Between 1852 and 1887 James William Wallack and his son, Lester, achieved arguably the most successful single management in the nation during the nineteenth century. Because both were starring actors of the first magnitude, they exploited their own popularity by playing starring engagements at other theatres about half the time. At the same time, their New York City theatre was occupied by an ensemble that was sufficiently talented and whose reper-tory was sufficiently attuned to the city's upper middle class that it could play profitably without them. Their achievement was unique because only New York City had a large enough class of managerial and professional peo-ple to support a theatre by itself.

Every aspect of Wallack's was fashioned for that audience. Each change of theatre was a move uptown, intended to keep the theatre near its audience. The original (Wallack's Lyceum) was at Broome Street on the west side of Broadway. Wallack's Theatre (1861) was on the corner of Broadway and Thir-teenth Street, and the third theatre (1882) was at Broadway and Thirtieth. The capacity never exceeded a modest seventeen hundred persons in an era when metropolitan theatres regularly seated between twenty-five hundred and thirty-five hundred, and ticket prices were always at the upper end of the scale, ranging from fifty cents to a dollar-fifty in 1870, double what they had been at the outset.

The repertory depended on a mixture of manners and romantic comedy, fulfilling J. W. Wallack's opening night promise "that his intent was to delight with laughter, not move to tears" (*New York Herald,* 9 October 1852). The older comedies of Sheridan and Goldsmith were combined with the more recent ones of Tom Taylor and T. W. Robertson as the heart of the repertory, but the melodramas of Boucicault always figured prominently, as did Lester's *Rosedale; or, the Rifle Ball* (1863).

To perform such a repertory, which depended on close interplay among characters, the Wallacks employed a company of about forty, with almost as many women as men. These were paid nearly twice what they would have been anywhere else. They were also rehearsed about twice as much. Younger players were tutored in their parts, especially by Lester, who went to great lengths to demonstrate exactly how lines should be read and business executed. Every actor who has written about being in the company has noted the civility and propriety with which everything was done. Although there were strict rules about being on time and prepared for rehearsal and performance and though there were stiff fines for altering dialogue or established stage business, Lester (who from the first was the active manager, and who became sole proprietor upon his father's death in 1864) was accessible to everyone and treated them all with equal fairness. As a consequence many actors and stage employees were with the theatre for ten to twenty years, and the theatre grossed between seven hundred and a thousand dollars a night.

The normal Wallack season was a series of new productions in the fall, each one performed for as many consecutive nights as possible, followed by a series of revivals in the late spring and early summer. The policy of the longer run was economically inspired. Once the play was mounted and the investment made, the more performances the better. Thus, in 1857–58 Boucicault's *The Poor of New York* ran for six weeks, and in 1863–64 *Rosedale* ran for sixty-seven nights when premiered. The longer run reduced the number of plays produced each season (and therefore the number of new parts an actor had to learn) and led to the abolition of benefits in 1867. Benefits always demeaned the actor, and they interrupted profitable runs. Wallack dispensed with them to the delight of his actors, raising the average salary by ten dollars a week as compensation.

Wallack's was anachronistic. Secure with its audience, it sustained an older idea of theatre, engaging only an occasional star to replace either of the Wallacks when they were on tour, refusing to abolish afterpieces or introduce matinees (standard in New York City by 1860), and curtailing runs of consecutive performances of popular new pieces in order to revive old favorites.

Still, Wallack's set a pattern that actor-managers in other cities sought to emulate as much as possible in terms of order and stability. What was most subject to change was the repertory. Each theatre's offerings reflected both local audience taste and the manager's own line of parts as a star. In New

York City other managers who successfully achieved something of Wallack's stability with different repertories and audiences were William Mitchell (Mitchell's Olympic, 1839–50), William E. Burton (Burton's Theatre, 1848–58), and Augustin Daly (Daly's Theatre, 1869–99).

Portents of Change: Tom Maguire and Regional Monopoly

Apart from New York and New Orleans, San Francisco was not only the most complex, dynamic city in the country, it was also the center of the nation's fastest growing region. Its population of about thirty thousand in 1851 quintupled by 1870, and the state's population (almost all of it in the northern part and comprised largely of single males under the age of forty) multiplied by seven to over half a million. The emperor of its theatre (and that of most of the state) was a nearly illiterate New York City cab driver, saloon keeper, and initiate of Tammany Hall politics, Thomas Maguire. Like Stephen Price, he was not from the theatre. He had no experience of or interest in the art; he was devoted to the profitability of the business. His management was premised on the principle of monopoly. He attempted to exclude competition by filling as many theatres as possible with his attractions. Consequently, he operated on a larger scale, both in terms of geography and genre, than any other manager in the period. In this way he was an indicator of the future of theatrical management.

He became proprietor of San Francisco's Parker House Hotel in 1849. When he rebuilt it after the fire of 4 May 1850, he devoted its second floor to the Jenny Lind theatre, which was consumed by fire, rebuilt, and eventually sold as a city hall. He plunged his profits into San Francisco Hall, where Junius Brutus Booth, the younger, was his stage manager, and which he rebuilt and renamed Maguire's Opera House in 1856.

During the same period a major new theatre, the Metropolitan, had been built, and in March 1862 Maguire leased it and turned it over to Booth. A year later he purchased a minor theatre, the Eureka, for his San Francisco Minstrels, and in May 1864 opened his Academy of Music as a home for grand opera. His ambitions were not confined to San Francisco. Though the extent of his theatrical enterprise will never be fully known, he built and managed an opera house in Virginia City, Nevada, from 1863 to 1867, and at different times either owned or leased theatres in Marysville, Sacramento, Stockton, Nevada City, Grass Valley, and Los Angeles. Nor were his activities solely theatrical. He seems always to have had interests in various San Francisco saloons and gambling halls.

His prosperity declined by 1870. He had lost as much as $120,000 on ten years of grand opera, he was being sued for both contract and copyright violation, the California Theatre managed by Barrett and John McCullough was about to open, and Maguire's properties were being sold or auctioned to satisfy his creditors. When his wife died in 1870, it was widely thought that his career was finished. Consequently, his renaissance at the Baldwin Theatre in the 1880s was unexpected, but is outside the period of this volume.

Maguire relied on others (Charles Tibbetts, Sheridan Corbyn) to run his theatres. He concentrated on bringing attractions for them to California. Because of his extensive control of theatres, he could offer performers 150 nights of performances. Each of the nearly one hundred stars he engaged played an initial engagement of four to six weeks in San Francisco, made an interior tour of one to three months, and then played a two- to three-week farewell engagement in the city. He was not above elevating minor talents such as Avonia Jones and Annette Ince to star status, nor was he adverse to exploiting the local appeal of Lotta Crabtree (1862) or Adah Isaacs Menken (1863), but he also engaged Mr. and Mrs. J. W. Wallack (1858–59), Mr. and Mrs. Charles Kean (1864–65), Edwin Forrest (1866), Helen Western (1867), her sister, Lucille (1868), Lawrence Barrett (1868), and Mr. and Mrs. W. J. Florence (1869). To support the stars he maintained a stock company of about two dozen, dividing it, augmenting it, shifting it from place to place as necessary. He also organized and promoted minstrel and opera companies, and in 1867 he went to the Eastern states and Europe with a troupe of Japanese acrobats and tumblers he had imported.

Laura Keene and the Rise of the Combination Company

By 1870 access to America's continually increasing audience was facilitated by the rapid expansion of the railroads. The primary cause of the increase in railroad track mileage of a standard gauge was the Civil War. The Union had the industrial ability to execute the army's demand for more efficient rail transportation in order to supply its troops. Thus, while there had been less than ten thousand miles of track in 1850, there was over fifty thousand in 1870.

Not only did trains enable actors to move more quickly and less expensively, it enabled them to do so in a new way. They were able to return to something like the traveling company, complete with costumes and scenery that had been the norm when David Douglass had managed and that John Potter and others sustained on the frontier. Because they could move farther faster, these new companies needed only a small repertory at most, and some managers found that a single-play of sufficient popularity was adequate to sustain an entire season. These new companies were called combinations or single play combinations and were the basis for national theatrical monopolies that emerged in the last quarter of the century.

Laura Keene was one of the managers who pioneered the new mode of organization. Her career has been presented both as the result of an impetuous female personality and as the result of male opposition to a female player in a man's game. However, it is also possible to see her career as the result of a series of rational managerial decisions, some of which were more successful than others. She was not a conventional starring actor, so she had limited audience appeal. Her problem was constructing a management that would maximize her exposure to that audience. She experimented with geographic location and with repertory before abandoning the organization of the permanent company to experiment with the combination company.

From this perspective Keene seems remarkable for her ability to find alternative solutions and for her nerve in implementing them. If a particular strategy was not working, she was quick to change and protean in contriving options. Her career can be divided into four phases: developing actress (1851–53), provincial management (1853–55), New York City management (1855–63), and touring in combinations (1863–73).

The beginning of her career demonstrates her ability and willingness to embrace change. In March 1851 she was Mary Francis Taylor, wife of Henry Taylor and mother of his two daughters, living at a London public house, "The Plough", of which he was owner. On 8 October 1851 she appeared as Juliet at Emma Brougham's Theatre Royal, Richmond. In little over half a year she had left her husband of seven years and become an actress, the sole support of her mother and children. Her momentum did not slacken. After two short engagements in London, she emerged in less than a year as the ingenue of Wallack's Theatre, New York (20 September 1852).

Her rapid success was due in part to the Wallacks' need for an actress of her type, but it was also due to Keene's willingness to gamble everything on an audition with them after coming to this country without an engagement. During her first season at Wallack's she played thirty-four roles in 250 appearances. Reengaged for a second season at forty-five dollars a week and two half benefits, she brought her family to her new country.

For a young actor of her type she could not have been in a better situation. She was at her best in polite comedy featuring wit and imagination rather than emotion. One contemporary characterized her acting as "a water color sketch, full of light and grace" (Reignolds-Winslow, 67). Her greatest success was as Pauline opposite Lester Wallack's Claude Melnotte. She also appeared as Shakespeare's Beatrice and Rosalind, Sheridan's Lady Teazle and Lydia Languish, Goldsmith's Kate Hardcastle, and Boucicault's Lady Gay Spanker, in all of which, like all young actors in the company, she was carefully coached by Lester. She was ensconced in the one company in America that featured plays with good parts in her line, and she was well paid and receiving the best training she could have found anywhere. Her sudden, rancorous departure in the midst of her second season stunned everyone and seemed inexplicable except as temperamental caprice.

It was more probably a calculated risk intended to advance her professionally and personally. She left Wallack's in order to manage her own company at the St. Charles Theatre, Baltimore (24 December 1853 through 3 March 1854). By itself the move from actor to manager is a move from salary to possible profit, something that is rational though risky. The messy circumstances surrounding the move probably stem from personal considerations of which only the outlines survive.

Though married, she presented herself as a single woman raising two nieces. She had developed a social relationship with John Lutz, married with children and characterized as a professional gambler. His family was from Baltimore, and he signed the theatrical lease as her agent. Possibly Keene and Lutz simply decided to gamble on an available theatre in a place with which he was familiar and where his family and business connections could assist the launch of her managerial career.

In Baltimore she studiously repeated her successes from Wallack's, and she supported herself with two young actors (Charles Wheatleigh and Edward Askew Sothern), whose careers were to continue to be associated with hers. Although her initial management appears to have been profitable, both in terms of critical and popular response, she did not renew her lease. Instead, she returned to New York and sailed on 6 March for California, where her arrival was anticipated in the press.

Her move to California could have been motivated by the same combination of professional and personal motives as her arrival in Baltimore. Lutz seems to have been occupied with his wife's final illness (she died in June 1855). Keene may have decided to explore other possibilities by going west, where, it was said, amorous miners pelted actors with gold nuggets. Whatever the reason, she arrived in San Francisco 2 April 1854 with her family and without John Lutz.

From 6 April through 3 June 1854 she played engagements in San Francisco, Stockton, and Sacramento, deploying her standard repertory. Her reception was lukewarm compared to that given Matilda Heron, Kate Denin, and the Bateman sisters. California's audience liked its actors emotional and their effects broad. Struggling as a starring actress, she turned to management. The American, one of San Francisco's two major theatres, was to be torn down, so Keene leased a minor theatre, the Union (used once a month for performances by French-speaking amateurs) and opened on 22 June with actors dispossessed from the American.

It was a strong company, featuring local favorites William and Caroline Chapman and David "Doc" Robinson. However, it was not a group skilled in her repertory. Keene adapted herself, appearing in topical musical burlesques written for her by Robinson (*The Lioness of the North, The Camp at the Union*), slowly adding a few of her regular roles (Beatrice, Pauline) and experimenting for the first time with spectacular melodrama (*The Sea of Ice*). The theatre seemed to prosper through the end of July, and, though she was announced in the bills for 1 August, she did not appear, sailing instead for Australia with Edwin Booth and D. C. Anderson.

The reason for her departure given by her first biographer was that she had learned of her husband's presence in Australia and went there to seek a legal separation. While that is possible (at least two single men by the name of Henry Taylor emigrated to Victoria between 1851 and 1854), she had gone out of her way to conceal her relationship with him, so it is hard to imagine someone bringing her the news. Perhaps she was frustrated by the repertory she was compelled to use at the Union. Perhaps she was frustrated with the limited profit from a small theatre. Others (C. R. Thorne, Kate Denin) had recently gone to Australia, and there were several Australian actors active in California. Keene may have gambled on this second mining frontier as she had on the first. For whatever reason, it was certainly not intended to be a long stay, because she left her mother and daughters behind.

She had played briefly with Booth at the Metropolitan in San Francisco, and their repertories made an interesting combination. She could manage the female roles in his specialties (*Hamlet, Richard III, The Merchant of Venice*); he was a good Benedick and passable as Haller and Claude Melnotte, so they ought to have made an attractive combination. However, they managed a bare two weeks at Sydney's Theatre Royal and a week at the Queen's Theatre, Melbourne (24 October through 24 November 1854). Keene did not arrive back in San Francisco until 19 March, and three weeks of playing seems small return for an absence of seven and a half months.

She seems to have begun arrangements to lease the new American Theatre immediately. She assembled a strong company for polite comedy and melodrama (local favorites Mrs. Thoman, Mrs. Judah, John McCabe, Walter Leman, and featuring her former Baltimore leading man, Charles Wheatleigh), and the theatre had a prosperous season from 9 April through 30 July 1855. It was during this management that she produced spectacular revivals of *Twelfth Night* (six nights), *A Midsummer Night's Dream* (twelve), and *The Tempest* (four). This time her departure was orderly. Farewell benefits were organized, newspaper regrets expressed, and on the first of August she sailed for New York.

Her apprenticeship was over. In two years she had sucessfully managed three different companies in two cities. At the American her company had presented over forty main pieces in 98 nights of playing. She had added three Shakespearean roles to her repertory (Viola, Titania, and Miranda) and one new melodramatic heroine (Rose Fielding, *The Willow Copse*). However, her logical place was New York City. It was the biggest city, the biggest audience; it was the place where Keene was most likely to find support for the plays she excelled in: manners comedy and extravaganza. She had neither the emotional power of Matilda Heron or Julia Dean, nor did she have the flamboyant instinct of such clowns as Caroline Chapman and Lotta Crabtree. She belonged in an ensemble. It was the setting that enhanced her special skills, and she had the organization and attention to detail to manage it effectively. She was joined by John Lutz, whose wife had died, and who now resumed his relationship with her.

From 27 December 1855 through 4 May 1863 she managed a resident company in New York City, after the first season in a new intimate (1,700 seats) theatre built for her. It was a difficult time for theatres, encompassing the financial panic of 1857 and the disastrous early years of the Civil War. Her task was even more difficult because she had few friends in the theatre. Lester Wallack still held a grudge, and he was perhaps the most popular theatrical person in the city. W. E. Burton was probably next, and Keene hired most of his company away to open her theatre.

Moreover, she had to find plays that competed for Wallack's audience without duplicating his repertory. She succeeded several times. Her two new hits were Tom Taylor's *Our American Cousin* (140 consecutive performances, beginning 18 October 1858) and Thomas H. DeWalden's *The Seven Sisters* (253 performances beginning 26 November 1860, the longest run in New York up to that time). For the rest she relied on the comedies that had succeeded before, to which she added Taylor's *Still Waters Run Deep.* She strove for the longest runs possible, and relied increasingly on revivals because they were less expensive than mounting new productions.

Her greatest comic success, *Our American Cousin,* depended on the acting of Joseph Jefferson III as Asa Trenchard and of E. A. Sothern as Lord Dundreary. Her part, Florence Trenchard, was neither particularly comic nor challenging. Jefferson and Sothern left to become stars on the basis of their success in her company, and she discovered that she did not have the copyright control of the play she thought she had. She had paid Taylor $1,000 for the rights, and she had reason to believe that her ownership would be secure under the American copyright law of 1857, which recognized dramatic compositions for the first time.

Unfortunately, she was wrong. When Wheatleigh and John Sleeper Clarke produced the play in Philadelphia the court ruled that performance was a form of publication and that she was only entitled to royalties. She could not deny them the right to produce it. When Moses Kimball did it at the Boston Museum, she fared even worse. The Massachusetts court held that only property could be copyrighted and that only the printed text was property. She had no legal control over the spoken text. As long as Kimball didn't print the text, his production was legal and he owed her nothing. Keene was unable to profit from her investment to its fullest extent, though she continued to play the piece for the rest of her career. The matter was not finally settled until 1868, when Boucicault got a judge to acknowledge that dramatic copyright included performance as well as publication.

She looked for new material, and her audience responded most favorably to extravaganza, "operatic, spectacular, diabolical, musical, terpsichorean, farcical burletta" (Odell, VII, 313), a musical variety show with a female chorus and some plot continuity. In her final season of New York management she pioneered the single-play combination. Employing a double company, she planned to tour one while the other was resident. She took half her actors on the road in her standard comic repertory while Emma Broughton-Robinson starred at New York Theatre in a new burlesque, *Blondette.* The goal was to exploit the popularity of burlesque while keeping her legitimate repertory alive. Unfortunately, the profits of the one could not offset the losses of the other. She sold the theatre and went on the road in a combination for the rest of her life.

Boucicault seems to have initiated the combination system in England in 1860. In the United States his invention was imitated by both Keene and Henry C. Jarrett two years later. Keene seems to have been the most consistent pioneer, but by 1867–68 multiple combinations were on the road and had no trouble finding places and dates to play. Keene's first combination (1862–63) was her largest: a full company with sets and costumes in six plays, playing for half the gross receipts in New England. In subsequent years she reduced the repertory to two or three plays, a core of three to five actors, and relied on the scenery and resident company of the local theatre, thereby decreasing her cost and hopefully increasing her profit.

Though she followed no fixed pattern, she played most often and successfully in New England and New York State and in the South. She could always count on cordial receptions in Boston, Philadelphia, Washington, St. Louis, and Chicago. Her most frequent plays were *Our American Cousin, She Stoops to Conquer,* and (after 1866) Boucicault's *Hunted Down,* though *The Lady of Lyons* and *Masks and Faces* were sometimes added.

She was constantly innovating and revising, and season after season her management supported her family. Even her skill, however, was challenged by the accident of her presence at Lincoln's assassination. Arrested, she obtained her company's release and continued touring. Similarly, she was challenged by a progressively worsening illness (tuberculosis) and by the death of her long-time companion, John Lutz (1869). When her strength began to fail, she tried magazine publishing and the lecture circuit (1872), returning to the road until April 1873, when she hemorrhaged onstage. Efficient manager to the last, she returned to New York, paid her debts, and sold her property to provide for her daughters.

Conclusion

Mark Twain called his novel about America after the Civil War *The Gilded Age,* but the entire first half of the century had been infected with "the migratory and speculative instinct of our age" because, "To the . . . American . . . the paths to fortune are innumberable and all open; there is invitation in the air and success in all his wide horizon" (vol. 19, 112). The size and richness of the landscape was the foundation of the attitude. For those who made their living from playing, the essential condition was that the audience was increasing in number and expanding in new settlements faster than at any other time.

In attempts to capitalize on these unprecedented opportunities, theatrical managers experimented with the various conventions by means of which they articulated their performances with their audiences. Four of these experiments proved particularly profitable and were widely adopted. The first experiment was David Douglass's use of the length and breadth of the entire settled area, establishing headquarters in major regional cities: New York and Philadelphia in the North, while shifting from Williamsburg to Charleston in the South. Such change was sufficient to prosper in what was until the Revolution a geographically remote English home county.

Cultural homogeneity was one of the casualties of the Revolutionary War. It could not survive the combination of institutional change and unprecedented demographic shifts. Thus, the second experiment that worked, the star system, succeeded in adapting theatre as a social institution to both the cultural and the geographic map of the nation. At a practical level traveling stars were an economically more efficient way to supply constant variety to new audiences spread across a vast territory. At a mythic level they also supplied the new nation with popular heroes – figures who conquered insurmountable physical and emotional obstacles to establish or sustain a cultural identity. These gains, however, were not made without cost. To the extent the star became the reason the audience attended the theatre, the star legitimately took a greater share of the revenue. On the whole, this forced managers to pay supporting players no more and sometimes less than before, so their real income stagnated or declined. The consequence was that any actor who could went on the road as a star. Not only did this dilute the quality of starring actors, it watered down their support.

The third change, the long run in urban theatres, functioned in a similar way. Practically, it took advantage of increasing population to reduce the unit cost of the performance, thus increasing profit, while mythically each long-running play provided a narrative that supplied acceptable symbolic coherence for otherwise intractable social situations. As in all things, there was a price for the long run. The traditional repertory grounded in the plays of

Shakespeare gradually gave way to sensation melodrama and extravaganza because each had greater audience appeal. There came a time when not enough people shared cultural assumptions to which Shakespeare's plays or those that imitated them were relevant. The economic efficiency of the long run made it imperative to focus the repertory on those types of scripts that did articulate cultural assumptions that were more widely shared.

Two other changes, regional monopoly and the combination company, were introduced but were not widely adapted before 1870. Subsequently, each was to provide an effective new means of managing a profitable relationship between theatres and audiences. The aim of monopoly is to eliminate competition. Once that is accomplished, the monopoly can then do one or both of two things: it can lower cost by lowering quality and it can raise prices. Tom Maguire's monopoly was fragile and brief, but he experimented successfully with both strategies in a manner that anticipated later managerial practice. In the same way, Laura Keene's experiment with the combination company came at the end of her career, when her resources were diminished, but she demonstrated that a combination company without a star of the first magnitude could profit in both cities and small towns in different regions.

Perhaps the greatest change in structure and management during the entire period, however, is one that was almost unnoticed: the gradual shift in control of the theatre from those who were artists or who were motivated by a love of the art, to those who were not artists and who were motivated solely by profit. Any type of expansion requires capital. With only rare exceptions, David Douglass managed to find capital without surrendering control. So did the Wallacks. However, neither William Dunlap nor John Potter could; consequently, each lost control of his theatre. A similar fate befell John Ellsler and Laura Keene. So long as they managed within a capital structure they could pay for, they retained control of their theatres, but every time they couldn't pay for their own operations, every time they had to turn to commercial capital, they lost control, ceased to manage, and became salaried employees. Thus, the final irony was that Maguire's and Keene's management experiments, which in both cases were intended to allow them to retain control, later resulted in control of the theatre being concentrated in a small number of persons whose primary concern with theatre was to profit to the greatest degree possible from it.

Notes

1 Collier's famous attack appeared in *A Short View of the Immorality and Profaneness of the English Stage* (1698).
2 See Chapter 5, note 3.

Bibliography: Structure and Management

The only comprehensive study of the economics of the American theatre before 1870 is Bernheim's classic *The Business of the Theatre* (1932). However, Brooks, "The Development of American Theatre Management Practices between 1830 and 1896" is useful, and no one interested in the subject should miss Leavitt, *Fifty Years in Theatrical Management, 1859–1909* (1912). My views on the subject are contained in three articles: "The Development of Theatre on the American Frontier, 1750–1890," "The Theatre and Its Audience: Changing Modes of Social Organization in the American Theatre," and "The Impact of Working Conditions upon Acting Style," coauthored with Robert Sarlós. The cultural conservatism of migrants is documented in Wright, *Culture on the Moving Frontier.*

Dunlap's *History of the American Theatre* (1832) is not only the first attempt at narrative and analysis but is the closest thing to a primary source for Hallam and Douglass. However, Rankin's *The Theatre in Colonial America* is a masterful and indispensable secondary source. Two important recent studies are Peter A. Davis, "Puritan Mercantilism and the Politics of Anti-Theatrical Legislation in Colonial America" and Mays, "The Achievements of the Douglass Company in North America: 1758–1774." Bost also surveyed management in the early years in his *Monarchs of the Mimic World; or, the American Theatre of the Eighteenth Century Through the Managers – the Men Who Made It.*

The transition to the star system is chronicled by Dunlap, both in his *History* and in his diary, edited by Barck, and by Wood in *Personal Recollections of the Stage* (1855). Another useful primary source for the early nineteenth century is Wemyss, *Theatrical Biography; or, the Life of an Actor and Manager* (1848). The best secondary analyses of the transition to stars are Hewitt's, "'King Stephen' of the Park and Drury Lane" and Pritner's, "William Warren's Management of the Chestnut Street Theatre Company" and "William Warren's Financial Arrangements with Visiting Stars."

Literature on the frontier theatre in America is as vast as the geography itself. The best bibliography is Larson, *American Regional Theatre History to 1900: A Bibliography.* Two surveys are immensely useful: Dormon, *Theater in the Ante Bellum South, 1815–1861* and Rusk, *The Literature of the Middle Western Frontier.* The management that has been most completely documented is that of Noah Ludlow and Sol Smith. Both left important, useful autobiographies: Ludlow, *Dramatic Life as I Found It* (1880) and Smith, *Theatrical Management in the West and South for Thirty Years* (1868). Their early career has been studied by Carson in two books: *Managers in Distress* and *Theatre on the Frontier.* Their later career is the subject of Grisvard's "The Final Years: The Ludlow and Smith Theatrical Firms in St. Louis, 1845–1851." Among the other many autobiographies and memoirs, the most useful is *The Autobiography of Joseph Jefferson.*

My account of John Potter's career has been assembled from many sources. He is accorded an entry in T. Allston Brown's *History of the American Stage* and in Wemyss, *Chronology of the American Stage, 1752–1852.* Stories about him are found in Sol Smith (230–32); in Adair, "Stories of the Stage"; and in Dr. Judd's "The Old School of Actors."

For Potter's career in the South I used Free, "Studies in American Theatre History: The Theatre of Southwest Mississippi to 1840"; Gates, "The Theatre in Natchez"; Hunt, "The Nashville Theatre, 1830–1840"; Keeton, "The Theatre in Mississippi from 1840 to 1870"; Kendall, *The Golden Age of the New Orleans Theater;* Ritter, "The Theatre in Memphis, Tennessee, from Its Beginning to 1859"; and Stokes, "The First Theatrical Season in Arkansas: Little Rock, 1838–1839."

For Cleveland I used Gaiser, "The History of the Cleveland Theatre from the Beginnings to 1854."

For California I used these newspapers: *The Alta California* (San Francisco), *Daily Herald* (Marysville), *Daily California Express* (Marysville), and *The Mountain Democrat* (Placerville). Also useful are Hume, "The Sacramento Theatre, 1849–1885"; Noid, "History of the Theatre in Stockton, California, 1850–1892"; and Stewart, "The Drama in a Frontier Theater."

Sources on theatre in the Pacific Northwest include Eggers, "A History of Theatre in Boise, Idaho, from 1863 to 1963"; Elliott, "Annals of the Legitimate Theatre in Victoria, Canada from the Beginning to 1900"; Evans, *Frontier Theatre: A History of Nineteenth Century Theatrical Entertainment in the Canadian Far West and Alaska;* Herring, *In the Pathless West with Soldiers, Pioneers, Miners, and Savages;* Margetts, "A Study of the Theatrical Career of Julia Dean Hayne"; Schilling, "The History of Theatre in Portland, Oregon, 1846–1959"; and Schwarz, "Theatre on the Gold Frontier: A Cultural Study of Five Northwest Mining Towns, 1860–1870."

John A. Ellsler left autobiographical reminiscences that his granddaughter compiled: *The Stage Memories of John A. Ellsler,* edited by Effie Ellsler Weston, but an equally informative primary source is Clara Morris's, *My Life on the Stage: My Personal Experiences and Recollections* (1901). In addition to Gaiser's dissertation on Cleveland (cited under Potter), other sources on Ohio theatre are Dix, "The Theatre in Cleveland, Ohio, 1854–1875"; Burbick, "Columbus, Ohio: Theater From the Beginning of the Civil War to 1875"; and Utz, "Columbus, Ohio: Theatre Seasons, 1840–41 to 1860–61."

Those wishing to assess the typicality of Ellsler's management can compare it to that of Ludlow and Smith. It can also be compared to that of James McVicker in Chicago, Ben DeBar in St. Louis, and R. M. Field in Boston. The relevant sources are McVicker, *The Theatre: Its Early Days in Chicago;* Ludwig, "James H. McVicker and his Theatre" and "McVicker's Theatre: 1857–1896"; Herbstruth, "Benedict DeBar and the Grand Opera House in St. Louis, Missouri, from 1855 to 1879"; and Mammen, *The Old Stock Company School of Acting: A Study of the Boston Museum.*

The best firsthand account of California theatricals during and after the gold rush is Leman, *Memories of an Old Actor* (1886). The standard secondary sources are MacMinn, *Theater of the Golden Era in California* and Gagey, *The San Francisco Stage: A History.* Most recent books are neither as thorough nor as reliable. The definitive work on Maguire is Rodecape, "Tom Maguire: Napoleon of the Stage." There is also useful material in Wade, "The San Francisco Stage: 1859–1869."

The basic source for the study of Wallack's Theatre remains Odell's monumental *Annals of the New York Stage.* Useful analysis of Wallack's is provided by both Cecil Jones, "The Policies and Practices of Wallack's Theatre: 1852–88" and Swinney, "Production in the Wallack theatres: 1852–1888." Currently, the standard work on Laura Keene is Ben Henneke, *Laura Keene: A Biography.* It replaces earlier biographies, although the original one, Creahan, *The Life of Laura Keene: Actress, Artist, Manager and Scholar,* may still be consulted with caution for primary material. More reliable primary sources are Day, "An Early Combination: A Summer Tour with Laura Keene and Her New York Company" and Reignolds-Winslow, *Yesterdays With Actors.* Among the spate of recent studies, the following are worth consulting: Deutsch, "Laura Keene's Theatrical Management"; Dudden, *Women in the American Theatre: Actresses and Audiences: 1790–1870;* Morrell, "Laura Keene and Gold Country Theatricals"; and Taylor, "Laura Keene in America: 1852–1873." Finally, one should not ignore Irvin, "Laura Keene and Edwin Booth in Australia." Those seeking a context for Keene's activities may also wish to consult Curry, *Nineteenth-Century American Women Theatre Managers* and Roberts, "'Lady-managers' in Nineteenth-Century American Theatre."

For insight into the changing nature of the society and its repertory, beneficial are McConachie, *Melodramatic Formations: American Theatre and Society, 1820–1870* and the essays in Fisher and Watt, eds., *When They Weren't Doing Shakespeare: Essays on Nineteenth-Century British and American Theatre.*

3

The Plays and Playwrights

Plays and Playwrights to 1800

Peter A. Davis

Introduction

American culture before 1800 is not renowned for its theatre, and American theatre before 1800 is not known for its dramatic literature. The period is often characterized as a relatively barren era in which rare examples of theatrical writing appeared on odd occasions. Theatre historians describe long fallow stretches punctuated by sudden bursts of crude dramatic creativity, with plays remarkable only for their scarcity and inherent inferiority to European models. It is a perception that has influenced the development of American plays and playwrights since the first performances by Europeans more than four hundred years ago, and it still forms the basis of our present understanding of early American theatre.

A closer examination, of course, reveals a surprising number and variety of plays, written by an equally surprising assortment of playwrights, from politicians to preachers. Indeed, the seventeenth and eighteenth centuries produced a remarkable collection of scripts, dialogues, dramatic discourses, masques, and other dramatic and paratheatrical endeavors. Far from being a barren and unproductive period, pre-nineteenth-century America saw drama as an integral part of culture and society. Admittedly, the dramatic literature of this early period has received scant attention, its significance overlooked and perhaps deliberately shunned by social critics fearful of idle representations or even aesthetic patriots determined to distill a purified American drama by expunging those works deemed unworthy and inferior.

But the uneasy acceptance of American drama was not just the result of puritanical ire or nationalistic elitism. Economic and political events also conspired to prevent drama from establishing a firm and consistent foothold in the cultural milieu of pre-nineteenth-century America. The distinct role drama played in these early years would have a lasting influence on subsequent amusement forms, cultural tastes, and even the business of entertainment in America.

Non-English Beginnings

Most theatre historians agree that the earliest examples of Western theatrical literature in North America were written and performed by Spanish and French colonists in the late sixteenth and early seventeenth centuries. In June 1567 Spanish missionaries and soldiers in Tequesta, Florida, performed two religious plays. Neither scripts nor titles survive, but according to the description left by Francisco de Vallereal, the performances were probably in the tradition of medieval auto sacramentales, demonstrating the perpetual struggle between temptation and salvation. Whether these plays were composed for the occasion or were merely restagings of previously written material is unknown, but their existence reveals the relative importance theatre had among the early conquistadores and missionaries. Similarly, Joaquin Garcia Icazbalceta documents Spanish performances of plays in Mexico as early as 1538, when four sacred commedias were presented to educate the native population. It is also known that Cortez in his conquest of Honduras in 1524 included players and puppeteers among his personal staff. However, the extent of original dramatic writing associated with these performances and players is purely speculative.

More commonly known is the first documented play written in the New World – a comedy performed by the soldiers engaged in the conquest of New Mexico in 1598. The campaign was described in an epic historical poem published in 1610 by one of its participants, Capitán Gaspar de Villagrá, entitled *La Historia de la Nueva Mexico*. Again, the title of the work has not survived, but de Villagrá describes a play, written by a Capitán Marcos Farfan de los Godos, performed on 30 April by the soldiers in celebration of their arrival north of the Rio Grande. Though the script is lost, de Villagrá's account verifies the play as the first to be written and performed in what is now the United States.

Indeed, the Spanish continued their theatrical traditions during the seventeenth and eighteenth centuries, performing both secular and religious plays throughout the Americas. Among the last original pieces to be written and performed before the end of the eighteenth century is Fernando de Reygados's *Astucias por heredar un sobrino a su tío* ("A Nephew's Tricks to Inherit from His Uncle"), a three-act *capa y espada* drama that premiered in Monterey in 1789 and constituted the first play staged in California.

To the north, the French inhabitants of Acadia were also early creators of dramatic amusements. In 1606, the year before the founding of Jamestown, a masque was written and performed at Port Royal, Nova Scotia. Apparently designed to bolster the sagging spirits of the disheartened explorers, *Les Muses de la Nouvelle-France* (also known as *The Theatre of Neptune in New France*) was penned by Marc Lescarbot and served as a celebratory pageant welcoming back to camp an expedition led by Sieur de Poutrincourt. Although an edition was published in France in 1609, an English translation did not appear until 1927. It is, nonetheless, the earliest extant play to be written in the New World, and it represents the odd casualness that drama played among these earliest explorers.

Dramatic literature and performance of this kind are found scattered throughout the period of European colonization. But the extent of the work is minimal and its significance on later theatrical developments is negligible. What is important to note is that theatrical amusements were not ignored by these early European colonizers and in fact seemed integral to their cultural presence in an unfamiliar world. The theatrical expression through literature and performance appears to have served not only as a diversionary pastime, but as a reaffirmation of their European identity to themselves and perhaps to their victims as well.

The commonly held belief that theatre was slow to develop in the American colonies because the settlers were too busy struggling to survive in a hostile wilderness is clearly challenged by the efforts of the Spanish and French, who managed to write and produce theatre under very strenuous circumstances. Although these productions were few and modestly staged, their existence demonstrates that sparse populations in inhospitable locations do not necessarily dispense with idle frivolities such as theatre. The presence of dramatic entertainment is not contingent upon a leisure society and a comfortable environment. What these odd performances further demonstrate is how differently the English, compared to their European neighbors, viewed theatre and drama, indicating how theatre assumed a more complex place in English society.

British Traditions

English theatre crept into the New World. It may be more accurate to say that the New World crept first into English drama. English writers, recognizing early in the seventeenth century the growing importance of the New World, include hints of its vast potential as early as 1603 in Jonson and Chapman's *Eastward Ho!* and again in 1611 in Shakespeare's *The Tempest*. These early references, as well as a handful of comical allusions to the failed English settlements that made their way onto the London stage in the late Elizabethan era, present the New World as an exotic and mysterious land, fraught with danger both mortal and moral. This exposure also came at a time when England was beginning to challenge its European neighbors as a military and economic power. Additionally, English Protestantism, which had a natural fondness for mercantilism, bolstered the nation's economy through a Puritan zealousness unrivaled in Europe. This complex relationship between English mercantilism and Puritanism led to an equally complex attitude toward drama and the New World. Thus, the English, who had a merchant-class fervor to rival the Dutch, a skill for dramatic literature that equaled that of the Spanish, and a Protestant religiosity unmatched by anyone, found themselves in the early seventeenth century asserting their own prerogative for economic conquest in the New World while steadfastly denying their vast cultural heritage outside the confines of their island nation. The irony is astounding in retrospect, but entirely understandable when viewed in the context of English mercantilism and politics.

The peculiarities of this conflict are seen in the earliest political and literary documents from the Virginia colony. The English made several attempts to open commercial colonies in the Virginia region during the late sixteenth and early seventeenth centuries, including Sir Walter Raleigh's infamous "Lost Colony." Even before these merchant colonists left England, attempts were made to enforce Puritan morality on them. Prayers and sermons warning the first settlers of the dangers of harboring "players" and "idle persons" were written. Yet Sir William Berkeley, the royalist governor of Virginia beginning in 1642, was a staunch supporter of the arts, having close associations with London literati and the royal court. A playwright, among other things, he composed a popular comedy called *The Lost Lady* in 1637 and another play entitled *Cornelia* during the Restoration. Evidence of his writing plays during his thirty years in Virginia is lacking, but his fervent royalist attitude influenced Virginians' lenient attitudes toward the theatre. His support of the monarchy during the English Civil War allowed Virginia a virtual sovereignty unlike any other North American colony and promoted the immigration of royalists escaping Puritan persecution. By 1652, when Berkeley stepped down as governor, the succeeding administrators found the political die was cast, and Virginia remained firmly in the royalist camp. Although not exclusively Anglican and royalist, Virginia nonetheless became identified as such and it is there that theatre first appeared and would eventually flourish.

The production of *Ye Bear and Ye Cubb* in 1665 further illustrates Virginia's dichotomous reputation. The play survives only as a curious legal oddity, but it represents the humble origin of English playwriting in North America. Performed in Cowle's Tavern, near the village of Pungoteague on Virginia's eastern shore on 27 August, the play aroused the ire of at least one local citizen, Edward Martin, who filed charges against the three performer-playwrights – William Darby, Philip Howard, and Cornelius Watkinson. Accomoc County court records show that the three appeared before a local magistrate on 16 November, where they were asked to perform the show (presumably to determine whether it was in violation of the law). Apparently it was not, and the judge found in favor of the defendants. Martin was not so lucky, however. For his troubles, he was ordered to pay all court costs. Not much else is known about the play or its authors, but the play and the subsequent legal action hint at how divided the English were on the subject of theatre. Despite legal vindication, no other theatrical performance would be recorded in Virginia for almost forty years. Presumably, this performance was not an isolated case. There are hints of theatrical productions in several colonies during the latter decades of the seventeenth century, yet no indication of original dramatic composition can be found.

This is not to say that the English colonists were ignorant of dramatic literature. Their private libraries often contained examples of great dramatic literature, from classics to contemporary works. Even such stalwart Calvinists as the Mathers collected and read the plays of the ancient Greeks and Romans. Some historians even argue that the Puritan ministers themselves were acknowledged "actors" who deliberately used theatrical methods to attract worshipers. Cotton Mather frequently made use of theatrical terms to describe himself and his work, calling himself an actor and his pulpit a stage. Admittedly these acknowledgments were not meant to be taken literally, but their use reveals the extent to which theatre and dramatic terminology had influenced the colonial mind. It is this use of dramatic terms and descriptions that may be behind the growth of public disguisings and political street theatre that flourished during the years before the American Revolution, not to mention the eventual development of American drama. The phenomenon finds its roots in both the political and religious practices of the previous century.

To argue that the Puritans were inherently against theatre degrades the conflict to reductivist simplicity. Not only is it misleading, it ignores the extensive and complex reasons behind their attitudes. Indeed, even the term "Puritan" has become the focus of much debate about the nature of Puritanism and the Calvinist movement in Europe and America. Some argue that there was no such thing as a true Puritan, merely a fluid collection of Protestant nonconformists who opposed anything that might be construed as being papist. Their mission was to purify the Anglican church of Roman Catholic influences and to make it more accountable to local parishioners. But beyond that, most acknowledge that Puritanism defies definition. Even its socioeconomic boundaries are hard to define. Although many were part of the growing merchant (and eventual middle) class, the Calvinist influence was felt across English society, with some aristocrats adhering to the strictest Puritan creed, while many local merchants were staunch royalists. Those who emigrated to the American colonies were no less diverse. Thus, it is hard to generalize about American colonial attitudes toward theatre and drama. Admittedly, there was a strong antitheatrical sentiment throughout the seventeenth and eighteenth centuries. But there were also many who believed theatre was a harmless, if not worthwhile, diversion.

Objections to the drama are as diverse as the Puritans themselves. Much of the antitheatricalism can be classified into six basic categories. First, Puritans held a largely overrated spiritual objection: Theatre defied the second commandment against graven images – a much debated issue that added biblical weight to many antitheatrical treatises at the time, but that was generally ignored by most. Second, Puritans had an historical fear of theatre stemming from the use of playhouses just before and during the English Civil War as meeting places for royalists. Thus, theatre was seen by some as a royalist institution with dangerous political overtones. Third, most Puritans had long considered theatre a potentially subversive activity, beginning in the mid-sixteenth century, when the Jesuits spead Catholicism throughout central Europe with their well-funded and professionally staged productions. Although the earliest Calvinists also engaged in theatrical forms, they soon found themselves outdone by the better supported Jesuits. Thus theatre became a papist tool. Fourth, theatre was an economic threat to the merchant-class Puritans, who made their money from hard work and devotion to community. Theatre, being an idle amusement, was contrary to both the Puritan concept of communal industry and mercantilist ambition. Moreover, theatre in the colonies presented the additional threat of removing valuable specie from local circulation. At a time when coin was scarce due to restrictive monetary policies from abroad, colonists came to regard theatre as an inherently British institution, designed to reenforce their second-class status. Fifth, the theatre of the Restoration was perceived as licentious and immoral, a perception with some obvious merit. Finally, theatre – and indeed art in general – was just not a concern of the European middle class. Art and theatre were aristocratic amusements that did not fit in with the Calvinist work ethic and practical aesthetics that supported European mercantilism. For most Puritans, theatre was simply an elitist waste of time. Religious and moral objections, however, gathered attention.

William Prynne's *Histriomastix* (1633), Jeremy Collier's *Short View of the Immorality and Profaneness of the English Stage* (1698), and William Penn's *No Cross, No Crown* (1699) undoubtedly hindered the development of theatre and drama in the colonies. These tracts were widely read, and portions were repeated in antitheatrical arguments throughout the late seventeenth and early eighteenth centuries. Yet, despite such assaults, antitheatrical legislation in the colonies was virtually nonexistent before 1700. Most acts cited by modern scholars were laws designed to discourage idle behavior by forbidding "games and plays," but in this context, "plays" usually means gambling, not theatrical amusement. Only the Pennsylvania act of 1682 specifically mentions "Stage-plays, Masques, Revels," though it was eventually struck down by the Board of Trade. Pennsylvania attempted to reinstate the ban in 1700 and 1706, but again the Board of Trade held firm, and the laws were rejected. Not until the Massachusetts act of 1750 did a colony successfully ban theatrical performances, and although several other colonies soon followed suit, the laws were never energetically enforced. The probable reason was that most Puritan merchants recognized the value of theatre and paratheatrical amusements as enticements at local commodity fairs. The American colonies, following the lead from home, instituted a series of semi-annual fairs from Salem to Charleston beginning in the late 1690s. Although evidence that these fairs were ever held with the consistency of English fairs is scarce, certainly the wealthy London merchants who sat on the Board of Trade and who were directly responsible for ratifying all colonial legislation knew from firsthand experience the importance of entertainment at commercial gatherings such as fairs and markets. To them, any legislation that might hinder commerce was inappropriate. Thus, little effort was made to ban such amusements.

Dialogues and Discourses

Another awkward piece of evidence that lends confusion to the colonial sentiment against theatre was the appearance of numerous dialogues and discourses published by Puritan ministers and political leaders beginning in the early 1700s. More than two hundred such works are known to have been published between 1644 and 1800. Many are brief exchanges of dialogue around a moral or political theme – little more than a broadside in dialogue form. Few contain much evidence of theatrical knowledge. Stage directions or scene divisions are for the most part nonexistent. However, a handful of surviving manusripts exist that are written well, with obvious dramatic flair and theatrical skill. It is tempting to consider these simple dialectics as evidence of early American playwriting or, at the very least, suppose that Puritans were more theatrical than first thought. Although the latter may be a point worth debating, these moral dialogues were hardly drama. Their authors would be aghast at the comparison. In their view, these dialectical exercises were purely platonic arguments, designed to pursuade a political opponent or illustrate a moral point. Their influence on later drama is perhaps slight, though their importance as a cultural indicator should not be underestimated.

Although the very earliest examples of these dialogues are politically and morally neutral – Roger Williams's "Conference Between Truth and Peace" (1644), William Bradford's "A Dialogue or the Sume of a Conference Between

Som Younge Men Borne in New England and Sundrey Ancient Men that Came Out of Holland and Old England" (1648), and John Eliot's "Indian Dialogues" (1671) – the content changes in the first few decades of the eighteenth century, the dialogues now containing clear and powerful examples of either strict religious instruction or harsh political commentary. Although these documents lack skilled dramatic technique, they do contain a quality of dialogue that warrants critical consideration of the subtle influence of drama on the colonial mind. Ironically, one of the best and most popular writers of dramatic discourses was Cotton Mather. Evidence of his interest in drama and the dramatic is found throughout his writings. His use of theatrical terms as metaphors for his work is well documented. It was Mather who called his pulpit a stage and himself an actor, a comparison that would reach fuller realization during the Great Awakening under the greatest of all Puritan actors, George Whitefield.

Mather's dramatic tendencies are best exemplified in his famous piece "The Discourse of the Minister with James Morgan, on the Way to His Execution" (1704). Though less than four pages long, it is a dynamic expression of dramatic literature disguised as religious tract. The dialogue is brisk and witty, the characters well delineated, and the action moving. With very little effort, the piece could be effectively adapted to the stage. Of course, there is no evidence that it was ever performed, and certainly Mather would not have countenanced his work in theatrical form. However, the influence of dramatic literature on his literary style and technique is a valid concern. A longer piece, and more typical of the religious discourse of the time, was his 1705 dialogue "Baptistes; or, A Conference About the Subject and Manner of Baptism. Between C. M. and D. R." Although the manuscript is written in dialogue, it lacks the tension and dramatic elements of his earlier work. Much of the information is revealed through lengthy monologues that would be tedious onstage. Nonetheless, it demonstrates the extent to which dramatic dialogue influenced his work and, inevitably, the work of his colleagues and successors.

Over three dozen such discourses are extant, all written between 1705 and 1776. An equal number were composed during the Revolutionary War and in the years leading up to 1800. Apart from Mather's writings, few stand out as exemplary dramatic documents, though a small number reflect a similar knowledge of dramatic technique. Two discourses by Benjamin Wadsworth follow Mather's model and extend the practice of dramatic discourse into the 1720s, "Some Considerations about Baptism Managed by Way of a Dialogue between a Minister and His Neighbour" (1719) and "A Dialogue between a Minister and His Neighbour, about the Lord's Supper" (1724). The latter was popular enough to be reprinted posthumously in 1772. More prolific was Jonathan Dickinson, who authored several discourses between 1732 and 1746, including

"The Scripture-Bishop; or, The Divine Right of Presbyterian Ordination and Government, Consider'd in a Dialogue between Praelaticus and Eleutherius" (1732); "A Display of God's Special Grace. In a Familiar Dialogue between a Minister & a Gentleman of this Congregation . . . " (1742); "A Brief Illustration and Confirmation of the Divine Right of Infant Baptism; in a Plain and Familiar Dialogue between a Minister and One of His Parishioners" (1746); and "The Danger of the Present Times Represented in a Familiar Dialogue" (1746). Indicative of Dickinson's popularity, and perhaps an indirect result of the Great Awakening, his works were widely disseminated, prompting several published responses to his writings, all in dialogue form, including James Wetmore's "Eleutherius Enervatus; or, An Answer to a Pamphlet Intitled, the Divine Right of Presbyterian Ordination, etc. Argued. Done by Way of a Dialogue" (1733) and John Beach's "God's Sovereignty and His Universal Love to the Souls of Men Reconciled. In a Reply to Mr. Jonathan Dickinson's Remarks upon a Sermon, Intitled, Eternal Life God's Free Gift . . . " (1747) and "A Second Vindication of God's Sovereign Free Grace Indeed, In a Fair and Candid Examination of the Last Discourse of the Late Mr. Dickinson, Entitled a Second Vindication of God's Sovereign Free Grace. Done in a Friendly Debate between C. a Calvinist and B. a Believer of Mere Primative Christianity" (1748).

Religious discourses were popular throughout the rest of the eighteenth century. Joseph Bellamy, John Wesley, and John Witherspoon each wrote dialogues in this era, using the form to help define the fractious Calvinist churches and American morality in general. However, by the end of the century the form had also been adopted by educators who used the dramatic structure to instruct pupils in oratory, reading, and writing. By far the most prolific academic dialogue writer was Noah Webster, who was responsible for over two dozen published pieces and editions between 1786 and 1800. These are not to be confused, however, with the collegiate dialogues and dramas that appeared at the start of the century.

American colleges maintained the English tradition of using drama as a means not only to teach classical language, but to instruct young men in proper speech and social behavior. As a pedagogical tool, dramatic appeal was widespread, supported by both Anglican and Puritan educators on either side of the Atlantic. This tacit support of drama as pedagogy by Calvinists was reflected in higher education. Classical drama, though not plentiful, found its way into the libraries of America's first colleges. Students from New England to Virginia were exposed to dramatic literature, not all of it ancient, as a matter of course. Though the influence this exposure may have had is largely speculative, it is clear some persons were affected by the material. As early as 1690 Harvard students were performing original dramatic literature. In that year Benjamin Coleman's *Gustavus Vasa* was produced on campus. Whether this was an officially sanctioned production or an attempt to defy authority by a rebellious group of students cannot be determined. The lack of any further dramatic activity at the college may indicate the latter. Nevertheless, it demonstrates that drama and theatre were certainly available and attractive to a few adventurous students.

Further demonstration occurred in 1702 when a "Pastoral Colloquy" was performed by students at the College of William and Mary. And though no opposition to the production is known, it would be another thirty-four years before another production would be attempted. Taking up where the students left off, a small number of college educators embraced the regular use of dramatic pieces in commencement ceremonies around midcentury. Dr. William Smith, provost of the College of Philadelphia, encouraged the practice with his adaptation of *The Masque of Alfred* in 1756. Produced at the college, presumably by students during the Christmas holiday, it differed only slightly from the original, with Smith providing additional lines of blank verse and a new prologue. Despite opposition from the Pennsylvania Assembly, Smith continued to write and encourage dramatic productions at the college for almost twenty years. In 1761 Smith co-authored a commencement piece with Francis Hopkinson entitled "An Exercise consisting of a Dialogue and Ode Sacred to the Memory of his late Gracious Majesty, George II." This was followed the next year by "A Exercise containing a dialogue and ode on the accession of His Present Gracious Majesty, George III," written by Jacob Duché. The Reverend Nathanial Evans composed "An Exercise containing a dialogue and ode on peace" for the college commencement in 1763. And again in 1775 Smith presented an "Exercise, containing a dialogue and two odes set to music." Admittedly many of these exercises were exceedingly turgid endeavors, appealing to the esoteric nature of a purely scholastic audience.

But the form gained notoriety for its occasional lapses into charged political issues. Thomas Hopkinson's commencement exercise at the College of Philadelphia in 1766, though traditional in most aspects, contained a blatant message of support for the recent repeal of the Stamp Act. Its reception among the audience is not noted. Five years later, at the College of New Jersey, Philip Freneau and Hugh Henry Brackenridge penned "A Poem on the Rising Glory of America being an Exercise delivered at the public Commencement at Nassau-Hall." Though the extent of political controversy is largely summed up in the title alone, the piece implies the ascendancy of an independent America, where "freedom shall forever reign." Its importance in American literature is found in its timeliness, summing up in poetic subtleties the rising frustrations of a colonial population engaged in economic rebellion as the anti-importation movement reached its peak. Additionally, the piece served as a literary introduction for Freneau and Brackenridge, who would both go on to greater renown in the belles-lettres.

The trend that Dr. Smith began and encouraged at the College of Philadelphia, despite strong public opposition and moral condemnation, would continue to build throughout the century. His influence was felt on colonial campuses from Dartmouth to William and Mary. Whether genuine theatre or pedantic demonstration, the commencement dialogue became a common activity and an influential method of public commentary. More than any other educator, Smith was directly responsible for the growth of collegiate exercises and dialogues. And though his intention may not have been to encourage theatrical endeavors beyond the confines of academia, his influence was great among the early playwrights and largely overlooked by students of early American theatre.

Equally popular as religious dialogues were those with a purely political theme. Though the dramatic quality of these pieces is as inconsistent as the religious work, a few stand out as curious examples of political theatre. And it is quite possible that some may have had grander theatrical pretensions. The oldest known political dialogue is also renowned for being America's earliest extant play, *Androboros* (c. 1715) by Robert Hunter and Lewis Morris. This three-act farce scatalogically satirizes the political intrigues that surrounded the early years of Hunter's administration as New York's colonial governor. Between 1710 and 1714, Hunter encountered especially harsh criticism on several fronts. Separatists on Long Island representing the booming whaling industry were threatening to join the Connecticut colony, and the Rector of Trinity Church in New York, the Reverend William Vesey, was furious over Hunter's appropriation of church land up along the Hudson for the settlement of Palatine immigrants. But the culminating event was the intended arrival in New York of Governor Francis Nicholson, appointed "governor of governors" in the North American colonies, a man of the highest connections and an infamous temper. Nicholson's complaint stems from being snubbed for the New York governorship upon Hunter's appointment, and it was widely assumed there was great enmity between the two men. Nicholson never arrived, but the threat of an official visit to investigate Hunter's abilities as governor was enough to set the governor to pen the first play published in the New World.

Though crude and at times scatalogocial, the play is actually well constructed, with reasonably drawn characters and a passable plot. Even the humor works, and satire is strongly reflective of Hunter's literary associates in London, which included Arbuthnot, Pope, and Swift. The work shows an author well acquainted with contemporary theatrical conventions, and there are a number of literary allusions that testify to a wider knowledge of current theatre than most colonials. It is likely that Hunter was assisted by his close friend, and soon to be the first governor of New Jersey, Lewis Morris. Morris, though perhaps not as dramatically literate as Hunter, had a persistent poetic streak that appears in the play on occasion in allegorical songs and verses hinting at events that only Morris would know about. There is no indication the play was performed in its own day. However, the only surviving copy in the Huntington Library is filled with handwritten notations indicating who the characters represent and clarifying the political meaning behind particular passages. It is likely the script was passed among the author's closest allies and read privately.

Most of the earliest political dialogues were harsh satires and parodies that were generally read and rarely performed, though their political stances may have varied. Just a few years after *Androboros,* a short discourse appeared in manuscript form. Dated 1732, the piece had a most unlikely place of origin – Massachusetts. Only recently rediscovered, the anonymous work sat in the archives of the Massachusetts Historical Society for decades before being uncovered by Robert E. Moody in 1980 and discussed in a brief note in the *Proceedings of the Massachusetts Historical Society.* His take was decidedly untheatrical, missing the significance of its existence to American theatre historians. Although untitled, the piece is often referred to as *Belcher the Apostate.* Later docketing on the last page indictates "Copy play wrote at Boston 1732." Like its predecessor, it is a harsh political satire. And moreover, it has a clear theatrical structure that distinguishes it from other dialogues. Though not quite as sophisticated as *Androboros,* the play nevertheless shows an author who was familiar with dialogue, dramatic development, characterization, and staging technique. It tells the story of Jonathan Belcher, a colonial merchant who rose within local political circles to become eventually the first colonial-born royal governor of Massachusetts. But unlike *Androboros*'s royalist line, this play is decidedly colonial in attitude. As the adopted title implies, Belcher was perceived by some as a turncoat, who claimed to be on the side of the colonials as he achieved increasing political stature, but once appointed governor, he became a staunch supporter of the crown and oppressive British colonial policies. There is little balance in the characterization, though his portrayal in the first act as a compassionate colonial advocate contrasts effectively with his sudden conversion to Whitehall's harsh policies after his appointment. The play also differs in tone. It lacks any substantial amount of humor, and the general effect hovers between polemic and melodrama. Its lack of songs and poems is also different, making it closer in form to the religious dialogues. Still, its innate theatricality separates it from the dry discourses of the Mathers and other Calvinvist writers. Its existence shows the extent to which drama influenced the literate colonial mind, and its very form this early in such a hostile colony as Massachusettes may be a sign in its own right. Writing political satire in dramatic dialogue not only thumbs a nose at the object of ridicule, it challenges the spiritual foundations of the colony. If we acknowledge, however, that theatre was not as evil an endeavor to the Puritans as previously thought, then its challenge might be only superficial.

Two other important dramatic documents, often overlooked, are Lewis Morris's "Dialogue Concerning Trade" composed in 1726 and "A Dialogue between a South and a North Countryman" written the following year. Morris wrote a number of poems and dialogues following his collaboration with Hunter. Apparently, *Androboros* was not the end of Morris' theatrical endeavors. His papers at Rutgers University contain the manuscripts of these two dialogues plus a collection of poems. A third dramatic piece, dated 1743, in the archives of the Philadelphia Library Company, may be a Morris composition, though its authenticity has not been proved. These short works are perhaps more typical of the political dialogue of the early eighteenth century. They lack most theatrical trappings and focus primarily on current political issues and arguments. Their purpose appears to be primarily informative and may have offered Morris an amusing method of laying out the debate in a literary format. Lacking scene and act divisions, like most dialogues, the first piece includes an unusual nine characters. Most of these characters provide a colorful introduction to the main action, which eventually revolves around an extended debate about intercolonial trade between a merchant and a countryman who are staying the night at a roadside inn.

Although "Dialogue Concerning Trade" may not be a producible play and is more important as an historical footnote to the political history of New Jersey, its dramatic elements distinguish it from other similar documents. The dialogue is occasionally lively, and the initial pages display an element of wit. Character development is poor to nonexistent, and, by the middle of the eighteen-page manuscript, the action is reduced to a lengthy debate between the two principle characters. Nonetheless, it has an underlying spark that is lacking in many other contemporary pieces. Whether through his friendship with Hunter or through a liberal education, Morris gained an appreciation of dramatic literature that is demonstrated in his writings. Examples like this indicate the subtle influence of drama on the early colonial mind and how it may have affected the rise of theatre and a theatrical sensibility later in the century.

Morris's other piece is less impressive. Though longer, a full forty pages, the dialogue is strictly limited to the two title characters and eventually settles into the north countryman lecturing the south countryman almost nonstop for twenty pages on the political manipulations within a fictional government chamber (presumably the New Jersey Assembly). Again, there is some wit and life to the dialogue, especially in the early pages, but this document was clearly not intended for theatrical production. Though later than his other work, it appears to be sheer political venting rather than a serious attempt at a viable piece of theatre. But, like his earlier work, it stands out as a clear example of the influence of drama on politicians and writers of early-eighteenth-century America.

Between 1715 and 1764, when *The Paxton Boys* was published, more than fifty dialogues were printed or disseminated in manuscript form within the North American colonies. Some were mere political or religious diatribes demonstrating little or no dramatic skill. Many were anonymously written, possibly passed from hand to hand, and a few were staged at college commencements or private readings. Nonetheless, drama on the whole was a consistent if not overwhelming form of literary expression. By midcentury, however, things began to change, and over the twenty-five years leading up to the American Revolution, the colonies saw a decided increase in theatrical writing. Much of the increase can be attributed to simple demographics. From 1720 to 1760 the population of the colonies more than tripled, from 474,000 to over 1.6 million; it nearly doubled again during the next decade. Some degree of cultural diversity alone may account for the larger number of people with theatrical inclinations, but that reveals only part of the story. The fuller picture shows a complex series of events, people, and influences that contributed to a greater interest in theatrical writing and performance.

Perhaps least recognized as a theatrical antecedent was the gradual liberalizing of printing laws that contributed to the concept of a free press and a movement against censorship. Although this may seem contrary to Calvinist principles on the surface, it is in fact entirely consistent with the Puritan concept of literacy stemming from a fundamental concern for a vernacular Bible accessible to all. Literacy was a basic tenet of Puritanism. From this tenet rose both a compelling need to express ideas in print and an equally compelling desire to censor them. By 1765 more than forty newspapers had been founded in the North American colonies, a number that remained fairly constant for the next twenty years. The rise parallels a similar growth in the English press, brought about in part by the deliberate termination in 1695 of the Stationers' Company monopoly on printing.

With the criminality of unauthorized printing eliminated, the publishing industry flourished during the early eighteenth century. Political satire became especially popular through the craft and wit of such brilliant writers as Swift, Pope, Steele, and Addison. Unfortunately, the English drama was not similarly affected by the change in law, with the notable exception of Henry Fielding, whose plays bitterly criticized the Walpole administration and led directly to the infamous Licensing Act of 1737. In the colonies, the influence was less evident, though some of the early dialogues and political discourses may be in part responses to the general liberalizing of the printing laws. Certainly the colonial press benefited from the change and its independence was reinforced by the aquittal in 1735 of New York newspaper editor John Peter Zenger, who had been charged ten months earlier by the governor of the colony, William Cosby, with seditious libel. By midcentury, American colonists were well aware of the power of a free and vibrant press.

Changes in the printing laws may have encouraged some American dramatists to venture out into the public eye. But receptive audiences were still hard to find. Ironically, this situation may have been partially remedied through a most unlikely influence. Hard on the heels of the Zenger trial was the arrival in 1738 of George Whitefield, the English Methodist evangelist, who brought the Great Awakening to the colonies as he toured from Georgia to New England, drawing throngs of followers to his revivalist sermons. Whitefield's charismatic style was characterized by many as theatrical, and indeed his meetings were as much theatre as they were theology, though such a comparison would have horrified him. Though it may be tenuous to argue that the Great Awakening and George Whitefield helped to create a theatrical audience in America, the connection is not unreasonable, and certainly his popularity coincides with the rise of a commercial theatre in the colonies.

A third influence stems from the changes in British colonial policy. As the North American colonies grew, Britain became increasingly concerned about maintaining them primarily as sources for raw materials, necessary to feed the growing industries at home. Independence was unthinkable. The North American colonies existed strictly to support British industrialization. Beginning with the Navigation Acts in the seventeenth century, British policy continued to refine and restrict what liberties the colonies could pursue. The British view of the colonies as mere suppliers of industrial material is embodied in the governing council that oversaw all colonial activities – the Board of Trade. Established originally as the Lords of Trade under William and Mary, the Board of Trade – as it eventually became known – was composed of a select number of Privy Council members and an equal number of wealthy London merchants. The Privy Council members rarely attended meetings and thus the entire responsibility of governing the American colonies fell to a clique of England's wealthiest merchants, whose explicit purpose was the encouragement and protection of trade, not the protection of individual and community rights. The efficacy and composition of the board varied from year to year, but by the middle of the eighteenth century, there was little doubt that the Board had lost some of its earlier thoroughness. At times it was little more than a rubber stamp and the colonial assemblies took full advantage. So too did colonial editors and writers, who regularly included criticisms of British policy in broadsides and dialogues.

But the mid-eighteenth century saw a flurry of political changes and new trading policies that helped spawn increased political writing. In 1750, Parliament passed the Iron Act, which was designed to restrict the growth of the iron-finishing industry in the colonies by banning the construction of steel furnaces, rolling mills, and the like. This had the effect of protecting the iron-finishing industry in England while ensuring the continued supply of American pig iron to British factories. Needless to say, the American iron manufacturers were not pleased, and the enactment of the new policy signaled worse things to come.

Indeed, the very next year, 1751, saw the passage of the Currency Act – a disastrous attempt to prevent the printing of paper money in the colonies. By regulating the monetary supply, Whitehall hoped to keep the colonies' manufacturing ambitions in check while controlling the flow of coined money. The combination of these two policy changes prompted early indications of the growing resentment against British rule. Had it not been for the simultaneous expansion of colonizers into the Ohio River Valley, west of the Appalachians, and the start of hostilities with the French, the issue might have escalated sooner. As it was, colonial attentions were quickly diverted to war.

Despite the rising conflict, settlements to the western reaches of British control continued unabated. As the demographic map of North America shifted westward, away from the cities on the eastern seaboard, and new immigrants arrived from Europe, theatre saw a new era of tolerance and experiment. It is perhaps not surprising that it was during the late 1740s and early 1750s that professional players first appeared on the scene, with the appearance of the Murray–Kean troupe out of Philadelphia in 1749, followed by the Hallams from London in 1752. Despite (or perhaps because of) the influence of Whitefield and the Great Awakening, these early performers made some headway in an otherwise hostile environment. Even the early years of the French and Indian War did little to slow the Hallams' initial tours, and though little original drama appeared, apart from the occasional collegiate exercise, these companies must have had an aesthetic influence on future dramatists.

At the same time, the 1750s saw the first successful effort to legally banish theatre. In 1750, Massachusetts passed legislation forbidding "the many and great mischiefs which arise from publick stage-plays, interludes and other theatrical entertainments, which . . . occassion great and unecessary expences, and discourage industry and frugality. . . ." The effort was not substantially different from earlier attempts, but its unique appeal to business-related issues and concern for the impeding of commerce may have been enough to sway the merchant-minded members of the Board of Trade. Indeed, the bill's preamble was copied vebatim twelve years later by the General Assembly of Rhode Island in its first succeessful anti-theatrical act. Clearly, the business of theatre was now viewed as a potential impediment to business in general, at least from a colonial standpoint, but such a view was not universal by any means. Efforts to ban theatre in Virginia in 1752 failed, as did initial attempts in New York (1752) and Pennsylvania (1753), though both colonies eventually passed antitheatrical legislation as political tensions rose in the years immediately preceding the American Revolution. It may be stretching the point to argue that such legislation had an influence on dramatic literature. On the surface it may seem odd that original playwriting did not accompany the arrival of professional players. However, neither the Murray–Kean company nor the Hallam troupe was especially interested in producing original work during this period. Their strategy was to appear as "English" (and thus professional) as possible, so naturally their repertory consisted of major London hits. Wisely, Douglass eventually changed this strategy after returning to the mainland from the West Indies in 1758 as head of the revamped Hallam company. Still, it would be another nine years before he attempted to stage an original piece.

Despite the lack of original drama, the 1750s continued the tradition of discourse and dialogue forged fifty years earlier. An average of one to two pieces a year are recorded, including a piece entitled "A Dialogue Between X, Y, and Z Concerning the Present State of Affairs in Pennsylvania" printed in *The Pennsylvania Gazette* in 1755 by Benjamin Franklin. The American appetite for dialogue and para-dramatic literature was unaffected by both the military conflict arising in the West and the continued popularity of the Great Awakening. Yet no traditional forms of drama appeared until well after the Treaty of Paris.

Meanwhile, the French in New Orleans were developing a substantial colony, complete with their own transplanted forms of theatrical entertainment. LeBlanc de Villeneuve, an officer with the French garrison, wrote two plays on American themes, neither of which survive. The first, *Le Père-Indien* (1753), provides one of the earliest known dramatic characterizations of native Americans in its heroic protrayal of the Choctaw Indians. He apparently followed this play with another Indian tragedy, entitled *Poucha-Houmma*. These two pieces comprise the known extent of original francophone dramatic literature in this remote colonial outpost. Like much of what was appearing in the British colonies, these plays appear to be isolated examples of intellectual exercise, most likely performed by amateur players for the amusement of a culturally elite audience. Whether this small collection qualifies as "American" drama may be a debatable issue for some, but it is undoubtedly as much a part of the colonial European cultural endeavor as any English-language dialogue produced thus far on the Atlantic seaboard. Moreover, the sympathetic portrayals of Native Americans remain an unsual legacy and stand in stark contrast to what would soon become the common misperception of the "red savage" onstage.

Although professional players appeared first, original dramatic literature does not appear until the era of relative economic instability following the French–Indian War. The entire perspective of the American colonies changes after 1763, evidenced by the appointment of William Petty, Lord Shelburne (head of the Board of Trade), to draw up a postwar plan for the exploitation of the newly acquired lands in North America. Though he would be replaced within a year, Shelburne's appointment indicates the high commercial value the British government continued to place on the colonies in the wake of the Seven Years' War. Ironically, despite victory, the British found themselves burdened with a significant postwar debt. As a result, their attitude toward the colonies changes profoundly. With the institution of the Sugar Act in the spring of 1764, the colonies cease to be a strictly commercial source for raw materials and instead are legislated into a revenue-generating resource for the financially strapped government in Whitehall. This change would have far-reaching consequences, not the least of which would lead to the American Revolution. Another consequence would be an increase in original dramatic literature. It is misleading, of course, to pronounce all drama from 1764 to the Revolution to be the result of oppressive British revenue policies. Some may simply reflect the steady increase in new immigrants and their taste for the theatrical traditions of home. Certainly, an important number of plays written at this time were more sophisticated versions of the earlier political dialogues, many with a clear vision of theatrical staging, intent on stirring political controversy.

Perhaps the culmination of the American political dialogue is found in *The Paxton Boys* (1764). This odd little farce satirizes in genuine theatrical style an actual event from the previous year. As an indirect consequence of the recently concluded war, a murderously hysterical mob of settlers from Paxton and Donegal, Pennsylvania, fearful of continued raids by hostile Indians along their western border and angry at the lack of adequate protection during Chief Pontiac's rebellion, attacked and killed a group of about twenty peaceful Conestoga Indians in Lancaster County. Governor Penn demanded their immediate arrest and prosecution, but local authorities, sympathetic to their cause, acquitted them. This emboldened a group of more than six hundred armed frontiersmen to mount a march in January 1764 to Philadelphia, demanding protection and additional representation in the colonial assembly. Their arrival in the capital city was greatly anticipated and feared by many. However, with the diplomatic intercession of Benjamin Franklin, a settlement was negotiated and the rebellion averted.

Nonetheless, the entire episode became fodder for more than one dramatic discourse, beginning with an anonymous piece entitled "A Dialogue Between Andrew Trueman, and Thomas Zealot; About the Killing the Indians at Cannestogoe and Lancaster," with two editions published in 1764. This was followed the same year by a more detailed account with a harsh attack on sympathizers in "A Dialogue Containing Some Reflections on the Late Declaration and Remonstrance, on the Back-Inhabitants of Pennsylvania. With a Serious and Short Address, to Those Presbyterians, Who (To Their Dishonor)

Have Too Much Abettted, And Conniv'd at the Late Insurrection. By a Member of That Community." *The Paxton Boys* was just a more cleverly written extension of these critiques, exploiting a rather uncomfortable levity given the seriousness of the actual events. What distinguishes these pieces is the readiness with which they criticize colonial policy and the boldness of their rhetoric. The correlation between these pieces and the colonial anger over the recent Sugar Act bears consideration. In the final analysis, they may not have been directly influenced by British revenue schemes, but they mark a period of increasingly hostile writing against the British government that continues through the Revolution.

The Prince of Parthia

Spanning this period is a curious piece with multiple distinctions, Thomas Godfrey's *The Prince of Parthia* (1759). It is acknowledged by most historians as the first American tragedy and by others as the first play written by an American-born author to be performed in America by professional players. Its historical distinctions may outweigh its literary significance, however. Godfrey was a student of William Smith at the College of Philadelphia and had served briefly in the Pennsylvania militia during the campaign at Fort Duquesne, 1758–59. Godfrey's exposure to drama is, of course, attributed to Smith. And the influence of Smith's collegiate exercises is clearly evident in Godfrey's work. Though written in 1759, about the time Godfrey moved to Wilmington, North Carolina, the play was not produced until 1767, when Douglass, looking to find a suitable American piece to satisfy the chauvinist element in his Philadelphia audience, substituted Godfrey's work at the last minute for another American play deemed unsuitable for performance, *The Disappointment* by Thomas Forrest. Godfrey, who was only twenty-six when he died of a fever in 1763, had sent his play to Smith four years earlier, hoping to have it produced in Philadelphia. As a tribute to his friend and classmate, Nathaniel Evans collected Godfrey's works, consisting of assorted poems and the play, into a volume, which was published posthumously in 1765. How Douglass came to discover the play is unclear, though Smith may have been responsible.

Most critics agree that the play is an awkward effort. The five-act tragedy, written in archaic verse, is nominally an historic piece that tells the story of the treason and treachery within the royal family of Parthia, sometime during the early years of the Roman empire. Godfrey has borrowed liberally from Shakespeare for both plot and poetry, while infusing sentimental ideals and middle-class morality from Restoration and eighteenth-century models. Some have argued that the play's criticism of absolute monarchy as potentially

abusive is actually an indication of colonial sentiments toward British policies. Certainly, there are critics who see proto-revolutionary ideals embedded
in the turgid dialogue. However, such a theme is not unusual in post-Eliza-
bethan literature. Governments on both sides of the Atlantic were perenially
concerned about the misuse of royal power in the wake of Louis XIV and the
Puritan Interregnum. But American colonists in the late 1750s, when Godfrey
composed the play, were unlikely to criticize a monarch who at the time was
winning a crucial war against France. After 1763, however, opinions quickly
changed, so although Godfrey's view of his work as a subtle warning against
the potential abuses of a Georgian monarchy is unclear, Douglass, in the
unsettled atmosphere following the Sugar and Navigation Acts, may well have
seen the play for its political possibilities. In either case, the production was
unsuccessful. It was withdrawn after only one performance, and Douglass
never staged it again. Sadly, Godfrey's untimely death may have deprived the
North American colonies of their first substantial playwright.

By contrast, Forrest's *The Disappointment,* published in 1767 under the
pseudonym "Andrew Barton," is a far more interesting piece, satirizing the
fractious political squabbling in Philadelphia during the early years of the
anti-importation movement. Had it not been for Douglass's last-minute substitution, its place in American theatre history might be more visible. As it is, its
reputation is limited to being America's first ballad-opera – though it also
includes what many believe to be the earliest stage "Irishman" and "Negro" in
dialect. It was also the play that first introduced American audiences to the
tune "Yankee Doodle." Again, by most standards, the piece is simple and
basic, utilizing popular tunes in a fashion already perfected on London stages
years earlier. But as an American "first," it is an eminently producible work
that comes across as a light and enjoyable romp.

Pre-Revolutionary Drama

The years leading up to and during the American Revolution saw a remarkable flurry of dramatic activity, despite some serious restrictions placed on
the theatre, both real and perceived. The effects of the anti-importation
movement lasted well into the early 1770s, creating added resentment
against a form of cultural expression that was already considered elitist and
papist by many in the North American colonies. The occasional success of
the colonial legislatures in passing genuine and effective anti-theatrical laws
in the footsteps of the 1750 Massachusetts act furthered the legal difficulties
confronted by potential playwrights and their producers. By the fall of 1774,
when the Continental Congress passed its series of economic resolutions in
response to the highly unpopular Coersive Acts, including a call to restrict all

"exhibitions of shews, plays, and other expensive diversions and entertainments," the die was cast, and most professional entertainment ceased in the North American colonies. Yet the writing of plays seemed unaffected. In fact, the number of dramas written and published increased as war approached. As one would expect, many were political satires, arguing both for and against the rising tide of American independence, reflecting the long-standing traditions established almost seventy-five years earlier of dialogue and discourse as public commentary. But this later collection was generally bolder in both political content and – perhaps more significantly – aesthetic endeavor. The plays of the 1770s and early 1780s show a marked improvement in dramatic control and stage worthiness, as well as a certain political fearlessness.

But, significantly, one of the most important pieces written in the 1770s had nothing to do with the growing political and military conflict. The great Congregationalist writer and thinker Samuel Hopkinson published "A Dialogue Concerning the Slavery of the Africans" (1776). Inspired by the abolitionist arguments of Whitefield and John Wesley, Calvininst denominations in the colonies began earnestly projecting biblical foundations for their cause. Hopkinson's work places the new debate squarely on the traditional Calvinist doctrine of predestination – that they were the chosen people. Slavery, he argues, violates America's sacred covenant with God. Although not the first salvo fired in the battle for emancipation, Hopkinson's writing served to inspire many to the abolitionist cause, even in the face of more immediate events.

Pamphleteers and propagandists from both sides produced dialogues during the 1770s outlining their divergent points of view. Among those siding with the colonists, Thomas Paine's work is notable. Keeping up the tradition of discourse writing begun by Hunter and Morris, Paine created two dramatic pieces that helped articulate the patriots' position. Less than a year after emigrating to the colonies, Paine published "A Dialogue Between General Wolfe and General Gage in a Wood Near Boston." The piece appeared 4 January 1775 in the *Pennsylvania Journal,* a publication long associated with radical colonial politics. Though several topics are discussed in this hypothetical meeting between Wolfe (the British general whose defeat of Montcalm at Quebec City in 1759 signaled the end of French and Indian War) and Gage (the newly appointed governor of Massachusetts), the thrust of the work is an attack on the Quebec Act of 1774, which effectively cut westward expansion by the New England colonies. The imagery of these two generals discussing the fate of the English colonies was an obvious symbol to colonial radicals, though not as relentless as his following piece two years later, "A Dialogue Between the Ghost of General Montgomery, Just Arrived from the Elysian Fields, and an American Delegate, in a Wood near Philadelphia." By then, of course, he was gaining widespread renown for his political essay *Common Sense,* in which he urged his fellow colonists to declare their independence from Britain. Neither dialogue can be considered a viable play. Like many of the earlier examples, these two works are pure propaganda, written in the familiar form of a political discourse and intended for reading only. Any suggestion that these were dramatic plays obscures their importance not just as historical documents but as barometers of the rising opposition to British occupation. The fact that both dialogues straddle the publication of *Common Sense* prevails upon an evaluation of Paine's progress as an articulator of colonial unrest. Clearly, his resolve has been hardened by the publication of his second dialogue. Its uncompromising stance on British policy seals its author as a leader of the colonial opposition. But as a contributor to American drama, Paine remains as marginal as his predecessors.

Perhaps more germane to the discourse tradition of the early eighteenth century is the handful of loyalist works that began to appear in the months immediately preceding the Revolution. Like the early colonial pieces they are satirical and anonymously written. They were intended for a reading audience and copies certainly circulated among leading loyalists in New York and Boston. A telling aspect is that, unlike the patriot pieces, none of these Tory dialogues were published in newspapers. Instead, they were printed and distributed privately, much like the earliest dialogues a half-century before. "A Dialogue Between a Southern Delegate and His Spouse on His Return from the Grand Continental Congress" (1774) is an obvious satire on the effectiveness and legitimacy of the First Continental Congress, which had just met in Philadelphia. The action takes the form of an argument between a husband and wife, using the metaphor of marriage as a symbol of the divisiveness, both real and potential, that threatens the security of British North America. Typically, the work lacks substantial theatricality, and its characters are flat and uninteresting. Though its attempt at farce is reminiscent of *Androboros,* it is not enough to hold it together as a work of dramatic literature.

Similarly, "Debates at the Robin-Hood Society in the City of New York on Monday Night 19th of July, 1774" attempts to mollify the large Tory population in New York through an especially vicious portrayal of the patriot movement and its supporters. The significance of the date in the title is unknown, though it may signify New York's response to the series of legislative actions taken by Parliament in an effort to curtail colonial restlessness, including the Quebec Act, the Boston Port Act, and an amendment to the 1765 Quartering Act, all enacted between 20 May and 2 June 1774. Certainly, the content of the piece alludes to the agitated state of the New York Whigs, and it is reasonable to conclude that such actions were a motivating force behind the dialogue. Its allegorical characters and political lampooning are straight from the earlier part of the century.

Ironically, Boston is the publication site of what must be considered the most dramatic of all the Tory inspired dialogues of this period. *The Americans Roused in a Cure for the Spleen; or, Amusement for a Winter's Evening* (1775) was probably written by Jonathan Sewall, and as expected it proffers a negative view of the colonial position while setting forth a most reasoned argument in favor of British interests. The multiple-character play provides some insight into early American caricatures and may be a forerunner of the stereotypes more typical of the Federalist and Jacksonian periods.

Mercy Otis Warren

Undoubtedly, the most important dramatist of the age was a woman, Mercy Otis Warren. Of all the colonial American playwrights, the influence and importance of Warren on the development of American dramatic literature cannot be overemphasized. Her work over a relatively brief period of seven years established a new level of quality, intelligence, and dramatic insight that would set a new standard for subsequent writers. Between 1772 and 1779, she produced a collection of dramatic work unparalleled at that time in the colonies, notable not just for its prolificness but for its political boldness, aesthetic maturity, and dramatic durability. The consistently high quality of her work as well as the unusual breadth of her interests distinguish Warren as one of America's greatest writers of the eighteenth century.

Warren's first effort was a blank-verse tragedy in five acts entitled *The Adulateur* (1772). Taking a cue from earlier political farces, the author inserts thinly veiled characterizations of actual people in an equally transparent setting. In essence, the play is a call to arms in the aftermath of the Boston Massacre. Warren uses Samuel Adams (Cassius) and her brother, James Otis (Brutus), as patriot leaders who attempt to incite their fellow citizens to rebel against the bloody tyranny of the brutal dictator, Rapatio (Gov. Thomas Hutchinson of Massachusetts). Its abrupt and inconclusive ending is interpreted by some as a literary weakness. But in its own day, the effect may have signaled unresolved political or military action and the implication that the worst was yet to come.

Her next play, *The Defeat,* published the following year, gets slight attention from most drama historians largely because it lacks the cohesiveness of her first work. The abbreviated discourse may be merely an extension of her first play, in which peace is restored and Rapatio is finally brought down to face execution. Needless to say, the work reflects the crumbling political situation in Boston but is notable for its articulation of the contempt rebellious colonials had for British authority.

Warren's most celebrated play, *The Group,* appeared in 1775. Here she abandons her clumsy blank verse and turgid tragic themes and embarks on a two-act farcical romp that clearly tops all earlier dramatic efforts in British North America. Once again the echoes of Hunter and Lewis's *Androboros* can be discerned in the blasting of political scandal and intrigue. Her characters evoke the social and political parodies of R. B. Sheridan with names like Humbug, Hateall, Spendall, and Beau Trumps – each one, of course, based on actual people in contemporary Boston politics. Her effort is to ridicule the imposition of martial law by Governor Gage and the abrogation of the colonial charter earlier that year (following the battles of Lexington and Concord), when the governor's elected council was replaced by royal appointees. Though still criticized for its dramatic naïveté and awkward dialogue, most acknowledge this work as the pinnacle of colonial drama.

The authorship of Warren's next piece, *The Blockheads; or, The Affighted Officers* (1776), has been a source of some debate. Although recent scholarship proves that Warren did indeed pen this three-act farce, many argued that its crude language and scatological references were inconsistent with a female author. The play, published as a pamphlet, is the first to deal directly with an event from the Revolutionary War – the patriots' successful occupation of Dorchester Heights overlooking Boston Harbor. In this piece, Warren delivers a scathing attack on the British occupying forces and their Tory sympathizers while concluding with a rousing patriotic display for the victorious forces. The play never reaches the dramatic levels of its predecessor, but as political satire, it hits the mark.

By 1779, Warren's interest in drama as a medium for political expression appeared to be waning. Nonetheless, a published one-act farce, *The Motley Assembly,* possibly also a Warren effort, attacks the hypocrisy of patriots who verbally support the colonial war effort while enjoying the luxuries of British culture. Again, there are those who have challenged the play's authorship, citing its occasional coarse language as proof that Warren was not the author. As several historians note, the play reflects the winding down of the war and the new focus on defining a distinctly American culture. It is a theme that pervades American dramatic literature to this day.

Warren ceased writing plays until the late 1780s, when she constructed her last two dramatic efforts, *The Sack of Rome* and *The Ladies of Castille.* Though both plays were published in 1790, *The Sack of Rome* was probably written in 1787, when the author made a failed attempt to have the work produced in London. Neither tragedy received much attention, owing to their stilted verse and tired themes. Nevertheless, they mark the conclusion of a singular career in American drama. Warren, of course, did not retire from writing altogether. She continued to publish poetry, and in 1805 she produced one of the early histories of the war, the three-volume *History of the Rise, Progress and Termination of the American Revolution.*

Other Revolutionary Efforts

Warren was not the only writer to dramatize the rising conflict. A number of playwrights presented a variety of dramatic works during the war years. Among the leading patriot writers, Hugh Henry Brackenridge, John Leacock, and Robert Munford are most frequently mentioned – each building on the political satire and social farce that had become an American standard.

Hugh Henry Brackenridge was a prolific writer, having published numerous stories and poems. He also wrote *Modern Chivalry* (1792), the satiric novel for which he is best remembered. His contribution to drama is limited to two plays, *The Battle of Bunker's-Hill* (1776) and *The Death of General Montgomery in Storming the City of Quebec* (1777). What distinguishes these pieces is the effort to create relatively accurate historical dramas, rather than the usual political diatribe or farce. Both are based on actual events, as their titles suggest, and are constructed in blank verse. Though simplistic, the characters display a sincerity and dignity unique to colonial American drama. The first play was apparently produced at the Maryland Academy while Brackenridge was on the faculty; the second has no record of production, having been written while the author was serving in the Continental Army. Despite showing patriotic losses, the plays articulate the colonial cause – too much perhaps. Both have been criticized for lack of direct action. Each relies heavily on narrative with virtually all activity happening off-stage. The declamatory nature of the dialogue makes performance difficult, while the stage directions are sometimes utterly impossible. Yet, Brackenridge's contribution is another step toward a viable professional drama in America and enriches the scope of an innate dramatic literature.

Another major step was taken in 1776 with the publication in Philadelphia of John (or Joseph) Leacock's *The Fall of British Tyranny; or, American Liberty Triumphant.* This five-act extravaganza, which spans two continents, contains twenty-five scenes and an unusually large cast. It is also the first play to depict George Washington. In a series of loosely connected episodes, Leacock firmly places the blame for the Revolution on Parliament. Thus, his play opens with a parliamentary debate between Lord Paramount (Earl of Bute), who argues for stronger restrictions against the colonies, and Lord Wisdom (William Pitt), who predictably takes the other side, posing the colonial point of view and suggesting a conciliatory posture. The rest of the play moves from scene to scene in North America, detailing the early events of the war and the colonial resentment toward British oppression. The play concludes on a patriotic note as General Washington resolves to fight on despite an uncertain outcome. The heroic and episodic tone reveals Leacock's familiarity with the chronicle play, whereas the farcical dialogue indicates his connection with earlier political discourses. Despite its many weaknesses, the play remains one of the most ambitious works in early American drama.

Departing from the usual revolutionary rhetoric, Robert Munford, a Virginia farmer educated in England, crafted two comedies in the 1770s worth noting. *The Candidates; or, The Humours of a Virginia Election* (c. 1771) takes a critical look at the rudimentary democratic process involved in selecting members to the House of Burgesses. Rife with genuine comedy, wit, and slapstick, the play takes a somewhat equivocal stand on the effectivenesss of democratic government by exposing the corruption inherent in the system. Neither condoning nor condemning democracy, Munford seems to remain above the fray, allowing his characters to battle it out among themselves and letting the story unfold unencumbered. It is a distinctly mature example of playwriting from an American perspective. Similarly, his other play, *The Patriots* (1776), reveals the apostasy and hypocrisy of colonial patriotism. Munford uses the play to admonish his contemporaries against overzealousness and false patriotic behavior. Perhaps in anticipation of a British defeat and a new nation's reliance upon an old adversary, Munford condemns the pursuit of too harsh a victory. Despite having served as a soldier in the patriot cause, he espouses a measured pacifism. The humane equanimity of Munford's plays is itself a distinguishing factor when compared to the rest of colonial America's dramatic output. Yet the likelihood is that Munford was actually reflecting the benign neutrality the majority of colonials felt at the time. Though never performed on stage, both plays were eventually published in 1798.

Post-Revolutionary Drama

The years immediately following the Treaty of Paris saw a marked decline in original dramatic literature. There are many reasons – political, religious, and cultural – that may account for this unusual dearth. But one element not often discussed in histories of American drama was the economic chaos that affected all aspects of early American life from 1781 until 1789. Beginning with the victory at Yorktown and extending through 1785, spending grew uncontrollably. Americans, who had long suffered from a lack of currency under the British, were now exploiting their newfound financial freedom. However, the excitement resulted in states printing excess currency, which inevitably led to devaluation. By the end of 1785, the new nation was fully involved in its first great economic depression. States exerted almost exclusive and sovereign control of their affairs, leaving a weak federal government that had little authority over what was in essence a loosely formed confederation rather than a tightly managed centralized republic. Devaluation of the currency, coupled with unregulated profiteering and economic overexpansion, brought the nation's economy to a near halt. Such conditions did not bode well for theatre.

Even with the return of Douglass's company from the Caribbean, the pressure to make a profit required the playing of traditionally lucrative plays. New, untried works were generally ignored. As a result, what survives from this brief dark age is an odd assortment of amateurish endeavors that provide little insight into the era and probably deserve the scant attention they have received from most historians. Plays like Barnabas Bidwell's *The Mercenary Match* (1784), Peter Markoe's *The Patriot Chief* (1784), Samuel Low's *The Politician Outwitted* (1788), and *The Better Sort*, anonymously written in 1789, are really significant only in that they maintain the literary continuum. To say they represent a bridge between the earlier political farces and the more mature professional writing at the end of the century is misleading, for though they each may have been influenced by earlier works, little evidence of such influence exists. Certainly, their inconsistent literary quality provides no evidence of substantial progress toward dramatic excellence. Bidwell's piece, written while the author was a student at Yale, may be considered a refinement of the college commencement discourse; similarly, Markoe's poetic tragedy may be seen as a successor to *The Prince of Parthia* and Low's farce a continuation of *Androboros* and the writings of Warren. However, none made a lasting impression on American drama.

Royall Tyler

One play from this period did, however, leave a lasting impression – Royall Tyler's *The Contrast* (1787). Often mislabeled "America's first play," its importance has been exaggerated on occasion. Judging by its primacy among anthologies of early American drama, one can see why it has such a reputation. Tyler was born into a prominent Boston family. His father accumulated a modest fortune as a merchant and gained a respected political reputation as a member of the King's council. Appropriately, his son received the best education available to a Bostonian, earning a bachelor's degree from Harvard in 1776. After serving briefly in the colonial military under the command of John Hancock, Tyler received a master's from Harvard and was admitted to the Massachusetts Bar in 1780. Obviously, he was a man of considerable intellectual talent with connections at the highest levels of New England society. He served with distinction as state's attorney for seven years followed by six years as a justice on the Vermont Supreme Court. But it was a brief trip to New York City in the spring of 1787, where he was introduced to the performances of the American Company and the comic talents of Thomas Wignell, that led him to try his hand at dramatic composition. In less than a month he created his first play, *The Contrast*, most likely a direct result of his exposure

Frontispiece to Royall Tyler's *The Contrast;* engraved by William Dunlap. Thomas Wignell as the Yankee Jonathan is pictured at center. Don B. Wilmeth Collection.

to Sheridan's *The School for Scandal*, which was performed during the season. It was immediately picked by the American Company and successfully staged in April, making it the first comedy by a native-born American to be professionally produced.

As critics point out, *The Contrast* resembles Sheridan's work in a number of ways. It is a skillfully crafted five-act comedy containing great wit, amusing characters, and clever action. Tyler easily adopts the techniques of Sheridan's comedy of manners to produce a nationalistic play that juxtaposes the innate decency of American society with the corrupting influence of the British, hence the title. Tyler introduces two important characters to American literature – the effete, British-bred, Sheridanesque fop Billy Dimple and Jonathan, the "true born Yankee American son of liberty." Most of the action concerns the amorous machinations of Dimple and the play's earnest hero Colonel Manly. Charlotte, Manly's sister, and her friends, Maria and Letitia, are courted simultaneously by Dimple, who is eventually exposed and humiliated. Meanwhile, Jonathan, Manly's servant, gets involved in a parallel subplot with Jenny, a maid in the Van Rough household, and Jessamy, manservant to Dimple. Tyler uses the subplot most effectively to express the basic goodness inherent in American culture through the common sense and rural humanity of Jonathan's naive but well-intentioned character. The Jonathan character is one that would be repeated many times and in many forms over the next century, and it remains Tyler's greatest contribution to American drama.

Tyler's other plays are much less noteworthy but indicate that his dramatic avocation was more than just a passing fancy. A month after his triumphant premiere with *The Contrast*, Tyler saw his comic opera, *May-Day in Town; or, New York in an Uproar*, also performed at the John Street Theatre with great success. Almost ten years passed before he produced another play, an adaptation of J. P. Kemble's comedy by the same name, *The Farm House; or, The Female Duellists*. Although some doubt exists, it appears it was Tyler's play that was performed at the Boston Theatre that same year. Other works by Tyler include *A Georgia Spec; or, Land in the Moon*, a three-act comedy first performed at the Haymarket Theatre, Boston, in 1797, and another adaptation, *The Doctor in Spite of Himself*, based on Molière. Tyler also left four additional plays in manuscript form, a three-act farce entitled *The Island of Barrataria* and a trilogy of biblical dramas, *The Judgement of Solomon, The Origin of the Feast of Purim*, and *Joseph and His Brethren*. There is no record of these plays having been produced.

By 1790, the depression of 1785–86 had run its course. With the election of Washington as president and the creation of a central bank to pay off the accumulated war debt, the new nation experienced its first period of political stability and moderate economic growth. With this new security, the country saw a relaxation of its harsh antitheatrical laws. And with the easing of currency troubles, cultural luxuries, like theatre, experienced a new era of popularity and prosperity. There also began an attempt to define and extol a national identity – to discover just what America was. One of the first to do so was William Dunlap, renowned as artist, playwright, historian, novelist, and theatre manager.

William Dunlap

Often referred to by the patronizingly patriarchal title "father of American drama," Dunlap was a major cultural figure in Federalist America. Trained as a painter in London, the New Jersey-born artist soon discovered the wonder of theatre and quickly turned his attentions to the writing of plays. He wrote his first play, *The Modest Soldier; or, Love in New York,* in 1787 after returning from his London studies. Although he submitted the comedy to Hallam and Henry of the American Company, it was never produced. He persisted, nevertheless, and over the next forty years, Dunlap wrote, adapted, and translated nearly sixty plays for the professional stage. As America's first professional playwright, the significance of his work to the development of American theatre cannot be overestimated. Unfortunately, the scope of his contribution is too vast to be condensed into a single chapter.

Dunlap's first professional success came in 1789 with *The Father; or, American Shandyism.* It was produced at the John Street Theatre by John Henry and the American Company and was an immediate hit. Taking advantage of his sudden popularity, he wrote another original play that year, a short farce entitled *Darby's Return.* It too was professionally staged, and Dunlap was now an established playwright of some note. By the end of 1789, he had also translated August von Kotzebue's *Menschenhass und Reue* into *The Stranger,* a sentimental melodrama. Like his first two offerings, this too was a success, and Dunlap soon became the premiere translator and producer of Kotzebue's plays in America. He continued a steady stream of theatrical works, including *The Fatal Deception; or, the Progress of Guilt* (1794), *Fontainville Abbey* (1795), *The Archers; or, the Mountaineers of Switzerland* (1796), *The Italian Father* (1799), *Abaellino, the Great Bandit* (1801), *Yankee Chronology* (1812), and *A Trip to Niagara; or, Travellers in America* (1828). But his best-known play was a tragedy entitled *André* (1798), based on an actual event from the Revolutionary War. In the fall of 1780 the Continental Army hanged a British spy, Major John André, for his participation in the conspiracy to surrender West Point to the English forces under Sir Henry Clinton. Dunlap used this incident to explore the complexities of America's relationship with England by questioning the morality of the execution and the conflicting passions surrounding the efforts to prevent it. Though it is now considered one of the best plays of the early American stage, *André* was not so popular with its original audience. The very ambiguity that Dunlap effectively uses to illustrate the contradictory feelings that characterized the American attitude toward its recent foe was what the audience found most unsettling. Perhaps it was too soon after the war for a sympathetic portrayal of a British spy, or maybe Dunlap hit too close to home in a city that had recently been the center of loyalist sympathies.

Dunlap's early successes precipitated the first major movement toward native-born American playwrights. The 1790s saw a flurry of original American plays produced by major professional companies from Boston to Charleston. John Murdock, a barber-turned-playwright from Philadelphia, scored a hit with his first play, a comedy of manners entitled *The Triumphs of Love; or, Happy Reconciliation* (1795), which satirized Philadelphia society and popular customs. He followed it up with a political satire in 1798, called *The Politicians; or, a State of Things,* a farcical lampoon aimed at the controversial commercial agreement with Great Britain known as Jay's Treaty and signed in 1795. Other successful playwrights who helped define this era include John Beete of Charleston, who wrote *The Man of the Times; or, a Scarcity of Cash* (1797), William Brown of Boston, author of *West Point Preserved* (1797), and David Everett, whose historical play, *Daranzel; or, the Persian Patriot* (1798) was produced at Boston's Haymarket Theatre.

Murray and Rowson

Equally notable are two women playwrights who furthered the dramaturgical efforts initiated by Mercy Otis Warren. Judith Sargent Murray, who like Warren was from Boston, wrote two plays that received professional productions. *Virtue Triumphant* (1795) is a light domestic drama that presents a female character of uncommon resolve who firmly negotiates her marriage contract to her own satisfaction. Her second play, *The Traveller Returned,* staged at the Federal Street Theatre in 1796, employs the well-worn theme of the attempts to reconcile long-lost siblings before they marry. But in its structure and language it is recognized as an important advance in American literature.

English-born Susanna Haswell Rowson generally gets more attention from theatre historians than Murray, primarily because of the reputation of her lone surviving work, *Slaves in Algiers; or, a Struggle for Freedom* (1794). The drama played on the nationalist passions inflamed by a series of attacks on American merchant ships in the Mediterranean by Algerian pirates during the early 1790s. The horrors of these raids along the Barbary Coast made for exciting copy in the press. Undoubtedly, Rowson saw an opportunity to exploit a contemporary news item for dramatic effect. The play was first performed at the Chestnut Street Theatre in Philadelphia ten months before the United States signed a treaty with the Dey of Algiers agreeing to pay tribute to halt the attacks. Whether Rowson's play had any effect on the treaty is not known, but it proved a timely piece of political theatre. Sadly, only titles remain of her other works, which include *The Female Patriot* (1795), *The Volunteers* (1795), and *Americans in England* (1797).

John D. Burk

By the end of the century, the Federalists' hold on power was quickly slipping away under the administration of John Adams. In an attempt to control damaging partisan rhetoric and maintain power, the Federalists passed the Alien and Sedition acts in 1798. In essence, these acts put an immediate halt to all political opposition. Their passage had a chilling effect on freedom of speech and was reflected in the publication industry as well as in the literary arts. One of the few people to be prosecuted under the new laws was an Irish immigrant named John Daly Burk. Burk arrived in Boston in 1796 after having been expelled from Trinity College in Dublin. Pursuing his interest in journalism, he quickly developed a reputation for being both contentious and outspoken. Burk also displayed a fondness for drama, and in February 1797 his first play, *Bunker-Hill; or, the Death of General Warren,* opened at Boston's Haymarket Theatre. Despite generally miserable reviews, the play was revived numerous times and became a popular spectacle at Fourth of July celebrations. It received widespread fame for its climactic battle scene and heroic portrayals of American patriots. Burk's next play, produced the following year at New York's Park Theatre, did not fare as well. *Female Patriotism; or, the Death of Joan d'Arc* uses the famous event as a symbol of universal liberty and patriotic resolve. Lacking the spectacle of his first work, the play quickly disappeared, and, coincidentally, so did the playwright. Earlier in the year, Burk left Boston for New York to edit a newspaper, *Time-Piece.* While serving in this post, he was arrested for violating the sedition law of 1798, putting a temporary end to his theatrical career. With the repeal of the Alien and Sedition laws in 1802, Burk eventually ended up in Virginia, where he wrote at least one other drama, *Bethlam Gabor, Lord of Translyvania; or, the Man-Hating Palatine* (published in 1807). It is likely the play was produced as early as 1803 by an amateur company in Petersburg and again a few years later at the Richmond Theatre. The year after its publication Burk was killed in a duel.

Conclusion

Historians have a natural inclination to proclaim "firsts," and there are certainly many "firsts" in American drama before 1800 ("the first play produced," "the earliest extant play published," "the first comedy/tragedy by a native-born American," etc.). But counting these as "firsts" implies a pattern. That these firsts are somehow connected, related, or interdependent is misleading. Most are isolated occurrences that measure more subtle influences. They are symptomatic rather than progressional. They are indicators of a culture's depth and beliefs rather than direct references to linear and deliberate development. Yet from these odd and curious efforts we can begin to discern the future direction of theatre and more particularly American attitudes toward theatrical performance and dramatic literature. Contained within these earliest plays are the seeds of a distinct American aesthetic, founded on an aristocratic aesthetic, tempered by Puritan values, and driven by the commercial necessities of English mercantilism.

Bibliography: Plays and Playwrights to 1800

Published works on American drama before 1800 are rare. Most of what is available is contained in studies either devoted to the entire spectrum of American drama, from the colonial era to the present, or is integrated into generalized surveys of theatre history. Apart from the odd article or book, there has been little sustained publication on the topic and almost no extensive examinations of either a critical or historical nature. The lack of detailed research has led to the perpetuation of inaccuracies and a general failure to contextualize the material beyond the scope of theatre history.

In contrast, recent histories of colonial America abound and are revitalizing the narrative form through postcolonial examinations and forays into the realm of new historicism. At the same time, many of the older works have retained their validity and still serve as a basis for much of the current work in colonial life and American Puritanism. Perry Miller's writings, though increasingly vilified for their positivism and reductivist logic, remain crucial reading for anyone interested in colonial American culture and Puritanism. *The New England Mind* (1961) is perhaps his best-known work and serves as a vital introduction to the topic. Equally important as classic sources are Wright's *The Cultural Life of the American Colonies, 1607–1763,* Rutman's *American Puritanism,* Bailyn's *The New England Merchants in the Seventeenth Century* (as well as his *The Ideological Origins of the American Revolution*), and Hofstadter's *America at 1750.*

But arguably the greatest contributor to the cultural history of colonial America is Carl Bridenbaugh, who wrote two essential studies that still dominate the field: *Cities in the Wilderness* (1938) and *Cities in Revolt* (1955), which, combined, cover the years 1625 to 1776.

Among the more recent studies, Breen examines the transplantation of English customs in the New World in *Puritans and Adventurers.* He also articulates the growing anti-importation movement within a colonial cultural context in "Baubles of Britain." The foundations of a Puritan-American identity are traced by Bercovitch in *The Puritan Origins of the American Self.* The complexities of colonial demographics are brilliantly illuminated in Fischer's exhaustive and fascinating study, *Albion's Seed.* Ruland and Bradbury have co-authored an excellent critical overview of American literature that includes, in the first five chapters of *From Puritanism to Postmodernism,* an assessment of early American Puritan aesthetics and the drive toward a national identity. Another useful recent survey is volume one (1590–1820) of *The Cambridge History of American Literature* (edited by Bercovitch).

No published study deals exclusively with American drama before 1800, though Meserve's *An Emerging Entertainment* comes the closest. As praiseworthy as this work remains, its lack of a comprehensive index makes it difficult to use for reference purposes. Nevertheless, there has never been a work on early American drama as exhaustively researched as this and it continues to be a crucial study. Its only rival is Quinn's venerated study, *A History of the American Drama from the Beginning to the Civil War* (1943). As the first part of a two-volume set, it was the standard text in early American drama for much of this century. As such, however, it suffers from its dated historiography and critical methodology. For a short and quick overview (200 pages), Vaughn's *Early American Dramatists* gives a brief survey of the early highlights and is a good introduction. Equally useful is Meserve's *An Outline History of American Drama*. More recently, Richardson's *American Drama from the Colonial Period Through World War I,* though necessarily selective, provides more contemporary assessments of important American plays and covers a broader historical range beginning with the seventeenth century. Another standard in the field is *The Revels History of Drama in English* (Vol. VIII), edited by Bogard, Moody, and Meserve. Some details of early playwriting can be found in Rankin's classic study, *The Theatre of Colonial America.*

Two other useful resources, recently published, include Bryan's *American Theatrical Regulation, 1607–1900,* and *The Dawning of American Drama: American Dramatic Criticism, 1746–1915,* compiled and edited by Wolter. Both provide vital primary materials in accessible and indexed volumes. Aspects and Revolutionary War drama can be gleaned from Silverman's *A Cultural History of the American Revolution,* Winton's "The Theatre and Drama," and Jared Brown's *The Theatre in America during the Revolution.*

The rare but important studies of individual colonial playwrights include Canary's *William Dunlap,* Baine's *Robert Munford,* the Carsons' *Royall Tyler,* and Zagari's *A Woman's Dilemma* on Mercy Warren.

Also hard to come by are anthologies. Most are dated, and none focuses exclusively on dramas before 1800. The best include *America's Lost Plays,* Moody's *Dramas from the American Theatre,* Philbrick's *Trumpets Sounding,* and Quinn's *Representative American Plays.* A welcome addition to this group is *Plays by Early American Women, 1775–1850,* edited by Kritzer. In addition to containing plays by Warren, Rowson, and Murray, it offers a good introduction and an extensive bibliography.

Plays and Playwrights: 1800–1865

Gary A. Richardson

Introduction

For those living during the transition, more than a new century seemed to dawn with the year 1801. Twelve years of centralizing, pro-British Federalist government was giving way to a new era. The ascendant Democrat-Republicans promised a reorienting of the nation's political, economic, social, and cultural agendas. But despite Federalist fears of a wholesale dismantling of federal power and an embracing of radical French republicanism, the new cast of political leaders, epitomized by Thomas Jefferson, remained fundamentally committed to the established government infrastructure, to gentry governance, and to the preservation of republican virtue. As Robert Wiebe has noted, though members of both political parties saw their differences in stark contrasts, their dissimilarities were finally struggles "over the interior design of the same ideological house" (xiii). Though often distanced by both temperament and class from those they governed, this new leadership was destined to oversee a new wave of westward migration into the territories of the Old Northwest and the Louisiana Purchase, the United States's tentative forays into international politics, and a second war with Britain. In turn, Jackson and his successors would grapple with the shift of political power to the frontier, the expansion of a commercial economy, the "Indian question," an influx of new immigration and the consequent growth of cities, the emergence of irreconcilable sectional rivalries, and, eventually, a civil war that would irreversibly set the national course by ending slavery and establishing the primacy of the Union over the states.

Encompassing as they did enormous transformations in the nature of the national state and culture, these seventy years were a period of flux and persistent anxiety. While the vestigial remnants of John Winthrop's sectarian "city upon a hill" were being transmogrified into Lincoln's "last, best hope of earth," the new nation's peoples clung resolutely to the comforting old regional and national myths even as they lived a national identity constantly in the process of becoming. The nation's dramatists, both native born and immigrant, recorded the changes and, inevitably, helped to frame the realities they chronicled. As always, the theatre was both effect and cause. If at once the traditional mirror held up to reflect public and private realities, it was also an active agent, shaping – most often implicitly, occasionally explicitly –

the course of events. Like other writers, the nation's playwrights were consumed with describing, exploring, analyzing and, ultimately, defining what it meant to be "American." That their conclusions about the nation and its citizens seem retrospectively grounded too complacently in unexamined assumptions about gender, race, class, and culture is perhaps less surprising than the insistently broadening issues they examined and the energy with which they undertook those efforts. Searching constantly for continuity, more often than not American playwrights before the Civil War encountered disjunctions; implicitly asserting univocality, they found and reproduced polyphony; seeking to render a single, unifying cultural sign of a present national identity, they encountered the always receding traces of a mythic past and an impenetrable future. Their ultimate accomplishment was not any of the various answers they provided to the vexing question of American subjectivity but the multivalent process in which they engaged.

To Be or Not to Be:
Playwriting as Profession in the Early Republic

Ironically, few in 1801 would have recognized American dramatists' potential to serve such a pivotal cultural role, for playwriting as a profession arguably did not exist in early-nineteenth-century America. The revolutionary age dramatic propagandists had fallen silent, and the efforts of such Republican-era dramatists as Royall Tyler and William Dunlap did not immediately attract successors. The reluctance to write plays was grounded in a constellation of factors, including the cultural status and economic realities of authorship; the theatrical tastes of managers, critics, and audiences; and the theatrical practices of the period. Some of these circumstances they shared with American writers generally, but others were distinct to the situation of playwrights.

Writers of all genres confronted the reality that no matter how widely esteemed its cultural significance, literary production in the early decades of the nineteenth century was a distinctly marginal activity. Though the colonial period had produced instances of outstanding poetry and narrative, a playwriting tradition did not exist, and the process of building the country itself demanded the vast majority of the country's collective energy. Few had leisure to devote themselves to any type of literary career, and fewer still conceived of making their livelihoods with the pen. Members of the social elites, whose education and background had, perhaps, best prepared them for literary pursuits, sometimes saw literature as such a serious undertaking that a literary life seemed incompatible with more immediate civic responsibilities, which they conceived as concomitants of their social position. Members of that class who did write, often tellingly, cast their efforts as diversions from these "more important" duties. Thus, former Philadelphia mayor James Nelson Barker would rationalize his dramatic efforts between 1806 and 1824 to William Dunlap as the products of his idle hours, and Pennsylvania Supreme Court justice David Paul Brown, whose *Sertorius* was successfully mounted by Junius Brutus Booth in 1830, could write that his works "were written rather as matters of relief from the care and toils of an arduous profession, than with any view to their representation upon the stage."[1] This ostensible nonchalance about their literary activity may reflect oblique attempts by "amateur" male elites to distance themselves from the opprobrium that attached to professional authorship. Writing in 1788, frustrated satirist and poet Philip Freneau asserted that "authors are at present considered as the dregs of the community: their situation and prospects are truly humiliating" (46–47). Things had not changed markedly by the turn of the next century.

If authorship's general social status was dubious, the reputation of the theatre and, by extension, playwrights was particularly problematic. Widespread calls for a new national literature did not seem to encompass dramatic activity – at least if the results were actually to be publicly performed. The long-standing religious antipathy for the theatre was no longer sanctioned by law, but the attitudes of many citizens still reflected variants of the traditional bias, and even the stoutest proponents of a national literature often demurred in the case of drama. Noah Webster, a linguistic nationalist who argued for an American idiom to supplant its British antecedent, is a case in point. Although he asserted with vehemence that "an attention to literature must be the principal bulwark against the encroachments of civil and ecclesiastical tyrants," he was suspicious that theatre could inculcate values appropriate to the young republic (*Letters of Noah Webster,* 4). For Webster and for many others, the chasm between literature and mere entertainment loomed wide at the theatre door:

> What sort of entertainment is that in which a thin partition only separates the nobleman from his lackey and the dutchess from her kitchenmaid, in which the gentleman and the lady associate with the footman, the oysterman, the woman of the town, and all partake of the same fare! With what sentiments must superior beings look down upon this motley school of morality. (Webster, *Letter to a Young Gentleman,* 27)

Answers to such criticisms came not only from members of the theatrical community itself but also from friends who took up the pen in theatre's defense. Reminiscing in 1832 of his decision to become a manager and playwright, William Dunlap recalled his reasoning thirty years before by quoting from his diary of 1796 that "if the effects of the stage are as great as its friends and enemies have concurred in representing it, surely I should have the power to do much good" (*History,* I, 187). The handful of short-lived theatrical magazines that began in the new century's first decade also argued the theatre's case, often in moral terms remarkably similar to those Dunlap employed. Among others, Philadelphia's *Theatrical Censor* (1805–6); New York's *Thespian Mirror* (1805–6), written by future playwright John Howard Payne; and Boston's *Something* (1809) asserted the moral and civic desirability of a vital national drama. The opening number of the *Theatrical Censor* (9 December 1805) declared that under a careful manager, the stage "teaches all that enobles, all that embellishes human life. It teaches all the decencies of public and private intercourse. It is the School of Morals; it is the School of Arts; it is the School of Language; it is the School of *Piety.*" The cumulative effect of such arguments was to increase the conceptual possibility of entering into a respectable career as a dramatist. In the first half of the century, however, playwrights generally continued to fall into one of two social groupings: serious and talented elite amateurs whose playwriting was a minor part of their public lives – or professional actors and managers who saw writing as an entrepreneurial adjunct of their broader theatrical endeavors.

Beyond the writer-dramatist's problematic social position resided the economic obstacles to authorship. Bluntly put, there was little economic incentive to enter upon a career as a writer, and even less of one for becoming a playwright. The era's mercantile ideology wedded thrift and profit seeking to the older sectarian ideals of hard work, diligence, and moral probity. The combination was particularly pernicious for the arts, implicitly arguing as it did against indulgence in such extravagances as the purchasing of literature and attending the relatively costly theatre. Initially, the economic onus upon managers, actors, and playwrights was somewhat ameliorated by the infusion of monies from the upper class. But as Bruce McConachie has persuasively argued, the economic elite's involvement with theatre steadily diminished over the period, especially after the 1820s, as they increasingly switched their economic support and personal prestige to cultural enterprises such as opera, which reinforced more overtly their economic and social standing and segregated them from the intensifying intrusions of an emerging mercantile middle class.[2]

Paradoxically, larger middle-class audiences did little to improve the economic situation of dramatists and the theatres. Theatrical revenues were notoriously poor, and most managers were loath to pay American playwrights a premium for untried pieces when a ready repertoire of proven favorites and cheaply secured adaptations of French or German plays cost less. David Grimsted's tabulations of various types of plays' popularity between 1800 and 1850 suggest that the tragedies Americans saw were overwhelmingly English (and predominantly Shakespearean), that British melodramas outnumbered American originals by about five to one, and that the ratio of English to American social comedies was on the order of twelve to one.[3] Even having one's play accepted by a manager did not guarantee financial reward. Joseph's Hutton's Preface to the unperformed *Fashionable Follies* suggests that would-be dramatists who overcame managerial reluctance could nevertheless fall victim to the whims of stars who simply refused to act their roles. Nor did printing one's play provide an alternative means to economic reward. Not until the 18 April 1856 copyright statute was enacted did playwrights have "along with the right to present and publish the said composition, the sole right to act, perform or represent the same." For all authors before 1856 pirated editions represented lost revenue. For playwrights, this situation was aggravated by managers, who merely appropriated a published play without providing either royalties or the author's traditional benefit performances.

The tastes of audiences and theatre critics provided other challenges. Particularly pernicious for American playwrights was the colonial critical and theatrical legacy of neoclassicism. Especially in the early part of the period, neoclassical aesthetic models were constantly reinforced both by performances and theatre criticism. These dicta mandated versions of universal, timeless truths decorously presented in an appropriate form. While neoclassically construed Shakespearean tragedy – Joseph Addison's *Cato,* John Home's *Douglas,* and George Lillo's *The London Merchant* – dominated the canon of tragedy and Shakespeare's romantic and eighteenth-century sentimental comedies monopolized comedy, there was little chance that a distinctively new American drama would emerge. Despite the fact that many early-nineteenth-century American playwrights argued the inappropriateness of such standards, change came slowly. In the preface to his 1808 *The Indian Princess,* James Nelson Barker complained that American critics unfairly expected their native tragedies to "lisp the language of Shakespere [*sic*]."[4] In the main classically schooled, the critics, though asserting the need for a vital national theatre in the theatrical magazines, also, ironically enough, urged adherence to traditional subject matters, language, and style. Though in a series of dramatic criticisms for Philadelphia's *Democratic Press* (1816–17) Barker would sound a call for a distinctly and implicitly nonneoclassical American drama, his was a solitary voice. Tellingly, it was almost three decades before American subject matter was actively sought as dramatic material. In 1828, the popular actor Edwin Forrest signaled a new direction by placing an advertisement in the 22 November issue of the *Critic,* offering a $500 cash prize and a half-benefit for "the best tragedy in five acts, of which the hero, or principal character, shall be an aboriginal of this country." Until the emergence of romantic drama and melodrama, American playwrights confronted enormous managerial inertia to changing the repertoire, a reluctance reinforced by audiences' and critics' preference for the traditional dramatic canon.[5]

Beyond aesthetic and critical considerations were the period's theatrical practices, particularly acting styles. At the beginning of the century, many of the leading actors and actresses were British born and trained, and they brought to American theatres versions of the grand acting style associated with the Kembles, the preeminent English acting family of the day (see Chapter 4, "European Actors and the Star System in the American Theatre, 1752–1870"). Their repertoires consisted primarily of plays best adapted to this acting style, and when they crossed the Atlantic little changed. They merely transplanted those roles to America. Between 1810 and 1830 the next wave of actors introduced a more romantic acting style and, thus, paved the way for the acceptance of a more romantically inclined American drama. However, their performances were so profitable that American managers at once established a pattern of traveling "stars," whose limited repertoires undermined local repertory companies that had had the potential for introducing and nurturing American plays (see Chapter 2). During the 1830s, 1840s, and 1850s, touring British stars in the customary English canon remained commonplace but were increasingly counterbalanced by newer stars such as Charles Mathews, Tyrone Power, Agnes Robertson, and Dion Boucicault, who consciously adapted their work to American audiences, presenting Yankees, the increasingly familiar Irishman, and Native Americans. Though on balance the effect of these acting practices was liberating, the predominance of British actors and actresses at the top of the acting profession initially retarded the emergence of an American theatre by encouraging American authors to write plays whose subject matter and style seemed as much "British" as "American."

But acting style and repertoire were hardly the only factors that influenced the production and reception of American plays. Even if mounted, a play was as likely to be praised or damned for extratextual considerations as its own quality. In an age without formal acting training and when audiences and reviewers were concerned at least as much (and often more) with the performance rather than a play's intellectual matter, even quite good plays were wont to suffer because of a bad company. Similarly, pricing structure, attempts to include (or exclude) certain groups from a theatre, good/poor orchestras, new/worn backdrops and sets, or the comfort of patrons were as likely to influence a play's perceived merits as the play itself. And extratheatrical matters sometimes overwhelmed a play. The long and bitter rivalry between Edwin Forrest and William Macready, overlaid with nationalist and class antagonisms, is only the most notorious example. The Astor Place riot (occasioned by Forrest's and Macready's rival productions of Shakespeare and discussed elsewhere in this history) in which an estimated twenty-two died and one hundred and forty-four were injured suggests that occasionally even venerated plays were liable to receptions that had little to do with their literary worth.

Despite such formidable obstacles and lack of encouragement, Americans of all stripes took up the dramatic pen, venturing forth from law offices, parlors, and green rooms to give theatrical expression to the events, issues, and ideas surrounding and informing them at the century's beginning. Although the works testify to a consistent attempt to understand the complexities of nineteenth-century American life, to define the changing nature of being an American, and to give expression to the anxieties and hopes of a wide variety of writers and audiences, the plays can not finally be chronicled in a theatre history as a teleological progression toward either an ideological or artistic end. The points of view are too varied and the dramatic renderings too diverse to be simplified in such a manner. Moreover, the constant striving of managers and actors for successful vehicles within the repertory framework that dominated the era's theatres guaranteed that at least in metropolitan areas with multiple theatres, old plays often held the stage simultaneously with the latest material. Combined with the inevitable waxing and waning of audience taste and playwrights' interests, what emerges is less a narrative thread of steady progression than a tapestry with first one and then another element calling for the attention of historians and critics. Though broad patterns are discernible, the plays themselves ultimately resist convenient periodization or typology. Thus, what follows, though inevitably presented linearly, must be understood recursively.

Melodrama and the Emergence of the American Playwright

For prospective playwrights the inhibiting factors cited above became issues to be resolved in the course of composition. Thus, like twentieth-century postcolonial writers, nineteenth-century American playwrights contemplating the creation of a national theatre sought to reconcile a host of conflicting expectations. At their root were two complementary sets of considerations, one aesthetic-ideological, the other social-moral. The former presented the seemingly mutually exclusive alternatives of authoring plays without regard to historical considerations or of acceding to the equally compelling pull to write to the historical moment, to give expression to the new national dispensation. In essence, were "plays" or "American plays" to be written? If the answer was the former, playwrights might write without regard to the accident of their birth, embracing subject matters and artistic forms whose very utilization would lend credibility and artistic stature to their efforts. As the experience of John Howard Payne was to suggest, such an approach might well guarantee their acceptance with international and Europhile members of elite American audiences. But that strategy might also render their work suspect with domestic audience members and critics more nationalistically inclined. On the other hand, they could write in distinctly American idioms and of American experiences and in the process create plays that were formally and thematically suited to their new nation. However, this possibility also had limited viability, given acting troupes committed to the traditional repertoire, conservative drama critics, and elite patrons loath to accept untried, "provincial" wares or to embrace a more popularly grounded theatrical practice.

Complicating this issue was the moral-social debate over the claims of the theatre as temple of virtue and more pedestrian notions of it as a site of popular entertainment. Those arguing idealistically for the theatre as promulgator of virtue implicitly cast their lots with the cause of "high" art – conceived either aesthetically or politically. Managers and actors seeking profitable vehicles and audience members seeking pleasure of a less refined nature were more inclined to embrace "mere entertainments." As the century wore on, the proliferation of theatres, a narrowing of audiences in certain houses, and the emergence of pricing policies that segregated patrons economically, all diminished this conflict, allowing authors to tailor their plays more particularly to specific sets of playgoers; but in the century's early decades dramatists were compelled to write for a heterogeneous audience. American playwrights, therefore, tended to seek material and dramatic strategies that allowed them to satisfy sophisticated audience members well versed in the theatrical tradition as well as newer playgoers minimally grounded in the theatre's literature and practices.

Caught in this web of potentially conflicting critical standards, conservative theatrical practices, and varied audience expectations, playwrights explored numerous possibilities. The plays themselves testify to the ongoing search for a viable middle ground. Following the leads of Tyler and Dunlap, elite playwrights in the first three decades of the new century sought initially to use inherited dramatic structures to examine new social, economic, and political realities. Encompassing a wide variety of forms and stretching chronologically from the beginning of the century until the Civil War, their plays represent a variety of aesthetic nationalism, an assertion of Americans' capacity to write in a timeless vein for receptive American audiences. At first blush, the results often seem strangely at odds with the continual touting of these plays in prefaces and reviews as the latest (and usually finest) expression of American playwrighting. Often poetic, utilizing a foreign setting, and as apt to deal with aristocrats as with the types of common folk ostensibly populating the new, classless nation and theatre, these plays document both an implicit belief that American playwrights and theatregoers were the rightful heirs to the European dramatic legacy and the suspicion that the received tradition was ideologically suspect and in need of recuperation. Emerging side by side with these efforts, and occasionally produced by some of the same playwrights, was a growing repertoire of plays that focused overtly on an increasingly diverse catalogue of American characters, situations, manners, social questions, and reform movements. Whatever their genesis, almost all American plays in the period were marked by the emergence and popularity of the dominant dramatic form of the century – melodrama.

Fortuitously, melodrama's appearance at the century's beginning offered an immediate, workable solution to many of the dilemmas facing American playwrights. Unfortunately for an historical understanding of the work produced under its pervasive influence, the critical reputation of melodrama as a genre has suffered in the wake of realism's stylistic dominance since the end of the nineteenth century and has doomed most American plays of this period to critical oblivion, instances, so the traditional assessment goes, of "the same blight which afflicted playwrighting in England, Germany, and France."[6] But as recent scholarly reassessments demonstrate, melodrama emerged not as a falling away from the higher critical and artistic standards of earlier dramatic aesthetics, but as a theatrical response to rapidly changing social, political, economic, and cultural circumstances.[7] In effect, melodrama succeeded as a theatrical form and practice because it spoke more immediately and powerfully to nineteenth-century audiences than did older dramatic modes, and its very popularity testifies to the steady democratization of Western theatre during the period. An appreciation of melodrama's techniques and appeals provides an understanding of the audiences who watched it – their social, political, and economic attitudes, their aesthetic sensibilities, and the discourses that resonated for them within and without the theater – as well as the function of American plays within nineteenth-century culture.

Historically, the critical descriptor "*mélodrame*" was first used by Rousseau to describe his attempts to heighten the emotional expressivity of *Pygmalion* (1770) by adding musical accompaniment to the soliloquy and pantomime of his "*scène lyrique*." The term "melodrama" became popular in France at the beginning of the next century to describe the work of French playwrights (especially Pixérécourt, Caigniez, and Ducange) for the Parisian popular theatres. It eventually subsumed the earlier designation of "gothic," bringing into its critical ambit as "gothic melodrama" both the antecedent writings of August von Kotzebue and later reformulations of Thomas Holcroft. The circulation of plays and playwrights between Europe and the United States guaranteed that by midcentury melodrama had become the dominant genre in the contemporary repertoire on both sides of the Atlantic. Though there was a significant deficit in the American theatrical balance of payments at the century's beginning, the steadily increasing number of American melodramas crossing the Atlantic to successful mountings in Europe testifies to the emergence of a popular, international theatrical culture too often anachronistically represented as a phenomenon of the twentieth century. Overcoming, to this extent at least, their staunch nationalistic bias, American writers and audiences eagerly embraced melodrama, and its essential elements can be found to one degree or another in most of the plays of the period.

At its core, melodrama is at once both the assertion of the eternal battle between good and evil and a tacit admission that previously accepted constructs can no longer either explain the conflict's dynamics or guarantee virtue's inevitable triumph. While driven by other forces in England, in the United States and France, antecedent organizing principles had disappeared altogether or been radically reconfigured by revolution. Within the United States, no amount of holding "these truths to be self-evident," and no litany of reassurances by vestigial elites fighting a rearguard action for position and privilege could assuage the feeling that the world had become remarkably unstable, that turmoil and chaos were always only an unexpected circumstance away. Whereas this flux signified the new possibilities for which the revolution had been fought, the apprehension attending it reanimated a search for ordering principles beyond the influence of temporal events. Thus, on both the personal and community levels, the contest that melodrama enacted and thematized was, perforce, of some political and social moment. Through its dramatic universe, characters, languages, and stage devices, melodrama portrayed society's fractures, vented the age's anxieties, and lent support to the abiding hope that progress and a new, freer order were in fact the legacies of the American Revolution.

Read through the stylistic lens insinuated by a realistic dramaturgy at the end of the nineteenth century, the melodramatic universe seems neatly schematized, constructing for the audience what Peter Brooks has described as "an irreducible manichaeism, the conflict of good and evil as opposites not subject to compromise" (36). Presenting a world at once akin both to fantasy, and "the reality of the human condition as we all experience it most of the time," melodrama broadened the theatrical experience beyond its traditional elite social confines.[8] Whether conservative or radical in its social or political orientation, melodrama's representations are always evident to the entire audience. All its signifying systems contribute to the assertion of a fundamentally moral universe, to the recognition of that universe's valences by characters and audience members, and to the inevitable reassertion of the proper moral order. Despite temporary suffering by its central characters, melodrama does not entail the sanctifying sacrifice of tragedy. Simply put, melodrama, operating in a postsacred universe, cannot reconcile its characters to that which does not exist. While the universe is moral, it is no longer perceived as the extension of a manifest deity. For melodramatic audiences, the very concept of sanctity (as conceived in traditional religious thought) has been so problematized that it no longer has emotional or spiritual resonance. Melodrama also differs from comedy in that its concluding moral order is not that of a new society formed around a valorized couple who have overcome an older generation's irrational resistance but the reassertion of a virtuous order temporarily misprized by circumstance.

The principal characters in melodrama are often denigrated as mere factors set upon the stage to embody the concepts they represent. However, as Heilman has noted, the "monopathic" nature of melodrama's characters allows the audience to identify with them without having to confront and attempt to reconcile the types of internal divisions typical of tragedy or high comedy (85). Instead, interior conflict is projected outward, resulting in an action reflective of the anxieties generated by older ordering principles being cast into question. In the particular case of nineteenth-century America, anxiety about governmental authority materializes in plots of oppression in which innumerable malevolent rulers and aristocrats incessantly attempt to compromise virtuous women and to exile, imprison, or murder their beneficent protectors. Fraying paternalistic class structures are reflected as generational conflicts in which fathers (and occasionally mothers) either unwittingly or knowingly seek the destruction of their children. Fears of eroding religious faith are disclosed in hypocritical priests and pastors given to murderous sectarianism and worldly corruption. The virtuous characters, whose trials and persecutions at the hands of villains the audience is invited to vicariously share, are propelled through extremes of emotion with dizzying rapidity, often moving from one pole to its opposite in the space of a few lines or moments. Manifesting an exemplary integrity of being, these heroes and heroines doggedly seek throughout the play to have others comprehend and embrace their fundamental goodness, and the pivotal moment of their moral recognition (counterbalanced by the expulsion of evil) rights the universe. This interplay of virtue and villainy provides one of the primary means through which the moral nature of the melodramatic universe, a universe that is imaginatively projected to the world outside the theatre, is made evident to the audience.

The rhetoric of melodrama is perfectly suited to its "monopathic" speakers, for it refuses to indulge nuance. Its dominant figures – hyperbole, antithesis, and oxymoron – insist upon the capacity of language properly deployed to reveal both the moral quality of the conflict and the essential nature of its combatants. Inherently suspicious of previous linguistic codes, it either boldly resists conventional mediators of social intercourse – gender, class, filial and pietistic deference – in its attempt to speak in pure concepts or reveals them as mechanisms of unintentional or deliberate repression. Designed to appeal to audiences largely lacking an appreciation of poetic subtlety and inherently democratic in operation, melodrama's language asserts the virtuous characters' capacity to recognize and, if enabled, to resolve the moral chaos at the action's heart. But the moral confusion and corruption that permeates the melodramatic world has temporarily blunted language's efficacy, a circumstance implictly represented either by the momentarily successful attempts of evil to silence virtue or the incapacity of the uncorrupted to understand what they hear. Speech itself is often inhibited either by congenital defect or circumstances, and mute virtue often spends much of the play striving to speak its name. An interpreter, gestures, or action eventually suffices to right the world, but, more often than not, the travails of such muted characters are at the center of a play's commentary on the power (and limitations) of language. A telling example is found in Boucicault's *The Octoroon,* in which the Native American, Wahnotee, is falsely accused of murder because he cannot make himself understood, and only the timely discovery of the actual murderer through a miraculously self-developing photographic plate saves him from being lynched. Despite its temporary shortcomings, language remains the primary signifying sytem of the play, although by no means the only one.

Several devices that further make transparent the moral action supplement language. During this period, stylized acting gestures and facial expressions were "read" by audience members, who were often treated to the same or similar devices both in public readings or by political stump speakers. Resistant to the type of misinterpretation to which language might be subjected by evil, these mute testimonies to the emotional state of characters enhanced – and occasionally supplanted – speech, betokening a desired return to a pure signification traditionally believed to have preceded language's emergence. Similarly, the scenery of the play was put to expressive use. Dungeons, cozy parlors, ominous forests, and pastoral settings not only alerted the audience to the circumstances of the action but also elicited an emotional response, either generalized from conventional use or particularized through identification with a specific character's circumstance. The importance of setting increased during the century as melodrama's reliance upon evocative locale for establishing the emotional tone of the action was augmented and encouraged by continual improvements in stage decoration and machinery. Chariot races, exploding steamboats, burning tenements, and pitched naval battles became commonplace means of satisfying audience's rising expectations for the spectacular.

Melodrama's use of tableau provided a third visual insight into the moral situation of the play. The freezing of the action, most often at the ends of scenes and acts, furnished a spatial and pictorial distillation of a specific emotional moment, allowing the focusing arrangements of characters, their frozen attitudes, and the play of light and shadow to reiterate the participants' situations for an audience temporarily suspended from the emotional pull of language and action. Tableau's very nature had the added advantage of suggesting simultaneously both the flux of events and the timeless moral truths against which that action was taking place. These visual systems were complemented by music, the signifying system from which the genre derives its name. Incorporated as song or dance to vary the action, music also served to signal entrances, providing the audience clues as to a character's nature and the emotional coloring that he or she brought to the action. Music was also generously applied to scenes of mute action, especially those whose tensions or pathos might be heightened by appropriate accompaniment. Thus, Eliza's perilous dash across Ohio River ice floes in George Aiken's adaptation of *Uncle Tom's Cabin* (1852) or scenes of domestic despair in W. H. Smith's *The Drunkard* (1844) were liberally underscored by strains designed to effect the audience subconsciously.

Within the limitations of box-set staging, melodrama attempts to manipulate every sense, to create total theatre. Denied in large measure a homogenous audience educated in the received theatrical tradition, American melodrama constructed its audience from those finding their way into an increasingly democratic theatre. Valorizing its audiences' lives, it was the means through which the theatre became a venue wherein issues of social justice and democratic community might find immediate representation. Unlike the turbulent political and economic worlds outside the theatres, melodrama offered reassurance. The audience's cognitive abilities, engaged through language and plot, are driven inevitably toward the recognition of both the manichaen universe underpinning the action and the inevitability of virtue's fight for existence with those forces – political, economic, social – that would eradicate it. Relying upon archetypal familial patterns (Parent–Child, Lover–Beloved, Brother–Sister) *in extremis* (either literally or figuratively) to generate within the audience the broadest possible emotional identification, melodrama presented its imaginative universe in the stark terms in which most of the audience saw the postrevolutionary world. Equally as important, the expressive elements – primarily the visual and aural – effaced any cognitive elisions. The effect was emotionally powerful, and the persistence of melodrama on the stage for more than a hundred years (and its continuation in contemporary cinema and, arguably, in the theatre to the present) suggests that only by privileging our own temporarily constructed bias can we dismiss these plays and their audiences as culturally and theatrically naive.

American Drama as Transnational Negotiation

Although melodrama was becoming the preeminent form in an American theatre soon to be dominated by the rising middle and working classes, American playwrights were already serving patrician audiences who controlled the theatres for most of the century's first three decades. Wealthy, patriotic, but politically and socially conservative, these urban elites were wedded to ideologies that construed their control of political, social, economic, and cultural institutions both as obligations and as positive goods. Sustaining the theatrical enterprise by owning theatres, by hiring managers, by subsidizing the companies through season tickets and benefit performances, and by lending their prestige to playgoing as a social activity, these patrons sought and initially found confirmation of their roles as the guardians of the new republic in the plays they enjoyed. Written in large measure by fellow patricians, plays from James Nelson Barker's *Marmion* (1812) to George Henry Boker's *Francesca da Rimini* (1855) manifest the pleasures, assumptions, and shifting anxieties of the predominantly male elites who viewed them. Capitalizing on their audiences' knowledge of and interest in ancient and modern history, exotic locales, heightened action, and poetic language, these plays reflect the widespread transatlantic popularity of romantic drama at the turn of the century. At the same time, they neatly gloss in their displacements the emerging social and ideological conflicts within the United States that were eroding the overt power of the class whose point of view they espoused. Though most of these plays assumed the justness of paternalistic privilege, the enduring appropriateness of a modified republicanism as a political ordering principle, and the danger of rampant acquisitiveness to the public and private structures of the new nation, their operations betray the rising fear that neither older social and political constructions nor traditional dramatic art could preserve paternalistic republicanism.[9]

Paternalistic social configurations had already been compromised by the Revolutionary War's assertion of political equality. But republicanism had been sufficiently flexible to reconcile political and social spheres by reconfiguring the nation's political history as a family drama in which "founding fathers" had rescued the general citizenry from potential aristocratic oppression. The iconologizing of Washington as the "Father" of the country – a role represented dramatically in Dunlap's *André* (1798) and rendered more explicit in its reworking as a patriotic spectacle, *The Glory of Columbia: Her Yeomanry* (1803) – made the point visually arresting for audiences regularly treated to the spectacle for fifty years (see also the discussion of melodrama in Chapter 1). As republicanism steadily gave way to liberalism, and liberalism itself moved beyond its initial Jeffersonian incarnation toward a Jacksonian egalitarianism sustained and validated by a capitalistic economy's operation, these plays increasingly reflect the search for social, political, and artistic strategies that might buttress the elite's power against the encroachments of the rising acquisitive classes.

At the beginning of the new century, William Dunlap, James Nelson Barker, and John Howard Payne modulated their poetic dramas' actions to stress the popularly accepted linkages between orderly families and stable political states. Operating by indirection and displacement, their plays propel fathers or father figures to the center of the audience's attention and, while acknowledging its potential shortcomings, carefully reassert through both language and action paternalism's efficacy. Such limited assurance was short-lived. The election of Jackson in 1828 and the sense of waning parental control throughout the 1820s called for new strategies. Responding to more insistently democratic audiences, David Paul Brown, Robert Montgomery Bird, and Robert T. Conrad sought to bolster paternalistic republicanism by further romanticizing their republican heroes and embedding considerations of paternalism within celebrations of democratic ideals. While shoring up their allegiances to republican ideals and paying lip service to the inherent worth of a host of uncommon common men, these writers were careful to reinsinuate paternalism through their heroes' touching interactions with their nuclear families and with the political families that coalesced around them. Having indirectly reinforced the links between public and private orders, these writers subtly suggested that in lieu of the more widely dispersed leadership provided by traditional paternal republicanism only such heroes could preserve both public and private order. However, their title characters' seemingly inevitable deaths argued strongly for the audience's recognition of the vulnerabilities of charismatic leaders and the instability of the political and social formations to which their histories testified. Thus, they seem to assert, Jacksonian democracy's repudiation of customary deferential social and political ordering comes at some risk. Finally, the works of Nathaniel Parker Willis and George Henry Boker evidence a repudiation of the new, acquisitive public world and a retreat into an imaginative universe in which the virtues traditionally affiliated with elite social formations could be revalorized as a variety of internalized, romantic refinement.

English-language playwriting activity in the century's early decades understandably centered in New York and Philadelphia, the sites of most active theatrical companies, extending by way of tours and local repertory productions to secondary sites such as Boston, Charleston, New Orleans (after 1824), and the frontier. In New York, early national drama was associated with one man, William Dunlap. Although financially unsuccessful as the principal manager of the Park Theatre (1798–1805), Dunlap contributed pivotally to early American drama. While writing, translating, or adapting more than fifty plays, Dunlap laid the groundwork for both the international and domestic orientations that were to characterize American drama until after the Civil War. At the end of the eighteenth century, his work tended to have an overtly American cast. *Darby's Return* (1789), *André* (1798), and *The Father; or, American Shandyism* (1799) reflect a keen desire to graft American subject matter onto established dramatic forms or literary styles. Pressed by the Park Theatre's downward economic spiral, however, he turned to adaptations, particularly the melodramatic works of the German playwright Kotzebue – *The Stranger* (1798), *False Shame* (1799), and *Pizzaro in Peru* (1800). In 1799–1800, his most financially successful season, the ninety-four performances at the Park Theater were dominated by French and German plays – fifty-two of Kotzebue's melodramas alone. Although returning to American events and places, later works such as *The Glory of Columbia* (1803) – with its transparency of George Washington crowned with a wreath of victory – and *A Trip to Niagara; or, Travellers in America* (1828) – with an eighteen-scene diorama of sights along the Hudson River – seem more an occasion for theatrical spectacle than an examination of historical or contemporary events and domestic manners. Nevertheless, Dunlap's early work argued forcefully for American dramatists to seize rather than repudiate the dramatic legacy of the English stage and to transform that heritage into something distinctly American. His successors, including Barker, Payne, Bird, Willis, Conrad, and Boker, were to heed his call and press ahead.

If Dunlap's fate revealed the tenuous life that the theatre offered the would-be professional, others, relieved of immediate commercial concerns, gave vent to more artistic impulses. In Philadelphia, James Nelson Barker was to make marked progress in creating American plays within the parameters established by Tyler and Dunlap. In his comedy *Tears and Smiles* (1807), Barker sets his sights on domestic folly, excoriating contemporary American fascination with French fashion. The next year, Barker turned his attention to the continent's indigenous population in *The Indian Princess; or, La Belle Sauvage,* the first produced play in the United States with Native Americans as its central characters and the first dramatic rendering of the Pocahontas myth. Having shown his willingness to utilize native materials, Barker sought in *Marmion* (1812) to give expression to his belief that a democratic drama must "keep alive the spirit of freedom; . . . and unite conflicting parties in a common love of liberty and devotedness of country" while at the same time indicating one manner in which seemingly alien matter might be made compelling for American audiences.[10]

Adapted from Sir Walter Scott's poem of the same name, the play examines England's subjugation of sixteenth-century Scotland. Though concerned fundamentally with the undemocratic issue of the fates of competing aristocrats, the play is replete with rousing speeches on liberty and defiance of tyranny that resonated for American audiences on the brink of the War of 1812:

> My lord, my lord, under such injuries,
> How shall a free and gallant nation act?
> Still lay its sovereignty at England's feet –
> Still basely ask a boon from England's bounty –
> Still vainly hope redress from England's justice?
> No! by our martyred fathers' memories,
> The land may sink – but, like a glorious wreck,
> 'Twill keep its colours flying to the last. (*Marmion,* 55)

For Barker the linking of paternity ("martyred fathers") and patriotism ("colours flying") is a natural reflection of how the ordering principles of a free society are perpetuated. When the weak and gullible Scottish king fails in his fatherly duties to the nation, the result is inevitably slaughter and subjugation. Tellingly, Barker disguised the paternity of his play, allowing his original audience to believe the play an English import. When the truth emerged, attendance decreased, suggesting that even when American playwrights spoke on timely issues in the elevated blank verse of their artistic forebearers, the elite patrons of Philadelphia's Chestnut Street Theatre remained skeptical of American dramatic wares.

As historically interesting as these plays are, *Superstition* (1824), Barker's masterpiece, represents a quantum advance in American playwriting. Again relying upon a domestic subject, Barker refuses to downplay the shortcomings of his colonial American characters, in the process creating a penetrating history play as opposed to the celebratory English versions of the genre that he had decried in his indictment of Scott. Set in late-seventeenth-century New England, the play examines the oppressive power of superstition in its tale of a Puritan minister's destruction of a woman and her son who refuse to accede to his narrowly sectarian authority. It also serves as a convenient means of displacing the growing tensions between children and paternal authority in 1820s America to an earlier age. The play presents three fathers: the absent Charles II, the rakish king who has seduced and impregnated Isabella Fitzroy; Isabella's regicide father who as the "Unknown" disguises his true identity throughout most of the play; and the heartless minister, Ravensworth. Motivated by sensual, political, and religious passion, respectively, each has neglected his role as father, precipitating destruction upon his house and endangering the body politic. It is tempting, and somewhat accurate, to read the play as a critique of paternalism. But the choric figure Walford's assertion that Ravensworth succeeds only through his ability to manipulate "The unthinking crowd, in whom credulity / Is ever the first born of ignorance" ironically reasserts the necessity for a tempered paternalistic republicanism to act as a brake on liberalism's too hasty elevation of the masses (*Superstition,* in Quinn, *Plays,* 130).

If Barker's works reveal some sense of the problems attending to paternalism's continuing force as the social glue holding together American society, John Howard Payne's plays seem generally more assured. The American-born Payne began writing plays when his acting career in England did not achieve the success of his earlier New York efforts. Written primarily abroad (though widely praised and performed in America), his works provide an interesting example of the points of affiliation between European and American theatres and audiences while at the same time suggesting the possibility of different bases for their receptions. On the whole his plays reflect the popularity of romantic drama on both sides of the Atlantic. Certainly, there can be little doubt that plays such as *Thérèse; or, The Orphan of Geneva* (1821, Drury Lane) and *Clari, the Maid of Milan* (1823, Covent Garden), with its signature song "Home, Sweet Home," reflect growing concerns with decreasing paternal authority among both British and American elite audiences. As is typical of the fairytales from which their structures are derived, in both plays a father or father figure exercising the traditional paternal role of protector proves the agent for righting the world and relieving the suffering of the title characters who can then be embraced on stage as they have been long before by their audiences. Incredibly popular before the mid-1830s, these plays' exteriorization of the fantasy lives of urban male elites represents the most unproblematic expressions of their audiences' abiding faith in paternalism.

On the other hand, *Brutus; or, The Fall of Tarquin* (1818, Drury Lane), the play that first brought Payne notoriety, reveals nagging suspicion of paternalism's viability in the public arena. While for British audiences *Brutus* represented merely another in a long line of verse tragedies with classical settings, for American audiences the play provided a telling commentary on the tensions between republicanism's allegiance to civic freedom and paternalism's devotion to family. In some senses harkening back to Dunlap's *André* in its evocation of the torments of a national hero in time of crisis, *Brutus* also looks forward to the later works of Bird and Conrad in questioning whether pulls of blood and civic duty might ultimately be irreconcilable. On its surface the play reiterates Dunlap's eighteenth-century vision of the *pater patriae*'s civic responsibility by having Brutus painfully elevate his desire to free Rome from Tarquin despotism above his paternal duties and affections for his misguided son, Titus. Though politically successful, Brutus's liberation of Rome comes with the concomitant sacrifice of Titus's life, an emotional cost that precipitates his father's death. Payne, thus, carefully counterposes the audience's recognition of Brutus's personal tragedy with its simultaneous perception that Brutus's actions have brought into being the Roman republic, a precursor of the new American state. Although the action seems to suggest the necessary dismantling of existing social and political orders, Brutus's constant reiteration of his own father's vain attempts to preserve Roman liberty argues that Brutus's revolt will merely re-establish a noble, antecedent world. For American elites conditioned by Whig historiography to read the American Revolution as the reassertion of traditional Englishmen's liberties against potential tyranny, the play's picture of a conservatiave rebellion proved compelling and guranteed the play's enduring popularity.

The heroic plays of Brown, Bird, and Conrad ushered in a new era in patrician drama. Brown's *Sertorius* (1830) charts Sertorius's defeat of Pompey and his eventual death at the hands of an envious and corrupt group of Roman colonists in Spain. Bird's *The Gladiator* (1831) and *Oralloosa* (1832) trace the

attempts of Spartacus to gain and Oralloosa to retain freedom for themselves
and their families against the imperial abuses of classical Rome and Spanish
conquistadors, respectively. Bird's domestic tragedy *The Broker of Bogota*
(1834) displaces fears of America's growing acquisitiveness to a popular New
World setting. Conrad's *Jack Cade* (1835) draws upon Wat Tyler's 1450 rebellion in England to reindict the world of aristocratic privilege and dignify the
common man's fight for freedom. Drawing together disparate ideological elements from classical republicanism, from the romantic constructions of the
New World "noble savage," and from English popular history, these writers'
public tragedies provided a telling critique of the political and social direction of the nation at the height of Jacksonian democracy's veneration of the
common man. Bird's domestic tragedy adds a new wrinkle in its explicit
indictment of the new cult of wealth that was growing with the rising bourgeoisie. Collectively these plays also suggest the depth of anxiety that
plagued urban male elites, who increasingly saw themselves as martyrs to a
set of virtues quickly disappearing from the American scene.

The public tragedies of Brown, Bird, and Conrad all begin from the shared
premise that historical representation retains its suasive power even within a
society radically reconfiguring the venerated institutions on which liberty has
been grounded. Following the path blazed by Barker, these plays seem to construct an historical drama emphasizing shared democratic ideals with import
for an America conceived as the latest, and most nearly perfect, incarnation of
common men's struggles against aristocratic oppressions. But the fates of the
heroes and their followers also strike a cautionary note, illuminating and
warning against Jacksonian America's proclivity for mindless hero worship.
For patrician writers confronted with the specter of Andrew Jackson and his
backwoods and urban underclass followers, such concerns were more than
theoretical. To accomplish these somewhat antithetical goals, the plays all follow a common structural pattern in which a figure who strives against the
forces of oppression seeks to return himself, his family, and his followers to a
pre-existent Arcadian world of egalitarian freedom. After aristocratic villains
prevent this return, the charismatic leader leads a temporarily successful
revolt only to be deserted or betrayed by his followers. Seizing this moment to
counterattack, the aristocrats reassert their control, and the hero, deprived of
supporters and spurred by the loss of family, falls in a final spasm of resistance, a martyr to egalitarian republican liberty.[11] Combined with an elevated
language that propelled their common heroes into the realm formerly occupied only by aristocrats, these plays' actions seem at first blush to provide
confirmation of popularly held Jacksonian beliefs in the inherent dignity of
even the lowliest of men and the redemptive power of a charismatic leader.

Ironically, as they celebrate the ideals embodied by the hero and elevate
for veneration the martyr to freedom, these plays subvert the impulse

toward hero worship. The stirring speeches and thrilling actions of these plays (especially as performed by their master impersonator, Edwin Forrest) never failed to rouse American audiences, but an individual audience member's impulse toward identification with the hero was always counterbalanced by the spectacle of the hero's betrayal by his followers. In play after play, the petty bickering and self-serving acquisitiveness of followers rendered the hero's lot a problematic one. While each man might well see himself as Spartacus or Jack Cade, he also inevitably had to confront the real possibility that his neighbors would, in the moment of crisis, fail through egotism or greed to adhere to the very ideals to which they had pledged themselves. Though rousing speeches on liberty and a martyr's death had obvious appeals for Jacksonian male audience members, the playwrights' insistent representations of the deaths of wives and children that attended the hero's destruction preached a special caution. For patrician writers their protagonists seemed more cautionary emblems of what might be necessary if freedom is not preserved than models for contemporary political emulation. Far better, the plays subversively suggest, to lessen individual danger and to better guarantee the safety and freedom of one's family by recognizing the necessity of collective resistance to encroaching tyranny and the efficacy of a shared leadership. Though Forrest and his audience devotees might see Spartacus and Cade as unsuccessful precursors of Andrew Jackson, there seems little doubt that the patrician writers of these plays were more than wary of such a reading. Thus, despite their surface endorsement of Jacksonian hero worship, the plays themselves – if not their performances – assert a countermovement toward traditional social and political formations.[12]

The disguised conservatism of these plays becomes more apparent when the plays are read in conjunction with the best domestic tragedy of the period, Bird's *The Broker of Bogota*. Whereas the public tragedies embrace the political ideals of democracy – if not their specific Jacksonian configurations – *The Broker of Bogota* offers a warning of the dangers inherent in the economic program attendant on the period's governmental transformations. The play's language, which is dominated by images of mining, gold, and, more generally, wealth, links father and son and points to the competing economic and social ideologies that lie at the play's heart. Avatar of a vestigial aristocratic class system, the merchant Febro tragically internalizes an inappropriate code, ruling his children with the iron hand of the traditional autocratic patriarch. On the other hand, caught in the machinations of the new mercantile economic dispensation and sinking into a quagmire of debt and attendant social marginalization, his son, Ramon, reluctantly surrenders to the call of ruthless acquisition propounded by the villain Cabarero. For Bird, the tragedy of Febro and Ramon nicely emblematizes the potential tragedy of the United States, which by the 1830s had seemingly given itself over to a new materialist ethic. The increasingly evident failure of the new acquisitive classes to internalize older social ordering principles and the simultaneous fragmentation of elite families in the drive for wealth was, to Bird's mind, eroding the glue that had held both family and state together. Although the play can hardly be read as a full-blown endorsement of traditional paternalism, there is little doubt that it strikes a cautionary note about the social and economic directions of the country.

The conservative gestures of Brown, Bird, and Conrad were effectively made moot by the economic, social, and political events of the later 1830s and 1840s, during which elite authority and power steadily diminished. The effective dissolution of the National Bank; the plunging value of patricians' western land investments; the financial crash of 1837; the increasing clout of frontier voters; westward expansion into Texas, California, and Oregon; the influx of immigrants into eastern elites' urban bastions; and the increasing importance and autonomy of western and southern agricultural markets all combined to compromise elite influence and forced the elite to seek new mechanisms to retain its power. Although the emergence of corporations and the command of transportation networks provided some measure of economic control in the North, and the solidification of planter culture in the South guaranteed a still greater influence in that region, there is little doubt that by the mid-1830s the day of uncontested elite domination was passing from the American scene.

Like most of the other institutions that bore the elite's imprint, the theatre reflected the alteration of circumstance. Willis's *Tortesa, The Usurer* (1839) and Boker's *Francesca da Rimini* (1855) provide convenient examples of attempts to reconfigure elite subjectivity in ways that carved out imaginative space for the perpetuation of a radically reconstitued hegemony. Rejecting the public arena that had consumed the heroic tragedies, these plays propel their audiences inward toward a refinement of personal sensibility unavailable to the bourgeoisie and working classes consumed with materialist acquisition. Ironically refashioning foreign aristocrats as models of sensibility, these plays evidence both the dawning recognition that the battles for overt social control had been lost and an assertion of a world that transcended both the power of the new money and the corruption of the new politics.

In his choices of a verse comedy form, in his construction of a plot reconciling upper and lower classes, and in his introduction of an artistic romantic hero, Willis reveals the waning hopes of elites in the late 1830s for a social rapprochement with the rising bourgeoisie. Willis's use of verse in a comedy serves to elevate the characters, dignifying even the lower-class clown Tomaso and the glover's daughter, Zippa. But this egalitarian gesture is somewhat militated by action. On the surface, Tortesa's attempts at revenge against the Italian aristocracy that has slighted him are reminiscent of both

Shakespeare's Shylock and characters in American verse tragedies who suf-
fered unwarranted oppression. But Willis carefully differentiates Tortesa from
Spartacus or Jack Cade by circumscribing his injuries to those of pride.
Tortesa's motives and parvenu attitudes also place him outside the audi-
ence's sympathy until the very end of the play. His desire to marry Isabella
Falcone for revenge rather than love, his inability to distinguish the painter
Angelo's artistic genius, and his desire to destroy Count Falcone when his
marriage plans are thwarted all serve to alienate him from an audience asked
to sanction the love of the sprightly Isabella and the artistically intense
Angelo. Only in the play's last act, when Tortesa reveals his capacity to love
Isabella as she deserves, is the audience allowed compassion for a man who
discovers too late that true affection is more personally fulfilling than amass-
ing wealth. Despite his transformation, Tortesa is consigned to a socially
appropriate match with Zippa. Willis's most intriguing social commentary is
focused on Isabella and Angelo. The stultifying corruption of traditional aristocratic patriarchy is, of course, embodied by Count Falcone's desire to
marry his daughter in order to square accounts with Tortesa. Though forced
to rely upon a series of contrived plot devices to give Isabella freedom to
choose her husband, Willis is finally able to suggest that her refined character and aesthetic sensibility are available only to those removed from the
struggle for money or power. Similarly, though Angelo handles a sword as
adeptly as he does his brushes, it is his ability to see and venerate beauty
that makes him a worthy husband for Isabella. For Willis this marriage is less
an infusion of new democratic blood into a desiccated aristocracy than a
revitalization of the aristocracy's traditional role as preservers of cultural
ideals. Removed from the threat of poverty, Angelo will be free to produce
great art and, with Isabella, progeny who will appreciate, patronize, and preserve such sublime artistic achievement.

By 1855, such optimism seems to have been beyond the grasp of Boker
whose *Francesca da Rimini* retells the familiar story of Francesca of Ravenna
and Paolo of Rimini. Like *Calaynos* (1848) and *Leonor de Guzman* (1853),
Francesca reveals Boker's abiding interest in romantic dramatic subjects. But
unlike his earlier efforts, *Francesca* proved the means for both a sympathetic
assessment of the passing of American elites from power and an examination
of the implications of an American society deprived of their virtues. For Boker,
the Guelfs and Ghibelins who seek wealth and power without regard to their
broader social responsibilites seem to sadly foreshadow the situation of midcentury elites fighting to regain social and political control even as they were
being drawn ever more deeply into a materialistic America. Indeed, several
critics have read Bebbo Pepe as an anachronistic democrat prophesying the
doom of the forces of repression. The duplicity and sacrifice of its worthiest
elements to the demands of policy in many ways vindicate the call for a new

order made by Pepe, into whose mouth Boker places the play's democratic indictment. But the ill-disguised personal spite that motivates Pepe undercuts his democratic critique. His first-act declaration of revenge is firmly grounded in a sense of individual insult and barely hidden envy. However, Boker's reluctance to accede to Pepe's commentary is revealed most pointedly in the fates of the three sympathetically drawn central characters, who collectively suggest a nobility unavailable to the lower-class fool. Lanciotto's expressed sympathy for his people vitiates Pepe's assertion of a callous aristocracy, and Lanciotto's valor, sensitivity, and philosophical disposition mark him as an extraordinary person, no matter what his class background. Paolo and Francesca's romantic passion tellingly contrasts with both the base political motives of their fathers and Pepe's lust. At the same time, the guilt that Paolo and Francesca feel and their eager embracing of death as relief from lives too painful to endure evinces a moral refinement that, though betrayed in practice through their adultery, remains a vital and, ultimately, determinative aspect of their characters. For Boker, *Francesca da Rimini* represents a tragedy on both a personal and social level. Without the palliative influences of his central characters, the world would sink further into corruption until overwhelmed by the self-serving ideological heirs of Pepe.

The failure of *Francesca da Rimini* with its original audiences signaled both the death knell of romantic verse drama in nineteenth-century America and the final passing from the scene of the cadre of writers devoted to elite dramatic entertainment. Their plays, as often misconceived by their contemporary audiences as by later critics, nevertheless served to assert the American playwright as a force on the international stage. Accepting the challenges of producing plays in the aesthetically sanctioned forms that they inherited from their European dramatic forebearers, these writers demonstrated to both domestic and international audiences a depth of imagination, a literary accomplishment, and a dramatic facility that few would have anticipated at the beginning of the century. Their works were to be performed only fitfully after the Civil War, but their contributions paved the way for later American playwrights such as Percy MacKaye and William Vaughn Moody, who were committed to an examination of issues both current and perennial in elevated language.

Constructing an American Identity: Popular Drama, 1800–1865

While patrician playwrights were delineating and sharing their visions of themselves and their cohorts, other writers were addressing increasingly popular audiences. Forbearing the poetic language, exotic settings, and aristocratic trappings, the popular drama set about a broadly conceived national stock taking. The repudiation of patrician poetic drama in favor of more immediately acccessible forms combined with an embracing of working- and business-class audiences provided writers of popular, primarily melodramatic, plays the imaginative space to interrogate and provide tentative answers to several fundamental issues: Who are we Americans; from whence did we emerge and what do we make of our history; what is the impact of the growth of cities and the expansion of the frontier on the nation; what is our relationship both to indigenous populations and to immigrants; what beliefs (if any) do we collectively share; what are the problems – social, economic, political, moral – that we face; where are we as a nation headed? More often than not, the answers to these and other questions are given scant overt attention, for like most popular entertainments, American theatre in this period responded by implication, by the kinds of characters and actions it presented. But by conflating identity issues with questions of political policy and social attitude, these plays often juxtapose various character types in actions that highlight the concerns that consumed the theatrical audiences outside the theatres. In their totality, the era's popular plays provide a fascinating chronicle of the changing faces of America, of the process of creating America itself.

The question of national identity is confronted most overtly by a host of plays that seek to examine categorized individuals as outside a tacit norm. Native Americans, frontiersmen, Yankees, the urban underclass, and immigrants all found representation on the stage, either as the central characters of plays devoted to them or as secondary figures in broader canvases. Rarely providing anything beyond a reinforcement of popular stereotypes, these plays nevertheless reveal the ongoing audience anxiety to understand the differences and similarities of the peoples of the country, to investigate the possibility of a unified American identity, to appropriate for broader ideological purposes these stereotypical characterizations, and to assert, implicitly, what the national character might entail.

The earliest group to consume these writers' attentions was Native Americans. Whereas eighteenth-century plays such as Robert Rogers's unperformed *Ponteach* (1766), Thomas Morton's *Columbus; or, A World Discovered* (1792), and Anne Kemble Hatton's *America Discovered; or, Tammany, the Indian Chief* (1794) had dealt with America's indigenous population, the period from the turn of the century to the Civil War marked the apex of representations of Native Americans on the American stage. Plays such as Barker's *The Indian Princess* (1808), Mordechai Noah's *She Would Be Soldier; or, The Plains of Chippewa* (1819), Henry J. Finn's *Montgomery* (1825), and George Washington Parke Custis's *The Indian Prophecy* (1827) usually subordinated concern for Indian character to the fates of proto-Americans. In Barker's opera, the fate of British colonialism in the face of native opposition and the crossed love of Pochahontas and Rolfe form the plot's mainsprings. In his play, Custis uses Native Americans as the anachronistic agents of destiny to deliver the message of George Washington's future greatness. Despite their limited roles in these plays, their popularity with audiences prompted Forrest's famous call for a play built around an Indian protagonist. The resulting play, John Augustus Stone's *Metamora; or, The Last of the Wampanoags* (1829), was an enormous hit and guaranteed a spate of imitations.

Domesticating elements of poetic drama in its tale of Metacom or King Philip and his seventeenth-century war against New England settlers, *Metamora* arguably begins the imaginative process of incorporating stereotypical Native American characteristics into a more broadly conceived American identity. As a paragon of the Rousseauesque natural man, Metamora embodies many of the traits that Americans perceived as their own. A natural gentleman, devoted to family, fiercely independent, brave in war, and courteous in peace, Metamora proves a ferocious opponent to the colonists, who seek to displace him from his native land. But it is, ironically, this very relationship with the land that provided audiences the emotional warrant for effacing his cultural otherness and assimilating his "essential" character into their own sense of identity. Metamora's presentation as a savage superman, while conceptually analogous to such characters as Spartacus, is grounded in the popular belief in the uniqueness of the American environment. Although modifying the older sectarian vision of America as the "new Eden," Metamora's wilderness remains the force that has shaped him. As the heirs of those who defeated him and seized his land, American audiences who applauded Metamora's doomed struggles were invited at once both to sanction his defeat as the rightful fate of a non-Christian savage and to recognize the elevating natural legacy that now formed them. This divisibility of mind was not without its ironies. As Jeffrey Mason has noted, *Metamora* is one of the early instances of the creation of a theatrical myth whose idealizations paved the way for a brutalization of the living instances of its subject. Even while celebrating the virtues of their stage hero, most members of the audience were equally passionate in favoring the removal of Native Americans from their traditional lands to reservations beyond the Mississippi River.[13]

In the wake of *Metamora* a veritable tribe of Indian plays emerged. Like Stone's play, works such as Richard Penn Smith's *William Penn* (1829), Nathaniel Deering's *Carabasset* (1830), Robert Montgomery Bird's Inca tragedy *Oralloosa* (1832), Richard Emmon's *Techumseh* (1836), Alexander Macomb's *Pontiac* (1836), and Nathaniel Bannister's *Putnam* (1844) sought to present historical figures. But with no Native American dramatists to temper the vision they presented (and with few Native Americans to lend these representations credibility), these plays tend to see and render the Indians either as exemplars of nobility or as embodiments of treachery and barbarism. An interesting exception is Charlotte Barnes Connor's *The Forest*

Princess (1848), which minimizes the usual romance in favor of a carefully crafted retelling of the Pocahontas story noteworthy for its respectful treatment of Native Americans. But as clashes between Indians and settlers expanding westward intensified, Native Americans increasingly assumed a negative cast. Louisa Medina's adaptation of Robert Montgomery Bird's novel *Nick of the Woods* (1839) is typical in its reduction of the Indian characters to bloodthirsty brutes who murder and pillage until eradicated by Reginald Ashburn, who survives a massacre that claims his family to wreak revenge upon the native population, a pattern of settler retribution. However, shifting theatrical tastes as much as changing attitudes toward Native Americans spelled the doom of the Indian play vogue. The Irish American playwright John Brougham punctured the dignity of the noble savage plays in a series of burlesques, including *Po-ca-hon-tas; or, The Gentle Savage* (1855) and *Metamora; or, The Last of the Pollywogs* (1857).[14] By the Civil War, Native Americans had in large measure faded from both the national stage and the national consciousness. Though they reappeared in the wake of post-Civil War westward expansion, Native Americans would never again rise to the level of prominence they had occupied between 1830 and 1850.

At about the same time that the Indian plays were rising to their peak, a white counterpart emerged in the figure of the frontiersman. Though these characters were to achieve their greatest popularity after the Civil War, plays such as James Kirke Paulding's *The Lion of the West* (1831), Medina's *Nick of the Woods,* Mordecai Noah's *The Frontier Maid* (1840), and W. R. Derr's *Kit Carson, The Hero of the Prairie* (1850) alerted urban audiences to the emergence of a new American type. The popularity of *The Lion of the West* at the height of Jacksonian power presents an interesting instance of the ways in which the popular stage adapted itself to changing political and social circumstances by providing popular audiences the opportunity to examine their new champions in action. On its surface, the play is all rollicking action as Nimrod Wildfire (the "lion" of the title) brings his particular brand of backwoods, ringtail roaring to New York City. For all of its rambunctious energy, centered primarily on Wildfire's ludicrous pursuit of Amelia Wollope (a thinly diguised Frances Trollope), the play provides a reassertion of an American identity that spans both class and geography and is sufficiently secure in itself to contemplate reconciliation with its former colonial oppressor. The satire of English and patrician American social pretensions and the triumph of merchant probity over the mercenary designs of a fake English aristocrat permit the audience to firmly align itself with the clear-sighted, democratic merchant Freeman, who asserts that integrity, talent, and hard work will confer the only titles to which Americans should aspire. Freeman's gracious indulgence of his country nephew's extravagances, his willingness to sanction his daughter's marriage to an honorable English merchant, and his ultimate reassertion of authority over his social-climbing wife suggest a model for harmonizing the international, sectional, generational, and familial discords the play exposes. While such reconciliations were to prove only temporary, their very prospect suggests the sense of limitless possibility that characterized attitudes of many Americans in the 1830s.

Whereas dramatizations of frontier residents reflected the importance of the wilderness to midcentury American identity, the appearance of Yankee characters implied that the more settled areas of the country continued to spawn unique brands of Americans. With the frontier dramas, the Yankee plays represent some of the earliest attempts to engage the multiplicities of the dominant white culture. Like their Indian counterpoints, stage Yankees first appeared in the eighteenth century. Royall Tyler's Jonathan in *The Contrast* (1787) established the type, and in the early years of the next century Lazarus Beach's *Jonathan Postfree* (1807) and A. B. Lindsley's *Love and Friendship; or, Yankee Notions* (1809) centered on Yankee characters. Ironically, however, it was the English comedian Charles Mathews who first realized the theatrical gold mine that the character represented, establishing the vogue for Yankee parts in two plays, *Trip to America* (1824) and *Jonathan in England* (1824). Between 1825 and 1855 the entire population of New England seemed to be migrating to urban stages as one Yankee after another sallied forth to amuse and enlighten his city cousins. Following Mathews's lead, four American actors – James H. Hackett, George Handel "Yankee" Hill, Danforth Marble, and Joshua Silsbee – mined the vein for the next thirty years. Figures such as Hackett's title character in *Sylvester Daggerwood* (1826), Jonathan in Samuel Woodworth's *The Forest Rose* (1832), Jedediah Homebread in Joseph S. Jones's *The Green Mountain Boy* (1833), Lot Sap Sago in Cornelius A. Logan's *Yankee Land* (1834) and *The Wag of Maine* (1842), Sy Saco in John Augustus Stone's *The Knight of the Golden Fleece; or, The Yankee in Spain* (1834), and Solon Shingle in Jones's *The People's Lawyer* (1839) became staples of the American stage. Quickly identifiable to audiences by name and increasingly by costuming and language, these characters were primarily comic creations whose mixture of simplicity, confusion, patriotism, shrewdness, and sentimentality made them perfect instruments for deflating the sophisticated pretensions and moral lapses of the foreigners or city denizens with whom they interacted.

Although figures such as Deuteronomy Dutiful in Logan's *The Vermont Wool Dealer* (1838) occasionally occupied center stage in farces, more often the Yankee was relegated to a secondary position in the action. Typical in this regard is Solon Shingle in *The People's Lawyer.* On its surface, the play's plot has little to do with the Yankee, concerning itself instead with the successful efforts of Robert Howard, the title character, to exonerate an innocent clerk, Charles Otis, of charges of theft lodged by his dishonest former employer.

Shingle almost literally stumbles into the courtroom action, having come to Boston to defend himself in a lawsuit that he has refused to settle dishonestly. The farcical antics and linguistic blunders that attend Shingle's courtroom appearance late in the play both enliven the otherwise rather standard moralizing action and tend to vitiate working-class and bourgeois fears of the law as a mechanism of elite control. But it is on the symbolic level that Shingle functions most powerfully, providing as he does a gesture toward national unity. Shingle's suit unites him with the innocent Otis, and his class links him to Howard, who spends most of the play disguised as a simple mechanic. The point is driven home in the play's dénouement when Shingle reveals that as a soldier in the Revolution and the War of 1812 he has shared friendships with the fathers of both Otis and Howard. As a "founding father," Shingle stands as testament to the ideals that have grounded both the nation's revolutionary struggle and its continuing resistance to potential new oppressions.

If the Yankee characters humorously provided a means of recovering the urban audience's rural roots and imaginatively reuniting city and country citizens, then the plays of metropolitan life and the underclass in the late 1840s and 1850s presented the same audiences both the opportunity to laugh at and to palliate fears of an increasingly rough-and-tumble city existence. Initiated and sustained mainly through the efforts of actor-manager-playwright Benjamin A. Baker, these plays purport to give the audience insights into the life of urban lower classes during an era in which increasing Irish and German immigration and migrations from the countryside were remaking the social faces of the Northeast metropolises. *A Glance at New York in 1848* (1848), Barker's first effort in this vein, brought before its original New York audiences Mose, the Bowery B'hoy, and turned Frank Chanfrau, who acted the part, into a local celebrity. With his red shirt, plug hat, and turned-up trousers, Mose became the darling of the Olympic Theatre pit, who saw in him the quintessential representation of volunteer firemen whose activities were both a boon and bane to lower-class areas of the city. Like his counterparts outside the theatre, Mose was a hard-drinking, pugnacious rapscallion whose saving of lives and property from the ever-present urban danger of fire was somewhat offset by his willingness to brawl with competing fire companies and react violently to those of any class who transgressed his sense of honor. Although the models from whom Mose was drawn were often little more than criminals, Baker's play presents a more beneficent picture. Fighting a fire, taking care of an abandoned child, and wooing his working-class sweetheart, Mose manages to recoup, to a significant degree, the Bowery B'hoy's reputation, in the process allaying nascent class fears. The respectable business-class hero of the piece, Harry Gordon, turns out to be Mose's old school chum, and Mose extends his protective presence to George Parsells, Gordon's visiting country friend. In a scene of the classless solidarity of the good-hearted, Mose and his girl join the more obviously respectable members of the play's cast for a night of entertainment at the Vauxhall Garden. But Baker's attempts to domesticate him hilariously collapse as Mose leaves to help a firefighting friend caught in a "muss" off-stage. While finally untamable, Mose's actions solicit the audience's indulgence if not sanction. Baker quickly capitalized on Mose's popularity in sequels such as *New York as It Is* (1848), *Three Years After* (1849), and *Mose in China* (1850), and the character soon took on a life of his own, becoming the centerpiece of such plays as Henry W. Plunkett's *The Mysteries and Miseries of New York* (1848). Though short-lived as a theatrical character, Mose's success suggested a growing interest among some middle- and working-class audiences in characters drawn from their daily experience. With the door opened, newer citizens of the cities soon found themselves the subjects of dramatists' attention.

Although Northeastern metropolitan areas had long drawn immigrants to their concentrated labor and housing markets, the later 1840s and 1850s saw a staggering increase in foreign immigration, primarily from Ireland and Germany, whose inhabitants had been driven forth by the dual forces of famine and political oppression. Settling in the tenements and slums, these newest arrivals quickly became a fixture in urban locales, where brute strength and willingness to labor in demanding and dangerous jobs were more important than their deficiencies in English and education. Although they adapted as best they could to new circumstances, their eagerness for work drove down wages and brought them into conflict with working-class Americans with whom they competed for jobs. For American elites, this wave of immigrants – predominately Catholic in religion and perceived as clannish, unfamiliar with American ideals, and uncommitted to the assumed democratic operations of American government – transformed previous class anxieties about loss of social control into fears about the continued existence of the republic. Collectively, American fears about this influx took many forms at midcentury. The emergence of the Know-Nothing Party and a virulent nativist campaign against continued immigration were merely the most obvious public manifestations. Unsurprisingly, concern with these immigrants spilled into the theatre. While the language barrier induced some German immigrants to form German-language theatre troupes (most notably New York's Stadt Company founded in 1854) and thereby to control in part their representation, Anglo-American playwrights in the 1850s also drew portraits of the Germans in such farces as S. Barry's *The Persecuted Dutchman; or, The Original John Schmidt* (1854) and *The Dutchman's Ghost* (1857). As was typical of such ethnic farces, *The Persecuted Dutchman* relied upon supposed universal traits of German immigrants – poor English, superstition, love of beer, and penny-pinching thrift – to amuse and reassure Anglo-American audiences.

If Germans on the American stage were primarily buffoons, the theatrical portaits of the Irish were somewhat more complex. The long English tradition of comic Irish characters had been imported to the American stage both indirectly through American refashionings, such as John Murdock's *The Triumphs of Love* (1795), William Dunlap's *Darby's Return* (1798), and John Minshull's *Rural Felicity* (1801), and directly through the staging of plays, such as Samuel Lover's *Rory O'More,* J. R. Planché's *The Irish Post,* and J. B. Buckstone's *The Irish Lion.* However, the increasing visibility of the Irish at midcentury attracted Irish "delineators," actor-playwrights such as the first Tyrone Power, John Brougham, Barney Williams, and James Pilgrim, whose principle roles were almost exclusively Irishmen. Combined with the widespread audience mix of dread and fascination with the Irish outside the theatres, these actors' skills go a long way toward explaining the increasing popularity of the Irish character on the American stage during the period. Interestingly, though all were native-born Irish, all except Williams came to the American stage by way of theatre work in London, where deprecatory versions of the Irish had long been a staple of both East End and West End theatres. Thus, it is not surprising that all of them wrote plays that carried on a campaign of ethnic rehabilitation while ostensibly acceding to the anti-Irish prejudices of their Anglo-American audiences. Typical in the strategies Williams deployed was James Pilgrim.

One of the era's most prolific playwrights, Pilgrim wrote a number of Irish plays both as vehicles for himself and for others. A cursory reading of standard acting editions of his early plays suggests that Pilgrim's works are firmly situated in the mainstream of traditional English versions of Ireland and the stage Irishman. Early works such as *Paddy Miles; or, The Limmerick Boy,* which premiered at London's Sadler's Wells Theatre in 1836, reflect the conventional hard-drinking, blarney-spouting, shillelagh-wielding stage Irishman. When Pilgrim arrived in the United States in the 1840s, he unpacked this character and found ready acceptance of him in working-class theatres such as the Arch Street in Philadelphia and the Bowery and the National in New York. However, over the course of the next decade or so, a subtle transformation is detectable in his figurations. Pilgrim's earlier portrayals of Ireland as an impoverished wilderness is gradually displaced by an altogether more romanticized landscape, and his farce versions of roistering Irish peasants are more and more often counterbalanced by the emergence of a newer, proto-middle-class Irishman.

The genesis of these transformations makes for interesting speculation. Part of the answer lies, no doubt, in the changing audiences of the decade. By the early 1850s, the traditional working-class audiences of Philadelphia's Arch Street and New York's Bowery and National theatres were gradually being infiltrated by new Irish immigrants. Although the number of Irish ensconced in costlier boxes was probably minimal, the gallery provided ready access to those who wished to indulge themselves in an evening of nostalgia for the "old sod." Another factor resides in Pilgrim's newest clients for his works, the husband-and-wife acting team of Barney and Maria Williams. After 1850, when Pilgrim began to write for the Williamses with great frequency, he seems to have embraced the conventions of domestic melodrama, which accorded substantial male and female roles. Finally, the conventions of the domestic melodrama itself, with its perennial plot emphases on a heroine's endangered honor and a parallel anxiety about the economic stability of middle-class life, tended to redirect the dramatic focus away from farcical physical actions to more serious concerns. Although it is unreasonable to suppose that he consciously turned his back completely on the expectations of his original Anglo-American working-class audiences, Pilgrim is clearly seeking in his later plays to present actions more appealing to audiences who were leavened by Irish immigrants and who were collectively striving to embrace an increasingly ubiquitous middle-class ideology.

In *Shandy Maguire* (1851), Pilgrim deploys a carefully constructed domestic melodrama upon the vexed political landscape of Ireland, attempting in obvious fashion to placate his Irish auditors without alienating Anglo-Americans, who may well have felt some sympathy with British colonizers surrounded by potentially dangerous Paddys. By elevating the Irish heroes and heroines while carefully restricting his critique of the English to the villainous son of an honorable English magistrate, Pilgrim is able to accommodate both audience expectations simultaneously. Pilgrim's sensitivity to the political subtext of the plays carries over to his major characterizations. Although the play has a wealth of singing, rollicking peasants, its central character, Maguire, is presented more as a lighthearted melodramatic hero than as a peasant trickster. Although he retains many of the exuberant characteristics of his stage ancestors – including singing often and engaging in running banter with his lady love and fellow villagers – Maguire's shenanigans are primarily reserved for more serious purposes than might be anticipated. For example, adapting an oft-employed farce device, Pilgrim uses disguise (including three cross-dressing episodes) to enhance his central character's heroic stature. Rather than duping those around him for his and the audience's general amusement, Maguire uses the opportunities to beat corrupt police, to retrieve stolen papers from the villain and temporarily save the heroine's father's livelihood, and to rescue the heroine from the clutches of the villain intent upon compromising her honor. The play ends, of course, with the villain dead and Maguire united with the heroine, Mary O'Connor. In a thinly veiled attempt to distance his Irish hero from the residual legacy of violence so often ascribed to Irish protagonists, Pilgrim has the villain dispatched by a village boy (Maria Williams in drag) to avenge the death of a dishonored local maiden.

In *Eveleen Wilson; or, The Flower of Erin* (1853), a vehicle for himself, Pilgrim's revamping of Irish representations becomes even more apparent. In action ranging from Dublin, across the Irish countryside, to New York, a complex metaphoric characterization crossing ethnic and class lines emerges as Pilgrim attempts to capitalize fully on domestic melodrama's emotional range. Fundamentally a classic melodrama of greed and lust, the play shifts the audience's attention from the hero to the villain who alternately attempts to seduce and/or murder his cousin so that she cannot supplant him in his father's will. The beset heroine of the piece, Eveleen Wilson, is in some senses the prototype of Dion Boucicault's *Colleen Bawn*. A standard embodiment of melodramatic virtue on the one hand, Eveleen is also the quintessence of Irish beauty. But, as is typical in such plays, her exterior beauty is also a curse, exciting as it does the lust of the villain, who determines either to possess that beauty or to besmirch it, compromising, in the warped logic of domestic melodrama, her interior virtue as well. This idealized Catholic beauty becomes, of course, a metaphoric representation of Ireland itself, the focus of the struggle between a resurgent Irish middle-class manhood and rapacious Irish collaborators who manipulate their countrymen for English-inspired profit. For most of the play, Eveleen does little more than faint on cue and wring her hands at the prospect of losing her new love. But in the play's third act, Eveleen, transported to New York by the villain's henchmen, strives valiantly, and ultimately successfully, against the villain's treachery.

Eveleen's dual saviors, the heroic Haviland and the comic Barney O'Slashem, embody the logical extension of the pattern seen in *Shandy Maguire*. Haviland, the successful gentleman farmer, personifies the standard middle-class hero – sober, courteous, educated, frugal, and brave. But Pilgrim goes to some pains to overlay his hero with at least a veneer of Irishness. Accused of spying for the British authorities, Haviland characterizes such reports as "foul calumny" and, contemplating his fate to wander America in search of Eveleen, he strikes a note of pathos at his and Ireland's fallen fortunes that must have resonated with the play's Irish-American audience. The speech's affiliation of the Irish with ancient knowledge and a heroic past seems designed to render Haviland as the legatee of a very different Irishness than that associated with Barney. And the sentiment's placement immediately prior to the play's climax suggests that this particular version of the Irish character remains a possibility that widespread adoption of standard middle-class virtues might well revive.

But Pilgrim was not willing to vault wholly into the realm of middle-class idealism, as his inclusion of Barney O'Slashem testifies. A stage Irishman of the first water, Barney points the way toward Boucicault's Myles, Shaun, and Conn. A blarney-spouting servant, Barney spends the early part of the play complaining in thick brogue about the hardships of his life and wielding his shillelagh against those who threaten his domestic order or offer violence against Eveleen. The most colorful character of the play, Barney becomes the embodied wrath of the Irish peasantry who runs the villain to ground in New York and effects the heroine's escape. Tellingly, however, he is excluded from the play's concluding episode, apparently too pointed a reminder for the audience of the very Irishness that Pilgrim wishes to efface. Nevertheless, within the confines of the melodramatic plot, he serves as the good-hearted energy needed to confront the villain in his own violent turns and pave the way for the triumph of the middle-class hero.

The strategies for dealing with Irish characters developed by Pilgrim would be refined by Boucicault and John Brougham, and, after the Civil War, comic and tragic visions of Irish ethnic identity would be further transformed by playwrights from Edward Harrigan and Edward Sheldon to Eugene O'Neill and Philip Barry. More generally, immigrant characters would become part of the canvas of the American theatre, available to add ethnic color to broader portraits of the American scene and, occasionally, to step center stage as the focal point of the action. The tensions between immigrant and native-born evident in these plays continue to play themselves out both on the contemporary American stage and in the social and political worlds. And the attempts of playwrights to speak for marginalized groups seems a phenomenon that will continue until Americans at large can resolve the question of American identity that these plays both enact and thematize.

If American playwrights were concerned with questions of identity configured as the relationship between an overt or implicit cultural other and an assumed dominant culture, they also sought to illuminate the genesis of the dominant culture's identity and to reinforce its ostensible solidarity. The primary expression of this project is to be found in the various types of history plays that were popular throughout the century. Whether reconstructing an imaginary past, providing theatrical biographies for emulation, or dramatizing national events, these plays served as one of the primary means by which popular theatre educated its audiences to a supposedly unitary national identity. Ranging formally from interludes and historical spectacles to domestic melodramas and comedies, these plays served the needs of rising middle and lower classes and immigrants in giving them a sense of America as both ideal and social-political entity.

Serious considerations of the nation's historical past were limited to the work of James Nelson Barker, whose attempts in *Superstition* to use the colonial period to earnest didactic purpose were neglected by subsequent American playwrights. On the whole, romanticism's pervasive influence tended to relegate history to the realm of quaint locale. But in one instance, folkloric history became the basis for one of the most successful plays of the century. In 1819, Washington Irving published the story "Rip Van Winkle," ostensibly based upon notes of Diedrich Knickerbocker, Irving's New York Dutch alter

Joseph Jefferson III (1829–1905) in his starring vehicle of Rip Van Winkle, pictured with Miss Godsall as his grown daughter Meenie in a London production. Photography by W. Walker and Sons, London. Laurence Senelick Collection.

ego. In 1828 a version of the play (penned by an anonymous "Albanian") was staged in Albany, New York. John Kerr produced a second version in 1829, and Charles Burke rewrote the play in 1850. After the Englishman Thomas Lacy provided a fourth variation for the London stage, Joseph Jefferson III commissioned the master adapter of his age, Dion Boucicault, to furnish another. Completed in 1865, the Boucicault–Jefferson collaboration held the stage until Jefferson's death in 1905. Over the course of its adaptations, Irving's familiar story eventually centered on Rip's suffering at his shrewish wife's hands and the parallel plot of Derrick Von Beekman's attempts to swindle Rip out of his lands. Rip's pathetic departure into the stormy night, his magical interlude with the ghosts of Henry Hudson and his crew, his fantastic return to his lately Americanized village, and his sentimental reunion with his daughter and chastened wife wedded New York Dutch folk history to domestic melodrama in a thoroughly appealing manner. When combined with Jefferson's understated acting, the play's evocation of rural verities and simple homespun wisdom proved a powerful mechanism for linking nineteenth-century audiences with a romanticized past.

More conventional versions of the history play falling primarily into democratic hagiography and chronicles of various pivotal events in the nation's history also drew audience enthusiasm. The already mentioned *André* and *The Glory of Columbia* powerfully situated Washington in the national imagination, a process repeated by some dozen forgettable plays on the same subject produced between 1830 and 1855. But Washington's power as national symbol transcended his life. Even Washington's 1799 death proved an occasion for theatrical commemoration, if not full-blown drama, with New York's Park Theatre producing a scene in which the American eagle wept tears of blood over the tomb of Washington while holding in its mouth a scroll inscribed "A Nation's Tears." Other colonial and revolutionary heroes also provided theatrical material. Richard Penn Smith, the prolific writer of history plays, provided Philadelphia audiences the opportunity to honor the title character in *William Penn* (1829), which traced Penn's reconciliation of warring factions in a play otherwise given over to the blood and thunder of Indian drama. In *Putnam, The Iron Son of '76* (1844) N. H. Bannister incorporates various melodramatic elements, including songs, tableaux, and breakneck action to celebrate the exploits of one of the Revolutionary War's major figures. Somewhat more stately is John Brougham's *Franklin* (1856), which details Franklin's life from his youth to his days as the American emmisary to the court of France's Louis XVI. Although all of these plays idealize the nation's heroes, they also suggest the legacy of the founders of the nation that each audience member is invited to internalize.

More numerous than the dramatized biographies are works dealing with political events and chronicle plays of the nation's military exploits. Establishing a pattern that would culminate in the slavery plays, the popular theatre was quick to interject itself into national questions. The 1800 presidential contest generated J. H. Nichols's satire of Federalist candidate John Adams and the apotheosis of Jefferson in *Jefferson and Liberty; or, Celebration of the Fourth of March* (1801). Barker rallied support for Jefferson's 1807 Embargo Act in *The Embargo; or, What News?* (1808). Similarly, in 1835 Henry J. Finn's farce *Removing the Deposits* evoked for New York's Bowery Theatre's working-class audience Jackson's decision to no longer utilize the Bank of the United States as the federal depository. Boundary disputes with Canada also occasioned comment, figuring prominently in N. H. Bannister's *The Maine Question* (1839) and Joseph M. Field's *Oregon; or, The Disputed Territory* (1846). But dramatizations of political controversies receded before a tide of plays dealing with America's martial endeavors. Like their patrician counterparts, popular plays dealing with military matters tended initially to keep actual fighting off stage, but unlike *André, Marmion,* or even *The Gladiator,* in which the clash of competing ideologies consumes much of the dialogue, the popular dramas tended to emblematize the agon as a romantic conflict. In plays such as Dunlap's *Yankee Chronology* (1812), Noah's *She Would Be a Soldier* (1819), Clifton W. Tayleure's *Horseshoe Robinson* (1856), and Oliver Bunce's *Love in '76* (1857), the military action is either narrated or reduced to the backdrop against which the contested romantic loyalties of the characters play themselves out. Plays about later military episodes, including Richard Penn Smith's *The Eighth of January* (1829) and *Triumph at Plattsburg* (1830), both of which deal with events in the War of 1812, Mordecai Noah's Barbary War play *The Siege of Tripoli* (1828) and John P. Adams's Mexican War play *The Battle of Buena Vista* (1847) tend toward celebrations of American manhood, but in most cases retain a love interest as a secondary plot line. In all cases, a broadly conceived democratic ideology underpins an action focused on the fates of common heroes rather than the general staff. And, unlike the patrician plays' supermen, popular plays tended to see wars from the "underside," with the heroism of the common man distributed widely throughout the cast. Intriguingly, the pattern of linking generalized love stories to national politics is retained in plays written in midcentury and after the Civil War, when improved stage machinery made depictions of stage combat more possible and when stirring battle scenes appeared more regularly in response to audiences who had grown accustomed to melodramatic spectacle.

While history and particular political events provided perennial material, manners and broad social issues also proved popular subjects. Addressing from different perspectives the abiding search for a normative definition of America and the character of its people and institutions, these plays sought to redress what they saw as the country's failures in social organization. Whether satirically reflecting upon social pretensions or campaigning against the evils of "demon rum" or slavery, plays as diverse as *Fashion, The Drunkard,* and *Uncle Tom's Cabin* argued forcefully for a reassertion of abiding American ideals, ideals that by the 1840s and 1850s had become synonymous with rationality, moderation, patriotism, and love of the family – in other words, the ideology of sentimental domesticity for women and liberal bourgeois respectability for men. Operating through melodrama's reductive bipolarities and reflecting unexamined class, race, gender, and economic biases, these plays in their very blindnesses, omissions, and unself-conscious reflections of the period's ideologies, provide a fascinating insight into the ways in which the popular theatre simultaneously confronted and effaced the issues of its day.

Social comedy was not generally explored during the first half of the nineteenth century. Though Tyler's *The Contrast* had domesticated the form for American use and the success of Barker's *Tears and Smiles* had demonstrated its theatrical potential, few American playwrights evidenced interest in anatomizing the upper classes until after the Jacksonian ascendancy propelled the elites from the theatre. Perhaps fearful of offending their patrons or disgracing their social group, patrician playwrights, whose knowledge of their fellows would have provided the most telling insights, rarely turned their attentions to the foibles of their own class. Popular playwrights, such as James Kirke Paulding, in the process of creating a different audience occasionally imported upper-class characters as butts for the robust humor of the lower classes, but until Anna Cora Mowatt's *Fashion* (1845), social comedy remained an undiscovered country on the American stage. In the wake of *Fashion,* a few playwrights chose to send their Americans abroad. Utilizing the easily recognizable class trappings of the old world, the contrasts between Americans and Europeans played themselves out in plays such as Oliver S. Leland's *Caprice; or, A Woman's Heart* (1857) and William Henry Hubert's *Americans in Paris* (1858). The majority of the social comedies, however, chose to focus on American elites, importing Europeans to enliven the action and somewhat mitigate the satire on Americans. Like *Fashion,* Henry Oake Pardey's *Nature Nobleman* (1851), Mrs. Sidney J. Bateman's *Self* (1856), and E. G. P. Wilkins's *Young New York* (1856) all use American fascination with European aristocrats as an indication of elite America's falling away from egalitarian republican virtues. Despite their occasional charms, all of these efforts pale in comparison with their inspiration.

Mowatt's *Fashion* (1845) represents the high-water mark of social comedy in nineteenth-century America. The story of the parvenu Tiffany family, their respectable governess, Gertrude, and their rural savior, Adam Trueman, the play is a sprightly examination of fashionable pretenders to New York high society and of the concept of fashion itself. As a product of the very American upper class to which her satiric butts aspire, Mowatt brought to her action insights that made her critique devastating. Reiterating many of the oppositions deployed in *The Contrast, Fashion* explores the seeming persistent need of nouveau riche Americans to attain a veneer of culture usually ascribed in the period to Europeans and perceived as obtainable through marriage. The centerpiece of the satire on class pretensions is the duo of Mrs. Tiffany and her daughter Seraphina, who set about to lead the New York "ee-light" out of the cultural wilderness of American boorishness into the promised land of a Europeanized gentility. Mrs. Tiffany's lack of refinement, her insistence upon living beyond her family's means, her mangled French, her inability to recognize the bogus Count Jolimaitre for a chef in disguise, and her willingness to bargain her daughter's hand for a spurious title provides for a complex set of critiques, both conservative and liberal in its import. On the one hand, the play exposes the social pretensions of the nouveau riche, whose acquisitiveness provided the economic basis but not the refined taste to become members of the upper class. As such, the play surely buttressed the biases of upper-class audience members such as Epes Sargent and Nathaniel Parke Willis, who loudly applauded the opening-night performance at New York City's Park Theatre. Adam Trueman, the rural patriarch who saves his old friend Tiffany from a charge of forgery and oversees the uniting of Gertrude with the doughty Colonel Howard, serves on one level an even more conservative function. By insisting that Mrs. Tiffany and Seraphina be sent into the country to be re-educated in republican political virtues and in their proper roles in the domestic order, Trueman becomes one of the last traditional republican patriarchs to be seen on the American stage arguing the moral superiority of the country over the city. On the other hand, Trueman may well have been reconceived by part of the post-Jacksonian audience as a refined version of the Jacksonian common man rather than a Jeffersonian yeoman patriarch and, thus, served as a critique of the very class lines that the play ostensibly reinforces. From another perspective, Mrs. Tiffany's longing for European sophistication lays bare the persisting cultural colonization against which democratically inspired contemporary writers such as Emerson were railing. Beyond these socially and politically determined readings resides the point made by Edgar Allan Poe in his review for the *Broadway Journal* (April 5, 1845) that the play satirizes the very concept of fashion. A rich text transformed by an able original cast into a successful play, *Fashion* held the stage throughout most of the nineteenth century and has regularly been revived. The perennial appeal of the play was recognized by the seminal American modernist company, the Provincetown Players, which under the leadership of Kenneth Macgowan, Robert Edmond Jones, and Eugene O'Neill mounted a production that ran for 235 performances in 1924.

If *Fashion* evidences an enduring concern for questions of social position and the humorous aspects of America's ostensibly permeable class lines, the temperance melodramas that became popular in the antebellum period reflect the more serious issue of alcohol abuse and the broader question of respectability, a lynchpin of a bourgeois liberal ideology increasingly deployed across class lines.[15] British temperance plays such as Douglas Jerrold's *Fifteen Years of a Drunkard's Life* and T. P. Taylor's *The Bottle* had found American audiences in the early part of the century at the same time that patrician organizations such as the Massachusetts Society for the Suppression of Intemperance and the American Society for the Promotion of Temperance sought initially to extend patrician control over the working classes by discouraging alcohol abuse and later by arguing that only total abstinence would preserve one's immortal soul and avoid the ruin awaiting the slide from moderate drinking to drunkenness. The wave of reform that swept through the working classes in the 1830s and 1840s also addressed the plague of alcohol abuse. Organizations such as New York City's Apprentices' Temperance Union and the Washingtonian Temperance Society embraced teetotalism and offered a challenge to patrician leadership of the movement. The Washingtonian Temperance Society was particularly effective, harboring among its initial membership former drinkers who were dedicated to using their personal testimonies to rehabilitate drunkards. Unsurprisingly, perhaps, many working-class theatres embraced temperance melodramas. But others saw the potential of these plays as well. Museum theatre owners such as P. T. Barnum and Moses Kimball, seeking to recoup the reputation of the theatre and expand audiences to include the middle-class families, turned to morally uplifting plays such as W. H. Smith's *The Drunkard* (1844). Thus, Smith's play provides telling insights not only into the strategies utilized to effect reform across broad segments of the American theatregoing public but also into the ways in which the ideology of bourgeois liberalism extended its influence through two different types of theatres.

The Drunkard enacts one of the conventional temperance narratives. Forgoing the alternative chronicle of a drunkard's slide from respectability to death, *The Drunkard* details the descent into intemperance and resurrection into sobriety of Edward Middleton, a young man seduced from hearth and home by a combination of personal weakness and the machinations of Lawyer Cribbs. Cribbs is driven by a pathological hatred of good grounded in his own avarice and the fact that Edward's father had discovered Cribbs in a "vile atrocity" and forgiven him. For audiences already attuned to such villains, Cribbs situates the action straightforwardly in the melodramatic universe, in which liquor merely becomes another weapon in evil's arsenal in its ongoing battle against earnest, middle-class respectability. Middleton's descent into drunkenness argues against the evils of drink, for his fundamentally good character proves no match for the unforeseen and derationalizing effects of alcohol. But, more generally, Middleton's fate reinforces the pervasive audience anxiety that evil was ever watchful for the opportunity of transforming the slightest digression from upright behavior into destruction. As is typical in temperance plays, Edward moves from social drinker to drunkard with dismaying rapidity, propelling both himself and his family from middle-class decency and economic security to destitution. Using Middleton's wife, Mary, and daughter, Julia, as markers of his descent, Smith delivers scenes of increasing pathos as Mary and Julia are driven by poverty and shame from their secure rural domesticity to rag-bedecked subsistence in a New York City tenement. Reinforcing conventional links among drunkenness, urban poverty, and moral degeneracy, Smith completes his moral fable by having the reformed drinker and now upright merchant Arden Rencelaw save Edward from suicide, oversee the exposure of Lawyer Cribbs, and reunite the Middleton family in rural domestic felicity. In the play's final scene, Edward and Julia combine in a duet of "Home, Sweet Home," followed by the formation of a tableau in which Edward prays with one hand on the Bible and the other pointed toward heaven. As his family gathers around him, Middleton becomes again the embodiment of ideal middle-class respectability grounded upon a sentimental domesticity.

For audiences in working-class theatres, the play was a powerful ideological statement of the perils that attended aspirations to middle-class status. The smallest moral lapse might well put one's ambitions forever beyond one's reach, and indulgence on the order of Edward Middleton could possibly drive one into the ranks of the poor again. For middle-class museum theatre audiences, the play's messages were somewhat different. On the most overt level, *The Drunkard* served to reinforce middle-class fears of their tenuous hold upon respectability and to argue the evils of drink. Beyond that, however, resided the even greater fear of losing hold upon reason itself. Middleton's terrifying delirium tremens scene compelled museum audiences to realize how quickly rationality, the foundation of middle-class belief in personal perfectability and the cornerstone of their ordered, self-controlled, and self-reliant lives, might be lost. While *The Drunkard* holds out the possibility of benevolence's intervention and reiterates the power of religious faith and a nuturing family to restore the fallen to society, the spectacle of Middleton with poison vial in hand powerfully suggested that the stake in the contest between self-controlled, rational good and indulgent, sensual evil was life itself. Collaterally, the play argued both the need for and efficacy of such men of principle as Rencelaw. With reason, faith, and overt action, the play argues, Americans can confront and overcome the most persistent social evils.

No evil in nineteenth-century America was more invidious and divisive than slavery. As the nation stumbled toward the Civil War, the popular theatre was drawn irresistibly into the public debate, and African American characters appeared in increasing numbers. African Americans had long been associated with the American theatre and had been represented in both stage plays and in more popular entertainments such as minstrel shows. In 1821, William Henry Brown, a retired African American seaman, founded the African Grove Theatre at which his African American troupe performed such plays as Shakespeare's *Richard III* and W. T. Moncrieff's melodramatic adaptation of Pierce Egan's *Tom and Jerry; or, Life in London*. Having fallen afoul of Mordecai Noah, who was waging a campaign to have restrictions on African American voting written into the New York state constitution, Brown conducted a two-year battle to keep his theatre open. Although he eventually lost that fight and disappeared from the New York City theatre scene, Brown in the interim managed to produce his own play, *The Drama of King Shotaway* (1823), the first play by an American to elevate a black man to heroic stature. Mainstream playwrights typically restricted their black characters to secondary roles. In plays such as Dunlap's *A Trip to Niagara,* Paulding's *The Lion of the West,* and Mowatt's *Fashion,* African Americans had usually been portrayed as buffoonish servants. But African American characters (played by whites in blackface) were thrust center stage in the spate of slavery plays that appeared in the wake of Harriet Beecher Stowe's 1852 novel *Uncle Tom's Cabin.* Even as the novel's serialization was appearing, *The Southern Uncle Tom* appeared at the Baltimore Museum, followed in short order by C. W. Taylor's adaptation presented at Purdy's National Theatre in New York City. These were quickly succeeded by numerous other versions, the most famous being George Aiken's, written originally for the Troy Museum company in Troy, New York, and Henry J. Conway's, produced by P. T. Barnum at his American Museum in New York City. The play quickly found audiences abroad, with multiple stagings becoming commonplace in most major European cities. During the remainder of the century, at least a dozen renderings reached print as literally hundreds of companies crisscrossed the country, performing the play in almost every city, town, and hamlet. Though the timeliness of its political critique had been eclipsed by the Civil War, the play's melodramatic and theatrical appeals continued to pack in audiences. In fact, the heyday of "Tomming" did not occur until the century's last two decades.

But if *Uncle Tom's Cabin* dominated the stage and public imagination, it was not the only play to tackle the slavery issue. The escaped-slave and abolitionist speaker William Wells Brown produced a loosely constructed dramatic indictment of slavery in *The Escape; or, A Leap for Freedom* (1858). Displaying the physical and emotional degradations of slavery in the pattern of the *Uncle Tom's Cabin* adaptations, Wells's piece centers the action on the attempts of the morally refined slaves Melinda and Glen to escape through the underground railroad to freedom in Canada. Less politically pointed, but more polished dramatically, is Boucicault's *The Octoroon* (1859). Within a spectacular melodrama framework, Boucicault tells the story of the doomed love of Zoe, the title character, and George Peyton, the European-educated scion of a southern plantation family. Unable to reconcile her love and fearing her fate at the hands of the lustful villain, Zoe kills herself, rendering the essential questions surrounding slavery moot, if draped in pathos. Mrs. J. C. Swayze's *Ossawattomie Brown* (1859) lionizes John Brown's commitment to the abolition of slavery, weaving an improbable love story into the fabric of Brown's raid on Harper's Ferry and his eventual capture. Finally, Stowe's second novel, *Dred,* provided the title, if little else, for three 1856 adaptations.

Aiken's *Uncle Tom's Cabin* partakes of several of the strategies that we have already seen in popular dramas dealing with social issues and institutions. Its primary strategy is a two-pronged attempt to resituate African Americans within the category of humanity as understood by its contemporary audiences. To accomplish this, Aiken, following Stowe's lead, selects two male heroes, George Harris and Uncle Tom, on which to focus the audience's attention. To the mulatto Harris, Aiken ascribes the conventional attributes of

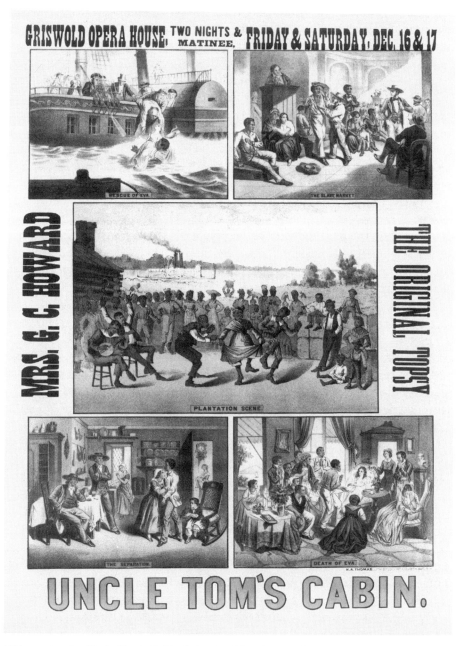

This poster for *Uncle Tom's Cabin,* featuring Mrs. George C. Howard as Topsy, includes a series of key scenes from the play. Harvard Theatre Collection.

the middle-class domestic hero – refined sensibility, self-reliance, self-control, and love of family. Having humanized Harris in white terms, it is a relatively simple matter to persuade the audience that slavery is intolerable for a man of Harris's obvious character and abilities. In carefully wrought scenes in which George makes his case for freedom in terms redolent with American truisms about humanity's inherent desire for freedom, Aiken prepares the audience for the action-packed escape of this slave's holy family to Canada. The coalescing of staunch southern businessmen, Quaker abolitionists, and reformed slave owners around Harris and his family provides a steadily mounting sense of the inevitability of slavery's demise. Counterpointing this plot line is the pathos of Uncle Tom, the martyr to the evils of slavery. Tom's downward spiral to death at the hands of the Yankee Simon Legree furnishes Aiken his second line of attack. With the exception of Eva St. Clare, Tom is the purest soul in the play, the very embodiment of Christian virtue. His long-suffering devotion to the welfare of his fellow slaves and his concern for the spiritual fate of even Simon Legree align Tom with the domestic heroines, whose faith and fate call for protection against the forces of evil. The play's final tableau – an apotheosis of Tom in the company of the Protestant Virgin, Eva St. Clare – drives home the point that before transcendent divinity, race is of no consequence. Coinciding with this strategy of humanization, resides a scathing indictment of the economic underpinnings of slavery. Although some whites are portrayed as ineffectually mitigating the worst excesses of slavery, the majority are rendered as conscienceless exploiters of cheap labor silencing their better angels with the sounds of profits. Even for working-class audiences chary of competition from freed blacks, such men were easily recognizable and universally loathed as the southern counterparts of victimizing northern shop and factory owners. Little surprise, then, that the play spoke powerfully to the entire range of antebellum northern audiences. Nevertheless, Aiken's racial politics are less radical than they appear – African Americans receive their humanity as a dispensation from a privileged class, whose final guilt is avoided in the scapegoating death of its vilest member. As an institution producing consumable entertainments, the popular theatre's final object was not political insight or even disinterested art but rather profit, and, despite its most determined attempts, nineteenth-century American popular theatre did not often outdistance its audience's social biases.

The popular plays of the antebellum period ranged across the face of the American landscape, searching continuously for material that would enlighten its audiences to the changing complexities of the nation and its peoples. By confronting issues of individual and collective identity, examining the effects of growing cities and westward expansion, probing the social, political, moral, and economic problems of the day, the popular theatre became the common man's window on a changing world. In an era of enormous flux, it was simultaneously a site of entertainment and edification, an avenue toward tentative acculturation for a populace in the process of forging often conflicting self-conceptions. Though the chronicle of antebellum American popular theatre is filled with the twists and turns of popular taste and the appearance and disappearance of plays that addressed only briefly a barely conceived collective need, its aggregate provides a powerful reminder of the capacity of the theatre to both shape and reflect, however tentatively, however imperfectly, a people and an age.

Dion Boucicault: Popular Dramatist Par Excellence

Ironically, the situation of the nineteenth-century American playwright finds its finest example in the career of Dublin-born Dion Boucicault, already a successful playwright and theatrical adapter in Paris and London, who disembarked in New York City in September 1853 and quickly became a fixture of the American theatre scene. Though it would be twenty years before Boucicault would become a citizen, his career until his death in 1890 was firmly linked to his adopted country. Through public success and personal disappointment, Boucicault came to symbolize for would-be playwrights the glamor and economic possibilities (and dangers) of a life in the theatre. For the modernist critics who later excoriated his melodramas, he became the quintessence of a degenerate theatrical age. For students of American theatre, he has remained the epitomal playwright of his era.

Throughout most of his career, Boucicault was linked to his second wife, the fine actress Agnes Robertson. Indeed, when Boucicault arrived in America, he served almost exclusively as Agnes's manager. But he quickly realized that Agnes's extraordinary popularity would not guarantee long-term success. Inevitably family responsibilites (they were to have six children together) would demand Agnes's departure from the stage. To shore up his growing family's economic security, Boucicault undertook several theatrical occupations. He was the manager of various American theatres (Gaiety in New Orleans, 1855–56; Washington in Washington, D.C., 1858; and Winter Garden in New York City, 1859), an actor, acting teacher, producer/director, and, most notably, playwright. Driven constantly by his need for money and a desire to control the efforts of his labors, Boucicault sought to reform the economics of playwriting on several fronts. Along with George Henry Boker, he was instrumental in securing passage of a revised copyright bill in 1856 that provided playwrights greater rewards for productions of their plays. Seeking to guarantee the highest quality of performances (and, thereby, the greatest possible profits from his play's productions), Boucicault assumed the director's role in the mountings he produced. Although Boucicault was too much a man of his time to reconceive drama radically, his insistence upon his coherent artistic vision had the effect of reducing conventional acting "lines," unifying the tone of his pieces, and of increasing the illusion of his characters' individuality. More immediately influential was his revolution of touring companies. Previously, stars toured after a successful play's closing, supported by the local repertory company. In the wake of *The Colleen Bawn*'s (1860) success, however, Boucicault introduced the practice of granting production licenses only to managers willing to hire touring companies that Boucicault had personally formed and supervised. As impressive and long-lasting as these efforts were, it is primarily as a playwright that Boucicault is remembered today.

Boucicault's English career prepared him admirably for his American tenure. Having been a provincial actor, he arrived in London only to find his acting talents generally unappreciated by the audiences or managers. He quickly changed directions, churning out a host of plays, primarily for Charles Mathews and Madame Vestris and, later, Charles Kean. His efforts spanned the gamut, from adaptations of French pieces to farces to five-act comedies such as the enormously successful *London Assurance* (1841), *The Irish Heiress* (1842), and *Old Heads and Young Hearts* (1844) to melodramas such as *Sixtus V* (1851), *The Corsican Brothers* (1852), and *The Vampire* (1852). His output was prodigious. In the five-year period (1842–46) after the production of his first hit, *London Assurance,* London saw twenty-four new works from Boucicault's pen. By the time he arrived in America, Boucicault was an established playwright of some renown.

Boucicault's primary talent as a playwright was an uncanny sense of the public mood and his ability to translate social undercurrents into exciting theatre. Never a deep or philosophical thinker, Boucicault was nevertheless able to write works in whose hands the master actors of the period, including himself, could express a humanity that immediately captured their audiences. In the United States Boucicault turned his facility for acute social observation and his desire to give popular audiences plays that spoke with immediacy to their concerns into works that transformed the American stage. The first of these was *The Poor of New York* (1857). Having toured with Agnes from 1853 to 1857, Boucicault returned to New York City determined to expand his playlist beyond vehicles for his wife's ample talents. Linking contemporary interest in a financial panic with a similar occurrence twenty years before, Boucicault borrowed the essential plot from a French original, *Les Pauvres de Paris,* and produced a work that touched the economic fears of his business- and middle-class audience. A fairly typical melodrama, the play centers on the fate of the Fairweather family, who are impoverished in 1837 by the villainy of Gideon Bloodgood. Twenty years later, his reformed accomplice Badger reveals his former boss's crime, and virtue triumphs. The pivotal scene of the play is the on-stage "burning" of a tenement building, a meticulously choreographed action that riveted the audience as an actual city fire engine was pulled onto the stage to fight the blaze. The "sensation" created by this scene lent its name to the form, and "sensation" melodramas became Boucicault's trademark: In *The Octoroon,* a riverboat burns onstage; in *The Colleen Bawn,* the heroine is thrown into and must be rescued from a lake; in *Arrah-na-Pogue* (1864), the comic hero scales the exterior of a prison tower; and in *Formosa* (1869), a boat race occurs onstage. Though he was a master of such scenes, Boucicault was careful to integrate them into the action, making them crucial to the plot's development, not the raison d'être of the play itself. For all of their spectacular appeal, these scenes serve, more often than not, to further elucidate the heroism or villainy of the characters by providing an unambiguous visual expression of the natures of those involved in its action.

Although Boucicault recognized the box office appeal of sensation scenes, he astutely situated them within actions whose exoticism or timely appeal promised to draw audiences. Following on the success of *The Poor of New York,* he capitalized on interest in the 1858 Indian Sepoy uprising in *Jessie Brown; or, The Relief of Lucknow* (1858), providing Agnes one of her most successful roles as a young Scots girl who bolsters a garrison's morale until the arrival of a relief column of bagpipe-playing Campbell Highlanders. However great the appeal of foreign subjects, Boucicault recognized that nothing drew American audiences like plays centered on hotly contested contemporary American issues, and in *The Octoroon; or Life in Louisiana* Boucicault touched the pulse of his New York City audience again. Performed on the heels of John Brown's execution and the New York City election of a Copperhead mayor, the play brought together a cross section of American types – an Indian, numerous slaves, two Yankees, and members of the southern gentility – forming them into a whole that allowed Boucicault to examine the moral and legal implications of slavery within the framework of a sensation melodrama spiced with romance. The accuracy of his depiction of southern manners, his carefully modulated treatment of slavery designed to appeal to both abolitionist and pro-slavery sympathizers, the carefully constructed love story whose resolution hinges on Zoe's blackness, and the sensation scene already mentioned deflected attention from his more serious consideration of the law as the grounding concept of American society. But the combination was powerful enough to guarantee the play's success with his American audiences.

However, if contemporary events in America overtly grounded a significant part of his work, Boucicault was also sensitive to issues that flowed beneath the surface of urban American life. As a member of the class himself, he was drawn to the plight of Irish immigrants, whose status remained equivocal in their new American urban environment. Boucicault had long recognized the comic potential of the Irish, writing such pieces as *The Irish Heiress* and *A Soldier of Fortune; or, The Irish Settler* during his London tenure. In America, the increasing visibility of poor Irish immigrants, the popularity of Irish "delineators," growing numbers of immigrant Irish theatregoers, and his latent nationalism combined to precipitate a spate of Irish plays including: *Andy Blake* (1854), *The Colleen Bawn, Arrah-na-Pogue, Daddy O'Dowd* (1873), *The Shaughraun* (1874), and *Robert Emmet* (1884). Though many of these lie beyond the scope of this study, it is important to recognize the way in which Boucicault utilized the popular theatre as a mechanism of cultural intervention by reworking the conventions of nineteenth-century American theatre, specifically, the Irish American plays discussed above. Though he was to refine these techniques in his later plays, his 1860 hit *The Colleen Bawn* provides a convenient overview of the strategies he employed.

Ignoring for a moment his decision to put an Irish play before a middle-class audience at all, Boucicault's most daring ploy is to provide his audience with two interwoven plots, complete with two sets of heroes and heroines. Constrained perhaps more than he should have been by the play's source, Boucicault nevertheless managed, finally, to subordinate fully the trickster Irishman to a serious action centered on the Irish middle class. At the same time, by suggesting an ennobled Irish peasant as the central romantic interest in the play and paralleling the cross-class romance of Hardress Cregan and Eily O'Connor with the conventional middle-class love of the witty Ann Chute and the properly sober Kyrle Daly, Boucicault took a giant step toward the construction of the noble peasant tradition that was to figure so prominently in later attempts of Irish writers to wrench their representations from the forces of colonialism. Within the context of America's receptions of the Irish, *The Colleen Bawn* stands as a landmark instance in which Irish representations were finally able to tap successfully into America's noble commoner myth, and thus to pave the way for a positive theatrical reassessment of the Irish. Moreover, by restricting the action primarily to the Irish countryside, Boucicault was able at once to use the setting for both its picturesque appeals and as the basis for an implied affinity between Irish peasants and rural Americans. Finally, by presenting several middle-class Irish characters, Boucicault was able to counterbalance the popular stereotype of the poor "Paddy" with elevated figures who conformed to America's dominant middle-class ideology. In plays written during and after the Civil War, he was to augment these appeals by playing upon resurgent anti-British sentiments among American audiences, drawing more explicit links between nationalism in contemporary Ireland and Revolutionary-era America. As the antebellum period drew to a close, however, Boucicault, taking a cue from Pilgrim, had struck a note that would fundamentally reorder nineteenth-century dramatic representations of the Irish in America.

Though his career would continue well into the 1880s, Dion Boucicault established himself as the preeminent American popular playwright in the eight short years between his arrival in New York City and the beginning of the Civil War. In his assertion of the playwright's proprietary rights over his labor, Boucicault helped secure the economic futures of American writers. In his devotion to the Irish and through the representational strategies he developed and refined, Boucicault provided a model for successful ethnic playwriting that allowed ethnic characters to speak to a broad American audience. In his capacity to move with ease among the major centers of English-language theatrical activity in the United States, England, and Ireland, Boucicault almost singlehandedly established American playwrights as members of an international fraternity and dispelled the lingering sense of American dramatists as mere provincials. Finally, in his ability to read the public and to consistently produce works that touched the nation's subconscious concerns and abiding questions, Boucicault testified to the popular theatre's capability simultaneously to entertain and edify the nation.

Conclusion: Toward a New Professionalism

By the end of the Civil War, the theatre had emerged from the margins of American society to assume a position of central cultural importance for many – particularly urban – Americans. Arguably more democratic by 1865, the theatre and its writers reflected the rapidly changing face of America. Although a few of the patrician playwrights remained active after the 1830s, the new middle-, business-, and working-class audiences were addressed primarily by a new, semiprofessional, popularly oriented group of playwrights. Most often actors or managers (or both), these men and women rarely had the economic freedom to live solely by their pens and, as often as not, saw their work as an extension of their other theatrical activities. Plays were often composed to fill the specific needs of star actors, whose influence, despite their sponsorships of playwriting contests, acted generally as an inhibiting force to the growth of independent playwrights. Nevertheless, over the period under discussion, American playwrights' economic status improved somewhat with the passage of a new copyright bill providing at least a modicum of protection against unrecompensed productions of their plays. For those who were not also actors or managers, however, the theatre still did not provide the basis for a secure living.

With the advent of actor-writers such as Boucicault, actor-playwrights also began to achieve slightly greater control over their material within the theatre. Ironically, the theatrical rather than literary aspirations of the period's popular playwrights had a paradoxical impact upon the development of American playwriting. On the one hand, the popular playwrights' situation within the theatres more often than not provided knowledge of what worked on a stage, assuring that their plays were effective theatre pieces. On the other hand, by being located within the theatrical establishment itself, they were hard pressed to evoke the sanctioning authority of "literature" to elevate their efforts beyond workaday theatrical endeavors. The persistence of acting "lines," the jealously guarded autonomy of star actors and entrepreneurial managers, and traditional divisions between play and playscript resisted the assertion of authorial control. In the post–Civil War era of Augustin Daly and David Belasco, changing acting techniques and the localization of power within the hands of author-managers would finally elevate the author to a position of preeminence in the theatre, but that day had yet to arrive.

Nevertheless, the changing faces of American plays testified to the emergence of a new class of writers. Their tactics were straightforward and aptly suited to their age. They eagerly dismantled the received dramatic tradition and reconfigured it to fit the needs of a growing country in the process of understanding its various elements. Older casts of characters were quickly reworked to reflect American types. Wily servants and lower-class figures were soon speaking with Yankee or Irish or African American accents. Heroes and villains were as likely to carry bows or rifles as swords or canes. Settings and actions moved steadily away from the ancient battlefields of Greece or Rome or the fashionable salons of Europe to the frontiers and parlors of America. Tragedy gave way to melodrama, and class-based social comedy was soon leavened by the rough-and-tumble humor of frontiersmen and urban immigrants. In sum, this new group of playwrights was determinedly creating a national theatre worthy of the name. Though in some ways the "American" element of the phrase "American theatre" continued to strive toward full articulation, there is little doubt that by 1865 "American theatre" could no longer be considered an oxymoron.

Notes

1 See Barker's letter to Dunlap, reprinted in *A History of the American Theatre* (II, 308–16).
2 See McConachie, *Melodramatic Formations* (61–62).
3 See the appendixes to Grimsted's *Melodrama Unveiled* (249–61).
4 Barker, *The Indian Princess* in *Representative Plays by American Dramatists*, Moses, ed. (I, 576).
5 This issue is discussed in Nichols, "The Prejudice against Native American Drama from 1778 to 1830."
6 The phrase is Garff B. Wilson's in *Three Hundred Years of American Drama and Theatre* (104), but similar sentiments will be found in Grimsted's *Melodrama Unveiled* (xv), in which he calls melodrama "the most banal of dramatic forms."

For a particularly telling critique of such aesthetic assessments, see McConachie's *Melodramatic Formations* (ix-xiv).

7 On the general subject of melodrama see Booth, *English Melodrama;* Heilman, *Tragedy and Melodrama;* and, particularly, Peter Brooks, *The Melodramatic Imagination.* Grimsted; McConachie; and Mason, *Melodrama and the Myth of America* are particularly useful on melodrama in a specifically American context.

8 On the relationship of melodrama and fantasy, see Bentley, "Melodrama," in *The Life of the Drama* (195–218). The quotation is from James L. Smith, *Melodrama,* 11.

9 For a more thorough discussion of these issues, see McConachie, 1–63.

10 In "The Drama," [Philadelphia] *Democratic Press,* 18 December 1816: 2.

11 McConachie provides a detailed analysis of this pattern (91–118).

12 The disparity between the views of playwrights and contemporary audiences is hinted at by a letter that Bird wrote while visiting England three years after composing *The Gladiator.* Decrying the corruption and misery he saw, Bird worried, "I am afraid if I stay here much longer, I shall become a Jackson man! I begin to feel like a democrat, and for the first time in my life to think that God will lead the foot of the poor man to the neck of the rich, and that, in this, there will be justice . . ." (quoted. in Moody, *Dramas from the American Theatre,* 236).

13 Mason provides a detailed analysis of *Metamora* in the context of Jacksonian resettlement policy (23–59). For an overview of the changing image of Native Americans onstage, see Wilmeth, "Noble or Ruthless Savage?"

14 Brougham's burlesque has recently been reprinted in *Staging the Nation,* edited by Wilmeth.

15 On the temperance movement background to *The Drunkard,* see Mason (61–87).

Bibliography: Plays and Playwrights, 1800–1865

The following is intended to complement the notes in the chapter. Although theses, dissertations, and journal/serial essays often provide helpful and authoritative materials, limitations of space have precluded inclusion here of sources other than published books. For convenient bibliographical information on dissertations, see Litto's *American Dissertations on the Drama and Theatre: A Bibliography* (1969), supplemented by the subsequent yearly lists in *Theatre Journal* and *American Literature.* The following journals regularly publish on American theatre before the Civil War: *American Drama, Journal of American Drama and Theatre, Theatre History Studies, Nineteenth Century Theatre,* and *Theatre Journal.*

Increasing interest in earlier American theatre is reflected in the numerous reference works dealing in part or in whole with this period. Convenient one-volume encyclopedias are Gerald Bordman's *Oxford Companion to American Theatre,* which restricts itself primarily to "legitimate theatre," and the more comprehensive and essential *Cambridge Guide to American Theatre,* edited by Wilmeth and Miller. Among the most useful general bibliographies are: Gohdes, *Literature and Theatre of the States and Regions of the USA: An Historical Bibliography;* Hatch, *The Black Image on the American Stage;* Long, *American Drama from Its Beginnings to the Present;* Meserve, *American Drama to 1900;* Stratman, *Bibliography of the American Theatre Excluding New York City;* and Wilmeth, *The American Stage to World War I: A Guide to Information Sources.* As many of the playwrights discussed were also actors and actresses, general biographies on thespians as well as in volumes devoted specifically to playwrights can prove useful. Besides the individual biographies listed later, the most applicable general biographical resources are T. Allston Brown, *History of the American Stage: Containing Biographical Sketches of Nearly Every Member of the Profession from 1733 to 1870;* Applebaum, ed., *Great Actors and Actresses of the American Stage in Historic Photographs,* which includes material from 1850–1865; Arata and Rotoli, *Black American Playwrights, 1800 to the Present;* Archer, *American Actors and Actresses: A Guide to Information Sources;* Bryan, *Stage Lives: A Biographical and Index to Theatrical Biographies;* Matthews and Hutton, eds., *Actors and Actresses of Great Britain and the United States: From the Days of Garrick to the Present Time;* McNeil and Herbert, eds., *Performing Arts Biography Master Index;* Rigdon, ed., *The Biographical Encyclopedia and Who's Who of the American Theatre* and *Notable Names in the American Theatre;* Robinson, Roberts, and Barranger, *Notable Women in the American Theatre;* and Wearing, *American and British Theatrical Biography.* See also the sources discussed in Chapter 4.

The most comprehensive work dealing with theatre companies in this period is the first volume of Durham's *American Theatre Companies,* covering the years 1749–1887. On theatre periodicals, see the somewhat incomplete Stratman, *American Theatrical Periodicals, 1798–1967: A Bibliographical Guide.* A convenient, if slight, collection of reviews of selected plays in this period can be found in Montrose J. Moses and John Mason Brown, eds., *The American Theatre as Seen by Its Critics, 1752–1934* (New York: Norton, 1934). On manuscript and special collections devoted to theatre see the dated (1971) but worthwhile (though quite incomplete) Young, *American Theatrical Arts: A Guide to Manuscript and Special Collections in the United States and Canada.*

Many plays discussed above can still be found in the inexpensive contemporary acting editions published by French, Lacy, and Dick, which often provide interesting insights into the casts and contemporary staging. The most comprehensive collection of texts of American plays written in this period are found in two collections published by Readex Microprint, "Three Centuries of Drama" (to 1830) and "English and American Drama of the Nineteenth Century" (1830–1900). The latter collection has been indexed by Hixon and Hennessee, *Nineteenth-Century American Drama: A Finding Guide.* The most expansive assembly of rarely reprinted texts is the twenty-volume *America's Lost Plays,* Barrett H. Clark, general editor (1940–41). This work was reissued in ten double-volumes with an additional twenty-first volume in 1969. Several editors have devoted works exclusively to nineteenth-century drama: Booth, *Hiss the Villain;* Clark, *Favorite American Plays of the Nineteenth Century;* Matlaw, *The Black Crook and Other Nineteenth-Century American Plays* (1967) and *Nineteenth-Century American Plays* (1985); Meserve, *On Stage, America!;* and Wilmeth, *Staging the Nation.* Although general anthologies of American drama usually devote space to plays written before 1865, the only volume currently in print is Watt and Richardson, *American Drama, Colonial to Contemporary* (1995).

General histories and critical works devoting substantial space to discussions of American plays and playwrights in this period are numerous. Older anecdotal histories provide information on plays and players and, despite the lack of scholarly accuracy, are still worthwhile for the occasionally reprinted letters, handbills, illustrations, and other materials. Besides Dunlap's *History,* the most noteworthy of this group are Coad and Mims, *The American Stage* (1929); Hornblow, *A History of the Theatre in America* (1919); Moses, *The American Dramatist* (1925); Power, *Impressions of America During the Years 1833, 1834, and 1835* (1836); and Wemyss, *Chronology of the American Stage* (1852). The first truly scholarly history is Quinn, *A History of the American Drama from the Beginning to the Civil War* (1943), whose extensive playlist and comprehensive assessment of plays, movements, and writers makes this a valuable, if dated, work on the history of the text. Still useful, though methodologically out-moded, are volumes that examine American drama divorced from cultural, political, and social history: Bogard, Moody, and Meserve, *The Revels History of Drama in English*, Vol. VIII, *American Drama;* Downer, *American Drama;* Henderson's lavishly illustrated *Theatre in America: 200 Years of Plays, Players, and Productions,* recently updated; Hewitt, *Theatre U.S.A., 1668–1957;* Hughes, *A History of the American Theatre, 1700–1950;* Meserve, *An Outline History of American Drama;* and Wilson, *Three Hundred Years of American Drama and Theatre.* The most comprehensive theatre histories devoted to the period under discussion are Meserve's *An Emerging Entertainment: The Drama of the American People to 1828* and *Heralds of Promise: The Drama of the American People During the Age of Jackson, 1829–1849.* Recent works situating American plays in broader social, political, and economic contexts include the works by Grimsted, Mason, and McConachie, already cited in the notes, as well as Richardson, *American Drama from the Colonial Period Through World War I: A Critical History,* and Bank, *Theatre Culture in America, 1825–1860.*

Several local or regional histories provide insight into the production histories of the plays discussed here. A helpful bibliography of such materials is Larson, *American Regional Theatre History to 1900: A Bibliography.* As the center of theatrical activity during the period, New York City has received the most attention. The most notable efforts include Brown, *History of the New York Stage, From the First Performance in 1732 to 1901;* Ireland, *Records of the New York Stage from 1750 to 1860;* and the exhaustive Odell, *Annals of the New York Stage.* Other eastern and southern centers of theatrical activity have also received attention. Particularly important are Durang, *The Philadelphia Stage for the Years 1749–1855;* A. H. Wilson, *History of the Philadelphia Theatre, 1835–1855;* Ryan, *Old Boston Museum Days;* Dorman, *Theatre in the Ante Bellum South;* Hoole, *The Ante-Bellum Charleston Theatre;* and Smither, *A History of the English Theatre in New Orleans, 1806–1842.*

The elite drama and patrician playwrights have been the subject of numerous, primarily biographical, studies: On William Dunlap, Coad, *William Dunlap* and Canary, *William Dunlap.* James Nelson Barker's life is detailed by Musser, *James Nelson Barker.* For the acting and writing career of John Howard Payne, see Overmyer, *America's First Hamlet.* Robert Montgomery Bird's varied life has been the subject of Faust's *The Life and Dramatic Works of Robert Montgomery Bird* and Dahl, *Robert Montgomery Bird.* The most insistently literary American dramatist of the nineteenth century, George Henry Boker, has attracted considerable attention. Most noteworthy are: Bradley, *George Henry Boker, Poet and Patriot;* Evans, *George Henry Boker;* and Kitts, *The Theatrical Life of George Henry Boker.* Finally, on the life and works of Nathaniel Parker Willis, see Beers, *Nathaniel Parker Willis,* and Auser, *Nathaniel Parker Willis.*

Scholarly literature on the popular theatre has proliferated in the last few decades, with several specialized studies examining particular facets of American popular drama in the period. Romanticism's impact on early American drama/theatre is examined by Moody in *America Takes the Stage: Romanticism in American Drama and Theatre, 1750–1900.* On comedy see Hartman, *The Development of American Social Comedy, 1787–1936* and Havens, *The Columbian Muse of Comedy: The Development of a Native Tradition of Early American Social Comedy, 1787–1845.* Gallagher's *The Foreigner in Early American Drama* touches on the presentation of foreigners during the early years of the nineteenth century. On the Yankee play, see Hodge, *Yankee Theatre: The Image of American on the Stage, 1825–1850* and Morgan, *An American Icon: Brother*

Jonathan and American Identity. A survey of immigrant theatre organized by ethnic group is available in Seller, ed., *Ethnic Theatre in the United States.* A more detailed study of New York German theatre is Frederick Leuchs, *The Early German Theatre in New York, 1840–1872.* The slavery plays as a whole have yet to be examined, but *Uncle Tom's Cabin* has been the subject of two book-length studies: Birdoff, *The World's Greatest Hit: Uncle Tom's Cabin,* and Gossett, *Uncle Tom's Cabin and American Culture.*

Biographies of popular playwrights have been sporadic and of uneven quality. Much work remains to be done in this arena. On Mordecai Noah see Goldberg's *Major Noah: American Jewish Pioneer* and Sama, *Jacksonian Jew: The Two Worlds of Mordecai Noah.* The prolific Richard Penn Smith is the subject of McCullough's *The Life and Writings of Richard Penn Smith with a Reprint of His Play "The Deformed," 1830.* The satirical writer and actor John Brougham is still served only by Winter, ed., *Life, Stories, and Poems of John Brougham.* On James Kirke Paulding see Herold, *James Kirke Paulding: Versatile American,* Reynolds, *James Kirke Paulding,* and Ratner, *James Kirke Paulding.* The life of African American playwright and abolitionist William Wells Brown has been the subject of both his own autobiographies, *From Fugitive Slave to Free Man: The Autobiographies of William Wells Brown,* edited by William L. Andrews, and Farrison, *William Wells Brown, Author and Reformer.* On Anna Cora Ogden Mowatt Ritchie, see her *Autobiography of an Actress* supplemented by Barnes, *The Lady of Fashion.* For Dion Boucicault the standard works are Walsh, *The Career of Dion Boucicault;* Hogan, *Dion Boucicault;* Molin and Goodfellowe, comp., *Dion Boucicualt, the Shaughraun: A Documentary Life, Letters, and Selected Works;* and Fawkes, *Dion Boucicault.*

4

The Actors

European Actors and the Star System in the American Theatre, 1752–1870

Simon Williams

When trying to account for actors who have had a substantial impact on the history of the theatre, we frequently resort to metaphors of royalty. We refer to the finest performers of past generations as "player kings" or "queens" and allude to the stage and auditoriums over which they preside as personal "realms," as if such spaces are determined primarily by the powerful allure displayed by the actor. We speak of the leading clans of the theatre world – the Kembles, the Booths, the Sotherns, or the Barrymores – as the "royal families" of the theatre. No doubt we do this in part because we feel the magnetism exercised by the most powerful actors' calls for an unquestioning acceptance and loyalty, akin to the allegiance expected by monarchical authority, an appeal incidentally that few actors do much to counter. But our desire to make monarchs of stage performers may also have historical roots, in the close identity, especially strong in the eighteenth century, of acting troupes with royal patrons. In Europe, most actors who wished to achieve the social stature and respect that would ensure professional survival could do so only if they received the sanction of royalty. Their appearance on royally patented stages was even seen as a surrogate for the power of the prince himself.

In the early years of the American republic, this sense that actorial authority is somehow monarchical in nature casts the theatre into intriguingly anomalous light. As the newly independent nation grew, it emphatically asserted its freedom from royal shackles and assiduously constructed a political system, the principle aim of which was to ensure that relations between ruler and ruled were subject to constitutional limitations that guaranteed the rights of the individual citizen. The authority and ethos emanating from the stage were therefore contrary to those that informed the culture as a whole. Added to this, theatre in America was one of those few institutions that was

untouched by the revolutionary experience. As scholars have almost universally acknowledged, for the first century of its existence, the early American
theatre was essentially an offshoot of the British theatre, and therefore it
might be argued that the institution was largely tangential to the life of the
nation as a whole.

English-Speaking Traditions

The first actors that traveled to the American colonies with the specific intention of establishing a professional circuit did so because they had been
excluded from the royal privileges that both guaranteed and circumscribed
theatrical activity in their own country. The troupe of London actors that
opened the first season of professional theatre in the American Colonies at
Williamsburg in September 1752 had been financed and outfitted by William
Hallam (d. 1758) out of the remnants of the New Wells Theatre in Goodman's
Fields, which had been closed in 1751 precisely because it lacked the royal
patents that legitimized theatrical performance in England. Nevertheless, the
company did not come to America in the spirit of their Puritan forebears, in
rejection of a society that had excluded them. Instead, they continued to con-
ceive of themselves as ambassadors for that society and as advocates of its
values, a function clearly announced by Lewis Hallam, their leader, in the prologue that initiated the opening night in Williamsburg:

> To this New World, from famed Britannia's shore,
> Through boist'rous seas where foaming billows roar,
> The Muse, who Britons charm'd for many an age,
> Now sends her servants forth to tread your stage;
> Britain's own race, though far removed, to shew
> Patterns of every virtue they should know. (Quoted in Dunlap, *History,* I, 17)

Hallam's pronouncement was characteristically European, combining the
widely held Enlightenment idea of the theatre as a model of social grace and
virtue with a clear assertion of the cultural ascendancy of the mother country. The actors arrived on colonial shores, it would appear, to spread the
virtues of royal civilization.

The values and loyalties the statement implies seem to have changed little
over the twenty-five years leading up to the Revolution. For the first three
years of their existence, the company performed only in Williamsburg, New
York, Philadelphia, and Charleston. They then removed to Jamaica, a theatrically vigorous community where, after Hallam's death in 1755, the management was taken over by another British actor-manager, David Douglass. The
company returned to the eastern seaboard in 1758, under their old title of the
"London Company of Comedians," altering their name to the "American Com-

pany of Comedians" only in 1763. But this was a change in name only. The company, composed exclusively of English actors, continued to invoke the British monarch in their announcements, and at the opening of their season in Annapolis in 1772, pleaded eloquently to sustain a harmony between Britain and America that political tensions had long been tearing apart:

> Long may blest Concord here maintain her Sway,
> And radiant Science gild each rising Day:
> Whilst Patriots plead, without one private View,
> And glorious Liberty alone pursue!
> So shall the Mother Isles with joy approve,
> And aid their Offspring with parental love. (Quoted in Rankin, 167)

The American Company avoided the Revolutionary War by returning to Jamaica in 1775. When it reappeared in the United States in 1782, it did so in a country in which the theatre was not a high priority. Those who wished to influence the course of public events in the new republic found a more effective arena in the political world, whereas the general public, if they thought of the theatre at all, hardly associated it with the national cause. So for several decades after their return, the American Company, from 1786 under the management of Lewis Hallam Jr. and the Irish-born comedian John Henry, carried with it a touch of anachronism that characterized the profession as a whole. Theatre benefited from the general prosperity that resulted from the conclusion of the war, so that by the end of the eighteenth century there were permanent theatres occupied by resident companies in New York, Philadelphia, Boston, Baltimore, and Charleston, but the actors and other personnel that staffed them were almost exclusively British. For example, in 1792 Hallam's American Company settled in New York, occupying first the John Street Theatre, later the Park Theatre. When Thomas Wignell broke from Hallam to set up the Chestnut Street Theatre in Philadelphia in 1794, there were no native-born Americans he could call upon, so he returned to London to recruit the entire company from British theatres, a practice managers would continue well into the nineteenth century. Not surprisingly, the structure of an American theatre company was almost identical to a British one; in the early days of the Hallams, actors held shares in the communal enterprise, but toward the end of the eighteenth century as companies came to be held privately, actors were remunerated by salary and by the ubiquitous custom of benefit performances, in which a significant proportion of a given night's proceeds would go to the actor whose benefit had been designated. Furthermore, given the extreme dearth of American plays, the repertoire virtually duplicated that of the British theatre.

In significant ways, however, the American theatre did differ from the British. For a start, it was a more demanding place to work. By 1794, the American Company, ensconced in the John Street Theatre in New York, had grown to thirty-two personnel from the mere handful of actors that had returned to the States twelve years before. Nevertheless, it performed a repertoire as extensive as that of Drury Lane in London, which had almost six times the number of personnel. This placed greater strain on the memory and stamina of actors, who were called upon to play more roles than their English counterparts. But it would be a mistake to assume that because the American theatre had fewer resources than the British the quality of its performances was automatically poorer. It has been customary to dismiss the Hallams and their associates as theatrical inferiors; Hewitt speculates that they were "close to the bottom of their profession" (*Theatre U.S.A,* 14), but it should be remembered that in mid-eighteenth-century England the acting profession was minuscule and incapable of absorbing all who aspired to be part of it;[1] indeed, since Shakespeare's time, several talented actors who had found it impossible to establish a stage career in Britain took to the European continent to find audiences. In the latter half of the eighteenth century, Britain developed a widespread network of provincial theatres, but the prestige of London was such that professional success was measured mainly by whether one could acquire an engagement with Covent Garden or Drury Lane. As only a handful of actors could sustain a complete career at these theatres, most submitted to the obscurity of the provinces. Under these circumstances, a career in the American theatre, which by the start of the nineteenth century was beginning to flourish, could appear attractive to the actor who had just failed to make it to the top in London. Indeed, John Bernard claimed that when he traveled to London in 1806 to recruit actors for the Boston Theatre, managers there were already offering contracts to British actors in America to return home (see Clapp, 85–86).

By the turn of the century, then, a steady stream of actors, several of whom were far from undistinguished, were making the journey across the Atlantic. John Hodgkinson, for example, had initiated such a promising career in England, playing major roles opposite Sarah Siddons, that when he joined Hallam in New York in 1792, he could be regarded as "the first actor who visited the Western World in possession of a transatlantic reputation as a man of considerable ability" (Clapp, 29). Later in the decade, Thomas Wignell succeeded in acquiring for the Chestnut Street Theatre in Philadelphia a group of British actors that formed an ensemble of exceptional cohesion and quality, including Anne Merry, who had already had six successful seasons at Covent Garden, James Fennell, a noted Othello, and Thomas Abthorpe Cooper, an intensely ambitious man, who turned to the United States when he failed to receive the recognition he felt he deserved in London. Cooper, who had been educated by William Godwin, was advised by both Godwin and the playwright Thomas Holcroft not to go to America, because, in the words of Holcroft, "as an actor you would be extinct and the very season of energy and improvement would be for ever passed" (quoted in Dunlap, *History,* I, 349). As it turned out, Cooper had an exceptional career in which he endowed the American theatre with his own "energy and improvement."

Dramatic criticism was not highly developed in the early years of the American theatre, so it is difficult to determine precisely the style and quality of the acting practiced there. It is reasonable to surmise that actors would have imitated those models associated with the leading performers of the London theatre. For much of the eighteenth century, two British actors in particular crafted modes of representation that served as paradigms for the profession. The first half of the eighteenth century was dominated by James Quin (1693–1766), who practiced a heroic mode of acting composed of grand gestures, stentorian utterance, and a general lack of attention to the inner life of the character. In essence, a holdover from the Restoration theatre, Quin's influence over the English stage was beginning to wane by the mid-eighteenth century, when the Hallams came to America. Into his place stepped David Garrick (1717–79), who dominated the English stage from 1741 until his retirement from the managership of Drury Lane in 1776. As an actor, Garrick was light and fluent, even in tragic roles. He revealed facets of multiple and complex characters in a way that embodied the Enlightenment notion of the artist as one whose function is to celebrate the richness, harmony, and variety of the human condition. But while Garrick eclipsed Quin in England, the older actor's mannerisms were easier to imitate, and to adopt the grandeur of his style invested actors with a stature that both lent them stage presence and gave them a consequence that seemed to belie their lowly social status. Lewis Hallam Jr., who acquired almost legendary status during his long career, adopted Quin rather than Garrick as his model. A contemporary who saw him act in Philadelphia suggests that he had both the strengths and failings of the grand style of acting: "his declamation was either mouthing or ranting, yet [he was] a thorough master of all the tricks and finesse of his trade, his manner was both graceful and impressive" (Graydon, 77). However, for those who had seen Garrick perform, Hallam was neither imposing nor gracious, as is clear from the comments of another Philadelphia critic:

> I am sorry Mr. Hallam, who is genteel in his Person and Actions, could not take Copy from the inimitable Garrick, and speak plain English, whenever he assumes a character that may be supposed to understand the language. There is no necessity of destroying the least articulate Beauty of language, thro' Fury, Eagerness, or Passion.[2]

Ironically, the first major influence on acting in the New World may have been a style that had already lost its force in the Old.

In the American theatre, David Garrick's influence was felt more as a touchstone of reputed excellence than as an effective model for others to adopt. In fact, he was probably more influential as the director of London's Drury Lane Theatre, where he developed a company in which all parts, from leads through supporting roles to the smallest walk-ons, were acted with equal application and skill. Such a company was a rarity in eighteenth-century Europe and, until Garrick, virtually unheard of in England, where displaying the graces of the leading actors was the priority in most performances. Most actors in the early American theatre had had some contact with Garrick, and some, like Thomas Wignell, had been familiar with the Drury Lane company since childhood. No doubt, Drury Lane was a model for Wignell as he proceeded in 1794 to recruit personnel for the Chestnut Street Theatre, hence founding a company that was to stand at the forefront of the American theatre for the next twenty-five years. But even at this date, cooperation among actors was not unknown in the American theatre. The conditions of privation under which they had initially had to work and the comparatively minuscule size of the earliest troupes meant that the equal energies of each member were required to sustain a regular repertoire, and although the early troupes tended to maintain the casting system of the English theatre, possession of roles was not as rigorously maintained as it was in England. From the accounts of the early actor-managers, especially William Dunlap, who directed the Park Theatre, New York, between 1798 and 1811, and William Wood, who took over joint managership of the Chestnut Street Theatre in Philadelphia soon after Wignell's death in 1803, one gains the impression that as the profession diversified and theatres opened up in the major cities of the eastern seaboard, the independent stock company in which all actors made an equal contribution and all plays were performed against the same "stock" scenery was the norm. Indeed, to judge from the reminiscences of John Bernard, the turn of the century was a halcyon period in the early days of the American theatre, not only in the artistic sense but as regards the well-being of the actors, all of whom could maintain a fair standard of living (263). Dunlap actually maintains that the conditions of the profession, which were beginning to reflect the democratic ideals of the country, were such that the United States seemed preferable to Britain. In America, actors had greater status, they were "not degraded by the presence of a privileged order; and if the mere moneyed aristocrat assumes airs of superiority, they feel authorized to resist the assumption" (Dunlap, *History,* I, 365).

Although these sanguine views of the past were no doubt tempered by nostalgia and national pride, the stock system (see Chapter 2) was firmly established in America early in the nineteenth century and seems to have served actors and audiences well. However, at precisely the juncture at which the system had reached its prime, symptoms of its decline were already apparent, specifically in the rise of the star actor as the preeminent figure of the theatrical profession.

Historians are divided as to precisely which actors are responsible for initiating the star system, but the arrival of John Hodgkinson at the John Street Theatre in 1792 is as good a point as any to mark the decline of the stock companies. Hodgkinson was a protean actor with little patience for the system of lines of acting, discussed in Chapter 2, that still prevailed in the American theatre; he was also ruthless, with an immoderate appetite for any role that came his way. Soon after being hired by Hallam and Henry, he engineered Henry's departure from the company and effectively commandeered all of Hallam's leading roles. By 1794, he assumed joint managership of the John Street Theatre with Hallam and some years later, in 1798, welcomed Cooper to New York, that actor having become dissatisfied with his treatment in Philadelphia, where James Fennell played most of the major roles. Cooper soon drove out Hodgkinson, who spent the rest of his years touring the eastern seaboard. Later, Cooper divided his energies between New York and Philadelphia until 1815; then he in turn severed all ties with any specific company in order to play individual engagements in the network of theatres that were proliferating as a result of the rapid expansion of the nation. Over the next decades, any actor who had the skill and presence to stand out from run-of-the-mill company actors, and hundreds did, took to the roads.

Economic conditions at the start of the nineteenth century were ripe for the foundation of the star system, by which the organization of theatre companies, choice of repertoire, and box office appeal to the public were determined primarily by the lure of a single famous actor rather than the attraction of the play itself or of the company performing it. The reasons for this transformation were various. No doubt, economics played a large part. Salaries for star actors were much greater than they were for regular members of the company. Cooper, for example, as a company actor, was paid a salary of $25 a week for the 1798–99 season at the Park Theatre, $32 for the next season, and $50 by 1801. He played most of 1803–4 in Britain, where his success at Drury Lane was indifferent, but he returned to the States a celebrity and was able to attract a house of $1,080 to his Hamlet at the Park Theatre. A decade later he was paid $1,878.62 for ten performances in Boston and by the early 1820s could command $200 a night in New Orleans.[3] British actors, in particular, were lured by the financial rewards of America, as they were substantially greater than those in their own country. By the middle of the nineteenth century "the star network," as McConachie has put it, "turned stars into protocapitalists and stock actors into workers" (*Melodramatic Formations,* 80).

The other capitalists were, of course, the managers, who quickly realized that full houses could be ensured only by the appearance of stars; consequently their efforts were directed mainly toward guaranteeing a continual stream of visiting stars on the stages they managed. They were helped in this endeavor by the entrepreneurship of Stephen Price, manager of the Park Theatre between 1808 and 1840 and, briefly, between 1826 and 1830, of Drury Lane Theatre itself. Price used his position to serve as an agent for English and subsequently European actors, dancers, and singers who wished to come to America, some to make a career, others to blaze briefly across the theatrical firmament and then return home flush with money. To make the prospect of an American tour more tempting, Price organized the managers of the major theatres outside New York into a circuit, so that foreign actors would be guaranteed performances in the major cities of Boston, Providence, Philadelphia, Baltimore, and Charleston and, as the country grew, in Cincinnati, St. Louis, Mobile, and New Orleans as well.

Because it effectively destroyed the stock system by demoralizing the companies, restricting the repertoire, lowering production and performance standards through the elimination of rehearsals, and encouraging mechanical acting even from the stars, several of whom were of doubtful eminence, theatre historians have almost universally condemned the star system.[4] Nevertheless, there must have been compelling reasons beyond the purely economic for its domination of the American theatre in the first half of the nineteenth century. One can be found in the nature of the contemporary repertoire. Because all companies were organized on a repertory model in which plays changed from night to night, the actual repertoire known to any company was relatively limited and tended to be the same from theatre to theatre. Furthermore, Shakespeare was central to that repertoire. As Lawrence Levine has demonstrated in *Highbrow/Lowbrow,* Shakespeare was even more part of popular culture in the United States than he was in Britain. Shakespearean language was woven into contemporary colloquial idiom, and theatre audiences were intimately familiar with the major works. Stars tended to have the same repertoire, with Shakespeare in the center, followed by a handful of roles from classic plays and a substantial number from popular contemporary works. Therefore, the interest in each star did not arise merely from a curiosity to see a famous face, or to be touched by what today we weakly label "celebrity," but from an interest in how the same text was subject to different interpretations. New "points" in classic roles were welcomed or hissed at according to how effective the audience sensed them to be, whereas a totally novel interpretation was a major event in the theatrical year. Regular theatregoers would have the opportunity to see several, widely different realizations of roles such as Richard III, Hamlet, Macbeth, Juliet, Rosalind, Lady Macbeth, Sir Giles Overreach, Virginius, Claude Melnotte, and several dozen others, so that their understanding of a play would not come mainly from reading the verbal text and seeing a handful of performances over a lifetime; instead they would encounter constantly changing versions of the play, or at least of its central role, that could result in a deep appreciation of the complexity and richness of the total text.

Of course, the lure of powerful personality and physical beauty did much to help stars become the pivotal figures of the early nineteenth century, and here we can identify continuation of the theme of the actor as a surrogate figure for monarchy. But the authority exercised by the star performer onstage, far from being understood as irrelevant or unattractive, in the nineteenth century became a *raison d'être* for theatre. It even evolved into a means of defining opposing concepts of American, British, and later European national identities and of distinguishing the mythical concepts on which they were built. Hence, the royal aura of the actor served ultimately to tie the theatre to the mainstream of American social and political life rather than isolate it as an irrelevancy.

Although Quin and Garrick were the dominant influences in the eighteenth century, during the turn of the century, actors found a more authoritative model. Even though Sarah Siddons (1755–1831) and her brother John Philip Kemble (1757–1823) never visited the United States, their acting had the most far-reaching influence on American theatre. For well over three decades, these statuesque actors had presided over the stages of both London patent theatres and had won national celebrity on British provincial circuits. Their acting can most productively be viewed as the final and most polished phase of an Enlightenment theatre that strove toward heightened representation of noble, human qualities rather than a realistic depiction of them. As Kemble's supernal presence and the quasi-metaphysical aura of Siddons's tragic characters had been achieved primarily through the adoption of rhetorical principles already established in the English theatre, the grandeur and pathos of their presence onstage appeared to lesser actors to be within their grasp. Though none of them achieved the exalted status of the originals, by the end of the eighteenth century, the ubiquitous high neo-classicism of the Kemble–Siddons school had provided a discipline for American acting that it had previously lacked, and the principles upon which it was built enabled actors to assume a mantle of majestic authority onstage that would have eluded them had they been left to their own resources.

Nowhere is this more apparent than in the rise of Cooper. When Holcroft warned Cooper against traveling to America, he also complained that his "rhodomante heroics" were "discordant, grating, and degrading'"(quoted in Dunlap, *History* I, 348), which suggests the young man to have been an epigone of the Quin tradition. In America, however, his acting matured. He was endowed with looks, personality, voice, and bearing, which allowed him to assume successfully the model of a Kemble actor, and his deliberate cultivation of the rhetorical principles of the Kemble–Siddons school enabled him systematically to ensure a fair degree of consistency in his performances:

> Mr. Cooper in his prime possessed from nature the primary accomplishments of a pleasing actor; a fine person, a voice of great compass, of most melodious silver tone, and susceptible of the greatest variety of modula-

tion; and eye of the most wonderful expression; and his whole face expressive, at his will, of the deepest terror or the most exalted complacency, the
direst revenge or the softest pity. His form in anger was that of a demon, his
smile in affability that of an angel. (Clapp, 65)

The range of his acting is described in the most ideal of terms, the impression of harmony and grandeur, even in the representation of violence and
misery, being of greater significance than a detailed representation of the
inner life of the character. The actor is imaged as the serene master of all
phases of human experience. Although Cooper was notoriously uneven – his
concentration in major roles often lapsed disastrously, and he rarely bothered to learn his lines in secondary roles – he still acquired a formidable reputation; indeed, until well into the 1830s, he above all others sustained the
idea of the actor as the paragon of majesty, as is clear from an ecstatic, nostalgic address, written to celebrate his appearance in New Orleans in 1833:

> For when in life's bright noon the stage he trod
> In majesty and grace, a demi-god;
> With form, and mien, and attitude, and air,
> Which modern kings might envy in despair;
> When his stern brow and awe-inspiring eye
> Bore sign of an imperial majesty;
> Then – in the zenith of his glory – then
> He moved a model for the first of men![5]

Sadly, by the time this magniloquent verse was penned, Cooper was striking audiences as wearisomely dated. Twenty years earlier, the neoclassical
values on which such acting was based had already been seriously shaken,
though never entirely dislodged, by one of the most turbulent ruptures ever
to have occurred in the history of acting. Because the American stage experienced this rupture more fiercely than did theatres elsewhere, it quickly
became central to the development of Western theatre, in the process losing
its status as a sideshow to its more prestigious European counterpart. At the
same time, this rupture affirmed the star system even more strongly as the
dominant order of the American theatre.

The three actors most responsible for the rupture with neoclassicism in
the English-speaking world all had significant careers in the American theatre. The first, George Frederick Cooke, spent the last two years of his life in
America and, because he died there, might be claimed by the Americans as
one of their own; the second, Edmund Kean (1789–1833), completed two
stormy tours of the United States, but he returned to Britain, with whose theatre he has always been identified; the third, Junius Brutus Booth (1796–
1852), emigrated to America in 1821 and, except for a couple of brief visits to
Britain in later years, remained there. Theatre historians have not been
wrong to associate these three actors. Broadly speaking, all represented

The Irish-born English actor George Frederick Cooke (1756–1812), the first major foreign star on the American stage, as Richard III as painted by Philadelphia artist Thomas Sully (original at the Pennsylvania Academy of Fine Arts). Don B. Wilmeth Collection.

phases of Romanticism that challenged the culture of the European Enlightenment. After the carefully structured, heroic presentations of neoclassical actors, Cooke, Kean, and Booth appeared to be spontaneous and volatile, acting free of any restraint. Although the imagination of the audience was contained and circumscribed by the neoclassical actor, the Romantic actors released that imagination into a world of tumultuous emotion that undercut confidence in the very possibility of a rational and harmonious human condition, exposing its essential wildness.[6] All three explored the extremes of emotional experience, thus earning the reputation of insanity. "There was frequently little difference," the actor Walter Leman reminisced, "between the excesses of their imagination and the freaks of the madman" (56). And all three were notorious alcoholics; indeed, Cooke's and Kean's lives were cut short because of the staggering amount of liquor they imbibed. It would be misleading, it would in fact betray the specific nature of the appeal exercised by these actors, to class them as a school, in the way one can class the neo-classicists. Moreover, as originality and individuality were the essence of their work, their differences were as vital as their similarities.

George Frederick Cooke was the first "great English star" with an established reputation to visit the United States, which has led one of his modern biographers, Don Wilmeth, credibly to identify the initiation of the star system with his arrival in New York in November 1810. Because Cooke came to America blazing trails of glory, Dunlap could claim his advent "caused a greater sensation than the arrival of any individual not connected with the political welfare of the country" (*Cooke*, II, 174). Cooke had acted for well over thirty years, first on the provincial circuit in Britain, then at Covent Garden, where he became a formidable rival of John Philip Kemble. He was persuaded by Cooper to come to America at short notice, for his fortunes, financial and artistic, were at an especially low ebb in Britain. Public enthusiasm in America was immense; his first appearance at the Park Theatre attracted a record box office of $1,820, and although the parlous state of Cooke's health meant that his performances were uneven and he could not always be relied on to appear, for the next twenty-two months audiences in New York, Philadelphia, Boston, and Providence were generally large and demonstrative. He died in New York in September 1812 of cirrhosis of the liver.

By the time Cooke arrived in America, dramatic criticism was becoming not only more frequent in the press but also more accomplished and detailed. One of the most consistent themes in the critical reception of Cooke was the surprise about how unimpressive he was physically.

> Nature has been by no means lavish in her bounties to the person or voice of this eminent tragedian [wrote "Thespis" in the *Columbian*]. His figure is neither majestic nor symmetrically proportioned: his voice, though not deficient in compass, is neither mellow nor varied: his gesticulation is more expressive than elegant: his gait is less distinguished for grace than ease and freedom; and it may be greatly questioned whether his stage-walk is always compatible with the dignity of a hero. (Quoted in Odell, II, 356)

Although the statuesque neoclassical hero represented an unreachable ideal, Cooke was more like members of the audience themselves. He did not appeal by vocal and physical power. Instead, he drew people in through simplicity, lack of ornament in his acting, quietness in his speech, and absence of all rhetorical flourish. It was said he rewrote Shakespeare's verse in prose in order to discover the human experience it articulated. He provided audiences with uncommonly direct access to the characters he portrayed; in fact at times they almost forgot he was an actor. "You did not see Cooke," wrote Charles Durang, "you only saw the character" (Quoted in Hewitt, *Theatre U.S.A.*, 84), which indicates that Cooke, who had an unusual respect for the playwright's text, presented the actor as a medium for the role rather than an object of admiration in himself. He had a subtle understanding of character, a resourceful imagination to bring that understanding to light, and flexible means to realize it onstage.

However, perhaps the most singular aspect of his acting was its lack of idealism. The tragic heroes he represented were no longer admirable; indeed, as John Bernard observed, his forte was the representation of the "insinuating villain" (368). While several found the access Cooke offered them to the mind of scheming villainy absorbing, even exhilarating, others found him more prosaic, lacking a breadth and generosity that belongs to the finest theatre. This was best expressed, not by an American critic, but by the Englishman Leigh Hunt, who found Cooke questionable:

> He was too entirely the satirist, the hypocrite, the villain. He loved too fondly his own caustic and rascally words. . . . As to his vaunted tragedy, it was a mere reduction of Shakespeare's poetry into indignant prose. He limited every character to its worst qualities, and had no idealism, no affection, no verse. (Quoted in Matthews and Hutton, *Kembles and Their Contemporaries*, 3)

Despite some reservations, Cooke's character-oriented acting made a substantial impact on the American theatre, but after his death, the neoclassicism of Cooper remained the preeminent style, which went unchallenged by the minor stars whom Price continued to bring over from Britain. Then, in 1820, Price landed Edmund Kean, who arrived in the United States with an even greater reputation than Cooke. Whereas Cooke had had to spend twenty-five years in the English provinces struggling to achieve stardom, and when he did, he never dislodged Kemble, Kean seemed to have achieved both ends with little trouble. From the moment he burst onto the Drury Lane stage with his remarkably human but vituperative Shylock in January 1814, he had been the most lauded actor in the British Isles, and he precipitated Kemble's retirement, which occurred in 1817. By the time he traveled to the States, there were signs his popularity was on the wane; indeed he may have undertaken the tour precisely to rouse the flagging enthusiasm of his London audience. But in New York, his reception equaled that enjoyed by Cooke, and, with one significant and fatal exception, it continued throughout his tour of the eastern cities.

Kean is a difficult actor to characterize. He was the antithesis of majesty onstage, and yet he convinced audiences of the magnitude and power of the characters he portrayed. He was smaller than Cooke and even less endowed with the physical and vocal prerequisites for tragedy. His voice could be "harsh and broken" (Hillebrand, 368), and his English champion, William Hazlitt, claimed Kean had "the eye of an eagle with the voice of a raven" (V, 176), but John Keats could praise "the elegance, gracefulness, and music of [his] elocution," which he considered invested Shakespeare's poetry with a "sensual grandeur" (229). Kean surprised audiences by the way in which he emphasized unfamiliar aspects of the roles he played; some found this invigorating and even beautiful, others considered it merely sensationalistic. Above all, he fastened on the emotional life of the character, through vivid contrasts representing the extremes of passion and violent conflicts that destroy all possibility of integration in the character. Kean was the poet of anarchy and alienation rather than of harmony and disorder. He was never ingratiating. "He did not," observed Leigh Hunt wryly, "seduce us into fondness" (*The Examiner*, Feb. 13, 1814).

American critics showed the same ambivalence to Kean as had their British counterparts; audiences, however, were ecstatic. For a start, they could trust him. During his first tour, Kean was significantly more temperate in his drinking than he had been in Britain, so he played with greater consistency, and could be relied on to turn up, until his second appearance in Boston. His first visit to that city had been particularly successful and he wished to return. He could do so, however, only late in May, when theatre audiences customarily declined. Despite warnings, he insisted on playing Boston. The first two nights attracted a moderate attendance, but when, before playing Richard III on the third night, he looked out into the auditorium and saw only a handful of people, he determined to cancel the performance. Soon after that, the auditorium filled up quite rapidly. Kean, however, had left the theatre and refused the pleas of the management to return. Next day, the trust he had built up with his American audiences vanished; in its place was a firestorm in the press. His insult to the Bostonians was "too foul and dishonoring to be overlooked – the actor too unprincipled not to be noticed with the finger of scorn." Kean was dismissed as nothing but a "second rate actor of the London stage" and an "inflated, self conceited, unprincipled vagabond" (press comments, quoted in Hillebrand, 217). Despite his attempts to apologize, Kean's defection swelled to a national scandal in the press and a few days later he was forced to set sail for Britain.

He undertook his second tour in 1825, when his career was seriously unraveling in Britain because of his declining powers and his involvement in a notorious divorce suit. He hoped this, and the memory of the Boston debacle, would not be on the minds of his audiences. Unfortunately they were. His first appearance at the Park was seriously disrupted by protesters, probably Bostonians, and when he went to Boston ostensibly to apologize, a furious audience refused even to let him speak. When they heard he had left the theatre, they proceeded to trash the auditorium. With the exception of a few

Romantic English actor Edmund Kean (1789?–1833), who appeared in the United States in 1820–21 and 1825–26, as Richard III. Nineteenth-century oil painting by unidentified artist. Don B. Wilmeth Collection.

protests in Charleston and another major riot in Baltimore, the rest of Kean's tour, which lasted a good year, was relatively undisturbed, after which he returned to London to face the gloomy final years of his career.

Hillebrand, Kean's biographer, claims to find no good reason for the protest. He merely argues that there was "a virus at work" (218) and says no more. Contemporaries expressed surprise at the vehemence of the outburst against Kean, as Cooke had frequently stood up his audiences without a word of protest. But to see no cause behind the riots is to view the theatre in a vacuum. Kean arrived in the States ten years after Cooke and in that time the political climate had changed. Not only had Britain and the United States fought another war, those years saw the first stirrings of militant American nationalism that was to have a profound effect on the theatre in the coming decades. Kean had insulted national pride and, to add insult to injury, he was not even an impressive figure. Cooke, despite his lack of conventional majesty, had a distinct touch of grandeur about him; Kean had none. The personally demeaning tone of the press attacks on him were not, therefore, fortuitous. They indicated American audiences and press were discovering their own "majesty."

Junius Brutus Booth began his American career in 1821 without the fanfare that had heralded Cooke and Kean. He was not brought over by Stephen Price. In fact, his departure from England was motivated mainly by failure in the past rather than in anticipation of future conquests; Kean's implacable opposition to Booth had made it impossible to establish himself as a star in the London theatre. He soon found eager enough audiences in America and was quickly established as one of the most celebrated of American actors in an erratic career that lasted until his death in 1852. Because of the competition between Booth and Kean when both were playing in London, Booth has always been compared to the English actor, generally to his disadvantage. Although both actors centered on the passions of their characters, there were distinct qualitative differences in their acting styles. Booth was more capable of appealing to those who still prized the Kemble-Siddons school. His voice was more musical than Kean's, and it expressed "the more elevated and ennobling sentiments of his author," particularly as Booth aimed at a "consistent and beautifully graduated order of vocal effects" (Murdoch, *The Stage*, 177–79). Contemporary accounts suggest he was less theatrically self-conscious than Kean, there was more totality to his performances, and he did not resort to "stage tricks." He was particularly intense in his representation of emotions and skilled in the manipulation of telling detail. According to Thomas Gould, to see Booth act Shakespeare was not as it was supposed to be with Kean, as if one read him by flashes of lightning; instead it was "rather like reading him by the sunlight of a summer's day, a light which casts deep shadows, gives play to glorious harmonies of color, and shows all objects in vivid light and true relations" (31).

Booth, it would appear, might have combined, historically, the conflicting styles of acting, the romantic and the neoclassical, the emotional and the restrained, but he failed to do this and to achieve preeminence in the American theatre because of his eccentricity and unreliability. Despite his siring of one of the "royal" families of the American theatre, he could not settle down, and the opportunities of a vagrant life offered by the star system kept him restlessly on the road. On the stage he could be temperamental – the star system encouraged egotistical indulgence – and he would infuriate audiences by walking through the first two or three acts of *Richard III* and then deliver an unforgettable performance at the end. He, far more frequently than Kean, failed to turn up for performances and walked out of them for purely personal reasons. But as he quickly became identified with the American rather than the British theatre, such conduct never caused riots that hit the national headlines.

By the 1830s, Booth, like Cooper, may have seemed dated to audiences, as styles in acting continued to change. Cooke and Kean remained in the collective memory as touchstones of a deeply personal, often moving, always disturbing approach to acting; like Booth, they provided no models, because as

The English actor Junius Brutus Booth (1796–1852) as Richard III in a widely reproduced illustration of the actor who emigrated to America in 1821 and became the
progenitor of one of America's greatest acting dynasties. Don B. Wilmeth Collection.

they laid claim to total originality onstage, any imitation would violate the
spirit of their work and result in bathetic imitation. But their Romantic mode
of acting was also displaced by the onset of Victorianism in the theatre. Aptly
enough, the British harbingers of Victorian acting were Charles Kemble
(1775–1854), the younger brother of John Philip Kemble and Sarah Siddons,
and his daughter, Fanny (1809–93), who embarked on a tour of the States in
1832 in order to revive the family fortunes, seriously depleted by years of
unprofitable management of Covent Garden.

In essence, father and daughter represented a continuation of the high
classical tradition reduced from heroic to domestic dimensions. Charles had
never achieved the eminence of his brother and sister, it being often said that
he was more successful in lighter-weight supporting roles, such as Mercutio,
rather than in heavier leads. It was uniformly agreed that Charles was acutely
conscientious in his reading of his roles; he was always "polished, critically

studied and impressive" (Hewitt, *Theatre U.S.A.,*111), and in all his appearances onstage produced "truly finished and graceful specimens of refined acting, replete with the dignity and elegance of high life" (Odell, III, 1832). Leigh
Hunt found him to be what later generations would call a matinee idol: "In
theatrical lovers, in that complaining softness with which the fancies of
young ladies adorn their imagination, Mr. Charles Kemble is certainly the first
performer" (quoted in Matthews and Hutton, xx). He lacked stage life, however. Fanny, always his most searching critic, appreciated the artistry of his
acting but found that in contrast to Kean, he wanted "depth and power"
(*Records,* 477). He displayed an admirably "minute accuracy and refinement"
in his characterizations, but this very accuracy made them unsuitable for the
stage, which meant that the whole occasion of performance could be tire-
some for audience and actor alike.

> the whole [is] a most laborious and minute study, toilsome in the concep-
> tion and acquirement; and most toilsome in the execution. But the result,
> though the natural one, is not such as he expects as the reward of so much
> labour. Few persons are able to follow such a performance with the neces-
> sary attention, and it is almost as great an exertion to see it *understandingly,*
> as it is to act it. (Quoted in Williamson, 68)

By the time the Kembles arrived in America, Charles was fifty-seven and the
lack of spontaneity in his acting was pronounced. In contrast, Fanny was a
tremendous hit. Her coming to America had been heralded by the media as
little short of a divine manifestation. She was not, however, the first woman
to achieve stardom in the American theatre – throughout the 1820s Mary Ann
Duff had achieved national celebrity for the physical allure of her performances and for moving audiences by her "gentle grief" – but Fanny had the
force of the Kemble name behind her, and she was the niece of the legendary
Siddons. It says much for her that she does not seem to have disappointed
expectations. Audiences in the eastern cities were ecstatic. Fanny combined
an illusion of great beauty with that of intense refinement and purity, so that
any sexual nuance or gesture was nullified by the air of mannerliness that
surrounded her performances: "If ever passion gave [her attitudes] a half
voluptuous ardor," wrote a critic for the New York *Mirror,* "innocence and
high love chastened them to simple grace" (quoted in Hewitt, *Theatre U.S.A.,*
114). There was always a danger that restraint and poise could result in performances as studied as her father's, but she had the capacity to construct
moments of great power, when the emotional pressures that drive the character toward her tragic end erupted onto the stage. As a result, she swept audiences away. Philip Hone, the diarist, records that when Charles debuted at
the Park as Hamlet, he was "listened to with great attention" by a "critical and
discerning audience." But the next night, Fanny, playing in Milman's *Fazio,*
brought the house down: "I have never witnessed an audience so moved,

astonished, and delighted. Her display of the strong feelings which belong to the part was great beyond description . . . . we have never seen her equal on the American stage" (Hone, 77–78).

Fanny Kemble achieved much. She helped diffuse, at least for a time, the whiff of prurience that always hangs around the theatre and that was a serious impediment in its acceptance as an integral part of a society that was becoming increasingly concerned, in the United States as well as Britain, with the "Victorian" virtues of domesticity and respectability. Furthermore, as Faye Dudden has recently phrased it, she set a "new standard of excellence" for women actors, not only onstage but as "an exemplar of freedom, achievement, and self-confidence" (37). Nevertheless, at the very time when Fanny was enjoying unparalleled popularity in America, there were signs of growing national resentment at the seeming monopoly of British stars in the American theatre.

America had never accepted completely the foreign tenancy of their theatre. As far back as 1764, Dunlap records, the playhouse in Beekman Street, New York, was destroyed, possibly because of "the predilection of the actors for monarchy" (*History,* I, 49–50). Although nationalist demonstrations did not increase after the Revolution, they still occurred. In November 1796, for example, two sea captains caused a riot at the John Street Theatre when they demanded the orchestra play "Yankee-Doodle," but whether outraged nationalism or alcohol was to blame is impossible to tell. There were moments when the stage offended nationalist sentiments; Cooper, for example, was hissed in 1798 when, as part of his role of Bland in Dunlap's *André,* he threw an American cockade to the ground. By the end of the century, the press was also demanding that more native-born Americans be hired into the theatre. Despite military and political tensions between the United States and Britain, which culminated in the War of 1812, there was still no organized campaign against the theatre. However, by the 1830s, when the threat of military confrontation between the two countries had almost disappeared and the United States was beginning to enjoy the same degree of leisured civilization that Europe itself did, cultural tensions appeared more persistently. Their origin is commonly identified in the publication of travel books and memoirs by foreigners who were critical of the United States. By and large, memoirs from earlier periods, particularly those written by actors, tended to be positive, even enthusiastic in their evaluation of the political and social experiment of the new republic. But by the 1830s a more judgmental tone colored descriptions of the young country and the most widely read and publicized travel books, such as Frances Trollope's *Domestic Manners of the Americans* (1832), Captain Marryat's *Diary in America* (1839), and, most notoriously, Charles Dickens's *American Notes* (1842), were considered, somewhat over-sensitively, perhaps, to contain malicious attacks on the national character.

Fanny Kemble herself had entered the fray by publishing a journal of her travels in 1835. Prior to leaving England, Fanny had expressed great agitation at the very idea of traveling to "that dreadful America" and was beset by homesickness the moment her ship left Liverpool. Though she probably did not find that America confirmed her worst expectations, her fears were, on the whole, corroborated. Her *Journal* contains several passages that indicate she was capable of intellectual vigor and generosity, but they comprise a litany of complaints against all aspects of American life. Women age more quickly in America than in England; hotels are inadequate, travel conditions poor, the aesthetic judgment of American audiences, particularly when it comes to the appraisal of bad acting, is frequently awry; and the democratic way of life is the cause of unbearable coarseness in the population as a whole: "The mixture of the republican feeling of equality peculiar to this country, and the usual want of refinement common to the lower classes of most countries, forms a singular felicitous union of impudence and vulgarity to be met with nowhere but in America" (106). Although the *Journal* was published, over the heated objections of her American husband, only after she had left the stage, Fanny had not been silent about her anti-Americanism while she still acted. When she appeared in Washington, D.C., threats were made to hiss her off the stage for insulting Americans, and in Philadelphia handbills were passed out demanding she suffer the same fate there. Significantly, these were threats only. She met with only friendly audiences during her tour of America.

That Fanny Kemble was not hissed off stage is characteristic of developing nationalist tensions in the American theatre. Threats were made of dire actions, but on most occasions a substantially larger portion of the audience took sides with the offending actor rather than with the nationalist protest. This tendency suggests that cultural vectors tending to isolate the British actor were as much class-based as they were nationalist in origins. During this period, the American theatre was becoming progressively stratified in terms of class,[7] with different classes becoming identified with different theatres. Hence, in New York, the Bowery Theatre became associated with the American nationalist cause and populist politics, whereas the Park Theatre retained an almost exclusively upper-middle-class audience that favored the British visitors. No doubt, several in that audience would have agreed with Fanny's strictures on American life and as that segment of audience was invariably present in a substantial majority whenever she played, nationalist protest was silenced.

However, the upper middle class could not always prevail in the auditorium. Joshua Anderson, a minor English actor, suffered an anti-British riot when he appeared at the Park in October 1831 and, at the same time, the Bowery Theatre accused Stephen Price, the Park manager, then still living in England, of anti-American views.[8] Two years later, the British comic actor Charles Mathews (1776–1835) returned to the States for the first time since his tour of 1822–23. The tour had been highly successful because of the versatility and finish of his acting; he was even considered by some to have been a finer artist than Kean himself. But on his return to London after his first tour, he presented *A Trip to America* at one of his famous "At Home" evenings, a show in which he impersonated a staggeringly wide variety of people with, apparently, complete credibility. Word had it this show was hostile to Americans, and when he returned in 1834, he found the following bill posted outside the theatre:

> We understand chs. [*sic*] Mathews is to play on Monday evening, the 13th inst. The scoundrell [*sic*] ought to be pelted from an American stage after his writing that which he did about six years ago called Mathews Carricature [*sic*] in America. This insult apont [*sic*] Americans ought to be met with the contempt it deserves. After using the most vilest language against the 'TOO EASILY DUPED YANKEES' as he calls us, he thinks to repay us for our kindness towards him. But we hope they will show him that we are not so easily duped this time, as we were then. And drive the ungrateful slanderer from our stage forever.[9]

In any event, Mathews was allowed to show *A Trip to America* to American audiences, and once they realized the satire was more good-humored than tender nationalist susceptibilities had anticipated, he went on to a moderately successful tour, though nothing like the triumph he had enjoyed a decade earlier.

He had it easier than his son, Charles James Mathews, who hoped to make a fortune in 1838 when he came over with his wife, the celebrated singer and comic actress Mme. Vestris. The failure of their tour may have been due to moral scruples, because the two, who had been associated for years, got married in a hurry, probably to make things easier in America. However, Mathews claimed the actual reason stemmed from an affront the couple unwittingly committed against the guests of a Catskill hotel where they had stayed prior to their tour; they had refused to take tea with the company and left the hotel secretly to avoid more public notice. As a result, they acquired the reputation of being hostile to Americans, and meeting everywhere only a lukewarm reception, they determined to cut their tour short after only two months, having made a mere £1,750 where they had expected £20,000. They were, of course, given a rousingly warm send-off at their final performance at the Park.

A more general cause for the ambivalence felt by audiences toward visiting actors may be identified with the growing sense of the need for a national theatre. General Morris, drama critic for the New York *Mirror* in the late 1820s, conducted a critical campaign for a theatre that centered its efforts on the good production of American drama and turned away from its constant preoccupation with London. Americans, Morris asserted, should turn to acting, especially now that other professions are becoming overcrowded.[10] This achieved little practical change. In 1828 James Fenimore Cooper reproached the American theatre for its failure to exercise influence on "morals, politics or anything else" and insisted that it was still "decidedly English" (112), and almost twenty years later, Walt Whitman still could argue that the best theatre in New York, the Park, was "but a third-rate imitation of the best London theatres, [giving us] the cast off dramas and unengaged players of Great Britain; and of these dramas and players, like garments which come second hand from gentleman to valet, everything fits awkwardly" (quoted in Hewitt, *Theatre U.S.A.*, 144). Things were, however, about to change.

Edwin Forrest was the first American-born actor to achieve unquestioned star stature in the American theatre and consequently national celebrity. As a young man he had initially modeled his acting on Cooper, but he also had the opportunity to act with Kean, playing Iago to his Othello, when the English tragedian visited Albany on his second tour. Kean praised Forrest as the "one actor in this country . . . who gave proofs of a decided genius in his profession and will . . . rise to great eminence" (Moody, *Edwin Forrest,* 56). Kean, by his very nature, was more an inspiration than a model to Forrest; he directed him toward an understanding that embodying the emotional experience of the role was the primary purpose of the actor. Unlike the small and wiry Kean, Forrest was a man of imposing physique with an immense voice, hence the emotion of the role expressed itself not so much as the agonized conflict of a diminutive man with forces larger than himself, as it did with Kean, but in an overpowering rush of feeling that engulfed the spectator, "like the falls of Niagara, in its tremendous down-sweeping cadence: it was a whirlwind, a tornado, a cataract of illimitable rage!" (Vandenhoff, 201).

Forrest was not a polished actor; his deliberately cultivated roughness and harshness was the opposite of refinement. As he rose to prominence in the theatre, Forrest became an icon for the growing American nationalism of the Jacksonian and post-Jacksonian eras, materializing a mode of representation that was clearly different from the demure and stately conduct that still passed for acting on most American stages. As the critic for the *Albion* put it in 1848,

> the courtly guise, the old world conventionalism, which "hedge in the divinity of kings," and the polished graces that surround the great and high born – are not held by Mr. Forrest as the imperative auxiliaries of his acting. His graces and dignity have been founded on other models – the free aboriginal of his country, erect and fearless in the freedom with which nature has endowed him, has afforded to this great actor lessons in the histrionic art, which the finished artists of Europe take only from the Court or the Salons. (Quoted in Hewitt, *Theatre U.S.A.,* 109)

Though it is appropriate that Forrest was associated with the one major civic disturbance in which nationalist tensions came to a head, it is partly ironic that his opponent was the most eminent of all Victorian visitors,

William Charles Macready (1793–1873), who became the icon of resentment against visiting stars. More than most visiting stars, Macready was familiar with the United States, undertaking three tours in the course of his career, 1826–27, 1843–44, and 1848–49. He was also more sympathetic to the country than were most British people of his generation. Although his diaries reveal an impatience with America similar to that expressed by Fanny Kemble, he had an acute appreciation of the political system. In fact, his political opinions were closer to those of a republican than a monarchist. Even at the start of his last tour, when he was aware of nationalist resentment against him, he still considered retiring to the States.

His mode of acting suited these values and beliefs.[11] As a young man he had freed himself first from dependence on a Quin-like rhetoric, still practiced by his actor-father, and then from a tendency to imitate Kean, which inevitably threatened to degenerate into mannerism. He devoted his energies to developing characterizations in which the contribution of the role to the thematic and intellectual unity of the play became apparent. To do this he used a number of techniques, such as the famous "Macready pause," carefully prepared transitions, and attention to psychological details. He also, more consciously than Charles Kemble, introduced a domestic dimension to his roles. His Lear was more an injured father than a turbulent and tyrannical monarch, and though this role, like several others, lacked intensity and power, it formed a pleasing whole. From his first appearance in America in 1826, he was also hailed by audiences for the uprightness of his private life. Macready aimed to bring respectability to the theatre.

In fairness, it must be admitted there were strongly negative sides to his character, so that the symbolic role into which he was eventually cast was not entirely undeserved. He was immensely egotistical. Although he claimed always to be concerned with the artistic quality of the whole production, he insisted that he be the center of attention. Furthermore, he despised the profession he found himself in, which encouraged him to maintain a distance between himself and his colleagues; this, and his frequently pompous demeanor in front of audiences, earned him a reputation for stuffiness and coldness. Moreover, his clearly stated aspirations to live the life of a gentleman undermined his more populist beliefs.

Macready first met Forrest when the American actor called on him during a tour he was making of Britain in 1836. He was impressed by the young man and defended him against what he considered to be the unduly negative criticism his acting encountered in the London press. Despite this, Forrest's British tour was not a success. The two men renewed acquaintance during Macready's second U.S. tour in 1843–44, but though Macready continued to like Forrest personally, he began to develop serious doubts about the quality and integrity of his acting. Macready seems to have thought Forrest failed for specifically American reasons. He ruined himself, he claims, by not acquiring the taste that can be acquired only in Britain. He allowed the applause of audiences and his stature as a national celebrity to mislead him. "He has great physical power," Macready confided to his diary after seeing him act Lear. "But I could discern no imagination, no original thought, no poetry at all in his acting." He lacked all grandeur and pathos, and "there was no character laid out." However, though Macready disliked Forrest as an artist who acted only for "the less intelligent of the Americans," he still admired him as "an upright and well-intentioned man." But "he is not an artist. Let him be an American actor – and a great American actor – but keep on this side of the Atlantic, and no one will gainsay his comparative excellence" (*Diaries*, II, 229–31). Macready's writing was not, of course, for public consumption, but his doubts about Forrest's acting nonetheless found their way to Forrest's ears. By the end of Macready's tour in the fall of 1844, the two men were engaged in a very personal rivalry on a very public plane.

They were no longer on speaking terms when Forrest visited London in 1845. This tour of Britain was not a success either. A combination of bad press coverage and intense competition from other actors meant that he could not arrange a tour as triumphant as the one that Macready had recently enjoyed in America, and he blamed Macready, probably without cause, for much of the bad coverage. Then in March 1846 he saw Macready act Hamlet in Edinburgh. At a point at which Macready engaged in a rather elaborate, and possibly gratuitous piece of business with his handkerchief, Forrest hissed. The injury to Macready's dignity was immense, and it was exacerbated a few days later by Forrest openly admitting in a letter to the *Times* that he was the guilty party.

Macready's final tour of the United States began with ominous signs of opposition from Forrest personally, from some audiences, and from the press. He was greeted, for example, by a defamatory article in the Boston *Mail,* while the New York *Herald* insisted that "we prefer the unsophisticated energy of the darling child of nature to the more glossy polish of the artificial European civilian" (quoted in Moody, *Astor Place Riot,* 94). After a rocky start in New York, where there was some hostility in the audience, true to the form of most encounters between British stars and a divided American public, most of Macready's appearances on an extended tour, which went as far south and west as New Orleans and St. Louis, met with a warm reception. Matters came to a head, however, when he returned to New York. Here, he was to act at the Astor Place Opera House, a building that stood in the popular imagination as the "English Aristocratic Opera House." Forrest, meanwhile, was appearing in an opposing engagement at the Bowery. On 7 May

Astor Place Opera House riot, 1849. Triggered by a feud between the English actor William Charles Macready and the American star Edwin Forrest and fed by anti-British sentiment among Irish groups of the Bowery area, this was one of the major riots in nineteenth-century America. In 1852 the theatre was renamed the New York Theatre to rid it of its tainted past. Library of Congress, Prints and Photographs Division.

Macready acted Macbeth at Astor Place to an audience that had been heavily stacked with the Bowery B'hoys, who, objecting vociferously to the British actor and the "codfish aristocracy" who supported him, eventually drove Macready from the stage. Macready was prepared to leave the States at once, his erstwhile sympathy for the country now being turned into implacable hatred, but members of the city's intelligentsia, appalled at the discourteous treatment he had received at the hands of the mob, urged him to appear once more. Macready gave way and on 10 May appeared once more as Macbeth at the Astor Place Opera House. The house was packed with well-wishers, and the one organized protest in the auditorium was soon quashed by a few strategic arrests by the police. A massive crowd had gathered, however, outside the theatre, and indignant at the news of the arrests, stormed it. The building itself held, but in a resulting confrontation with the militia in the square outside the theatre, twenty-two people were killed and one hundred and forty-four were injured (based on named individuals), one of the largest tolls ever exacted by a riot in New York. Macready, who finished the performance, was smuggled out of the theatre and left the country a few days later, to return to Britain a national hero.

Forrest was probably not the chief instigator of the riot, but he did little to assuage people's tempers and benefited greatly in his future career from the event, as the champion of American national identity. Though it has been customary for theatre historians to play down its importance – Joseph Jefferson III considered it to be aberrational and an offense to "the spirit of free play [that] circulates freely in Anglo-Saxon blood on both sides of the Atlantic" (*Autobiography,* 256) – the nativist versus anti-European rhetoric that fueled the riot masked broader class tensions that were developing in New York City and the industrial Northeast as a whole. The aftermath of the riot revealed deep class divisions in that society. Captain Rynders of the Empire Club, one of the ringleaders, in a speech in City Hall Park on the day after the riot, claimed that murder was done "to please the aristocracy of the city at the expense of the lives of inoffending citizens – to please an aristocratic Englishman, backed by a few sympathetic Americans." Macready he dismissed as being "full of his country's prejudices," which by this time was probably not far from the truth, and, less credibly, called the militia that shot down the people, "the slaves of her Majesty of England" (Moody, *Astor Place Riot,* 190–91). The nationalist tensions that had underlain the development of the star system in the American theatre had reached an unexpectedly bloody climax.

In several ways, the period of the Astor Place Riot represents a watershed for the American theatre. Macready had acted at the Astor Place Opera House because the Park Theatre no longer existed. After Stephen Price's death in 1840, the theatre had remained under the management of Price's partner, Edmund Simpson, but competition from other institutions in the expanding New York theatre meant that it no longer enjoyed the prestige of earlier years. When it burned down soon after Simpson sold it, it was not rebuilt. The demise of the Park Theatre and the Astor Place Riot did not, of course, put an end to the old star system, but they were among those forces at work that shifted it from being the central organizing principle of the American theatre.

Indicative of the gradual move away from sole dependence on stars to attract audiences was a return to the old stock company, at least in New York City. This move is associated first with William E. Burton, a celebrated comic actor, who arrived in the States from Britain in 1834. Burton was as skilled a manager as he was an actor, and at the high point of his career, between 1848 and 1856, he directed, at his own Chambers Street Theatre, one of the most accomplished ensembles of actors the city had seen. However, this was still not substantially an American affair, for when he had to replenish his company in 1852 he found he had to depend largely on the London theatre as the source for most of his actors. Burton's preeminence as the leader of a successful stock company, was challenged by James W. Wallack, the most distinguished member of a British-born family that controlled several American theatres in the course of the century. For the first thirty or so years of his career, Wallack shuttled between London and New York, but in 1851 he settled in New York, taking over the Broadway Lyceum Theatre, which he renamed Wallack's. Here, for the next decade, he would manage the most accomplished ensemble of actors that had until that time been known to the American public. Significantly, Wallack proved that theatre could be interesting without the presence of a star at each performance; the repertory, which remained primarily British, and the company, which was a mixture of British and American actors, were capable of attracting large audiences. The company continued to flourish, under the direction of Wallack's nephew Lester, until late into the century.

The interests of some of the star actors themselves were also diverted from pure performance into the field of production. Charles Kean (1811–68) had tried to cash in on the reputation of his father by touring the States in 1830, but his success was limited. He lacked the power of his father, and as a teenager he was quite incapable of doing justice to heavy roles such as Othello. Nevertheless, he persisted, and on several later tours, aided no doubt by the charms of his wife Ellen Tree (1806–80), he developed a fair reputation as an actor in the old, polished style, with "a grace and finish that gave repose and beauty to what would otherwise have been a mere copy" (Murdoch, *The Stage,* 145). In 1850, however, he went into management, producing, in the 1850s at the Princess Theatre in London, a celebrated series of Shakespeare productions, researched to the smallest detail for "historical accuracy" in design and stage presentation. As a director, Kean did not have much impact on the American theatre, though his production of *King John* at the Park in 1846 was seen as a precursor of the more celebrated Princess Theatre productions, and in the 1850s his concern for historical accuracy clearly influenced Burton's productions of Shakespeare. However, his choice to take up direction in lieu of or in addition to acting was symptomatic of the theatre as a whole.

The Irish-born Dion Boucicault was one of the most versatile theatrical figures of the century, as noted in the previous chapter, being equally successful as a playwright, actor, and manager. As a young man, he had all the physical and vocal qualifications to become a star in the old style, and Joseph Jefferson writes of him as having "the form of an Apollo with the strength of a Hercules; his deep musical voice was under perfect control . . . . As a melodramatic actor, he stood ahead of all his competitors" (*Autobiography,* 121). But the increasing sophistication of stage machinery and his celebrated use of spectacle in his melodramas led him to turn his attention to the technical aspects of staging and to the development of companies that would be devoted to the effective realization of the stage production. Although individual roles within these productions might require skilled acting – Boucicault himself was celebrated for his interpretation of the comic roles, especially stage Irishmen, that he wrote for himself – the production rather than an individual actor was the star.

The old star system had been made possible by the existence of theatres in which the repertoire changed nightly, so that, over a two to three week period, visiting stars could display the majority of their roles. Although the repertory theatre remained the prime model for the American theatre until 1870, from 1825 on some plays started running for several nights. As production costs grew with the innovations of Kean, Boucicault, and others, long runs became necessary to recoup the large initial investment that had made the production possible in the first case. As the run tended to replace repertory in New York as the prime means of organizing theatre production and as the combination companies came to dominate the theatre circuits, the artistic and financial basis of the old star system crumbled.

Despite these changes and despite the Forrest–Macready riots, there was no stemming the tide of stars from Britain. They made less impact than they had in the past. In part, this was because the events of 1849 had clearly defined the American theatre as the legitimate terrain of the American actor, hence American-born stars such as Forrest, Charlotte Cushman, and Edwin Booth now ruled the roost; in part, it was also because there was a distinct decline in the quality of British acting following the retirement of Macready in 1851. As a result, Gustavus Vaughan Brooke (1816–66) who arrived in the early 1850s was hailed as another Kean, but met with a cool reception from critics and audiences; a few years later, Barry Sullivan (1821–91), "a finished and elegant actor," made virtually no impact. Although their unpopularity was partially due to a decline in the authority of British visitors and an increased critical skepticism toward them as a result of the Macready affair, it may also have been because, if stars were still to visit America, there was "metal more attractive" to be found elsewhere.

Non-English-Speaking Influences

For the first hundred years of its existence, the language of the American theatre was exclusively English. Actors originating from outside English-speaking countries, such as the famous Placide family, which came from France, had to abandon their native language on stage. Hence, the only non-English stars who had great potential were those in musical forms of theatre, such as the Austrian dancer Fanny Elssler (1810–84), who enjoyed a fabulously successful tour in 1840–41, and the opera singers Maria Malibran (1808–36) and Jenny Lind (1820–87). Theatre had been given in French in New Orleans from the turn of the century, and visits of that French company became a regular feature of the New York season; from 1840 on, German-language plays were also staged regularly in New York, first under amateur, then professional auspices. Foreign-language theatres opened sporadically in other cities in which there was a sufficiently large immigrant community to provide an audience, but none of these operations were part of the English-language mainstream of American theatre. The situation has not, of course, changed much today, but from 1850 on, there were signs of a growing interest in America in theatre from more places than just Britain.

The first of the eminent foreign-language stars to visit the American theatre was the French actress Rachel (1820–58), who arrived with all the advance publicity and puffery normally reserved for dancers, singers, and British actors. Rachel is a crucial figure in the history of acting. Born into a family of peddlers, she rose from singing in the streets to become the unquestioned star of the Comédie Française. She did this not by adopting the statuesque style normally employed in the performance of Corneille and Racine, which bore much similarity to the neoclassicism of Kemble and Siddons, but by developing a mode of acting in which the marmoreal exterior of the character was eroded by the deep tensions resulting from emotional conflict. Representing sexual dementia, psychological decline, and physical degeneration, she did so not in the open, declarative style of neoclassicism, nor with the overt theatricality of the Romantic actor, but by suggestion and understatement in a manner foreshadowing the naturalism of some decades later.

Rachel's career at the Comédie Française and her tours of Europe had won her great acclaim, but she was less successful in the United States in 1855. Though audiences were intrigued by this unusual woman, they were put off not only by the foreign language, but by the high prices she charged; moreover, her muted acting did not carry well in the large theatres in which she performed. Consequently, although her opening night was packed, audiences soon fell off and continued to do so, even though prices were lowered. Nevertheless, Rachel did well, which indicates the U.S. theatre was still a major financial draw for Europeans. The $15,600 she received for fourteen performances was higher than anything she had been paid elsewhere. Nevertheless, popularity was elusive. Matters were not helped by the threatened eruption of another faceoff between democratic America and aristocratic Europe, this time through an article by the French drama critic Jules Janin, which was published in English translation in New York during the tour. Janin described America as "essentially democratic" and found this a menace to Rachel. She, he argued, is essentially aristocratic. Great artists, like great playwrights, only "address themselves to the chosen few, to the élite, to passion with elegance, to greatness, to power, to majesty." Janin continued in a paean to French culture, "it is an error, perhaps almost a crime, to offer to [democracy's] unintelligence, to its disdain, works written two and a half centuries ago with such artistry, such judgment, that no century has ever produced anything more exquisite, more rare, or more perfect." To appreciate such work, he insists, one needs to have had ancestors and been born into "benevolent idleness." Americans, however, have no such sense of the past or taste for elegant leisure. They prefer "tame bears, circus clowns, boxing, and the spectacular feats of acrobats."[12] While Janin's estimate of American tastes may not have been far wrong, the article displays a more overt cultural arrogance than any that Macready had expressed. Rachel had the good sense to dissociate herself from Janin, and the New Yorkers, now accustomed to slights on their national character, wisely chose to ignore it.

Rachel may have found the popularity for which she was searching had her health held out, but in her case life imitated art. She gave one performance in Philadelphia and then went on to Charleston, where it was clear that she was seriously ill with tuberculosis. After one appearance in that city, the last of her career, she returned to Europe, where she later died. The potential she could have found in America became clear only when her rival, the Italian actress Adelaide Ristori (1822–1906), initiated her first tour of the United States at the Théâtre Français, New York, in September 1866. Where Rachel met with reserve, Ristori was phenomenally successful. Her statuesque appearance on stage was reminiscent of Sarah Siddons, but in accord with the taste of the times, she reduced the poetry even of her classic roles and related the life of her characters to that of the everyday world. On her first tour of twenty-one cities alone she made a profit of $270,000 (cited in Morley, 333), so not surprisingly the following year she came back for more. Interestingly, although she learned to deliver some roles in English – later in life her Lady Macbeth was very highly regarded – she mainly spoke in Italian, usually with a supporting company of Italian speakers, and performed a repertoire that was French and Italian in origin. Few audiences could have been conversant enough with the language to follow her closely or even grasp clearly the plot of the play. Their interest in her was therefore different in nature from that of earlier audiences' attachment to the stars. Whereas earlier in the century the artistic justification for stars was the differing lights they threw on familiar roles, with Ristori it was clearly the "celebrity" of the woman who drew them rather than her contribution to a continuing artistic process. With her, the modern star system might be said to have begun.

It began too with the arrival of another foreign actor, the Polish-German tragedian Bogumil Dawison (1818–72), whose debut at the Stadttheater in New York took place on the same day as Ristori's. Dawison was known in Germany as the virtuoso actor who challenged the prevailing style of courtly acting embodied by Emile Devrient, itself a mannered version of high neoclassicism, much as Charles Kemble's acting related to that of his brother John

Rachel (1820–58), French actress, first major non-English-speaking star on the American stage, who gave her final performance in the United States. Despite her superb acting, her U.S. tour in 1855 was not a critical success. Miniature painting on ivory by "Alain" of Rachel as Phèdre. Don B. Wilmeth Collection.

Philip. Dawison, therefore, like Rachel – to whom he was occasionally compared – and Ristori brought a new realism, at times an earthiness, into acting that helped change the image of European actors as epigones of a past age of elegance. As the first major German-speaking actor to tour the United States, Dawison did well to attract audiences large enough to enable managers to guarantee him $1,000 a performance. The critical reception was not, however, ecstatic; several writers, like William Winter, found his interpretation of Shakespearean roles such as Shylock to be too studied, too technically self-conscious, and strangely conceived, "an able and effective display of an incorrect and inadequate ideal" (*Shakespeare on the Stage,* 164). Nevertheless, Dawison was capable of moments of great pathos with which audiences, despite the language barrier, could empathize. Perhaps the most curious occasion on his tour of the United States came when for three evenings he acted Othello to the Iago of Edwin Booth at the Thaliatheater in New York. Dawison spoke German, Booth and the rest of the cast English; Dawison considered "these evenings as one of the great experiences of his artistic life" (quoted in Kollek, 146). Audiences do not seem to have been much disturbed by the linguistic anomaly of the performance, which suggests that increased exposure to foreign-language actors trained them to sense the rhythm of the action rather than the language of the dialogue as the unifying force of the play (though texts in translation were often distributed to the audience). These events clearly served as preparation for the more celebrated tours of the Italian actors Ernesto Rossi and Tommaso Salvini in the coming decades.

Perhaps the changes that occurred in the two decades after the Astor Place Riot were most completely typified in the career of Charles Albert Fechter (1824–79). Born in London of a German father and an English mother, his first language was French, and he began his career as an actor of romantic melodrama in Paris prior to returning to London, where he spent the middle portion of his career. He ended in the States, to which he migrated in 1869. By the time he encountered American audiences, his middle-aged proportions made several of the heroes he represented onstage absurd. Furthermore, he had never fully mastered the English language, so he was often difficult to understand. Nevertheless, he acquired an enthusiastic following for the pictorial quality of his acting and for the directness and delicacy with which he could represent emotional flux within the character. He lacked all majesty and dignity and held his audiences by suggestion rather than bald statement: "Fechter," wrote John Ranken Towse, "had the special capacity, or genius, which enabled him . . . to establish the incredible by circumstantial evidence" (77).

Conclusion

If a pattern can be discerned in the development of modes of acting practiced by European visitors to the American stage in the first 120 years of its existence, it is probably that of an increasing dismantling of formality. The imperative of representing authority and majesty, so closely tied to the actor's function in the middle decades of the eighteenth century, took a long time to lose its hold; as late as the 1830s Charles and Fanny Kemble still held their audiences through the nobility and grace of their demeanor, and Macready himself, though not a monarchist at heart, undoubtedly cultivated an aura of elevation and detachment that could be read as being within the royal tradition of acting. The romantic actors invested the roles they played with an emotional urgency that made neoclassicism appear stilted and archaic. Their own representations were, however, still highly theatrical, in a way that struck subsequent generations as artificial, even shrill. But whatever their differences, the modes of acting practiced on the spectrum between the two poles of romanticism and neoclassicism suited the image of the actor as a star, as one who stands out from the surrounding world of the stage as a cynosure, drawing all eyes to the heroic struggle of the central figure. After the mid-nineteenth century, as the star system itself began to change, star actors themselves adjusted their relationship to the theatre of which they were a part. Their acting implied as much as it stated, and, as it focused increasingly on the borders of personality that interrelate with the exterior world, they gradually attuned themselves to a world in which the experience of the whole rather than that of a single actor alone become the prevailing goal of the theatre. Of course, the star did not disappear overnight; some of the most splendid, and regal, foreign actors were still to visit America – Tommaso Salvini, Henry Irving, Sarah Bernhardt, Joseph Kainz – but the old system whereby the star alone dominated the economy and the artistry of the theatre had, by 1870, disappeared, almost for good.

Notes

1 Philip Highfill Jr., in his article "The British Background of the American Hallams," *Theatre Survey* 11, no. 1 (May 1970): 1–35, demonstrates convincingly that the Hallam family had had vast experience in the British theatre and had even acted with some success at the patent theatres.

2 From a letter to the *Pennsylvania Gazette* (1767), quoted in Pollock, *The Philadelphia Theatre in the Eighteenth Century,* 21.

3 These figures are taken from Ireland, *A Memoir of the Professional Life of Thomas Abthorpe Cooper.*

4 William B. Wood provides an extensive analysis of the damage wrought by the star system on the American theatre in the penultimate chapter of his *Personal Recollections of the Stage.*

5 Verse address by Samuel Woodworth, quoted in Ireland, 61.

6 See Charles H. Shattuck's designation of Cooke, Kean, and Booth as "the Wild Ones" in *Shakespeare on the American Stage: From the Hallams to Edwin Booth,* 32–50.

7 See especially McConachie, *Melodramatic Formations* and Levine, *Highbrow/Lowbrow,* for extended discussions of the class divisions of American theatre.

8 See Barnard Hewitt, "King Stephen of the Park and Drury Lane," *The Theatrical Manager in England and America,* 134.

9 From an unpublished playbill cited in Richard L. Klepac, *Mr. Mathews at Home,* 20.

10 Morris's campaign is well described by Hodge in *Yankee Theatre,* 31–37.

11 In this paragraph I am particularly indebted to Downer, *The Eminent Tragedian: William Charles Macready,* 69–80.

12 The article is included complete in Léon Beauvallet, *Rachel and the New World,* 126–37.

Bibliography: European Actors

Acting, being ephemeral, is difficult to write about. All records of it exist in the memory, and writings about it are based mainly on people's impressions of performances that have moved or enraged them. Hence, documents of acting are often as much records of the writer's subjectivity as they are objective accounts of historical events. For this reason, good histories of acting are few and far between. Garff B. Wilson's *History of American Acting* is the only book that attempts to determine "schools of acting" in America, a concept with which the Europeans are more at home, and Richard Moody provides a useful survey of American acting in Chapter 2 of *American Drama, Volume VIII* in *The Revels History of Drama* series (see Bogard in Bibliography). However, no general surveys exist of the impact of European actors on the American theatre in the period covered by my chapter. Barnard Hewitt's *Theatre U.S.A.: 1665–1957* contains hard-to-find, invaluable documentation on their performances, as does the recent *Theatre in the Colonies and United States* (see Witham). Histories that examine in detail several of the issues that are raised in this chapter and also provide excellent surveys of their chosen period include Rankin, *The Theater in Colonial America;* Part I of Francis Hodge's *Yankee Theatre: The Image of America on the Stage, 1825–1850;* and McConachie's refreshingly polemical *Melodramatic Formations: American Theatre and Society, 1820–1870.* Burge, *Lines of Business: Casting Practice and Policy in the American Theatre, 1752–1899* provides a finely researched and clearly conceived account of the structure of the acting profession prior to the twentieth century.

Like its European counterparts, the American theatre has produced a rich literature of memoirs and diaries; those written by Europeans who came to settle in America are often distinctive for the vigor and excitement with which they encounter an unfamiliar society and theatre in the process of their formation. Especially enlightening, anecdotally informative, and often highly entertaining are the following: *An Apology for the Life of James Fennell, Written by Himself* (1814); Wemyss, *Twenty-Six Years of the Life of an Actor and Manager* (1847); Bernard, *Retrospections of America, 1797–1811* (1887); Wood, *Personal Recollections of the Stage* (1855); and Vandenhoff, *Leaves from an Actor's Notebook* (1860). Léon Beauvallet's *Rachel and the New World* tends to be more useful as a foreigner's view of America than as an account of Rachel's acting. Not always enthusiastic, but nonetheless mines of information about the theatre are Frances Ann Kemble, *Records of a Girlhood,* and *The Diaries of William Charles Macready.* Of the several collections of essays by contemporary critics and actors, I found Murdoch's *The Stage* (1880) most helpful in its understanding of the basic principles of acting and most generous in its appreciation of the contribution made by European stars to the American theatre.

Several of the major European actors discussed in this chapter have often been the subject of biography, but it is surprising how much work still needs to be done in this important field. Brief biographical sketches and analyses of major figures in the early years are offered in Bost, *Monarchs of the Mimic World,* and Stephen Price is the subject of an informative chapter by Barnard Hewitt in *The Theatrical Manager in England and America,* edited by Joseph W. Donohue, Jr. Ireland wrote a brief *Memoir of the Professional Life of Thomas Abthorpe Cooper* (1888), but the most substantial biography is in an as yet unpublished dissertation by Fairlie Arant, "A Biography of the Actor Thomas Abthorpe Cooper," although the recent biography by Geddeth Smith helps to fill the void. Doty's *The Career of Mrs. Anne Brunton Merry in the American Theatre* gives an excellent account of this important actress, but the only biography of the equally important Mary Ann Duff is Ireland's outdated *Mrs. Duff* (1882). The three great Romantic actors have, of course, been the subject of much critical and biographical writing. George Frederick Cooke has been well served. Dunlap's *Life of George Frederick Cooke* (1815) is still worth consulting, but the standard biography is now Wilmeth's *George Frederick Cooke: Machiavel of the Stage.* Oddly enough, though writers have been attracted to Edmund Kean more than they have to most actors, there is no satisfactory modern biography of him. One must, therefore, still depend on Hillebrand's *Edmund Kean* (1933), which possesses much valuable documentation and is saner in its evaluation than any other book on the actor, though its understanding of Kean in his broader cultural context is limited. Archer has recently produced a full-dress biography of Junius Brutus Booth.

Furnas provides an extended biography in *Fanny Kemble: Leading Lady of the Nineteenth-Century Stage,* but Dudden's chapter on Kemble in *Women in the American Theatre* is particularly recommended for its evaluation of her impact on women in American society as well as on the theatre. Williamson provides a reliable account of the life of Fanny's father in *Charles Kemble: Man of the Theatre.* The best modern account of Macready can be found in Alan S. Downer's superb biography, *The Eminent Tragedian: William Charles Macready.* Downer covers the events leading up to the Forrest–Macready riot in detail, but reference should also be made to Richard Moody's *Astor Place Riot,* which goes into great documentary detail and is admirably impartial, and Buckley's "To the Opera House." Of the later actors covered in this essay, only Rachel has attracted English-language biographers, and most of them deal mainly with her career in Europe. However, Brownstein's recent book, *Tragic Muse: Rachel of the Comédie Française,* is highly recommended for its refreshingly novel approach to the writing of an actor's biography.

As during its first hundred years, American theatre was less centralized than it became early in the twentieth century; books that cover the theatre of individual cities provide much valuable information about touring stars. Among these volumes, pride of place must go to Odell's monumental *Annals of the New York Stage,* still an indispensable resource for anyone working in pre-twentieth-century American theatre. Foreign-language theatre in New York is covered by Mason in *The French Theatre in New York* and Leuchs in *The Early German Theatre in New York: 1840–1872.* Philadelphia, for a time the rival to New York as the theatrical capital of America, has been well served by the six volumes of Durang's *History of the Philadelphia Stage,* Clark's *The Philadelphia Theatre in the Eighteenth Century,* and James's *Cradle of Culture.* Information on the stars' appearances in other eastern cities can be found in William W. Clapp Jr., *A Record of the Boston Stage;* Phelps, *Players of a Century: A Record of the Albany Stage;* Ritchey, *A Guide to the Baltimore Stage in the Eighteenth Century;* and Willard, *A History of the Providence Stage, 1762–1891.* Theatre and actors in the South have also received extensive coverage. In this regard, the major sources for European stars are Dormon, *Theatre in the Ante-Bellum South, 1815–1861;* Willis, *The Charleston Stage in the XVIII Century;* Hoole, *The Ante-Bellum Charleston Theatre,* and Smither, *A History of the English Theatre in New Orleans, 1806–1842.*

As Shakespeare featured so prominently in the repertoire of the European stars, much information can be found in books devoted to the performance of his plays. Among the substantial literature in this field, the most comprehensive volume is Charles H. Shattuck, *Shakespeare on the American Stage: From the Hallams to Edwin Booth.* The first chapter of Lawrence W. Levine's *Highbrow/Lowbrow: The Emergence of Cultural Hierarchy in America* provides a stimulating discussion of Shakespeare in popular American culture and has much to say about the function of Shakespearean performance in the theatre.

The Emergence of the American Actor

Joseph Roach

Rounding the bend three-quarters of a mile up river from a one-horse town in Arkansas, the raft on which Huckleberry Finn floats is "a most uncommon lively place." At that point in Huck's narrative, the makeshift showboat carries on its crowded deck a boy (Huck), a runaway slave (Jim), a "king," a "duke," and all their worldly possessions. These include the theatrical prerequisites, human and material, sufficient to rehearse a multitude of roles, which the travelers are prepared to perform for one another as well as for a larger public. The fact that Huck knows the truth about the purported royals – "that these liars warn't no kings nor dukes, at all" – detracts not at all from their urgent preparations for the forthcoming stage show:

Shakespearean Revival!!!
Wonderful Attraction!
For One Night Only!
The world renowned tragedians,
David Garrick the younger, of Drury Lane Theatre, London
and
Edmund Kean the elder, of the Royal Haymarket Theatre, White-
chapel, Pudding Lane, Piccadilly, London, and the
Royal Continental Theatres, in their sublime
Shakespearean Spectacle

Following the balcony scene from *Romeo and Juliet,* featuring Mr. Garrick as Romeo and Mr. Kean as Juliet, "assisted by the whole strength of the company," and the "thrilling, masterly, and blood-curdling broad-sword conflict" from *Richard III,* the playbill promises that the evening will conclude with Mr. Kean's rendering of "Hamlet's Immortal Soliloquy." Adult admission was set at a quarter, a dime for children and slaves (Twain, 141–42).

Such histrionics, performed along one of the many turns in the big river that Mark Twain remembered in *Huckleberry Finn* (1885), revived scenes from an America that no longer existed – and may never have existed – except in memory. They also evoked, in their own satiric and yet oddly nostalgic way, more than one version of the emergence of the American actor.

Acting is an art of collective recollection, involving both the performer and the public. The kind of cultural work that actors do often nominates them as caretakers of memory. In the intensity and evanescence of theatrical performance, actors sound what Abraham Lincoln, in his first inaugural address, termed "the mystic chords of memory" that may impart a sense of cohesion to the fractious body politic (Lincoln, 224). Actors may do this because nightly they transfer their version of the accumulating stock of invented social identities from the past into the future. The paradox of that transfer, however, as Alexis de Tocqueville noted in *Democracy in America* (1835), is that the conditions of nightly performance, in the midst of which no spectator can ask his minister's advice or refer to a dusty conduct book, make the theatre the most propitious forum for a revolutionary society: "The spectator at a dramatic piece is, to a certain extent, taken by surprise by the impression it conveys. He has not time to refer to his memory or to consult those more able to judge than himself. It does not occur to him to resist the new literary tendencies which begin to be felt by him; he yields to them before he knows what they are" (II, 79). In this way, by mediating between the transmission and the transformation of tradition, actors tend to embody the contradiction, at the heart of many American self-conceptions, between nostalgia and progress (see Kammen 702–3).

I want to introduce the principal themes of this chapter by citing Mark Twain's novel as a rich archive of cultural performances, especially, but not exclusively, performances onstage. In *Acting Naturally* (1995), Randall Knoper places Mark Twain in a "culture of performance" that embraced the frequently contradictory ideals of calculated effect and sincerity of spontaneous expression (76–80). When William Dean Howells, for instance, praised Twain's writing as both "dramatic and unconscious," he set forth the terms that had also come to define the paradoxical demands placed upon the performer in America (*Correspondence,* II, 780). These demands were based on what many authorities discovered in the actor and then generalized to the social performance of any citizen – a core identity at the heart of every real American, against which the authenticity of performances in a variety of roles could be measured. Self-conscious public expression of inner feeling – Howells's "dramatic" – must somehow derive from a legitimating source of "unconscious" truth, an innocence beyond the reach of art but nevertheless fundamental to its authority.

Three issues highlighted by the mordant ironies and nostalgic evocations of *Huckleberry Finn* are particularly important to the understanding of the emergence of the American actor in this "culture of performance": (1) the spectral presence of British actors or their imitators in the self-conceptions of Americans, onstage and off, with particular regard to the opposition, sometimes violent, of cosmopolitan center and frontier margin; (2) the inculcation of "double consciousness" in strategies of American self-invention by constructing categories of human difference through imitative performances; (3) the importance of proper expression in language, speech, and comportment to adjudicate standards of inclusion and exclusion in American life as represented (and re-created) on the stage.

The first and most pointed butt of Mark Twain's ridicule of the earlier history of the American theatre is its bogus and sycophantic anglophilia. The satirist aligns himself with a self-consciously American hatred of tyranny, of which snobbery is a particularly obnoxious subcategory. Even on the edge of the world – the trans-Mississippi frontier before the ubiquity of steam propulsion – the legitimating aura of the London theatre exerts its monocultural sway. Names like "Garrick" and "Kean" vie for pride of place as inflated signifiers of cultural capital, with spurious titles like "duke" and "king." Over and above a satirical hit on the abuses of the "star system" (the point of embarkation for boatloads of overpuffed barnstormers as well as charismatic celebrities), the joke here is that the names of long-dead English actors continue to work their magic on the lively citizens of a dynamic interculture represented by many nations, peoples, and their burgeoning progeny.

For this state of affairs, Shakespeare, rightly or wrongly, bore – and continues to bear – a significant share of the blame. The fun that Mark Twain pokes at anglophiles, in fact, would not be entirely misdirected at some of the most worthy histories of the American theatre. "In its beginning the art of theatre in America, including Shakespearean theatre," writes Charles Shattuck in *Shakespeare on the American Stage* (1976), "was entirely an importation from the mother country. From 1752 when Lewis Hallam led his London Company of Comedians to Virginia until well into the 1820s, very few native-born Americans took to the stage and none rose to eminence" (xi). Such a formulation, though it is generally accepted by theatre historians as a commonplace,[1] also rests upon at least three deeply problematic fictions: first, that as early as 1752 a discrete and autonomously coherent national entity called America existed separately from "the mother country"; second, that the only real Americans are "native-born Americans"; and third, that there is only one possible mother country.

In fact, the borders of America were more porous, contested, and improvisatory than such fictions allow, and the lives of the early actors record these fluidities. When Hallam's original London Company of Comedians, for instance, reimagined itself during the Revolutionary War as "The American Company," the center of operations for what actors like Lewis Hallam Jr. and David Douglass understood to constitute America was Kingston, Jamaica (see Hill, *The Jamaican Stage,* 76–80). In the 1790s, as English actors such as Thomas Wignell, Eliza Whitlock Kemble, and Anne Brunton Merry helped to establish Philadelphia as the dominant anglophone theatre center,[2] and as the Irishman John Henry gave way to the ambitious "provincial Garrick" John Hodgkinson in New York City, Monterey, California was the continuing scene of a Spanish-language theatre in North America that dated back to the Conquest. At the same time, following the Haitian Revolution, francophone theatre flourished in the Caribbean-oriented southern port cities of Charleston and New Orleans. The versatile and bilingual Alexandre Placide, for instance, a Parisian pantomimist-acrobat-actor-manager, was a major force in the Charleston theatre from 1794 to 1812 (see Willis, 466–68). Beginning in 1792, New Orleans welcomed metropolitan French actor-managers Louis-Alexandre Henry, Jean-Baptiste Fournier, and Haitian Louis Tabary as well as the sensational quadroon actress Minette. (See Allain and St. Martin, 139–174.)

The custom of defining what is or is not American by comparison to Great Britain, improvised in the revolutionary and postrevolutionary period, later takes on the golden penumbra of a creation myth, tempting theatre historians to forget that different origins are what most Americans have in common. At another bend in the river, "Nigger Jim," the runaway slave in *Huckleberry Finn,* whose mother country was certainly not Britain, asks Huck: "Is a Frenchman a man?" (95). Huck's answer in the affirmative reminds historians that not all men or even all Americans who claim the same nationality also claim the same descent, the same interests, or the same memory. The myth of American exceptionalism, predicated on the providential singularity of white, English-speaking Protestant entitlement in the New World, has continually encountered the reality of ethnic and racial difference as the real condition of life in America. This encounter generates a volatile, explosive practice of cultural containment and reformation: the negotiation of difference through the medium of mimicry. Mimicry characterizes performances of many kinds in the repertoire of the emerging American actor, who raised it to the level of a national art form. In this foundational practice, the theatre may rightly be seen to have been historically central – not marginal, as it is so often portrayed – among American institutions.

As Tocqueville's astute aristocratic vigilance predicted, in fact, the theatre became a site of the transformation as well as the transmission of American identities. This process, which significantly overlaps the emergence of the American actor in the first half of the nineteenth century, is perhaps sufficiently well defined to constitute what Bruce McConachie, in *Melodramatic Formations,* has termed "a theatrical formation, the mutual elaboration over time of historically specific audience groups and theatre practitioners participating in certain shared patterns of dramatic and theatrical action" (xii). The most obvious evidence for such a formation resides in the infusion of the strongly traditional actors' "lines of business" with new or newly elaborated stock characters based on ethnic stereotypes.

In *Lines of Business* Burge documents the transfer of casting and theatrical employment practices largely intact from English provincial companies in the eighteenth century to the colonial and early postrevolutionary American theatre. Lines of business – the established categories of types or roles – included "leading business" (the company's principal tragedian and/or comedian), the "leading lady," the "light comedy and eccentric business" (male), "juvenile lady" (ingenue), "1st and second low comedy" (male), "chambermaid," "1st and 2nd heavy business" (villains), "1st and 2nd old women," the "walking gentleman" and the "walking gentlewoman" (Burge, 297). Intelligible to actors, playwrights, managers, and publics, such a division of labor allowed a company to shape its forces to meet the needs of a relatively stable repertoire and to fulfill a set of largely conventionalized expectations. Usually, as long as he or she continued to play it successfully, a role remained in the actor's possession, and normally a line represented a career-long investment for the actor who filled it. The designation "walking" gentleman or gentlewoman meant that the assigned roles of this line contributed to the development of the plot of the play but carried little or no responsibility for representing the psychological or emotional consequences of its action. The latter responsibility fell to the players of "leading business" in the stock company, leaving a large opening in the network of theatrical relations through which the star would irresistibly enter. "Eccentric business," however, suggested that the actor's line consisted of humorous types, subordinated to and yet absolutely necessary for the normative definition of the conventional leading roles. (See also Chapter 2.)

Assigning the roles among the lines of business could be a delicate and perilous matter, however, and Mark Twain has a great deal of fun with the catastrophic miscasting of the superannuated "Mr. Kean" in the definitive juvenile lady role of Shakespeare's Juliet. The scope of such a theatrical transgression is perhaps best suggested by the words of the American actress and playwright Anna Cora Mowatt, herself a compelling Juliet after her stage debut in 1845, when she describes in *Autobiography of an Actress* (1854) the binding power of lines of business in a stock company: "The members of a company, in a well-organized theatre, resemble the men on a chess board. Each has his appointed place, and fights his battle for distinction in a fixed direction" (320). The stringent prerequisites of a real juvenile lady were helpfully delineated by Edgar Allan Poe in his tenderly prurient description of Anna Cora Mowatt's charms from *The Broadway Journal* (19 July 1845). Graceful movement is an important accomplishment in the perfect ingenue: "Her step is very graceful and assured – indeed all her movements evince the practised elocutionist." The voice must likewise be polished but not affected: "Her utterance is singularly distinct – its sole blemish being an occasional Anglicism of accent, adopted probably from her instructor." But above all, her face, body, and expressive countenance must fit within the fairly narrow limits of the type:

> Her figure is slight – even fragile – but eminently graceful. Her face is a remarkably fine one, and of that precise character best adapted to the stage. The forehead is the least prepossessing feature, although it is by no means an unintellectual one. The eyes are gray, brilliant and expressive, without being full. The nose is well formed, with the Roman curve, and strongly indicative of energy; this quality is also shown in the quality of the

Mrs. Mowatt, as Rosalind.

Anna Cora Mowatt (1819–70) as Rosalind in *As You Like It.* Actress, public reader, and playwright, best known today as the author of *Fashion* (1845) but in her day equally admired as an actress. Don B. Wilmeth Collection.

chin. The mouth is somewhat large, with brilliant and even teeth, and flexible lips, capable of the most effective variations of expression. A more radiantly beautiful smile we never remember having seen. Mrs. Mowatt has also the personal advantage of a profusion of rich auburn hair. (187–88)

In the line and in the role, which tended to fuse physical attributes and psychological capacities, Mowatt followed such winsomely sentimental English actresses as Anne Bellamy, Susanna Cibber, and the transatlantic Anne Brunton Merry. Through such theatrical simulacra – as clear as chess pieces on a board – lines of business allowed a traditional society to communicate its desired moves to the players on the stage with an unseen hand.

At the same time, however, lines of business were also vulnerable to the pressures of novelty. Their expandability allowed a revolutionary society to cope with the accelerating velocity of its cultural transformation. Such a transformation often brings with it a certain violence or threat of violence focused on those whose differences seem to point the way to an unsettled future. The emergence of the American actor was marked by the expansion of the eccentric business line as varieties of ethnic, racial, religious, and linguistic difference proliferated. In English and colonial stock companies, the line might include the Frenchman, the Irishman, and the Jew. In the Federal and Jacksonian periods, the line expanded to include the Yankee Jonathan, the stage Indian, the immigrant Irishman, the German, the "Sambo" darkie, and more. Adepts of the line learned how to emphasize the eccentricities of the characters through mimicry of their speech. The skills required of an actor called upon to sustain eccentric business included an excellent ear for the rhythms and inflections of spoken dialects, a radiant comic persona, and the intangible gift of creating a certain amount of sympathy for the risible oddities of alien behavior. Whether the eccentric character is foreign or native born, whether its fate is to be assimilated or excluded, eccentric business draws the constantly redrawn line between "us" and "them."

Unsurprisingly, the earliest postrevolutionary addition to the repertoire of eccentric business was the Yankee Jonathan, a homespun character written by the American dramatist Royall Tyler in *The Contrast* (1787) but created for the stage by the British comedian Thomas Wignell in the line of an English country rustic. Wignell's bumpkin Jonathan was followed by Joseph Jefferson I's characterization of Nathan Yank in *Tears and Smiles* (1807) and by the glossary of Jonathaniana published as an appendix to David Humphrey's *The Yankey in England* (1815). The definitive early consolidation of the Yankee Jonathan character – homespun but shrewd, taciturn yet colorful of speech – was achieved by English actor Charles Mathews, who made a number of immensely popular studies of American types in his transatlanticly famous "At Homes." In *Trip to America* (1824) Mathews measured the laconic Yankee against dialect burlesques of Scots, Irish, Dutch, French, and African Americans. In *Jonathan in England* (1824) Mathews further exploited dialect humor to satirize, among other American institutions, the contradiction between slavery and democracy, a well-publicized affront that contributed to the increasingly phobic responses of the American public to British actors.

The first "native-born" American actor to add substantially to the Yankee character was James H. Hackett, a New York trader who first appropriated Mathews's material into his own storytelling act and then developed a series of dramatic pieces, including *Down East; or, the Village Gazette* (1830), in which the Yankee figures centrally. Hackett was followed by George Handel "Yankee" Hill, the first New England native to play the Yankee, and Dan Marble, the "Western" Yankee, who developed the role further on tour as "Yankee Sam Patch" to suit the tastes of audiences of the American West, exemplified by the cliff-hanging sensation scenes of *Sam Patch, the Yankee Jumper* in 1844.

Phlegmatic Yankee Jonathan played himself off against more floridly

English actor-playwright Charles Mathews (1776–1835) in an 1824 engraving of the many characters he played in *Trip to America,* an important stimulus for Yankee plays and characters. Don B. Wilmeth Collection.

demonstrative types, the stage Irishman and the "Sambo," who occupied a liminal space between native and alien identities. The concept of liminality – the threshold space betwixt and between the inside and outside of a culture – is basic to the understanding of how performers mediate in a process that includes or excludes candidates for assimilation, while at the same time it also works to shore up the necessary fiction of a core identity around which boundaries can be fixed and patrolled. "The Americans," observed Francis Grund, the Austrian Tocqueville, in 1837, "do not laugh at honest bluntness, or good natured simplicity. . . . If Jonathan is to laugh, he must have a point given to him, or, in other words, [Americans] must laugh at the expense of their neighbors." Following other immigrant communities in suffering "the stings of American wit," Grund continues, "the Irish of late have become very popular" (79–80). Hapless, bumbling, accident-prone, quarrelsome, grandiloquent, and happily ignorant, the stage Irishman helped to define the fictive perimeters of the American core identity by walking with a drunken swagger along the fine line between its sympathy and contempt. From the 1820s to the

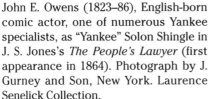

John E. Owens (1823–86), English-born comic actor, one of numerous Yankee specialists, as "Yankee" Solon Shingle in J. S. Jones's *The People's Lawyer* (first appearance in 1864). Photograph by J. Gurney and Son, New York. Laurence Senelick Collection.

James H. Hackett (1800–1871), known for Yankee and frontiersman characters, in particular, as seen here, Colonel Nimrod Wildfire (first seen in 1831) in J. Kirke Paulding's *The Lion of the West,* a role loosely modeled on Davy Crockett and played by Hackett for more than twenty years. Don B. Wilmeth Collection.

1850s, a series of actors succeeded in exploiting the stage Irishman specialty: Tyrone Power, John Brougham, William J. Florence, Barney Williams, the originator of "unlucky Pat," and his wife Maria Pray, and Dion Boucicault.

Boucicault, after a London debut as Teddy Rodent, the Irish rat catcher, shrewdly capitalized as a playwright on the appeal of Irish romantic nationalism and the relations between Irish ethnicity and social class in America. The burgeoning of a working-class urban subculture centered on Irish American characters coalesced in the 1840s around the immensely popular Mose the Fireboy, a "Bowery B'hoy" in the eccentric line perfected by Frank Chanfrau: "boaster and brawler, heroic fire fighter, and guardian angel of the greenhorns and of Linda the Cigar Girl" (Murphy, 222–24). Although the ostensible whiteness of the Irish imposed an acute crisis of visibility on Anglo-American

Know-Nothings in dealing with the "niggers of Europe," the actor in the line of eccentric business seemed to reduce this anxiety by substituting caricatured behaviors for caricatured physiognomies.

The convergence of Irish and African identities as laborers, servants, and slaves emerged as a popular racist and nativist trope (see Knobel, 92–93). Appearing in America with the "cheeky servant" character of Mungo in the transatlantic favorite *The Padlock* (1769) and lapsing into the shuffling "Sambo" in John Murdock's *The Triumph of Love* (1795), the blackfaced stereotype on the so-called legitimate stage prepared the way for the overwhelming proliferation of minstrelsy in the nineteenth century. The popular success of the minstrel shows, in which the American penchant for self-definition by mimicry and mockery attained its definitive form, made the careers of generations of white American actors from the 1830s on, including Thomas D. "Daddy" Rice, who claimed to have introduced the "Jim Crow" song and dance, Barney Williams, Jack Diamond, Barney Burns, and Bob Farrell, among others. For the next hundred years, minstrelsy would directly or indirectly provide many of the principal forms of American popular entertainment as well as many opportunities for the employment of American actors, singers, and dancers.

In the face of the perceived weakness of what Andrew Ross in *No Respect* calls "formations of prestige" (62–63) among native high-culture venues, American popular culture turned to Shakespeare, on the one hand, and to minstrelsy, on the other, and sometimes to both of them together, in order to accumulate its own cultural capital by framing that of others in contradictory juxtapositions of ridicule and sentimentality. As Eric Lott explains in *Love and Theft* (1993), the dynamism and insecurity of American identity, the unresolved questions of nationality and class, coalesced around the emergence of the American actor in blackface:

> What I mean to suggest about the character of popular culture in America is how unstable an entity it has been – a site of conflicting interests, appropriations, impersonations, indeed "nationalities," even in its allegedly national forms. Little wonder, then, that the question of whose "national" culture best expressed American life emerged around the popularity of the minstrel show, or that one sees a constant struggle for control – encompassing black, white, immigrant Irish, and other cultures – within blackface forms themselves. (92)

In the context of Lott's trenchant analysis of blackface minstrelsy and its various publics, it seems useful to reiterate McConachie's formulation of a "theatrical formation," the collaboration of stage practitioners and audiences in using performance to do the work of cultural memory and invention. This concept of a theatrical formation in and for antebellum America is indebted to Raymond Williams's distinction between "residual" and "emergent" culture

(121–27): The former descends as an active legacy from the past to the present, such as the dominance of British traditions on the early American stage; the latter introduces elements that are "substantially alternative or oppositional," such as the transformation of lines of business into a Babel of specialized antitypes and liminal demitypes in contrast to which a core identity may be collectively invented and imaginatively sustained. The American actor was emergent in this specialized sense of the word, and as such his or her very success posed a potential social threat.

Through the liminal personae of the "king" and the "duke" in *Huckleberry Finn*, Mark Twain plays upon a generally phobic response to theatricality, which was especially prevalent in the middle years of the nineteenth century and which associates the actor, potentially any actor, with the confidence man. In an emerging culture of self-inventing strangers, as Halttunen argues in *Confidence Men and Painted Women,* hypocrisy and fraud represent particularly powerful menaces. At the same time, however, the very necessity of self-invention in a new world and among new relations inspires calculated performances in the presence of potential collaborators or competitors – hence the paradoxical midcentury preoccupation with conduct books, including manuals of stage deportment, as guides to the rehearsal of sincerity, perfect transparency of sentiment, and authenticity of expression. One extremely useful obfuscation achieved by such a double move is the denial of class as the basis of social exclusion: "Sentimentalism," as Halttunen points out, "offered an unconscious strategy for middle-class Americans to distinguish themselves as a class while still denying the class structure even as they insisted they were merely distinguishing themselves from vulgar hypocrites" (195). In the face of such sentimental contingencies of value, the emergence of the American actor was both impelled and inhibited by the obligation to produce in public the sincere and spontaneous expression of inner emotion. Such a test of real feeling denied the imputation of hypocrisy even as the actor's histrionic skills drew attention to the potent menace of dissembled emotions: Deceit is the helpmate not only of fraud but also of tyranny.

For actors in such a culture of performance, style poses a fundamental problem. Where the "dramatic," in Howells's formulation, appears unsupported by the "unconscious," the potential contradictions between competence and sincerity are exposed. All the people, nevertheless, can be fooled some of the time. The shrewdly innocent Huckleberry Finn quickly sees through the fraudulent claims of royal origin made by the king and the duke, but he lets himself be taken in by the scenery-chewing style of the duke's Hamlet. The irony behind Huck's description highlights the proliferation of bad acting in American life, onstage and off:

> So he went to marching up and down, thinking, and frowning horrible every
> now and then; then he would hoist up his eyebrows; next he would squeeze

his hand on his forehead and stagger back and kind of moan; next he would sigh, and next he'd let drop a tear. It was beautiful to see him. By-and-by he got it. He told us to give attention. Then he strikes a most noble attitude, with one leg shoved forwards, and his arms stretched away up, and his head tilted back, looking up at the sky; and then he begins to rip and rave and grit his teeth; and after that, all through his speech he howled, and spread around, and swelled up his chest, and just knocked the spots out of any acting ever *I* see before. (140)

Here the comic reassurance to the sophisticated reader is that the difference between true expression and vulgar hypocrisy is or ought to be obvious: The king and the duke are classed among the vagabonds not because they are insolvent but because they are insincere. In that light, however, the duplicitous performance of Huck in the matter of Jim's escape, which troubles his conscience but upon which the slave's freedom and perhaps his life depend, sets up the ironic counter-example of self-inventing lies that seep out unbidden from a deep source in the most anguished inner truths.

From the lips of confidence men and painted women America heard its hypocrisy enunciated and exposed, but beneath that epidermal layer, in the interstices of the imagined community that Walt Whitman called a race of races, performance constructed human difference out of the contradictory expectations of the performers themselves. From the eighteenth century on, theorists of the stage developed the idea of double consciousness as a psychological explanation for the paradox of acting. As Denis Diderot put it in his famous dialogue, which has inspired or provoked many of the essays on the art of acting written since its publication in 1830, including those on American acting: "One is oneself by nature; one is another by imitation; the heart you imagine for yourself is not the heart you have" (140). As translated into the language of the American stage in a lecture called "The Art of Acting" (1882) by Dion Boucicault, Diderot's paradox divides the consciousness of the social performer into three parts:

We are all free men, in one sense, speaking, of course, of our inner life; but we have three characters. First there is the man by himself – as he is to himself – as he is to his God. That is one man, the inner man, as he is when alone; the unclothed man. Then there is the native man, the domestic man, as he is to his family. Still there is a certain amount of disguise. He is not as he is to other men. Then there is the man as he stands before the world at large; as he is outside in society. Those are the three characters. They are all in one man, and [the actor] does not know his business unless he puts them into one character. (158)

Professional actors like Boucicault rendered this phenomenon visible as a daily condition of employment, but civilians also felt its dichotomizing pressure – a pressure rendered all the more formidable by the insistence on the existence of a core identity. Boucicault's confidence that "we are all free men" at least as far as "our inner life" is concerned stands starkly juxtaposed to the most searingly eloquent description of divided consciousness in American history and criticism. As defined by W. E. B. Du Bois in *The Souls of Black Folk* (1903), "double-consciousness" expresses the bifurcating pressures exerted by slavery, race hatred, and segregation on the descendants of the African diaspora in the United States: "It is a peculiar sensation, this double-consciousness, this sense of always looking at one's self through the eyes of others, of measuring one's soul by the tape of a world that looks on in amused contempt and pity. One ever feels this two-ness, – an American, a Negro; two souls, two thoughts, two unreconciled strivings, two warring ideals in one dark body, whose dogged strength alone keeps it from being torn asunder" (8–9). Although it is the black folks who are defined as the "problem," white folks in America must also live with the bitter consequences of their jury-rigged fictions of race. As an example of tormented double consciousness in the performance of whiteness, one could do much worse than to observe the palpitations of Huck's bad conscience over his role in Jim's escape, which can only be stilled by the specious reassurance of a core identity at the heart of obvious difference: "I knowed he was white inside" (251).

By his detailed staging of the unpromising rehearsals for the king and the duke's one-night stand, Mark Twain dramatizes the importance of standardized speech and language, inscribed under the general rubric of eloquence, to the emergence of the American actor and, by implication, of the respectable American citizen. Pretension was a form of hypocrisy, one overt sign of divided consciousness, but the true native speaker spoke from the heart in well-tuned numbers, evincing a "Natural Theatricality" (Fliegelman, 79–94). Nineteenth-century audiences never seemed to stop taking delight in the stage malaprops whereby they could measure their own rectitude of speech by reference to the negative examples culled from the offending lips of clowns, minstrels, mountebanks, immigrants, and rubes. In *Highbrow, Lowbrow* Lawrence Levine opens his discussion of an American cultural hierarchy that is both mapped and produced by such bloopers with a citation from *Huckleberry Finn,* the duke's rendition of Hamlet's "sublime" soliloquy, spastically heaved up aboard the raft, fished "from recollection's vaults":

> . . . But soft you, the fair Ophelia:
> Ope not thy ponderous and marble jaws,
> But get thee to a nunnery – go![3]

Refinement and propriety of utterance in language are problems that traverse the most contested space of American identities in the culture of performance. Indeed, as Mark Twain clearly understood, the emergence of the American actor is historically linked to the conception of an American speech.

Stage acting, a suspect activity in the minds of many Americans, first authorized itself and then periodically rehabilitated itself as elocution, a privileged activity in the minds of most. Theatre in America typically justified itself by allying itself to something more respectable – a concert, a museum, a learned exhibition, especially an oration. Oratory offered itself as a "formation of prestige." The power of eloquence – what it is, who possesses it, and how it may be acquired by some or denied to others – is a unifying theme in the complex and often contradictory national self-consciousness about performance, especially, but by no means solely, performance on the stage.

Among the key texts in what has been termed "The Elocutionary Revolution" of the eighteenth century are William Stevenson, *Dialogues Concerning Eloquence in General* (1722); Thomas Sheridan, *A Course of Lectures on Elocution* (1762); James Burgh, *The Art of Speaking* (1764); Joshua Steele, *An Essay toward Establishing the Melody and Measure of Speech* (1775); and John Walker, *The Melody of Speaking Delineated; or, Elocution Taught like Music, by Visible Signs* (1787). Several of these transatlantic manuals, like Sheridan's and Steele's, and to some extent Burgh's, were the product of extensive theatrical experience or observation. They had lives of their own in colonial and revolutionary America, but they also informed native productions such as George Fisher's *The American Instructor; or, The Young Man's Best Companion* (1775) and Noah Webster's *American Selection of Lessons in Reading* (1785). What this elocutionary revolution supposedly accomplished was the overthrow of the notion of scholastic argumentation as the basis of rhetorical persuasion and its replacement with a doctrine of passionate expression, founded in natural sentiment, but cultivated by assiduous attention to what later came to be called "vocal culture" (Fliegelman, 28–35).

The founder of the vocal culture movement in nineteenth-century America was Dr. James Rush, who consolidated his teachings in *The Philosophy of the Voice* (1827). Drawing on the work of the elocutionary revolution of the previous century, Rush set out to adapt what he took to be the universal science of natural speech to the exceptional circumstances of the United States. The American originality of Rush's "system," as well as its indebtedness to prior elocutionists and its symbiotic relationship to the theatre, were chronicled by the popular actor James E. Murdoch in *A Plea for Spoken Language* (1883). In the matter of fine-tuning what he called the "national voice," Murdoch believed that the revolutionary potential of vocal culture was boundless:

> In the onward march of the American spirit of inquiry and improvement in the science of education, the time must come when the claims of an advanced state of elocutionary training will meet with the appreciation and support of a generous public opinion. Then, as foreshadowed by the eloquence of a Chatham or a Webster, our grand old Saxon syllables, rounded by the developed powers of a *national voice,* shall be heard from ocean to ocean, rivaling in vocal beauty the far-famed honors of the notes of song. (133)

The "old Saxon syllables," previously promoted by Thomas Jefferson as the essential linguistic foundation of law and liberty (see Frantzen 203–7), are to form the memorial basis for the national voice but not the future of its "developed powers." Although Murdoch leaves the authenticating origins of this exceptionalist national voice unplumbed, Thomas Jefferson himself had proposed Native American public speech as surpassing in excellence the eloquence of the "whole orations of Demosthenes and Cicero" and indeed all of European oratory (62). The symbolic role of Native Americans, as displaced but sacred authenticators of American exceptionalism, goes beyond their imputed eloquence, but any account of the "developed powers" of a "national voice" must also reckon with the contributions of African American speech, generally disavowed by historians in the past, which was filtered into the mainstream through the voice of the American performer.

At this juncture, the general tendencies remarked in the preceding glosses on *Huckleberry Finn* and the culture of performance may be more clearly delineated by a look at the careers of three prominent and immensely successful performers. Their lives embody the emergence of the American actor in the crucible of national legitimation. They are the close contemporaries Edwin Forrest (1806–72), Ira Aldridge (1807–67), and Thomas D. "Daddy" Rice (1808–60).

Edwin Forrest

Forrest, whose definitive biographer claims him as the "first star of the American stage" (Moody, *Edwin Forrest*), might, with greater amplitude of reference, in view of the earlier claim on international repute by the African American Aldridge, be called the first native-born white American to star on the stage in the United States. Celebrity (or notoriety) means that an individual's name and image circulate positively (or negatively) independently of his or her own person. Stardom is more than that. Attracting to itself the energies of both celebrity and notoriety, stardom not only circulates within but saturates the popular imagination; it raises contradictory passions of adulation and resentment; it lends itself to the public articulation of cultural moments and forces. The restructuring of stardom to accommodate the emergence of the American actor might be described as a conflation of the lines of leading business and eccentric business. The difference is that with stardom the eccentricities reflect less the stereotypical characteristics of a type than the idiosyncrasies of a single, dominating personality. This personality is strong enough to embody not only the most cherished dreams of the audience, but also its deepest anxieties. This personality is strong enough to perform not only *for* an audience but also *instead* of it. This personality is strong enough to bring the audience face-to-face with itself. Edwin Forrest was a star in that sense. Self-consciously representing the ideal of Jacksonian democratization (he was once invited to run for Congress), Forrest infused American stardom with a touch of the charismatic authority that other traditions had set aside for absolute monarchs. This was an authority that Forrest's public both violently loved and violently feared, unstable as it was in the face of the dual threats of tyranny and fraud.

Born into a poor but respectable family in Philadelphia, Forrest made his unofficial debut in 1817 at the South Street Theatre in drag when the actress playing the odalisque in John D. Turnbull's *Rudolph; or, the Robber of Calabria* fell ill. His ambition for self-improvement toward the goal of expressive declamation led him to study with the Philadelphia elocutionist Lemuel G. White, a contemporary of James Rush. He also built up his physique with daily exercise, which developed into a lifelong system: doing handstands, lifting dumbbells, and practicing postures. Later, the display of his well-conditioned body would come to characterize Forrest as a dynamic American actor (as opposed to an effete English one), but when Edmund Kean, who was not noted for his muscletone, played the Walnut Street Theatre in 1821, the dumbbell-hefting neophyte attended every performance, and in his subsequent amateur appearances he "out-Keaned Kean" (Moody, *Edwin Forrest,* 19). Unable to secure a sufficient number of paying engagements in his native Philadelphia, Forrest headed west, joining the company of Joshua Collins and William Jones, whose river-borne circuit took in Pittsburgh, Lexington, and Cincinnati. With Shakespeare's *Richard III* in his repertoire for benefit nights, Forrest began to headline for the company, but the tour failed to make its expenses in Cincinnati. Critics praised the sixteen-year-old Forrest in nativist terms, fearing he would depart to seek his fortune before European audiences, but the rag-tag members of the disbanded company took off to barnstorm Hamilton, Lebanon, and Dayton instead, literally playing in a barn on at least one occasion. On his return to Lexington, Forrest added Othello to his repertoire, a role he was never to relinquish, and then accepted an engagement at the American Theatre in New Orleans, a seven-day voyage away, down the Ohio and the Mississippi.

New Orleans in the 1820s offered Forrest and other visitors from Anglo America an eye-opening vista on the cultural complexity of what their country was becoming. Home to multilingual professional theatres and opera houses, as well as to a richly textured musical and festive life bound up in French, Spanish, Irish, African, and Native American traditions, the Crescent City presented the emergent American actor with a variety of competition that was both "substantially alternative or oppositional," in Raymond Williams's terms and, at the same time, stubbornly "residual." The use that Forrest made of his opportunity (or later said he did) is most instructive.

After quarreling with James H. Caldwell, manager of the American Theatre on Camp Street, he fled into the wilderness in the company of a Choctaw chieftain named Push-ma-ta-ha. For two months, Forrest later told his official biographer William Rounseville Alger, he lived among the Indians, wearing their clothes, learning their lore and customs, performing their rituals and dances, singing their songs, and studying their gestures and speeches.

Forrest professed to be especially awed by the eloquence and physical expressiveness of Push-ma-ta-ha, whose beautiful body the actor longed to study in the nude. One lambent Louisiana evening, the Indian edified the actor by stripping and posing majestically, clad only in firelight and moonlight: "The young chief, without a word, cast aside his Choctaw garb and stepped forth with a dainty tread, a living statue of Apollo in glowing bronze" (Alger, I, 138–39). Forrest's description of the Native American chief's physique, relayed through Alger, sounds like many later descriptions of the actor's own body in the role of Metamora, the Wompanoag sachem in John Augustus Stone's play of 1829. Forrest remembered Push-ma-ta-ha

> in the bloom of opening manhood, erect as a column, graceful and sinewy as a stag, with eyes of piercing brilliancy, a voice of guttural music like gurgling waters, the motions of his limbs as easy and darting as those of a squirrel. His muscular tissue in its tremulous quickness seemed made of woven lightnings. His hair was long, fine, and thick, and of the glossiest blackness; his skin, mantled with blood, was of the color of ruddy gold, and his form one of faultless proportions. (Alger, I, 126–27)

Here the transparent meanings of "Natural Theatricality" unfold in front of an elaborately painted backdrop of nostalgia and genocide. Behind it the producers had already cast Push-ma-ta-ha and the Choctaws, along with the other "Five Civilized Tribes," as the tragic heroes of the Trail of Tears, strengthening a dramaturgical link, forged much earlier in American memory, between the profound eloquence of marginalized peoples and the extreme violence of their fates.

Whether the tone of American mimicry is one of celebratory embrace, as in Forrest's bayou idyll, or vicious caricature, as in his occasional blackface parodies, the mimetic performer inevitably embodies within himself or herself some of the behaviors of the object of aspiration or ridicule. There is no certain way to measure the effects of imitative performance on the performers themselves and certainly no warrant to predict that the results will include deepened understanding or appreciation. In the recurrent actions of many American representations, however, the utopian vision of mutual assimilation or accommodation is figured in and through such liaisons, real and imagined, between the races. One version of this phenomenon was memorably described by Leslie Fiedler, who was thinking of Huck and Jim in *Love and Death in the American Novel,* but who could have been describing Forrest

Edwin Forrest (1806–72), first American-born star and dominant stage figure until mid-century, pictured as Metamora, first seen in 1829, in an engraving by Rawdon Wright from a painting by S. Agate. Although not the most realistic likeness, this image, as McConachie has noted, "emphasizes Forrest's sublime and Napoleonic qualities." Harvard Theatre Collection.

and Push-ma-ta-ha, as "the relationship between sentimental life in America and the archetypal image, found in our favorite books, in which a white and a colored male flee from civilization into each other's arms" (xii). The homoerotic and homosocial dimensions of Forrest's excursion among the Choctaws do not contradict his overall ethnological project, which is one of American mimicry in search of a core identity: In the eloquence of a Native American, Edwin Forrest, like Thomas Jefferson before him, professed to find what Howells later described in Mark Twain – the "dramatic" fused with the "unconscious."

The next year, in 1826, Forrest chose one role for three momentous occa-

sions – his New York City debut at the Park Theatre, his first starring engagement at Philadelphia's Chestnut Street Theatre, and his triumphant appearance
at the Bowery Theatre in New York. That role was Othello. Charles Durang
wrote an account of the Park Theatre debut that puts the audience in the spec-
tatorial position that Forrest had enjoyed when he beheld the naked Indian:

> Forrest entered with a calm mien and a dignified manner and took the cen-
> ter of the stage. His figure and manner elicited hearty applause at once. His
> youthful manly form – symmetrical as the Apollo Belvidere with all that fig-
> ure's repose – devoid of all superfluous flesh – an expressive youthful face,
> rather thin in its outline – a flashing hazel eye that foreshadowed vivid intel-
> lect – deportment and action naturally graceful and well costumed, made a
> *tout-ensemble* that at once struck like an electrical chord of harmony from
> the actor to the audience as he bowed to their warm greetings. (Quoted in
> Moody, *Forrest,* 63)

The shade of Othello's blackness was the subject of much speculation and
commentary in the nineteenth century (see Hunter, 31–59), and the white
actor had a range of tints to choose from. Critics seemed to enjoy torturing
themselves with learned disquisitions on the appropriateness of "tawny
Moor" as opposed to the "coal-black Negro." Eschewing the crudities of the
traditional burnt cork, Forrest blacked up with a special mixture of burnt
sienna, unburnt sienna, and ivory black combined with almond oil – erring, if
he erred at all, on the side of the tawny. As with most of his roles, he drew
attention to his physique, in this case the dangerous and ambiguous body of
the colored man. Forrest seems never to have met the actor who was his
greatest American contemporary and rival in the Shakespearean repertoire,
an actor who required no special makeup for Othello, though he did avail
himself of whiteface for Shylock, Macbeth, and King Lear.

Ira Aldridge

Born the son of a minister in New York City in 1807, Ira Aldridge, who
regarded Senegal as his mother country, matriculated in the African Free
School, which had been established in 1787 by the "Society for the Promotion
of the Manumission of Slaves and Protecting Such of Them As Have Been or
May Be Liberated" (Marshall and Stock, 25). In accordance with the principles of the elocutionary revolution, the excellent curriculum of the African
Free School included declamation. The concept, which young Edwin Forrest
was then imbibing from White and Rush in Philadelphia, was that the principles and the practices underlying true eloquence were available to everyone.
Implicitly, this meant that what Murdoch called the "national voice" represented the practical means of implementing the promise of the United States

Ira Aldridge (1807–67), African American actor who moved to England at age seventeen, becoming an international star, but who was unable to succeed in the United States. He is pictured here as Mungo, the slave of a West Indian planter, in Isaac Bickerstaffe's *The Padlock,* written in 1768 and first performed by Aldrige in the 1820s. Don B. Wilmeth Collection.

that it is a nation "dedicated to the proposition that all men are created equal." As Gary Wills has shown in *Lincoln at Gettysburg,* the elocutionary revolution had momentous long-term consequences, an outcome made possible to no trivial degree by the fact that Abraham Lincoln numbered himself among its moral and rhetorical heirs. But remaking America cost more than words. The special reverence with which Lincoln is regarded in retrospect should not be allowed to obscure the violent hatreds that his encumbency, and especially his attitudes toward the equality of men, unleashed among his contemporaries. His rhetorical skills as an orator marked him in the eyes of some as a demagogue and confidence man, just as his powers of persuasion (not to mention his assumption of war powers, such as the suspension of habeas corpus) marked him as a dangerous tyrant.

Like Lincoln, Ira Aldridge was able to put the ideals of the elocutionary revolution to a premature test when he made his theatrical debut with the short-lived African Company. This extraordinary ensemble opened in 1821 at the Mercer Street Theatre in New York under the management of William Henry Brown, who accommodated white patrons in a special section at the back of the theatre. The company's first star had been James Hewlett, a West Indian mulatto whose most celebrated role was Richard III. Aldridge made his debut with the African Company at the age of fifteen as Rolla in Sheridan's *Pizzaro.* The management of the Park Theatre and allied interests, however, found the success of the African Company intolerable, and its actors were arrested and released only on the understanding that they would cease playing Shakespeare. The company folded in 1824, and Aldridge departed for England and the Continent, never to return to the United States. (See Hill, *Shakespeare in Sable,* 11–16.)

Billed as the "African Roscius," but acting under the name of Keene, Ira Aldridge made his British debut in 1825 in the starring role of Oroonoko. In 1826 – the same year that Forrest made his New York debut as Othello – Aldridge first represented Shakespeare's Moor in London. When the African Roscius took his Othello to Scarborough, a local critic recorded his impressions in a pamphlet:

> The African Roscius is certainly an actor of genius. His complexion is deeply tinctured with Afric's ray of shade; his figure is tall, manly and muscular; and he is in the very vigour of manhood, being only in his 25th year. His pronunciation of the English language is as perfectly correct as that of a native, and his voice possesses great power, with intonations of an intuitive order, and which genius only can display; indeed, it is our opinion, that for every variety of intonation and inflection of the voice, there cannot be rules given, for the orator of true genius can throw out from the feelings of the soul such refrangibility of reflection (if we may be allowed to use these optical allusions) as beggars the rules of art. (Quoted in Marshall and Stock, 92)

The manliness and energy attributed to Aldridge's Othello recall the similar qualities praised in Forrest's rendering of this and other roles. The insistence on the importance of "intuition" in a performance that was clearly prepared carefully in the light of elocutionary technique might easily be read as racism (with which British reviews of Aldridge abound). But it may also record the effects of a search by both actor and critic for the authenticating power of a core identity, the ethos that Americans sought in themselves and attempted to project to foreigners, particularly the British, as an assertion of cultural sovereignty. In that, as in so many other ways, Aldridge was a representative American actor – the innocent abroad – in much the same way that American political life has been internally shaped by a search for a pure sincerity – the log-cabin candidate.

On the crucial question of mimicry, Aldridge's practices were complex. The playing of whiteface roles rendered the African Company's Shakespearean performance particularly obnoxious to their Park Theatre rivals, but Aldridge played them with success throughout Europe, especially in Russia. His Lear in St. Petersburg, for instance, was hailed by critics as the "real" British monarch (Marshall and Stock, 236). But expectations driven by the insatiable hunger for "Ethiopian" delineation drove the African Roscius into another repertoire, one that lurked behind the abjection of the king and duke's grotesque pastiche, "The King's Camelopard; or, The Royal Nonesuch," on which thespians fall back when they discover that "these Arkansas lunkheads couldn't come up to Shakespeare; what they wanted was low comedy – and maybe something ruther worse than low comedy" (151). Aldridge relates how Charles Mathews claimed to have attended a performance of Hamlet at the African Theatre during his New York tour of 1822:

> He says that on the occasion alluded to, I played Hamlet, and in the celebrated soliloquy, "To be or not to be" the similarity of the sound of the words reminding the audience of the Negro melody, "Opossum Up a Gum Tree," they loudly called for it, and this polite request Mr. Mathews makes me accede to in the following language: "Well, den, ladies and gemmen, you like 'Opossum Up a Gum Tree' better den you like *Hamlet?* Me sing him to you," which I, according to the anecdote, did three or four times, much to the exquisite edification of my black hearers, and then resumed my part of the pensive prince. (Quoted in Marshall and Stock, 44)

With cool dignity Aldridge observes that he never undertook the role of Hamlet, but he also thereafter incorporated a rendition of "Opossum Up a Gum Tree" into his performances as an olio. In this bit of double-edged minstrelsy, he mimicked Charles Mathews's version of the dialect song that Mathews claimed to have learned from him. As in the duke's fractured version of "To be or not to be," Shakespeare serves as the touchstone whereby propriety of speech may be tested and authenticated. He also serves as the keystone to the formation of prestige wherein the abject may be ridiculed.

Thomas Dartmouth Rice

In the late 1820s, as Forrest and Aldridge were establishing their careers as Shakespeareans on opposite sides of the Atlantic, Thomas Dartmouth "Daddy" Rice was taking credit for being the original "Ethiopian Delineator," the father of minstrelsy. In *Dramatic Life as I Found It* (1880), the great frontier theatrical manager Noah Ludlow recounted (392) that Rice, waiting for his cue during a rehearsal at the Louisville Theatre, heard a black stable boy singing the song "Jump, Jim Crow." Captivated by the singer, Rice paid him to repeat the song as many times as it took for the white actor to learn it. This famous story, repeated and elaborated in a number of versions, set in various cities, and featuring different accounts of the actual transaction, consistently

Thomas Dartmouth "Daddy" Rice (1806–60) as the original Jim Crow (c. 1830). Laurence Senelick Collection.

features the idea that American minstrelsy, like Forrest's rustic life class among the Choctaw, is drawn from authentic models:

> Turn about an' wheel about and do jis so,
> An' ebery time I turn about I jump Jim Crow.

The insinuation of minstrelsy into the "national voice" was extensive and profound. The language of *Huckleberry Finn,* for instance, as Ralph Ellison so presciently observed (104–12), is permeated by cadences, turns of phrase, metaphors, and sounds that derive their musicality from African American speech. Recent research has established the likelihood that Mark Twain based the expressive language and more than a little of the character of Huckleberry Finn on the remarkable performances of a black child he encountered in 1871–72, a child he called "Sociable Jimmy" (Fishkin, 13–15). Jimmy's character seems to have divided itself into Huck and Jim, who thereafter long to reunite on the raft, but the subtle pervasiveness of his speech animates the address of almost all the characters, except perhaps the lines in which the duke is trying to talk like an English tragedian on tour in America.

The most significant single event concerning the emergence of the American actor as the avatar of authenticity in the culture of performance was the Astor Place Riot in 1849, a central image and turning point as noted throughout this history. The fact most often repeated about this riot is that a mob of working-class Bowery B'hoys, incensed by the pretensions of the English tragedian William Charles Macready at the Astor Place "Opera House," rallied violently in the name of brawny Edwin Forrest, who was then playing the Broadway Theatre as an American rival to the effete foreign star. The resentments between the two actors had been increasing for decades, exacerbated when Forrest hissed Macready during a performance of *Hamlet* at the Theatre Royal in Edinburgh. For a disagreement over acting styles, however, the stakes were very high indeed: as "the worst riot in the history of the theatre" (Moody, *Astor Place Riot,* 12), Astor Place claimed the lives of at least twenty-two citizens with approximately one hundred and forty-four wounded, when the militia, provoked by cascades of paving stones, fired point-blank into the mob.

The dynamics of the events that led to the bloodshed at Astor Place were already present fifteen years earlier during the Farren Riots of 1834. In the midst of antiabolitionist violence directed primarily at "amalgamationist" churches in several cities in the Northeast, William Farren, the English-born stage manager of the Bowery Theatre, tactlessly assumed the role of the confidence man: "Damn the Yankees; they are a damn set of jackasses and fit to be gulled," he allegedly said (quoted in McConachie, 144), anticipating the duke's cynical attitude toward his potential audience for the Royal Nonesuch, "If that don't fetch them, I dont know Arkansaw!" (151). A disgruntled actor fired by the management of the Bowery further aroused nativist sympathy against the theatre, and on 9 July 1834, a mob of antiabolitionists demanding the punishment of Farren and the deportation of blacks, invaded the theatre. They were mollified only by the manager's apology, the display of American flags, and the singing of "Yankee Doodle" and "Zip Coon" in blackface (Lott, 132). The national ambivalence over the continued preeminence of celebrities from what Mark Twain ridicules as "Pudding Lane" highlights the symbolic struggle between self-sameness and difference through public performance. The resentment of the British, however, aggravated though it may have been by Britain's antislavery stand, nevertheless stood in for deeper anxieties about displacement founded on racial and ethnic nativism. In *Strangers in the Land,* John Higham describes this process of imagining a community by identifying what it must at all costs exclude: "[The nativist] believed – whether he was trembling at a Catholic menace to American liberty, fearing an invasion of pauper labor, or simply rioting against the great

English actor William Macready – that some influence originating abroad threatened the very life of the nation from within" (4). In the actor's supposed duplicity and false airs, the collective memory and hatred of tyranny (which was the polite way of saying the hatred of outsiders) found its condensational object.

In advance of the Astor Place Riot, the forces aligned with both Macready and Forrest carried on an inflammatory campaign in the newspapers to promote the causes of the rival stars. Forrest was heralded as the exemplar of Native American virtue, an honor he never deprecated or minimized, though there is no reason to believe he was directly involved in inciting the riot. As at the Farren Riots, the leadership of the mob of B'hoys used the occasion of silencing Macready at Astor Place to settle other nativist scores: They broke up a meeting of the American Anti-Slavery Society and attempted to do the same to a meeting of the provocatively entitled American and Foreign Anti-Slavery Society (see Moody, *Astor Place Riot,* 114). The rioters first silenced Macready and then drove him from the country, but what they accomplished for their cause was to confirm the foreign or affectedly foreign-sounding actor as a readily accessible effigy for symbolic burning. The flames of his immolation served as a source of general illumination, and the titanic figure that basked in its glow belonged to the statuesque Edwin Forrest. What the rioters thought they saw emerge from the tremulous body of the burning Englishman was the core persona of the authentic American – manly, defiant, democratic, and white – whose "unconscious" feelings existed in perfectly harmonious relationship to his "dramatic" expression. What they saw in fact, though they could have had no way of knowing consciously what they were looking at, was the sacrificial doubling of Forrest by Ira Aldridge, exiled for life, invisible to much of theatre history, but no less authentic an American for that.

In the second half of the nineteenth century, the position of the actor in American life became at once more complex, more elaborately documented, and less interesting. In *Actors and American Culture,* Benjamin McArthur tells the story of an increasingly sophisticated professionalization of the career of acting, including the evolution of the stock company and itinerant star into an array of touring ensembles, combination companies, syndicates, agents, and producers in the modern sense of that term. Yet McArthur concludes with an acknowledgment of the continuation of the liminal status of the actor as a messenger between the past and the future, which he calls "the paradox of the actor, a contradiction rooted in the mysterious social drama of which he is a part" (236).

Among the innovations McArthur sees in the critical approach to the actor's art, which might also be seen as a continuation and complication of the idea of double consciousness, is a new depth psychology that takes as its premise the importance of unconscious motivations in the creation of spontaneity, variety, and believability in characterization. What is striking about such a formulation is that it seems to represent the privatization of the actor's unconscious. It foregrounds the psychological rather than the social paradox of the actor in the culture of performance. This privatization encourages the cult of the star by stressing the importance of the idiosyncratic personality. The public craving for information about celebrities was apparently insatiable. A flourishing genre of nineteenth-century theatricana was the star biography or autobiography. Another less august genre was the newspaper scandal predicated on the private lapses of actor or actress (one of the most unsavory of these, Edwin Forrest's divorce, was predicated on both). In such a formation, the stage and the backstage collaborate to encourage a particularly complicated kind of fetishism, one focused not on a particular bodily part but on the whole soul of the performer. The larger-than-life emotions of the characters portrayed are traced to their source in the larger-than-life personality that portrays them.

In his oft-cited essay called "The Illusion of the First Time in Acting" (1915), William Gillette offers a retrospective account of the impact of this mode of production:

> The actors of recent times who have been universally acknowledged to be great have invariably been so because of their successful use of their own strong and compelling Personalities in the roles which they made famous. And when they undertook parts, as they occasionally did, unsuited to their Personalities, they were great no longer and frequently quite the reverse. (134–35)

The cult of personality that Gillette describes seems to be the natural consequence of the pressure exerted on behalf of authenticity, although the cultural work of memory that the actor does under the aegis of personality is carefully mystified – by Gillette certainly, but also by the consumers of the public performance of private psychologies. Perhaps the most extraordinary instance of the fusion of personality, role, and public expectation in American theatrical history was the association of Joseph Jefferson III with the part of Rip Van Winkle: it might be said without exaggeration that the role did not exist in the absence of Jefferson's embodiment of it. Another famous or infamous instance was the popular association of James O'Neill, the father of the playwright, with the role of the Count of Monte Cristo. The consequent psychic pressure on the American actor took its toll, exemplified by the kind of psychic drain on the spirit so poignantly dramatized in the character of James Tyrone in Eugene O'Neill's *Long Day's Journey into Night* (1957): it is potentially exhausting to embody nightly what the audience expects; it is potentially devastating to embody nightly what the audience deeply but insatiably needs.

The work of three American actors in particular, though they had very different theatrical careers in other ways, shows the apparent atomization of the culture of performance into tests of dominant personality: Charlotte Saunders Cushman (1816–76), George L. Fox (1825–77), and Edwin Booth (1833–93).

Charlotte Cushman

Born in Boston to a well-descended but impecunious family, Charlotte Cushman began her career as an opera singer. She made her acting debut in 1835, the same year that the beloved English-born actress Mary Ann Duff gave her farewell performance: Historians mark this date as a significant moment in the emergence of the American actress (see Wilson, *History of American Acting*, 47). At the outset of her singing career, Cushman ruined her instrument by trying to fill the huge St. Charles Theatre in New Orleans. The resulting timbre of her voice was dark and haunting. Her temperament was no less so. In *Bright Particular Star*, Joseph Leach recounts the customary collapse of the star after a climactic emotional outburst: "At the end of the scene, she felt herself so completely overcome with the passion of the scene and with sheer nervous agitation that she could only lie still for a time, too weak and disturbed to respond to the ringing 'bravos' that burst over her" (145).

Cushman's swoons did not originate in a frail constitution. As with Edwin Forrest, critics frequently used metaphors of electricity to describe the effects of her acting on her audience and on herself. Large-framed and physically imposing, she excelled in parts that required the representation of strong "masculine" attributes, like Lady Macbeth and perhaps most notably Meg Merriles in *Guy Mannering*. She also played the male roles of Cardinal Wolsey, Hamlet, and Romeo to her sister Susan's Juliet. She intimidated more than a few of her associates, one of whom was James E. Murdoch, the actor and elocutionist, whose account of Cushman's psychological and vocal power in *The Stage* (1880) is one of the most revealing documents concerning her acting:

> There was always in Miss Cushman's vocal effects a quality of aspiration and a woody or veiled tone more becoming the expression of wilful passion suppressed and restrained than that emotion which seeks a sympathetic recognition of outspoken vocality, pure, ringing, and elastic – the former being Nature's mode of utterance for the evil passions, while the latter speaks of the noble, pure, and bright. (237)

In most accounts of gendered sexuality on the stage in the nineteenth century, not a great deal of room is usually provided to accommodate a personality as far outside the norm as Charlotte Cushman's. But not only was it accommodated by her audiences, it was embraced and celebrated. In such a career, the efficacy of the process of the formation of stars out of the nebulae of eccentric business is revealed.

Charlotte Cushman (1816–76) as Lady Macbeth, her debut role in 1836 in New Orleans, repeated the same year at The Bowery Theatre in New York. Cushman was the first native-born actress to gain true stardom and acclaim. Don B. Wilmeth Collection.

George L. Fox

George Washington Lafayette Fox had no face, but he had an extraordinary personality. Illustrated by the lithographer Henry Thomas at the center of a poster composed of six clown countenances, Fox's real face looks vacantly back at the artist, who struggles to represent him as "a respectable Victorian gentleman," but who succeeds in fixing his visage as a neutral mask. Born into a theatrical family in Boston, that most unpromising of theatrical cities, which nonetheless also produced Charlotte Cushman, Fox made his debut as a trainbearer in Junius Brutus Booth's *King Lear* in 1832 and ended his career by going mad onstage at his farewell performance. This last calamity has been ascribed, appallingly enough, to the deleterious effects of his lead-based

Pantomime artist George L. Fox (1825–77) as "The Original Humpty Dumpty." Lithographed poster by Henry A. Thomas, New York, and copyrighted by Fox in 1875. Laurence Senelick Collection.

clown-white makeup, which he used daily to "put on his face." If so, he would not be the only actor ever to have been poisoned by his persona, but he may well be one of the most unsettlingly protean.

Onstage "Laff" Fox had many faces. His comic repertoire ranged from roles in straight plays, such as Salem Scudder in Boucicault's *The Octoroon,* to Shakespearean travesties. He was a cunning and accurate mimic, but his signature creation was the title role in the hugely successful pantomime *Humpty Dumpty.* In this guise, bald-pated and white-faced, the popular image of the clown, he peers with seeming innocence from Thomas's portraits, his ovoid countenance variously enlivened by six bubbles of impudence. The first American pantomime in two acts, *Humpty Dumpty* opened on 10 March 1867, and it thereafter became one of "the sights of New York," which, like the long-run musicals a century later, could draw upon a seemingly inexhaustible audience of curiosity seekers and out-of-towners above and beyond the usual run of New York theatregoers. Fox's comedy, marked by rapid and highly skilled physical business, was played at the velocity at which everything threatens to disintegrate – a distinctive tempo that marks what may be an indigenous brand of American comedy: "In his ingenuousness and his enterprise, his assumed innocence and his sly malice, his selfish aggression and his unbridled appetites," writes Laurence Senelick in his definitive biography, "Humpty Dumpty was not simply a naturalized Arlecchino" (222). Karen Halttunen has described the composition of a society of self-fashioners that "ascribed to most Americans a permanent condition of liminality" (29). Fox, the liminal figure par excellence, suggests the depth of the cultural motives behind the clown's popular success, his appeal to all levels of society. In a society that sought to repress the public acknowledgment of the existence of levels, however, while it simultaneously invented new ways to insist upon them, the clown personality had a very demanding job. In the end, after ranting incoherently and attacking his audience with the stage properties, Fox was institutionalized with the diagnosis of "progressive dementia accompanied by paresis" (Senelick, 209). Of all the visages formed by double consciousness, as the character of Huckleberry Finn attests, perhaps the mask of comic innocence is the hardest one to wear.

Edwin Booth

In a nostalgic essay on the theatre called "About Play-Acting" (1898), Mark Twain remembers the emergence of the actor into a more dynamic society before the closing of the American frontier. Reviewing the theatre advertisements in a New York newspaper, he notes the limited diet of "mental sugar" that the stage now offers, and he recollects the vitality of "serious" acting in those now-receding days that began with the old stock companies and ended with the apogee of the career of Edwin Booth: "Thirty years ago Edwin Booth played 'Hamlet' a hundred nights in New York," he notes, and in "the first half of this century tragedies and great tragedians were as common with us as farce and comedy" (quoted in Knoper, 147). Letting slide the memory of his own portrayal of itinerant tragedians turning tragedy into farce, Mark Twain eulogizes the Palmy Days. Appointing Edwin Booth's Hamlet, which ran for 100 nights in 1865, as the culminating event in a theatrical formation, he constructs the history of American "Play-Acting" around its dominant and its most conflicted personality.

Born into the theatrical household of Junius Brutus Booth, whose genius and instability were legendary, the melancholic but prolific Edwin once explained how the tortures of double consciousness were a family heirloom. In a sad, tender note about his father that he never published, the most devoted of Junius's sons, though not the one who in the end most resembled him, described his father's mental symptoms as they surfaced during demanding emotional scenes:

> At the moment of intense emotion, when the spectators were enthralled by his magnetic influence, the tragedian's overwrought brain would take refuge from its own threatening storm beneath the jester's hood, and, while turned from the audience, he would whisper some silliness or "make a face"; but when he left the stage no allusion to such seeming levity was permitted. His fellow-actors, who perceived these trivialities, ignorantly attributed his conduct at such times to lack of feeling, whereas it was the very excess of feeling which thus forced his brain back from its utmost verge of reason. Only those who have known the torture of severe mental tension can appreciate the value of that one little step from the sublime to the ridiculous. (Quoted in Archer, 235)

Edwin Booth made his debut in 1849, the year of the Astor Place Riot, when his father needed a supernumerary to play the part of Tressel in Colley Cibber's version of *Richard III.* In his early career, he made it his business to prepare for tragic roles by taking on comic ones in the line of the "walking gentleman." This had the salutary effect of relaxing his body and mind for the larger efforts, but it also recapitulated as a general technique what he described in his father as "that one little step from the sublime to the ridiculous," which stops the actor just one step short of plunging over the edge.

In the category of the sublime, contemporaries and historians alike have classed Edwin Booth's Hamlet as his greatest role and as the definitive achievement of American acting in its time and perhaps of all time. Delicate, haunted, complicated, and eerily conversational, Booth's Hamlet was the work of a lifetime. He played the role for forty years, from 1853 to 1893. His acting in the part held his contemporaries in such a thrall that three of them, Charles Clarke, Hamlin Garland, and Mary Isabella Stone, attended multiple performances and recorded their impressions of his interpretation line by line. Stone's evocation of Hamlet's hands-on eulogy of Yorick records a representative moment from Booth's Hamlet – melancholic, tender in an almost feminine way, and vivid as an instance of the actor's work as a caretaker of memory. For

Edwin Booth (1833–93) in his most famous role, Hamlet, performed periodically from 1852 until 1891. The definitive performance, seen here, was in 1870, though he is also remembered for his 100 Nights Hamlet in 1864–65 at the Winter Garden Theatre. Harvard Theatre Collection.

Hamlet is an actor, no less than Edwin Booth, recovering the souvenirs of performances long past among the detritus of his father's household:

> Holding [Yorick's skull] up before him in both hands and gazing on it with a strange earnestness shining from his deep, dark, melancholy eyes. You can see his mind going back thro' the long years to the days of his careless childhood and the merry times he had then, contrasting them with the present, and thinking of Yorick's former life and where he is now. A long pause.
> "*Alas, poor Yorick!*"

O the melodious pathos of the "Alas!" and the world of meaning Booth puts into it! The pity and the fondness in his "poor Yorick"! It seems to me this is *the* most exquisitely beautiful thing *said* by Booth. Though it is well-nigh impossible, if not quite so, to select *the one* from so many fine things. Moonlight again upon his face striking it sidewise; he stands fronting toward left front corner of stage, and at foot of grave. (124–25)

The role of a melancholic prince who is charged by his father's spirit to carry out an impossible task – to serve as caretaker of memory for uncomprehending contemporaries – obviously found its way into Edwin Booth's heart.

Another, perverted version of this charge found its way into the heart of John Wilkes Booth, Edwin's brother and the assassin of Abraham Lincoln. In *Assassin on Stage* (1991), Albert Furtwangler points out that the Booth family's proclivity for playing tyrannicides created the dramatic action in the shape of a wish that lent its sinister form to John Wilkes's plot to murder the president in a theatre with histrionic flourish: "Thus always unto tyrants!" These are actions that a man might play: Raised on the family's farm in Maryland around slaveholding neighbors, John Wilkes Booth came to see himself as the avenger of the supposed wrongs, past and present, that Lincoln was perpetrating on the South, on Maryland, and on the body politic generally by freeing the slaves. He regarded white supremacy as enshrined in the constitution and in nature. "The country," Booth wrote, invoking the martyred patriots of the American Revolution in justification of what he regarded as an heroic tyrannicide, "is not what it *was*" (quoted in Furtwangler, 110).

At the heart of the actor's mad scheme was his sense of what America ought to have been, a question that other actors had posed, in one form or another, on every stage since colonial times – trying to enact sincerity of motive and transparency of character for the better edification of a race of races. The violent contention of nostalgia and progress in this vast improvisation of a country tends to coalesce in melodramatic gestures. Lincoln's own words foresaw his murderer's desperate lunge at authenticity within a tradition invented in double consciousness and at continuity within a culture sustained by violent change: "The mystic chords of memory, stretching from every battle-field, and patriot grave, to every living heart and hearthstone, all over this broad land, will yet swell the chorus of the Union, when again touched, as surely they will be, by the better angels of our nature" (224). In the culture of performance, the relationship between the "dramatic" and the "unconscious" has been fraught with the potential for the most terrible tragedies as well as for the most dynamic achievements of collective self-invention in human history. As Huck puts it, reiterating the terms of Lincoln's first inaugural address with the poignancy of naive allegory – every sentiment of which is heart-felt, every word of which is loaded – "for what you want, above all things, on a raft, is everybody to be satisfied, and feel right and kind towards the others" (131).

Notes

1 The standard single-volume account remains Wilson, *History of American Acting* (1966), which sets the scene for Edwin Forrest's debut in 1820 as follows: "At that time . . . the American theatre was dominated by English actors, English managers, and English dramaturgy. Political independence had been won some forty years before, but culturally the United States was largely dependent upon Great Britain" (19). More recently, Dudden, in *Women in the American Theatre* (1994), has illuminated the emergence of the American actress.
2 For an exemplary biographical account of the transatlantic actress on the Philadelphia stage, see Doty, *The Career of Mrs. Anne Brunton Merry in the American Theatre.*
3 Mark Twain, 141. See Levine, *Highbrow, Lowbrow* (13).

Bibliography: The Emergence of the American Actor

No one bibliographic source can encompass this subject, but a good place to begin research on American acting is with Archer's *American Actors and Actresses: A Guide to Information Sources* (1983), especially when its entries are supplemented by the excellent biographical articles in the *Cambridge Guide to the American Theatre* (1993), edited by Wilmeth and Miller. The researcher will find that the wealth of citations on the subject is located in the biographies and autobiographies of individual artists, and I will not attempt to survey this extensive literature here. An astringent introduction to the issues of using such materials is provided by Thomas Postlewait in "Autobiography and Theatre History" in *Interpreting the Theatrical Past: Essays in the Historiography of Performance,* which offers a good orientation to the kind of work that theatre historians do.

General histories that survey the field of acting specifically include Duerr, *The Length and Depth of Acting;* Wilson, *A History of American Acting;* McArthur, *Actors and American Culture, 1880–1920;* and, more recently, Faye Dudden, *Women in the American Theatre: Actresses and Audiences, 1790–1870.* Among the numerous general histories of the American theatre that also contain useful accounts of actors and acting must be numbered Hornblow, *A History of Theatre in America;* Hughes, *A History of the American Theatre, 1700–1950;* and Hewitt, *Theatre U.S.A., 1688–1957* (1959). These pioneering but rigorously anglocentric histories should be supplemented by perspectives such as those of Nicholas Kanellos in *A History of Hispanic Theatre in the United States* (1990), the various contributors to Maxine Schwartz Seller, ed., *Ethnic Theatre in the United States* (1983), and Errol Hill and James Hatch in their forthcoming history of African American theatre (projected for 2000). Generally speaking, the relationship between the study of dramatic literature and American theatrical history is vexed (see *Critical Theory and Performance,* edited by Reinelt and Roach, pp. 293–98), but three studies of melodrama are exemplary in the reciprocity they demonstrate between stage and page: Grimsted, *Melodrama Unveiled: American Theater and Culture, 1800–1850;* McConachie, *Melodramatic Formations: American Theatre and Society, 1820–1870* (1992); and Mason, *Melodrama and the Myth of America.* In this context, it is important to draw attention to the useful preliminary work of James Burge in *Lines of Business: Casting Practices and Policy in the American Theatre 1752–1899,* a subject that remains particularly promising for further research.

Pathbreaking studies of more specialized topics that pertain to American acting up to Edwin Booth include Carson, *The Theatre on the Frontier;* Hodge, *Yankee Theatre: The Image of America on the Stage, 1825–1850;* Shattuck, *Shakespeare on the American Stage;* Hill, *Shakespeare in Sable: A History of Black Shakespearean Actors;* and Lott, *Love and Theft: Blackface Minstrelsy and the American Working Class* (1993). Lott makes a number of significant methodological contributions, not the least of which is to bring a strong theoretical critique to bear on the imposed dichotomy of "high" and "popular" culture. This dichotomy, with performers on the cusp, has also been illuminated by Levine in *Highbrow/Lowbrow: The Emergence of Cultural Hierarchy in America.* No theatre historian should ignore the recent developments in American cultural studies pertaining to performance, particularly Halttunen, *Confidence Men and Painted Women: A Study of Middle-class Culture in America, 1830–1870;* Fliegelman, *Declaring Independence: Jefferson, Natural Language and the Culture of Performance;* Knoper, *Acting Naturally: Mark Twain in the Culture of Performance;* and Roach, *Cities of the Dead: Circum-Atlantic Peformance.*

(Related sources are discussed in Chapter 7.)

5

Scenography, Stagecraft, and Architecture in the American Theatre

Beginnings to 1870

Mary C. Henderson

The Colonial Period

Until the arrival, in 1749, of identifiable actors and managers in the eastern part of the American continent, the nature and practice of theatrical performance are matters almost entirely of historical conjecture.[1] What records exist of theatrical activity make little or no mention of playhouses, scenery, or modes of performance. We know from at least one instance in the sparse chronicles of colonial theatre that, in 1665, three young men, who were accused of "acting a play of ye Bare and ye Cubb, on ye 27th of August" (quoted in Odell, I, 4), were ordered to appear in court in "those habilments that they acted in" before the judge in Accomac County, Virginia. Whether it was the costumes they wore or the excerpts from the play they recited for the judge's edification, we know that he was persuaded to find them not guilty.

If the young men at the College of William and Mary in Williamsburg, Virginia, indulged in theatrical activities (as some believe), they left little evidence of their efforts, but a few historians have read into these intimations a sense that the Virginia colony, and the South in general, was somewhat more tolerant of theatrical practice than its northern counterparts. Their position is strengthened by the discovery of the foundations of a playhouse, built sometime between 1716 and 1718, in Williamsburg. Erected by William Levingston, a merchant of New Kent County, the playhouse was probably nothing more than a large barn built with wood posts and beams with joists carrying the weight of the floor and ceiling. It measured approximately 86½ by 30 feet and in all probability would have been arranged into the bare rudiments of stage and auditorium in the interior. Charles and Mary Stagg, two of Levingston's servants, had been associated with the playhouse from the beginning and appear to have been active in the theatre for some years, either as performers, managers, or sometime lessees. The playhouse changed hands several times and was probably used intermittently by amateur thespians and remnants of Levingston's ragtag "professional" imported troupe from London – although history reveals few clues. At some point, the playhouse was converted into the Court of Hustings. In 1745, a notice in *The Virginia Gazette* advertised proposed changes in the building to make it suitable for its new purpose.

More concrete evidence of theatrical activities in the southern colonies arrives with the advent of a theatre in Charleston, South Carolina. In 1735, a playhouse was built for the town's amateur players on the south side of Dock (or Queen) Street just west of Church (Meeting) Street, but it was not opened until the following year. Since the *South Carolina Gazette* advertised Joseph Addison's *Cato* on 24 January 1736 (the second season) with tickets to be purchased from Mr. Charles Sheppeard's at thirty shillings for stage and balcony boxes, twenty-five shillings for pit seats, and five shillings for the gallery, it is now possible to state with a degree of certainty that the auditorium was arranged in the familiar English pit-box-and-gallery, but there is no review of the actual performance nor any description of the scenery or the stage. The theatre was probably destroyed by fire in 1740 but was rebuilt twice thereafter in the same location.

As the colonies, both north and south, prospered, inevitably the accumulation of money and the expansion of leisure time created opportunities for expending both in pursuit of cultural outlets beyond business and home. There are tantalizing bits of information transmitted through newspapers, letters, and personal accounts of events such as fairs, puppet shows, circus acts, concerts, not to mention such less edifying activities as horse racing, cock fighting, and card playing. Side by side with these were attacks against all of them from the pulpit and/or from conservative official sources. Although the early colonial years did not offer fertile ground for establishing permanent structures for a unique colonial theatre, there is enough information to conclude that a substantial population was ready – if not eager – to support limited theatrical activity.

New York, the most cosmopolitan of the rapidly developing urban colonial centers, presented the most relaxed atmosphere in which theatrical activity could be launched. The early impetus, however, did not come from the Dutch, the original settlers, who had little theatrical heritage of their own, but from the English, who wrested the city from them in 1664. Although there are fragmentary bits of information in journals and official records in the early years of the English colony suggesting theatrical activity, concrete evidence does not surface until the 1730s. According to an item published in the *New England and Boston Gazette* on 1 January 1733, a playhouse called "the New Theatre" was opened in a building on Nassau Street owned by Rip Van Dam with a performance of *The Recruiting Officer* on 11 December 1732. Rip Van Dam, a prosperous merchant who had previously served as acting governor of the New York colony, had property on Nassau Street, which probably included a large warehouse, part of which could have been converted into a playhouse.

Historians have been confounded, however, by the placement on a 1735 map of a playhouse that is nowhere near Nassau Street. This seems to bespeak the existence of another playhouse to rival Van Dam's at the same approximate time. There are enough doubts about the 1735 map, however, to suggest that if there *was* a second theatre in 1732, it was probably nothing more than the great room of Abraham Corbett's tavern, which existed on the east side of Broadway between Beaver and Garden streets. Because the political controversy between Van Dam and Governor William Cosby, his court-appointed successor, factionalized the city, it is perfectly possible that the Van Dam supporters would not have ventured into Cosby's domain. The Corbett Tavern was near the English fort and the Governor's Palace and would have been frequented by the military and royalists attached to the court.

Several things appear to be incontrovertible. If there were two theatres in New York at the same time, both would have housed amateur productions, and both would have been makeshift playhouses within other structures. Of the two, the Van Dam warehouse theatre could have been more easily converted into pit, box, and gallery than the low-ceilinged public room of the Corbett Tavern. In both cases, the playhouses were functional and understated. How long either functioned as a theatre is not known, but it is certainly possible that the Corbett Tavern was the less permanent of the two and that the theatrical activity in both was intermittent at best. We may surmise that the site used by the professional troupe led by Walter Murray and Thomas Kean, who in 1749 took up residence "At the Theatre in Nassau Street" in one of the buildings "lately belonging to the Hon. Rip Van Dam, Esq., lately deceased," was the 1732 playhouse. It is interesting to note that the company advertised seats for sale in the pit and gallery. Can we assume that the few boxes that could be encompassed in the hall were set aside for the town's dignitaries?

To return to historical conjecture, before the arrival of the professional companies, the colonials made do with amateur productions in playhouses – with the exception of Levingston's Williamsburg Theatre and the Dock Street Theatre in Charleston – that were converted from large spaces within existing buildings. Taverns, inns, and warehouses could have afforded unencumbered architecture to surround a makeshift stage and auditorium. Whether built from the bottom up or converted from other uses, the playhouses of the early colonial era were functional, with little charm or adornment. Colonial morality, north and south, would not allow ostentation in playhouses. Lighting would have been simple candlepower, adapted from the prevalent mode of illuminating home and business. Sconces, simple chandeliers, and existing windows would have provided the necessary light. Since the performances began during late daylight hours and auditoriums would have been lit throughout the dramatic events, there would have been little opportunity to indulge in any special effects. Scenery would have been minimal – paper wings and a drop curtain, perhaps – and would have most likely been painted by the performers themselves. It is conceivable that the most elaborate element in the productions would have been the costumes. Since almost everyone was handy with a needle and thread in those times, it would have been incumbent upon the performers to dress their individual parts to optimize the most in visual enjoyment. But what mattered most was the play itself and the communion of the colonial audience with the performers, who may well have been friends and neighbors.

With the opportune arrival of the theatre professionals in 1749, colonial culture was ready to accept changes in the conduct of theatrical entertainment, which could at last begin to shed its air of amateurism and impermanence. The colonists had arrived in the New World carrying with them conservative Old World models and traditions of a previous age. These were gradually being revised and reassessed in the flush of colonial prosperity and permanence. Once the colonists began to find it necessary to return to their roots in England and Europe for business and familial visits, they saw with their own eyes intimations of the industrial revolution that was to explode with full force in the next century. Back in the Old World, they were exposed again to the constantly evolving cultures of their motherlands. They were not immune to the changes that were occurring and adapted what they observed to the different conditions of the New World. With an expanding trade between the two continents, the colonists had a greater array of imported materials, not to mention *ideas,* from which to choose. When these were combined with the rich natural and human resources of the American continent, an amalgam of the two inevitably shaped the lives of the colonists. It touched every aspect of colonial society, up to and including its theatre.

It is not improbable that many of the colonial visitors to London frequented one of the London theatres, where, at midcentury, they could have seen the great David Garrick, then the reigning actor at the Drury Lane Theatre. Since the Licensing Act of 1737 had severely curtailed the proliferation of theatres in London and the English provinces, the managers of the "patent" houses had what amounted to a monopoly of theatrical performance in the country. They could count on full houses for most of the performances. Both Drury Lane and Covent Garden playhouses could seat approximately two thousand people in physical enclosures that were nonetheless in close enough proximity to the stage to allow everyone to see the facial expressions of the actors. The spectators were packed onto benches in front of the stage (pit); into tiers of boxes around the side walls surmounted by galleries; and finally, into "slips" placed high in the rafters under the roof.

Eighteenth-century English theatres were unheated and depended on the body heat of the packed audience to provide warmth in winter. Lighting was supplied by candles in sconces and chandeliers in the auditorium and spermacetti and wax candles together with oil lamps onstage. The Drury Lane stage in Garrick's time, which rose 15 inches from the apron to the farthest point upstage, was equipped with traps and grooves for wings and flats, combined with a counterweight system to lift backdrops, curtains, and borders. Garrick and rival managers paid their scene painters and machinists well, realizing that scenic display was an important element to the success of productions. The patent houses also had stores of costumes in their wardrobe rooms to complete the spectacle. Costumes for Restoration and contemporary comedies were as elegant as could be found or made, whereas period plays made do with historical touches: Roman togas, Greek robes, turbans, feathered headdresses, and so forth, as the plays demanded. Garrick was particularly interested in lighting effects and with his chief scenic artist, Philip de Loutherbourg, developed new techniques for producing moonlight, sunlight, mist, and ethereal effects, using transparent curtains and colored plates.

Witnessing a performance in London at midcentury, colonial American visitors could have only been impressed by what they saw and on their return home would have been much more receptive to any increase in professionalism in theatrical performance. A degree of professionalism arrived in 1749 when Walter Murray and Thomas Kean, two actors who were certainly more than amateurs, fitted up a warehouse on Water Street owned by William Plumstead of Philadelphia. "The New Theatre" was described as a tall "party-coloured or black glazed brick" building with a stage and an auditorium consisting of a pit, gallery, and boxes (Charles Durang, quoted in Pollock, 19). The company performed a repertory that was typical of an English itinerant company, a mixture of comedies, tragedies, and farces from Shakespeare to Colley Cibber and apparently had new scenery and properties sent from England. From Philadelphia, they journeyed to New York in early 1750 and moved into the old Van Dam playhouse in Nassau Street.

While more is known about the actors and their performances, information about the actual productions is still elusive. There is some evidence that Murray and Kean made a few improvements to the playhouse in Nassau Street, adding a new floor and perhaps a few boxes. The company was successful enough to return in the fall of 1750 for an additional season which

Plumstead's Warehouse (center), Philadelphia. Considered the first "professional" theatre in America, it was made into a performance space by the company of Walter Murray and Thomas Kean in 1749. Harry Ramsom Humanities Center, The University of
Texas at Austin.

lasted until July of the following year. When Thomas Kean decided to pull
out, he received a (second) benefit performance, which was intended to provide him with enough money to succor him in his new endeavors. In return
for *all* of the receipts of the evening, he turned over his share of the scenery,
costumes, and whatever else he shared mutually with Walter Murray. From
that piece of information, it can be inferred perhaps that the company had
accumulated a store of the accoutrements of production for their long
sojourn in New York. After the company disbanded, some of them went to
Williamsburg, whereas others preferred to remain in New York.

Theatrical activity continued a while longer in New York when Robert
Upton, an actor who had come to New York from England and joined the
Murray–Kean company, lingered on at the Nassau Street theatre with some of
the remnants of the troupe. Walter Murray, with his cache of costumes and
scenery, was enticed to Williamsburg by the promise of a new playhouse to
be erected by Alexander Finnie, the proprietor of the Raleigh Tavern. Finnie

tried to raise the money through subscriptions, a method that would be used time and again in the course of the development of the American theatre. When the money did not roll in as expected, he pushed the project ahead on his own and built a playhouse on the east side of Eastern (later Waller) Street on two lots that he had purchased. The plot could accommodate a building of at least 20 by 50 feet. Resembling a large wooden box, the theatre contained the essentials of stage, pit, boxes, and gallery minus any amenities for performers and audience, and the company opened their season on 21 October 1751 with *Richard III.* Soon after, an advertisement appeared in the *Virginia Gazette,* in which the actors solicited funds from the community for the purpose of purchasing "proper Scenes and Dresses." If it is safe to assume that if a few patrons responded to their pleas, the actors could have augmented their store of costumes and scenery at this time. It can also be theorized that the best that they could afford would be costumes made by local tailors and seamstresses. Whether they painted the scenery themselves or hired local talent (sign painters and itinerant artists), it is relatively safe to conclude that they would not have had the money to send to London for scenery painted by the artists at the patent theatres.

Despite their shoestring budget and their repeated solicitations for financial buttressing, the regrouped Murray-Kean troupe spent the next year (1752) traveling from Williamsburg to Annapolis and to outlying towns in a Virginia–Maryland circuit, playing in courthouses, warehouses, and generally makeshift playhouses with minimal stagecraft. Since they had to travel by wagon over rough terrain, whatever they used in their productions must have been rolled or folded and packed in trunks for easy stowage. Although they may have been aware that their acting alone would not have carried the performances, they could have provided at best only a few painted backdrops, a green baize curtain and floor covering, wings and costumes that would have had to suffice not only for their entire repertory of comedies, tragedies, farces, and afterpieces but for the crude theatres in which they played. Whatever the quality of their productions, they were the only show in town, and judging by the troupe's itinerary, their largely unsophisticated audiences would have been grateful for what they received. Despite their shortcomings, the Murray–Kean company succeeded in setting the stage for the arrival of more professionals from London.

In April 1752, Lewis Hallam, his wife and family, and a complement of actors set sail from London on *The Charming Sally,* at the urging of several Virginians then visiting London.[2] Along with a repertory of plays, they brought with them scenery, props, and trunks of costumes, all typical of an eighteenth-century minor theatre. (They came from William Hallam's New Wells Theatre in Goodman's Fields.) When the Hallam company finally reached Williamsburg, Lewis placed an advertisement in the *Virginia Gazette:*

THIS IS TO INFORM THE PUBLIC

That Mr. Hallam, from the New Theatre in Goodmansfields,
is daily expected here with a select Company of Comedians,
the Scenes, Cloaths and Decorations are all entirely new,
extremely rich, and finished in the highest Taste, the Scenes
being painted by the best hands in London are excell'd by none
in Beauty and Elegance, so that the Ladies and Gentlemen may
depend on being entertain'd in as polite a Manner as at the
Theatres in London, the company being perfected in all the
best Plays, Opera's [*sic*], Farces, and Pantomimes, that have been
exhibited in any of the Theatres for these past ten years. (12 June)

In an attempt to lure an audience, Hallam can be forgiven a touch of hyper-bole in his personal estimations of the strengths of his company. The scenes, costumes, and so forth, might be considered *nearly* new, since William Hallam had only recently had his theatre in Goodman's Fields shuttered for good by authorities after periodic closings prompted by complaints from the patent theatres. It is certainly possible, however, that the scenery was painted by George Lambert, John Inigo Richards, or Nicholas Thomas Dahl,[3] all of whom painted for the patent theatres at one time or another and might have been amenable to offers of work from the minor managers (such as William Hallam). Always in competition with the patent theatres, the managers of the lesser theatres would have been forced to expend as much as they could afford for scenery and spectacle just to attract audiences to their out-of-the-way locations.

When Lewis Hallam received permission from the colonial governor to perform, he purchased Alexander Finnie's playhouse, enlarged it, and finished the interior to make it more hospitable for his audiences. At best, the architecture was somewhat comparable to its English and European provincial counterparts. The English divisions of pit on the ground floor, boxes surrounding the pit but separated by metal spikes, and a raised gallery along the wall farthest from the stage, all prevailed in the colonial playhouse. What he did to improve the stage is open to conjecture, but it may be safe to say that he would have improved it to accept the kind of scenery that he brought from London. The stage, sloping gently from rear to front and extending into the pit, pulled actor and audience into close proximity. A row of iron spikes along the edge of the stage discouraged even closer intimacy.

Hard benches consituted pit and gallery seating, whereas the higher priced boxes may well have been provided with chairs. (The object of the colonial manager was to pack as many seats as possible within the enclosure, which more often than not measured 30 to 40 feet wide by 80 to 90 feet long.)

Illumination was supplied by chandeliers or "hoops" carrying candles over the stage and auditorium. As usual, dripless spermacetti candles brightened

Georgian Theatre, Richmond, Yorkshire, England (built 1788, restored 1962). Since no eighteenth- or early-nineteenth-century American theatre exists, this tiny English play-house (interior is just 24 feet wide) provides a visual suggestion of what a colonial theatre might have looked like. The benches in the pit would have been backless. Don B. Wilmeth Collection.

the stage above the actors' heads, whereas dripping tallow was good enough for the audience. The scenery itself may have consisted of at least three sets of wings and drops, painted on canvas and rolled for easy transport. Each set would be pressed into multiple duty to serve the plays in the repertory: per-haps an interior for Restoration and contemporary plays, a forest for Shake-speare's comedies, and a palace set for the tragedies of Shakespeare and other playwrights. The costumes would have certainly been more elegant and stylish than street dress, but it would have been largely contemporary, overlaid with period embellishments to fit the play and character.

After a successful stint in Williamsburg, Hallam moved on to New York in 1753, where (after the usual difficulties with the authorities) he took over the old theatre on Nassau Street, which he must have found too makeshift to play in. He razed it and built another playhouse on the site. Nothing in history suggests that Hallam built other than a facsimile of his Williamsburg theatre. He did, however, enlarge the boxes "For the better Accommodation of the Ladies" during his tenure, which lasted until March 1754, at which time he moved on to Philadelphia. The City of Brotherly Love proved to be a harder nut to crack than both New York and Williamsburg, but Hallam's tenacity saved the day, and he was allowed to perform in the old theatre in Plumstead's warehouse. Again, he renovated the extant playhouse to make it more playable for the performers and more comfortable for the patrons. After a brief season in Philadelphia, he sailed with his troupe and trunks to Charleston, where he constructed (or reconstructed) another theatre. From there, he and his company decamped early in 1755 for Jamaica, where Lewis died of yellow fever.

Three years were to elapse before the return of professional theatre in the colonies. In the fall of 1758, the London Company of Comedians under the management of David Douglass sailed from Jamaica to New York. Douglass, who had formed a troupe made up of remnants of the old Hallam company augmented by a few actors in his Jamaican company, became the Johnny Appleseed of American colonial theatre. Douglass, like Hallam before him, found the standing colonial playhouses unsuitable for his troupe. Wherever his troupe played, he built a theatre or converted an existing structure into a playhouse. When he arrived in New York, he discovered that no playhouse existed and immediately set to the task of building a theatre or improvising one in a building on Cruger's Wharf on the eastern side of the city between Coenties Slip and Old Slip, that was sandwiched by two busy markets. By day, the wharf and surrounding area must have presented a lively and busy scene; by night, it was dark, damp, and too far away from the residential city to the west and north. Douglass inadvertently compounded his error by arriving in New York at a time when the city's economy was depressed because of the French and Indian War. His season in New York was brief. By late spring of 1759, he was on his way to Philadelphia.

Douglass, having applied for the usual permits well in advance, contracted with local artisans to build a theatre on Society Hill, just outside of the Philadelphia city limits. Fortunately, he found a local artist, William Williams, mentor of the painter Benjamin West, and commissioned him to furnish new scenes for his company. Within a few months, the building was ready for occupancy, and Douglass began his season. For his production of *Theodosius; or, The Force of Love,* Williams supplied a "transparent Afterpiece, showing the Vision of Constantine the Great, before his Battle against the Christians. . . ." Douglass advertised that the decorations were entirely "new and proper" (quoted in Rankin, 83).

From Philadelphia, the company moved to Annapolis, where they found the playhouse first used by the old Murray–Kean troupe still in existence. From there, they went to Upper Marlborough, where they played in a "neat convenient tobacco-house, well fitted up for that purpose" (Rankin, 101). Between early July and October 1760, when they reached Williamsburg, they may have played in villages on their way south. Until May 1761, Douglass and his company remained in Virginia, playing mainly in the theatre built by Lewis Hallam in Williamsburg.

Seeking fresh opportunities, Douglass and his troupe headed by boat to New England. In the spring of 1761, they took over the public room of the Kings Arms Tavern in Newport, Rhode Island, for a series of "Moral Dialogues," which proved popular enough for the manager to contract for a playhouse to be built speedily on Easton's Point. Before leaving Newport, Douglass had arranged for a new playhouse to be built by Philip Miller in New York on the southwest corner of Nassau and Chapel (now Beekman) streets. The building was to be 40 by 90 feet to accommodate three hundred and twenty-five spectators, possibly the largest of the colonial theatres to date. It was built at a cost of £650. The location, just north of the original Nassau Street Theatre and south of the Common, was more fortunate than Cruger's Wharf, but the troupe again did not fare well in New York. He tried appealing to the aristocratic class by adding partitions between the boxes and making alterations to the playhouse to make it more attractive, but Douglass was forced to move on after a brief engagement in the city. He went north to Newport and from there to Providence, Rhode Island, where he again had a playhouse hastily constructed for their performances, which they just as hastily abandoned after a few performances in the chilly New England moral atmosphere.

In the fall of 1763, after spending a year in a tour of the hospitable theatre towns of Virginia, Douglass and his renamed "American Company of Comedians" arrived by boat in Charleston, South Carolina. In Queen Street, near the site of the older Dock Street Theatre, Douglass had another theatre built in six weeks and began a lengthy season. The new theatre measured 75 by 35 feet and was "completed in a very elegant manner" (cited in Rankin, 102). Sometime during their Charleston sojourn, David Douglass and Mrs. Douglass journeyed to England for the purpose of recruiting actors, finding stageworthy dramatic material, and commissioning new scenery from Nicholas Thomas Dahl, scene painter for Covent Garden. What these "superiour" scenes and decorations consisted of was, alas, not recorded. Because of the small size of the colonial playhouses, the drops could not have been much wider than 25 or 30 feet and no higher than 16 to 20 feet. If side wings were used, it is more likely that they were grommeted and hung from the rafters rather than nailed on flats and placed in grooves in the manner of the established playhouses of England. Because the company was constantly on the move, the curtains, drops, and wings would have been designed to be rolled or folded so that they could be stored on wagons or boats. Since the scenery was shifted in full view of the audience, it would further advance the theory that it was tied to ropes and pulleys. On both sides of the Atlantic, eighteenth-century actors played largely in front of rather than within the painted scenery, with the drops and wings serving mainly as background to the action and to establish locale in the most superficial ways. Because of the dim lighting, all the scenery must have been brightly colored and crudely outlined to make some visual impression on the audience. If Dahl painted to Douglass's specifications for small theatres, he may have been able to sketch in more detail than he would have been able to provide for the large London stages. Furniture, gates, false doorways, fences, walls, and so forth might well have been painted on the canvas or linen drops in trompe l'oeil perspective. Since painted transparent curtains had already been introduced on the London stages, Douglass may have come home with a few examples of the art to fit the ghost scene in *Hamlet* or the witches' scene in *Macbeth* for the delectation of his audiences. Whatever scenery that he brought back to the colonies, it would surely have represented an improvement over what must have become by this time worn, tattered, and discolored.

It must also be remembered that Douglass's theatres were hastily erected (sometimes in a matter of weeks) and must certainly have been constructed in post and beam, then the quickest way of building a barn or a box-shaped structure. Because they were completed so hastily, we can only conjecture about the interior finishing – if any. (In the northerly climate, he may have had the interior walls plastered over an insulation consisting of straw.) It is conceivable that Douglass made improvements to the theatres where he enjoyed longer seasons, as in Williamsburg, Charleston, and Annapolis, but the precariousness of the troupe's fortunes would have dictated how much – or how little – could have been expended on the actual playhouses.

After his tour of the south, Douglass returned to the West Indies until the fall of 1766. Fortified with new players and fresh scenery from London, he and his company sailed to the northern colonies to try their luck again. Wisely sidestepping New York, where an anti-British mob had effectively rendered useless his theatre on Chapel Street in the previous spring, Douglass made his way to Philadelphia to open his new theatre, the sturdiest and best- equipped house he had built so far. Over the repeated and vociferous objections of the Christian conservatives, the theatre was erected on Cedar (later South) Street, just over the city line in Southwark, a suburb of Philadelphia. Utilizing the prevalent and abundant building materials of the area, the contractor built the lower floor of crude red brick, on which sat a frame structure of wood for the upper story surmounted by a peaked roof and a cupola, which was probably added as much for ventilation purposes as for adornment. The wood was painted "barn red," the least expensive pigment of the time consisting of brick

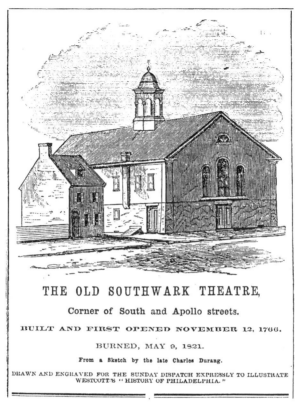

THE OLD SOUTHWARK THEATRE,

Corner of South and Apollo streets.

BUILT AND FIRST OPENED NOVEMBER 12, 1766.

BURNED, MAY 9, 1821.

From a Sketch by the late Charles Durang.

DRAWN AND ENGRAVED FOR THE SUNDAY DISPATCH EXPRESSLY TO ILLUSTRATE
WESTCOTT'S "HISTORY OF PHILADELPHIA."

Sketch of the Southwark Theatre, Philadelphia (based on drawing by Charles Durang), 1766. Engraved for the *Sunday Dispatch* to illustrate Westcott's "History of Philadelphia." Theatre Collection, Free Library of Philadelphia.

dust or red ocher mixed with skim milk. There were three rectangular windows in the upper story, each painted with a semicircular arch as a faux Palladian touch. The building's dimensions were approximately 95 feet by 50 feet and the structure cost about £360. In John F. Watson's *Annals of Philadelphia and Pennsylvania,* the interior was described thus in 1786:

> The building, compared with the new houses, was an ugly ill-conceived affair outside and inside. The stage was lighted by plain oil lamps without glasses. The view from the boxes was intercepted by large square wooden pillars, supporting the upper tier and roof. It was contended by many, at the time, that the front bench in the gallery was the best seat for a fair view of the stage. (Quoted in Rankin, 112)

The house was, of course, divided into the traditional pit, box, and gallery, but the earliest patrons of every rank had to walk through Cedar Street, muddy in inclement weather, to enter through the two doors. (Subsequently, a brick walk was laid to the theatre for the greater convenience of the playgoers.)

To complement the new theatre, new scenery was devised and painted by Philadelphia's William Williams and also ordered from Dahl in London. For his April 1767 production of *The Gamester,* Douglass advertised that "The Machinery, Deceptions [and] Decorations" (quoted in Rankin, 117) for the accompanying Harlequin were also new.

While enjoying a successful season in Philadelphia, Douglass contracted for a new playhouse in New York to open in early December 1767. Packing up his troupe and his scenery in wagons, he made his way overland to New York, where his new theatre had been completed in time for their arrival. The theatre was located on John Street, just east of Broadway, on the northernmost edge of the city. It was modeled on his Philadelphia theatre in Southwark except that it contained no brick work and was smaller. William Dunlap described it as "principally of wood, an unsightly object, painted red." For unexplained reasons, it was set about 60 feet back from the street, which made it difficult for patrons to enter the theatre during rainy or bad weather either by foot or carriage. Later, a wooden shed was added to protect playgoers.

Without further describing the interior of the Theatre on John Street, Dunlap reports that it had two rows of boxes, a pit, and a gallery and that the stage was "of good dimensions . . . equal to that of Colman's theatre, originally Foote's, in the Haymarket, London." A slightly more complete account of the interior occurs in Royall Tyler's play *The Contrast* (1787), in which one of the characters goes to the theatre unwittingly, telling of his experience:

> As I was going here and there, to and again, to find it [a magician's show], I saw a great crowd of folks going into a long entry that had lantherns over the door. . . . So I went right in, and they shewed me away, clean up to the garret, just like a meeting-house gallery. And so I saw a power of topping folks, all sitting around in little cabins, just like father's corn-cribs; and then there was such a squeaking with the fiddles, and such a tarnal blaze with the lights, my head was near turned. (III, i)

The John Street Theatre underwent changes during its thirty-year history – notably, an outbuilding was added for dressing rooms and storage – but it endured, a testament to its better construction and the more tolerant temper of the times.

Douglass added contemporary plays to the repertory, which may have necessitated adjustments to his scenic stock, but what they were and when they were introduced were never noted. Whatever reviews of his offerings survive, they invariably comment upon the play, the performers, and the performance rather than the mode of presentation, which leads to the conclusion that audiences became accustomed to the stock scenes and did not expect any spectacular scenic display on the early stages. That was to change after the American Revolution.

David Douglass built two other playhouses before decamping to the West Indies on the eve of the war. The more impressive of the two arose in Annapolis, Maryland. Built entirely of brick (a construction material abundant in the region), it was located on West Street. One of the leading citizens of the town, William Eddis in *Letters from America* (1792), left a description of the theatre that is frustratingly lacking in detail:

> The structure is not inelegant, but, in my opinion, on too narrow a scale for its length; the boxes are commodious, and neatly decorated; the pit and gallery are calculated to hold a number of people without incommoding each other; the stage is well adapted for dramatic and pantomimical exhibitions, and several of the scenes reflect great credit on the ability of the painter. (Quoted in Rankin, 162)

Douglass had again sent to London for new scenery by Dahl, which unfortunately did not arrive in time for the opening of the theatre in September 1771. The following spring, the manager introduced new plays from London and new scenery from the hand of John Inigo Richards, probably London's finest scene painter. In describing the scenery for Irish playwright Hugh Kelly's latest London comedy, *A Word to the Wise,* Eddis (at last) provided more specific information:

> the Curtain drew up, the new Scenes painted by Mr. Richards presented themselves to us, and exhibited a View of a superb Apartment, at the end of a fine Colonade of Pilars of the Ionic Order, which, by the happy Disposition of the Lights, had a most pleasing Effect. (Quoted in Rankin, 167)

Like most of the theatres that Douglass built in the colonies, funds for the new Charleston theatre, the last of his architectural contributions to colonial culture, were raised by subscription from well-to-do interested citizens of the town. Whether out of civic pride or actual fact, the *South Carolina Gazette* reported that the theatre in Church Street was the largest and most elegant of the colonial theatres. Douglass brought down his new scenery from Annapolis for *A Word to the Wise* to open the house, and audiences seem to have been well pleased with the theatre, the scenery, and the costumes. For the next year, Douglass and his company continued touring, stopping in the towns and cities where he had built his sturdy theatres. In October 1774, when the resolution passed by the Continental Congress "discountenanced and discouraged . . . exhibition of shews, plays, and other expensive diversions and entertainments," Douglass and his company set sail for Jamaica, and the era of colonial theatre was at an end.

What Murray and Kean, the Hallams, and David Douglass accomplished in a quarter-century was to establish theatre in the emerging American society as part of the cultural life of the citizens of the New World. The odds against success were enormous in the face of vocal religious opposition from the conservative Christian factions, particularly in the northern colonies, but the troupers prevailed, both north and south, exposing in their persistence the overarching moral and political principle that people (particularly the majority) have the fundamental right to choose. By any standards, the playhouses themselves were crude affairs with few, if any, amenities, but they continued to improve in comfort and attractiveness, largely through the efforts of David Douglass and his wisdom in tapping civic pride to make them better built and each architecturally superior to the one previously erected. The few recorded comments about the scenery, lighting, and costumes reveal that the emphasis for unsophisticated playgoing audiences continued to be on the players and the play and not on the production. Douglass was canny enough to realize that periodically he had to introduce new scenery and costumes (as well as new faces) to revitalize his repertory and advertised them whenever he could to maintain the level of interest in his offerings.

Mirroring the only kind of physical arrangement that they knew, the itinerant actor-managers divided their theatres into pit, box, and gallery, which explicitly segregated audiences in the Old World by rank and class. In the New World, however, the arrangement was made more pragmatic and, therefore democratic: Whoever could afford the best seats got them. (The "best" seats in the boxes within a rectangular auditorium were not necessarily the best seats for viewing the stage, but the cachet persisted into the nineteenth century.) Douglass's "permanent" theatres met with various ends. The John Street Theatre in New York and the Southwark Theatre in Philadelphia endured through the Revolution and beyond, but were supplanted eventually by better theatres in their respective cities. The theatre in Annapolis was converted into a church, but the Church Street Theatre in Charleston did not survive the war. It burned down in 1782. What was not destroyed, however, in any of the cities and towns of Douglass's itinerary was the thirst for dramatic entertainment. Although suspended by edict and necessity during the war, it arose again after hostilities ceased.

The Early Republic Era (1783–1825)

There was not a complete cessation of dramatic activity during the war despite the resolutions of the Continental Congress. Several of Douglass's theatres were reopened by the British to combat the ennui of military occupation during the Revolutionary War, notably, the Southwark in Philadelphia and the John Street in New York. (As testament to the talents of the officers, the infamous Major John André left behind several pieces of scenery that he had painted at the Southwark.) General Burgoyne's troops shattered the sacred precincts of Boston by presenting entertainments at none other than Faneuil Hall to the outrage of its citizens. In Baltimore, the first theatre in its history was built in 1781 by an actor who had once belonged to the old American Company, and for nearly two years, performances were held there before the end of the war. When the remnants of Douglass's old company began returning in the months after the cessation of military action, they, of course, gravitated to the cities in which there were extant playhouses and a theatregoing public from the prewar years. Although their first maneuvers were tentative (to test the political waters), the returning actors were nevertheless determined to reestablish themselves in the early years of the republic. As the country emerged from the political and economic turmoil immediately following the war, they sensed that the profound changes would inevitably affect the course of theatrical entertainment in the new country. They were right.

For approximately the next forty years, the time it took not only to reestablish the theatre and expand its limits geographically but to begin to acquire a distinctively American feeling, the theatrical practice progressed from being a small and contained event dominated by a resourceful but itinerant actor-manager to a large and ever-expanding enterprise. Because of the exploding population, each of the former colonial cities would acquire a new and improved playhouse with a resident company, which eventually no longer needed a far-flung and arduous itinerary to other towns and cities to survive. All of the prewar playhouses were soon outgrown and eventually abandoned. In their place stood handsome (to the eyes of the new Americans) theatres no longer relegated to the outskirts of the cities but close to their centers. For the first time in history, they were planned by architects and were built to reflect civic pride on money provided by well-to-do citizens. They were bigger, more comfortable for patrons and actors alike, and frequently adorned by decorations, both inside and out, that bespoke their mission. Many of them had ornate "presidential boxes," draped in red, white, and blue, for the visits of presidents and other officials. Although the pit-box-and-gallery plan of the Old World continued to dominate, auditoriums were curved into a flat ellipse to provide better sight lines from the side portions of the room. Whereas the largest of the colonial playhouses could seat fewer than five hundred patrons, the newer theatres could hold as many as two thousand.

With a resident company in each of the major playhouses, it became necessary to hire and retain a resident scene painter, who might have one or more assistants. Each theatre became a training ground not only for future native-born performers and managers but also scene painters, stage carpenters, machinists, and other technical staff. No longer was it necessary to send periodically for new scenes and costumes from London, since they could now be supplied locally. Because the company and theatre were permanent, the scenery no longer had to be made with an eye toward trouping it with the actors. Beginning with recruits from London, the profession of scene painting was established, and native talent was being trained in the art. Stages were routinely grooved to accept side wings permanently covered with painted canvas, and the green baize transportable curtain was supplanted by a permanent decorative act curtain. As a result of these changes, each company was subjected to a closer scrutiny by critics on the quality of their scenic display.

As the new century dawned, a new kind of play was imported from Europe, the melodrama, which often demanded special and frequently more elaborate scenery than ever seen before. No longer could the stock scenery suit all of the scenes and situations of all the plays in the company's repertory. The stock interior scenery, which could suffice for almost any Restoration comedy, did not suit the humble cottage of a peasant at the end of a forest for a domestic drama nor could the stock exterior scenes fit battlefields, exotic places, or wild and savage backgrounds for melodramas. The managers' purses had to open wide to accommodate the scenic changes of their plays.

Finally, audiences approached their experiences in the theatre with greater expectations. When the plots of the melodramas became more and more predictable, they looked to the spectacle for their delectation.

Predictably, it was the South that saw the first expansion of theatrical activity as actors explored possibilities in the burgeoning towns of Savannah, Atlanta, and Richmond. It was in Charleston that the first of the postwar playhouses, Harmony Hall, was built in 1786. Although it was described as "a beautiful little theatre" (quoted in McNamara, 74) within a spacious garden in the suburbs of the city, it harked back to the prewar playhouses in size, plan, and money expended. Unfortunately, the manager could not keep it afloat without a steady audience, which his offerings failed to attract, and the theatre was closed after the first season.

A few years later, in 1793, a larger and more elaborate theatre for Charleston was planned by the actor-managers Thomas Wade West and John Bignall. The construction budget of £2500, which they had raised, did not begin to cover the large and handsome playhouse that they envisioned, and the playhouse had to be scaled back and completed at a later time. Fronting on Broad Street, it was 125 feet long by 56 feet wide and 37 feet high with a stage 56 feet in depth. There were three tiers of boxes, each equipped with a window covered by a venetian blind. It is doubtful that the managers could have included the other interior embellishments they had planned, because the opening-night reviewer of the *Charleston Gazette and Daily Advertiser* (18 Oct. 1794) commented only on its "neatness and simple elegance." However, a year later the managers found enough money to refurbish the interior, probably adding what had been planned, and in 1830, the large columned portico of the original plans was finally added to the exterior. The Charleston Theatre may also have been the first theatre in America to have installed a prototype air-conditioning system in 1794. An air pump, of the kind that was used aboard British warships of the time to recirculate air, was placed in the gallery and apparently afforded some relief from the Charleston heat.

Although theatres were still being converted from buildings formerly used for other purposes, as soon as enough capital was raised by subscriptions from well-to-do supporters, managers quickly erected new theatres and tried to equip them with the latest technology available. Probably the finest theatre of the early republic years was built in Boston, the fortress of Puritanism, which represented the triumph of democracy over minority opinion in the exercising of prerogatives bestowed by the Constitution and Bill of Rights. In 1793, on the heels of the repeal of the 1750 law banning the theatre in Massachusetts, money was subscribed to build a theatre on the corner of Federal and Franklin streets in Boston. Designed by the architect Charles Bulfinch, it was a large playhouse built of brick with "stone facings, iron posts and pillars," 140 feet long by 61 feet wide by 40 feet high. There were separate entrances for pit, box, and gallery and a porte-cochère to allow carriages to drive up to the main entrance in inclement weather. Box holders passed through a lobby heated by two fireplaces at either end to reach the staircases that led to their seats. The interior was described by an anonymous writer of the time:

> The interior was circular in form, the ceiling composed of elliptical arches resting on Corinthian pillars. There were two rows of boxes, the second suspended by invisible means. The stage opening was thirty-one feet wide, ornamented on either side by two columns, between which was a stage door opening on a projecting iron balcony. Above the columns a cornice and a balustrade were carried over the stage openings; and above these was painted a flow of crimson drapery and the armys of the United States and the commonwealth blended with emblems tragic and comic. A ribbon depending from the arms bore the motto, "All the world's a stage." (Quoted in Crawford, 114–15)

The boxes were festooned with crimson silk and gilt and painted in shades of blue, straw, and lilac. The building also contained a dancing pavillion, tea rooms, and kitchens for the further entertainment of patrons. The theatre was inaugurated in early February 1794 as the Boston Theatre, but was later known as the Federal Street.

Unfortunately, no contemporary account exists of the productions themselves, but the manager, Charles Stuart Powell, an English-born actor, may well have commissioned scenery from London scene painters while he was recruiting a company in England for the theatre. His repertory, plays all new to the Boston audiences, was the standard repertory fare for any provincial company and ranged from Shakespeare to works from such contemporaneous English playwrights as R. B. Sheridan, Oliver Goldsmith, John O'Keeffe, and Mrs. Elizabeth Inchbald. It was varied enough to conclude that Powell must have had to provide more than stock scenery – even when his audiences might not have known better. The theatre burned down in 1798, was quickly rebuilt, and remained in operation until almost the mid-nineteenth century.

The city of Philadelphia rivaled Boston in the elegance of its new theatre, but descriptions from two sources are at variance. Built on Chestnut Street, near Sixth Street, and known as the Chestnut Street Theatre, the playhouse was completed early in 1793, but because of the periodic epidemics of yellow fever, it was not officially opened until February 1794. Its managers were the actor Thomas Wignell and the musician Alexander Reinagle, who leased the house from the subscriber-stock holders. Supposedly designed by John Inigo Richards, Wignell's brother-in-law, it was modeled after the Theatre Royal in Bath, England. As in the case of other theatres of the time, the construction money ran out before the house was completed, and parts of it were finished over a period of years. In 1804 or 1805, Benjamin Latrobe designed the imposing facade, which stretched 90 feet along Chestnut Street and included two projecting wings of 15 feet each. They were connected by a colonnade of ten Corinthian columns on which rested a classical entablature. The center of the building contained a large Palladian window, flanked by two niches, in which were placed figures of comedy and tragedy executed by Benjamin Rush. Other classical details graced the facade, to which marble facing was added to the brick. There were, of course, three separate entrances to the various parts of the house. Philadelphians were proud of their new theatre.

A French emigré, Moreau de Saint-Méry, saw the theatre through different eyes. He was unimpressed with its facade and its size – it held close to two thousand people, making it the country's largest. He pronounced the interior "quite handsome" with its color scheme of gray and gilt. Three tiers of boxes were arranged around a semielliptical pit, but Saint-Méry was unhappy with the partially obstructed view from the boxes and their red wallpaper. He described the other elements: a large stage (36 by 71 feet), a capacious orchestra pit that could hold thirty musicians, up-to-date lighting (oil lamps that could be dimmed for day and night scenes), and satisfactory acoustics. He was impressed with the new and well-painted scenery (see Young, *Playhouses,* I, 18).

In addition to recruiting a first-rate company from England, Wignell wisely brought along an English scene painter, Cotton (or Charles) Milbourne, to create new scenery for the playhouse. (A few years later, he recruited John Joseph Holland, who with Milbourne trained a generation of native scene painters, all of whom served theatres throughout the country and established the American scene painting tradition reaching into the twentieth century.) Milbourne and Holland and their assistants, one of whom was Hugh Reinagle, the son of the manager Reinagle, were very busy during the early years of the Chestnut Street. Wignell's expanding repertory, which included

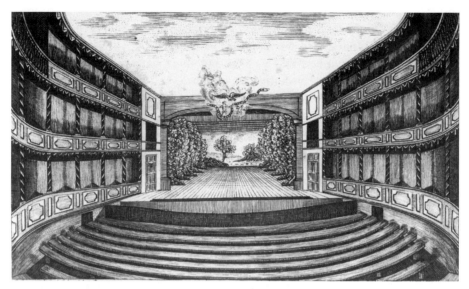

Chestnut Street Theatre, Philadelphia, completed in 1793, but opening delayed a year because of a yellow fever outbreak. Engraving by W. Ralph after a drawing by S. Lewis; published in *New York Magazine* (1794). Original in the Cooper-Hewitt Museum of Decorative Arts and Design (Smithsonian Institution) in New York. Theatre Collection, Free Library of Philadelphia.

the newest importations from London as well as translations of melodramas from Europe, demanded from their talented hands such scenes as a Turkish village, a blue magic chamber, a temple of the sun, caverns and dungeons, papier-mâché elephants and other wild creatures, German forests, snow-covered mountains, marriage bowers, turreted castles, and so forth, many of which were accompanied by "machines" to create natural disasters and move scenery onstage. The excellence of the scenery at the Chestnut Street continued unbroken when the stewardship of the theatre passed to William Warren Sr. and William B. Wood.

In 1816, the Chestnut Street became the first theatre in the country to be lit by gaslight, which not only introduced better illumination but had the potential to create future possibilities for altering light in intensity and color onstage as well as making the painter's art more precise. The theatre burned down in 1820 and was rebuilt by the architect William Strickland in a version that did not resemble the original. The glory years of the Chestnut Street ended in 1828 when Wood and Warren left its management.

The theatre that became the premiere theatre of America – but not because of the beauty of its architecture – was the New Theatre in New York, which came to be known as the Park. Built on Park Row, just north of the most populous area, it was soon to be at the heart of the burgeoning city. (Park Row formed the eastern leg of a triangle that joined Broadway as the western leg at its apex and Chambers Street as the northern boundary. This area eventually enclosed a small park, into which in 1811 was set City Hall at the northern end.) The cornerstone was laid in 1795, but the theatre was not completed until early 1798 and bore slight resemblance to the structure that was designed originally by the architect, a French emigré named Joseph Mangin. (Joseph Ireland writes that the theatre was first planned by Marc Isambard Brunel, a French engineer and builder of the Thames Tunnel. The New-York Historical Society has in its archives a ground plan that has been attributed to Brunel.) For the construction one hundred and thirteen shares were sold for $375 each, but they did not begin to cover the cost overruns, which nearly tripled the original estimate. The theatre had a frontage of 80 feet on Park Row and a depth of 165 feet to a rear alleyway (later named Theatre Alley), where a shed was eventually built for storage. The semi-circular auditorium originally could hold approximately two thousand patrons in three tiers of boxes, a large pit, and a gallery at the rear of the auditorium above the lower and largest box, but, after the fire of 1820, the seating capacity was enlarged to about twenty-five hundred when the playhouse was rebuilt. According to William Dunlap's description, the boxes were cantilevered in the original building but were propped by columns in the later version of the house.

Opened in a largely unfinished state, the interior of the theatre lacked, according to a review of the opening in the *Daily Advertiser* (31 Jan. 1798), "the brilliant decorations which the artists have designed for it, yet exhibited a neatness and simplicity which were highly agreeable." It was probably painted in white (or near white) and accented in gold. (The actor-managers John Hodgkinson and Lewis Hallam Jr. eventually finished the decorations for the auditorium later in the year, which was pronounced "the most superb and stately spectacle" in America.) The account in the *Commercial Advertiser* goes on to describe the double columns on either side of the stage painted to resemble marble, the flat ceiling to look like an azure dome "with floating clouds, between which celestial forms are visible, a green and gold canopy over the stage and each tier of boxes, a glass chandelier suspended from the dome, and a blue mohair curtain fringed with gold bearing a center decoration of a lyre of muses, surrounded by the usual symbols." The curtain bore the words: "To hold the Mirror up to Nature." (Before its final fiery end in 1848, the interior was redecorated several more times.)

Seven arched doorways were cut into the facade of the building, with the center five reserved for the box holders, who mounted a set of steps into the lobby, where fireplaces at either end warmed patrons in cold weather. The other two doors at street level led separately to the pit and the gallery. (The raked pit was reached through a subterranean passageway.) In the early days of the Park, there was apparently a wing described as a "rude extension" to

Park Theatre, New York. This is the interior of the restored Park, 1822, after it was burned to its exterior walls in 1820. Painting by John Searle (1783–1834). Collection of The New-York Historical Society.

the left (north) of the theatre, which was used as a green room. (It was later replaced by a more substantial structure as the area grew more popular for builders.) Lighting for the auditorium was provided by three chandeliers.

From the moment of its opening, the Park's facade evoked scathing criticism from New Yorkers, but most pointedly from foreign visitors. It was in truth an ugly building from the start and was not improved in the rebuilt version following the fire of 1820. The earliest iconography shows a brick face in the upper stories over the arched portico, Palladian-type windows in the second story, and a pilastrade extending to the cornice, which was topped by a pediment. A statue of Shakespeare was set into the facade and may or may not have been placed in the center of the pediment. (A small iron balcony appears in front of the pilasters in a watercolor version by Milbourne dated

1798 but is absent in later iconography, as is a strange pyramidal structure on the roof.) When the theatre was rebuilt after the fire, the facade became even plainer. It was now covered with stucco and scored to resemble either granite or marble. In 1831 (*New York Mirror,* 25 Feb.), it was described tongue-in-cheek by Basil Hall:

> The beauty of the outside is a matter of serious astonishment, consisting of the best quality of colored plaster variegated by straight lines, which are ingeniously intended to imitate cracks. This gives it an appearance of venerable grandeur, calculated to strike the beholder with silent awe. Indeed, the munificence of its owners has spared neither plaster nor brown paint to impart to it a sombre cast, and anxious for improvement, they have changed it from its former color, which was yellow, here and there blackened with smoke, to one of becoming and unvaried brown.

Writing in the same year, Walt Whitman described it as "the most villainous specimen of architecture you ever beheld." Horrendous architecture notwithstanding, the Park offered, under the management of Edmund Simpson and Stephen Price in the middle years of its fifty-year-long history, the finest acting in the best productions that had yet to be seen on the American continent.

The building of the new and better theatres in the closing years of the eighteenth century and the ascendancy of the melodrama in popular favor in the next century brought necessary changes in stagecraft. In 1798, actor-manager John Hodgkinson, in a letter to the trustees of the (rebuilt) Federal Street Theatre, stated his needs for the repertory of "all old stock plays" he was planning to present for them: "5 chambers varied, 1 Library, 1 Wood, 1 Grove, 1 Garden, 1 Cut Wood, 1 Village, 1 Camp flat, 2 Streets, 1 Palace, 2 Palace apartments, 1 Castle with Gates, 1 Kitchen, 1 Rustic Chamber, 1 interior of a Cave, 1 Prison and arch, Horizon, Waves, etc., etc." (quoted by Stoddard in *Theatre Survey,* 102). All of these, for a repertory of seventy-five to a hundred different plays! Add to these the unending flow of melodramas with a variety of backgrounds that could not be served by the stock scenery. Moreover, the demands of melodramas began to pull the acting area *within* the scenic environment, not merely in front of painted wings and drops, as was customary for the old repertory. Canvas-covered hills were built onstage along with ramps and suggestions of bridges to suit the needs of the dramas, which were often filled with historical events and exotic backgrounds. Melodramas were also prop-heavy, which added to the burdens of the heads of the scenic departments.

In an 1806 letter to Thomas Abthorpe Cooper, who managed the Park Theatre for several years, his predecessor William Dunlap tried to explain the work of the scene painter, justifying the high salaries that they received. He reminded Cooper of a conversation that both had had with John Joseph Holland, the scene painter from the Chestnut Street Theatre, whom they were trying to lure to New York. Holland explained that he was an artist and "not bound to work by the hour like a mechanick [*sic*]." Dunlap's sympathy was clearly with him and his colleagues, as he continued his own defense of the profession, which continues to have modern resonances:

> Where is the man who shall judge of the time required for designing a picture, or the number of hours necessary for the artist to execute his design? Where is the article that can bind a man to promote your interest at the sacrifice of his own ease? . . . The Actor will exert himself before the public for the recompense of public approbation . . . but there is no reward for the thousand services render'd in secret by your Scene painter & Machinist except what springs from the consciousness of doing right & the pleasure of promoting the interests of his employer. (*Diary,* 402)

The best of the scene painters were well paid by the standards of the time, frequently receiving almost as much as the leading actors and managers of the companies, but they earned their money. Not only did they design and paint the scenes, they were usually called upon to paint the decorations for the auditorium. They were also peripatetic, moving about from city to city in search of greater rewards and better opportunities, and frequently working with and for each other. Although they are known mostly by surname and are mentioned infrequently in the playbills (usually only when managers announced "new scenes" for productions), they began to form a sizable corps within the growing native theatrical profession. Fuller biographical details for at least two of them, Charles Ciceri and John Joseph Holland, have been recorded, but the majority of them passed quietly into history.

Ciceri's life, according to Dunlap, was "a romance of real life." He was born in Milan, probably during the last quarter of the eighteenth century, and educated in Paris, where he learned the rudiments of landscape drawing. After a troubled and rebellious youth, he joined a military regiment that eventually landed in Santo Domingo. During service there, he moonlighted as a scene painter at the local theatre, discovering in himself a talent for theatrical art. He eventually made his way to Paris and Bordeaux, thence to London, finding employment as an assistant scene painter at theatres wherever he went. After several misadventures, he returned to North America, where he worked first in Philadelphia at the Chestnut Street and Southwark theatres and then, finally, in New York at the John Street and the Park. Dunlap appreciated his talents and considered him not only a fine scene painter and excellent machinist but "a most valuable auxiliary to the *corps dramatique.*" After a falling out with the Park's management in 1807 over the redecoration of the Park's interior (a job that was given to Holland), Ciceri left the theatre and returned to Europe.

During his dozen or so years as a scene painter in America, Ciceri made his mark on the art. Although no detailed descriptions of his scenery exist, copious compliments for his efforts abound. He painted the scenes for the

Park's opening production of *As You Like It,* which was, according to one New York reviewer, "surpassing for elegance and effect, everything of the kind heretofore seen in America." According to another: "The scenery was of itself worth a visit to the theatre" (quoted in Duerr, "Charles Ciceri"). During his years at the Park, Ciceri's work elevated scenery to a higher plane than had been customary in America. How he did it will never be known, but his important place in the development of an indigenous art must be inferred from the commendations of his contemporaries.

The agent responsible for Ciceri's departure from the Park was John Joseph Holland (1776–1820), born in London and trained by Gaetano Marinari, the chief artist of the Haymarket Theatre. In 1796, Thomas Wignell, then in London recruiting actors for his company in Philadelphia, hired him for the Chestnut Street Theatre. At first, he served as assistant to Milbourne, already at work on scenery for the new theatre, but, in 1805, Holland replaced him as chief scene painter. In 1807, he was hired to redecorate the Park Theatre in New York and stayed on to join Milbourne in the scenic department. He remained at the Park until 1813, then left to pursue other activities for a few years, returning to the theatre in 1816, probably finishing his career there until his death in 1820.

Like Ciceri, Holland was a skillful machinist, receiving praise from a Philadelphia critic for his deft transformation of mice to horses and a pumpkin to a carriage for a production of *Cinderella* at the Chestnut Street Theatre in 1806. Like Ciceri, he was a painstaking artist, who used the limited means of his time to create the best effects that he could. Like all the scene painters, he used a full range of colors from bright white to deep blues, which he mixed with water and size (a light glue) and painted on various weights of linen, muslin, and canvas stretched on wooden frames. The wings and moving shutters, combined with curtains, some of which were transparent, constituted the stock-in-trade of the early nineteenth-century artist for the stage. He and his assistants – some of whom obviously developed specialties within the art – were responsible for building and painting three-dimensional pieces and props as well. Add to this the creation of devices (machines) to move clouds down from the flyloft, ships across the horizon, ocean waves of painted canvas for stormy seas, together with special lighting effects for rising suns and moons, smoke and gunfire for battles, and sounds for thunder and waterfalls, and whatever else was required for the plays, and it is understandable why the scene painter was much more than his name implies and was worth the generous salaries that he received.

With a thriving theatrical profession permanently established, with architect-designed playhouses, and with the art of scene painting brought to new heights, theatrical entertainment followed the growth of the nation and began to move westward with the population.

Frontier Theatres and Stagecraft

While theatre building and dramatic performances were spreading rapidly along the Atlantic coast from Massachusetts to Georgia, events in history were determining the next phase of American theatrical history. By 1800, Tennessee and Kentucky had been added to the Union, and three years later, with a stroke of a pen, the area of the United States was doubled with the purchase of the Louisiana territory from France. It extended from the Mississippi River to the Rocky Mountains and from the Gulf of Mexico to Canada and launched the westward movement that would take up the entire century and help form a new and enduring national identity. From simple encampments sprang settlements; from settlements, villages; and from villages, towns and cities. In the wake of the westward flow, first came the actors and, eventually, the theatres that they founded. Their story was a repetition of the efforts and accomplishments of the first pioneering theatrical troupes to the colonies but with several significant twists.

Frontier theatre was largely unaffected by the fervor of religious scruples against playacting that was in colonial cities. Although there were occasional fierce condemnations from the pulpit in the West, they were almost always ignored by the entertainment-thirsty populace of the burgeoning towns and cities in the new territories. Almost everywhere they went, the early barnstormers found a makeshift theatre that had been fitted up by the local Thespian Society, which they were able to use for their own performances. Rather than hostility, the pioneering troupes could count upon support from the officialdom of whatever rank they found. Like David Douglass, they discovered that a call on the head of the constabulary to ask for permission to perform (or to inquire whether there was a local tax on performance) was a part of the ritual even though they knew it would be forthcoming with the customary free tickets to the performances. When the actors were secure enough to build theatres from the ground up, they realized that the buildings, far from being regarded as the "devil's playroom," were welcomed by the town and its citizens. When James H. Caldwell, one of the most successful of the frontier entrepreneurs, contemplated building a theatre on unpaved Camp Street in New Orleans, many warned him that its location on the outskirts of the city would be a deterrent to an audience. Caldwell persisted in his belief that people would come despite the inconvenience and predicted that his theatre would become the magnet for drawing other kinds of business. He was correct on both counts.

The early frontier managers were aware that the population in the western territories was overwhelmingly native born. Whatever theatrical performances the audiences may have enjoyed in the settled eastern part of the country, they had no direct knowledge of the London playhouses. Consequently, although they may have brought with them a predilection for theatrical entertainment from past experience, their standards of comparison were lower and their enjoyment of even the roughest, crudest productions in the most makeshift of playhouses was unalloyed by faulty prejudice. Of course, that was to change as both audiences and performers matured and the productions and the theatres in which they took place became more sophisticated. Like their eastern counterparts, audiences eventually tired of mismatched scenery and costumes and cheerless theatres and demanded something better

Audiences in the West also differed in several other respects from their eastern brethren. There was no landed aristocracy on the frontier. Almost everyone began on an equal footing. If anything defined the new American at this time (and for all time), it was the hardworking and independent frontiersmen (and women), who toiled on farms, set up small businesses, and pursued the kinds of livelihoods that were available to them in the raw territories. Eventually, an affluent class emerged from them, which had both the money and the inclination to fund the building of substantial and permanent theatres not only to house their entertainment but to mark their rising status to the American world. As in the East, the erection of playhouses was financed by subscriptions. Hastily built wooden barns that cost a few hundred dollars and could seat fewer than five hundred people in the early decades of the nineteenth century were supplanted by impressive structures like the St. Charles Theatre in New Orleans, which cost more than $100,000 dollars to build in 1835 and was considered the handsomest theatre in America to that date. Once the playhouse became an important part of frontier life, it grew and flourished unhampered by the restraints that it had in the East.

The history of the frontier theatre is found in the biographies of the men who brought it to the newly opened territories: Samuel Drake, Noble Luke Usher, Noah Ludlow, Solomon Smith, and James H. Caldwell. The first of them, Samuel Drake, an English-born actor and stage manager, was middle-aged when he was urged by the itinerant actor Noble Luke Usher to lead a troupe to Kentucky, where he was assured of finding a welcoming audience and a circuit of theatres managed by Luke Usher (either his father or uncle). Leaving Albany, New York, in May 1815, Drake's troupe traveled overland and by flat-bottom boat to reach Frankfort, Kentucky, by December. Along the way, they stopped and presented plays in whatever large space was available in each of the small villages. One of the members of Drake's company was Noah Ludlow, who was to set down all of his reminiscences in a later chronicle. He describes the improvised productions:

> The stage adjuncts consisted of but six scenes, a wood, street, parlor, kitchen, palace, and garden. The wings, or side-scenes, consisted of three of a side, to be stationary in one sense, but to be so arranged with flaps or

aprons as to present, when required, an out-door view adapted to correspond with garden or street; an in-door view to suit parlor or palace; with a third, to match the kitchen. The proscenium was a painted drapery, made so as to be expanded or contracted to suit the dimensions of the places occupied by our performances. These and a neat drop-curtain, and green baize carpet, constituted our stage facilities. The scenery could be put in place, or taken down and packed, in two or three hours. (7–8)

At Pittsburgh, they found a theatre at the edge of town, which was, according to Ludlow, "the poorest apology for one I had then ever seen" (55). Covered with coal dust, the playhouse contained a pit and one tier of boxes and had been probably erected and used by amateurs with an occasional foray by strolling actors. As they made their way west, the company had to hire local help not only as supernumeraries for the plays but also for scene shifting and backstage work, often with humorous and sometimes disastrous results. When the company reached Frankfort, Kentucky, in the late fall of 1815, they found a theatre located on the second floor of a building on Broadway and St. Clair Street. It was small, probably not seating more than three hundred, and was divided into pit, box, and gallery. Managed by Luke Usher, it had been used by the local amateur group and a traveling troupe for several years. In Louisville, his next stop, Drake found the theatre in such bad condition that he had to hire a local painter to refurbish the interior while he and his son worked to improve the scenery. In June 1816, the troupe moved on to Lexington. The theatre, part of a former brewery owned by Luke Usher, was situated on a small hill, which forced the audience to enter from a street nearly on a level with the floor of the second story. The interior of the auditorium was arranged, according to Ludlow, "upon the amphitheatre plan, – [with seats] gradually rising from the floor, one above the other, to the back, these back seats being reached by a sloping platform at one side" (90). Again, the troupe found the house scenery in short supply and badly painted, and, again, everything had to be cleaned and repainted before they could give their performances. After Drake finished his circuit, he lent Ludlow and other members of the troupe a small supply of scenery for a barnstorming tour of the villages around Lexington.

Ludlow then joined another troupe that was making its way to Nashville, Tennessee, where they arrived in early summer 1817. Finding no available theatre – not even a makeshift playhouse – they converted an old salt house on Market Street into a playhouse with the help of local carpenters, provided it with benches in an improvised stepped-up auditorium, and opened for business. After a successful season, Ludlow decided to try his luck in New Orleans, where he was told by scene painter Richard Jones (then in New Orleans) that the time was ripe for a season of English-language plays for the growing English-speaking population. Ludlow sent part of the troupe to New

Orleans, while he and the rest of the troupe made their way down river, stopping at Natchez, Mississippi. They found what had been described to them as a "very nice little theatre" (134) on a bluff in the upper part of the city, which had been built on subscription for amateur performances. It was a small house, seating about five hundred people, which Ludlow and his players were able to fill every night of their engagement.

When Ludlow reached New Orleans, he immediately made arrangements to rent the St. Philip Street Theatre (Théâtre St. Phillipe), a small brick building with a seating capacity of seven hundred, which had previously been home to French-speaking actors alternating with several American troupes. (The other theatre in New Orleans, the Théâtre Orleans, usually referred to as the French Theatre, had burned to the ground in 1813.) He hired Richard Jones to touch up the scenery and paint the interior of the theatre, which consisted of two tiers of boxes and a parquet (the French name for the English pit) and could hold seven hundred patrons, and began his season.

Although Ludlow claimed to have introduced English-language theatre to New Orleans, he was not correct. From 1806 to 1817, itinerant players and troupes had presented theatrical performances in English. In 1811, one William Duff and his American Company alternated with a French company at the St. Philip Street Theatre on a weekly basis for a month, and, for a number of years, the local Thespian Society presented plays sporadically at the theatre. But it was Ludlow's arrival that established English theatre in New Orleans and broke ground for the professionals who followed him.

It was not long after Ludow's departure that James H. Caldwell, recognizing the possibilities of a permanent theatre with its own company in a prospering southern city, took over the St. Philip Street playhouse and later the rebuilt French Theatre in Orleans Street when it was not engaged by the French-speaking troupe. Caldwell, although advertising himself as "native American," was a British-born actor, who arrived in Charleston in 1816. Sensing the opportunities in the southwestern territory, he assembled a company of actors and struck out on his own, first in Virginia, then moving to Kentucky and, eventually, New Orleans in 1820. With competent actors and a strong repertory of plays, he was to become Ludlow's principal rival. One of his actors, William McCafferty, doubled as a scene painter and was responsible for the high quality of Caldwell's scenery and effects.

Caldwell's success in managing his company in New Orleans was highly profitable, and he returned for successive seasons, always holding his ground against competition from other troupes, both English and French. Finally, in 1823, Caldwell was sufficiently secure to build his own theatre to house his company. Early in 1824, he opened the Camp Street Theatre, erected at a cost of $70,000 and with a seating capacity of a thousand in a structure that measured 160 feet long by 60 feet wide. It was a solid brick building, three stories high, with Doric touches in the facade and a set of marble steps across the front intersected by four marble piers from which extended cast iron lighting fixtures. The auditorium – divided into pit (now known as the parquet) and three rows of boxes – was considered well proportioned and commodious. According to one of the actors who played in it, Joe Cowell, it was "better adapted to the peculiar climate of New Orleans than any he had ever seen" (quoted in Smither, 39), which may have meant that Caldwell achieved better ventilation. Although no detailed descriptions of the interior exist, it was notable in being the first theatre in the Southwest to be illuminated by gas both onstage and in the auditorium with its own gasworks. (The enterprising Caldwell eventually founded a gas company in New Orleans not only to light his theatres but the entire city.)

Caldwell's staff at the Camp Street Theatre included a full-time scene painter, Antonio (or Antoine) Mondelli; a stage machinist, John Varden; and an engineer for the gas table, Mr. Symons, all of whom were such valuable adjuncts to his theatre that they received benefit nights. Together with the stage carpenters, they produced effects for the succession of melodramas that Caldwell was offering his public. For *Cataract of the Ganges,* in April 1825, the scenic and machine departments delighted audiences with a real waterfall onstage.

Enjoying great success in New Orleans, Caldwell made ready to strike out in other directions and was later to compete head-on with Noah Ludlow, who left Caldwell's acting company in New Orleans again "to try [his] fortune as a manager" (254). Ludlow journeyed to Alabama, where he discovered that citizens in Mobile and Huntsville, Alabama, were sufficiently dedicated to theatrical entertainment to provide playhouses at their own expense – on the subscription basis as usual – and lease the buildings to him. Finding no scene painter for his scenery in Mobile, Ludlow trained a local artist in the mixing and application of distemper and made use of him for an entire season before engaging Antonio Mondelli, "a thoroughbred artist" (262), who had worked for Caldwell in New Orleans. Mondelli was engaged for six months to paint six stock scenes, wings, borders, and "other necessary appurtenances" for Ludlow's next engagement in Mobile. The artist also decorated the auditorium of the Mobile theatre in 1825, improving its appearance, according to Ludlow, to make it look lighter and more cheerful.

But the enterprising Ludlow was often reduced to having his company play in temporary and makeshift theatres just to break ground in the southern towns. In Montgomery, the only place he found was in the attic of a hotel, which had been fitted up as a theatre by an amateur group. The single entrance into the theatre (for both actors and audience alike) was by an outdoor flight of steps at the top of which was a window, through which everyone had to pass. With no backstage or wings, actors had to thread their way through the audience for their entrances and exits onstage. Once the theatrical appetites had been whetted, however, more substantial structures rapidly replaced the temporary theatres on Ludlow's circuit.

Meanwhile, with Ludlow mining the towns in the lower Mississippi Valley, Caldwell decided to try his luck in St. Louis, which had been incorporated as a city in 1823 and where Ludlow and Samuel Drake had introduced dramatic entertainment on a regular basis in 1819. Finding that the only suitable building for his purposes was an old salt house ("a melancholy structure altogether" [292]), Caldwell took it, added a 40-foot structure to serve as a stage, and began performances in 1825. From there he took his troupe to Nashville, where he found the Cherry Street Theatre (which had been erected by a Frenchman in 1819), but considered it unsatisfactory and contracted to have a new playhouse built on Summerville Street. When Ludlow took it over some five years later, he found Caldwell's theatre a very rough and plain structure with few conveniences for the audience. Scenes for the actors were few, and Ludlow found them to be of "the plainest character" (380).

With the backing of some of St. Louis's prominent citizens, Ludlow was determined to build a better theatre in St. Louis. He raised the capital, $65,000, and work began in the fall of 1836. He also hired John Rowson Smith to create eight pairs of shutters (or center scenes) and appropriate wings to be placed in grooves on the stage to be ready for the opening of the theatre. Smith also painted the dome in sections to be lifted up and put into place when the auditorium was in an advanced state of completion. Ludlow gives an account of the lighting to be put into the house:

> We also had to make arrangements for lighting the house, which had to be done by spirit-gas, coal-gas not having at that time been introduced into the city of St. Louis. This lighting was effected by means of branch-lamps suspended around the front of the boxes; the stage having for the "foot-lights" (front lights), square tin boxes, with large burners for spirit gas, a similar kind of box, only of triangular shape, being used behind each wing, with reflectors attached, to throw the light to the centre of the stage. (476)

Because of its importance to him and the town, Ludlow engaged a local architect, George S. Barrett, to draw up the plans, but relied on his stage carpenters to correct any errors in design they saw. The house could hold fifteen hundred patrons and opened in July 1837. Because the construction and painting was not quite finished, scaffolding was being thrown out of side windows as the audience was entering at the front doors.

Wise enough to perceive the growing sophistication of their audiences, both Caldwell and Ludlow supplanted the rough structures and plain scenery and effects with increasingly finished playhouses and better scenery. In Cincinnati, Caldwell erected a well-built playhouse on the corner of Third Street and Broadway, which measured 137 feet deep by 70 feet wide and contained a large pit and three tiers of boxes to seat about eight hundred patrons.

Both managers hired professional scene painters and machinists for the growing repertory of melodramas, many immigrating from France and Italy to work in the southern theatres. The names of Mondelli, John Rowson Smith, Joseph Cowell Jr., James Forster, and others regularly appeared in advertisments as having prepared "new scenery and effects" as an added lure to the audience.

Only in rare cases is it possible to find biographical information about these artists. One of the most successful scene painters, Russell Smith, left behind a memoir and designs that have been preserved. Born in Scotland in 1812, his parents settled in southwestern Pennsylvania while he was still a boy. Showing artistic talent, he was given instruction as a portrait painter. In 1833, the actor-manager Francis Wemyss appeared in Pittsburgh and hired Smith to paint new scenes for his company. Smith took to the art almost instantly and became a member of Wemyss's company, which traveled through Pennsylvania and West Virginia. In 1835, he followed Wemyss to Philadelphia when the manager leased the Walnut Street Theatre and completely redecorated the auditorium using a patriotic theme, depicting celebrated battles, portraits of presidents, generals, and naval heroes. Wemyss thought it "the most pleasing interior I ever saw" (*Twenty-Six Years,* 235).

Although Smith continued to travel up and down the eastern United States, he kept Philadelphia as his home base for the rest of his career. He was not a designer in the contemporary sense, but his extant drawings and paintings reveal a creative imagination and first-rate painting technique.

As in the East, the scene painters were paid handsome salaries to equal (and sometimes surpass) those paid to the leading actors of the companies. Unfortunately, very few descriptions of what they created have been found. The newspaper reviews were usually complimentary (or excoriating) without being specific. Sol Smith, later Ludlow's partner for eighteen years, described a production of a musical extravaganza, *The Deep, Deep Sea; or, the Great American Sea Serpent* in an 1838 letter:

> It went smoothly, and is done very well – *every dress new* – . . . and the scenery consists of a flat composed of coral wings (which takes six) – three coral wings each side, and two rock wings – the coral drop hoisted up above the flat – so as to match – the Sea Serpent *gets over the flat* and *comes down a rope,* instead of the usual way of having winding stairs – the last scene – Coral Scene of Cinderella, without the waters. (Quoted in Carson, *Theatre on the Frontier,* 240)

The rivalry between Caldwell and the partnership of Noah Ludlow and Sol Smith heated up when both began to schedule tours to the same cities in the southwest. Because each was vying for the same audiences, the laurel went to the company that provided the better theatre, the better company, and the better scenery and effects, all of which tended to make the productions of higher quality than they had been before. In 1835, James Caldwell built in

New Orleans what many considered the finest theatre in *all* America to that date. Having renovated the Camp Street or American Theatre in 1828 with a lavish hand, the manager was ready to give the city another magnificent structure. At a reputed cost of $350,000, the St. Charles Theatre inevitably dominated the theatrical activity of the city. It was described in a 1838 guide to Louisiana:

> This magnificent structure, erected by the unassisted energies of one man [Caldwell], has a frontage of one hundred and thirty-two feet, and a depth of a hundred and seventy-five. Its capacity, and accommodations within, correspond with the magnitude of its exterior. The grand saloon is 129 feet by 26; it has four tiers of boxes, surmounted with enormous galleries: at the back of 47 of its boxes, are convenient *boudoirs,* or retiring rooms. In the center of the dome is suspended a magnificent chandelier – twelve feet in height, thirty-six feet in circumference, weighing 4200 weight and illuminated with 176 gas jets. . . . From the curtain to the back of the boxes is 78 feet; across the boxes, 71 feet. The proscenium is 50 feet, with an opening of 44 feet. From the pit floor to the ceiling, is 54 feet; and from the stage to the roof, 62 feet. The scenery is 44 feet high, and 48 feet wide, with the wings; and from wall to wall, the stage is 96 feet wide, and 78 feet deep, from the Orchestra line. (Quoted in Young, *Playhouses,* I, 137)

On the exterior ten Corinthian columns supported the portico, which ran across the front between the second and third floors. Over this was a balustrade decorated with statues of Apollo and the muses. There was a liberal use of Classic Revival in the interior, Ionic columns supporting the vestibule on the main floor, and Corinthian columns on either side of the proscenium. Behind the huge stage were a large paint shop and greenrooms; below it were twenty-six dressing rooms as well as rooms for props, wardrobe, and scenery. The entire structure as well as its scenery was designed by Antonio Mondelli, Caldwell's longtime scene painter.

Unfortunately, all of this grandeur was consumed by fire, the fate of many of the pioneer theatres in the Southwest, in 1842. It was rebuilt but not on Caldwell's scale.

From 1815 to 1830, theatre was firmly established from western Pennsylvania down to New Orleans and was further aided by the improved transportation both by land and water from east to west. Stars had already invaded the theatres in the cities along the Atlantic coast, and they were soon to make their way south and west. Although the theatres had not yet established permanent companies, it was just a matter of time when the troupes would take up residence in one of the cities where they had formerly toured. Each resident company would have its complement of scene painters, stage machinists, and gas technicians as part of the regular staff, which resulted in the expansion of the profession by leaps and bounds during this period. The major theatre towns in chronological development were Pittsburgh;

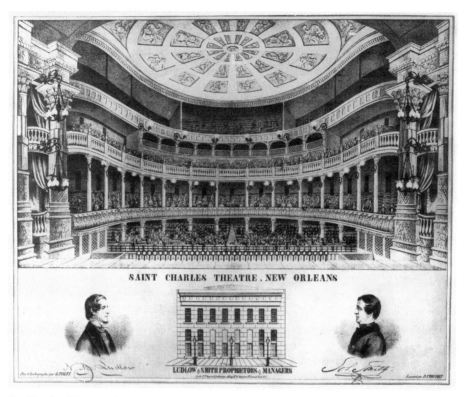

SAINT CHARLES THEATRE, NEW ORLEANS

LUDLOW & SMITH PROPRIETORS & MANAGERS

St. Charles Theatre, New Orleans. Built by James Caldwell in 1835, it was at the time the largest and handsomest theatre in America. It burned in 1842, was replaced by a lesser structure (seen here), and eventually passed to Caldwell's rivals, Ludlow and Smith (pictured at the bottom). Library of Congress, Prints and Photographs Division.

Louisville, Frankfort, and Lexington, Kentucky; Cincinnati; Nashville; New Orleans; Huntsville, Mobile, and Montgomery, Alabama; and St. Louis.

In the northern tier of the western territory, roughly from the Allegheny Mountains to the Great Lakes, theatrical entertainment was slower in arriving. The sparse population, the difficult roads to traverse, the less than hospitable climate – all these factors may have played a role in the delay in theatre's intro-duction, but it was inevitable that troupes would make their way west and north. Albany had an established theatre and Buffalo the beginning of one, when, in 1838, Joseph Jefferson II received a letter from his uncle to join him in the management of a theatre in Chicago, then just a village. Jefferson, a mid-dling actor but a better scene painter, packed up his family and made the trip by land and lake boat to Chicago to open the new theatre that had supplanted the improvised one in the dining room of the Sauganash Hotel. Jefferson's son, Joseph III, recounted the Rialto Theatre in his autobiography:

And now for the new theatre, newly painted canvas, tack-hammer at work on stuffed seats in the dress-circle, planing boards in the pit, new drop-curtain let down for inspection, "beautiful!" – a medallion of Shakspere, suffering from a severe pain in his stomach, over the center, with "One touch of nature makes the whole world kin" written under him, and a large, painted, brick-red drapery looped up by Justice, with sword and scales, showing an arena with a large number of gladiators hacking away at one another in the distance to a delighted Roman public; . . . There were two private boxes with little white-and-gold balustrades and turkey-red curtains, over one box a portrait of Beethoven and over the other a portrait of Handel. . . . The dome was pale blue, with pink-and-white clouds, on which reposed four ungraceful ballet girls. . . . (21–22)

The Rialto, which had formerly been an auction room, was fortunate in being located in the center of the town, on Dearborn Street, between Lake and South Water streets. It was described as looking more like a dismantled gristmill than a playhouse, but it was a real theatre and served the town for several years.

Theatrical troupes opened up the small towns of Ohio, Illinois, Indiana, and Iowa, playing in the usual run of improvised playhouses in hotels, warehouses, courthouses, and even a pork house. When the town and the troupe could afford a theatre, it gave the appearance, according to Jefferson, of a "large dry-goods box with a roof," as he describes:

The building of a theater in those days did not require the amount of capital that it does now. Folding opera-chairs were unknown. Gas was an occult mystery, not yet acknowledged as a fact by the unscientific world in the West; a second-class quality of sperm-oil was the height of any manager's ambition. The footlights of the best theatres in the Western country were composed of lamps set in a "float" with the counter-weights. (26–27)

When the Rialto Theatre closed in 1840, Chicago was without a theatre for seven years. In 1847, the actor-manager John B. Rice arrived from Buffalo, and with the blessings of town and Common Council, built a little theatre on the corner of Dearborn and Randolph streets. It probably did not seat more than two or three hundred patrons, but, according to a newspaper report of the day, the interior was "admirable," with unobstructed views of the stage from all seats, which were arranged on "the plan of the old Coliseum." The boxes were furnished with carpets and settees and were said to be elegant. The scenery for the presentations was all newly painted and was the "joint production of two distinguished artists," who were unfortunately not identified (see Young, *Playhouses*, I, 155–57). The theatre burned to the ground in 1850.

The name most associated with Chicago's theatre is James H. McVicker, whose career had taken him all over the frontier territory, from the New St. Charles in New Orleans as a call boy for Ludlow and Smith to St. Louis as an actor-manager and finally to Chicago as a leading actor in John Rice's com-

McVicker's Theatre, Chicago, built in 1857 by actor-manager James H. McVicker, was considered for many years the best theatre in the West. Rebuilt four times, the final structure was razed in 1922. This lithograph of the first McVicker's (after a drawing by Louis Kurz) was published in James W. Sheahan's *Chicago Illustrated* (October 1866). Don B. Wilmeth Collection.

pany. At this point in its history, McVicker realized that the city offered fertile ground for a permanent theatre, so he bought two lots in its center. Establishing itself rapidly as a hub for the agricultural products of the farm belt, Chicago had leaped from village to the most populous city (eighty-four thousand people) in the West in a very short time. With a developing urban pride, its leading citizens felt the need of a first-class theatre and entrusted it to the management of McVicker. Finally, in 1857, McVicker opened his theatre (bearing his name) on Madison near State Street. It was a commodious clapboard version of an Italianate palazzo with a seating capacity of twenty-five hundred, and built at a cost of $85,000. Although Chicagoans were proud of it, the *Chicago Tribune* (6 Nov. 1857) was restrained in its praise: "The Theatre is neither remarkable for brilliancy of decoration or grandeur of design, but is beyond question exceedingly graceful." The auditorium measured 60 by 97 feet and was painted white and gilt and dressed with crimson and white lace draperies. The stage was 30 by 80 feet with a proscenium height of 33 feet. One of the more interesting aspects of the theatre was the inclusion of stores and offices in the front part of the building, the rent from which would help to support the theatrical activity occurring in the rear part. The theatre had the added distinction of having been designed by an architect, Otis Wheelock.

Until 1871 and the Great Chicago Fire, McVicker's Theatre reigned supreme in the Midwest. It was destroyed and rebuilt four times in its history, but not on the original plan, and survived until 1922.

But for the discovery of gold in upper California in 1848, theatrical entertainment would have inched westward in the wake of waves of enterprising frontiersmen and women, who formed new settlements, established permanent homes, and eventually became ready to receive cultural amenities. For the theatrical pioneers, the pattern of setting up makeshift theatres, of traveling from village and town to the next village and town, and of inevitably building better and more sophisticated structures while widening their offerings to ever-growing audiences – the pattern that had been established over the course of one hundred years – would have been again repeated. Instead, theatrical entertainers leapfrogged half a continent to a land of bustling energy and brimming dollars. Very quickly after the California gold rush came the professional acting companies.

In the fall of 1849, Z. Hubbard built the first playhouse in California, the Eagle Theatre, as an adjunct to a saloon in Sacramento. Costing (by varying estimates) somewhere in the range of $75,000, it was little more than a canvas tent affixed to a rectangular wooden frame, 30 feet wide by 65 feet long, with a tin roof. At one end of the "auditorium," which was bare ground, there was a box-tier or gallery reached by means of an outside stepladder. (The actor Walter Leman wrote in his memoir that canvas was nailed to the underside of the ladder "in deference to ladies" [231].) The pit held approximately three hundred persons and the gallery another hundred. Admission was steep (box: three dollars; pit: two dollars), but because it was the only show in town, the actors had no trouble finding an audience. At least for a few months.

The stage of the Eagle, about 16 feet deep, was made from pieces of packing boxes and the scenery consisted of three drop curtains to represent a wood, a street, and an interior, to cover all eventualities. The act curtain was described by Bayard Taylor as exhibiting "a glaring landscape with dark-brown trees in the foreground, and lilac-colored mountains against a yellow sky" (quoted in Young, *Playhouses* I, 158). There were no dressing rooms for the actors, and entrance to both the stage and the "parquet" was through the saloon. Amenities for the patrons – except for the liquid refreshments from the saloon – were nonexistent. Everyone sat on benches. Unfortunately for the Eagle, it was located on a flood plain and was inundated by the January flood of 1850. The actors decamped for higher ground and fled to San Francisco, and the Eagle was no more. It was followed, however, by several other theatres during the next ten years. In 1855, an "elegant brick" theatre, the Forrest, was built in Sacramento and endured until 1859.

During the boom years of the 1850s, theatrical activity in California was centered south of Sacramento in San Francisco and advanced rapidly through the forceful efforts of one man, Thomas Maguire, toughened on the streets of New York City. Although makeshift theatres had sprung up in San Francisco to accommodate the entertainment-starved populace after the Gold Rush, it was Maguire who built bigger and better theatres to capitalize on both the appetite for amusements and the deep pockets of his patrons. His first theatre, named the Jenny Lind in honor of the famous soprano (who, incidentally, never ventured to California), was part of his Parker House Saloon on Kearny Street. Seating about eight hundred persons, it was described in the *Alta California* (27 Oct. 1850) as having a "neat and pretty stage" and an auditorium fitted with "commodious settees." The walls and ceilings were decorated with painted frescoes, and the entire theatre was pronounced handsome. It opened in the fall of 1850 and burned to the ground in the spring of 1851, but from its ashes sprang a newer, larger, and more elegant Jenny Lind. Advertised as being fireproof, the second theatre was 150 feet deep and built of brick with a stage depth of 75 feet. Refuting its advertisements, the second Jenny Lind, with a capacity of three thousand, was also destroyed by fire shortly after it opened.

Undaunted by his ill fortune, Maguire built the third Jenny Lind and ushered in a new period in the dramatic activity in San Francisco. Set in a ramshackle neighborhood, Maguire's large theatre with its white Australian sandstone facade seemed out of place with its surroundings. With a frontage of 75 feet, a height of 60 feet, and a depth of 140 feet, it could seat approximately two thousand and cost $150,000 to build. Seven arched doors marked the entrances, and seven more in the interior lobby led to the seats. There were seven windows reaching from floor to ceiling in the second and third stories, seven smaller windows in the upper story, and a cupola atop the building, which encased a ventillating system to allow the rising warm air from the auditorium to pass through an opening. The auditorium was decorated in understated light pink touched by gold paint and was divided into a parterre, orchestra stalls, a dress circle, a balcony, three galleries, and a few boxes behind the balcony, which was an unusual arrangement for a theatre of this time. It opened in the fall of 1851, was purchased by the city of San Francisco for $200,000 in the summer of 1852, and was promptly gutted and converted to use as a city hall.

The most reasonable explanation for the quick demise of the Jenny Lind III was in the building of the American Theatre just weeks after Maguire opened the doors of his own theatre. The American (also seating around two thousand) surpassed the Jenny Lind in comfort and in the quality of the productions. A French journalist passing through San Francisco wrote:

> I always preferred the American, which is extremely agreeable. It has two balconies and a gallery, a dress-circle, orchestra seats, and several stage boxes.

> There is a great deal of typical English or American comfort. The carpets are thick and soft, and deaden your footsteps. . . . The house is nicely decorated with paintings and gilt-work. The boxes have red velvet curtains and the seats are upholstered in red plush. (Quoted in Young, *Documents*, I, 168)

A bright revolving sun ornamented the ceiling, and two spread eagles on either side of the proscenium held chandeliers suspended from their beaks. The fact that the scenery for the mix of Shakespeare and melodramas in the company's repertory had been freshly painted on a huge paint frame backstage meant that itinerant professional scene painters had found their way to San Francisco to ply their trade profitably. By 1853, San Francisco had four other theatres in addition to the American. Fire, always the plague of the city, meant that most of the theatres had short lives because of it.

Not to be outdone by his rivals, Maguire sprang back with another theatre, Maguire's Opera House, which he opened in the fall of 1856. He razed the San Francisco Hall on Washington Street, which he had been operating in the interim, in order to build his new playhouse. Eventually enlarged to seat seventeen hundred, his theatre was 55 feet wide by 137 feet long and 50 feet high. On each side of the proscenium were two large boxes, one above the other, ornamented with gilded mouldings and crimson and gold draperies. The orchestra floor, reached by descending stairs from the lobby, was unbroken by columns except to support the dress circle tier, which curved around the interior. Each row of seats in the dress circle, reached by an ascending staircase from the lobby, rose gradually from front to back to give the audience an uninterruped view of the stage. Brightly colored cushions broke up the white and gold interior. The entire house was lit by gas, including the chandelier (imported from New York), which was suspended from the dome. A grandiose scene of Venice was depicted on the large act curtain.

One interesting statistic was the depth of the stage – only 35 feet – of Maguire's Opera House. Although Maguire was booking minstrel companies into the theatre, which would not have required a deep stage, he was also providing dramatic entertainment. Throughout most of the nineteenth century to that date, the production of melodramas, domestic tragedies, and Shakespearean plays necessitated scenic spectacle and a deep stage to encompass both a prominent forestage and upstage space for the scenery. The shallowness of Maguire's stage bespeaks, perhaps, a change in the kind of scenery that was coming into use. Both of Maguire's scene painters, John W. Fairchild and Charles Rogers, had previously worked in the East.

Although San Francisco's theatre dominated upper California, dramatic entertainment continued to flow into the mining towns. In the space of one decade, theatres had proliferated more rapidly in California than in any other area of the country. San Francisco, with one-sixth the population of Philadelphia, had almost as many theatres by the end of the fifties.

Even though religious opponents of the "Devil's playroom" had not been completely stilled (and would never totally disappear from the American scene), playhouses continued to be built from the east coast to the western frontier during the first half of the nineteenth century. Never had a religious group in America not only espoused theatrical entertainment as beneficial to the morality of the community but built a temple to the Muses of Drama almost alongside their Temple to God. So it was in the Mormon community in Salt Lake City. Brigham Young, the spiritual leader of the sect, dispatched one of his associates to an auction conducted by the departing United States Army troops to buy up any and all building supplies they were leaving behind so that a theatre could be erected. For 10 percent of original costs, his representative came back with nails, glass, and assorted building materials, and the work was commenced in the summer of 1861. Using adobe bricks made locally, the architect William H. Folsom designed and supervised the erection of the Salt Lake City Theatre.

Only partially completed when it opened the following March, the theatre was closed for several months to finish the interior before reopening on Christmas night 1862. Built on the corner of the State Road and First South Street, in the heart of the city, the playhouse measured 140 feet long by 80 feet wide by 40 feet high. It had a hipped roof with a promenade on top that measured 40 by 90 feet. Two Doric columns supported the main entrance in a facade that was vaguely Greek Revival in feeling. Inside were a parquette and four circles (no balcony and no gallery) and proscenium boxes: two parquette boxes surmounted by two others on each side. Two columns flanked the proscenium, and a dome covered the auditorum. (Because the dome caused acoustical problems, a ceiling was later built over the auditorium.) The stage opening was 31 feet wide by 28 feet high with a depth of 62 feet. Before the arrival of gas and incandescent lighting, illumination was supplied by coal oil lamps and candles. The building also contained ample dressing rooms for the performers and a large, comfortable greenroom as well as studios for the scene painters, prop makers, and costumers.

E. L. T. Harrison, a London architect, was engaged to design the interior and used metal filigree in the front boxes and white, pale green, and gold paint throughout the rest of the auditorium to set off the elaborately decorated ceilings and the scarlet plush of the seats. The scene painter George Martin Ottinger arrived to paint the scenery and was assisted by Henry Maiben, the Welsh-born London designer; William Morris; and Alfred Lambourne for a number of years. Painting drops and wings, staples of the nineteenth-century playhouse and repertory, were their domain.

The theatre endured until 1928, when it was no longer the most imposing building in the city. Throughout its long history, its stage was occupied by the most famous stars of the late nineteenth century.

Theatre Buildings and Stagecraft to 1870

In 1868, in the epilogue to his reminiscences, *Theatrical Management in the West and South,* actor-manager Sol Smith noted that the "number of buildings for dramatic purposes had increased at an astonishing rate," but lamented that they were no longer "theatres." "Where *are* the theatres?" he asked. "They seem to have nearly all vanished, and in their places we have 'Academies of Music,' 'Olympics,' 'Varieties,' 'Gaieties,' 'Atheneums,' and 'Opera Houses'" (237–38). Smith had correctly assessed his theatrical age. By 1870, a profound change both in social custom and in the theatrical practice had occurred in the approximately fifty-year period following the conclusion of the War of 1812. The war had momentarily inhibited the spread of theatrical entertainment and had temporaily suspended the spate of theatre building that had begun at the beginning of the new century. The Civil War had many of the same effects in the 1860s, but in those intervening decades, theatres and their attractions had proliferated beyond anyone's prediction.

The social climate had changed significantly. The theatre, inherently an urban institution – and in America, a democratic one – serves the greater population that inhabits cities and towns, and it was precisely this broadening population for whom managers had to gear their attractions. Justly or unjustly, Stephen Price, manager of the Park Theatre in New York in its peak years in the 1820s and 1830s, was accused of ushering in the age of the star to the ruination, some thought, of the tightly knit "company of twelve," comprised of an acting troupe that could assay all roles. Other managers bewailed the lowering of taste of the expanded audiences. Their thirst for melodramas, domestic dramas, sentimental comedies, spectacles, and bowdlerized Shakespeare appeared unquenchable, and the managers gave them a steady diet, adding novelties to the theatrical menu.

The names given to playhouses (to the consternation of Sol Smith) was another indication both of their new respectability and an advertisement of their wares. An "academy of music" or "opera house" or "museum" lent cachet to an institution that had to hide in previous generations on the city's outskirts but that now was accepted – indeed, vaunted – by the population as one of the most important buildings in the city's center. The change in location also brought a change in size. Theatres kept getting larger throughout the period. No longer "designed" by the managers on familiar plans and hastily put together by local carpenters and masons, they were works by recognized architects, who supervised the construction, and were built by contractors, who employed specialty artisans, frequently imported from Europe, for increasingly sophisticated structures. One thing did not change: Managers relied on well-to-do interested citizens, in most of the important theatre cities and towns, to provide the money through subscription to build their magnificent edifices. They were rewarded, in most cases, with access to boxes in the first tier of the auditorium, where, dressed in handsome evening clothes, they could be seen as well as see.

Stagecraft during this period was affected by the change in illumination (gaslight) and the alteration in the size and shape of the stage. Gaslight, being brighter, caused scene painters to reduce their broad strokes to fine brush stokes and trompe l'oeil painting became much more precise. Once the men who controlled the gas table learned how to adjust the feeding of gas to the jets, they discovered an ability to dim or brighten illumination by tightening or loosening valves. Eventually, it became possible to dim (but not darken) the auditorium significantly, which affected not only acting styles but audience behavior. Gas lamps could be covered by colored glass mantles to alter moods for individual scenes. Special effects were made more plausible with gas light: Rising and setting suns and moonlight could be achieved more easily and with greater realism. Further, the introduction of the limelight during this period allowed actors to be picked out onstage by a halo of bright, white light. The intense light was achieved by heating a cylinder of lime to incandescence within a metal box fitted with a lens. The light it emitted could be directed to the stage from a perch above the audience's head. The limelight was forever the province of a skilled technician with a steady hand and eye, and it persisted into the age of electricity.

The plays of the populist nineteenth century, particularly the domestic dramas, demanded a different kind of production. The melodramas of the late eighteenth and early nineteenth centuries took place mostly outdoors on heaths or within gardens, in front of palaces, on battlefields, on mountaintops, and so forth, with occasional anonymous interior scenes in great halls or throne rooms, but the later plays focused more on familial conflicts and took place in kitchens or specific areas of the characters' living quarters. As the actors moved closer to the proscenium to play intimate scenes within intimate spaces, so did the large stage aprons. Proscenium boxes and doors were either entirely omitted in the newer playhouses or, when they did survive, not used as extensively as they had been in a previous era. Toward the end of this era, the apron eventually became vestigial, as the action continued to move behind the proscenium and the actors played within, not in front of, the scenery, as the scripts demanded.

More and more, theatrical activity was centered in New York City. By 1825, it was not only the most populous city in America, it was also the leading mercantile and financial matrix for the entire nation. With the opening of the Erie Canal in 1825, the city could export its goods by ship to the burgeoning West while carrying on trade with Europe from its bustling port. With its population topping one hundred and sixty-six thousand and a rising middle class, the city could afford cultural amenities – and more than one theatre. It did not take long for the Park Theatre, which had enjoyed a hegemony over theatrical activity from the turn of the century, to receive strong competition. In October 1826, wealthy patrons of theatrical art welcomed the New York Theatre (soon to be rechristened the Bowery) on the Bowery, a main thoroughfare that led to the Boston Post Road and New England. Many of its well-to-do subscribers, including the Astor family, lived within walking distance of the theatre, when the Lower East Side of New York was still a respectable neighborhood.

The subscribers engaged the Connecticut-born architect Ithiel Town, then the most prominent designer of buildings in the northeast, to plan the theatre. Although he had been trained as a carpenter, he quickly advanced to architectural assistant, and when he was proficient in the study and practice of architecture, he opened his own office. He was an advocate of classic design, preferring the Greek Revival style, and received commissions for many important buildings in New York and the Northeast. The new theatre was the largest in America, with a seating capacity of close to three thousand. The facade consisted of tall columns and pilasters with the "similitude of white marble" supporting an entablature and pediment and flanking the entrance doors, which were reached by a set of steps through a spacious portico. The interior was described as elegant, but no detailed descriptions of the original theatre have survived. That it was divided into pit, tiers of boxes, and gallery is borne out by the price structure of the seats. The scenery department was headed by Boudet and Ferry, who were considered among the finest painters in America. Gas lines had been installed during construction, and even the footlights were fed by gas. In 1831, after attending the Bowery Theatre, Mrs. Frances Trollope wrote that she considered its scenery and machinery "equal to any in London" (*Domestic Manners of Americans,* quoted in Henderson, *City and the Theatre,* 339).

Unfortunately, the theatre was destined to be plagued by a series of unhappy events, the first of which was the steady deterioration of the neighborhood in which it was built. Within a few years, the gentry moved away, and the surrounding streets were filled with new immigrants, most of them too poor to attend the theatre at its regular prices. (The succession of managers lowered the prices and changed the forms of entertainment to appeal to its new audiences.) The playhouse itself burned to the ground in 1828 and was rebuilt quickly with an enlarged auditorium and a more ornate front of lofty Corinthian columns designed by John Trimble. (The theatre underwent further alterations and enlargements when it burned again in 1830, 1836, 1838, and 1845. It miraculously endured until 1929 as the Thalia Theatre, when, reduced to ashes, its life ended permanently.)

There is a story that the size of the stage and auditorium of the Bowery tested the lungs of the actors, some of whom had to shout in order to be heard in its farthest reaches. The "Bowery rant" described the acting style that was necessary for the blood-and-thunder melodramas that were its specialty, but it was said to have exacted its toll on many actors' voices.

A number of other theatres, some short-lived or consumed by fire, arose to challenge the Park and the Bowery in New York. Some grew out of pleasure gardens as temporary structures made permanent. By 1836, New York could boast five theatres, which were far more than the city's population could support, but the building of playhouses continued unabated. In the 1840s, P. T. Barnum added a lecture room to his American Museum on Ann Street and Broadway, which he enlarged in 1850 to create an auditorium seating three thousand. Another playhouse, the Broadway Theatre, which stood on Broadway between Pearl and Worth Streets, was designed by John Trimble, who used London's Haymarket Theatre as a model but enlarging it to a capacity of forty-five hundred seats, the largest in America to 1847.

John Trimble was again called into service to design the new theatre intended for the much admired Wallack family of actors. Wallack's Theatre, at the corner of Broadway and Thirteenth Street, was built at the rear "of a peculiar-looking new building late erected on Broadway by Mr. Gibson."[4] (Because either Greek or Roman Revival had dominated urban architecture for almost a half-century, whatever was *not* in the neoclassical mode might very well have appeared "peculiar-looking.") The architecture for the building that enclosed Wallack's Theatre owed much to French and Italianate influences in its mansard roof and arched windows. The auditorium was 95 feet deep by 72 feet wide with a stage measuring 50 feet deep and 72 feet wide behind the curtain. A contemporary reporter recorded the plans for the interior:

> The seats will be much more comfortable than in most theaters, plenty of room being left between them, and deep sofas being provided, instead of the narrow benches now offered to the suffering public. The upholstery will be plain, but rich, and all the decorations of the theater will be modest and tasteful, the gaudy steamboat style being entirely eschewed.

He went on to describe the stage:

> Those pieces of stage machinery technically designated *grooves* and *wings,* will be arranged on a new plan, which will admit of the setting of scenery without the obtrusion on the eye of the unsightly skeleton framework that supports the beautiful canvas landscapes, lakes, and parlor. Every modern device for perfecting the scenic illusion and concealing the machinist's art will be adopted.

Precisely what was meant by "modern device" to change the scenery is difficult to assess, but it certainly represented an attempt to achieve greater verisimilitude.

The theatre that incorporated all of the architectural advances made in the first half of the nineteenth century and the technical improvements in stage-craft that were evolving at the same time was Booth's Theatre, which opened in early February 1869. At an unprecedented cost of $1,500,000, it was considered the finest theatre ever built in the United States and rivaled some of the great playhouses of Europe. Designed by James Renwick Jr., of the prestigious architectural firm of Renwick and Sands, in French Second Empire style, the playhouse measured 70 feet from the ground to the cornice under the mansard roof and 149 feet in length along West Twenty-third Street off Sixth Avenue. Iron joists and balloon wood framing comprised the inner structure and granite covered the facade. There were seven entrances on the Twenty-third Street side and one on Sixth Avenue. The theatre had a seating capacity of nearly eighteen hundred with standing room for another three hundred patrons.

The interior lobbies, all thickly carpeted, led to the orchestra floor (formerly known as the pit, parterre, or parquet[te]) and three curved, gently receding galleries in a horseshoe configuration. Six boxes were pushed outside the proscenium, three on either side, and the large forestage typical of early nineteenth-century theatres was reduced to a sliver. The pit for musicians was depressed partially under the stage and presented no obstruction for those seated in the orchestra.

The theatre was heated by forced-air furnaces in the winter and cooled in the summer by means of a fan blowing cooled air throughout the theatre. The interior was a marvel of plush, gilt, iron filigree, and painted plaster. Lit by gas, a special electrical device sparked the illuminant so that all of the auditorium lights could be ignited simultaneously. There was even an early version of a sprinkler system installed in the house to allay the ever-present threat of fire.

In a five-story wing attached to the theatre were studios for the scenic, machine, and costume departments as well as Booth's private flat on the top floor. On the ground floor, shops were leased to provide income for the maintenance of the theatre.

The scenic department was headed by Charles Witham, who became one of the renowned scenic artists of his time. Born in Portland, Maine, Witham apprenticed under Gaspard Maeder, who later became the principal designer at Niblo's Garden in New York. In 1863, Witham was hired by the Boston Theatre, where Edwin Booth was so impressed with his work that he snatched him away to become the chief designer at the Winter Garden in New York, then at his own theatre in 1869. Witham was responsible for all of the scenic improvements incorporated in the new playhouse, some of which eventually proved impossible to operate. He began by eliminating the raked stage and forestage, raising the stage house to a height of 76 feet so that whole scenes could be flown into the fly loft. Eschewing the old wing-and-groove system, he had the mechanics brace the flats to the flat stage floor in whatever configuration was necessary for the scenes. He was clearly influenced by the emerging

Booth's Theatre. In this watercolor by the theatre's scenic designer, Charles W. Witham, the interior is pictured with the set for the first act of *Romeo and Juliet,* the theatre's inaugural production on 3 February 1869. Museum of the City of New York.

"box set," which created three walls of a room by means of a series of flats lashed together, since he used it in several productions for Booth. He installed an elaborate hydraulic system to move platforms vertically, which presaged Steele MacKaye's use of the elevated stage, and to raise and lower trapdoors in the stage floor. Although most of these improvements in stagecraft had already been made, Witham was the first to include them all in one theatre.

Because of his fine scene painting technique and inventiveness, Witham was in great demand after he left Booth in 1873, working for Augustin Daly until 1880, then for Edward Harrigan until 1890. He continued as a scene painter until 1909. Because Witham reconstructed many of the scenes that he had designed for Booth and Harrigan in his later years (which have been preserved), they constitute important historical documentation of scenic design. Whether they are typical of the work of his contemporaries cannot be ascertained without examples of their work with which to compare them. But they reflect a growing attention to detail, particularly authentic historical detail, and an expanded use of color, a result of continuing improvements in lighting. Freed from the old wing-and-groove system, his extant designs reveal a strong architectural quality as well as continuing attempts to achieve greater realistic illusion.

Because of overspending on his theatre and his productions, Edwin Booth was forced to relinquish control of his theatre to other managements after just four years. Following the course of contemporaneous theatres, Booth's passed into history in 1883, only fourteen years after it opened its doors. With the exception of the Walnut Street Theatre built in 1809 in Philadelphia, the theatres built between 1800 and 1870 were either destroyed by fire (often to arise again in the same place and burn again) or abandoned when they became declassé or outmoded, or were converted to other uses. (The Walnut Street Theatre continues in use today but in a much altered, rebuilt version.) Unlike the Park Theatre in New York, which enjoyed a fifty-year lifespan, most theatres could have a longevity as short as a few months and as long as thirty years.

Throughout the period, entrepreneurs continued to carve theatres out of other large buildings (banks, churches, hotels), and one or two of the most resourceful hit upon the idea to mount a playhouse on a river boat, thus launching both literally and figuratively, the era of the showboat. From simple shacks built atop a floating flatboat, they evolved into steamboats plying the rivers (from the Hudson to the Mississippi) with proper theatres and well-equipped stages modified to fit into the confines of what ordinarily would have been the grand saloon. The early boats, which could seat perhaps two hundred patrons, were superceded by grandiose floating palaces with a capacity of more than one thousand. With the outbreak of the Civil War, showboating was suspended, but it was revived with renewed vigor in the postwar years.

Conclusion

From the moment that theatrical activity took root in America, there was a slow, steady development from immigrant art to native art, which necessarily embraced the structures that housed the entertainments and the manner in which they were presented to the public. The earliest playhouses were pragmatic structures built on plans that the managers carried in their minds from England, always adapted to local circumstances, local materials, and local labor. In the early years of the republic, architects were commissioned to build more elaborate and deliberately planned theatres, some with elegant interiors and commodious stages, to serve not merely for the entertainment and the entertained but to stand for the aspirations of the community. The theatre was fast becoming a special edifice that could speak to the level of culture and the sophistication of the citizens, who were more frequently than not asked to underwrite the costs of construction in their towns and cities. Theatres proliferated as the population moved westward to establish more American cities, frequently springing up in the unlikeliest of places that were blessed, sometimes for the briefest of periods, with sudden wealth and prosperity, as in the mining towns of California, Nevada, and (later) Colorado. The day was arriving that would see at least one playhouse in almost every town and city in America.

Colonial audiences were extraordinarily tolerant of the way in which the plays were presented, accepting the bare essentials of scenery without question. If the play was, however, the thing that drew them to the often unheated, under-illumined, wooden boxes that were the theatres of the time, that was to change, too. The popularity of melodrama and theatrical novelties brought about an escalation in stagecraft in the early decades of the nineteenth century. The "painted stage" of wings, shutters, and drops that had been the hallmark of eighteenth-century theatre both here and abroad was supplanted by a more illusionistic display, still painted, but now augmented with necessary props and furniture, and moving scenery. The box set, consisting of three walls of flats to form a room enclosure, was used as early as 1862 by the Boston Museum stock company, and was destined to supplant the centuries-old wing-and-drop in the closing decades of the nineteenth century. As lighting improved from candlepower to gaslight, painting techniques also improved. It is interesting to note that many scene painters of this era worked for Henry and William Hanington, who specialized in producing realistic panoramas and moving dioramas, which were the rage during the first half of the nineteenth century. As the wing-and-groove and border system was gradually giving way to more flexible staging to suit the increasingly more realistic plays of the period, the era of the box set was at hand, which was to pull the action behind the proscenium and reduce the forestage to an apron. Like the playhouse itself, stagecraft was on the verge of serious change. In the next era, both would continue to evolve to serve the dramatic event.

Notes

1 For the purposes of this chapter, only English-language theatre will be examined. Although dramatic activity in French and Spanish settlements has been documented, as noted elsewhere in this history, it made no lasting impact on the development of American theatres.
2 Editors' note: Recent research by Peter Davis – as yet unpublished – indicates that the Hallams arrived about four weeks earlier than previously believed on a brig called *The Sally* (not *The Charming Sally*). A small intercoastal sloop called *The Charming Sally* did operate between Bermuda and South Carolina for several years in the late 1750s, but it never landed in Virginia.
3 This surname has been variously spelled Doll or Dall in American accounts.
4 This and subsequent descriptions of Wallack's are from unidentified and undated clippings in the Wallack's Theatre file, New York Public Library of the Performing Arts, Theatre Collection.

Bibliography: Scenography, Stagecraft, and Architecture

Two general bibliographic sources for the subject are Stoddard's *Stage Scenery, Machinery, and Lighting* and *Theatre and Cinema Architecture,* both somewhat dated but nonetheless with numerous sources listed on American theatre. For English backgrounds, see *The London Stage 1747–1776, A Critical Introduction* by George Winchester Stone Jr. and *Box, Pit, and Gallery,* by Thomas J. Lynch. Although it is incomplete for scene painters, the New-York Historical Society's *Dictionary of Artists in America, 1564–1860* by Groce and Wallace is still valuable as a checklist for names. Approximately ninety artists are identified as having worked in theatres throughout the country. Useful background sources are Rifkind, *A Field Guide to American Architecture* and Burchard and Bush-Brown, *The Architecture of America.*

Primary sources for the colonial period include Dunlap's *History of the American Theatre* (1832) and his *Diary* (1766–1839); secondary sources, all of which quote primary source documents from contemporaneous newspapers and records, are Seilhamer's *History of the American Theatre;* Rankin's *The Theatre in Colonial America;* McNamara's *The American Playhouse in the Eighteenth Century;* Odell's *Annals of the New York Stage,* Vol. I; Young's *Documents of the American Theatre,* Vol. I; Pollock's *The Philadelphia Theatre in the Eighteenth Century;* Glazer's *Philadelphia Theaters: A Pictorial and Architectural History;* and Willis's *The Charleston Stage in the XVIII Century.* Some feeling for an early colonial theatre can be gleaned from the extant Georgian Theatre, Richmond, Yorkshire, England, described in Rosenfeld's *The Georgian Theatre of Richmond Yorkshire* and Leacroft's *The Development of the English Playhouse.*

For the early republic era, see Odell's *Annals,* Vols. II–III; Seilhamer's *History;* Dunlap's *History* and *Diary;* Young's *Documents;* also Grimsted's *Melodrama Unveiled: American Theater and Culture 1800–1850;* James's *Cradle of Culture: The Philadelphia Stage 1800–1810; The Memoir of John Durang, American Actor, 1787–1816,* edited by

Downer; Clapp's *A Record of the Boston Stage;* Henderson's *The City and the Theatre* and her chapters on design and architecture in *Theater in America.* Also useful are "Charles Ciceri and the Background of American Scene Design" by Duerr and "Notes on John Joseph Holland, With a Design for the Baltimore Theatre, 1802" by Stoddard.

For frontier theatres and stagecraft, the best primary sources are still Ludlow's *Dramatic Life as I Found It* (1880); Sol Smith's *Theatrical Management in the West and South for Thirty Years* (1868); Cowell's *Thirty Years Passed Among the Players* (1844); *The Autobiography of Joseph Jefferson* (1890); and Lambourne's *A Play-House.* Other secondary histories include *The Theatre in Early Kentucky 1790–1820* by Hill; *The San Francisco Stage* by Gagey; *The Theatre of the Golden Era in California* by MacMinn; *The Theatre on the Frontier* by Carson; *History of the Theatre in Salt Lake City* by Henderson; *A History of the English Theatre in New Orleans* by Smither; and *Showboats* by Graham.

For New York theatre buildings and stagecraft to 1870, see *The City and the Theatre;* Odell's *Annals,* Vol. III; Ireland's *Records of the New York Stage;* and *A History of the New York Stage* by Brown. Other primary and secondary sources include Cowell's *Thirty Years; Personal Recollections of the Stage* by Wood; Jefferson's *Autobiography; America Takes the Stage* by Moody; and chapters on theatre architecture and scenography in *The American Theatre: A Sum of Its Parts,* edited by Williams.

6

Paratheatricals and Popular Stage Entertainment

Peter G. Buckley

Introduction

The actress Olive Logan, reviewing the state of American theatre in 1866, found much about which to complain. The New York stage, once the home to Kean's Shakespeare, was now filled with blood-and-thunder melodramas, appealing only to "Bowery B'hoys," and with fantastic, fairy amazonia, drawing rows of "Bald Heads." Since managers were only interested in cash rather than "the drama," few standards remained. Everything, Logan claimed, "from educated dogs, performing fleas to the sermons of Henry Ward Beecher now comprises the show business." As the rest of her essay made clear, Logan was only trying to make a salutary, pointed joke. As an aspiring author for the legitimate stage, she thought it possible that firm boundaries between frivolous, minor amusement and edifying drama might be reestablished. Yet, in giving us such an encompassing definition of the show business, even in irony, she exposed an important truth about the development of commercial amusements in America that would have been unthinkable only thirty years before. No matter how ludicrous the juxtaposition of secular fleas and the priestly Beecher, their respective performances were now fueled by the same energies of profit, fame, and celebrity. All forms of performance achieved their value on the same level ground of commercial return.

Logan's remarks allow us to take a conveniently broad definition of what constitutes popular entertainment and paratheatricality. Over the last thirty years or so, scholars have expanded the definition of the "theatre" to include many nonlegitimate forms such as tent shows, the circus, children's theatre, and ethnic acts, and the term "paratheatricality" suggests something even more far-ranging. Rather than limiting its purview to commercial forms and to those theatrical forms with a known relation between performers and a seated audience, paratheatricality borders on signaling an anthropological interest in the enactment of social roles in public and even gestures toward

Ladies of the ballet preparing "to fly" in *The Black Crook* (1866), considered by many the precursor of American musical comedy and burlesque. Billy Rose Theatre Collection, The New York Public Library for the Performing Arts. Astor, Lenox, and Tilden Foundations.

the work of Irving Goffman with his observations about the theatricality of everyday life.

So boundless is the potential subject area that this essay has to be self-limiting. Here I wish to extend "theatre" to include forms of ritual drama and public display, but only those that shed some ambient light upon the general context of theatrical amusements. It is necessary to cast the net fairly wide for two reasons. First, it is useful to counter the idea that early American culture was sadly deficient in ritual and theatrical forms of expression. Almost every foreign visitor to America's shore until the 1830s remarked upon the paucity of amusement life in general and Americans' overwhelming absorption in the productivist ethos. Contemporary historians of colonial and early national society have continued this gloomy assessment of the settlers' capacity for celebration and unproductive leisure. David Freeman Hawke states that the early American festival calendar was "the dullest in Western Civilization" (*Early Life,* 23), and Richard L. Bushman offers the following rhetorical lament: "Where were the Morris dancers, the wassailing, the annual wakes, the crafts holidays, maypoles" (351)?

Largely absent is the inevitable reply. The sparse settlement, the vast distances, and the absence of an historically dense web of institutional life limited severely the old practices of folk customs, games, and fairs that formed the ground for popular theatricality and ritual inversions in Europe. "One hardly sees any villages," observed Alexis de Tocqueville as late as 1830, "the cultivators' homes are scattered in the midst of woods" (*Journey,* 226). Of all kinds of cultural production the theatre and its ancillary arts were the least developed and the most scorned. In the third quarter of the eighteenth century, small English theatrical troupes eked out a living in the southern colonies and in New York, but elsewhere theatrical performers faced a welter of petitions banning their presence. Sundry itinerant entertainers appeared in American towns, yet the records, compared to European evidence, do not indicate much depth. Rope dancers show up in Philadelphia in 1724, a slack-wire and tight-rope performer appears in New York in 1753, tumblers and dancers in Boston in 1792; and though there is something no doubt heroic in the way that David Douglass's reorganized Hallam company managed to sustain their troupe after 1758, their productions illustrate the conservative features of a provincial culture in maintaining forms long out of fashion at the metropolitan core. This subordination, at the legitimate level, of the American theatre to European cities continued throughout the first half of the nineteenth century as well. Most of the new enthusiasms and genres were established abroad, and star European performers had the habit of treating the United States, Havana, and Jamaica as a terrain to be mined by using the capital of a reputation made in the courts and theatres of Europe. Foreign celebrities made little attempt to address the autochthonous interests of the various regions of the Americas, and, if they accommodated local taste and political sentiment at all, this meant little more than the inclusion of the ubiquitous "Yankee Doodle" somewhere within the program.

If one looks at the streets, the markets, plantation yards, religious campgrounds, summer gardens, and museums, however, a different, and I would argue more vital, theatrical tradition comes into view. America gained its cultural identity on the terrain of the popular and the vernacular. It elevated minor forms into major commercial successes. The tremendously popular novels of James Fenimore Cooper (the only American to make a living by pen alone) established one particular identity for the United States among the European reading public, yet many more people on the other side of the Atlantic must have encountered America as a cultural artifact through the

travels of P. T. Barnum, the dancing of T. D. Rice, or the singing (
son family. As other colonial cultures have done, and conti
United States cultivated the "homespun" as a way of correc
imbalance in luxury items.

A second reason to cast a wide net over a sea of paratheatrical sources runs somewhat counter to the commercial emphasis of the first. The story of the development of a distinct American show business has never been just determined by markets or by the ability of capitalism, to paraphrase Marcuse, to interpose a product between the itch and the scratch. As Logan indicates, issues of value, other than monetary, always emerge. American colonial culture began with protestations against any form of acting. By 1870, the United States was saturated with forms of political performance and acts of religious testimony and was in love with commercial entertainments. How the culture worked through and with this transformation is not a matter of a lineal growth of a market but rather of a series of transgressions and containments, the constant redrawing of the boundaries between the legitimate and illegitimate, high and low, travesty and affirmation. Perhaps because American popular entertainment, in contrast to Europe, developed with so little state or municipal interference, "culture wars" fought in the press or from the pulpit have been endemic and remain hotly politicized issues today.

First, however, one might be cautious about the use of the term "American," for it is difficult to identify a distinctively Americanized culture until the first quarter of the nineteenth century. English North America formed a thin spine of settlement east of the Alleghenies until 1800. The Dutch in New York successfully maintained much community ritual, the practice of keeping a "continental" Sunday, replete with drinking, card playing, and dancing. The French in the Mississippi Valley and the Spanish during their reign over Louisiana also kept to older agricultural patterns in which settlers consented to work the common fields and where royal land grants made for a more seignorial order, along with those "entertainments" with which social superiors were supposed to treat the common folk. European theatre in the New World began, one might note, with demonstrations of power and inequality. The Spanish devised "comedies" as part of their celebrations of conquest such as the one conducted by Don Juan de Oñate in 1598 after reaching the Rio Grande, and the French worked up masques for similar purposes in New France. In 1606, *Les Muses de la Nouvelle-France,* a two-hundred-and-forty-two-line effort written by the explorer Marc Lescarbot, featured Neptune dispensing his blessing upon the new dominion and four Indians (played by the colonists) bearing tribute. Though both instances might claim the designation of early American drama, they are best seen within a different tradition, as entremets within ritual feasts. The settlers clothed themselves in the regalias of power and enacted imaginatively the deference due them by the conquered.

This maintenance of aristocratic, kingly, and military ritual, to which much European theatre was tied, was exactly what most of the early British colonial leaders found distasteful. In the Northeast, Puritans abhorred the theatre not just because of its age-old connections with lewdness and drunkenness but because it was part of a whole range of cultural forms – masques, court ritual, peasant revelry, and processions – that bore the stamp of pagan, pre-Christian belief and practice. For strict Congregationalists there was only one power authorized to make representations in a redeemed world – the Word of God – and only one stage for its exercise, the pulpit. All other places and modes were essentially secular and emptied of religious significance; these included marriage ceremonies and funerals, and even the interior of church buildings. Or conversely, it is possible to claim that Puritans saw all days as equally holy, and all places as equally theatrical – the *theatrum mundi* – for which the script was set by God's predestinations. Whichever way they perceived the ritual landscape, the effect was to disperse entirely the older calendrical organization of festivities and to eradicate most forms of the carnivalesque.

Colonial Rituals and Civic Entertainment

The colonists retained, however, a rhythmic pattern of fast and thanksgiving that expressed the theological cycle of sin and repentance. Fast and "humiliation" days in New England were marked not only by the absence of food but also by the presence of public prayer, confession (in courts and churches, or even open ground), and public execution. As David Hall has pointed out, the erection of scaffolds, the naming of witches, and the renewal of covenants were all rituals of reversal to make the sick healthy and the hidden visible. Public confessions were fully "staged" to the extent that penitents might wear rags, kneel before those they had wronged, and offer an emotional recounting of their sins. If the public did not witness the expiation of sins, it was certain, of course, that God would know about them, and Puritans turned to a remarkable number of folk beliefs – bleeding bodies, disturbed animals, monster births, storms, and so forth – that revealed God's distant hand in exposing an accused person's guilt.

Of all colonial ritual, executions drew the largest crowds everywhere, sometimes in excess of three thousand people, and contained the greatest drama, even though the conclusion, so to speak, was predetermined. In New England, hangings were protracted affairs, ideally with the slow progress of the cart, the scaffold speech of the guilty (in the form, it was hoped, of a confession), parting prayers, and a ministerial sermon. Every gesture of the victims upon the stage (the only legal stage) of the scaffold was examined – their manner; their gait; the quality of their repentance; and, much more rarely, their protestations of innocence. Though the hanging led to death, the dramaturgy was one of religious conversion, and the words of the condemned were circulated and used later by the clergy to aid in their work among the living.

There was one notable, early crisis in Puritan authority that illustrates to what lengths congregational divines might go to maintain control over the improper forms of ritual. In 1626 the Anglican Thomas Morton took charge of a small settlement that he renamed Mare Mount. There he established a self-consciously pastoral community – detailed in his *New England Canaan* (1637) – where the land would not only flow with milk and honey, but also wine, women, and Indians. The theatrical centerpiece to this Arcadia, in which pleasure would outdistance mortification, was the maypole, and the sight of such an obviously sacral spot – around which Morton had gathered his "boyes," "bottles," and "maidens" – drew the full weight of Governor Endicott's wrath.

Puritans have, however, gained unjustly a monopolistic reputation for joylessness, in part because the term "Puritan" became a general term of abuse (directed at the excesses of Victorianism) by the urban sophisticates in the 1920s. Pennsylvania's Quakers were just as keen to eliminate the revelries of traditional holidays and rituals. They forbade the wearing of masks, card playing, and noise making, as well as drinking and feasting at Christmas and Whitsuntide. Theatrical representations of any form, as in Boston, were banned within the city limits of Philadelphia. Yet Puritans, unlike the plain, formal Quakers, set feast days on the occasion of military and religious victories. Feasting was common, perhaps excessive given the amount of available rum, at weddings and at funerals, and even at ordinations copious amounts of food and drink were allowed. The colonists may have been religious reformers, but they were still Elizabethan in their appetites. Puritans danced and got drunk in taverns despite the edicts of the Massachusetts General Court. In the eighteenth century, as ministerial watchfulness and control fell away, older forms returned. There were cases of youthful charivaris directed against inappropriate marriages, and active Pope's Day (5 November) celebrations in Boston seldom bothered the authorities, despite the firing of guns, the lighting of bonfires, and a good deal of mumming.

Two new forms of socializing appeared in the British colonies to fill the calendrical void. The first kind of ritual – the bee or frolic – evolved as a way to combine work with pleasure. At barn raisings and corn-husking bees, the language and practices of the pastoral returned. Though most of the more elaborate features of Harvest Home – the corn dollies, the processions, and the election of a harvest lord – appear to have been flattened out in the egalitarianism of the American context, the traditional late fall feast refocused on the natural, indigenous plenitude of "Indian" corn. At husking times it was considered normal for "swains," should they find a red ear of corn, to claim a kiss from any damsel, and this practice led to the kinds of excesses that are registered in court records. "There is now a custom amongst us," noted Nathaniel Ames in 1766, "of making an Entertainment at husking of Indian Corne whereunto all the neighbouring Swains are invited, and after the Corn is finished they, like the Hottentots, give three cheers or huzzas, but cannot carry in the husks without a Rhum bottle. They feign great exertion, but do nothing until the Rhum enlivens them, when all is done in a trice" (quoted in Dulles, 26).

The reference to Hottentots in this often-used quotation has gone unexamined, though it is surely telling that already inversions and ritual license were identified with, and symbolically handed over to, an exotic "other." This was hardly unique to the American context, for "gypsies" had played a similar role within English mumming; indeed "gypsies" along with "moors" were one of the racial identifications given to Indians by the settlers. From the early colonial period on, then, a distinctive American theatricality would be freighted with both the images and presence of unruly blacks and Indians who were allowed to dance and sing in ways that transgressed the transparent, productive, and Protestant landscape of colonial culture. Indian and African ritual forms appeared bestial and licentious, but they also suggested, in ways that would be important in the postrevolutionary period, "freedom." Protestant belief in the power of the Word, the individuality of salvation, and the inscrutability of their god was to have profound effects on how the colonists viewed both Native American and African ritual. Both the slaves and the Indians practiced forms of spiritual collectivism – enactments of myths and dreams – whose meaning remained impenetrable to those colonists imbued with the doctrines of original sin, in which salvation was deferred and mediated through the church teaching the Bible.

The second occasion for socializing evolved out of civil and military gatherings. From 1693 on in Massachusetts an election day was fixed. Over time other public and church functions were added to the last week in May so that by the 1720s, "election" had become a full popular festival, with booths for liquor and food, drawing many people from the outlying settlements. Within this loose structure of election week, slaves conducted their own "Lection" ceremonies in which they chose a king or governor to rule over them. It was a declared holiday for slaves, and they would be allowed the liberty of the commons in Boston and other public sites elsewhere. Such freedom also extended to Native Americans, and accounts make reference to Indian women collecting roots and bark for brewing the election beer. In Massachusetts, candidates for election would engage before the main event in parmateering (parliamenteering), perhaps in parody of official election procedure. Whites certainly considered these stump speeches conscious "shams," and they may have figured in the later development of mock electioneering in blackface minstrelsy. In the allied Pinkster Day (after Pentecost) in New York and New Jersey, kings were more hereditary. In Albany, King Charles, a slave owned by the mayor Volckert Douw, had an uninterrupted reign of more than thirty years, and hundreds of blacks through the 1790s awaited his annual coronation on Pinkster Hill.

Whatever the political reference, these festivities, as Shane White has argued, became the central cultural fixture for blacks in the north. They provided the main occasion to circulate among their own kind, and in a region with few concentrations of slave population, they offered the chance to gamble and socialize at paw-paw, and to gain commercial profit with the sale of cakes and beer. Above all, they offered the chance for display and extended dancing. Slaves would wear elaborate, colorful clothes in a bricolage of high fashion, sometimes supplied by masters, and after a brief processional would set about dancing and drinking with music supplied by the fiddle, Jew's harp, and Guinea drums. The merriment might continue for two full days. Whites viewed the proceedings as "entertainment," whereas the blacks themselves continued the forms of dance and music that spoke of community.

Yet Pinkster and Election day appear to have quickly died away in the first decade of the nineteenth century. Reform came from two directions: One emerged from ministerial concern about the increasing presence of "beastly whites" in the motley assemblies. The second form of suppression came from the leaders of black societies and churches who considered that such unruly antics hardly corresponded to the passage of manumission acts throughout the northern states. Their new citizen status required the adoption of more formal, respectable parades that matched white civic processionals. In 1808, two hundred free blacks first celebrated the abolition of the slave trade with a march to the African meeting house in Boston, and one year later the African Society for Mutual Relief processed in New York. Parades with marshalls and society banners claimed the town in more politically legitimate ways than could a black presence, no matter how multifaceted, limited to a liminal spot. In the North, the dominant political thrust of black public activism in the Jacksonian period would be to meet the gaze of white onlookers not with entertainment but with the rituals of citizenship.

Southern colonies had a deeper, or at least more recognizable, tradition of civic entertainment. In Colonial Williamsburg the "publick times" – the fairs held in April and December to coincide with the meeting of the assembly and court sessions – might swell the population threefold. These would be the occasion for displays of fashion, crafts, and horseflesh as well as lawn fetes and banquets, despite the fact that laws against "idleness," as draconic as any in New England, remained on the books. Civic ceremony arising from the appointment of governors or royal birthdays clearly matched in pomp, though not in scale, traditional English court ritual. These were "public" events but also still largely "private" entertainments in the sense that the governor covered much of the cost. The coronation of Queen Anne (1702), for instance, produced the regular pageant of buglers, fireworks, collegiate exercises, and troop movement, including, more interestingly, the "rightful" incorporation of the local Indian leadership within the orders of the day. The final assembly included a dance with the Tidewater Indian chiefs following their own observances, though what ceremonial meaning had been invoked remained entirely unclear to the colonists:

> When the Indian King himself is present, the Governor gives him the right hand. Then they began to play, but the queen danced so wonderfully, yea barbarously, that everyone was astonished and laughed. It has no similarity to dancing. They make such wonderful movements with body, eyes and mouth, as if they were with the evil one. At one time they rave as if they were angry, then bite their arms and other parts with their teeth, or else they are entirely quiet. In short it is impossible to describe this mad and ludicrous dance. (Quoted in Hinke, 134)

Incomprehension worked in reverse as well. According to the *Virginia Gazette* (17 November 1752), when the Cherokee chiefs witnessed Hallam's rendition of Othello, performed for the king's birthday in 1752, the sight of naked sword play shocked the Indian "queen" to such an extent that she asked her followers to intervene to prevent bloodshed. Without the frame of cultural legitimacy any display of violence may appear "evil," and the colonists, in this case, not only had the advantage of knowing the conventions of the stage but also that the whole event – fireworks, parades, and theatre – was a demonstration of authority and the law.

These occasions of festive entertainment and the honor of "treating" in southern colonies survived the revolutionary period; indeed they became a self-defining feature of southern life underwritten at every point by the presence of chattel slavery. One does not need to be a Nietzschean to agree that much of the festive has its origin in "blood" and in demonstrations of inequality. Large landowners adopted the ideals of the English gentry to the extent that the enjoyment of leisure was the mark of social prestige. The provision of entertainments to guests and workers conferred a sense of honor, and from the mid-eighteenth century on, writers such as John Hammond promoted the South as a region given over to leisure and material abundance.

In hunting, the southern planter class differentiated themselves from the commoners by emphasizing the "chase" rather than "the kill" and by preferring those sports, especially horsemanship and fencing, previously tied to aristocratic accomplishment. The most glaring archaism was the popularity of ring tournaments, which referred back to the medieval pageantry of royal jousts. "Knights," often military cadets, had to scoop up rings suspended from posts with their lances, with the most skilled performer ending up as a "king."

The gentry were certainly not above promoting and enjoying rougher sports; indeed their position as judges and patrons of wrestling matches, cockfights, and eye-gouging contests only further emphasized their social standing.

Even allowing for the hyperbole from later apologists and memorialists, many planters did "entertain" their slaves with a form of patriarchal benevolence. Most owners granted slaves the traditional Christian holidays and the Sabbath, as well as Saturday afternoons and extra time after harvesting and planting. In addition, the provision of extra meat and drink for celebratory barbecues appears to have been customary. The works of Genovese and Blassingame detail the ways in which slaves used this free time: in the securing of passes to visit towns and other plantations, the exercise of normal rural sports, and the maintenance of distinctive styles of music and dance. Disagreement arises, however, over the social and psychological consequences of such treating. From Frederick Douglass onward, many commentators have taken the provision of leisure to be little more than cynical social control. For Genovese, the grant of "entertainment" generated a curious double bind, characteristic of other aspects of master-slave (and indeed class) relationships. On the one hand, "treating" permitted the masters to claim their notions of benevolence and allowed slaves the social space to develop their own oppositional culture as well; on the other hand, and more problematic, the slaves' "acceptance" of entertainment tied them to their own domination.

The extent to which West African religious belief and ritual informed slave culture is also subject to active debate, but there is general agreement that whatever carryovers took root, the most important cultural forms were forged within the plantation system and in answer to it. Apart from Louisiana, the ceremonies of voodoo never gained an internal coherence, and most conjuring remained at the level of unorganized, imitative magic – charms, nails, potions, and fetishes. Usually, however, a particular slave – an oracle – was marked with greater power, and it was this figure who drew both white suspicion and perhaps assent for it. Not until the 1820s were whites actively discouraged from seeking the help of black "herbal" doctors.

The form of slave religious celebration that was most noticeably different and disturbing to the white settlers occurred at funerals. West African beliefs in reincarnation made funerals less an expression of grief than a celebration of existence; they were the avenue for the departed spirit to enter the world of rest and required processionals, solemn to the grave and festive afterward. Here strong carryovers existed: burying with food, strewing the site with broken earthenware, and marching three times around the plot. The most problematic difference in these funerals from white religious practice, however, was the desire for burials at night, complete with torchlight processions, in part to allow slaves from other farms to attend, in part to help the spirit into the dark world of rest. As early as 1687, public slave funerals were banned in

Virginia because of their presumed role in fostering revolt, and in 1772 New York City required funerals to be held during the day and with a limit of twelve participants.

Though this is not the place to describe in any detail slave dancing and singing, it is worth noting that some of the features would later pass into more general possession within urban commercial culture through such avenues as the minstrel show. Slaves continued the multimetrical musical forms of their homelands with their call-and-response phrasing and their antiphonal and contrapuntal effects. In dance, commentators observed that in contrast to white styles, slaves exhibited a great fluidity of form and used their whole body, especially the torso; patting legs and arms became the most recognizable form, as in "patting Juba." From the earliest accounts it seems that dancing and musicianship among slaves possessed a competitive side. Participants tried to outdistance each other in the complexity and rapidity of movement, and either the musicians or dancers would set metrical challenges for the other.

Though such feats of competition within the slave community were geared to keeping up the pace and spirit of work or worship, they gained different meanings as masters began to wager on the results. In the late fall festival of corn shucking, for instance, masters would assemble two piles of corn and "invite" slaves from neighboring plantations and their owners to see which gang could shuck the corn with greater speed. The competing groups would be managed by callers, who used songs, tales, and percussive music to set the rhythm and regulate the work. A good deal of repartee was traded between the masters on the verandah and the slaves in the liminal space of the yard. Masters saw before them the innocent "happy" pleasures of the chattel confirming their self-image of paternalism. This certainly became one of the recurring images in American culture, not just among the apologists for slavery, but also in genre painting, sheet-music covers, and northern minstrelsy through Reconstruction and beyond. Yet at the same time the festivals offered the opportunity for slaves to celebrate community cohesion and to gain a religious affirmation of their own expressive talents.

By the 1830s some of the slave dance forms – the chalkline, the "jig," and the Pigeon Wing – had developed in response to white spectatorship, or, in the case of the cakewalk, in conscious parodic imitation of the stiff upper-body movement of white cotillions. In addition single feats of showmanship – cutting and breakdowns – appear to have drawn white sponsorship and betting in northern cities as well. Dancing for eels in Catherine and Fulton markets, New York, was a recognized practice by the first decade of the nineteenth century. Here a short board provided a percussive stage for the dancer to strut his stuff, and the limitations to movement it imposed provided the field play for gambling among the onlookers. Already once removed from the slave community, these hyper-athletic, flashy forms of dance, or rather parodies of them, probably formed models for the kind of choreographic antics that ended up in the northern minstrel show.

With the rapid Christianization of the slave population after 1800, new forms evolved, at first of importance to the slaves themselves and later to American popular culture in general. In order, for instance, to conform to Methodist injunctions to stop dancing, slaves developed the "ring shout," in which three or four people would stand still while the other participants would move counterclockwise in leaping movements. The ring shout managed to integrate many forms of expression, body movement, voice, harmony, call and response directly into Christian worship, and, together with the simplicity of the Methodist gospel and stress on equality, the spirit of religious collectivism as well. White observers noticed, however, that there remained something theologically suspicious about the way slaves approached divine worship, that the music seemed to express more than Christian joy. Indeed, there were signs that God and the devil continued to be part of the same supernaturalism, not rendered as discrete figures. As many blues songs later celebrated, the devil brought pain and mirth, and God brought suffering and salvation.

One regional variation deserves to be noted in any account of the South's popular culture. In Spanish Louisiana, slavery was structurally more akin to serfdom than to the chattel slavery existing in the rest of the region. Slaves were allowed to congregate en masse to hold public festivals and outdoor fandangos. In addition, the existence of a large class of free blacks encouraged the evolution of Africanized music and dance as well as the preservation of syncretism in religion and medicine. Slaves contrived to exhibit their skills at dancing, especially during parades and funerals, and in order to confine the exercise of ritual and magic, the Place Square was designated as the official arena for displays of the calenda, the bamboula, and the chica. Entrepreneurs, after 1750, tried to privatize these dance gatherings by charging admission to quadroon balls and other events that admitted the free black (usually women) and the white Creole populations. Through such commercialized mixing, Africanized forms rapidly crossed the thresholds of race.

Religious rituals also manifested a high degree of hybridity more characteristic of Caribbean than North American culture. Both Catholicism and voodoo provided wide spaces for the exercise of the occult. Indeed, the rites of African conjuring proved so attractive to whites that Governor Miro, in 1788, tried to restrict these oblations to the slave population, largely without success. Even after the incorporation of Louisiana into the Union, the streets of the Vieux Carré exhibited a kind of public license unknown to the rest of North America, and inevitably their control became a hotly contested issue. The year after annexation (1803) witnessed several fracases between the Creole and American populations over the proper forms of dance and display at the Carnival balls. The Mardi Gras procession itself appears to have been modeled directly on French carnival masking, perhaps organized by informal "abbeys" of young men, who also carried on the tradition of perpetrating charivaris on newly married couples with inappropriate age differences. By 1837, large processions, complete with floats, grotesque costuming, and transvestite revelry had become an annual event, though the extent to which it emerged entirely out of some folk memory of the Creole population is questionable, because the famous acrobatic Ravels were performing their own "Venetian Carnival" on the commercial stage of New Orleans at the same time.

Street Theatre and Public Festivities

Not every group in America has loved a parade, nor have the themes, emblems, and participants always drawn the assent of the general public. For most of the colonial period, street ceremonials representing the power of the Crown, especially military parades, were treated with hostility, and the support of the British Army for the stage was instrumental in the Continental Congress banning all forms of theatrical representation. Though the Revolution spelled the temporary demise of the legitimate theatre – at least in the hands of non-military professionals – it was an active period for the revival of vernacular street theatricals, now safely harnessed to the republican cause. Ritual techniques of crowd justice included hangings in effigy of Tories and merchants who aimed at profiteering, burnings of stamp men in effigy, mock funerals for the demise of liberty, and tarring and feathering. In each case the genre was a burlesqued extension of official punishment, whether civil, maritime, or military in origin, and most arose spontaneously from the popular classes, without the official sponsorship of the mercantile elite.

With the evacuation of British troops and the eventual signing of the Constitution, residents of the seaboard cities reinvented forms of British civic and guild pageantry, overcoming, now they were sovereigns, a deep mistrust of traditional religious and court pageantry. The grandest and best documented parade of the Early National Period – Philadelphia's constitutional celebrations of 1788 – provides some idea of the enthusiasm with which Americans used the streets and of the passage of national iconography into popular consciousness. According to writer and musician Francis Hopkinson, chairman of the event, more than five thousand people marched (about one-quarter of the city's male population) in a one-mile line that took three hours to pass by. First came twelve "axe men" representing the pioneer spirit; these were followed by various military groups on foot and horse parading to Alexander Reinagle's new "federal march." Next came the Constitution float, decorated with liberty caps and supporting a thirteen-foot-high eagle; immediately behind this was the "Grand Federal Edifice" surrounded by four hundred and fifty carpenters and builders and many emblem-holding farmers dispensing seeds. The next section contained forty different trades, all with allegorical floats stuffed with the paraphernalia of their craft. Dumb-shows displayed the work of the trade – spinning machines for weavers, mariners peering through telescopes, barbers cutting hair, and so forth. The printer's float carried a press that distributed copies of Hopkinson's ode, and on top of an adjacent platform the dancer and actor John Durang, dressed as Mercury, dispatched carrier pigeons bearing toasts. In the van, came members of Congress; representatives of the professions; the clergy; and, finally, professors and students, supposedly symbolizing the rising generation.

Such processions proved useful, at a time of heightened antitheatrical sentiment, in keeping alive a number of the theatrical arts – miming, machinery, painting, music, and dance – as well as introducing a pantheon of republican characters – frontiersmen, farmers, common soldiers, tars, firemen, and mechanics – who on the legitimate (English) stage would be most likely to appear in the role of comic fools. These parades attempted to construct a new patriotism in which the vernacular could be blended with the classical and in which the common folk could ascend to ideal status.

The grandest and most perennial festival of American republicanism, however, was the Fourth of July, a ritualized *E Pluribus Unum,* creating a sense of common purpose and future out of diverse elements. Almost everywhere in the United States, Fourth of July observances adhered to the same basic pattern. At midday participants would gather in front of some public building, a city hall, courthouse, tavern, or church, to hear an oration or address. They would then proceed, often wearing the costumes or holding the paraphernalia designating their citizen status, toward the site of a celebratory dinner. After the reading of the Declaration, which appropriately took the place of a religious blessing, and more oration, everyone sat down to eat. At the end of the meal, the "cloth" was removed – an act dating back to medieval banquet custom – and toasts were then offered: first, official toasts given by members of the organizing committee (and invariably to Washington and the flag), then volunteer toasts to the bravery of revolutionary figures and to the patriotism of contemporaries. The day would thus offer a benediction upon the town and a consecration that the blood of the revolutionary martyrs would renew the republican spirit for the following year.

This sequence speaks to notions of community cohesion, yet any celebration, when claiming to enact political legitimacy, may end up by providing the occasion for displays of social power and inequality rather than demonstrations of togetherness. In rural districts, the beneficent proprietors of estates and plantations offered their houses as gathering sites, thereby maintaining the patterns of preindustrial largesse. In cities, occupational groupings, voluntary associations, and political parties strove to make their particular versions of the republican spirit felt. Urban festivities would proceed in parallel with threads of the population proceeding from their districts or associations to a central site before taking up their own closing rituals. In the 1830s, workers in the General Trades Union held their own celebrations; in the 1840s many reform groups chose to make the Fourth of July a celebration of liberty, not from British colonial rule, but rather from other threats to the course of republican virtue – irreligion, immigrants, or drink. As the Sons of Temperance proclaimed in Pittsburgh in 1847, their Fourth was about a "better freedom – a freedom not alone from foreign shackles, but from a more deadly and dangerous foe to man" (*Washington Examiner,* 10 July 1847, quoted in Scott Martin, 215).

Most divisive of all, perhaps, was the calendrical convenience of the Fourth to political parties for the business of nomination routines leading up to November elections. Indeed, after the rise of Jackson, it is striking how many elements of community and national ritual could be turned to partisan purpose: effigies, banners, triumphal arches, chowder parties, barbecues, and husking bees were all employed to gather the faithful. Though Democrats had long been the leaders in establishing new election routines and working the politics of expediency, it was the Whigs, with their famous Log Cabin campaign of 1840, who finally outpaced their Democratic rivals and set the standards for political campaigning for the rest of the century. Every aspect of civic and community ritual was marshaled to present the Whig platform in a popular light. Indian motifs were drawn from Harrison's claimed credit for the victory over the Northwestern Indians at Tippecanoe in 1811, and from his running mate, John Tyler, all the barbecue accoutrements of Virginia largesse. Above all, because the Democrats had joked that Harrison would be content with just a log cabin and hard cider, the Whigs developed these icons assiduously. Throughout the country, Whigs encouraged their supporters to raise an emblematic "barn" and to liberally treat participants and onlookers to the native drink. Though these scenes referred to ideas of community, their significance was now totally changed, as ironically noted in William Sidney Mount's famous genre picture *Cider Making the Old Fashioned Way.* However obviously "staged," such rituals of participation worked: Four out of five white males voted. Even the aristocratic Daniel Webster felt like declaring that he was "a plain man . . . a farmer," and Philip Hone, who hated popular crowds, "went [one] evening . . . to the great Whig Meeting in Hudson Street. There was an immense crowd and a vast deal of fun and banners – bonfire – the Old Hero [William Henry Harrison] staring glumly in plaster of Paris – and 'Tippecanoe and Tyler Too' in grand chorus, given with more effect that any effort of the Sacred Music Society."[1]

Once again the activities of the street overflowed onto commercial stages. The popular Whig dramatist Silas Steele was forced to abandon the run of his *Battle of Tippecanoe* (1840) when members of the Democracy threatened to close the Chestnut Street Theatre. The presence of music in campaigning was equally important. Even minority parties, such as the nativist American party of 1844, used free or inexpensive popular concerts to drive the message home. De La Ree, a New York mechanic and the "Apollo of the American Party," gave twenty concerts gratis in support of Henry Clay that featured jingoistic ditties such as "Come, natives arouse" and "Rise, ye sons of Freedom." Popular politics, more than any other cultural form, inaugurated the new technology of reputation and fame. Through combining the power of the popular press, the parade, song, and eventually the photographic likeness, parties manipulated reputations and manufactured constituencies. Popular politics shared personnel, as well as routines, with the infant entertainment industry. In 1836, the famous American actor, Edwin Forrest, was asked by the "loco-foco" wing of the Democrats to run for the Senate. The fact that he declined the nomination is of less importance than noting that an actor was already seen as a "natural" for high political office. Both actors and politicians had begun to see their road to success, not in patronage but in a show of hands; both worked the crowd and possessed a vision of a career that moved on to larger and larger "stages."

In addition to the Fourth of July, other republican uses of the street fell prey to the same story of declension. Militias offer the clearest case. In most states until the Civil War there was a legal requirement for those enrolled in militia to drill. Militia Day took on the coloration of a "jubilee of idleness," for what should have been, by law, only a march and drill spread out, since work was suspended, into a full day of target excursions, chowder parties, ox roasts, and general drinking. This public centerpiece of republican equality, in which all male citizens strove to protect the nation, instead expressed the social and economic divisions characteristic of industrializing society. The wealthy sponsored and enrolled in particular private companies, usually tagged "silk stocking" – that were known for the gorgeousness of uniform and excellence of horse flesh and tack. This was especially marked in Pennsylvania, where state law required service in either a volunteer or public militia company. For elite volunteers it was suggested that the uniform was "useful as common wearing apparel upon Sundays and days of festivity" (quoted in Scott Martin, 189). Liberal amounts of cash also permitted the hiring of bands and private instructors to help them drill in complex evolutions and marches. The poor were left with inadequately funded companies and, in addition, faced the burden of fines for nonattendance and the cost of removing themselves from work. Such inequalities gave rise in the 1830s to a particular piece of street theatre in which protesting workers paraded in mock arms and dress as the "invincible fantasticals" with broomsticks for rifles and brushes for epaulettes. These cornstalk brigades took on a life of their own beyond the occasion of the seasonal muster. In Philadelphia, they reappeared at Christmas and New Year's Day as vehicles for young working men to poke fun at aristocratic pretension and for the sheer delight at dressing up and behaving in ludicrous ways; by the 1840s bands of mummers descended even further into outright gang violence.

Another form of popular street theatre, allied to militia antics, emerged out of volunteer fire brigades. Before the arrival of the professionalized force most cities allowed particular companies to establish their own esprit de corps by developing their own iconography, choosing their own names taken from the heroes and heroines of the republic, the theatre, or the turf. They commissioned painters (even members of the National Academy of Design) to draw elaborately painted engine backs, and fire-company banners were in evidence at every municipal celebration. Rivalry between companies was intense and somewhat institutionalized. Fierce street races took place on route to fires. There were publicly staged "hosings" in which a group would attempt to wash away another's "virgin" status, and companies raided houses to capture a rival's miscellaneous iconography.

Company life extended far beyond the firehouse itself. Certain bars and oyster houses were recognized as ateliers of companies, and the association of the fire "B'hoys" with theatres was especially evident. In New York, the most obvious link between stage and firehouse was the propensity of the theatres to burn down; the Bowery had to be totally rebuilt four times (1828, 1836, 1838, and 1845), the Chatham twice (1839 and 1841), and the National and Olympic once. For insurance, managers commonly offered benefit nights for the firemen's widows and orphans fund. In addition, they commemorated heroic deeds through the staging of interludes and tableaux, and, after 1830, manager Thomas Hamblin at the Bowery gave the space gratis for the annual firemen's ball.

In return, certain companies declared their allegiances. At the Croton Water celebration of 1840 the Eagle Hose Co. No. 1 displayed a banner illustrating the burning of the National Theatre. Chatham Engine Co. No. 2 possessed a portrait of James Wallack as Rolla and a banner of the burning of the Bowery in 1838. Forrest Engine Company No. 3 machines depicted their hero's last scene in *Metamora,* whereas Mazeppa Engine Co. No. 48 illustrated the famous hippodramatic ride across the Bowery's boards. Firemen thus presented a theatricalized, militant public presence in the city, yet many companies, like the militias, fell foul of the municipal authorities by the 1840s. Races to fires often ended up in gang violence, and the firehouse itself, especially in immigrant wards, was frequently used by popular politicians as a base of operations.

This divisive usage of public space was intensified by substantial changes in the character of urban morphology. As cities grew in population and geographic reach, urban space became more differentiated by class and by ethnicity. The appearance of relatively expensive horse-drawn street cars after 1830 allowed the affluent to create suburbs, leaving wage workers, who had to walk to work, within close proximity to the congested commercial and industrial "downtown." In the 1830s most northern cities introduced measures to suppress, among other things, street vendors' cries, unlicensed hucksters, the wanderings of vaguely domesticated pigs, and the keeping of poultry. Much of this modernizing reform issued from a new and necessary concern with public health; however, it is also clear that the physical proximity of plebeian life to the city center prompted new perceptions by the elite of unregulated street performances and the ominous presence of the mob. Old public squares were fenced, Fourth of July booths were banned; public executions ceased to exist in any northern city after 1837, the last one being in Philadelphia. Propertied gentlemen certainly expressed rising anxiety over the potential for ceremonious and legal occasions to get out of hand. The labor strikes, antiabolitionist agitation, political riots, and new forms of religious conflict in the mid-1830s tested the customary manner of dispersing crowds by an informal reading of the "riot act," and all municipalities by the 1840s had extended and amplified their police powers to use the state militia to control public gatherings as well as to establish a professional day watch.

Popular Religious Ritual

That parades and politics formed an important source for American popular entertainments is perhaps self-evident. The case for evangelical religion as a conduit for theatricality may, on the surface, seem much more difficult to sustain. The arrival of George Whitfield and the Great Awakening of the 1740s emphasized in quite a new way the emotional and personal side of salvation and was committed to a more active monitoring of personal pleasure. Evangelicals therefore reenergized the criticism of many amusements as a waste of time and a dissolution of self-control. It would only be in the beginning of the twentieth century that the notion of consuming pleasures or products meant anything other than the "using up" of resources that would be better saved for later.

Nevertheless, it is possible to claim that evangelical revivalism accelerated the making of a national, popular, and theatricalized culture. Both amusement entrepreneurs and evangelicals stressed American innovation over European tradition and competition over orthodoxy. George Whitfield's use of advance publicity, paid puffs, and cheap pamphlets set new standards for the infant amusement business. Since evangelicals did not allow Christian status to rest on baptism, a secession of public declarations of faith was required. Revivals were seldom spontaneous; they had to be worked up by using the most modern forms of promotion available.

Many aspects of the new popular religion thus worked directly toward an accommodation with theatrical practice. The clearest case was the development of a new type of camp meeting in the South at the end of the eighteenth century. On 6 August 1801, more than twenty thousand people converged on Cane Ridge, Bourbon County, Kentucky, for six full days and nights of prayer and sermonizing. "The noise was like the roar of Niagara," wrote James Finley. "The vast sea of human beings seemed to be agitated as if by a storm. I counted seven ministers, all preaching at one time, some on stumps, others in wagons, and one standing on a tree that had, in falling, lodged against another" (166). Before these multiple points of preaching new kinds of behaviors were witnessed among the believers: barking, jerking, clapping, howling, rolling in the dust, and the rending of clothes. Many commentators saw in all this the work of heathen "misrule" rather than God's calming grace. The most problematic aspect of all was that men and women, whites and black slaves, appeared to be blended in a promiscuous mix of enthusiastic dancing, vocalizing, and prayer; indeed, there was promiscuity in more than just a figurative sense, because a woman of easy virtue was detained at Cane Ridge after entertaining six men beneath a preaching platform. Though there is no evidence of staged performances, other than the preaching itself, camp meetings took on the aspect of traditional fairs, with horse trading and other forms of hucksterism – booths for food and even liquor – set up on the periphery. Over the next decade, even itinerant preachers were forced to give such meetings a spatial arrangement and a manageable order of service in order to bring the proceedings firmly back to the work of salvation. Manuals recommended that a roofed preaching platform be erected at the northern end of the chosen ground, and before it an "altar," which was no more than a fenced enclosure or "pen," with seats for anxious "mourners." Beyond the pen, seats spread out for many rows: women on the left, men on the right. Blacks were resegregated within the grove in an area set aside for their own preaching, dancing, and prayer, though there is evidence that in camp meetings the practices of ring shouts and call-and-response singing passed into the white congregation.

Camp meetings remained seasonal religious festivals within rural areas, so it was left to Charles Grandison Finney to institutionalize such practices within New Light Protestantism and to provide them with a permanent urban setting. Nothing about Finney was small. He possessed a powerful, sonorous voice, piercing blue eyes, and a towering six-foot-two frame. Regular New Light ministers complained not just about his antinomian theology but about the ways in which his homespun "Yankee" lawyer's style dissolved the dignity of the priesthood. He used colloquialisms and shouted out "hell" to engender fear and embellished God's word with homespun analogies. Finney's legal training made him appreciate the drama of the courtroom, and he wished that potential believers, like juries, would come to an immediate decision about their salvation. This required from the preacher a direct, unmediated appeal to people's "animal feelings," and this undercut traditional Protestant belief in the power of God's word alone, for it foregrounded the preacher's skill at delivery. The pen of the camp meeting now became an anxious bench on which the "mourners" were placed before his commanding presence.

A second worrying development in Finneyite evangelicalism arose from his belief in the equality of all people before God. His gatherings offered one space in public culture where women mixed freely with men and antinomian stirrings led to the first wave of all female benevolent organization in rural districts. Women visited homes, set up prayer meetings, and brought the faithful out. Ironically, the rhetoric of domestic piety was spread throughout the Northeast by activist women who stressed the virtues of female silence, physical modesty, and nontheatrical behavior. By the late 1820s, Finney and his female volunteers had ignited revivals in Lancaster, Philadelphia, Boston, and most famously in Rochester, where for six months in 1830 he conducted a series of five-day, sunrise-to-sunset protracted meetings. In 1835 he estimated that he had brought over a hundred thousand people into regular church attendance.

With so much popular, though peripatetic, success behind him, Finney, with help from the wealthy Tappan brothers, tackled the final outpost of ungodliness, New York. In 1832, he took over the Chatham Theatre and converted it into a free Presbyterian Church, free, that is, from customary pew rents. There, to be overmaterialistic in description, he offered the cheapest and largest show in town with continuous performances on Sunday and standard revivals three nights a week. To accommodate ever larger crowds, he built a new Broadway Tabernacle, with three thousand seats (the biggest auditorium in the city), to his own specifications. Breaking with the design of an elevated "proscenium" pulpit, he placed the lectern at the center of a rotunda with rows of pews rising steeply toward the walls. This church-in-the round permitted a new scenography of conversion. It focused the audience's attention directly on the attitudes of the preacher and on the manifestations of the reborn. The anxious bench became an anxious circle, and wide rows allowed an easy processional passage down to the point of conversion.

Thus, at the very same time that melodramas flooded the popular stage and the second party system transformed the nature of American politics, Finney developed an actor's appreciation of technique and a modern political understanding of working a constituency. In his *Lectures on Revivals of Religion,* which became the standard manual of evangelical revival all the way through to Billy Graham, Finney considered the relation of his craft to the parallel successes of the stage and platform and found that it had much to learn from them. Since the "theatres will be thronged every night" it was no use for a preacher to offer only "sanctimonious starch . . . the common-sense people will be entertained." And as for politicians:

> What do politicians do? They get up meetings, circulate handbills and pamphlets, blaze away in the newspapers, send ships about the streets on wheels with flags and sailors, send conveyances all over the town, with handbills, to bring people up to the polls – all to gain attention to their cause, and elect their candidate . . . The object is to get up an excitement, and bring people out. They know that unless there can be an excitement it is in vain to push their end. I do not mean to say that their measures are pious, right, but only that they are wise, in the sense that they are the appropriate application of means to the end.[2]

Finney was truly revolutionary in that he explicitly rejected the traditional ministerial denial of theatre and politics but rather sought their direct incorporation in the business of salvation. By the 1830s he recognized the impossibility of using the pulpit for the suppression of theatricality and ungodly representation; evangelists had to rival and outpace the popularity of the new commercial culture. It was a lesson never forgotten.

Yet Finney had a crisis of conscience. At the very height of his popularity he relinquished the Broadway Tabernacle. He realized that he had focused too much on the "practical skill in the art of bringing about an excitement" and that in becoming a specialist of means he had forgotten the ends. In 1835 he moved to the quiet outpost of Oberlin College to take up radical and unpopular antislavery positions.

One further example of the theatricality of American popular religion may be drawn from the other end of the antinomian spectrum, again from the burnt (by fires of religious enthusiasm) district of Upstate New York and Vermont. Facing new kinds of commercial pressures, the area became a remarkable seedbed for the apocalyptic imagination, including one belonging to one Walters or Wingate, who spread the idea locally that hidden treasures might be found in the mountains by using a sacred rod of St. John. Divination was rife. One local digger, Joseph Smith Jr., was lucky enough to extract in 1828 some golden plates on Hill Cumorah along with a pair of seer stones that enabled him to read the inscriptions on the tablet. For two years, supported by wealthier farmers, Joseph, covered by a sheet to hide the sacred tablets, translated and dictated a "book of Mormon" to his wife and another digger, Oliver Cowdery. The resulting mix of fantasy, trickery, and mysticism detailed battles that had once occurred between the lost Jews, Nephites, and the Amanite forerunners of the bad Indians. The new latter-day-saints were to move to the West, where, with converted descendants of the Amanites, they would await the return of Christ.

A fusion of popular religion and theatrical technique thus gave birth to Mormonism, and this stress on the performative and on divination makes sense if we accept John L. Brooks's recent argument that Mormonism, far from being a strange offshoot of New England Puritanism, is part of the sectarian tradition of the radical reformation, blending together hermetic and Gnostic ingredients. Ritual, even comic turns, could be used to attract believers, and early Mormons were known to disavow the repressive moralism of the newer evangelicalism. In 1839, hoping to find converts for the newly established settlement at Nauvoo, Illinois, Joseph Smith used the services of none other than Dan Rice, the circus performer, to bring out the people along the upper Mississippi, at a fee of fifty dollars per month. When the temple was completed in 1842, Mormon initiation rituals were developed bearing remarkable similarities to the Masonic endowment rite in which elders "play" the roles of God, Adam, and Satan, among other figures. In the central Mormon initiation ceremony initiates are led through rooms where the great cosmological wars between God and Satan are performed before being led to a place where the spirit world is reincorporated into human life and labor. Every aspect of conversion was performative. As may be guessed, Smith was personally interested in professional theatrical technique, and there were no warnings issued against dancing or public entertainments. Indeed, in 1844, when Smith faced substantial legal bills, a benefit performance of Kotzebue's tragedy *Pizarro* was enacted under the direction of Thomas A. Lyne using church elders in some key parts. None other than Brigham Young played the high priest, a role that he was later to assume in real life after Smith's demise.

Mormonism provides, it seems to me, only one case of a half-buried strain of hermetic perfectionism that encouraged the belief that it was possible for people to actually enact or invoke the divine in their daily practices and worship rather than struggle toward grace through the Bible and the institutions of the Church. As established Protestant divines lost their monopoly over the presentation of the word, theatrical representations of godliness returned in sundry "come-outer" enthusiasms, whether in Shaker dancing and singing, Charismatic vocalization, or even Masonic rite. Such outbreaks had perhaps been a regular feature of the Reformation, yet what appears new to the American context was the way such beliefs spread, through the democracy of evangelicalism, to grant a broad permission for acts of personal testimony. Everyone had a story to tell.

The strongest development in acts of personal testimony occurred later within the temperance movement. Most of the early temperance activity was directed from the pulpits of New Light ministers and was strongly averse to using the new means of popular culture to spread its message, but with the arrival of the Washingtonians in 1840, all of the elements of public theatricality came to play – parades, "shilling" concerts, testimonial lectures, and group confessions. Grand tours of temperance specialists were inaugurated, such as the one organized by Father Mathews, the Catholic temperance worker, who in eighteen months traveled thirty-seven thousand miles, visiting twenty-five states. The most famous temperance "act" of all was the ever popular John B. Gough, who set new standards for platform emotionalism. Gough had started as a singer, and like many of the theatrical cohort, enjoyed a drink or three. In contrast to earlier New Light ministerial addresses Gough "preached" by recounting the highly personal story of his fall into drunkenness and the stages of recovery. Both the decline and ascent were enacted over the course of about two hours in an "unbroken succession of contortions and antics," comic and serious by turns, including a knockabout rendition of delirium tremens. Part of his hold over the audience may have been due to his reputation as a backslider, which he did little to counter; there was always the expectation for the audience that he was not simply acting during his phase of inebriation. Gough thus commercialized the evangelical stress on testifying and dramatized the particularities of occupational failure and self-redemption; perhaps he should be viewed as the progenitor of that form of theatricalized personal narrative that ends up in today's performance art of Spalding Gray and Claudia Schear.[3]

The peculiar feature of American popular religion, dating back to Finney's time, is the easy accommodation of technical professionalism with piety. So important is the business of salvation that any means from the commercial and theatrical worlds may be incorporated with a justified, if not entirely clean, conscience. The rhetoric traded between ministers and amusement entrepreneurs was so hostile because both forged, and claimed, the new American public of social actors who could be equally "recreated" regardless of class or background. When ways were found eventually to link piety and commercial entertainment, through the 1840s, as in P. T. Barnum's moral plays, or Timothy Shay Arthur's temperance tales, a profitable and enduring amalgam was developed that remains a distinctive hallmark of American popular entertainments today.

Although the evangelical pulpit formed one conduit for America's passage into quotidian theatricality, the development of three popular sites, all allied to the theatre, formed another axis: the circus, summer garden, and the museum. All three elaborated versions of the visual "spectacle," of republican and natural imagery, that would become a distinguishing feature of American staged entertainments.

Circus, Garden, and Museum

Of the three, the circus most closely followed English theatrical practice. The history of the circus in America begins with the arrival from England of John Ricketts in 1792. Though there had been earlier equestrian shows – John Sharp in Boston (1771), a Mr. Faulk in Philadelphia (1771) and Williamsburg

Spalding and Rogers's Floating Palace, built on a flat-bottomed barge, opened March 1852. This lithograph provides an interior view at center, the barge itself at bottom, and various equestrian acts around the center image. Don B. Wilmeth Collection.

(1772), and Thomas Pool[e] in New York and Boston (1786) – Ricketts was the first to offer multipart entertainments featuring equestrian feats, clowning, and various tumbling and slack-wire entr'actes. Moreover, Ricketts' performances were judged from the outset as "elegant" (and his horses "sagacious") in contrast to the rough, rural tricks of previous riders. During his first season in Philadelphia in the spring of 1793, he introduced tricks such as picking caps off the ground at full speed, spearing oranges with swords, and drinking a glass of wine while straddling two horses, all the while assuming attitudes of urbanity and classicality. By the end of the season Ricketts had expanded the show to include simple pantomimes with spoken dialogue and the barest of plots, probably modeled on Philip Astley's London hippodramas. In touring, Ricketts had to change constantly the nature of his featured acts to keep the audience's appetite whetted, and the whole of the performance, lasting roughly two hours, was fleshed out with band music, processions, comic dances, and songs. By the time he opened a new, purpose-built amphitheater in Philadelphia in 1795, the various entr'actes had become stable features, and he made a point of advertising the extensive use of machinery and scenery.

Though the circus later developed into a totally independent form of amusement structured around the anthropomorphic acts of animals and clowning, for most of the period under discussion it remained closely allied to regular theatrical practice. It specialized in the hippodramatic, with singing, dancing, clowning, strongman feats, and tumbling taking accessory roles. By the 1830s theatrical elements were strengthened with the incorporation of truncated *Mazeppa*'s or other allegorical spectacles into which chargers might be worked. There might also be room found for a brief pantomime. The circus, in other words, was closer genealogically to drama than to the menageries that developed in eastern cities after 1830. The theatre proper also incorporated horses whenever possible. Hippodrama first appeared in America at the Park Theatre on 15 June 1803, when three real horses, marshaled by Signor Manfredi, performed that favorite hippodramatic mount of London and Paris, *La Fille Hussard,* and by the 1830s every theatre worth its salt staged equestrian pieces such as the Asiatic melodrama *El Hyder, Timour the Tartar,* and, most enduring of all, *Mazeppa; or, the Wild Horse or Tartary* (American premiere, 1833). It was not until the circus took to the road that it began to slough off its theatrical side and, though the first elephant appeared in 1812, on a brief visit from a museum, it was not until the Barnum–Van Amburg combination of 1862 and his even more famous three-ring venture (first with W. C. Coup in 1871 and then with Bailey in 1880) that all the elements of the museum, menagerie, circus, and hippodrama were combined.

The American enthusiasm for museums in the early national period was underwritten by the role that natural history played in forging a distinct national identity. Lacking the trace of history to be found in the built environment in Europe, and assuming that Indian burial grounds were evidence of a civilization entirely lost, American intellectuals turned to the evidence of a pristine nature to find national symbols: the buffalo, the mammoth, the bald eagle. That they were all big animals formed a convenient reply to Buffon's theory of westward degeneration. In 1793, New York City's first collection of curiosities opened to the public – the American Museum advertised "A Tooth of the American nondescribed animal called the Mammoth, supposed to be four or five times as large as the modern elephant" (cited in McClung, 158). New Yorkers had to wait three further years before seeing the first live imported elephant paraded through the streets. In 1801 Charles Willson Peale exhumed two complete skeletons of this mammoth (renamed mastodon), from Newburgh, New York, one of which was reassembled to form the centerpiece of his museum in Philadelphia.

Early American museums aimed at something more than mere display but rather arranged their materials in ways that demonstrated the gradation of life forms in the great chain of being. In Peale's museum this ran from minerals to a portrait of Thomas Jefferson – that is from low to high. More problematic were the exhibits and illustrations of supposed gradations within the higher primates. After 1810 it was possible to see cranial sequences that moved through orangutan, African, American Indian, Asiatic, and European. As George Mosse has suggested, this was a powerfully available visual ideology, made by artists and anatomists, that did not rely on any bookish theory for its powerful racist message.

Museums were sites for the promotion and dissemination of the ideology of a national, natural history but were also lead institutions in the introduction of new technologies of display and graphic arts, many of which flowed into theatrical practice. The American Museum in New York, founded by Gardiner Baker and John Pintard in 1791, contained a mixture of visual exhibits that would later find their own specialized sites. A 1793 Broadside in the collection of the New-York Historical Society catalogues some live animals, including a porcupine, some stuffed curiosities – a lamb with two heads – mounted birds, a collection of wax figures, an air gun, coins, and Indian war implements. The whole room was elaborately painted with exotic scenes, a sky blue ceiling, and an area devoted to copies of history paintings. When the museum moved into its new quarters in the Old Almshouse, the pictorial side of the business was extended with a small cosmorama, transparencies of natural subjects, and next door (in 1817) John Vanderlyn opened his purpose-built rotunda in which to house his panoramas of Paris and Versailles. The exhibition of transparencies was also a part of regular theatrical practice through the period, especially in historical dramas with national themes, such as H. J. Finn's ever popular *Montgomery; or, the Falls of Montmorency.* In such plays transparencies would be worked into the drama as well as being displayed as an entr'acte complete with an address and patriotic song. There were also scenic burlettas, such as Moncrieff's *Paris and London; or, a Trip to both Cities,* featuring a moving diorama that presented a journey from Calais to London, and, finally, requiring all of the machinist's art, there were the disaster pieces that led up to cataclysmic finales, as with the ubiquitous *Masaniello:* "A View of the Bay of Naples, bordering on Portici and Tore Del Greco. VIEW OF VESUVIUS. Terrific explosion!! Forked lightnings rend the sky; the burning lava impetuously flows down the side of the mountain and the whole country becomes AWFULLY ILLUMINATED" (cited in Smither, 81).

The work of illusionists in the museum and the theatre deserves to be seen in the context of a general expansion in the visual exhibition business, and, for all of the nineteenth century, close connections existed between the theatre and the graphic arts. The museums fed Americans' unquenchable interest in the details of natural creation, and the pictorial side of drama was enhanced through the importation of visual wonders directly from these sites. In addition, museums attracted an emerging industry of pictorial representation around its periphery. Scudder's elegant five-story, marble-fronted structure near City Hall in New York (opened in 1830, captured by Barnum in 1841) had, in 1838, Nathaniel Currier's glass-fronted store for his popular prints two blocks to the south, and six years later Mathew Brady established a sumptuous daguerreotype gallery across the street that contained not only pictures of famous politicians and criminals but also the human oddities that Barnum had gathered.

The attraction of summer gardens, apart from offering a cool site for light performances, was that they allowed the simultaneous enjoyment of two different worlds, both the exotic and the urban. The "urban" was preserved through the ability of the "fashion" to promenade in circles around a centrally placed bandshell and to engage in formal kinds of socializing – balls, cotillions, and so forth – whereas the exotic could be found in all of the orientalist elements, the little alhambras, and the hundreds of lamps hanging from the trees, which brought the fairy tale elements of the pantomime into the open air. The Chatham Garden in 1810 advertised the best assortment of statuary, fountains, grottoes, and cascades.

The gardens provided regular employment for all of the novelty acts that appeared on the legitimate stages during their regular seasons. There were ventriloquists; fire-eaters; Antipodeans; and Polyphonists (who would imitate dog barks, locomotives, bees, and so forth); Parisian or Grecian posture masters (such as Mathis, who regaled American audiences through the mid-1820s with spectacular leaps, bending, tumbling, and tightrope dancing); Italian and Chinese shades; and, finally, puppets.

Two forms that were impossible to maintain in regular theatres and found their natural home in the gardens were balloon ascensions and elaborate displays of pyrotechnics. Because of improvements in rocketry, we now tend to look up at fireworks, but in the early nineteenth century more focus was given to earthbound displays, with showers of sparks and roman candles emerging in front of painted scenery, or from freestanding architectural and topographical models in the form of a theatrical setting. Judging by the records, pyrotechnics were ubiquitous through the summer months in all the American cities, with sites, such as New York's Castle Garden after 1835, holding shows every other night. To make the price of attendance (twenty-five cents) worthwhile, orchestral music usually accompanied the shows, and sometimes displays of light and sound were worked up into full-length fireworks epics, as in "The Grand Eruption of Mount Vesuvius."

Summer gardens, aside from pyrotechnics and ascensions, specialized in all forms of spectacle: dances, pantomimes, poses plastique, pageants. Among the most distinctive were tableaux vivants, living representations usually taken from famous prints, paintings, or statuary. Living statuary first shows up in the Vauxhall Gardens in 1826, where a "posture master" assumed a succession of classical attitudes covered in flour to suggest plaster of Paris or marble. The first advertised instances of poses plastique on the regular stage were in September 1831 at New York's Park Theatre, where Ada Barrymore held the pose of Scheffer's "The Soldier's Widow" for a few minutes.

The growing enthusiasm for this genre in theatres and gardens through the 1840s may seem a little difficult to understand, yet it was commensurate with the acting practice of striking attitudes within the course of a legitimate play, to freeze the action to "make a point." This was especially common in melodramas, in which the plot proceeded through acts of nomination and discovery ("You are my long lost daughter," and so forth) and the audience's reception of which was dependent on the comfortable recognition of character types. A character's dress, gait, demeanor, and name instantly disclosed his or her relation to the forces of good or evil. As Peter Brooks has suggested, the root of melodrama is "excess," the fear that something may be left unsaid. Frozen tableaux were a way of highlighting the hinges in the narrative. The most famous stage tableau of all – the apotheosis of little Eva – certainly overdetermined the message: "Glorious clouds, tinted with sunlight. EVA, robed in white, is discovered on the back of a milk-white dove, with expanded wings, as if just soaring upward. Her hands are extended in benediction over ST. CLARE and UNCLE TOM, who are kneeling and gazing up to her" (vi, vii).

Tableaux within dramatic action were only one way in which "living" pictures were utilized. During the famous Boz ball in 1842 to fete Charles Dickens, for instance, actors represented still-life scenes from illustrations in the novels. In the late 1840s, enterprising managers, often under the sobriquet of professors, began to exploit the resources of tableaux vivant, not for verisimilitude to art but for exposure of the body itself. A Dr. Collyer, about whom nothing is known, began to present "Model personifications" in September 1847 at a fairly respectable house called The Apollo Rooms. Though he presented male performers in such politically correct poses as "A monument to Washington," the greatest draw were the women who sculpted, thinly draped, "The Three Graces." Many imitators followed, at each stage with less propriety, until "model artistes" exhibitions flooded side-street houses such as the Hall of Novelty, the Temple of the Muses, and the Anatomical Museum. "Biblical" scenes were much in evidence, such as "Esther in the Persian Hot Bath" and "Eve in the Garden of Eden." The New York *Herald* (2 Dec. 1847) reported that there were a dozen "taverns, hotels, saloons, and other drinking houses – where young men and women are exhibiting, in every form and shape, and for every price, from sixpence up to fifty cents." The final development, before the police cracked down, was an exhibition of totally naked, dancing women viewed through a portal of stretched gauze at the Eagle Hotel on Canal Street; 22 March 1848 thus stands as the first documented instance of nude dancing, a prelude to the striptease (see McCullough, 165, n. 44).

On an entirely different and respectable track, summer gardens, even more than the theatre, offered a hospitable venue for the development of musical culture. Public concerts were a rarity in the United States until the 1790s when a host of immigrant musicians appeared on the scene, many in flight from the revolutionary disturbances in Europe. Musicians had to job together a variety of employments to make a living, as theatre folk (not only before the performances but also during intermissions when they supplied large amounts of "act music"), as teachers, as "originators of subscription concerts" usually containing a ball or assembly within the package, and as merchants of musical and luxury wares to supply the demand they had a hand in creating.

It was through music rather than theatrical displays that U.S. cities developed an infrastructure of "refined" culture, often French in coloration. Brillat-Savarin, the famous gastronomic writer, tried to introduce New Yorkers to the delights of French cuisine as well as play in the Park Theatre's orchestra, whereas the lead violinist Charles Collet introduced brioche at a local bakery. French immigrants also opened dancing and fencing establishments throughout the 1790s. Newly organized musical societies attempted to refine the tastes of the American public even further by introducing uncut compositions of Handel and Haydn. New York possessed its first, and certainly not last, philharmonic society as early as 1799, and in 1804, George Jackson conducted the first sacred music performances of oratorios. Well-known merchants usually led in the organization of such efforts through the formation of institutions whose bylaws actually forbade the presence of professionals on their boards. Perhaps because of such exclusivity the attempts to introduce regularly scheduled "classical" performances met with little success in any city until the late 1820s. Though there were obvious differences between a five-cent tavern entertainment and a three-dollar subscription concert the performances themselves were not thought to require a different sensibility, a special education, or distinct forms of attention and critique. Even secular musical concerts, until the 1830s, contained a loose mixture of material – overtures, glees, comic songs, single movements from symphonies, and so forth – that would tax the imagination of contemporary orchestral conductors and would, because of their undisciplined variety, fall squarely within today's "popular" categorization.

One of the most interesting, and least explored, forms that arose in gardens and theatres after about 1790 were the staged patriotic spectacles that drew both on street processions and the pantomime tradition and undoubtedly helped to install republican iconography in the minds of the public. There were grand history and military pantomimes – with music but without words – such as "American Independence" (Charleston, 1795) and patriotic sketches such as "America: Commerce and Freedom" (New York, 1812). Almost every theatre and garden in the Early National Period managed to stage simple one-act effusions celebrating the heroic activities of tars and soldiers, whereas the Revolutionary leaders, as they died, were feted with grand allegorical finales, as with "The Apotheosis of Franklin: His Reception in the Elysian Fields" (Charleston, 1796). Black and Indian figures show up in these vehicles, as they did in front of target company excursions, as symbols of American "natural" exceptionalism and as trademarks of political republicanism. Though they were not full citizens, they were evidence of American sovereignty. On 14 June 1815, for instance, a grand spectacle entitled *4th of July; or, America, Commerce and Freedom* featured a set of transparencies of revolutionary subjects, a few military convolutions, and a song about the battle of Champlain and Plattsburg (Micah Hawkins?) performed in the character of a black sailor. A recurrent tension existed then, between freedom and foolishness, between using these types for comic purposes and their employment in the scenography of republican virtue.

Early Native Types

One local character was definitely pulled in a virtuous direction. The stage Yankee, when he first appears, is no more than a regular rural buffoon no different in kind from English or Irish rustic types. Early delineators, including Wignell's figuring of Jonathan in Tyler's *The Contrast* (1787), employed bright-red wigs, a prop that may be traced back to various "Toby" figures such as Toby Allspice in Thomas Morton's *The Way to Get Married* and symptomatic of his subversive, servant status. The first Yankee peddler appears in a small afterpiece by A. B Lindsey entitled *Yankee Notions* (1808), but it is not until he is integrated into longer works that his commercial character is sealed. The Chatham Garden in New York, for instance, produced the first two American operas: Micah Hawkins's short-lived *The Sawmill* (1824) and Samuel Woodworth's *The Forest Rose* (1825), which, without its music by John Davies, had a long run as a regular play. Out of these vehicles emerged a more rounded character of the "Yankee" as a wise rural rube and a straight vernacular type, innocent of the mirth he created in the audience. He was further stabilized and fleshed out by James H. Hackett, who achieved success in a Yankee adaptation of Colman's *Who Wants a Guinea?,* emerging as one Solomon Swap in *Jonathan in England* (1827) and as Industrious Doolittle, "a busy talkative speculating Yankee," in *The Times; or, Travels in America.* After Hackett's success, other comedic actors developed greater specialization in native parts. George Handel Hill covered the same roles as well as adding Jedediah Homebred in J. S. Jones's *The Green*

Mountain Boy (1833); Thomas Dartmouth Rice and Dan Marble also worked the enthusiasm. (See Chapter 3, for more discussion of the Yankee.)

These new pieces were innovative in that the Yankee's initial servant or farm-boy status gave way to a self-activating, garrulous, entrepreneurial character. He still possessed the physical awkwardness and verbal peculiarities of a low-comic type, yet he gained in narrative strength – spinning out tales in an endless thread of neologisms – and despite his gentle blasphemy a preternatural moral and political virtue as well. His new "Jacksonian" independence was also heightened by his placement in an international setting, either as a traveler or as a gentleman encountering foreign visitors. Indeed, after about 1830, the Yankee is seldom found on his own New England turf but is rather dispatched to London, China, New Orleans (most amusingly in H. A. Buckingham's *A Day in France; or, the Yankee at Calais* [1838]) – anywhere his regional and national distinctiveness is thrown into sharp relief. From being a comic type, subverting civic dignity, the Yankee rose to being a social type representing national ideals. This elevation also required more low-others as a butt for his natural smarts. In the vehicle plays written for Marble, Hackett, Rice, and Hill, dramatists seldom restricted themselves to one America type. Cornelius Logan's *The Vermont Wool Dealer* (1838), for instance, included two comic black figures and an Irish servant. Black–Yankee comic confrontations were indeed a near requirement in vehicle plays, perhaps as a device to aid the Yankee's ascent from his vernacular origins.

Indians were useful in this regard, though their ideological placement worked against humorous characterizations. Real Indians began to play themselves, devoid of ritual context, in "war" dance entr'actes during the 1820s. Six Seneca appeared at the Chatham Garden in the fall of 1824, and six Oneidans at the Lafayette Amphitheater in 1827. Already by those dates a modest transatlantic museum trade in Indians had taken place (five showed up in Bristol in 1818). These performances had little connection to the sentimental and dignified stage Indian who was evolving in heroic melodrama and who made his presence felt most strongly in Forrest's tremendously popular rendition of Metamora (Augustus Stone, 1829); the other obvious and perennial case of a figure elevated onto the high moral plain of tragedy was Pocahontas, who in George Custis's play (1830) showed the necessary mixture of mercy and bravery in her struggles with Powhatan.

Most Indians parts, however, remained marginal figures. Nathaniel H. Bannister's *The Fall of San Antonio; or, Texas Victorious* (1836) featured an Indian Dance and vanquished Mexicans as affirmative subjects of American uniqueness and as objects of inferiority to white republican government. When *Oceloa; or, the Death of Dade* (L. F. Thomas, 1837) was produced in New Orleans, the rampant heroism of the chief was severely criticized in the *New Orleans Courier* (24 Dec. 1836): "The Indian character is not dramatic, and this subject is doubly unfortunate in being the story of our defeat and disgrace. The triumph of our enemies over ourselves can never be represented with success on any stage." Indian characters could thus be worked for their heroic potential but preferably only in settings that left them solitary, taciturn, and defeated. The much more popular *Nick of the Woods* (1838) by Louisa Medina specialized in the pure, bloody revenge of a frontiersman against Indians who had killed his family.

The most enduring native type, however, was the black character portrayed by whites in burnt cork. Here the most important early delineator was Thomas Dartmouth Rice, who claimed to have witnessed in 1828 a disabled black stable hand perform a strange hopping dance, possibly in Louisville. The figure ended his dance with the verse:

> Weel about, and turn about
> and do jis so:
> Eb'-ry time I weel about
> I jump Jim Crow.

Rice's debut of this kinetic skit at the Bowery Theatre, in 1832, before the vigorous plebeian audience that the Bowery was then attracting, caused an enormous sensation. Rice was encouraged to extend the piece by developing other figures – Ginger Blue, Jumbo Jim, and Zip Larkin – and incorporating them into "Ethiopian Operas," knockabout travesties of the refined Italian forms. By the mid-thirties other comedic actors who were active in Yankee work, especially Barney Williams, joined the Ethiopian craze, and Jack Diamond made a specialty of appropriating black dance forms that could be seen in urban markets: hornpipes, pigeon wings, and double shuffles.

By the 1830s, then, a range of vernacular types, elaborated by talented performers, had begun to make their passage from their emblematic status in parades or from their liminal status in street, forest, or farm onto the commercial stage. Yet this stage, in the process of appropriating such common types, was obviously a more "popular" place than it had been in 1810. To read notices for Ricketts's circus from that date recommending that servants retain seats for their masters before the performance, or to encounter the theatrical criticism of a Washington Irving regretting the antics of the artisan "gods," in the upper gallery, is to encounter a theatrical milieu no different in kind from that of Astley's or Covent Garden in late-eighteenth-century London. The social metaphor for the composition of the theatre audience as late as 1825 remained the "town" to which all grades and ranks were admitted even though they were distributed by price within the auditorium. Until the early 1830s public places of resort did not reflect or, better, amplify social stratification. Taverns, inns, circuses, gardens, museums, and theatres potentially accommodated most grades of society, and those people who stayed away from them probably did so for religious or ethnocultural reasons. The poor, of course, were excluded by price; many rural dwellers did not possess much access; and respectable women, as we have seen, had to have the protection of male company. Nevertheless, the cultural elaboration of social distinction was relatively mute; social stratification still remained rooted in family, land ownership, political appointments, and preferment but not, in a way so obvious later, cultural taste.

Stratification of Performance

By the 1830s, however, as all eastern port cities began to sustain several permanent places of amusement, it was obvious to residents and visitors alike that a hierarchy of sites was beginning to form and with it a differentiation of genres by site. In New York nearly everyone agreed that the Park attracted a more fashionable audience than the Bowery, even though many of the plays remained the same, and, moreover, that differing relationships existed between the audience and the stage, depending on what grade of performance was being offered.

The expansion in popular entertainments and the entry of the popular classes encouraged members of the haute bourgeoisie to relinquish their patronage of staged drama and to turn to the support of orchestral and sacred music, as well as to Italian Opera. As the New York *Herald* observed on 31 March 1841, "the taste of the intelligent and educated classes has merged into music of the very highest order."

The order referred to here was of two kinds: First, a new hierarchy of musical genres developed, with the orchestral and vocal music of Handel, Haydn, and Beethoven, now termed classical, overshadowing the older English and Irish theatrical and ballad forms of Tom Moore and the like. Second, a new order of performance values arose to accommodate this "taste of the intelligent and educated classes." Longer musical forms and the complexities of Italian opera required strict and assured standards of production in which one person could be held responsible for the aesthetic results. At the same time that actor-managers, such as Englishman William Charles Macready, were beginning to assume responsibilities equivalent to today's director, orchestra leaders stopped playing the fiddle and began to wave their bows in the manner of modern conductors. In both cases a single authority developed who conceived of a work in its entirety in advance of the performance. The audience received, in addition to an evening of edification, one man's interpretation of a known classic, and this was confirmed or questioned, for the first time, by a cadre of professional critics employed by the popular and monthly press. The process of reception, one might say, was extended on either side of the performance itself and thus became part of a broader acquisition of taste, discrimination, and refinement. The project of "culture," in the Arnoldian sense, had begun.

This aesthetic of reception, which was shown by Michael Broyles to owe its origins to German Romanticism and which was first broadcast through music journals, ratified and made plain older distinctions between amusement and edification. Amusement was the evanescent, vigorous, and immediate world of minstrelsy; travesty; spectacle; and, by the 1850s, vaudeville. On the other, refined, side lay orchestral music; oratorio; opera; lectures; and, by midcentury, Shakespeare in his historically authenticated versions. The first category presented the most fertile ground for the development of national characters and themes; the second evidenced the desire for supranational, or at least transatlantic, notions of "civilization" and "culture."

It was, ironically, a downturn in growth that produced even more innovation in American popular amusements and that gave rise to further forms of a distinctly national character. The long depression of 1837–44 was a disaster for established legitimate houses, whereas minor places of resort, those that could think of fare to offer at twenty-five cents or less, did spectacularly well. As the *New York Express* noted on 25 March 1841, "The failure of the large houses and success of the minor ones presents an anomaly which it is difficult to reconcile. Public taste has been diverted from its usual course, and it will require time, skill, and judgment to bring it back again."

The major, legitimate houses did recover by 1845, and yet public taste, if measured by predepression standards, never "recovered" its old course. New sections of the public had been brought into the world of amusements during the Panic, and the demand for an extended range of cheap shows never abated. In addition, the depression accelerated the division of forms by site; it siphoned off the remunerative, light occasional pieces from the legitimate stage to which they were never entirely to return. The structure and conditions of show business were irrevocably changed.

One of the more interesting developments in the towns throughout the depression was the appearance of small drinking places offering entertainments on the free-and-easy principle. Malachi Fallon's Ivy Green Saloon (72 Elm Street), for instance, became a home of Irish folktales, songs, and instrumental music. At the once genteel Vauxhall Garden in 1841, an energetic manager named P. T. Barnum advertised "Grand Trials of Skill at Negro Dancing" and asked the public to witness enactments of such city types as "The Fireman" and "The Fulton Market Roarer and the Catherine Market Screamer." Prizes for amateur slack-rope walking and beauty contests rounded out the bill. Barnum and others thus began to appropriate, at very low cost, entertainments that had previously had their life in the streets and markets of the cities. Placed in the context of the commercial stage, these acts became part affirmation, part travesty of people's obvious idiosyncrasies of character and occupation.

Travesty, indeed, was the "legitimate," though overtly popular, theatrical form through which these occupational and ethnic identities passed finally onto the formal stage. The home of American travesty through the middle years of the century was William Mitchell's tiny Olympic Theatre (1837) at 444 Broadway, New York, modeled on Madame Vestris's legendary house of that name in London. Using the resources of his main writer and sometime dentist Dr. William K. Northall, the orchestra leader George Loder, and a dedicated stock company, Mitchell managed to produce a remarkable run of hits following the London modes of extravaganza and burlesque. His theatre became the main American outlet for James Robinson Planché's musical extravaganzas such as *The Bee and the Orange Tree,* and he kept alive the traditions of holiday pantomime with long runs of *Cinderella* (1844). Almost all of these creations, under his management, were absurdist in their use of strange juxtapositions of scene and in the way they drew attention to their own artifice through asides, prologues, and choruses. The pace of production at the Olympic was furious: Odell counts 109 separate shows for the 1846 season alone. In return for his efforts he recruited a dedicated audience of "pit-tites," whose antics and spontaneous wit was as much part of the show as what transpired on stage, and his ability to interpolate comic line, double entendres, and bad puns brought him the name the "Prince of Gag."

Though Mitchell is known as an importer of the Vestris style of rhymed burlesque, it was his near-instantaneous send-ups of local events that sealed his reputation. Charles Kean's Richard III became "Richard III to kill" within a week of the actor's debut in New York. *The Upper Row House on Disaster Place* (1847) appeared less than four days after the new opera house opened to dismal revues on Astor Place. A take-off of *Lucia di Lammermoor,* called *Lucy Did Sham Amour,* emerged as a farcical feud between two rival pill manufacturers. Here scenes included the fountain in City Hall Park, Moffat's Broadway building, and the Broadway Tabernacle, and the characters ranged from Mr. Puff, the newspaper man (James Gordon Bennett); Mr. Nabob, the codfish aristocrat; and, usually, the insufferable verbose cultural critic N. P. Willis, who emerged simply as Mr. N. P. Willis. Throughout the late 1840s, Mitchell developed his plays with a repeatable inventory of local stock types, from market women through pretentious wealthy folk. His "hits," in the sense of apt imitation, hit local targets.

This introduces a more general point. Though most popular genres, plots, and bits of stage business were imported, it required only modest effort and no legal struggle (in the absence of an international copyright law) to adapt them to local conditions. A "low" setting of Billingsgate easily transferred to the Bowery and the question posed by J. Stirling Coyne's ever popular "Did you ever send your wife to Wapping?" could quickly be answered, as it was, in terms of Sacramento, Hoboken, or Philadelphia. Indeed, because the absur-

Frank Chanfrau (1824–84), who specialized in the role of Mose the Fire B'hoy, first in 1848 in Benjamin Baker's *A Glance at New York,* but seen as the "lion" of the town with his red shirt, plug hat, soap-lock curls, and turned-up trousers, in other subsequent "Mose" plays. Don B. Wilmeth Collection.

dist comedy of travesty and burlesque proceeds best with a density of local allusion and instant topicality, the truly successful plays often ended up offering a topographical realism.

This is certainly the case with one old English vehicle, *Tom and Jerry; or, Life in London,* a stage adaptation of Pierce Egan's illustrated serial from 1820. For many years a *Life in New York* had been trotted out as an afterpiece to legitimate plays, frequently on the occasion of the volunteer firemen's regular benefit night at the Park Theatre and later at the Bowery. Its loose plot line, no more than a series of "sprees" conducted by Corinthian Tom and Bob Logic through the high and low life of the city, offered generous opportunities for the incorporation of local color. To produce a "Life of" some city became almost a required test of an actor's and author's abilities to work the local audience. John Brougham's first recorded American play was *Life in New York* in 1843, complete with Irish interpolations, and Thomas D. Rice managed to jump Jim Crow in Burns's *Life in Philadelphia* (1836). Nathaniel Bannister, during his New Orleans sojourn, added a real black street vendor, "Old Corn Meal," into his *Life in New Orleans* (1837) to great acclaim and surprising little protest given the racial feeling in the city.

Thus, it would not have required a great leap in imagination for Benjamin Baker, the Olympic's prompter, to translate the plot of *Tom and Jerry* into *A Glance at New York in 1848* as a simple afterpiece for his benefit night. Baker took a young Connecticut greenhorn named George Parsells into New York City, where he experiences a series of "scrapes" with loafers and sharpers. Instead of being guided by the original Corinthian Tom, George is escorted by no other than "Mose, a true specimen of one of the B'hoys." When Mose, played by Frank Chanfrau, appeared in the second scene he was "received with shouts of delight from the thousand originals of the pit." Realizing that they had a winner, Chanfrau, Baker, and Mitchell redrafted the piece with Mose as the central protagonist, relegating Parsells to a minor role. Two further weeks of playing to crowded houses convinced Chanfrau to move Mose to the Chatham Theatre, under his own management, where the "stove-pipe hat literati" filled the whole theatre rather than just the pit. In this new version, called *New York As It Is,* plebeian life was given an even larger canvas. Mose received a new sidekick named Joe, "a Catherine Market Loafer," and Harry Gordon (previously a rather old-fashioned "Gothamite") became Charlie Meadows, "a New Yorker"; Parsells, the rural type who was a carry-over from the Tom and Jerry plot, shrank into the tiny character of William Twill. New scenes included the Chatham Theatre itself, the interior of a soup house, a "nigger" dancing for eels in Catherine Market, and a burning house in the Bowery. Over the next forty-seven consecutive nights, *New York As It Is* became the most popular play ever performed on an American stage. David Rinear has estimated that between 15 April 1848 and 6 July 1850, Chanfrau appeared at least three hundred and eighty-five times in seven different Mose plays.

Continuing the many transactions between stage and street, "Mose" escaped from Chanfrau's delineation. Children took to shouting "Sykesy, take de butt" outside the engine houses, and the whole play was reenacted by real "B'hoys" at the North River Docks. Lithographers reproduced all of the scenes from *New York As It Is* and turned out sketches of the heroic fire laddie relieving oppression in all parts of the globe. This outpouring of Mose plays, prints, and personifications did not meet with universal approval. William K. Northall now thought that the "illegitimate" style had been taken far enough. He called *A Glance at New York in 1848* an "unmitigated conglomeration of vulgarity and illiteracy . . . low in design, vulgar in language and improbable in plot." He blamed the entire declension of popular drama on this single production – "the boxes no longer shone with the elite of the city; the character of the audiences was entirely changed, and Mose, instead of appearing on the stage, was in the pit, the boxes and the gallery" (91–92). The *Herald* (28 April

1848), however, saw in Mose and his stage success proof positive that democracy offered the best system for the cultivation of art and commerce:

> It has formerly been the policy of the rulers of the people on the continent of Europe to grant large sums annually for the support of the theatres, and thus, by keeping these establishments open at low prices, they provided abundant amusement for the many, and hoped to keep them from paying too much attention to the acts of their rulers. This system was all very well for a time, but seems to have broken down lately, as if the folks of Europe are all performing real melodramas, in which the hurried exits of kings and potentates are the chief incidents. But what we want to come at is this, that here, in our happy and free country, the sovereigns also make large contributions to the support of the theatres – the sovereign people we mean.

From Mitchell's house, this kind of localized burlesque rooted in the figures and concerns of the street moved in many directions. More than a particular property of one manager and writer, "burlesque" is best viewed as a persistent modality in American popular theatre, one that informed the creation of minstrelsy, the further development of pantomime, and, after 1850, the rise of the leg show and of musical comedy.

Pantomime and the Minstrel Show

Pantomime took a decidedly popular direction in the hands of George L. Fox, who was the reigning hero of the Bowery until after the Civil War. Fox's genius was to blend the rough realism of the "Mose" style of vernacular drama with the absurdist elements of the pantomime, especially the absurdist elements of the harlequinade. Unlike the contemporary English pantos, which were built around stars, Fox's works employed a remarkable range of local talent from Barnum's giants to champion roller skaters. Fox's chief innovation with the pantomime form was to establish it as a self-standing, two-act drama, rather than an auxiliary piece. The rough magic of the harlequinade spread throughout the show. The vehicle *Humpty Dumpty,* penned by Clifton Tayleure in 1867 and clearing over $1.4 million in its first season, was unbelievably parochial in its allusions and scene settings. Apart from the usual range of jokes made at the expense of New Jersey, which was personified in the prologue, almost all of the written humor requires detailed historical elucidation. The scenes included a German billiard saloon, Wild's candy store on Broadway, and the yet unfinished Tweed Court House on Chambers Street. The force of the piece, literally, issued from Fox's kinetic abilities at knockabout comedy. Humpty, on his wall, has plenty of bricks at hand, and these were dispatched, with increasing velocity and at shortened intervals toward the head of an upper-class New York fop. Other acts of unrestrained brutality and vandalism followed: Humpty steals a pig, turns over carts, and kidnaps babies. This perhaps wore the aspect of a charivari, a world turned upside down, except that such ritual inversions are supposed to serve the moral function of pointing out the regular order of society. In *Humpty Dumpty* there is no order, just an amoral frenzy, and the action unfolds as a fantastic recreation of unpoliced streets, or worse. It was inevitable, perhaps, that Fox should appear toward the end of the show dressed as one of New York's finest, beating the rest of the characters around the head with a nightstick. The *Times* detected in Humpty a "picture of hundreds of young mischievous youths who are daily suffered to wander about too little guarded for their years and their propensities" (quoted in Senelick, 143). Though rough antics had always been part of panto and the earlier Joe Grimaldi tradition of clowning in England, to Fox perhaps we may trace back a line of popular stage cartoon-like violence, unframed by either the tragedy of thwarted love or the comedy of families reunited. (For another perspective on Fox, see Chapter 4, "The Emergence of the American Actor.")

Apart from Fox, pantomime remained a minor form in America after 1850. Most of the transgressive energies of popular theatre had already been siphoned off into new forms of Ethiopian delineation. The history of blackface minstrelsy has one clear date, an interesting set of precursors, and a long trail of development and interpretation. The date, 6 February 1843, is when the Virginia minstrels debuted at the Bowery Amphitheatre. This was the first time that a quartet of veteran blackface performers – William Whitlock, R. W. Pelham, Frank Brower, and the famous Dan Emmett – decided to pool their resources and establish a loosely structured evening of variety entertainment. They had gathered together, apparently without much rehearsal, to perform what Emmett called a charivari. The first evening offered no more than a series of songs played discordantly, but so successful was the idea that soon they, and their imitators, incorporated or burlesqued almost all of the available theatrical forms in a kind of blackface shorthand.

The first thing to be noticed about minstrelsy, therefore, is that it was a very open, malleable form and that its popularity, at the simplest level, may be accounted for by its spontaneity, the quickness and freshness of the improvisation, as well as being a novel, unstructured way in which to frame and collect older routines and pieces of stage business. Among the standard skits taken up by nearly all troupes in the first decade were locomotive impressions, wench acts (not only of the "Lucy Long" variety but also mock women's rights lectures), a break for conundrums (offered by the audience for prizes as well as by the performers themselves), and finally travesties (usually either of Shakespeare or of Italian opera). To confuse matters even further, not all of the acts in early minstrelsy were in burnt cork. Room was found for Irish and Yankee skits, and within a year there were "real" African Americans – the Apolyons from Brooklyn – performing before mixed-race audiences.

Though minstrelsy began as an interchangeable sequence of song-and-dance numbers it soon gained a distinctive three-part structure, though a recent interpretation by William Maher is based on a number of structural variants in antebellum minstrel shows. The first part featured a line of players often seated in semicircle. The end-men Bruder Tambo and Bruder Bones played two racial stereotypes, either the plantation darky or the free black urban dandy. They served as the mischievous, vernacular low-other, the ends able to spin out of control. The master of ceremonies, the middleman or interlocutor, tried as best he could through high-flown diction and upper-class manner to keep control of the performance, always with dismal success. There were many opportunities, within the gradient of class represented in the line, for puns, double entendres, and malapropisms – for great social and behavioral misunderstanding. The second part contained the "olio," or variety, entertainment, which ranged from sentimental songs to a standard "stump" speech. The evening often ended with a short one-act skit, usually of an Ethiopian opera variety, and often located in the South. Commentators have detected in this three-part structure a loose narrative of return and nostalgia running through the show, but it is also clear that the excitement of the show depended on the expectation of the structure breaking down and the possibilities of irruption.

As Charles Haswell noted, later generations would "fail to understand the extent and the power of the minstrel 'craze' when it was at its height . . . . 'New Negro songs' were sent out almost daily from the publishers' presses and were sung all over the land. . . . Households that had amused themselves with singing English opera (which had been greatly in fashion) and English glees and part-songs, turned to the new melodies." Besides the original compositions, Haswell notes that a crowd of parodies appeared: "'The Mellow Horn' became the 'The Yellow Corn': Balf's air, 'I Dreamt that I Dwelt in Marble Halls' was Africanized into 'I Dreamt that I Dwelt in Hotel Walls . . .'" (447).

What did "Africanized" mean in this context? As Haswell's two brief examples indicate, much of the subject matter ignored plantation life and the conditions of slavery: urban topicality, travesties of opera following Mitchell, and popular airs formed much of the minstrels' diet. Nevertheless, most of the early minstrel show performers established stories that seem to testify to their direct observation of African American culture. E. P. Christy claimed to be "the first to catch our native airs as they floated wildly, or hummed in the balmy breezes of the sunny south," and he made a point of stressing his use of authentic plantation instruments – the banjo, bone castanets, tambourine, and violin. Yet claims about the plantation origin of minstrelsy had less to do with the authenticity of musical and dance forms than the need to present something distinctively American during a time of overwhelming foreign influence in popular musical culture. Minstrelsy was touted as being "truly national and truly democratic." It had after all "its home among the slaves and fairly represents their amusements, character, and social condition" (*Broadway Journal,* 12 July 1845). As Mark Twain noted in his autobiography, "I remember the first Negro musical show I ever saw. It must have been in the early forties. It was a new institution. In our village of Hannibal . . . it burst upon us as a glad and stunning surprise" (59). What was no doubt stunning to Twain was not the novelty of seeing black dance forms but the arrival of a developed urban entertainment of a distinctly national kind. Moreover, as many scholars have shown, almost all of early delineators were born in cities in the middle Atlantic states, and most had previous careers in circuses or variety or as supernumerary actors: Christy's southern experiences were with a traveling circus; Stephen Foster, born in Pittsburgh, wandered south only as far as Cincinnati; Dan Emmett's longest stay south of Mason–Dixon was as an underage drummer in the army. The minstrel show became these actors' chosen vehicle to propel them onto the lucrative stages of the eastern cities.

The black mask of minstrelsy did prove useful in dulling the sharp edges of all kinds of issues – sex, class, and race – without totally denying them. In the same way that blacks had "performed" themselves in northern markets and plantation yards in order to express joy, suffering, and resistance, so northern minstrels could employ the resources of blackface to poke fun at "aristocratic" pretension, to suggest sexual desire, and to simply enjoy the freedom of "misrule." That they also were overtly racist at the same time need not be a contradiction. The meanings of the minstrel show were as unruly as its style of performance. Ways still have to be developed to allow for the ideological capaciousness of popular forms. This is especially true in the use of racial humor, in which there was obviously the possibility of laughing at blackface and with blackface at the same time. In what is certainly the most imaginative and close reading of early minstrelsy to date, Eric Lott, in *Love and Theft,* shows the ways in which minstrel routines could elaborate northern themes in southern guise. Songs such as Foster's "De Blue Tail Fly" (1844), in which a master is jubilantly killed off, spoke to male workers' apprehensions of boss power, whereas songs in which the master retained the loyalty of slaves might have addressed the patriarchial imaginings of workers about their fractured household arrangements.

Minstrelsy also worked well at elaborating southern themes in northern guise. Minstrel depiction of southern life, such as it was, was of a timeless rural Arcadia with simple virtues and needs, not a place of forced commercial agriculture. Slaves were sorrowful, but also domestic and contented. This form of domestic piety matched well with the images of the peculiar institution advanced by southern apologists and more specifically with the needs of the

Boston Minstrels, illustrating two stereotypes ("dandyism" of the North and "Ethiopians of the South"). This 1843 Endicott lithograph sheet music cover for "Cudjo's Wild Hunt" by Anthony Winnemore shows the six members of the company in both types of roles with Winnemore (playing banjo) second from left in both rows. Brown University Library.

Democratic party to maintain their North-South alliance in the face of a rising Republican Party. Most minstrel showmen, in the early period, had known alliances with the Democratic Party, and as Alexander Saxton has observed, the shows effectively propagandized, in rather general ways, an alliance between white workers in the North and plantation interests. Several examples of the interrelationship between the Democratic Party and minstrelsy may be offered. E. P. Christy was the personal favorite of many Democratic Party politicians in New York, in part because of his partnership with Henry Wood, Mayor Fernando Wood's brother. The song featured in Dan Emmett's famous "Dixie's Land" walk-around finale became the unofficial Confederate anthem, and Stephen Foster was heavily involved in the Buchanan, anti-abolitionist wing of the party and penned songs about the unifying ethos of the South:

> We'll not outlaw the land that holds
> The bones of Washington,
> Where Jackson fought and Marion bled
> And the battles of the brave were won.

The connections between the new range of commercial entertainments and the Democratic Party were not just partisan in the narrow sense. Whig Party rhetoric through the 1840s stressed the benefits of temperance, self-regulation, and piety, and, usually, to include nativists, adopted a hostile stance toward recent and continued European immigration, especially the Irish influx. Promoters of popular amusement were hardly likely to embrace a party that threatened to limit their profits, either at the bar or at the ticket office. Even melodramatic versions of *Uncle Tom's Cabin* became heated matters of political correctness, as when Aiken's sentimental, anti-slavery version played at the same time Conway's happy, jokey, version, in which Tom not only lives but finds his freedom and family, played at Barnum's.

Minstrelsy spread out along many routes, not all of them low by any means. Despite the novelty of the routines, the burnt-cork faces, and the "Africanized" instrumentation, audiences were receiving a completely regular diet of variety entertainment. Palmo's legitimate opera company, staffed largely by Italians, appeared in blackface for a season (1845) of Ethiopian operas, in which, for instance, Fra Diavolo became Black Diabolo. Minstrelsy invaded almost all grades of performance sites through the late 1840s and attracted, in ways not yet appreciated by scholars, audiences of respectable families. As a writer in the *Musical Times* (13 Oct. 1849) noted:

> In looking at the so-called Negro music, we have often thought of the peculiar taste of this country in patronizing Negro minstrelsy to such an extent, while in reality the music is of the same character as all the other ballads. We were forcibly reminded of this while we attended a performance of the New Orleans Serenaders at the Philadelphia Melodeon. The program announced to us Negro melodies of various characters; but to our astonishment, we were

regaled with the all-popular ballad of "Jeanette and Jeannot" [from the Olympic's *The Conscription Bride*, 1848], "Vi ravviso" from *La sonnambula*, and several other gems of operas. The audience consisted of the very elite of Philadelphia society and could not have numbered less than a thousand.

Here it seems that to "Africanize" served as a mask to allow respectable families to enter into the new world of variety entertainment much as, in our own time, the Beatles, in whiteface, presented to many middle-class youth a channel of accessibility into subversive "black" music. Racial transpositions can disguise and transgress class barriers in both directions.

The Greatest Showman

If minstrelsy presents a form of contained, commercialized transgression, then our enduring fascination with P. T. Barnum makes sense. It is difficult to offer a balanced, critical assessment of Barnum, in part because he was so insistent, in his many autobiographical endeavors, about the terms of his greatness. His own reputation was surely his largest and most enduring humbug. In the many photographic portraits he commissioned, one sees a garrulous Yankee half-winking at the camera with his mirthful bulk barely contained in a respectable urban suit. So it first becomes necessary to cut him down to manageable size. He was not, for instance, the "father of American advertising." Extensive puffing had been a feature of the penny press since its inception in 1833, and the Bowery Theatre, as early as 1826, had employed a full-time "write-up" man. Neither was he especially innovative with the contents of his various shows and displays. The series of "transient attractions" that he brought to the American Museum, opened in 1842 – Joice Heth, Tom Thumb, bearded ladies, and so forth – had been the mainstay of itinerant showmen for decades. One of his first successes, the Fejee mermaid, that odd collection of sewn-together animal parts, had an exhibition record dating back to 1822.

Barnum's genius, if it may be called that, lay in his directorial energies, especially the manner in which he orchestrated existing elements within amusement culture to produce some deliberately discordant notes. He found new ways to represent material to cater to the public's thirst for novelty. First, there was the building itself. Barnum claimed, when he bought Scudder's existing building and stock, that he was purchasing a moribund institution, though in fact its cabinets, waxworks, and dioramas drew a stable clientele. After the purchase, however, Barnum began to change the relationship of the building to its respectable locale near City Hall and mercantile Broadway. Much of the Bowery flash, in terms of style and audience, that he had learned with his Vauxhall Garden management, traveled with him down to this respectable location. He festooned the front of the museum with glaring

A vigorous P. T. Barnum (1810–91) as he appeared in an 1851 daguerreotype. Don B. Wilmeth Collection.

transparencies that illustrated the permanent attractions. He placed a Drummond lamp, with a power usually reserved for lighthouses, on the roof, thereby dividing New York, according to guidebooks, into "above" and "below" Barnum's. He also employed a dreadful wind and brass ensemble to play on the balcony in the hope of driving customers inside. General Tom Thumb, during his tenure, was contracted to parade along Broadway everyday in his diminutive carriage drawn by miniature horses. No commercial venture had so imposed itself visually on an American city before.

Within the building Barnum centralized all branches of the exhibition business that in London had their own specialized sites. The automata, panoramas, transparencies, waxworks, and stuffed curiosities, as well as the regular series of cabinets, alternated with the transient attractions jobbed in for the week. Now, however, elements of popular performance were bound to a "museum" complex that also claimed to educate citizens in the wonders of natural creation. The Linnean categories, which had informed American museum arrangements from Peale's onward, were punctuated with a host of oddities in a way that the typical oscillated with the merely idiosyncratic.

Barnum's American Museum (formerly Scudder's), Broadway and Ann Street, as it appeared in 1850. Historical Collections, Bridgeport Public Library.

Barnum thus created a department store of amusement that answered to as wide a range of desires as possible. As with his adjustment of the building to its location, the museum's content was designed to appeal to both the rough and the respectable.

Barnum fashioned this mixed bag in the language of radical democracy and, because he was a univeralist, antinomian salvation as well. Everyone could come to his museum to see how things worked and to exercise his or her right to knowledge and amusement. He published claims to an object's authenticity and counterclaims to its falsity; that is, his famed "humbugs" were not simply tricks of outright deception but rather a generous, twenty-five-cent invitation to the audience to test its credulity. This method of somehow implicating an audience in its own deception extended beyond his exhibitions of mechanicals and individual curiosities: Everything he offered was placed in a skewed frame of reference. Barnum played with the ambiguities of categorization. For instance, when the public was enamored with singing families, Barnum put together a group of ex-Shakers who, in costume, and billed as "The Shaking Quakers" (1846), were willing to show the public "the customs and usages of their former co-religionists." There is no reason to believe that the performers danced or sang in anything other than authentic ways, and yet, under Barnum's management, the act must have appeared as the exposure of secrecy and an exhibition of the exotic.

Although the above changes produced almost a travesty of the museum form, Barnum's efforts were always directed at creating a blend of moral piety and instant excitement in which all people, regardless of gender or class, could feel at home. In 1844, he opened a "lecture room" intended for "all those who disapprove of the dissipations, debaucheries, profanity, vulgarity, and other abominations, which characterize our modern theatres." Into this theatre he imported the proven vehicles of the temperance cause such as singing families (eleven in all) and W. H. Smith's *The Drunkard;* he also admitted Shakespeare and minstrelsy "shorn of their objectionable features." The most remarkable innovation lay not in the forms themselves but again in their mode of presentation. In 1846, he invented the practice of matinees and continuous performances so as to attract a new public, which he tagged as "the family audience." The terms of entry into this new public were generous yet exact: No alcohol or profanity was to be allowed. Barnum's development of "unceasing fun" shows the extent to which entertainments had now become unyoked from any ceremonial or calendrical purpose; the commercial carnivalesque took on its current diurnal character.

Barnum's unending search for the largest, though respectable, audience found its greatest success in his management of Jenny Lind's tour in 1850–51. Many European stars had traveled to the United States in search of cash before, yet almost all fell prey, in an era of heightened cultural nationalism, to their "Old World" and potentially corrupt, origins. The dancer Fanny Ellsler (1840) was criticized for her "aristocratic" sexual relations; Ole Bull (1845), the violinist, apparently pandered to the elite; and the British tragedian, William Charles Macready, was driven from the country for making antirepublican statements as a result of the Astor Place Riot of 1849. In Jenny Lind, however, Barnum found a perfect vacant object for his promotional genius, for though she possessed a fine operatic voice, she had developed an open reputation for feminine piety and republican feeling, made all the greater in Barnum's advance publicity. On arrival, he carefully steered his valuable property to all of the important New York institutions in a conscious orchestration of the city's competing cultures; he restricted the elite's access to her, while allowing fire companies to parade before her hotel. To further forestall accusations of "favoritism" and unequal access, he came up with the idea of auctioning the tickets to the concerts, and, of course, he also sold tickets to the auction itself.

By the standards of the time, the Lind tour was a phenomenal success, producing over a half million dollars in revenue for Barnum alone. Above all,

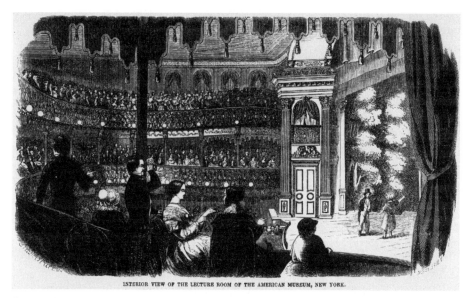

INTERIOR VIEW OF THE LECTURE ROOM OF THE AMERICAN MUSEUM, NEW YORK.

Barnum's Lecture Room (euphemism for "theatre") was expanded in 1849 into a full-scale playhouse for dramatic performances; in 1850 the seating was increased to three thousand for *The Drunkard.* This wood engraving appeared on 29 January 1853 in *Gleason's Pictorial.* Laurence Senelick Collection.

it proved the possibility that such mammoth productions would neither offend the respectable nor attract the rowdy. Lind's image and her repertoire remained remarkably stable throughout her tour. She brought assured standards of production and moral value to a host of local stages. Lind attracted around her an aura of both accessibility and elevated status that demanded the use of that ancient religious word – "celebrity." With the advent of such international celebrities, together with the touring musical virtuoso, such as Ole Bull or Henri Vieuxtemps, new professional standards for entertainment were set for the whole nation.

That Barnum worked his grab for respectability on the terrain of musical performance is hardly surprising, given the remaining suspicions of the theatre among the middle classes. So consistent was the demand for such wholesome amusement that entrepreneurs built ever larger halls through the 1840s and 1850s that boasted enormous capacities. The Broadway Tabernacle, Tripler, and Stuyvesant halls in New York each claimed to seat three thousand, and, even allowing for exaggeration, this number represented roughly a sixfold increase in capacity over the converted halls or chapels and hotel spaces that had housed the occasional entertainments of the 1830s. All of these new spaces were what today would be called multipurpose, though they were careful to distinguish themselves from theatrical sites. The stage could be used for lectures and music, and if necessary the orchestra pit could be boarded over and the seats removed to provide areas for dancing, assembly, and exhibition. With steam-driven fans and other forms of ventilation and cooling, including Cooper Union's Great Hall's subbasement location, as well as improved gas lighting, these halls further eroded whatever seasonality remained in the staging of urban amusements.

Other entrepreneurs attempted to make even more elaborate combinations. William Niblo, after his original garden burned, rebuilt (1849) the site as an all-season entertainment complex that included a hotel, a theatre, and a saloon, all with separate entrances. Most of the open spaces in gardens disappeared. The Italian impresario Ferdinand Palmo cobbled together perhaps the most remarkable complex of all on Chambers Street in New York by linking an old public bath, Stoppani's, an oriental saloon, and a small opera house. As the *Herald* (15 Jan. 1844) declared, "Palmo's establishment will contain everything – you can have baths, opera, cherry cobblers, sandwiches, comedy, scandal, wit, and theology on the Sunday nights."

The new halls were only one way in which commercial leisure created a range of semipublic spaces. In the early 1840s, Philadelphia, Boston, and New York all witnessed the importation of the enormously popular promenade concerts of light music given in Paris and London by Philippe Musard and later by Louis Antoine Jullien. Concerts d'hiver à la Musard, as they were billed in the papers (called "dee highver" locally), took place in winter in closed halls such as Niblo's Garden, and concerts d'été filled the summer evenings, usually interspersed with fireworks presentations. Promenade concerts, as the name suggests, included a long break, still accompanied by music in the background, to allow listeners to walk about, view other members of the fashion, and engage in forms of polite sociabilty. Newspaper accounts suggest that such gatherings may have served as training grounds in politeness, for they included advice about the best way to acknowledge others and the appropriate times to remove or retain one's hat. As an indication that the public commercial spaces were still subject to unseemly behavior, advertisements frequently assured patrons that police would be on hand.

A new development within this expanded musical culture was the appearance of "ethnic acts," not as a parody of some low comic other but rather as a celebration of origin. "Scottish musical entertainments" appeared in the mid-1840s, as did Irish concerts including favorite songs such as "The Irish Mother's Lament," "The Last Rose of Summer", "Kate Kearny," and so forth. The actor and playwright John Brougham produced fairly involved Irish evenings, perhaps modeled after Samuel Lover's success in England, usually entitled "Pat's Peculiarities" (1846), which consisted of stories, sketches, poems, and the usual required songs. The final ethnicity to appear in this musical mix was "American" itself, which in the context of the period invariably meant Yankee. The most popular and profitable ensemble was undoubtedly the singing Hutchinson Family – Judson, John, Asa, and sister Abby, who hailed from the Granite State of New Hampshire. Their homespun image was worked up to suggest an America free from the perils of immigration and the problems of urban vice. "My Mother's Bible" (George Pope Morris) and "The Old Granite State" became their signature tunes. Over time, they also specialized in incorporating songs advocating temperance, abolitionism, women's rights, and the avoidance of a multitude of sins ("The Gambler's Wife"). Though they proudly announced that their show had been tested in the small towns of New England, their greatest success came in New York after 1843 and during an extended tour of England in 1845 from which they netted over $100,000.

Other singing families multiplied: the Wardens from Philadelphia, the Orpheans from upstate New York, the Washburns from Fishkill, the Cheneys from Vermont. This last ensemble drew a favorable review from a novice music critic in the *Broadway Journal* (1846), one Walter Whitman, entitled "Art-Singing and Heart Singing." Whitman used the occasion to blast the current enthusiasm among the wealthy for Italian operas and imported culture in general. On hearing the Cheneys, he had at last found the original, unadorned "American Voice": "This, said we, in our heart, is the true method which must become popular in the United States – which must supplant the stale, second-hand, foreign method, with its flourishes, its ridulous sentimentality, its anti-republican spirit, and its sycophantic influence, tainting the young taste of the republic."

The vogue for singing families forms the clearest case of establishing this middle ground of amusment, suitable for both domestic and public consumption and free from the taint of the theatre. These families may appear in retrospect to be heavy in Victorian sentimentality, but their shows were amusing as well as pious, light rather than mawkish in their effects. The Hutchinson's program carefully blended the comic, gothic, moral, and the sentimental – in equal parts. They established, onstage, a particular American specialty of wholesome family humor that remains a good export commodity.

The Lecture Platform and the Parlor

Besides musical concerts, middle-class audiences also flocked to lectures. Though in large cities there was an unusually "free" market in lecturing, with "professors" hawking their talks to Mercantile Library Associations and Literary Unions on every subject from dietary reform to exotic travel, most performances were organized through a network of lyceum associations. The lyceum movement, the brainchild of Josiah Holbrook, had been founded in 1821 as a way of energizing the New England propensity to earnest self-improvement. The lyceum, in Holbrook's initial scheme, was supposed to be a locally based voluntary association, meeting in the village hall or church basement, that would encourage the knowledge needed for internal improvement by building a cabinet of scientific apparatus – the orrery, a few geological specimens, and a few books of practical science and mechanics. Within a decade of the movement's founding, however, the notion of mutual improvement began to give way to the practice of drawing outside speakers, at first by offering expenses, and then by the late 1830s through the payment of fees. Most of the early speakers were drawn gratis from local pulpits and the fledging state educational systems. However, Carl Bode's count of disbursements from the Salem and Concord, Massachusetts, lyceums show a progressive escalation in fees between 1840 and 1860, capped by the fabulous sum of $100 given in 1848 to Daniel Webster for his wonderful and rather self-serving "History and Constitution of the United States."

Attendance at lectures usually cost about twenty-five cents, roughly comparable to popular musical performances and cheap theatre. Local lyceums thus had to face similar pressures of drawing a crowd, which had the effect of making the corresponding secretary little more than a manager who had to worry about house receipts. By the late 1840s, aided by the railroad, lyceum lecturing had developed circuits of considerable complexity and reach. After 1852, S. D. Ward, secretary of the Chicago Young Men's Association, arranged tours for Illinois and Wisconsin platforms, block-booking eastern stars into the far Midwest. By that time, Emerson and the rest of the eastern illuminati were demanding in excess of fifty dollars plus expenses as a lecture fee.

Theodore Parker, Henry Ward Beecher, Mark Hopkins, John B. Gough, Edward Everett, R. W. Emerson, and Bayard Taylor thus became as much "stars" as their theatrical counterparts. They flitted from place to place, drawing crowds and profits. They used lecture agents to handle their bookings and finances and became as mercenary in their business correspondence as their lectures were spiritually uplifting. S. D. Ward, having being rebuffed yet again by Beecher's booking agent, sarcastically reflected, "Oh! most noble Mr. Beecher! . . . generous, kindhearted man, the young man's true friend! . . . Money has no charms for thee; never dost thou debase thyself by letting thyself out to be exhibited by a showman as would a lion, bear, or monkey. Richly dost thou merit canonizing for all thy virtues" (quoted in Bode, 198–99). The commercial development of the lyceum clearly substantiates Olive Logan's claim that the godly were caught up in the same mechanisms of fame, reputation, and celebrity as politicans and actors. Because part of Beecher's moral reputation was founded on his early lectures (1844) warning young men of the dangers of commercial amusement, it is extraordinary that within a decade he should embrace those very forces. At least Logan's apocryphal fleas were not open to charges of hypocrisy.

The second development, implicit in the notion of star billing, was the ascendancy of individualized style over general moral content. Many lecturers – Emerson; his West Coast doppelgänger, Thomas Starr King; and Parke Godwin – did well by maintaining the high-flown, abstract Unitarian style; yet by midcentury wit was prized over measured orotundity, literary quality over scientific rationalism. Park Benjamin delivered addresses in rhymed couplets, and Bayard Taylor, often dressed in Arab costume, did much to popularize orientalism in his narratives of travel through Egypt and Palestine. Taylor, according to Bode, cleared $5,000 a year in fees after 1854. As these figures suggest, the lecture circuit became the intellectual and then commercialized ground that underwrote much of the New England Renaissance. Lucrative opportunities in lecturing must have factored in the discussions of many liberal ministers, Emerson included, to relinquish or ignore their local pastoral duties and then to set off on regional, then national careers of eloquence. Lectures in turn became the building blocks for published books, though it is likely that book publication, until about 1870, seldom produced the financial returns of the lecture tour.

Though lectures and musical concerts drew pietistic middle-class folk from their houses to experience stage performances, theatrical amusements were also entering through the open parlor doors. In examining the vogue for parlor theatricals after 1850, Karen Halttunen has detected a growing, worldly accommodation with fashion, self-display, and the rituals of social life. In Anna Cora Mowatt's popular and genteel satire *Fashion* (1845), which drew elite audiences back into the theatre after the depression, it is not wealth and material comfort that poses a moral threat to family and political life so much as the sham pretensions of new, uninformed cash, as represented by the aptly named Tiffany family. The question became for urban dwellers not whether one should dress, dine, and display oneself in the street but rather how one should do it in a seemly, respectable manner. Articles in *Godey's Lady's Book* and a host of other etiquette publications offered plenty of answers. However, once it was admitted that one could actually aim for simplicity of manner and appearance, then "naturalness" itself became a style to be cultivated as a property of personal taste rather than as the expression of inner virtue.

The theatrical arts of cosmetics, hairstyling, and costuming were thus naturalized into everyday life, and as Halttunen has convincingly shown, everyday death as well. As towns gained "rural" cemeteries, funeral processions became elaborate long affairs with a parade of glass-sided hearse, flowers, pallbearers, and family. The corpse itself was on display in a coffin, now a casket, with split lids or glass tops, and made to appear as in life. Even under the most difficult circumstances the corpse had to remain respectable, odorless, coiffured, and at peace. As a cap to this transformation of the funeral into a public event, the undertaker emerged by 1870 as a funeral director whose main functions were to stage manage the mourners and arrange for this proliferation of ceremonial detail.

The most literal intrusion of theatricality into middle-class domestic life was the vogue of parlor theatricals. These developed out of the eighteenth-century French word game "charades," in which clues to the syllables of a word were given through literary allusion rather than mime. By midcentury "living charades" had become a popular parlor pastime, opening the door to acting proverbs, *tableaux vivants*, shadow pantomimes, and, by 1860, burlesques, farces, and one-act skits. Dozens of guides to these "home performances" poured off the presses. All stressed that drama, within the confines of the home, offered wholesome, innocent amusement and that anything like "style" could be avoided. Yet immediately after offering such assurances, the guides went into great detail about the construction of a stage, the wearing of makeup, the use of backcloths, or screens for shadow work, the employment of sound effects, and the use of colored lighting. The recommended subjects for parlor staging also show a self-conscious attention to the business of acting, in a sense making a parody of theatricality itself. Melodramatic scenes of disguise and unmasking were popular, as were greenroom conversations between Shakespearean actors. Most surprising of all, given the origins of American arguments against the theatre, was the focus on rituals, such as the celebrations of May Day, in which peasants danced around the maypole and crowned a queen, or even more pagan, magic-mirror work, in which magicians were frightened by the image of a lovely woman. Even the rituals of Catholicism, as in tableaux of "The Penitent" and the "The Novice," were recommended. What had been the objects of Puritan radicalism now became the subjects of bourgeois entertainment. It was not the case, of course, that these middle-class folk were being transformed into either actors or medieval Catholics. The parlor allowed for a strict division of space between the real world of authentic, domestic sentiment and the fabulous world on stage: the theatricality of parlor performances was heightened just to make that distinction evident. Nevertheless, the entry of theatrical technique into the parlor must have suggested to all of the players and audience that middle-class life was hardly transparent and that society worked through conventions of performance rather than the unmediated action of the sentiments. In 1840, notions of respectability for the middle classes required an aversion from all forms of commerical amusement. By 1860 one's respectability was marked by the ways in which you chose your entertainments. Work and family still remained the most important social values, yet the registration of one's status took place in the sites you chose to visit and the fashions you wished to adopt. Knowledge of the proper forms of consumption became more important than their denial.

Conclusion

Perhaps, then, Olive Logan had underestimated the extent of "the show business." Rather than stopping with Beecher's pulpit, Logan might have included the whole culture of consumption – the restaurants, hotels, and dry-goods stores and the semipublic spaces of the domestic parlor – in which her potential audience performed their own ideas of respectability. However, this telescopes more than a century of further transactions between stage and the street and overlooks the many changes in the form and economics of the business itself. In 1866, popular commercial amusement could still be avoided by the pious and had yet to reach into the daily diet of most Americans. Show business, whether fleas or Beecher, was still composed of individual operators, and the most innovative managers – P. T. Barnum and Tony Pastor – never controlled more than one site at a time. Not until the 1880s did enterprising capitalists manage to vertically integrate their operations, pushing show material, frequently not of their own devising, through chains of theatres. The huge circuits of E. F. Albee, B. F. Keith, Marcus Loew, or F. F. Proctor or the empire of the Shuberts spelled the final death of the "Jacksonian" period of innovation. Olive Logan could never have anticipated that distribution would become more important than production in the shaping of American show business, or that the business itself would eventually cover the world.

Notes

1 Taken from the manuscript diary of Philip Hone, 23 October 1840, New-York Historical Society.
2 Quoted in Lee Krahenbuhl's "The Actor, the Prophet, and the City: Religion as Theatre/Theatre as Religion in the Earliest Mormon Metropolis, 1830–1870." Unpublished paper delivered at the Interdisciplinary Nineteenth-Century Studies Conference, University of California-Santa Cruz, March 1995.
3 See John Pond, *Eccentricities of Genius,* quoted by Bode, 212, and also John F. Quinn, "Father Mathew's American Tour 1849–1851," *Eire-Ireland* 30 (Spring 1995): 91–104.

Bibliography: Paratheatricals and Popular Stage Entertainment

A wealth of material exists on variety entertainments, popular theatre, and public ritual, but until recently it has been so widely scattered across a range of scholarly, local, and various enthusiast publications that it has been difficult to get a sense of the whole. New histories, bibliographies, and indexes are appearing all the time. Among the most useful are Wilmeth's *American and English Popular Entertainment* and his *Variety Entertainment and Outdoor Amusements.* The latter book contains brief summaries of all of the "major" kinds of so-called minor amusements, as well as extensive bibliographical treatments of every form. A watershed in the scholarly treatment of amusements was the Conference on the History of American Popular Entertainment in 1977, the proceedings of which were collected in *American Popular Entertainment,* edited by Myron Matlaw. To receive a quick overview of the relations between spectacular theatre and popular culture readers can do no better than to read Michael Booth's concise *Prefaces to English Nineteenth-Century Theatre* (Manchester: Manchester University Press, 1976). Though this work examines only the English stage, almost all of the categories and developments apply equally well to the United States.

Among the older surveys of popular recreation, Dulles's *A History of Recreation* is still the best. Another garrulous account, Minnigerode's *The Fabulous Forties, 1840–1850, A Presentation of Private Life* is also worth consulting. The person to whom every scholar of American amusements owes a debt is Constance Rourke. Her two books, *American Humor* and *The Roots of American Culture, and Other Essays,* together form the first attempt to take popular culture seriously, even though her reification of the American "mind" as a single entity now seems rather limiting and cumbersome. Unfortunately, we still await a more general synthetic account of the development of rural commercial entertainments in the United States. Nothing, for instance, is equivalent to Malcolmson's *Popular Recreations in English Society, 1700–1850.* Two studies, however, make promising local contributions: Click, *The Spirit of the Times: Amusements in Nineteenth Century Baltimore, Norfolk, and Richmond* and Scott Martin, "Leisure in Southern Pennsylvania, 1800–1850."

Approaching the subject with theoretical and comparative interests, one might note that much of the most innovative work in the history of popular amusements has emerged out of the British schools of social history and cultural studies. This work has been led by literary and social historians interested in finding new ways of capturing the concerns and class consciousness of subordinate groups. Three essays one will find invariably referenced are Yeos, "Ways of Seeing: Control and Leisure versus Class and Struggle"; Bailey, "A Mingled Mass of Perfectly Legitimate Pleasures: The Victorian Middle Class and the Problem of Leisure"; and Gareth Stedman Jones, "Class Expression versus Social Control? A Critique of Recent Trends in the Social History of 'Leisure.'" These essays, and many more like them, all critique, praise, enlarge upon, but in no way ignore, the pathbreaking work of Raymond Williams and Richard Hoggart, who, together with Stuart Hall, are usually taken to be the founding fathers of "cultural studies." It is worth noting, however, that "cultural studies" has now escaped far beyond any concrete meaning it might have once possessed. Having completed its original mission, to break open the confinements of English literature teaching at Cambridge and Oxford, it expanded to meet new resistances, and in the United States it has so far met few immovable, conservative targets. It now includes new versions of literary history, cinema studies, and heavy, rather indigestible doses of continental philosophy.

The study of Native American cultures has been transformed since the 1960s. Many new works have followed the line of ethnohistory in stressing the uniqueness of cultural patterning. The most influential model has been Anthony Wallace's *The Death and Rebirth of the Seneca.* Though most are focused on the changing ritual practices of the later nineteenth and early twentieth centuries, some effort has been made to unearth the character of Pre-Columbian cultures, as in Josephy, *America in 1492* and Hudson and Tesser, eds., *The Forgotten Centuries.* For work on particular regions with some cultural content see White, *The Middle Ground* and Joel Martin, *Sacred Revolt.* Students interested in tribal ritual and resistance should consult three new journals: *American Indian Historian, American Indian Quarterly,* and *American Indian Culture and*

Research Journal. The ways in which Indians were represented in popular culture are ably surveyed in Stedman's *Shadows of the Indian.* Sheehan has looked at the way colonists in Virginia could not see beyond the notion of the "noble savage" in his *Savagism and Civility.* Deloria, in "Playing the Indian: Otherness and Authenticity in the Assumption of American Indian Identity" looks at a number of instances, including the Boston Tea Party, when social actors assumed "Indian" identities. For related sources, see the bibliographical essay for Chapter 1.

A sense of the colonial landscape for ritual and amusement is best acquired by looking at individual regions. New England is brilliantly surveyed in *Worlds of Wonder, Days of Judgment* by David D. Hall. The famous maypole incident may be read about in Zuckerman, "Pilgrim in the Wilderness: Community, Modernity, and the Maypole at Merry Mount." The greatest repository of hints and clues for further work remains Earle's work, especially *Customs and Fashions in Old New England* (1893).

The mid-Atlantic region, for some reason, has never attracted the close attention lavished on its neighbors to the north and south, yet Fletcher's *Pennsylvania Agriculture and Country Life, 1640–1840* (1950) covers our period well. Other aspects may be found in the classic collection of colonial studies edited by Greene and Pole, *Colonial British America* (1984). Two essays in that volume have proved especially influential: Breen, "Creative Adaptations: Peoples and Cultures" and Bushman, "American High Style and Vernacular Cultures."

Material on the old South is abundant: The Rutmans' *A Place in Time* provides a good understanding of the texture of everyday life, but for the special case of early shows see Roeber, "Authority, Law and Custom: The Rituals of Court Day in Tidewater Virginia, 1720–1750"; Wyatt-Brown's *Southern Honor* is also recommended.

Work on Afro-U.S. ritual and popular culture has grown considerably in the last two decades. It has moved past the stage of simply recovering forms to the presentation of complex analysis. For the southern plantation culture a good place to start is Blassingame's *The Slave Community,* before moving on to *Roll, Jordan, Roll* by Genovese. Both reference a host of sources and draw on Puckett's venerable *Folk Beliefs of the Southern Negroes* (1926). The most exciting of the new works blending social history, anthropology, and folk life studies are Abrahams's *Singing the Master* and Kinser's *Carnival, American Style: Mardi Gras at New Orleans and Mobile.* Another good book on Mardi Gras is *All on a Mardi Gras Day* by Mitchell. The particularities of the delta are examined in Gwendolyn Midlo Hall, *Africans in Colonial Louisiana.* For matters even further to the south, though still within the American orbit, see Errol Hill's exhaustive *The Jamaican Stage, 1655–1900.*

Among the best studies on Afro-U.S. culture in the North are Shane White, "'It Was a Proud Day': African Americans, Festivals, and Parades in the North, 1741–1834"; Melvin Wade, "'Shining in Borrowed Plumage'": Affirmation of Community in the Black Coronation Festivals of New England, ca. 1750–1850"; and Piersen, "Black Yankees."

For parades and street theatricals, the standard account is Davis's wonderful *Parades and Power,* though McNamara's *Day of Jubilee* is equally important for these phenomena in New York City. The ideas in Ryan's article "The American Parade: Representations of the Nineteenth-Century Social Order" are extended in her book *Women in Public: Between Banners and Ballots, 1825–1880.* A couple of sources relate the development and decline of the Fourth: Cohn, "A National Celebration: The Fourth of July in American History" and Robert Hay, "Freedom's Jubilee: One Hundred Years of the Fourth of July."

On religious ritual, evangelical and otherwise, the first book to consult is Brooks's truly astonishing *The Refiner's Fire: The Making of Mormon Cosmology 1644–1844.* For

Finneyite evangelicalism, Johnson's *A Shopkeeper's Millennium* remains the best account, especially in its attention to the details of drawing a crowd.

For minstrelsy, Carl Wittke's standard *Tambo and Bones* has largely been superseded by a new range of studies beginning with Toll's comprehensive *Blacking Up*, which contains a large bibliography and a useful listing of minstrel troupes. For attention to matters of musical composition and origin, Nathan's *Dan Emmett and the Rise of Early Negro Minstrelsy* remains unsurpassed, as does Epstein's *Sinful Tunes and Spirituals*. Other efforts useful to consult are Zanger, "The Minstrel Show as Theater of Misrule" and Rehin, "The Darker Image: American Negro Minstrelsy through the Historian's Lens." Winter in "Juba and American Minstrelsy" provides the story of the most important black dancer of the period who rode the minstrel craze, and Sampson has done wonderful work by tracking down other black troupes in *Blacks in Blackface*. Boskin's *Sambo: The Rise and Demise of an American Jester* surveys that powerful image as it appeared in many forms, whereas Lott's *Love and Theft* is clearly the most innovative and historically contextual account of the development of early minstrelsy to date, though forthcoming books by Cockrell and Mahar provide new perspectives on minstrelsy's origin and antebellum forms. A useful collection of essays is Bean, Hatch, and McNamara, *Inside the Minstrel Mask*.

For the minor forms of musical and spectacular theatre one might begin with Porter's compendious *With an Air Debonair: Musical Theatre in America, 1785–1815* before moving on to Root's *American Popular Stage Music 1860–1880*. The intervening gap may be filled, to some extent, with Broyles's *"Music of the Highest Class": Elitism and Populism in Ante-bellum Boston* and Lawrence's *Strong on Music: The New York Music Scene in the Days of George Templeton Strong, 1836–1875*. The latter is extraordinary in its even coverage of high and low musical forms. For the feminization of the American stage, one book is especially useful: Dudden, *Women in the American Theatre: Actresses and Audiences, 1790–1870.*

Museum culture, both before and during the Barnum period, has attracted much new work. Anyone interested in any branch of the exhibition business should first consult Altick's *The Shows of London*. Local developments are well handled in Orosz, *Curators and Culture*. Two older studies of the museum in New York remain valuable: Haberly, "The American Museum from Baker to Barnum," and McClung, "Tammany's Remarkable Gardiner Baker." Sellars's *Mr. Pearle's Museum* covers the important early museum in Philadelphia. For more general interpretative accounts see Stewart, *On Longing: Narratives of the Miniature, the Gigantic, the Souvenir, the Collection* and Bogdan, *Freak Show*. Ricky Jay's *Learned Pigs and Fireproof Women* also provides good reading, especially on dime museums.

On P. T. Barnum in particular, see Harris's pathbreaking *Humbug: The Art of P. T. Barnum;* Saxon's *P. T. Barnum: The Legend and the Man;* and the Kunhardts' *P. T. Barnum: America's Greatest Showman,* as well as more detailed studies such as Betts's "P. T. Barnum and the Popularization of Natural History."

For the circus, a good place to start further inquiry is Wilmeth (cited earlier) and Flint's "A Selected Guide to Source Material on the American Circus." The origins of the form are brilliantly surveyed in Saxon's *Enter Foot and Horse*. For precursors in America to Ricketts's arrival, see Greenwood, *The Circus and Its Origins and Growth Prior to 1835,* though a more accurate and scholarly survey may be found in Thayer's *Annals of the American Circus 1793–1829* and its sequel, covering the years 1830–1847.

A considerable number of studies are now devoted to particular forms that had their moment in the early nineteenth century before losing out in novelty value. McCullough's *Living Pictures on the New York Stage* traces *tableaux vivants* from their introduction in the 1830s to their demise in the 1890s. Jordan's *Singin' Yankees* remains the only book-length account of the important vogue for singing families. A notable essay to consult is Nathan's "The Tyrolese Family Rainer, and the Vogue of Singing Mountain Troupes in Europe and America."

Riverboat theatre is traversed in Graham's *Showboats;* however, readers may find more to wade through in Reeds's unpublished dissertation "A History of Showboats on the Western Rivers" and Schick's "Early Showboats and Circus in the Upper Valley." Two books should be consulted for the history of the lyceum movement, both somewhat tired but equally serviceable: Bode's *The American Lyceum* and Mead's *Yankee Eloquence in the Middle West.* Horner, *The Life of James Redpath and the Development of the Modern Lyceum,* provides many insights into the business side of the form but is weak on the nature of the presentations themselves. New studies of popular lecturing are badly needed, and at least two are promised. A new direction in the study of popular oratory has been established in Cmiel's wonderful *Democratic Eloquence.* For other middle-class forms of theatricality, readers need go no further than to consult Halttunen's superb *Confidence Men and Painted Women: A Study of Middle-Class Culture in America, 1830–1870.*

Bibliography

(The sources below include those mentioned in the text, in notes, and in bibliographical essays at the conclusion of each chapter.)

Abrahams, Roger D. *Singing the Master: The Emergence of African American Culture in the Plantation South.* New York: Pantheon, 1992.

Adair. "Stories of the Stage." *New York Dramatic Mirror,* 3 Jan. 1903: 8.

Alger, William Rounseville. *Life of Edwin Forrest, the American Tragedian.* 2 vols. Philadelphia: J. B. Lippincott, 1877.

Allain, Mathé, and Adele Cornay St. Martin. "French Theatre in Louisiana." In Seller, *Ethnic Theatre in the United States,* 139–74.

Allen, Robert C. *Horrible Prettiness: Burlesque and American Culture.* Chapel Hill: University of North Carolina Press, 1991.

Altick, Richard D. *The Shows of London.* Cambridge: Harvard University Press, 1978.

The American Theatre: A Sum of its Parts. See Henry B. Williams.

Anthony, M. Susan. "'This Sort of Thing . . . ': Productions of Gothic Plays in America." *Journal of American Drama and Theatre* 6 (1994): 81–92.

Applebaum, Stanley, ed. *Great Actors and Actresses of the American Stage in Historic Photographs.* New York: Dover, 1983.

Appleby, Joyce, ed. *American Quarterly, Special Issue: Republicanism in the History and Historiography of the United States* 37 (1985): 461–598.

   Capitalism and a New Social Order: The Republican Vision of the 1790s. New York: New York University Press, 1984.

Arant, Fairlie. "A Biography of the Actor Thomas Abthorpe Cooper." Diss., University of Minnesota, 1971.

Arata, Esther S., and Nicholas John Rotoli. *Black American Playwrights, 1800 to the Present.* Metuchen, N.J.: Scarecrow Press, 1976.

Archer, Stephen M. *American Actors and Actresses: A Guide to Information Sources.* Detroit: Gale Research, 1983.

   Junius Brutus Booth: Theatrical Prometheus. Carbondale and Edwardsville: University of Southern Illinois Press, 1992.

Auser, Courtland P. *Nathaniel Parker Willis.* New York: Twayne, 1969.

Axtell, James. *The Invasion Within: The Contest of Cultures in Colonial North America.* New York: Oxford University Press, 1985.

Bailey, Peter. "A Mingled Mass of Perfectly Legitimate Pleasures: The Victorian Middle Class and the Problem of Leisure." *Victorian Studies* 21 (1977): 7–28.

Bailyn, Bernard. *The New England Merchants in the Seventeenth Century.* Cambridge: Harvard University Press, 1955.

    The Ideological Origins of the American Revolution. Cambridge: Harvard University Press, 1967.

    The Peopling of British North America: An Introduction. New York: Knopf, 1986.

Baine, Rodney M. *Robert Munford.* Athens: University of Georgia Press, 1967.

Bank, Rosemarie K. "Staging the 'Native': Making History in American Theatre Culture, 1828–1838." *Theatre Journal* 45 (1993): 461–86.

Bank, Rosemarie K. *Theatre Culture in America, 1825–1860.* New York and Cambridge: Cambridge University Press, 1997.

Barck, Dorothy C., ed. *The Diary of William Dunlap.* 3 vols. New York: New-York Historical Society, 1930. Rpt. New York: Benjamin Blom, 1969.

Barker, James Nelson. *Marmion.* New York: Longworth, 1816.

Barnes, Eric W. *The Lady of Fashion.* New York: Charles Scribner's Sons, 1954.

Bean, Ann-Marie, James V. Hatch, Brooks McNamara, eds. *Inside the Minstrel Mask.* Hanover, N.H.: Wesleyan University Press (University Press of New England), 1996.

Beauvallet, Leon. *Rachel and the New World.* Trans. and ed. Colin Clair. London and New York: Abelard Schuman, 1967.

Beeman, Richard R. *Patrick Henry: A Biography.* New York: McGraw-Hill, 1974.

Beers, Henry A. *Nathaniel Parker Willis.* Boston: Houghton Mifflin, 1885.

Bell, Michael D. *The Development of American Romance: The Sacrifice of Relation.* Chicago: University of Chicago Press, 1980.

Bentley, Eric. *The Life of the Drama.* New York: Atheneum, 1964.

Bercovitch, Sacvan. *The Puritan Origins of the American Self.* New Haven and London: Yale University Press, 1975.

Bercovitch, Sacvan, ed. *Reconstructing American Literary History.* Cambridge: Harvard University Press, 1986.

Bercovitch, Sacvan, gen. ed. *The Cambridge History of American Literature. Volume One: 1590–1820.* New York and Cambridge/UK: Cambridge University Press, 1994.

Bergquist, James M. "German-Americans." In John D. Buenker and Lorman A. Ratner, eds., *Multiculturalism in the United States: A Comparative Guide to Acculturation and Ethnicity.* Westport, Conn.: Greenwood Press, 1992, 53–76.

Berkhofer, Robert F. *The White Man's Indian: Images of the American Indian from Columbus to the Present.* New York: Random House, 1978.

Bernard, John. *Retrospections of America, 1797–1811.* New York: Harper, 1887.

Bernheim, Alfred. *The Business of the Theatre.* 1932. Rpt. New York: Benjamin Blom, 1964.

Berson, Misha. *The San Francisco Stage, 1849–1869.* San Francisco: San Francisco Performing Arts Library and Museum, 1990.

Betts, John R. "P. T. Barnum and the Popularization of Natural History." *Journal of the History of Ideas* 20 (1959): 353–68.

Bierhorst, John. *The Mythology of North America.* New York: Morrow, 1985.

Birdoff, Harry. *The World's Greatest Hit: Uncle Tom's Cabin.* New York: Vanni, 1947.

Blassingame, John. *The Slave Community: Plantation Life in the Ante-Bellum South.* New York: Oxford University Press, 1972.

Blumin, Stuart. *The Emergence of the Middle Class: Social Experience in the American City, 1790–1900.* Cambridge: Cambridge University Press, 1989.

Bode, Carl. *The American Lyceum; Town Meeting of the Mind.* New York: Oxford University Press, 1956.

Bogard, Travis, Richard Moody, and Walter J. Meserve. *The Revels History of Drama in English,* Vol. VIII. *American Drama.* London: Methuen, 1977.

Bogdan, Robert. *Freak Show: Presenting Human Oddities for Amusement and Profit.* Chicago: University of Chicago Press, 1988.

Boorstin, Daniel J. *The Americans: The National Experience.* New York: Random House, 1965.

Booth, Michael, ed. *Hiss the Villain.* New York: Benjamin Blom, 1964.

English Melodrama. London: Herbert Jenkins, 1965.

Prefaces to English Nineteenth-Century Theatre. Manchester: Manchester University Press, 1976.

Bordman, Gerald. *Oxford Companion to American Theatre.* 2nd ed. New York: Oxford University Press, 1992.

Boskin, Joseph. *Sambo: The Rise and Demise of an American Jester.* New York: Oxford University Press, 1986.

Bost, James. *Monarchs of the Mimic World; or, The American Theatre of the Eighteenth Century Through the Managers – the Men Who Made It.* Orono: University of Maine, 1977.

Boucicault, Dion. "The Art of Acting." In Mathews, *Papers on Acting,* 137–60.

Boyer, Paul S. *Urban Masses and Moral Order in America, 1820–1920.* Cambridge: Harvard University Press, 1978.

Boyer, Paul S., et al. *The Enduring Vision: A History of the American People,* 2nd ed. Lexington: D. C. Heath, 1993.

Bradley, Edward Sculley. *George Henry Boker, Poet and Patriot.* Philadelphia: University of Pennsylvania Press, 1927.

Braudy, Leo. *The Frenzy of Renown: Fame and Its History.* New York: Oxford University Press, 1986.

Breen, T. H. *Puritans and Adventurers: Change and Persistence in Early America.* New York: Oxford University Press, 1980.

"Creative Adaptations: Peoples and Cultures." In Greene and Pole, *Colonial British America: Essays in the New History of the Early Modern Era,* 195–232.

"'Baubles of Britain': The American and Consumer Revolutions of the Eighteenth Century." *Past and Present* 119 (May 1988): 73–104.

Bridenbaugh, Carl. *Cities in the Wilderness: The First Century of Urban Life in America, 1625–1742.* New York: Ronald Press, 1938.

Cities in Revolt: Urban Life in America, 1743–1776. New York: Capricorn Books, 1955.

Brooks, John L. *The Refiner's Fire: The Making of Mormon Cosmology 1644–1844.* Cambridge: Cambridge University Press, 1995.

Brooks, Mona. "The Development of American Theatre Management Practices between 1830 and 1896." Diss., Texas Technical University, 1981.

Brooks, Peter. *The Melodramatic Imagination.* New Haven: Yale University Press, 1976.

Brown, Jared. *The Theatre in America during the Revolution.* New York and Cambridge: Cambridge University Press, 1995.

Brown, Richard D. *Knowledge Is Power: The Diffusion of Information in Early America, 1700–1865.* New York: Oxford University Press, 1989.

Brown, T. Allston. *A History of the New York Stage.* 3 vols. New York: Dick and Fitzgerald, 1870.

Brown, William Wells. *From Fugitive Slave to Free Man: The Autobiographies of William Wells Brown.* Ed. William L. Andrews. New York: Mentor Books, 1993.

Brownlee, W. Elliot. *Dynamics of Ascent: A History of the American Economy.* New York: Knopf, 1974.

Brownstein, Rachel M. *Tragic Muse: Rachel of the Comédie-Française.* New York: Knopf, 1993.

Broyles, Michael. *"Music of the Highest Class": Elitism and Populism in Ante-bellum Boston.* New Haven: Yale University Press, 1992.

Bryan, George B. *Stage Lives: A Bibliography and Index to Theatrical Biographies.* Westport, Conn.: Greenwood, 1985.

    American Theatrical Regulation, 1607–1900: Conspectus and Texts. Metuchen, N.J., and London: Scarecrow Press, 1993.

Buchard, John, and Albert Bush-Brown. *The Architecture of America: A Social and Cultural History.* Boston: Little, Brown, 1961.

Buckley, Peter. "To the Opera House: Culture and Society in New York City, 1820–1860." Diss., State University of New York, Stony Brook, 1984.

Burbick, William. "Columbus, Ohio: Theater from the Beginning of the Civil War to 1875." Diss., Ohio State U, 1963.

Burge, James C. *Lines of Business: Casting Practice and Policy in the American Theatre 1752–1899.* New York: Peter Lang, 1986.

Bushman, Richard L. "American High Style and Vernacular Cultures." In Greene and Pole, *Colonial British America: Essays in the New History of the Early Modern Era,* 345–83.

    The Refinement of America: Persons, Houses, Cities. New York: Knopf, 1992.

Butsch, Richard. "American Theatre Riots and Class Relations, 1754–1849." *Theatre Annual* 48 (1995): 41–59.

    "Bowery B'hoys and Matinee Ladies: The Re-Gendering of Nineteenth-Century Theater Audiences." *American Quarterly* 46 (1994): 374–405.

Canary, Robert H. *William Dunlap.* New York: Twayne, 1970.

Carson, Ada Lou, and Herbert L. Carson. *Royall Tyler.* Boston: Twayne Publishers, 1979.

Carson, Jane. *Colonial Virginians at Play.* Williamsburg: Colonial Williamsburg Foundation, 1989.

Carson, William G. B. *Managers in Distress.* St. Louis, Mo.: St. Louis Historical Documents Foundation, 1949. Rpt. New York: Benjamin Blom, 1965.

    The Theatre on the Frontier; the Early Years of the St. Louis Stage. Chicago: University of Chicago Press, 1932.

Chandler, Alfred. *The Visible Hand: The Managerial Revolution in American Business.* Cambridge: Belknap Press of Harvard University Press, 1977.

Clapp, William W. *A Record of the Boston Stage.* Boston: J. Munroe, 1853.

Clark, Barrett H., gen. ed. *America's Lost Plays.* 20 vols. Princeton: Princeton University Press, 1940–41. Rpt. Bloomington: Indiana University Press, 1963–65.

    Favorite American Plays of the Nineteenth Century. Princeton: Princeton University Press, 1943.

Clark, Dennis. "Irish-Americans." In John D. Buenker and Lorman A. Ratner, eds. *Multiculturalism in the United States: A Comparative Guide to Acculturation and Ethnicity.* Westport, Conn.: Greenwood Press, 1992, 77–102.

Click, Patricia C. *The Spirit of the Times: Amusements in Nineteenth Century Baltimore, Norfolk, and Richmond.* Charlottesville: University Press of Virginia, 1989.

Cmiel, Kenneth. *Democratic Eloquence: The Fight over Popular Speech in Nineteenth-Century America.* New York: William Morrow, 1990.

Coad, Oral S. *William Dunlap.* New York: The Dunlap Society, 1917. Rpt. New York: Russell and Russell, 1962.

Coad, Oral S., and Edwin Mims Jr. *The American Stage.* New Haven: Yale University Press, 1929.

Cockrell, Dale. *Demons of Disorder: Early Blackface Minstrels and Their World.* New York and Cambridge: Cambridge University Press, 1997.

Cohn, William. "A National Celebration: The Fourth of July in American History." *Cultures* 3 (1976): 141–56.

Collins, Bruce. *White Society in the Antebellum South.* New York: Longman, 1985.

Conolly, L. W., ed. *Theatrical Touring and Founding in North America.* Westport, Conn.: Greenwood, 1982.

Cooper, James Fenimore. *Notions of the Americans.* Philadelphia: Carey, Lea and Carey, 1828.

The Correpondence of Samuel L. Clemens and William Dean Howells, 1872–1910, Vol. 2. Ed. Henry Nash Smith and William M. Gibson. Cambridge: Belknap Press of Harvard University Press, 1960.

Cott, Nancy F. *The Bonds of Womanhood: "Woman's Sphere" in New England, 1780–1835.* New Haven: Yale University Press, 1977.

Cowell, Joe. *Thirty Years Passed Among the Players in England and America.* 2 vols. New York: Harper, 1844.

Cox, Jeffrey N. "Introduction." *Seven Gothic Dramas, 1789–1825.* Athens: Ohio University Press, 1992.

Crawford, Mary Caroline. *The Romance of the American Theatre.* New York: Halcyon House, 1940.

Creahan, John. *The Life of Laura Keene: Actress, Artist, Manager and Scholar.* Philadelphia: Rodgers, 1897.

Cronon, William. *Changes in the Land: Indians, Colonists and the Ecology of New England.* New York: Hill and Wang, 1983.

Cross, Gilbert B. *Next Week – East Lynne: Domestic Drama in Performance, 1820–1874.* London: Associated University Press, 1977.

Culhane, John. *The American Circus: An Illustrated History.* New York: Henry Holt, 1990.

Curry, Jane Kathleen. *Nineteenth-Century American Women Theatre Managers.* Westport, Conn.: Greenwood, 1994.

Dahl, Curtis. *Robert Montgomery Bird.* New York: Twayne, 1963.

Davidson, Cathy N. *Revolution and the Word: The Rise of the Novel in America.* New York: Oxford University Press, 1987.

Davis, Peter A. "Puritan Mercantilism and the Politics of Anti-theatrical Legislation in Colonial America." In Engle and Miller, eds., *The American Stage: Social and Economic Issues from the Colonial Period to the Present,* 18–29.

Davis, Susan G. *Parades and Power: Street Theatre in Nineteenth Century Philadelphia.* Philadelphia: Temple University Press, 1986.

Day, Charles. "An Early Combination: A Summer Tour with Laura Keene and Her New York Company." *New York Dramatic Mirror,* 31 August 1901.

Deloria, Philip. "Playing the Indian: Otherness and Authenticity in the Assumption of American Indian Identity." Diss., Yale University, 1994.

D'Emilio, John, and Freedman, Estelle. *Intimate Matters: A History of Sexuality in America.* New York: Harper and Row, 1988.

Denning, Michael. *Mechanic Accents: Dime Novels and Working-Class Culture in America.* London: Verso, 1987.

Deutsch, Helen. "Laura Keene's Theatrical Management." Diss., Tufts U, 1992.

Diderot, Denis. "The Paradox of the Actor." In *Selected Writings on Art and Literature.* Ed. Geoffrey Bremmer. London: Penguin, 1994, 98–158.

Dix, William S. "The Theatre in Cleveland, Ohio, 1854–1875." Diss., University of Chicago, 1946.

Dizikes, John. *Opera in America: A Cultural History.* New Haven: Yale University Press, 1993.

Donohue, Joseph W., Jr., ed. *The Theatrical Manager in England and America.* Princeton: Princeton University Press, 1971.

Dormon, James H. *Theater in the Ante Bellum South, 1815–1861.* Chapel Hill: University of North Carolina Press, 1967.

Doty, Gresdna A. *The Career of Mrs. Anne Brunton Merry in the American Theatre.* Baton Rouge: Louisiana State University Press, 1971.

Dowd, Gregory Evans. *A Spirited Resistance: The North American Struggle for Unity, 1745–1815.* Baltimore and London: Johns Hopkins University Press, 1992.

Downer, Alan S. *American Drama.* New York: Thomas Y. Crowell, 1960.

　　The Eminent Tragedian: William Charles Macready. Cambridge: Harvard University Press, 1966.

Du Bois, W. E. B. *The Souls of Black Folk.* New York: Vintage Books, 1903. Rpt., 1986.

Dudden, Faye E. *Women in the American Theatre: Actresses and Audiences, 1790–1870.* New Haven: Yale University Press, 1994.

Duerr, Edwin. "Charles Ciceri and the Background of American Scene Design." *Theatre Arts Monthly* 16 (1932): 983–94.

　　The Length and Depth of Acting. New York: Holt, Rinehart and Winston, 1962.

Dulles, Foster Rhea. *A History of Recreation: America Learns to Play,* 2nd ed. New York: Meredith, 1965.

Dunlap, William. *Diary of William Dunlap (1766–1839): The Memoirs of a Dramatist, Theatrical Manager, Painter, Critic, Novelist, and Historian.* See Barck.

　　A History of the American Theatre. 2 vols. New York: Harper, 1832. Rpt. in 1 vol., New York: Burt Franklin, 1963.

　　Life of George Frederick Cooke. 2 vols. London: H. Colburn, 1815.

Durang, Charles. *The Philadelphia Stage from 1749–1855.* 7 vols. Philadelphia: Philadelphia Sunday Dispatch, 1854–55 (arranged and illus. by Thompson Westcott, 1868).

Durang, John. *The Memoir of John Durang, American Actor, 1787–1816.* Ed. Alan S. Downer. Pittsburgh: University of Pittsburgh Press, 1966.

Durham, Weldon B., ed. *American Theatre Companies, 1749–1887.* Westport, Conn.: Greenwood Press, 1986.

Dyer, Richard. *Heavenly Bodies: Film Stars and Society.* New York: St. Martin's Press, 1986.

Eagleton, Terry. *The Ideology of the Aesthetic.* Oxford: Basil Blackwell, 1990.

Earle, Alice Morse. *Customs and Fashions in Old New England.* New York: Scribner's, 1893.

Eggers, Robert Franklin. "A History of Theatre in Boise, Idaho, from 1863 to 1963." Thesis, University of Oregon, 1963.

Elliott, Craig. "Annals of the Legitimate Theatre in Victoria, Canada from the Beginning to 1900." Diss., University of Washington, 1969.

Ellison, Ralph. "What America Would Be Like Without Blacks." In *Going to the Territory.* New York: Random House, 1987, 104–12.

Ellsler, John A. *The Stage Memories of John A. Ellsler.* Ed. Effie Ellsler Weston. Cleveland: Rowfant Club, 1950.

Emerson, Everett, ed. *American Literature, 1764–1789: The Revolutionary Years.* Madison: University of Wisconsin Press, 1977.

Engle, Ron, and Tice L. Miller, eds. *The American Stage: Social and Economic Issues from the Colonial Period to the Present.* New York: Cambridge University Press, 1993.

Epstein, Dena J. *Sinful Tunes and Spirituals: Black Folk Music to the Civil War.* Urbana: University of Illinois Press, 1978.

Evans, Chad. *Frontier Theatre: A History of Nineteenth Century Theatrical Entertainment in the Canadian Far West and Alaska.* Victoria: Sono Nis, 1983.

Evans, Oliver H. *George Henry Boker.* Boston: Twayne, 1964.

Faron, Henry Bradshaw. *Sketches of America.* London: Longman, Rees, Orme, and Brown, 1818.

Farrison, W. E. *William Wells Brown, Author and Reformer.* Chicago: University of Chicago Press, 1969.

Faust, Clement E. *The Life and Dramatic Works of Robert Montgomery Bird.* New York: Knickerbocker, 1919.

Fawkes, Richard. *Dion Boucicault.* London: Quartet Books, 1979.

Fearnow, Mark. "American Colonial Disturbances as Political Theatre." *Theatre Survey* 33 (1992): 53–64.

Felheim, Marvin. *The Theatre of Augustin Daly.* Cambridge: Harvard University Press, 1956.

Fiedler, Leslie. *Love and Death in the American Novel.* New York: Stein and Day, 1966.

Finley, James. *Sketches of Western Methodism.* Ed. W. P. Strickland. Cincinnati: Methodist Book Concern, 1854.

Finney, Charles Grandison. *Lectures on Revivals of Religion.* Ed. William G. McLoughlin. Cambridge: Belknap Press of Harvard University Press, 1960.

Fischer, David Hackett. *Albion's Seed: Four British Folkways in America.* New York and Oxford: Oxford University Press, 1989.

Fisher, Judith L., and Stephen Watts, eds. *When They Weren't Doing Shakespeare: Essays on Nineteenth-Century British and American Theatre.* Athens: University of Georgia Press, 1989.

Fishkin, Shelley Fisher. *Was Huck Black? Mark Twain and African-American Voices.* New York: Oxford University Press, 1993.

Fitzhugh, William W., ed. *Cultures in Contact: The Impact of European Contacts on Native American Cultural Institutions, A.D. 1000–1800.* Washington: Smithsonian Institution Press, 1985.

Fletcher, Stevenson. *Pennsylvania Agriculture and Country Life.* Harrisburg: Pennsylvania Historical and Museum Commission, 1950–55.

Fliegelman, Jay. *Declaring Independence: Jefferson, Natural Language and the Culture of Performance.* Stanford: Stanford University Press, 1993.

Flint, Richard. "A Selected Guide to Source Material on the American Circus." *Journal of Popular Culture* 6 (1972): 615–19.

Foner, Eric. *Free Soil, Free Labor, Free Men: The Ideology of the Republican Party before the Civil War.* Oxford: Oxford University Press, 1970.

Frantzen, Allen J. *Desire for Origins: New Language, Old English, and Teaching the Tradition.* New Brunswick: Rutgers University Press, 1990.

Free, Joseph Miller. "Studies in American Theatre History: The Theatre of Southwest Mississippi to 1840." Diss., University of Iowa, 1941.

Freneau, Philip. "Advice for Authors." In *Miscellaneous Works of Mr. Philip Freneau, Containing His Essays and Additional Poems.* Philadelphia, 1788.

Frick, John W. *New York's First Theatrical Center: The Rialto at Union Square.* Ann Arbor, Mich.: UMI Research Press, 1985.

Frisbie, Charlotte, ed. *Southwestern Indian Ritual Drama.* Albuquerque: University of New Mexico Press, 1980.

Furnas, J. C. *Fanny Kemble: Leading Lady of the Nineteenth-Century Stage.* New York: Dial Press, 1982.

Furtwangler, Albert. *Assassin on Stage: Brutus, Hamlet, and the Death of Lincoln.* Urbana: University of Illinois Press, 1991.

Gagey, Edmond M. *The San Francisco Stage.* New York: Columbia University Press, 1950.

Gaiser, Gerhard. "The History of the Cleveland Theatre from the Beginnings to 1854." Diss., University of Iowa, 1953.

Gallagher, Kent. *The Foreigner in Early American Drama.* The Hague: Mouton, 1966.

Galloway, Patricia, ed. *The Southeastern Ceremonial Complex: Artifacts and Analysis.* Lincoln: University of Nebraska Press, 1989.

Garrett, Kurt. "The Flexible Loyalties of American Actors in the Eighteenth Century." *Theatre Journal* 32 (1980): 223–34.

Gates, William B. "The Theatre in Natchez." *Journal of Mississippi History* 3 (1941): 71–129.

Genovese, Eugene D. *Roll, Jordan, Roll: The World the Slaves Made.* New York: Vintage, 1974.

Gilje, Paul L. *The Road to Mobocracy: Popular Disorder in New York City, 1763–1834.* Chapel Hill: University of North Carolina Press, 1987.

Gillette, William. "The Illusion of the First Time in Acting." In Mathews, *Papers on Acting,* 115–35.

Glazer, Irvin R. *Philadelphia Theaters: A Pictorial Architectural History.* New York: Dover, 1994.

Gohdes, Clarence. *Literature and Theatre of the States and Regions of the USA: An Historical Bibliography.* Durham: Duke University Press, 1967.

Goldberg, Issac. *Major Noah: American Jewish Pioneer.* New York: Knopf, 1936.

Goodfriend, Joyce D. *Before the Melting Pot: Society and Culture in Colonial New York City.* Princeton: Princeton University Press, 1991.

Gorn, Elliott J., and Warren Goldstein. *A Brief History of American Sports.* New York: Hill and Wang, 1993.

Gossett, T. F. *Uncle Tom's Cabin and American Culture.* Dallas: Southen Methodist University Press, 1985.

Gould, Thomas R. *The Tragedian: An Essay on the Histrionic Genius of Junius Brutus Booth.* New York: Hurd and Houghton, 1868.

Graham, Philip. *Showboats: The History of an American Institution.* Austin: University of Texas Press, 1951.

Graydon, Alexander. *Memoirs of a Life, Chiefly Passed in Pennsylvania, Within the Last Sixty Years.* Edinburgh: W. Blackwood, 1822.

Greenberg, Kenneth. *Masters and Statesmen: The Political Culture of American Slavery.* Baltimore: Johns Hopkins University Press, 1985.

Greene, Jack P. *Pursuits of Happiness: The Social Development of Early Modern British Colonies and the Formation of American Culture.* Chapel Hill: University of North Carolina Press, 1988.

Greene, Jack P., and J. R. Pole, eds. *Colonial British America: Essays in the New History of the Early Modern Era.* Baltimore: Johns Hopkins University Press, 1984.

Greenwood, Isaac J. *The Circus; Its Origins and Growth Prior to 1835. With a Sketch of Negro Minstrelsy,* 2nd ed. with additions. New York: William Abbatt, 1909.

Grimsted, David. *Melodrama Unveiled: American Theater and Culture 1800–1850.* Chicago: University of Chicago Press, 1968.

Grisvard, Larry. "The Final Years: The Ludlow and Smith Theatrical Firms in St. Louis, 1845–1851." Diss., Ohio State University, 1965.

Groce, George C., and David H. Wallace. *Dictionary of Artists in America, 1564–1860.* New Haven: Yale University Press, 1957.

Grund, Francis. *The Americans in Their Moral, Social, and Political Relations.* Boston, 1837.

Haberly, Lloyd. "The American Museum from Baker to Barnum." *New-York Historical Society Quarterly* 43 (1959): 273–87.

Hall, David D. *Worlds of Wonder, Days of Judgment: Popular Religious Belief in Early New England.* Cambridge: Harvard University Press, 1990.

Hall, Gwendolyn Midlo. *Africans in Colonial Louisiana: The Development of Afro-Creole Culture in the Eighteenth Century.* Baton Rouge: Louisiana State University Press, 1992.

Halttunen, Karen. *Confidence Men and Painted Women: A Study of Middle-Class Culture in America, 1830–1870.* New Haven: Yale University Press, 1982.

Hamm, Charles. *Music in the New World.* New York: W. W. Norton, 1983.

Hanson, Russell L. *The Democratic Imagination in America.* Princeton: Princeton University Press, 1985.

Harris, Neil. *The Artist in America: The Formative Years, 1790–1860.* New York: George Braziller, 1966.

Humbug: The Art of P. T. Barnum. Boston: Little, Brown, 1973.

Hartman, John Geoffrey. *The Development of American Social Comedy, 1787–1936.* New York: Octagon Books, 1971.

Haskell, Thomas. "Capitalism and the Origins of the Humanitarian Sensibility." *American Historical Review* 90 (1985): 339–61, 547–66.

Haswell, Charles. *Reminiscences of an Octogenarian.* New York: Harper and Bros., 1897.

Hatch, James V. *The Black Image on the American Stage.* New York: Drama Book Specialists, 1970.

"Some African Influences on the Afro-American Theatre." In *The Theatre of Black Americans: A Collection of Critical Essays.* New York: Applause Books, 1987.

Hatch, Nathan O. *The Democratization of American Christianity.* New Haven: Yale University Press, 1989.

Havens, Daniel F. *The Columbian Muse of Comedy: The Development of a Native Tradition of Early American Social Comedy, 1787–1845.* Carbondale: Southern Illinois University Press, 1973.

Hawke, David F. *Early Life in Everyday America.* New York: Harper and Row, 1988.

Hay, Robert. "Freedom's Jubilee: One Hundred Years of the Fourth of July." Diss., University of Kentucky, 1967.

Hay, Samuel A. *African American Theatre: A Historical and Critical Analysis.* New York and Cambridge: Cambridge University Press, 1994.

Hazlitt, William. *Complete Works.* 5 vols. London and Toronto: Dent, 1930.

Heilman, Robert B. *Tragedy and Melodrama.* Seattle: University of Washington, 1968.

Henderson, Mary C. *The City and the Theatre; New York Playhouses from Bowling Green to Times Square.* Clifton, N.J.: J. T. White, 1973.

Theater in America : 200 Years of Plays, Players, and Productions. H. N. Abrams, 1986; 2nd ed., 1996.

Henderson, Myrtle E. *A History of the Theatre in Salt Lake City from 1850 to 1870.* Salt Lake City: Deseret Book Co., 1941.

Henneke, Ben Graf. *Laura Keene: A Biography.* Tulsa: Council Oaks Books, 1990.

"The Playgoer in America (1752–1952)." Diss., University of Illinois, 1956.

Herbstruth, Grant. "Benedict DeBar and the Grand Opera House in St. Louis, Missouri, from 1855 to 1879." Diss., University of Iowa, 1954.

Herold, Amos L. *James Kirke Paulding: Versatile American.* New York: Columbia University Press, 1926.

Herring, Frances E. *In the Pathless West with Soldiers, Pioneers, Miners, and Savages.* London: T. Fisher Unwin, 1904.

Heth, Charlotte, ed. *Native American Dance: Ceremonies and Social Traditions.* Washington, D.C.: Smithsonian Institution with Starwood Publishing, 1993.

Hewitt, Barnard. "'King Stephen' of the Park and Drury Lane." *The Theatrical Manager in England and America, Player of a Perilous Game.* Ed. Joseph W. Donohue. 87–141.

———. *Theatre U.S.A., 1665–1957.* New York: McGraw-Hill, 1959.

Higham, John. *Strangers in the Land: Patterns of American Nativism 1860–1925.* New York: Atheneum, 1955; 2nd ed., 1963.

Highfill, Philip, Jr. "The British Background of the American Hallams." *Theatre Survey* 11 (1970): 1–35.

Higonnet, Patrice. *Sister Republics: The Origins of French and American Republicanism.* Cambridge: Harvard University Press, 1988.

Hill, Errol. *The Jamaican Stage 1655–1900: Profile of a Colonial Theatre.* Amherst: University of Massachusetts Press, 1992.

———. *Shakespeare in Sable: A History of Black Shakespearean Actors.* Amherst: University of Massachusetts Press, 1984.

Hill, Errol, ed. *The Theatre of Black Americans: A Collection of Critical Essays.* New York: Applause Theatre Books, 1987.

Hill, West T., Jr. *The Theatre in Early Kentucky 1790–1820.* Lexington: University Press of Kentucky, 1971.

Hillebrand, Harold Newcomb. *Edmund Kean.* New York: Columbia University Press, 1933.

Hinke, William J., ed. and trans. "Report of the Journey of Francis Louis Michel from Berne, Switzerland, to Virginia, October 2, 1701–December 1, 1702." *Virginia Magazine* 24 (1916).

Hixon, Don L., and Don A. Hennessee. *Nineteenth-Century American Drama: A Finding Guide.* Metuchen, N.J.: Scarecrow, 1977.

Hobsbawm, E. J. *The Age of Capital, 1848–1875.* New York: New American Library, 1979.

Hodge, Francis. *The Yankee Theatre: The Image of America on the Stage, 1825–1850.* Austin: University of Texas Press, 1964.

Hoffman, Ronald, and Peter J. Albert. *Women in the Age of the American Revolution.* Charlottesville: University of Virginia Press, 1989.

Hofstadter, Richard. *America at 1750: A Social Portrait.* New York: Vintage Books, 1973.

Hogan, Robert. *Dion Boucicault.* New York: Twayne, 1969.

Hone, Philip. *The Diary of Philip Hone, 1828–1851.* Ed. Allan Nevins. New York: Dodd, Mead, 1927.

Hoole, W. S. *The Ante-Bellum Charleston Theatre.* Tuscaloosa: University of Alabama Press, 1946.

Hornblow, Arthur. *A History of the Theatre in America.* 2 vols. Philadelphia: J. B. Lippincott, 1919.

Horner, Charles F. *The Life of James Redpath and the Development of the Modern Lyceum.* New York: Barse and Hopkins, 1926.

Horsman, Reginald. *Race and Manifest Destiny: The Origins of American Racial Anglo-Saxonism.* Cambridge: Harvard University Press, 1981.

Hudson, Charles, and Carmen Tesser, eds. *The Forgotten Centuries: Indians and Europeans in the American South, 1521–1704.* Athens: University of Georgia Press, 1994.

Hughes, Glenn. *A History of the American Theatre, 1700–1950.* New York: Samuel French, 1951.

Hultkrantz, Ake. *Belief and Worship in Native North America.* Syracuse: Syracuse University Press, 1981.

Native Religions of North America. San Francisco: Harper, 1987.

Hume, Charles. "The Sacramento Theatre, 1849–1885." Diss., Stanford, 1955.

Hunt, Douglas L. "The Nashville Theatre, 1830–1840." *Birmingham-Southern College Bulletin* 28 (1935): 1–89.

Hunter, G. K. "Othello and Colour Prejudice." In *Dramatic Identities and Cultural Tradition.* New York: Barnes and Noble, 1978, 31–59.

Ireland, Joseph N. *A Memoir of the Professional Life of Thomas Abthorpe Cooper.* New York: The Dunlap Society, 1888.

Mrs. Duff. Boston: J. R. Osgood, 1882.

Records of the New York Stage, from 1750 to 1860, 2 vols. New York: T. H. Morrell, 1866–67.

Irvin, Eric. "Laura Keene and Edwin Booth in Australia." *Theatre Notebook* 23 (1969): 95–100.

Isaac, Rhys. *The Transformation of Virginia, 1740–1790.* Chapel Hill: University of North Carolina Press, 1982.

Jaher, Fredric Cople. *The Urban Establishment: Upper Strata in Boston, New York, Charleston, Chicago, Los Angeles.* Urbana: University of Illinois Press, 1982.

James, Reese Davis. *Cradle of Culture, 1800–1810; The Philadelphia Stage.* Philadelphia: University of Pennsylvania Press, 1957.

Jay, Ricky. *Learned Pigs and Fireproof Women.* New York: Villard Books, 1986.

Jefferson, Joseph. *The Autobiography of Joseph Jefferson (*1890*).* Ed. Alan S. Downer. Cambridge: Belknap Press of Harvard University Press, 1964.

Jefferson, Thomas. *Notes on the State of Virginia.* Ed. William Peden. New York: Norton, 1972.

Jennings, Francis, ed. *The History and Culture of Iroquois Diplomacy.* Syracuse: Syracuse University Press, 1985.

The Invasion of America: Indians, Colonialism, and the Cant of Conquest. Chapel Hill: University of North Carolina Press, 1975.

Johnson, Claudia D. *American Actress: Perspective on the Nineteenth Century.* Chicago: Nelson-Hall, 1984.

Johnson, Paul E. *A Shopkeeper's Millennium: Society and Revivals in Rochester, New York, 1815–1837.* New York: Hill and Wang, 1978.

Jones, Cecil. "The Policies and Practices of Wallack's Theatre: 1852–88." Diss., University of Illinois, 1959.

Jones, Gareth Stedman. "Class Expression versus Social Control? A Critique of Recent Trends in the Social History of 'Leisure.'" *History Workshop* 4 (1977): 163–70.

Jordan, Cynthia S. "'Old Words' in 'New Circumstances': Language and Leadership in Post-Revolutionary America." *American Quarterly* 40 (1988): 491–513.

Jordan, Philip D. *Singin' Yankees.* Minneapolis: University of Minnesota Press, 1946.

Josephy, Alvin M., Jr., *500 Nations: An Illustrated History of North American Indians.* New York: Knopf, 1994.

America in 1492: The World of the Indian Peoples before the Arrival of Columbus. New York: Knopf, 1992.

Jowitt, Deborah. *Time and the Dancing Image.* New York: Morrow, 1988.

Judd, Doctor. "The Old School of Actors." *Billboard* 10 (September 1904). Reprinted in Joseph and June Csida, eds., *American Entertainment: A Unique History of Popular Show Business.* New York: Watson-Guptill, 1978, 33.

Kammen, Michael. *Mystic Chords of Memory: The Transformation of Tradition in American Culture.* New York: Knopf, 1991.

Kanellos, Nicholas. *A History of Hispanic Theatre in the United States: Origins to 1940.* Austin: University of Texas Press, 1990.

Kasson, John F. *Rudeness and Civility: Manners in Nineteenth-Century Urban America.* New York: Hill and Wang, 1990.

Keats, John. "On Edmund Kean as a Shakespearean Actor." *Poetical Works and Other Writings.* 8 vols. Ed. H. Buxton Forman. New York: Phaeton, 1970.

Keeton, Guy H. "The Theatre in Mississippi from 1840 to 1870." Diss., Louisiana State University, 1979.

Kemble, Fanny. *Fanny Kemble: Journal of a Young Actress.* Ed. Monica Gough. New York: Columbia University Press, 1990.

Records of a Girlhood. New York: Henry Holt, 1879.

Kendall, John S. *The Golden Age of the New Orleans Theater.* Baton Rouge: Louisiana State University Press, 1952.

Kerber, Linda. *Women of the Republic: Intellect and Ideology in Revolutionary America.* Chapel Hill: University of North Carolina Press, 1980.

Kinser, Samuel. *Carnival, American Style: Mardi Gras at New Orleans and Mobile.* Chicago: University of Chicago Press, 1990.

Kitts, Thomas M. *The Theatrical Life of George Henry Boker.* New York: Peter Lang, 1994.

Klepac, Richard L. *Mr. Mathews at Home.* London: Society for Theatre Research, 1979.

Knight, Stephen. *Form and Ideology in Crime Fiction.* Bloomington: Indiana University Press, 1980.

Knobel, Dale T. *Paddy and the Republic: Ethnicity and Nationality in Antebellum America.* Middletown: Wesleyan University Press, 1986.

Knoper, Randall. *Acting Naturally: Mark Twain in the Culture of Performance.* Berkeley: University of California Press, 1995.

Kohl, Lawrence F. *The Politics of Individualism: Parties and the American Character in the Jacksonian Era.* New York: Oxford University Press, 1989.

Kollek, Peter. *Bogumil Dawison: Porträt und Deutung eines genialen Schauspielers.* Kastellaun: Henn, 1978.

Kritzer, Amelia Howe, ed. *Plays by Early American Women, 1775–1850.* Ann Arbor: University of Michigan Press, 1995.

Kulikoff, Allan. *Tobacco and Slaves: The Development of Southern Culture in the Chesapeake, 1680–1800.* Chapel Hill: University of North Carolina Press, 1986.

Kunhardt, Philip B., Jr., Philip B. Kunhardt III, and Peter W. Kunhardt. *P. T. Barnum: America's Greatest Showman.* New York: Knopf, 1995.

Lambourne, Alfred. *A Trio of Sketches: Being Reminiscences of the Theater Green Room and the Scene-painter's Gallery from Suggestions in "A Play-house."* Salt Lake City, n.d.

Larkin, Jack. *The Reshaping of Everyday Life, 1790–1840.* New York: Harper and Row, 1988.

Larson, Carl F. W. *American Regional Theatre History to 1900: A Bibliography.* Metuchen, N.J.: Scarecrow Press, 1979.

Lascelles, E. C. P. *The Life of Charles James Fox.* New York: Oxford University Press, 1936.

Laubin, Reginald, and Gladys Laubin. *Indian Dances of North America: Their Importance to Indian Life.* Norman: University of Oklahoma Press, 1977.

Laurie, Bruce. *Artisans into Workers: Labor in Nineteenth-Century America.* New York: Hill and Wang, 1989.

Lawrence, Vera Brodsky. *Strong on Music: The New York Music Scene in the Days of George Templeton Strong, 1836–1875.* New York: Oxford University Press, 1988.

Leach, Joseph. *Bright Particular Star: The Life and Times of Charlotte Cushman.* New Haven: Yale University Press, 1970.

Leacroft, Richard. *The Development of the English Playhouse.* Ithaca, N.Y.: Cornell University Press, 1973.

Leavitt, Michael. *Fifty Years in Theatrical Management.* New York: Broadway Publishing, 1912.

Leech, Clifford, and T. W. Craik, eds. *The Revels History of Drama in English.* London: Methuen; New York: Barnes and Noble, 1976–83.

Leman, Walter. *Memories of an Old Actor.* San Francisco: A. Roman, 1886; Rpt. New York: Benjamin Blom, 1969.

Leuchs, Frederick. *The Early German Theatre in New York: 1840–1872.* New York: Columbia University Press, 1966.

Levine, Lawrence W. *Black Culture and Black Consciousness: Afro-American Folk Thought from Slavery to Freedom.* New York: Oxford University Press, 1977.

    Highbrow/Lowbrow: The Emergence of Cultural Hierarchy in America. Cambridge: Harvard University Press, 1986.

Lincoln, Abraham. *Speeches and Writings, 1859–1865.* Ed. Don E. Fehrenbacher. N.p: Library of America, 1989.

Litto, Fredrick M. *American Dissertations on the Drama and Theatre: A Bibliography.* Kent: Kent State University Press, 1969.

Long, Hudson E. *American Drama from Its Beginnings to the Present.* New York: Appleton-Century-Crofts, 1970.

Longmore, Paul K. *The Invention of George Washington.* Berkeley: University of California Press, 1988.

Lott, Eric. *Love and Theft: Blackface Minstrelsy and the American Working Class.* New York: Oxford University Press, 1977.

Ludlow, Noah M. *Dramatic Life as I Found It.* 1880; Rpt. New York: Benjamin Bloom, 1966.

Ludwig, Jay. "James H. McVicker and His Theatre." *Quarterly Journal of Speech* 46 (1960): 14–25.

    "McVicker's Theatre: 1857–1896." Diss., University of Illinois, 1958.

Lynch, James J. *Box, Pit and Gallery; Stage and Society in Johnson's London.* Berkeley: University of California Press, 1953.

Lystra, Karen. *Searching the Heart: Women, Men, and Romantic Love in Nineteenth-Century America.* New York: Oxford University Press, 1989.

MacMinn, George R. *The Theater of the Golden Era in California.* Caldwell: Caxton, 1941.

McArthur, Benjamin. *Actors and American Culture, 1880–1920.* Philadelphia: Temple University Press, 1984.

McClung, Gales S., and Robert M. McClung. "Tammany's Remarkable Gardiner Baker." *New-York Historical Society Quarterly* 43 (1958): 143–69.

McConachie, Bruce A. "The Cultural Politics of 'Paddy' on the Midcentury American Stage." *Studies in Popular Culture* 10 (1987): 1–13.

"Out of the Kitchen and into the Marketplace: Normalizing *Uncle Tom's Cabin* for the Antebellum Stage." *Journal of American Drama and Theatre* 3 (1991): 5–28.

Melodramatic Formations: American Theatre and Society, 1820–1870. Iowa City: University of Iowa Press, 1992.

McCoy, Drew. *The Elusive Republic: Political Economy in Jeffersonian America.* Chapel Hill: University of North Carolina Press, 1980.

McCullough, Bruce W. *The Life and Writings of Richard Penn Smith with a Reprint of His Play "The Deformed," 1830.* Menasha, Ala.: Banta, 1917.

McCullough, Jack W. *Living Pictures on the New York Stage.* Ann Arbor: UMI Research Press, 1983.

McDermott, Douglas. "The Development of Theatre on the American Frontier, 1750–1890." *Theatre Survey* 19 (1978): 63–78.

"The Theatre and Its Audience: Changing Modes of Social Organization in the American Theatre." In Engle and Miller, eds., *The American Stage,* 6–17.

McDermott, Douglas, and Robert Sarlos. "The Impact of Working Conditions upon Acting Style." *Theatre Research International* 20 (1995): 231–36.

McNamara, Brooks. *The American Playhouse in the Eighteenth Century.* Cambridge: Harvard University Press, 1969.

Day of Jubilee: The Great Age of Public Celebration in New York, 1788–1909. New Brunswick, N.J.: Rutgers University Press, 1997.

McNeil, Barbara, and Miranda C. Herbert, eds. *Performing Arts Biography Master Index,* 2nd ed. Detroit: Gale Research, 1981.

McPherson, James M. *Battle Cry of Freedom: The Civil War Era.* New York: Oxford University Press, 1988.

McVicker, James H. *The Theatre: Its Early Days in Chicago.* Chicago: Knight and Leonard, 1884.

Macready, William C. *The Diaries of William Charles Macready.* 2 vols. Ed. William Toynbee. London: Chapman and Hall, 1912.

Maher, William J. *Behind the Burnt Cork Mask: Early Blackface Minstrelsy and the Formation of Antebellum American Popular Culture.* Urbana: University of Illinois, forthcoming 1998.

Malcolmson, Robert. *Popular Recreations in English Society, 1700–1850.* Cambridge: Cambridge University Press, 1973.

Mammen, Edward William. *The Old Stock Company School of Acting: A Study of the Boston Museum.* Boston: Trustees of the Public Library, 1945.

Mankowitz, Wolf. *Mazeppa: The Lives, Loves, and Legends of Adah Isaacs Menken.* New York: Stein and Day, 1982.

Margetts, Ralph. "A Study of the Theatrical Career of Julia Dean Hayne." Diss., University of Utah, 1959.

Marshall, Herbert, and Mildred Stock. *Ira Aldridge: The Negro Tragedian.* Carbondale and Edwardsville: Southern Illinois University Press, 1958.

Martin, Joel. *Sacred Revolt: The Muskogees' Struggle for a New World.* Boston: Beacon Press, 1991.

Martin, Scott Christopher. "Leisure in Southern Pennsylvania, 1800–1850." Diss., University of Pittsburgh, 1990.

Mason, Alexander H.. *French Theatre in New York.* New York: Columbia University Press, 1940.

Mason, Jeffrey D. *Melodrama and the Myth of America.* Bloomington: Indiana University Press, 1993.

Matlaw, Myron, ed. *The Black Crook and Other Nineteenth-Century American Plays.* New York: Dutton, 1967.

Nineteenth-Century American Plays. New York: Applause Theatre Books, 1985.

American Popular Entertainment. Westport, Conn., and London: Greenwood Press, 1979.

Mathews, Charles James. *The Life of Charles James Mathews.* Ed. Charles Dickens. 2 vols. London, 1879.

Matthews, Brander, ed. *Papers on Acting.* New York: Hill and Wang, 1958.

Matthews, Brander, and Lawrence Hutton, eds. *Actors and Actresses of Great Britain and the United States: From the Days of Garrick to the Present Time.* 5 vols. New York: Cassell, 1886.

The Kembles and Their Contemporaries. Boston: L. C. Page, 1900.

Mays, David D. "The Achievements of the Douglass Company in North America: 1758–1774." *Theatre Survey* 23 (1982): 141–49.

Mead, David. *Yankee Eloquence in the Middle West; The Ohio Lyceum, 1850–1870.* East Lansing: Michigan State College Press, 1951. Rpt. Westport, Conn.: Greenwood Press, 1977.

Meinig, D. W. *The Shaping of America, Vol. 1: Atlantic America, 1492–1800.* New Haven: Yale University Press, 1986.

Meserve, Walter J. *An Emerging Entertainment: The Drama of the American People to 1828.* Bloomington: Indiana University Press, 1977.

American Drama to 1900. Detroit: Gale Research, 1980.

Heralds of Promise: The Drama of the American People in the Age of Jackson, 1829–1849. Westport, Conn.: Greenwood, 1986.

An Outline History of American Drama. Totowa: Littlefield, Adams, 1965; 2nd ed., New York: Freedback Theatrebooks and Prospero Press, 1994.

Meserve, Walter, ed. *On Stage, America!* New York: Feedback Theatrebooks, 1996.

Miller, Kerby. *Emigrants and Exiles: Ireland and the Irish Exodus to North America.* New York: Oxford University Press, 1985.

Miller, Perry. *The New England Mind: The Seventeenth Century.* Boston: Beacon Press, 1961.

Minnigerode, Meade. *The Fabulous Forties, 1840–1850: A Presentation of Private Life.* New York: G. P. Putnam's Sons, 1924.

Mintz, Sidney, and Richard Price. *The Birth of African-American Culture: An Anthropological Perspective.* Boston: Beacon Press, 1976.

Mintz, Steven. *A Prison of Expectations: The Family in Victorian Culture.* New York: New York University Press, 1983.

Mitchell, Reid. *All on a Mardi Gras Day: Episodes in the History of New Orleans Carnival.* Cambridge: Harvard University Press, 1995.

Molin, Sven Eric, and Robin Goodfellowe. *Dion Boucicault, the Shaughraun: A Documentary Life, Letters, and Selected Works.* Newark: Proscenium, 1979.

Monkkonen, Eric H. *America Becomes Urban: The Development of U.S. Cities and Towns, 1780–1980.* Berkeley: University of California Press, 1988.

Moody, Richard. *America Takes the Stage: Romanticism in American Drama and Theatre, 1750–1900.* Bloomington: Indiana University Press, 1955.

The Astor Place Riot. Bloomington: Indiana University Press, 1958.

Edwin Forrest: First Star of the American Stage. New York: Knopf, 1960.

Moody, Richard, ed. *Dramas from the American Theatre, 1762–1909.* Cleveland: World Publishing, 1966.

Morgan, Edmund S., and Helen M. Morgan. *The Stamp Act Crisis: Prologue to Revolution,* rev. ed. New York: Collier, 1963.

Morgan, Winifred. *An American Icon: Brother Jonathan and American Identity.* Dover: Delaware University Press, 1988.

Morley, Sheridan. *The Great Stage Stars.* New York: Facts on File, 1986.

Morrell, Elaine. "Laura Keene and Gold Country Theatrical." Thesis, University of Washington, 1960.

Morris, Clara. *Life on the Stage: My Personal Experiences and Recollections.* New York: McClure, Phillips, 1901.

Moses, Montrose J. *The American Dramatist.* Boston: Little, Brown, 1925.

Moses, Montrose J., ed. *Representative Plays by American Dramatists.* New York: E. P. Dutton, 1918–21.

Moses, Montrose J., and John Mason Brown, eds. *The American Theatre as Seen by Its Critics, 1752–1934.* New York: Norton, 1934.

Mosse, George. *The Nationalization of the Masses; Political Symbolism and Mass Movements in Germany from the Napoleonic Wars through the Third Reich.* New York: H. Fertig, 1975.

Mowatt, Anna Cora. *Autobiography of an Actress.* Boston: Ticknor, Reed and Fields, 1854.

Murdoch, James E. *A Plea for Spoken Language: An Essay upon Comparative Elocution.* Cincinnati and New York: Van Antwerp, Bragg, 1883.

The Stage: Recollections of Actors and Acting. Philadelphia: J. M. Stoddart, 1880.

Murphy, Maureen. "Irish-American Theatre." In Seller, *Ethnic Theatre in the United States,* 221–35.

Musser, Paul H. *James Nelson Barker.* Philadelphia: University of Pennsylvania Press, 1929.

Nash, Gary B. *The Urban Crucible: The Northern Seaports and the Origins of the American Revolution.* Cambridge: Harvard University Press, 1986.

Nathan, Hans. *Dan Emmett and the Rise of Early Negro Minstrelsy.* Norman: University of Oklahoma Press, 1962.

"The Tyrolese Family Rainer, and the Vogue of Singing Mountain Troupes in Europe and America." *Musical Quarterly* 32 (1946): 63–79.

Nichols, Harold. "The Prejudice Against Native American Drama from 1778 to 1830." *Quarterly Journal of Speech* 60 (1975): 279–88.

Noid, Benjamin. "History of the Theatre in Stockton, California, 1850–1892." Diss., University of Utah, 1968.

Northall, William K. *Behind the Curtain; or Fifteen Years Observations Among the Theatres of New York.* New York: W. F. Burgese, 1851.

Norton, Anne. *Alternative Americas: A Reading of Antebellum Political Culture.* Chicago: University of Chicago Press, 1986.

Notable Names in the American Theatre, 2nd ed. Ed. Raymond D. McGill. Clifton, N.J.: James T. White, 1976.

O'Malley, Michael. *Keeping Watch: A History of American Time.* New York: Viking, 1990.

Odell, George C. D. *Annals of the New York Stage.* 15 vols. New York: Columbia University Press, 1927–49.

Orosz, Joel J. *Curators and Culture: The Museum Movement in America, 1740–1870.* Tuscaloosa: University of Alabama Press, 1990.

Overmyer, Grace. *America's First Hamlet.* New York: New York University Press, 1953.

Patterson, Mark R. *Authority, Autonomy, and Representation in American Literature, 1776–1865.* Princeton: Princeton University Press, 1988.

——. *Jacksonian America: Society, Personality, and Politics.* Homewood, Ill.: Dorsey Press, 1969.

Pessen, Edward. *Riches, Class, and Power Before the Civil War.* Lexington: D. C. Heath, 1973.

Phelps, Henry Pitt. *Players of a Century: A Record of the Albany Stage.* Albany, N.Y.: J. McDonough, 1880.

Philbrick, Norman, ed. *Trumpets Sounding: Propaganda Plays of the American Revolution.* New York: Benjamin Blom, 1972.

Piersen, William D. *Black Yankees: The Development of an Afro-American Subculture in Eighteenth-Century New England.* Amherst: University of Massachusetts Press, 1988.

Poe, Edgar Allan. *The Broadway Journal* (July 19, 1845). In *The Complete Works.* Vol. 12. New York: AMS, 1902. Rpt., 1965, 187–88.

Pollock, Thomas C. *The Philadelphia Theatre in the Eighteenth Century Together with the Day Book of the Same Period.* Philadelphia: University of Pennsylvania Press, 1933.

Porter, Susan L. *With an Air Debonair: Musical Theatre in America, 1785–1815.* Washington, D.C.: Smithsonian Press, 1991.

Postlewait, Thomas, and Bruce A. McConachie, eds. *Interpreting the Theatrical Past.* Iowa City: University of Iowa Press, 1989.

Power, Tyrone. *Impressions of America During the Years 1833, 1834, and 1835.* 2 vols. Philadelphia: Carey, Lea, and Blandchard, 1836.

Pritner, Calvin. "William Warren's Management of the Chestnut Street Theatre Company." Diss., University of Illinois, 1964.

——. "William Warren's Financial Arrangements with Visiting Stars." *Theatre Survey* 6 (1965): 83–90.

Puckett, Newbell Niles. *Folk Beliefs of the Southern Negroes.* London: H. Milford, 1926. Rpt. Montclair, N.J.: Patterson Smith, 1968.

Quinn, Arthur Hobson. *A History of the American Drama from the Beginning to the Civil War,* 2nd ed. New York: Appleton-Century-Crofts, 1943.

Quinn, Arthur Hobson, ed. *Representative American Plays from 1767 to the Present Day,* 7th ed. New York: Appleton-Century-Crofts, 1957.

Quinn, John F. "Father Mathew's American Tour 1848–1851." *Eire-Ireland* 30 (Spring 1995): 91–104.

Raboteau, Albert J. *Slave Religion: The "Invisible Institution" in the Antebellum South.* New York: Oxford University Press, 1978.

Radin, Paul. *The Trickster: A Study in American Indian Mythology.* London: Routledge, 1972.

Ranger, Paul. *'Terror and Pity Reign in Every Breast': Gothic Drama in the London Patent Theatres, 1750–1820.* London: Society for Theatre Research, 1991.

Rankin, Hugh F. *The Theatre in Colonial America.* Chapel Hill: University of North Carolina Press, 1960; 2nd ed., 1965.

Ratner, Lorman. *James Kirke Paulding.* Westport, Conn.: Greenwood, 1992.

Reeds, Duane Eldon. "A History of Showboats on the Western Rivers." Diss., Michigan State University, 1978.

Rehin, George F. "The Darker Image: American Negro Minstrelsy through the Historian's Lens." *Journal of American Studies* 9 (1975): 365–73.

Reinelt, Janelle, and Joseph Roach, eds. *Critical Theory and Performance.* Ann Arbor: University of Michigan Press, 1992.

Reignolds-Winslow, Catherine Mary. *Yesterdays with Actors.* Boston: Cupples and Hurd, 1889.

Reynolds, David S. *Beneath the American Renaissance: The Subversive Imagination in the Age of Emerson and Melville.* New York: Knopf, 1988.

Reynolds, Larry J. *James Kirke Paulding.* Boston: Twayne, 1964.

Richardson, Gary A. *American Drama from the Colonial Period Through World War I: A Critical History.* New York: Twayne, 1993.

Rifkind, Carole. *A Field Guide to American Architecture.* New York: New American Library, 1980.

Rigdon, Walter, ed. *The Biographical Encyclopedia and Who's Who of the American Theatre.* New York: James H. Heineman, 1966.

Rinear, David. *The Temple of Momus: Mitchell's Olympic Theatre.* Metuchen, N.J.: Scarecrow Press, 1987.

Ritchie, Anna Cora Ogden Mowatt. *Autobiography of an Actress.* Boston: Ticknor, Reed and Fields, 1854.

Ritchey, David. *A Guide to the Baltimore Stage in the Eighteenth Century.* Westport, Conn., and London: Greenwood Press, 1982.

Ritter, Charles. "The Theatre in Memphis, Tennessee, from its Beginning to 1859." Diss., University of Iowa, 1956.

Roach, Joseph. *Cities of the Dead: Circum-Atlantic Performance.* New York: Columbia University Press, 1996.

Roberts, Vera Mowry. "'Lady-Managers' in Nineteenth-Century American Theatre." In Engle and Miller, *The American Stage,* 30–46.

Robinson, Alice M., Vera Mowry Roberts, and Milly S. Barranger, eds. *Notable Women in the American Theatre.* Westport, Conn.: Greenwood, 1989.

Rock, Howard B. *Artisans of the New Republic: The Tradesmen of New York City in the Age of Jefferson.* New York: New York University Press, 1979.

Rodecape, Lois Foster. "Tom Maguire: Napoleon of the Stage." *California Historical Society Quarterly* 20 (1941): 289–314; 21 (1942): 39–74, 141–82, 239–75.

Rodgers, Daniel T. *The Work Ethic in Victorian America, 1850–1920.* Chicago: University of Chicago Press, 1978.

Roeber, A. G. "Authority, Law and Custom: The Rituals of Court Day in Tidewater Virginia, 1720–1750." *William and Mary Quarterly* 37 (1980): 29–52.

Roediger, David. *The Wages of Whiteness: Race and the Making of the American Working Class.* London: Verso, 1991.

Rogin, Michael Paul. *Fathers and Children: Andrew Jackson and the Subjugation of the American Indian.* New York: Knopf, 1975.

Root, Deane L. *American Popular Stage Music 1860–1880.* Ann Arbor, Mich.: University of Michigan Research Press, 1981.

Rose, Anne C. *Victorian America and the Civil War.* New York and Cambridge: Cambridge University Press, 1992.

Rosenfeld, Sybil. *The Georgian Theatre of Richmond Yorkshire.* London: Society for Theatre Research, 1984.

Ross, Andrew. *No Respect: Intellectuals and Popular Culture.* New York: Routledge, 1989.

Rourke, Constance. *American Humor; a Study of the National Character.* Garden City: Doubleday, 1953.

The Roots of American Culture, and Other Essays. New York: Harcourt, Brace and World, 1942.

Ruggles, Eleanor. *Prince of Players: Edwin Booth.* New York: Norton, 1953.

Ruland, Richard, and Malcolm Bradbury, eds. *From Puritanism to Postmodern: A History of American Literature.* New York: Viking, 1991.

Rusk, Ralph Leslie. *The Literature of the Middle Western Frontier.* 2 vols. New York: Columbia University Press, 1925.

Russett, Cynthia Eagle. *Sexual Science: The Victorian Construction of Womanhood.* Cambridge: Harvard University Press, 1989.

Rutman, Darrett B. *American Puritanism: Faith and Practice.* Philadelphia and New York: Lippincott, 1970.

Rutman, Darrett B., and Anita H. Rutman. *A Place in Time: Middlesex County, Virginia, 1650–1750.* New York: Norton, 1984.

Ryan, Kate. *Old Boston Museum Days.* Boston: Little, Brown, 1915.

Ryan, Mary P. "The American Parade: Representations of the Nineteenth-Century Social Order." In Lynn Hunt, ed., *The New Cultural History.* Berkeley: University of California Press, 1989.

   The Empire of the Mother: American Writing About Domesticity. New York: Haworth Press, 1982.

   Women in Public: Between Banners and Ballots, 1825–1880. Baltimore: Johns Hopkins University Press, 1990.

Sarna, J. D. *Jacksonian Jew: The Two Worlds of Mordecai Noah.* New York: Holmes and Meier, 1981.

Sampson, Henry T. *Blacks in Blackface: A Source Book on Early Black Musical Shows.* Metuchen, N.J.: Scarecrow Press, 1980.

Saxon, A. H. *Enter Foot and Horse: A History of Hippodrama in England and France.* New Haven: Yale University Press, 1968.

   P. T. Barnum: The Legend and the Man. New York: Columbia University Press, 1989.

Saxton, Alexander. "Blackface Minstrelsy and Jacksonian Ideology." *American Quarterly* 27 (1975): 3–28.

Schick, Joseph S. "Early Showboats and Circus in the Upper Valley." *Mid-America* 32 (1950): 211–15.

Schilling, Lester. "The History of Theatre in Portland, Oregon, 1846–1959." Diss., University of Wisconsin, 1961.

Schudson, Michael. *Discovering the News: A Social History of American Newspapers.* New York: Basic Books, 1978.

Schultz, Ronald. *The Republic of Labor: Philadelphia Artisans and the Politics of Class.* New York: Oxford University Press, 1993.

Schwarz, Lyle. "Theatre on the Gold Frontier: A Cultural Study of Five Northwest Mining Towns, 1860–1870." Diss., Washington State University, 1975.

Seilhamer, George O. *History of the American Theatre.* 3 vols. Philadelphia: Globe Printing House, 1888–91.

Sellars, Charles Coleman. *Mr. Peale's Museum.* New York: W. W. Norton, 1980.

Seller, Maxine Schwartz, ed. *Ethnic Theatre in the United States.* Westport, Conn.: Greenwood, 1983.

Senelick, Laurence. *The Age and Stage of George L. Fox, 1825–1877.* Hanover, N.H.: University Press of New England, 1988.

Seymour, Bruce. *Lola Montez, A Life.* New Haven: Yale University Press, 1996.

Shattuck, Charles H. *The Hamlet of Edwin Booth.* Urbana: University of Illinois Press, 1969.

   Shakespeare on the American Stage: From the Hallams to Edwin Booth. Washington, D.C.: Folger Shakespeare Library, 1976.

Shaw, Peter. *American Patriots and the Rituals of Revolution.* Cambridge: Harvard University Press, 1981.

Sheehan, Bernard W. *Savagism and Civility: Indians and Englishmen in Colonial Virginia.* Cambridge: Cambridge University Press, 1980.

Silverman, Kenneth. *A Cultural History of the American Revolution.* New York: Thomas Y. Crowell, 1976.

Silvester, Robert. *United States Theatre: A Bibliography from the Beginnings to 1990.* Romsey, England: Motley Press, 1993.

Slotkin, Richard. *Fatal Environment: The Myth of the Frontier in the Age of Industrialization, 1800–1890.* Middletown, Conn.: Wesleyan University Press, 1986.

Smith, Geddeth. *Thomas Abthorpe Cooper: America's Premier Tragedian.* Madison, N.J.: Fairleigh Dickinson, 1996.

Smith, George W., and Charles Judah, eds. *Life in the North During the Civil War.* Albuquerque: University of New Mexico Press, 1966.

Smith, James L. *Melodrama.* London: Methuen, 1973.

Smith, Solomon. *Theatrical Management in the West and South for Thirty Years.* 1868. Rpt. New York: Benjamin Blom, 1968.

Smith, Susan Harris. *American Drama: The Bastard Art.* New York and Cambridge: Cambridge University Press, 1997.

Smith-Rosenberg, Carroll. *Disorderly Conduct: Visions of Gender in Victorian America.* New York: Oxford University Press, 1985.

Smither, Nelle. *A History of the English Theatre at New Orleans.* Philadelphia, 1944; Rpt. New York: Benjamin Blom, 1967.

Stansell, Christine. *City of Women: Sex and Class in New York, 1789–1860.* Urbana: University of Illinois Press, 1987.

Stedman, Raymond William. *Shadows of the Indian: Stereotypes in American Culture.* Norman: University of Oklahoma Press, 1982.

Stewart, George R. "The Drama in a Frontier Theater." *The Parrott Presentation Volume.* Ed. Hardin Craig. Princeton: Princeton University Press, 1935, 183–205.

Stewart, Susan. *On Longing: Narratives of the Miniature, the Gigantic, the Souvenir, the Collection.* Baltimore: Johns Hopkins University Press, 1984.

Stoddard, Richard. "The Haymarket Theatre, Boston." *Educational Theatre Journal* 27 (1975): 63–69.

Stage Scenery, Machinery, and Lighting : A Guide to Information Sources. Detroit: Gale Research, 1977.

Theatre and Cinema Architecture: A Guide to Information Sources. Detroit: Gale Research, 1978.

"Notes on John Joseph Holland, With a Design for the Baltimore Theatre, 1802." *Theatre Survey* 12 (1971): 58–66.

Stokes, D. Allen. "The First Theatrical Season in Arkansas: Little Rock, 1838–1839." *Arkansas Historical Quarterly* 23 (1964): 166–183.

Stone, George Winchester, Jr. *The London Stage 1747–1776, A Critical Introduction.* Carbondale: Southern Illinois University Press, 1968.

Stone, Mary Isabella. *Edwin Booth's Performances: The Mary Isabella Stone Commentaries.* Ed. Daniel J. Watermeier. Ann Arbor: University of Michigan Research Press, 1990.

Stott, Richard B. *Workers in the Metropolis: Class, Ethnicity, and Youth in Antebellum New York City.* Ithaca, N.Y.: Cornell University Press, 1990.

Stout, Harry S. *The New England Soul: Preaching and Religious Culture in Colonial New England.* New York: Oxford University Press, 1986.

Stratman, Carl J. *American Theatrical Periodicals, 1798–1967: A Bibliographical Guide.* Durham: Duke University Press, 1970.

    Bibliography of the American Theatre Excluding New York City. Chicago: Loyola University Press, 1965.

Stuckey, Sterling. *Slave Culture: Nationalist Theory and the Foundations of Black America.* New York: Oxford University Press, 1987.

Swinney, Donald. "Production in the Wallack Theatres: 1852–1888." Diss., Indiana University, 1962.

Takaki, Ronald. *Iron Cages: Race and Culture in 19th-Century America.* New York: Oxford University Press, 1990.

Taubman, Howard. *The Making of the American Theatre.* New York: Coward McCann, 1965.

Taylor, Dorothy Jean. "Laura Keene in America: 1852–1873." Diss., Tulane U, 1966.

Thayer, Stuart. *Annals of the American Circus, 1793–1829.* Manchester, Mich.: Thayer, 1976.

    Annals of the American Circus, 1830–1847. Seattle: Peanut Butter, 1986.

Thernstrom, Stephen, et al. *Harvard Encyclopedia of American Ethnic Groups.* Cambridge: Harvard University Press, 1980.

Tilton, Robert S. *Pocahontas: The Evolution of an American Narrative.* New York and Cambridge: Cambridge University Press, 1994.

Tocqueville, Alexis de. *Democracy in America.* Trans. Henry Reeve and Francis Bowen. Ed. Phillips Bradley. 2 vols. New York: Knopf, 1951.

    Journey to America. Trans. George Lawrence. Ed. J. P. Mayer. New Haven: Yale University Press, 1960.

Toll, Robert C. *Blacking Up: The Minstrel Show in Nineteenth Century America.* New York: Oxford University Press, 1974.

Tompkins, Jane. *Sensational Designs: The Cultural Work of American Fiction, 1790–1860.* New York: Oxford, 1985.

Towse, John Ranken. *Sixty Years of the Theater.* New York: Funk and Wagnalls, 1916.

Trachtenberg, Alan. *The Incorporation of America: Culture and Society in the Gilded Age.* New York: Hill and Wang, 1982.

Trussler, Simon. *The Cambridge Illustrated History of British Theatre.* Cambridge and New York: Cambridge University Press, 1994.

Twain, Mark. *The Adventures of Huckleberry Finn.* Ed. Gerald Graff and James Phelan. Boston: Bedford Books, 1995.

    The Gilded Age. Vols. 19 and 20 of *National Edition of the Writings of Mark Twain.* New York: Collier, 1922.

    The Autobiography of Mark Twain (1924). Ed. Charles Neider. New York: Harper and Row, 1959.

Tyrrel, Ian R. *Sobering Up: From Temperance to Prohibition in Antebellum America, 1800–1860.* Westport, Conn.: Greenwood Press, 1979.

Utz, Kathryn. "Columbus, Ohio: Theatre Seasons, 1840–41 to 1860–61." Diss., Ohio State University, 1952.

Vandenhoff, George. *Leaves from an Actor's Note-book.* New York: Appleton, 1860.

Vaughn, Jack A. *Early American Dramatists: From the Beginnings to 1900.* New York: Frederick Ungar, 1981.

Vecsey, Christopher. *Imagine Ourselves Richly: Mythic Narratives of North American Indians.* New York: Crossroad, 1988.

Wade, Jere D. "The San Francisco Stage: 1859–1869." Diss., University of Oregon, 1972.

Wade, Melvin. "'Shining in Borrowed Plumage': Affirmation of Community in the Black Coronation Festivals of New England, ca. 1750–1850." In Robert Blair St. George, ed., *Material Life in America, 1600–1860.* Boston: Northeastern University Press, 1988.

Wallace, Anthony. *The Death and Rebirth of the Seneca.* New York: Knopf, 1970.

Walsh, Townshend. *The Career of Dion Boucicault.* New York: Dunlap Society, 1915.

Ward, John William. *Andrew Jackson: Symbol for an Age.* New York: Oxford University Press, 1955.

Warner, Sam Bass. *The Private City: Philadelphia in Three Periods of Its Growth.* Philadelphia: University of Pennsylvania Press, 1968.

Watson, John F. *Annals of Philadelphia and Pennsylvania.* Philadelphia, 1786.

Watt, Stephen, and Gary A. Richardson, eds. *American Drama, Colonial to Contemporary.* Fort Worth, Tex.: Harcourt Brace, 1995.

Watts, Steven. *The Republic Reborn: War and the Making of Liberal America, 1790–1820.* Baltimore: Johns Hopkins University Press, 1987.

Wearing, J. P. *American and British Theatrical Biography.* Metuchen: Scarecrow Press, 1979.

Weber, David J. *The Spanish Frontier in North America.* New Haven: Yale University Press, 1992.

Webster, Noah. *The Letters of Noah Webster.* Ed. Harry Warfel. New York: Library Publishers, 1953.

Letters to a Young Gentleman Concerning His Education. Hartford, Conn., 1823.

Wemyss, Francis Courtney. *Chronology of the American Stage, 1752–1852.* New York: W. Taylor, 1852. Rpt. New York: Benjamin Blom, 1968.

Theatrical Biography; or, the Life of an Actor and Manager. Glasgow: R. Griffin, 1848.

Twenty-Six Years of the Life of an Actor and Manager. New York: Burgess, Stringer, 1847.

White, Richard. *The Middle Ground: Indians, Empires, and Republics in the Great Lakes Region, 1650–1815.* Cambridge and New York: Cambridge University Press, 1991.

White, Shane. "'It Was a Proud Day': African Americans, Festivals, and Parades in the North, 1741–1834." *Journal of American History* 81 (1994): 13–50.

Wiebe, Robert H. *The Opening of American Society: From the Adoption of the Constitution to the Eve of Disunion.* New York: Knopf, 1984.

Wilentz, Sean. *Chants Democratic: New York City and the Rise of the American Working Class, 1789–1860.* New York: Oxford University Press, 1984.

Willard, George. *A History of the Providence Stage, 1762–1891.* Providence: Rhode Island News, 1891.

Williams, Henry B. *The American Theatre: A Sum of Its Parts.* New York: Samuel French, 1971.

Williams, Raymond. *Marxism and Literature.* Oxford: Oxford University Press, 1977.

Williamson, Jane. *Charles Kemble: Man of the Theatre.* Lincoln: University of Nebraska Press, 1964.

Willis, Eola. *The Charleston Stage in the XVIII Century.* Columbia, S.C.: State Company, 1924.

Wills, Gary. *Lincoln at Gettysburg: The Words That Remade America.* New York: Simon and Schuster, 1992.

Wilmeth, Don B. *The American Stage to World War I: A Guide to Information Sources.* Detroit: Gale Research, 1978.

American and English Popular Entertainment: A Guide to Information Sources. Detroit: Gale Research Co., 1980.

George Frederick Cooke: Machiavel of the Stage. Westport, Conn.: Greenwood, 1980.

Variety Entertainment and Outdoor Amusements: A Reference Guide. Westport, Conn.: Greenwood Press, 1982.

"'Noble or Ruthless Savage?': The American Indian on Stage and in the Drama." *The Journal of American Drama and Theatre* 1 (Spring 1989): 39–78.

"Tentative Checklist of Indian Plays." *The Journal of American Drama and Theatre* 1 (Fall 1989): 34–54.

Wilmeth, Don B., ed., *Staging the Nation: Plays from the American Theatre, 1787–1909.* Boston: Bedford Books of St. Martin's Press, 1998.

Wilmeth, Don B., and Rosemary Cullen. "Introduction." In *Plays of Augustin Daly.* Cambridge and New York: Cambridge University Press, 1984.

Wilmeth, Don B., and Tice L. Miller, eds. *Cambridge Guide to American Theatre.* New York and Cambridge: Cambridge University Press, 1993.

Wilson, A. H. *History of the Philadelphia Theatre, 1835–1855.* Philadelphia: University of Pennsylvania Press, 1935.

Wilson, Garff B. *History of American Acting.* Bloomington: Indiana University Press, 1966.

Three Hundred Years of American Drama and Theatre. Englewood Cliffs, N.J.: Prentice-Hall, 1973.

Winslow, Catherine Mary Reignolds. See Reignolds-Winslow.

Winter, Marian Hannah. "Juba and American Minstrelsy." *Dance Index* 6 (1947): 28–47.

Winter, William, ed. *Life, Stories, and Poems of John Brougham.* Boston: James R. Osgood, 1881.

Shakespeare on the Stage. New York: Moffat, Yard, 1911.

Winton, Calhoun. "The Theatre and Drama." In Emerson, *American Literature, 1764–1789.*

Witham, Barry, ed. *Theatre in the United States: A Documentary History. Vol. I: 1750–1915, Theatre in the Colonies and United States.* Contributors Martha Mahard, David Rinear, and Don B. Wilmeth. New York and Cambridge: Cambridge University Press, 1996.

Wittke, Carl. *Tambo and Bones: A History of the Minstrel Show.* Durham: Duke University Press, 1930.

Wolter, J. C., ed. and comp. *The Dawning of American Drama: American Dramatic Criticism, 1746–1915.* Westport, Conn., and London: Greenwood Press, 1993.

Wood, Gordon. *The Creation of the American Republic, 1776–1789.* Chapel Hill: University of North Carolina Press, 1969.

Wood, William B. *Personal Recollections of the Stage.* Philadelphia: H. C. Baird, 1855.

Wright, Louis B. *Culture on the Moving Frontier.* Bloomington: Indiana University Press, 1955.

The Cultural Life of the American Colonies, 1607–1763. New York: Harper and Row, 1957.

Wyatt-Brown, Bertram. *Southern Honor: Ethics and Behavior in the Old South.* New York: Oxford University Press, 1982.

Yeo, Eileen, and Stephen Yeo. "Ways of Seeing: Control and Leisure versus Class and Struggle." In *Popular Culture and Class Conflict 1590–1914: Explorations in the History of Labour and Leisure.* Eds. Eileen Yeo and Stephen Yeo. Atlantic Highlands: Humanities Press, 1981.

Young, William C. *American Theatrical Arts: A Guide to Manuscript and Special Collections in the United States and Canada.* Chicago: American Library Association, 1971.

Young, William C., ed. *Documents of American Theatre History: Volume I, Famous American Playhouses, 1716–1899.* Chicago: American Library Assn., 1973.

   Famous Actors and Actresses of the New York Stage. 2 vols. New York: R. R. Bowker, 1975.

Zagari, Rosemarie. *A Woman's Dilemma: Mercy Otis Warren and the American Revolution.* Wheeling, Ill.: Harland Davidson, 1995.

Zanger, Jules. "The Minstrel Show as Theater of Misrule." *Quarterly Journal of Speech* 60 (1974): 33–38.

Zeidman, Irving. *The American Burlesque Show.* New York: Hawthorn Books, 1967.

Zelinsky, Wilber. *Nation into State: The Shifting Symbolic Foundations of American Nationalism.* Chapel Hill: University of North Carolina Press, 1989.

Zuckerman, Michael. "Pilgrim in the Wilderness: Community, Modernity, and the Maypole at Merry Mount." *New England Quarterly* 50 (1977): 255–77.

Index